DOGUICIMI

The First Dahomean Novel (1937)

Paul
Hazoumé

Translated from the French
by   -Richard Bjornson

An Original by Tl

©Richard Bjornson 1990

First English-Language Edition

Three Continents Press
1901 Pennsylvania Avenue, N.W.
Suite 407
Washington, D.C. 20006

This translation made from
Doguicimi, ©G.-P. Maisonneuve et Larose,
Mayenne, France, 1978
Originally published in 1938

Library of Congress Cataloging-in-Publication Data:

Hazoumé, Paul
[Doguicimi, English]
Doguicimi: the first Dahomean novel (1937) / Paul Hazoumé; translated from
the French by Richard Bjornson. —First English language edition.
    p.   cm.
"An original by Three Continents Press."
Includes bibliographical references.
ISBN 0-89410-405-5. —ISBN 0-89410-406-3 (pbk.)
1. Benin—History—Fiction. I. Title.
PQ 3989.H3D613   1989
843--dc20   89-20581
                CIP

Cover design by Max K. Winkler
©Three Continents Press 1990

Table of Contents

List of Illustrations

Paul Hazoumé

Prefatory Note

This work, which deals with the manners and customs of the traditional Kingdom of Dahomey, represents an attempt to depict a proud and powerful nation at a turning point in the history of its wars, its slave-trade and its human sacrifices which, in the civilized world, earned it a dubious renown for barbarity.

Through the intermediary of a novelistic fiction, conceived as entertainment and structured around lengthy excursions into that nation's past, the fundamental character of its people and the true countenance of its royal court will emerge clearly, despite the crimes into which it had been precipitated by a moment of madness and the greed of the slave-traders.

From its history, we have isolated one of the thousand virtuous actions performed by Dahomeyan women in order to show that they have been the model of fidelity, a fact which has, however, been called into question by certain men who always judge the opposite sex in light of the treachery practiced by those rare wives who have transgressed against marital duty.

In this novel slight changes have been introduced into the historical chronology, but each character retains the attitude and speaks the language appropriate to his station in life and to the spirit of his age (the first half of the nineteenth century); the story itself demonstrates that humanity is everywhere the same, for the sublime and the magnanimous exist side-by-side with mean-spiritedness and tyranny in traditional Dahomey just as they do in other parts of the world.

People embued with European culture and likely to value mechanical efficiency above honor while subscribing to the motto, "do it quickly," will undoubtedly encounter tedious passages in some chapters of this book. They have been motivated by our desire to provide an accurate image of a people who comprise but a single part of contemporary Dahomey – a people for whom life is palaver and war a celebration, a people who regard insouciance and imperturbability as the stamp of nobility.

The spelling of some indigenous names and the use of expressions which might appear unusual to the reader represent an accurate rendering of local pronunciation and a faithful translation of the picturesque speech of the Dahomeyans. We are convinced that this solemn manner of speaking will, by virtue of its rootedness in the land, succeed in imparting a seal of authenticity and exoticism to our documentation, for that is the constant concern of a true regionalist writer.

We are thus hoping that the reader who does not relish the fictional side of the work will at least appreciate the important anthropological and historical document which is contained in the following pages and which has resulted from twenty-five years of talking with the "elders" of Dahomey.

P. Hazoumé

King Guezo

Human Sacrifices the Ek-Gnee-noo-ah-toh, and the Battle at Dogba and the Death of Commander Faurax
King Toffa of Dahomey and his Royal Court

King Toffa of Dahomey and his Royal Court

Ministers of the Royal Court of Dahomey

Les amazones
au combat.

Dahomeyan Amazons in Combat

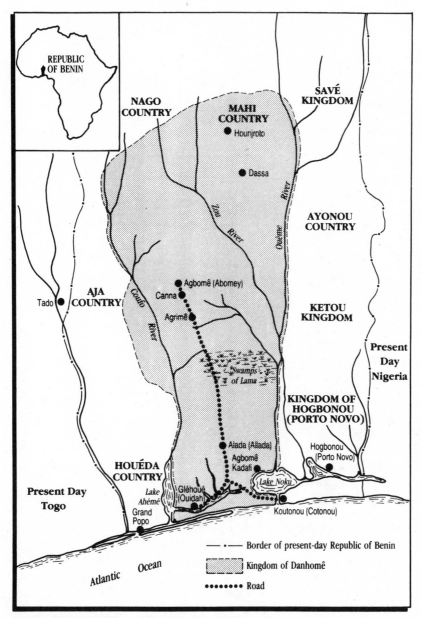

Map of the Kingdom of Danhomé

Geneological Table of the Kings of Danhomé

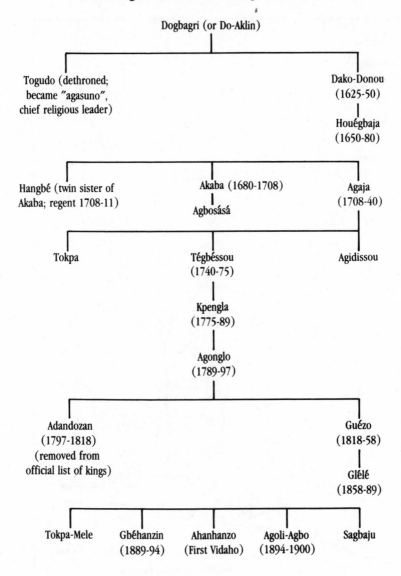

Figure 2.

Kpengla is often listed as the son of Agaja, but considering the length of Tégbéssou's reign, it is more likely that he was the son of Tégbéssou. There are some discrepancies in the dating of the reigns before Kpengla, but they are relatively slight. This list of kings was partly adapted from Maurice Glélé, *Le Danxome*.

Introduction[1]

Paul Hazoumé's *Doguicimi* is a neglected masterpiece. There are many reasons why it has never received the attention it deserves; indeed, it is quite different from what readers and critics have come to expect of African fiction. It is long, whereas the overwhelming majority of African novels are short. At a time when pre-independence African literature is valued largely for its anti-colonial stance or experimental style, Hazoumé seems like an anachronism. One of the first great intellectuals in francophone Africa, he was an ardent Catholic and a staunch supporter of the French colonial enterprise; moreover, his prose reads more like a sprawling nineteenth-century realistic narrative than a form-conscious, psychologically sophisticated twentieth-century novel.

Burdened with a superabundance of historical and ethnographic details, Hazoumé's text often strays from what modern readers would be most likely to regard as its principal line of narrative development – the story of Dogu-icimi, a courageous woman who maintains her honor and integrity under the most difficult circumstances. There are occasional stylistic lapses; some sections are overly melodramatic, and others seem only tangentially related to the main action. Scenes of extraordinary cruelty do not depict traditional Africa in a particularly favorable light, and more than one critic has admonished Hazoumé for pandering to a European taste for the exotic.

Nevertheless, *Doguicimi* is a masterpiece. Similar sorts of criticism might well be levelled against Western "classics" like the *Iliad*, *Don Quixote*, or *Moby Dick*. Each of these works depicts an individual whose experiences illuminate a crucial set of insights into the human condition as defined by the cultural assumptions of an entire people at a given moment in their history. This is precisely what Hazoumé has done. He effectively captured the soul of Danhomê (the traditional kingdom of Dahomey in what is today the People's Republic of Benin) by creating a character who embodies its ideal virtues and then placing this character in dramatic conflict with a corrupt society that merely pays lip service to them. For him, there was no contradiction between his admiration of these ideal virtues and his support for the "civilizing mission" of French colonialism. Furthermore, as an experienced ethnographer whose *Pacte du Sang au Dahomey* (Blood Oath in Dahomey) had been greeted with considerable praise when it was first published in 1937, Hazoumé was intimately familiar with oral story-telling techniques. When he wrote *Doguicimi*, he adopted a prose style that owed nearly as much to the influence of these techniques as to his reading in nineteenth-century French fiction. Essentially he created a medium suitable to the subject matter he had chosen to depict. The people of Danhomê had become notorious for their human sacrifices, their participation in the slave trade, and their army of Amazons, yet Hazoumé forged their history into an epic that reveals their profound humanity while respecting their unique cultural identity.

That Hazoumé should immortalize the collective consciousness of Danhomê in an epic fiction is not without a certain irony, for he viewed the historical Danhomê with a mixture of admiration and moral repugnance. Like the South African Sotho writer Thomas Mofolo, who made the legendary Zulu leader Chaka the central character in his epic masterpiece, Hazoumé was not from the kingdom about which he was writing. In fact, he was born in 1890 and raised in the kingdom of Porto Novo, which had been a major rival of Danhomê since the mid nineteenth century. Although Adja languages were spoken in both areas (Fon in Danhomé and Gun in Porto Novo), tensions between the two areas persisted well into the independence period. Hazoumé's grandfather Alomavô was a Yoruba who settled at Porto Novo and became a counsellor to King Sodji; Alomavô's son took the name Ha-zun-mê and became one of the most powerful "larris" (messengers, counsellors) in the court. Like nearly all Fon and Gun names, Ha-zun-mê contains part of a longer sentence that is intended to characterize the person who bears it. "Ha" refers to a kind of monkey whose shrill cry was regarded as unbearable, whereas "mê" means "in" and "zun" means "forest; the entire sentence suggested by his name is: "when Ha cries in the forest, no other creature dares cry." Hazoumé's father was said to have been the "eyes and ears" of Porto Novo's last king, Toffa, and the name he chose reflects the power of his word.[2]

Paul Hazoumé himself was sent to Catholic mission schools, where he came under the influence of two strong-willed, intelligent priests, Fr. Steinmetz and Fr. Aupiais, both of whom stimulated his interest in the study of psychology and religion. The church also embued Hazoumé with a Christian world view that unequivocally condemned the practices for which the people of Danhomê had become well known during the nineteenth century. One of the very few French-speaking West Africans to receive a secondary education at that time, he became a fellowship student at the Teacher Training School in Saint Louis (Senegal), where he graduated in 1910 at the head of his class. This school, which later moved to the island of Gorée and became the famous Ecole William Ponty, provided a unique training ground for the intellectual elites of francophone Africa. There was an extraordinary *esprit de corps* among the students at this school, and Hazoumé's experience there played a major role in his intellectual development.

When Hazoumé returned to Dahomey, he became a teacher and school director in Ouidah and then in Agbomê (Abomey), the capital of the former Kingdom of Danhomê. There he encountered customs that were very different from those he had known in Porto Novo. Fascinated by them, he began collecting the oral histories and ethnographic materials he would later use in his monograph on the blood oath. During the first world war, he and Louis Hunkarin edited one of the colony's first newspapers, the mimeographed *Le Recadère de Béhanzin*, which did not hesitate to attack the abuses of the colonial administration under the detested Governor Charles Noufflard. At the end of the war, Hazoumé became a French citizen. Although he was posted to a school in Cotonou and later served as a school inspector, Hazoumé continued to pursue his research into the history and social structure of the Danhomê kingdom. Despite his identification with Porto Novo, his Christian value system, and his integration into the French colonial service, he could not help but admire the nobility, the courage, the deeply religious sense of life, and the highly successful administrative system in a kingdom that had established itself as one of the most powerful in the history of West Africa.

Having read the accounts of nineteenth-century European travelers to Danhomê, Hazoumé felt they had completely misunderstood the human reality behind the customs they had described in such meticulous detail. *Doguicimi* is his attempt to convey a sense for that human reality. In some of his other writings, his moral disapproval of the oppression inflicted upon other peoples by the Kingdom of Danhomê is clearly expressed. For example, in the early 1940s, he transcribed and edited *Cinquante Ans d'apostalat au Dahomey: Souvenirs de S. E. Mgr. Fr. Steinmetz* (Fifty Years of Apostleship in Dahomey: Memories of H. E. Mgr. Fr. Steinmetz). Hazoumé was a great admirer of Steinmetz, whom he eulogized as "a living symbol of the church everlasting and of maternal France."[3] Throughout this pamphlet, Hazoumé lends support to Steinmetz's characterization of Danhomê as a bloodthirsty tyranny that had enslaved and persecuted Mahis, Nagonous, and other Africans for nearly four centuries. The kings of Danhomê are described as pillagers, and the last of them, Gbéhanzin, is dismissed as a "dethroned despot" justifiably punished for having disdained the generous peace offered him by the French. The people of Danhomê are repeatedly criticized for their servile acceptance of an unjust system, and the coming of the French is portrayed as the liberation of Africans who had been subjected to the oppression of Danhomê. Hazoumé believed in the French imperial ideal and was convinced it had helped bring peace and justice to his country. Such an attitude obviously implies a condemnation of nineteenth-century Danhomê, the principal subject of his novel *Doguicimi*; however, in his fascination with the kingdom, he was psychologically and emotionally incapable of portraying it in wholly negative terms. He sensed its greatness, and his own ambivalence contributed to the dramatic tension in his novel – a dramatic tension similar to the one that makes characters like Mofolo's Chaka and Melville's Captain Ahab so vividly memorable.

If Hazoumé was a proponent of French colonialism, he was not an uncritical one. Throughout the 1930s he contributed regularly to local newspapers, often attacking the arbitrariness of decisions made by the colonial authorities and pleading for a better understanding of the positive values that had held together traditional African society. When he was disciplined for refusing an order to reduce the teaching staff at his school by fifty per cent, he sued the colonial administration, and in an unprecedented decision, both the colonial governor and the French supervisor of schools were relieved of their duties for abuse of authority. What Hazoumé desired was that French ideals of justice and freedom be applied within an African context, although he knew such a goal could never be realized unless the humanity, wisdom, and nobility of traditional Africa were also recognized as a legitimate basis for defining one's own sense of identity, one's own philosophy of life.

One of the primary motivations behind Hazoumé's own ethnographic work was the hope of convincing others to share his belief in this ideal. During the late 1920s and early 1930s, he published a number of essays in the field, and after his study of the blood oath received a prize as the best work of the year in French West Africa, he received a fellowship to study ethnology at the Musée de l'Homme in Paris. Shortly afterwards he was appointed to the administrative board of IFAN (Institut Franais d'Afrique Noire), the principal research organization in francophone Africa. When he brought out *Doguicimi* in the following year (1938), he naturally drew upon the ethnographic materials he had been collecting for the past twenty-five years. The initial reviews of the novel were unanimously favorable, and it received three major literary prizes, including the French Academy's prestigious "Prix de Langue Franaise." Although pushed into the background by the outbreak of World War II and by the political preoccupations of the post-war period, *Doguicimi* continued to be admired by those who knew it. Until a second edition was published in 1978, however, it was not widely available because the relatively modest printing of the first edition had been out of print for a long time.

Just before the outbreak of the second world war, Hazoumé returned to Dahomey, where he traveled throughout the country delivering speeches against the German menace. His speeches were collected in a volume, *La France contre le racisme allemand* (France Opposed to German Racism), but it was never disseminated due to the fall of the Third Republic in France. After the war, he played a significant role in the political evolution of his country and became somewhat of an elder statesman in the francophone African intellectual community. He was a co-founder of the colony's first political party, and in 1947 he was elected to the legislative assembly of the French Union, where he served as vice-president for cultural affairs in the overseas territories. He was also a member of the Dahomeyan territorial assembly. An early sponsor of the publishing house Présence Africaine, he (along with Léopold Sédar Senghor and Alioune Diop) presided over the First Congress of Black Writers and Artists at the Sorbonne in 1956. Throughout his ten-year stay in Paris, he was unstinting in the encouragement he offered younger writers.

Upon his return to Dahomey in 1958, he wrote many newspaper articles in favor of national independence, but after Dahomey actually achieved it two years later under the presidency of Hubert Maga, Hazoumé became an outspoken opponent of the corrupt regime. Although more than seventy years old by this time, he continued to collect the oral tales, songs, and proverbs that he discussed in countless radio programs and newspaper articles. For years he sought unsuccessfully to create the first publishing house in his country. A man of legendary generosity and modesty, he embodied a wisdom that was officially recognized by his appointment as principal advisor to the newly constituted national counsel of elders in 1964. His favorite proverb – "the injustice that my brother does to my enemy makes me the enemy of my brother" – clearly encapsulates his own attitude toward oppression and tyranny. Hazoumé had a deep sense of attachment to his own extremely large family, and as a respected elder who spoke eloquently about the past, he came to be regarded with awe and reverence by many of his countrymen.

A novelist, ethnologist, historian, statesman, and journalist, Hazoumé forged a profoundly humanistic world view from his unique synthesis of African and French cultural values. This world view was already present in *Doguicimi*. In fact, it forms the background of all his writings, including the projects on which he was still working when he died in 1980: a history of Gbéhanzin, a treatise on traditional African beliefs, a study of Franco-African relations, and his own autobiography.[4] All these works remain in manuscript form; if they are ever edited and published, they will certainly provide new evidence for the breadth of Hazoumé's vision and for the profound respect he accorded traditional African values and the consciousness in which they are embedded.

In one sense, this consciousness is the true subject matter of *Doguicimi*. In a kingdom like Danhomê, the consciousness of the people is permeated with the history of the royal family. This history is recited for them each morning by the public crier as he makes his round of the city; it is carved in the bas-reliefs on the side of the Palace; it is an implicit component of their rituals and annual celebrations; and it is woven into the palavers where rhetorical effectiveness depends largely upon the facility with which a speaker can comment upon the meaning of historical events that are assumed to be known by everyone. This historical knowledge constitutes the narrative texture of *Doguicimi* and in general corresponds rather closely to the actual history of Danhomê. Much of this could be reconstructed through a careful reading of Hazoumé's novel, but readers unfamiliar with the reality upon which it is a probing commentary might find it useful to know a bit more about the remarkable story of Danhomê – how it came into being and how it prospered.

During the late sixteenth or early seventeenth century, the large Adja family migrated from Tado in present-day Togo to Allada (see fig. 1). According to legend, their common ancestor had been born of the liaison between a panther and a woman. When the family was wracked by a struggle for succession around 1620, one of the former chief's sons, Tê Agbanlin, left Allada and led his followers to the East, where they established Hogbonou, which later became known as Porto Novo. The youngest son, Dogbagri (or Do-Aklin), moved northward with his followers and the throne of Agassouvi (Son of Panther) to the plains area beyond the Lama swamps. Allada itself remained under the control of the former chief's brothers. Dogbagri settled near Canna, and his son, Dako-Donou (see fig. 2), became the first king of Danhomê in about 1625. Because Dako-Donou had paid the local chief Agri for the land on which he built his residence, the phrase, "to purchase (or acquire) Danhomê," later became a standard way of describing a new king's accession to the throne. When Dako-Donou desired to expand his land-holding to build a palace for his son, Agri objected, quipping that the answer to such a request could be found in his quiver; in response to this jibe, Dako-Donou killed the local chief and ordered the man's body entombed with his quiver in the foundations of the new palace, which he named Agrigomê (the quiver of Agri). In addition to establishing his people as a ruling aristocracy in the local area, Dako-Donou introduced an elaborate court etiquette and a complex administrative system that gradually evolved into the powerful state bureaucracy of the nineteenth-century kingdom.

Dako-Donou's son Houégbaja ascended to the throne in the middle of the seventeenth century, and he created the precedent of expanding the kingdom through warfare. Dan was the chief of a tribe living on the plateau before the arrival of the Agassouvis (or, as they are sometimes called, the Alladahonous or Adjahénous); he taunted Houégbaja that his aggressive people would never be happy until they had built in his stomach. Houégbaja took the local chief at his word. When he built his palace on the site of Agbomê (Abomey), he killed Dan and buried him in the foundations. The name of the kingdom derives from this incident, for Danhomê literally means "in the stomach of Dan."[5] Houégbaja's palace was truly impressive; it was completely encircled by walls that measured more than two and a half miles in circumference. Subsequent kings added more buildings, and by the nineteenth century, the walls had grown in length to eight miles, and a five-foot ditch had been dug around the outside of them. The name Agbomê was particularly appropriate for this site because it literally means "in the enclosure."

According to oral tradition, Houégbaja never lost a war. He assured his eastern borders by entering into a non-aggression pact with the Yoruba of Oyo, and he consolidated his control over the plain of Agbomê by the aggressive use of military force, by strengthening the administrative system introduced by Dako-Donou, and by imposing various taxes on the local inhabitants, who became known as Danhomênous (a term that was not used for members of the royal family). The word "Danhomênou" does refer to an individual who comes from Danhomê, but since "nou," when pronounced as a high tone, means "thing" in Fon, the term can also be translated as "thing of Danhomê." In actual fact, the "anato," or commoners, were regarded as being the property of the king. However, the "anato" were hardly reduced to peonage. They had considerable freedom to benefit from the fruits of their labor and even to rise to positions of great power, responsibility, and wealth. Even the heir to the throne had to be born of a queen who was not herself a member of the royal family by birth, and the principal ministerial positions at court were generally reserved for commoners who had distinguished themselves in some way.

There were actually four social classes in Danhomê – the royal family (the descendants of those who had originally come from Allada), the dignitaries (commoners who had been elevated by the king), the commoners (the original inhabitants of the area), and the slaves (those who had been captured in war or bought in the slave markets). A commoner could not be sold into slavery, and the children of slaves were not slaves but Danhomênous. Princes and princesses did enjoy significant privileges, but commoners too were generously rewarded for outstanding achievements. Along with the recognition that force is necessary for successful rule (as Dako-Donou and Houégbaja had amply demonstrated), this emphasis upon individual accomplishment helped make Danhomê into a dynamic, aggressive society. It also contributed to a growing popular loyalty toward the throne, for commoners believed they were solely dependent upon the king for any rewards they hoped to receive. By cultivating this belief, Houégbaja and his successors laid the groundwork for the emergence of a veritable nation in which people clearly identified with a state that was comprised of different ethnic groups. Houégbaja's reign was so successful in this respect that his name came to be employed as an honorific title for the sovereigns of Danhomê, which itself was frequently referred to as "the Danhomê of Houégbaja."

Akaba ruled over Danhomê for twenty-eight years, and he was succeeded by the renowned Agaja, who improved the efficiency of the administrative and military training systems, introduced the use of female warriors, and created a vast network of "Agbadjigbeto" (spies) both inside and outside the kingdom. With information gathered by these spies and incorporated into detailed cloth maps, Agaja and his advisers developed battle plans that enabled them to mount almost invariably successful surprise attacks – a tactic that Danhomê continued to utilize for nearly two hundred years.

At first Agaja opposed the slave trade, but developments that occurred during his reign ultimately pushed Danhomê into a greater involvement with it. Agaja's troops defeated the Aja to the East, but this victory placed Danhomê in direct conflict with the Yoruba of Oyo, who pillaged Agbomê and inflicted the only major defeat ever suffered by Agaja's armies. By agreeing to pay a heavy annual tribute to Oyo, Agaja was able to rebuild his capital and undertake successful military expeditions against Allada and Gléhoué (also called Whydah or Ouidah). The conquest of Allada was important for symbolic reasons because it was the city to which the royal family of Danhomê traced its origins, but Gléhoué (which means the hut, or house, of the fields and refers to the home of the peasant who had made the first contact with an European ship in this area) was even more important because it enabled Danhomê to trade directly with the Europeans who had settled there.

Oyo was favorable to the slave trade and exerted pressure on Agaja to allow it to be conducted at Gléhoué. Because Agaja's wars had resulted in the capture of many prisoners (over 8,000 at Allada alone), he had an abundant supply of the one commodity most coveted by the Europeans. Since he desired to purchase guns and other military supplies, he eventually did permit a resumption of the slave trade, but the conditions he laid down were so stringent that many traders avoided the port at Gléhoué. Agaja insisted that slaves could only be sold in his name and by his representatives; similarly, European goods could only be imported into the country by the king, who thus exercised a monopoly over all foreign trade, a practice that was rigorously enforced by his successors until the latter part of the nineteenth century.

By the end of Agaja's reign in about 1740, the chief ministers in the court had acquired most of the functions they and their successors would continue to perform for the next hundred and fifty years. The two most powerful ministers, the Migan and the Mêwou, had existed during previous reigns. Migan was a minister of justice who personally executed all death sentences; he was also responsible for performing the human sacrifices that were carried out for ritual purposes. After Agaja's successful military campaigns, the Migan was also entrusted with overseeing the governance of Allada. Mêwou served as a minister of the interior; he administered justice among the members of the extremely large royal family and was in charge of the royal messengers who assured communication between Agbomê and the other parts of the kingdom. In fact, all official messages for the king passed through him. Starting with Agaja's reign, Mêwou also supervised the administration of Gléhoué and the neighboring coastal provinces that were rapidly becoming the key to the kingdom's economic well-being.

The Ajaho was the chief fetishist. He served as administrator of the Palace, director of the secret police, and overseer of the extensive domestic spy network. He also presided over the trial by poison to determine the truthfulness of messengers, spies, witnesses, and people accused of crimes. During this procedure he would administer a potion to a cock that served as a surrogate for the person in question; if the cock survived the ordeal, the person was regarded as having spoken the truth, although, as becomes evident in *Doguicimi*, Ajaho had the capacity to prejudice the outcome of such trials. Gaou was the first minister of war. He supervised the spy network outside the kingdom and led the troops of Danhomê into battle. He was assisted by Possou, a second minister of war; both were generously rewarded after successful military campaigns, but neither was expected to return alive if Danhomê were defeated on the field of battle. Sogan was the guardian of the royal treasury and in particular of the slaves owned by the king (so = horse or beast of burden; gan = chief), and Tokpo was in charge of agriculture, land-holdings, and the "sacred waters" used for royal ceremonies.[6]Two important ministers did not live in Agbomê. The first was Akplogan, the high priest of the religious cult. He lived at Allada, where he was responsible for the local administration. The second was Yévogan, who administered the maritime provinces and supervised all transactions with Europeans; he lived at Gléhoué.

Throughout the history of Danhomê, the ministers tended not to be chosen from the royal family. However, one important member of the court was selected by the king from among his own sons. He was the Vidaho, or designated heir to the throne. Vidaho enjoyed a great number of privileges, and the respect due him was second only to that accorded the king.

Major decisions were made in the court counsel attended by the ministers, the court dignitaries, and the princes of the royal family; the Wives of Panther (queens) sometimes exercised considerable influence behind the scenes. Within this context, Agaja was a forceful and enlightened ruler; he was interested in European customs and even kept an Englishman, Bulfinch Lamb, at his court for many years. But more than anything else, he would be remembered as a military leader who vastly expanded the size of the kingdom and opened the way for direct trade with the Europeans.

The next four kings of Danhomê reigned for ninety years and labored under the humiliating necessity of paying tribute to Oyo. When Tégbéssou ascended to the throne in 1740, he had to face more than fifteen years of devastating raids by the neighboring Yoruba kingdom. Several times he had to abandon Agbomê and, like his predecessor, take refuge in the forests to the North. His revenues from customs duties and taxes diminished to almost nothing, and the slave trade at Gléhoué fell into complete disarray. Only at the price of a treaty in which he reaffirmed his willingness to pay the annual tribute to Oyo was Tégbéssou able to rebuild Agbomê and revive the kingdom's stagnating economy. His methods were often brutal. He named "king's traders" to conduct business with the Europeans and then executed anyone who traded privately with them. He eliminated many of his rivals in the royal family by selling them into slavery. Although he did succeed in restoring Danhomê to prosperity by increasing trade and regularizing the collection of taxes and customs duties, his economic policy was based on a contradiction that ultimately led to disaster. Tégbéssou believed that a flourishing slave trade was possible without constant war. As a result, he allowed the army and its store of weapons to deteriorate. His troops did subdue Houéda, but without a steady supply of war captives, his representatives at Gléhoué could not meet the European demand for slaves. Furthermore, European traders could easily abandon any port on the African coast, and the slave trade itself was subject to influences over which Tégbéssou had little control. By 1767 the weakness of his policy had become apparent, and Danhomê entered a period of economic depression from which it did not recover until Guézo ascended to the throne in 1818.

Tégbéssou was succeeded by Kpengla, who proved incapable of improving the situation. He sought to proclaim Danhomê's independence from Oyo, but he lacked the military force to sustain such aspirations. Even his slave-raiding expeditions often returned empty-handed, and because he failed to attract many European ships to Gléhoué, the kingdom's revenues from the slave trade declined precipitously, while rival ports like Porto Novo prospered. The neglect of farming and artisanry led to severe economic dislocations that resulted in famine and epidemic during the early 1780s. The situation was aggravated by an outbreak of thievery that made Europeans even less willing than before to conduct business at Gléhoué. Kpengla's son Agonglo became king in 1789, although his right to the throne was contested by a descendant of Agaja and many local chiefs were unhappy with his selection. Agonglo seems to have been somewhat of an idealist. His economic reforms and enlightened sense of justice made him popular among the Danhomênous, but some members of the royal family suspected him of sympathizing with the white man's religion, and he was allegedly poisoned by a woman from the Palace.

His son Adandozan ruled Danhomê for over twenty years, although his name was removed from the official list of kings after he was overthrown in 1818. There is some disagreement over the extent to which Adandozan's reign was oppressive. In *Doguicimi* he is consistently portrayed as a tyrant, but several historians have recently suggested that the reforms he proposed were actually quite progressive. He opposed the slave trade because he felt that the use of slaves on agricultural plantations would ultimately be more profitable for Danhomê; also, he did not accept the necessity of continually waging war to enlarge the size of the kingdom and to acquire captives who could subsequently be sold into slavery. Both policies appear enlightened when judged in retrospect, but they were extremely unpopular because many people, princes as well as commoners, felt that the greatness of Danhomê depended upon war and the slave trade.

Adandozan also alienated much of the royal family by depriving its members of their accustomed privileges and selling some of them into slavery; he even proposed to use them instead of slaves as the sacrificial victims during the traditional ceremonies. He further antagonized the people by refusing to hold the annual celebrations at which gifts were distributed among them and feasts provided for their benefit. This was also the time when the links with the ancestors were reaffirmed. During his entire reign, Adandozan never made offerings to his dead father, and his failure to do so was widely regarded as a sacrilege. In addition, he was notorious for acts of unusual cruelty: ripping open the wombs of pregnant women to determine the sex of their children or to obtain materials for preparing gris-gris, feeding prisoners to hyenas and panthers kept in cages at the court, castrating men suspected of imaginary crimes against the throne. Reputedly addicted to alcohol, Adandonzan came to be viewed as the personification of Lègba (spirit of evil), and when he was removed from the throne by a revolt of the princes, his fall was greeted with joy by most people in the kingdom.

The reign of his successor, Guézo, lasted forty years and proved to be the high point in the history of Danhomê. One mid-nineteenth-century British visitor to Agbomê described it as the "most powerful monarchy in West Africa,"[7] and Hazoumé reinforced this judgment by situating the action of *Doguicimi* during the early years of Guézo's reign. Kpengla and Adandozan had tried to defy Oyo, but Guézo was the first king of Danhomê to defeat his Yoruba neighbors and actually put an end to the hated annual tribute. For this reason, he came to be honored as the liberator of his people. Although Guézo himself was a perceptive and humane individual, he realized that his popular support and the economic prosperity of his kingdom depended upon practices of which he might disapprove (e.g., the slave trade and human sacrifice). He knew he could not eliminate them without jeopardizing his own position.

The irony of common nineteenth-century European perceptions of Guézo was the fact that people condemned him as a barbarian for practices he would have abolished if it had been in his power to do so. One of the major accomplishments of Hazoumé's novel is its depiction of the dramatic tension between Guézo's public persona and his private consciousness, for *Doguicimi* clearly reveals how the king's actions are circumscribed by a socio-religious context that is the culmination of previous history and tradition. Within this context, the practices that were interpreted in the so-called civilized world as evidence of senseless African brutality can be seen as part of a belief system in which such practices are comprehensible, even if one can not condone them, as Hazoumé most certainly did not. What he did succeed in doing was to convey a sense for the courage and nobility that were also made possible by this belief system.

One of the customs that most fascinated him was the blood oath, which he regarded as one avenue to noble action in Danhomê. According to an estimate in the scholarly monograph Hazoumé wrote on the subject, Guézo had recourse to the blood oath in contracting sworn friendships with more than 600 different people. In fact, the blood oath may well have been one of the keys to his success; it certainly played an essential role in his rise to power. After the death of Agonglo, according to some oral traditions, the supporters of Adandozan usurped the throne from Gakpé, who eventually assumed the throne under the name Guézo. Once Adandozan came to power, he paid little attention to his disenfranchised brother, who gradually acquired a reputation as a successful military leader, although he also spent a great deal of time working with his own hands on the royal plantations at Canna. He was an experienced hunter and had learned how to weave the local textiles. Although he did cultivate an ostentatious life style at court, as many of the royal princes did, Gakpé in addition gained valuable insights into the mentality of the people, and he developed a keen appreciation for the work that would be necessary for the economic well-being of the kingdom. He was so popular that the Danhomênous pleaded with him to replace Adandozan, but he refused their support because he regarded the masses as bloodthirsty and did not want to be in their debt.

He preferred to rely upon the sworn friendships he had contracted with particular individuals. Initially, the blood oath involved two people who drank each other's blood and swore absolute fidelity to each other; it eventually came to be associated with a ritual during which the blood of the contracting parties was mixed with a bit of earth, but the principle remained the same. If one repudiated the earth or the blood of the sworn friend, punishment was certain to follow. In a world of ambiguous appearances and widespread conspiracies, the blood oath was a powerful institution because it allowed an individual to act upon the knowledge that his confidence in another person could not be betrayed with impunity. When Ganpé became king in 1818, his success was due in large part to his sworn friendships with the Brazilian mulatto slave trader Francisco Felix da Souza and with the other princes of the royal family.

Da Souza had engaged in business dealings with Adandozan, who owed him a considerable amount of money. When he went to Agbomê to collect the debt, the king had him thrown into prison. Gakpé visited him there, and the two men swore a blood oath of friendship. The prince of Danhomê then rescued

A

B

Guezo and the Vidaho (Guachard, 1856), A; Chacha Ajinacou, King Guezo's Sworn Friend and Supporter in Ouidah (from 19th cent. drawing, 1931), B; A Man Who Had Sworn a Blood Oath with Behanzin, the Last Great King of Dahomey (drawing, 1931), C

C

the Brazilian trader and escorted him to Anécho in present-day Togo. As soon as Da Souza reestablished his trading stock, he sent guns, tobacco, alcohol, and European cloth to his "brother" in Agbomê. By judiciously distributing such items, Gakpé managed to attract a large number of supporters away from Adandozan, who had refused to share European goods with his subjects.

Gakpé also entered into sworn friendships with many of the princes, who had become totally disaffected with Adandozan as the result of his challenge to their privileges. In particular, he allied himself with Adouconou, who was the heart of the conspiracy, despite the fact that he was Adandozan's brother by the same mother. When the bloodless coup was carried out by the princes, Adandozan was simply taken prisoner inside the Palace and placed in Mêwou's custody. The Danhomênous were not even aware that a change had taken place. Although Adandozan had sold Gakpé's mother into slavery, the new king refused to execute anyone who had occupied the throne of Houégbaja, and his predecessor, confined to house arrest, actually outlived him. Building upon the network of sworn friendships that had enabled him to become king, Guézo (as he was known after his accession to the throne) broke with traditional precedent and named several princes to ministerial posts. This gesture of reconciliation clearly demonstrated the shrewd political sense that enabled him to consolidate the broad base of support he would need to revitalize a kingdom that had been in decline for more than half a century.

One of the first tasks to which Guézo turned his attention was the reform of the civilian bureaucracy and the army. He appointed Da Souza (henceforth known under the name Chacha Ajinacou) as his representative at Gléhoué and charged him to oversee all transactions with European traders. Chacha completely reorganized the collection of customs duties at the port and convinced Guézo to channel a good deal of slave labor into large palm-tree plantations in the coastal provinces, a decision that allowed Danhomê to prosper even after the abolition of the international trade in slaves around the middle of the century. In return for the privileges he received from Guézo, Chacha supplied the new king with an enormous number of guns to reequip an army that eventually became the largest standing military force in West Africa; estimates of its size range as high as 20,000. This army included a large number of women, for Guézo had transformed the Amazons, originally created by Agaja, into an elite fighting corps.

In addition to the standing army, Guézo could also call upon levies of troops from all the provinces in the kingdom. "Dénous" (customs offices) were located at strategic points along all major roads. During times of peace, the "dénougan" (customs officer) would collect duties on all goods that passed on the road and supervise the slave labor on nearby plantations; when the king needed troops for a military expedition, the "dénougan" would recruit them from the surrounding area and dispatch them to the capital. He was also responsible for expediting the transportation of guns and supplies to the battlefront and providing care for the wounded as they returned.

Such a system proved extremely efficient, but it was only part of Guézo's administrative network. He encouraged the organization of artisans, hunters, farmers, and fisherman, and he developed a cadre of messengers who assured constant communication between the capital and the outlying provinces. Even the provisioning of the Palace was a major undertaking, since there were as many as 10,000 people involved in its various activities. As a Nigerian scholar has remarked, nineteenth-century Danhomê was "an oasis of order and sound administration in a sea of surrounding chaos."[8]One of the reasons why this hierarchical system worked so smoothly was that Guézo had insisted upon imposing a uniform set of laws that guaranteed Danhomênous the right to enjoy the fruits of their labor. After the arbitrariness of Adandozan, such policies restored the people's confidence in their government and contributed to the loyalty with which they served Guézo.

This sense of allegiance to Danhomê was heightened by Guézo's scrupulous observance of the annual traditional celebrations and his willingness to undertake a large number of military campaigns. People looked forward to the lavish feasts and extravagant gift-giving of the celebrations, and they took pride in the conquests of their armies. However, war was not only a matter of national pride for Guézo; he obviously desired to expand the size of his realm, yet he also needed captives to supply victims for the human sacrifices he knew the people expected, particularly at the annual celebrations. Furthermore, the slave trade was still the kingdom's principal source of revenue, and the most feasible way to obtain slaves was to capture them in battle. For psychological and economic reasons, then, Guézo felt compelled to engage in at least one military action each year. This is the context in which the two wars against the Mahi kingdom of Hounjroto are carried out in *Doguicimi*.

These wars actually did take place, although Hazoumé embellishes upon his description of them in order to provide a more dramatic narrative framework for the action in his novel. The Mahis had originally inhabited the eastern portion of the Abomey plain, but they had been obliged to move northward after the arrival of the Agassouvis. During the two centuries before Guézo's time, they had been subject to numerous slave raids. As a result, the court at Agbomê did not anticipate any great difficulty in subduing them. The unexpected defeat during the first campaign contains an object lesson that Guézo was careful to heed in making lengthy preparations for the second attack, which resulted in the virtual annihilation of Hounjroto. The drama of *Doguicimi* thus plays itself out against a background that accurately reflects the prevailing atmosphere during the early years of Guézo's reign.

After the British succeeded in severely reducing the international slave trade during the 1840s, Danhomê maintained its prosperity largely through the sale of palm oil from the vast plantations that Guézo had developed at the urging of Chacha. Nevertheless, in the eyes of most Europeans, Danhomê remained the most notorious and barbarous slave state on the West African coast. Guézo did moderate the human sacrifices performed at the annual celebrations, but stories of these gruesome rituals continued to shock Europeans, and Britain alone sent sixteen diplomatic missions to Agbomê between 1843 and 1863 in the hope of persuading Guézo and his successor to abandon them and to cease exporting slaves, but these missions seem to have had little impact on the court.

The last fifteen years of Guézo's reign were marred by two unfortunate circumstances. First, a rift developed between him and Chacha, who had gone deeply into debt to supply the king with guns for his endless wars only to see his own trade privileges at Gléhoué withdrawn from him; Chacha died in 1849, and Guézo never again had a European trading partner whom he could trust. Second, his military ambitions led him to attack the Yoruba confederation of Abeokuta in 1844 and again in 1851; on both occasions his troops were soundly defeated. Although he lived for seven more years and presided over other campaigns, he had failed to win the battle he hoped would assure his everlasting glory.

After Guézo, the Kingdom of Danhomê declined and ultimately disintegrated under the pressure of French intrusions into the area. His successor Glélé was repulsed in repeated attempts to take Abeokuta, and when Porto Novo became a French protectorate in 1882, direct conflict with the European power became inevitable. The last legitimate king was Gbéhanzin, and he fought valiantly against the French. But when he was obliged to burn the Palace of Singboji and flee into the forest to live among the common people, the end of an era had arrived. Gbéhanzin's exile to the West Indies merely confirmed the fact. The mystique of the all-powerful ruler had disappeared, and the values embedded in the kingdom's long history were in danger of being extinguished. Hazoumé's awareness of this danger no doubt prompted him to write *Doguicimi*, in which he recaptured a specific moment near the high point of that history and created characters who exemplified those values to the highest degree. He was hardly an apologist for Danhomê. He depicted its cruelties, human sacrifices, and irrational actions in meticulous detail. Yet, by placing them into their cultural context and balancing them with the courage, nobility, and religious sense of life that also characterized Danhomê, he helped preserve the wholeness of a profoundly human phenomenon that had until then been described in partial and grotesquely biased terms by European observers.

The story line in Hazoumé's novel is quite straightforward. After several white men under Guézo's safe-conduct had been killed in the Mahi village of Kinglo at the instigation of young men from nearby Hounjroto, the council of the throne accedes to the wish of the king and decides to wage a war of reprisal against Hounjroto. Several of the royal princes who supported Guézo in his rise to power speak eloquently in opposition to the proposed campaign. Foremost among them is Toffa, the husband of Doguicimi. The night before the troops are to depart, Toffa harangues his favorite wife about the untrustworthiness of all women. He blames the wives of Guézo for persuading the king to undertake the expedition despite unfavorable omens and in the absence of any serious preparations for war. Offended by her husband's diatribe against women, Doguicimi insists that she is capable of absolute fidelity. The words she utters at this point define the self-image she so courageously defends during the rest of the novel.

At Hounjroto, although Toffa fights heroically for a cause he did not support in counsel, he is taken captive, and the troops of Danhomê are routed. When

Guézo makes his first public appearance in Agbomê after this defeat and again on the first day of the annual traditional celebrations, Doguicimi reviles him publicly and accuses him of having plotted to rid himself of Toffa and others who had helped him gain the throne. According to custom, no one is allowed to address the king directly, and such insults were considered blasphemies, immediately punishable by death. But Guézo is a wise, preceptive man, and, realizing that her angry words arise from her noble attachment to Toffa, he pardons her, much to the astonishment of the masses and against the wishes of his wives, who resent the implication that she is more virtuous than they are. At the conclusion of the celebrations, Guézo takes his son, the Vidaho, into his own father's death chamber to give him advice on how to carry out his future responsibilities as king. During the ensuing conversation, he explains his lenient treatment of Doguicimi and praises her as a woman worthy of being a queen. From this moment on, Vidaho develops a passionate obsession for Doguicimi. Assuming that his exalted position entitles him to anything he desires, he is surprised to encounter resistance to his advances, to his promises of wealth and privilege, and to the love potions he has prepared for her. Finally, humiliated by her refusals, he conspires with the king's jealous wives and the spy Zanbounou to make it appear as if Doguicimi had betrayed Danhomê.

Guézo knows the accusations to be false, but he allows the woman to be beaten viciously by Migan and then imprisoned in one of the royal gaols, where she is, however, treated with consideration. During her incarceration, Danhomê undertakes a second war against Hounjroto, and this one is completely successful, although the victors discover that Toffa had long ago been killed in captivity. Nevertheless, his fellow captive Assogbaou had managed to retrieve the dead hero's skull, and in a chilling final scene, Doguicimi demonstrates the absolute fidelity she had vowed to maintain by insisting upon being buried alive with it.

According to references in the text, the first war against Hounjroto took place in the fourth year of Guézo's reign, and the second one was undertaken in the eleventh year; therefore, Hazoumé specifically sets the action of his novel in the period 1822-28 (the apparent discrepancy in the latter date results from the fact that the second war was waged earlier in the year – during the rainy season). However, he does not hesitate to compress historic details from other parts of Guézo's reign into this relatively short time span. For example, Guézo did not name a Vidaho until 1848, so the role played by Doguicimi's scorned admirer is historically anachronistic. The conspiracy that brought Guézo to the throne did not occur exactly as it is described in the novel, and the Palace arson that supposedly triggered the revolt actually took place much later when Adandozan's son Dakpo sought to vent his rage at the naming of a new Vidaho. Details from the expeditions against Abeokuta are woven into Hazoumé's descriptions of the Hounjroto wars, and the fact that the greatest heroic feats in the book are ascribed to a man named Toffa suggests the possibility that, despite the difference between the Gun and Fon pronunciations of the name, the author could be making a veiled allusion to another Toffa, the last king of Porto Novo during the late nineteenth century when tensions between that kingdom and Danhomê culminated in the

French campaign against Gbéhanzin. And although Doguicimi's story is based on an actual historical incident, Hazoumé transplants it into a different time period and elaborates the self-consciousness with which she confronts her fate.

These alterations are imposed upon history for several reasons. In writing the novel, Hazoumé established three major points of focus – Doguicimi's struggle to remain faithful to her conception of herself, Guézo's attempt to act wisely and humanely in a cultural setting that often obliges him to sanction cruel and irrational practices, and the historical reality of Danhomê as a social and moral entity. Some changes are introduced to heighten the drama of the dilemmas confronting the two major characters, others to compress a sense for the values that emerged during Danhomê's more than 250-year history into a six-and-a-half-year period. At the same time, it must not be forgotten that Hazoumé poured much of himself into the writing of *Doguicimi*, for he was also leaving a record of what he himself thought and believed about human nature. He did not approve of the slave trade or human sacrifice, and as a native of Porto Novo, he felt a certain ambivalence toward the imperial ambitions of nineteenth-century Danhomê. Doguicimi and Guézo serve him as exemplars of virtue, whereas his characterizations of the feckless Vidaho and the bloodthirsty Migan reflect the abuses to which the culture of Danhomê could lead. Historical facts were thus raw materials for a mosaic that he pieced together in conformity with his own image of a fictional world capable of illustrating his belief in the possibility of modernizing traditional society while preserving what was valuable in it.

This mosaic became a novel of epic proportions. *Doguicimi* is an epic in the sense that its two main characters embody the heroic qualities of an entire people; the values according to which they live are ideals that could also be distilled from the long history of the kingdom itself. The greatness of Danhomê is thus symbolized by the moral character of Doguicimi and Guézo, just as the greatness of Rome is present in Virgil's depiction of Aeneas. The wealth of historical and cultural detail in Hazoumé's novel does provide the necessary context for a proper understanding of the dramas experienced by Guézo and Doguicimi, but it also has an epic quality of its own, for *Doguicimi* is the story of a people as much as it is the story of individual characters. These details contribute to the impression that Hazoumé has created the symbolic equivalent of an entire society at a crucial turning point in its history. The sense of wholeness he imparts to this depiction is heightened by the impression that the mundane realities of everyday life have been transmuted into significance through ritualization. This wholeness encompasses petty intrigues hatched behind masks of piety and obsequiousness, but it also subsumes the complex system of cultural values that lent coherence and integrity to traditional Danhomê society.

From Hazoumé's vantage point, the 1820s represented a turning point in the history of Danhomê because the people at that time still adhered to a rigidly defined, traditional way of life, while the enlightened Guézo already glimpsed the possibility of a changed society based upon knowledge, compassion, and justice. He knew he could not eliminate certain popular practices because they were intimately related to the beliefs that linked the people together in a unified state. For example, the hundreds of victims sacrificed at the annual traditional celebrations were regarded as messengers to the royal ancestors and as tributes to their memory. A belief in the real existence of these ancestors was a crucial component of popular allegiance to the state, and if it were called into question, the state itself would be in danger of fragmentation. Like the lavish distribution of gifts and the extended feasting at royal expense during these festivities, the human sacrifices were part of a ritual process that effectively renewed the people's faith in their national identity. However, the international context was changing, and it would require changes in Danhomê.

The great wealth of Agbomê was derived largely from its participation in the slave trade, but by 1807, the British had delared it an illegal activity, and a few years later they began to blockade the West African coast in an attempt to prevent others from engaging in it. Such opposition to the slave trade seemed hypocritical to the Danhomênous, since the Europeans had initiated it in the first place. Nevertheless, they would ultimately have to adapt themselves to a situation in which there was no longer a market for what had previously been their most valuable export commodity. Guézo had foreseen this eventuality and encouraged the production of palm-oil as a means of coping with it. Yet the problem was not an exclusively economic one, for the moral assumptions behind the elimination of the slave trade would necessarily lead to the condemnation of other established practices in Danhomê – human sacrifice, for example, and the use of slave labor in the palm plantations. With the increasing pressure of direct European intervention, the real question was whether Danhomê could retain the essence of its African identity while altering its customs sufficiently to survive in a rapidly changing world. Guézo was aware of this dilemma, and his attempt to deal with it was part of his heroic accomplishment.

In seeking to convey the collective psychology of Danhomê in an epic narrative, Hazoumé adopts many oral story-telling techniques. The fictive narrator in *Doguicimi* is an enlightened individual from the kingdom itself; he refers to the people of Danhomê as "we," and he clearly identifies with their victories and accomplishments. His use of poetic metaphor, his anthropomorphizing tendencies, and his interjection of historical anecdotes are all characteristic of oral narration. In general, he provides one of the finest examples in African written literature of the ways in which words are employed in traditional society: the skillful use of historical precedent to make a point in a palaver, the transformation of an individual's experience or emotion into a spontaneous song, the shaping of disparate events into a unified story. Certainly there are elements of nineteenth-century European novelistic strategies in *Doguicimi*, but Hazoumé's emphasis upon the word as used in African society establisnes an epic tone that is hardly characteristic of European fiction. This tone is admirably well suited to the book's heroic subject matter and to its focus upon the historical identity of an entire people.

This identity is symbolically embodied in the absolute authority of the king, whom the Danhomênous regard as the all-powerful "father of life" and "source of all wealth." All decisions are thought to emanate from him, and his status is so exalted that no one is allowed to watch him eat or drink, since kings are not supposed to have the same needs as ordinary mortals. But as Hazoumé's portrayal of Guézo makes clear, the reality of the king's situation is quite different. He must abide by the will of the ancestors as communicated through the voice of the oracle. He is bound to follow precedents established by his predecessors. Religious taboos circumscribe his actions. Even important political decisions are made by the royal council and only promulgated in his name. Toward allies, sworn friends, wives, and others who might have performed some service for him, he has invariably incurred obligations that he is not at liberty to disregard when they come to him with requests of various kinds.

As he himself laments at one point: "Imprisoned in tradition, obsessed with customs from which I must not stray by a single step, and petitioned by those in my entourage, I am, most of the time, no more than an instrument in a multitude of hands that are invisible to the people. The king is perhaps the person with the least freedom in this entire kingdom." By emphasizing the constraints that limit his discretionary power, Guézo is defining the tragic paradox of his situation: no matter how strongly he might condemn a particular course of action in private, he will have to appear in public as its author if it has been dictated to him by custom, by a decision of the council, or by some personal obligation. For example, although he himself is uncomfortable with the idea of human sacrifice, he knows he cannot discontinue it without jeopardizing his throne, yet because Danhomênous and Europeans alike assume that he exercises absolute control over his kingdom, nearly everyone holds him responsible for a practice of which he personally disapproves. In this situation, he is buoyed by the hope of gradually influencing Danhomê to abandon its more sanguinary customs and therefore contents himself with small victories – sparing an intended victim, rewarding a noble action, protecting an innocent person, redirecting people's energies toward more productive activities. Hazoumé's Guézo is a good and wise man caught in a web of obligations that prevent him from acting as he would have preferred to act. His heroism resides in the fact that he does not give up. He does what he can do under the circumstances.

His treatment of Doguicimi is a case in point. When she berated him in public, she was committing a sacrilege and could have been instantly put to death. In speaking with his son after her second attack upon him, he explains why he spared her, but his words are ambiguous. On the surface, he is saying that Doguicimi acted from an intense loyalty to her missing husband, that her words were uttered in anger, and that she had demonstrated courage in speaking out when she knew she was facing almost certain death. Because he could forgive insults spoken in the heat of passion and because he wanted to hold up her example of nobility and courage to the masses, he refrained from punishing her.

This explanation of his leniency is accurate but incomplete, for Guézo also expresses his regret at not having recognized Doguicimi's virtues earlier at a time when he could still have made her a Wife of Panther. He recognizes in her the female equivalent of his own wisdom and strength, and in referring to her love for Toffa, he adds that he too has felt the sentiment of love. In other words, the king is strongly attracted to Doguicimi and regrets not having selected her as one of his own wives. He has the strength and authority to appropriate her as his possession, but he knows that, if he were to do so, he would be creating problems for the future governance of Danhomê and acting in a fashion unworthy of himself. Recognizing the constraints of his position, he acts nobly by resisting the impulse to take what he wants and by continuing to protect Doguicimi from a distance. Because of his position in society he cannot intervene to prevent all the afflictions that are heaped upon her, but without his comprehension of her character, she could never have become the heroine of a national epic.

Guézo's treatment of Doguicimi is merely one manifestation of the kingly ideal he embodies: power exercised with wisdom. His power is actually of two kinds; the first is physical, and the second is social or institutional. Guézo himself is a remarkably strong person. At one point, he wrestles a captured enemy king and literally breaks the man's neck; like his predecessors on the throne of Houégbaja, he recognizes that an army's victory in battle is similar to single combat in the sense that it depends upon the effective use of force. The annual wars fought during his reign illustrate his success in marshalling the kingdom's strength and reaffirming its dominance in the surrounding area.

But Guézo's strength is not only physical; it is also a function of the respect accorded to his position in society. The Danhomênous did not regard their king as a deity, but rather as the incarnation of the power of the state. All justice was carried out in his name, and he could order the execution of anyone except Migan. All the wealth in the land was owned by him, and he distributed it at his will. He was even regarded as the one who gave being and existence to his subjects. This exalted status was symbolized by the distance that was maintained between himself and the people. He enjoyed extraordinary wealth and privilege; for example, in his kingdom he was the only person allowed to wear sandals and to be carried in a hammock. All messages were conveyed to him through an intermediary. In public, his subjects were always expected to prostrate themselves in his presence. The image that best corresponds to the power and brilliance of the king's position in society is the sun, which Hazoumé's narrator repeatedly describes in anthropomorphic terms. Like the sun, Guézo's brilliance is the outward appearance of power.

The inner workings of this power are far more pragmatic than most of his subjects realize. Guézo himself understands that political or military power is a combination of physical strength and the knowledge of how to apply that strength to greatest advantage. Just as Homer's Odysseus defeats physically stronger opponents by outwitting them, Guézo has no qualms about adopting ruses to conquer his enemies or to govern effectively. For example, during the second war against Hounjroto, his troops take elaborate precautions to surprise the Mahinous rather than confronting them on the battlefield as they had the first time. The result is a profitable victory that might not have been won in a simple test of physical strength.

In a similar way, Guézo skillfully uses Danhomê's rigid customs to maintain himself in power. Part of the loyalty that his subjects feel toward him derives from the belief that he is the continuator of a venerable tradition. This belief is reinforced at his enthronement when he is thought to communicate with his predecessors. And it is renewed each year during the traditional ceremonies when the people celebrate their common identity, momentarily forgetting social distinctions in a spate of eating, drinking, and dancing. Mountains of presents are thrown to them by the king, who also offers them the spectacle of war captives being brutally sacrificed. Guézo himself neither condones the sacrifices nor respects the commoners who scurry to snatch up the cloths and cowries he tosses in their midst, but he participates in such activities because he knows they consolidate his hold on the loyalty of the masses.

Similarly, he is always ready to mislead the people if he believes it is in the interest of the state to do so. On a quite practical level, he increased Danhomê's trade with the white men, but he shrewdly maintained the royal monopoly over all imports so that he could be regarded as the sole source of all European goods in his kingdom. Exploiting the rivalries among his ministers and seeking to prevent people from forming strong allegiances with anyone except himself, Guézo is a master at manipulating power.

Yet Guézo's heroic virtue is more than power; in fact, it resides primarily in his aspiration to exercise power with wisdom. In his soliloquies and in the solemn advice he gives Vidaho, he reveals that he wants to be a compassionate and just ruler who motivates his people to pursue excellence. To accomplish this goal, he feels he must understand his own society intimately. As he himself says, "Danhomê is no more than a profound knowledge of the very complex and mysterious soul of the Danhomênous." Having plumbed the depths of this soul, he realizes that the seed of potential failure lies in a widespread propensity to denigrate excellence rather than emulating it. His refusal to order the execution of Doguicimi for her blasphemies against him clearly reflects his attitude toward this tendency in Danhomê society, for he believes that her courage and loyalty are the moral virtues upon which the greatness of Danhomê depends. He also knows that those conspiring against her are acting largely out of jealousy; by protecting her against them, he is helping to create public acceptance for a model of the noble behavior he believes necessary for the future well-being of the state.

If Guézo is Hazoumé's portrait of an ideal king, his son Vidaho exemplifies the unworthiness to govern. Whereas Guézo sublimates his love of Doguicimi for the good of Danhomê, Vidaho single-mindedly pursues her for his personal gratification. As the designated successor to the throne, he is the second most powerful person in the kingdom, but unlike his father, he desires power for the prerogatives it brings, not for the opportunity of greatness it offers. While his father is absent during the first Hounjroto war, Vidaho hastens to persecute everyone he believes to have slighted him, and he at first hates Doguicimi because he feels himself implicated in her diatribes against his father. In neither case does he share his father's perceptiveness and sense of justice; he thinks only of himself.

The same is true of his feelings for Doguicimi after his father's praise of her have convinced him that she is the most noble woman in Danhomê. His immediate impulse is to take possession of her because he assumes he can have anything he wants. He also assumes that she or any other woman would quickly succumb to the lure of his wealth and status and to the love potions prepared for her at his behest by the local fetishists. After her initial rebuffs, he continues to regard her as an object to be attacked and conquered, not as a human being whose sorrow is aggravated by his solicitations. Preoccupied with his own selfish desires, Vidaho does not hesitate to lie and cheat in the hope of attaining his objective; he even participates in the conspiracy that results in Doguicimi's public beating, and he later pretends to have had nothing to do with it. Despite all his efforts, however, Doguicimi remains steadfast in her fidelity to Toffa.

In the end, she pays Vidaho the ultimate insult by allowing herself to be buried alive rather than accepting his offer of marriage. But whereas he is afraid of death, she is supremely indifferent to it. In this sense, she is stronger than he is, and his fear of death is merely one manifestation of his weakness. Essentially he is blind to all that his father sees so clearly, and his blindness suggests that he will be just as unsuccessful in the exercise of political and military power as he was in his pursuit of Doguicimi. A cowardly, indecisive man, he desires to enjoy the perquisites of power without assuming the moral responsibilities that are incumbent upon those who exercise it. Although fascinated by Doguicimi, he is incapable of understanding her because he lacks his father's conviction that courage and nobility are more valuable than possessions and empty titles.

In contrast, Doguicimi demonstrates how an individual can act in conformity with Guézo's ideal; her attitudes are just the opposite of Vidaho's. Whereas he is willing to compromise any principle in his pursuit of personal gratification, she exercises disciplined restraint to defend her belief in an ideal that transcends selfish desire. At one point she rejects Vidaho's invitation to come and live with him, saying, "no, Your Highness, I could not have a better life in any Palace." With these words, she is telling him there is something more important than anything he can offer her; it is the sense of honor that arises from the knowledge of having acted in accordance with an ideal that one has adopted as the hallmark of one's own character. Doguicimi's ideal is absolute fidelity to the man she loves.

At the beginning of Hazoumé's story, she has only been in Toffa's household for two years. One of his many wives, she was given to him by Guézo from among the batch of women he distributed each year in rewarding distinguished service to the kingdom; however, she has already become his favorite wife. He is attracted not only to her robust beauty, but also to her wise and noble temperament. When he has important decisions to make, he invariably seeks her counsel. And when he is in need of solace, he insists on being with her, although her co-wives soon grow jealous of the attention he lavishes on her.

Toffa is a strong and noble-spirited man who attaches less importance to material possessions than do most of his fellow princes, but he is also conservative in his adherence to traditional customs. During his speech against the first

Hounjroto war, he attacks the duplicity of all white men and decries the changes that are taking place in Danhomê. The misogynistic attitudes he expresses to Doguicimi on the night before he departs for battle reflect his frustration at being obliged to participate in a war he regards as unjust and ill-timed, but his remarks about "creatures with seven pairs of ribs" also reveal his fundamentally conservative view of the world.

But Doguicimi does not conform to such stereotyped notions of womanhood; for example, she knows that men and women have the same number of ribs because she has examined human skeletons in the ditches outside the walls of Agbomê. Despite differences of opinion, however, there is a strong emotional bond between Doguicimi and Toffa. Each respects the other's nobility, and they share the desire to pursue a life grounded in wisdom. Thus, when he attacks women in general and specifically calls her fidelity into question, Doguicimi understands Toffa and does not stop loving him. On the contrary, his words become a challenge to her, and she spends the rest of her life proving them wrong. He has obliged her to define an ideal image of herself, and during his absence, her honor consists of living in accordance with that image. Despite the pressures exerted on her by Vidaho and others, she maintains an unwavering allegiance to it. By remaining faithful to Toffa, then, she is actually being true to her own image of herself.

Doguicimi does commit blasphemy when she publicly attacks the king, and as she herself later admits, her accusations are based on an erroneous interpretation of appearances. What makes her gesture heroic is the courage with which she defends a passionately held ideal. Strong emotional involvement is a necessary prerequisite for heroic action, but strong emotions often blind people to the reality of the situation in which they are living. This happens to Doguicimi, and Guézo has the wisdom to recognize that her willingness to act in the face of death distinguishes her from the vast majority of his subjects, who lack the capacity for passionate engagement in a noble cause. Her defiance is a threat to the passive obedience that assures his control over the people of Danhomê, but Guézo is sufficiently far-sighted to realize that passive obedience can never produce the greatness to which he aspires. For this reason, he spares her life and holds her up as an example to others. Throughout the rest of the story, Doguicimi's passionate attachment to an ideal sustains her in adversities that parallel those of Toffa during his captivity among the Mahinous. She suffers Vidaho's importunities, the vicious public beating inflicted on her by Migan, and a lengthy imprisonment, but she never abandons her resolve to remain faithful to her husband. Once again she is acting courageously, although on a false premise: she lives in the hope of being reunited with Toffa at a time when he has already been slain by one of the Mahi regents.

However, the rightness or wrongness of her perception is of minor significance in comparison with the ennobling quality of her endeavor, which is no less than the unconditional defense of her idea of who she is. When the truth becomes clear to her, she embraces it with the same courage she has demonstrated in all her previous actions. The final scene of Doguicimi lying in Toffa's sepulchre, her eyes open and his skull cradled in her arms, represents the ultimate proof of her fidelity. Upon first marrying her, Toffa had given her the name Doguicimi, which means "distinguish me" or "do me honor." Her willingness to die and accompany him to the land of the spirits does do him honor, but it also distinguishes her and testifies to an extraordinary human capacity for shaping one's life according to a passionately held ideal. Doguicimi's final act transcends the specific circumstances in which it was performed and reaffirms the possibility of heroic behavior in a world that is often hostile to it.

Guézo and Doguicimi never engage in a face-to-face conversation during the course of the novel, but each of them exercises an important influence over the other. Guézo's understanding of Doguicimi's noble temperament allows her the opportunity to demonstrate her potential for heroic dignity, and her example draws out the best and most noble aspects of his character. Yet the moral qualities of both individuals ultimately derive from the cultural and historical context in which they are embedded. The final chapter of *Doguicimi* is entitled "A Danhomê Victory," even though the military victory over Hounjroto had taken place in the previous chapter. In many ways, the novel's center of focus is the historical reality of an entire kingdom, and by depicting Doguicimi's final heroic gesture as a victory for Danhomê, Hazoumé is identifying her and her positive qualities with the "true nature" of a people struggling to cope with a changing world.

In one of her long meditations, Doguicimi hopes that, if the French ever make Danhomê part of their colonial empire, they will preserve what is good in the kingdom. From Hazoumé's point of view, this goodness resides primarily in human relationships and modes of understanding. For example, Guézo at one point explains to his son Vidaho that the state is like a large pot riddled with holes; water can only be kept in the pot if each member of society maintains a finger over one of the holes. Implicit in this metaphor is the recognition that each member of society needs to accept partial responsibility for the well-being of the whole. Within the context of nineteenth-century Danhomê, this principle meant that each subject owed primary allegiance to the king, but in more general terms, it is also applicable to contemporary Africa, where a communal ethic represents the best hope for long-term survival. Historical Danhomê also manifested other virtues – a sense of personal dignity, an absolute integrity associated with institutions like the blood oath, a profoundly religious respect for the ultimate mystery of life – and Hazoumé was convinced that they offered a more suitable basis for modern African society than did the materialistic individualism of the West.

During the 1930s it would have been difficult for Hazoumé to publish a book that openly criticized the French colonial presence in Africa. Besides, he was not opposed to many aspects of the French system. But he was acutely aware of the abuses that characterized it, and when he portrayed a Glinci (British) mission to Guézo in the novel, his criticism of British hypocrisy and insensitivity could just as easily have been applied to the French, whom he took great pains not to offend in any explicit references he made to them. Both Guézo and Doguicimi

xl

recognize the contradiction between the self-righteous British condemnation of Danhomê's participation in the slave trade and the fact that the British had been among the first to encourage it along the West African coast. The novel's two major characters also censure the British ambassadors for failing to comprehend the complexity of Danhomê society and for dealing with it only in terms of their own preconceived notions. The latter point was one of the most common themes in Hazoumé's own journalistic writings, and it was undoubtedly one of the principal motivations behind his conceptualization of *Doguicimi*.

What Hazoumé admired about the French colonial system were the ideals it had brought to Africa: the principle of universal love in Christianity, a respect for individual rights, the scientific approach to useful knowledge, and the goal of peace among warring tribes. To a certain extent, Guézo and Doguicimi intuitively adopted these ideals long before the French actually occupied Danhomê. Both came to believe that the popular human sacrifices were futile and inhuman. Both aspired to kindliness and justice in their dealings with others. One might almost say that they were Christians before their time. In the book that Hazoumé wrote in collaboration with Msgr. Steinmetz, Africans are repeatedly portrayed as simple creatures with an innate vocation for religion. According to Steinmetz's missionary ideology, which is cited approvingly by Hazoumé, the introduction of Christianity would allow Africans to pursue such a vocation by sloughing off the "dross of reprehensible customs." In *Doguicimi*, Hazoumé presents both the African potential for greatness and the fetters that might prevent that greatness from being realized.

In fact, *Doguicimi* is as much a critique of traditional Danhomê as it is a eulogy to it. Much of the ethnographic material in the novel was part of the kingdom's secret history, and Hazooumé knew that some people reproached him for making it public. In his own mind, he justified the publication of such information as a means of establishing the truth on the basis of which progress toward a better society might be made. If the truth included ignorance, injustice, and unnecessary cruelty, Hazoumé felt they ought to be exposed for what they were. Nearly every character in the novel accepts the efficacy of fetishes, gris-gris, and love potions, but the attentive reader will notice that they generally fail to bring about the desired result; in fact, Hazoumé even describes instances in which the message of the oracle is falsely reported or the trial by poison dishonestly administered so that certain individuals can impose their will upon the people. For him, all these practices are part of a complex belief system that is intimately related to the positive values of traditional Danhomê. Parts of this system may be misguided, he agrees, but they cannot simply be eradicated without recognizing that they perform a vital function within the system. If the valuable qualities of Danhomê are to be retained, this function must be fulfilled in other ways, and that is precisely what Hazoumé hoped French colonialism would accomplish in Africa.

According to Hazoumé, another weakness of nineteenth-century Danhomê was its blindness to the truth about its own place in the world. The solipsistic attitudes of the Danhomênous were even reflected in the epithets they used in addressing the king. When they referred to him as "Master of the Universe," they were expressing confidence in his supposedly absolute power, but in reality his power was far from absolute, as his defeat during the first Hounjroto war and his inability to control the slave trade made abundantly clear. Hazoumé was certain that persistence in this false conception of Danhomê's place in the world could only exacerbate self-destructive tendencies already present in society. For example, human sacrifice might have been comprehensible within the context of ancestor worship in Danhomê, but it also represented a waste of valuable resources and isolated the kingdom from the rest of the world.

Most victims of these sacrifices were war captives, and they had been reduced to to the level of non-human "beasts" in the minds of the Danhomênous; however, Hazoumé repeatedly demonstrates that these beasts are just as human as the Danhomênous who rejoice in their dying agonies. A similar message is communicated by his depiction of the starving children who sift through the dust in search of cowries after the lavish traditional celebrations or by his portrayal of innocent young girls offering trays of drinks to the British mission minutes before their own heads would be served on the same trays to the horrified guests. Conversely, many aristocrats and commoners in Danhomê are revealed as corrupt, petty-minded, unreflective, or cruel. In other words, Hazoumé succeeded in portraying a great and powerful kingdom not from the vantage point of its own myths (although he made use of them in telling his story), but from a larger human perspective that illuminates its negative as well as its positive sides. This perspective is a projection of Hazoumé's own world view with all its breadth of vision and all its ambivalence. In a very real sense, then, the greatness of *Doguicimi* reflects the greatness of its author's soul.

Notes

[1] I would like to thank A. Joseph Djivo, Adrien Huannou, Abiola Irele, and Victor LeVine for their helpful comments and suggestions on this introductory essay. I am also deeply grateful to Donald Herdeck for his encouragement during the course of my work on *Doguicimi*. His contributions to the field of African literary studies are recognized by all those who have worked with him. Finally, I would like to express my sincere appreciation to G. Micheal Riley and the College of Humanities at The Ohio State University who have provided generous suppport for the completion of this project.

[2] Letter from A. Joseph Djivo, 21 January 1988.

[3] Paul Hazoumé, *Cinquante Ans d'apostolat au Dahomey: Souvenirs de S. E. Mgr. Fr. Steinmetz*. Lyon: Procure des Missions Africaines, n.d., p. 6.

[4] For this and other details about Hazoumé's life, I am endebted to Adrien Huannou's biographical references in "Paul Hazoumé: Romancier" (*Présence Africaine*, 105-06 [1978]: 203-15), "Hommage à un grand écrivain: Paul Hazoumé" (*Présence Africaine*, 114 [1980]: 204-08), and *La Littérature béninoise de langue franaise des origines à nos jours* (Paris: Karthala, 1984) *passim*.

[5] This is the popular etymology for the word, and Hazoumé alludes to it several times in *Doguicimi*. However, when "ho" is pronounced as a high tone rather than as a low one, it means house or residence; thus, "Danhomê" could be interpreted simply as "in the house of Dan." Letter from A. Joseph Djivo. February 21, 1988.

[6] For details about these ministerial responsibilities, I am indebted to A. Joseph Djivo. Letter of 21 February 1988.

[7] Frederick E. Forbes, *Dahomey and the Dahomeyans, Being the Journals of Two Missions to the King of Dahomey and Resdience at His Capital in the Years 1849 and 1850* (London: 1851), p. 6.

[8] I. A. Akinjo̱gbin, *Dahomey and Its Neighbors 1708-1818* (Cambridge: University Press, 1967), p. 4.

Exterior View of the King's Outer Palace Walls at Agbomê (Glelé, 1870)

Gates in the Wall around Agbomê (Forbes, 1850)

Procession of King Guezo's Wealth at Agbomé (Forbes, 1850)

Selected Bibliography

Works by Hazoumé:

Cinquante Ans d'apostalat au Dahomey: Souvenirs de Mgr. S. E. Fr. Steinmetz. Lyon: Procure des Missions Africaines, n. d. [1942 or 1943].

Doguicimi. 1938; rpt. Paris: G.-P. Maisonneuve et Larose, 1978.

Le Pacte du sang au Dahomey. 1937; rpt. Paris: Institut d'Ethnologie, 1956.

Historical and Ethnological Works About Danhomê:

Akinjogbin, J. A. *Dahomey and Its Neighbors: 1708-1818.* Cambridge: Cambridge University Press, 1967.

Argyle, W. J. *The Fon of Dahomey: A History and Ethnography of the Old Kingdom.* Oxford: Clarenden Press, 1966.

Baba Kaké, Ibrahima, "L'Armée dahoméenne aux XVIII et XIX siècles," in *Les Arméees traditionelles de l'Afrique.* Libreville (Gabon): Editions Lion, 1980. Pp. 164-73.

Burton, Sir Richard. *A Mission to Gelele, King of Dahome.* 1864; rpt. London: Routledge and Kegan Paul, 1966.

Djivo, Adrien Joseph. *Guézo: La Rénovation du Dahomey.* Paris: A. B. C. and Dakar, Abidjan: N. E. A., 1977.

Duncan, John. *Travels in Western Africa in 1845 and 1846.* 1847; rpt. London: Frank Cass, 1968. 2 Vols.

Forbes, Frederick E. *Dahomey and the Dahomeyans, Being the Journals of Two Missions to the King of Dahomey and Residence at His Capital in the Years 1849 and 1850.* 1851; rpt. London: Frank Cass, 1966.

Glélé, Maurice Ahanhanzo, *Le Danxome: Du Pouvoir aja à la nation fon.* Paris: Nubia, 1974.

Herskovits, Melville J. *Dahomey: An Ancient West African Kingdom.* 1938; rpt. Evanston: Northwestern University Press, 1967. 2 Vols.

Quénum, Maximilien. *Au Pays des Fons: Us et coutumes du Dahomey.* 1931; 3rd ed. Paris: Maisonneuve et Larose, 1983.

Verger, F. Pierre. *Flux et reflux de la traite des Nègres.* Paris: Mouton, 1908. Esp. pp. 171-72.

Works About Hazoumé and "Doguicimi":

Adande, Alexandre Sènou. "Paul Hazoumé: Ecrivain et chercheur," *Présence Africaine* 114 (1980): 197-203 (contains bibliography).

Blair, Dorothy. *African Literature in French: A History of Creative Writing in French from West and Equatorial Africa.* Cambridge: Cambridge University Press, 1976. Pp. 75-77.

Chemain, Roger. *La Ville dans le roman.* Paris: L'Harmattan, 1981. Pp. 26-52.

Chevrier, Jacques. *Littérature nègre.* Paris: Armand Colin, 1974. Pp. 34-35.

Clark, Priscilla P., "West African Prose Fiction," in Albert Gérard, ed. *European-Language Writing in Sub-Saharan Africa.* Budapest: Akadémiai Kiodó, 1986. I: 121-23.

Decraene, Philippe. "Paul Hazoumé, doyen des écrivains dahoméens." *L'Afrique Littéraire et Artistique* 23 (1972): 11-12.

Erickson, John D. *Nommo: African Fiction in French South of the Sahara.* York, S. C.: French Literature Publications, 1979. Pp. 127-28.

Fabre, Michel. "*Doguicimi*," in Ambroise Kom, ed., *Dictionnaire des oeuvres littéraires négro-africaines de langue franaise.* Sherbrooke: Editions Naaman, 1983. Pp. 194-95.

Gleason, Judith. *This Africa.* Evanston: Northwestern University Press, 1965. Pp. 48-54.

Huannou, Adrien. "Hommage à un grand écrivain: Paul Hazoumé," *Présence Africaine* 114 (1980): 204-08.

......*La Littérature béninoise de langue franaise des origines à nos jours.* Paris: Karthala, 1984. Pp. 73-78, 99- 103, 116-18, 136-45, 164-69, and *passim.*

...... "Paul Hazoumé: Romancier," *Présence Africaine* 105-6 (1978): 203-15.

...... "Pour saluer la réédition de *Doguicimi*," *Recherche, Pédagogie et Culture* 41-42 (1979): 59-60.

...... 'Reflexions sur l'oeuvre littéraire de Paul Hazoumé," *Culture Franaise* (1982): 37-43.

...... and Robert Mane. *"Doguicimi" de Paul Hazoumé*. Paris: L'Harmattan, 1987.

Kane, Mohamadou. *Roman africain et tradition*. Dakar: N. E. A., 1982. Pp. 71-76, 379-82, and *passim*.

Mayer, Jean. "Le Roman en Afrique noire francophone, Tendences et Structures," *Etudes Franaise* (Montreal) 3,2 (1967): 169-95 (esp. 172-73).

Pagéard, Robert. *Littérature négro-africaine*. Paris: Le Livre Africain, 1966. Pp. 56-57.

"Paul Hazoumé (1890-1980)," *Afrique Contemporaine* 109 (1980): 48.

Vignonde, Jean-Norbert. "Les Précurseurs: Felix Couchoro, Paul Hazoumé," *Notre Librairie* 69 (1983): 33-40.

The King of Dahomey (Danhomê) Granting an Audience

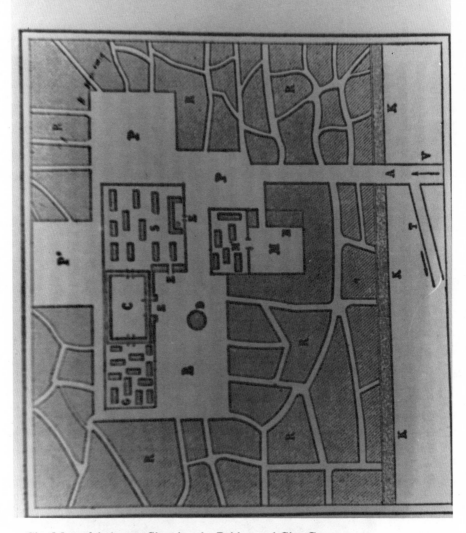

City Map of Agbomê, Showing the Bridge and City Gate
on the Road from Canna (A), the Main Courtyard (B), the
King's Palace (C), the Other Courtyards (P), the Homes
of the Royal Wives (S), the Residence of Mêwou (R), and
the Ditch and Wall Surrounding the City (Râpin, 1856)

Sculpture Wall of the Palace at Agbomè (Glélé)

Details in Sculpture Wall, Bas-Relief, Glélé Palace

Reception of the Troubadours in the Principal Courtyard
at Agbomê (Forbes, 1850), and Captured Slaves Being
Thrown from the Sacrificial Altar at Agbomê (Dalzel,
1793)

Reception of the Royal Wives at Agbomê (Forbes, 1850);

The Sepulchers of Agaja, Tégbéssou, Kpengla, and Agongló

Human Victims Being Led to Sacrifice at Agbomê

The Final Day of the Annual Celebrations as Witnessed
by European Ambassadors (Dalzel, 1793)

The King of Dahomey (Danhomê) Going to War at the
Head of a Column of Amazons (Dalzel, 1793)

The Royal Wives in Procession (Dalzel, 1793)

The Assens Representing the Illustrious Dead in the Kingdom of Dahomey (Hazoumé, 1931)

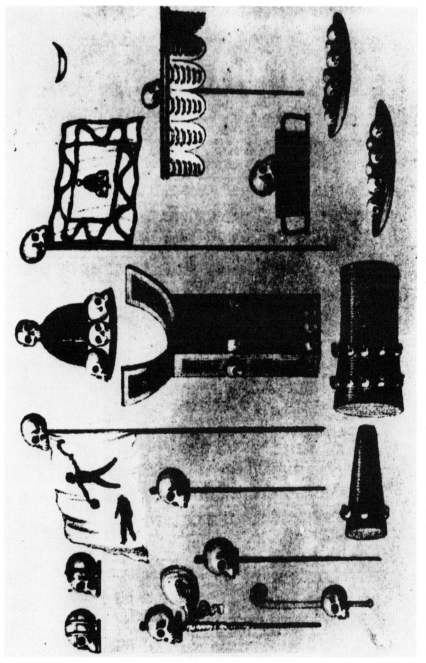

Skull Ornaments and Banners from the Kingdom of Dahomey (Forbes, 1850)

The Ceremonial Throne of Guezo (Glélé, 1970)

King Guezo's Ajalalazin, a Symbol of the Unity of Dahomey (Glélé, 1970)

A Soldier in the Dahomey Army (Forbes, 1850)

Amazon in the Service of the King of Dahomey

Chapter 1

A Plan for War

The cocks had concluded their second concert of crowings a short while ago. The "kro! kro! kro!" of the little bell on Panligan Déguénon Fonfi's large double bell tumbled forth, abrupt and drawn out, announcing that the public crier of this reign was rendering hommage to all his predecessors, living and dead, as he mentally enumerated their names and solicited their assistance before undertaking his perilous duty of extolling the reigns of the past and the present.

At regular intervals, the sounds of "kioun-go! kioun-go! kioun-go!" now interrupted the quavering voice of the public crier who was circling the Grand Palace (the work of nine reigns) and casting the proverbial epithets of the kings into the calm with which the night still enveloped the earth.

Upon the lips of those Danhomênous who heard him, fervent prayers addressed to the ancestors hastened to form, imploring their blessings for the Danhomê which they had founded, enlarged, and made as powerful as it was prosperous and which they should continue to protect.

Although he was more than four cubits tall, the head of the public crier did not reach a fourth of the way up the walls that rose majestically beside him and were crowned with a thick band of dry straw. Their haughty silhouette defied the rain which, if they had not had this head-covering, would indeed have brought them down eventually. Not the slightest crack marred these walls of beautiful red clay bricks, which presented a more lively appearance than the grey soil found near swamps and mountains.

In order to mould the clay in these walls on such an exceptionally dry plateau, the people had expended great pains and countless days of forced labor, during which, in the extreme heat, they had mixed their sweat with the water carried from a great distance by men, women, and adolescents under the vigilant supervision of overseers whose whips were constantly spurring on those who lagged behind.

The height and thickness of the walls, like the generous proportions of the

1

exclusively ironwood portals, were imposing and unquestionably reflected the grandiose conception that the people had of their king, a demi-god who, moreover, was regarded as the Lord of the Universe and could not therefore be housed in the low, cramped huts of simple mortals.

Each reign imposed upon itself an imperious duty to enlarge the Palace – a sacred patrimony – by erecting walls that rendered it inviolable as well as everything it contained: venerated ancestors sleeping their last sleep in tombs, to the maintenance of which descendants, selected for their advanced age and their virtue, devoted the last part of their lives; the throne of Houégbaja and the Idol of the Danhomênous who was presently reigning there; all the women who were obliged to live in seclusion from the defilement of men, because of the sacred aura that surrounded them as the result of certain religious rites performed in their honor – they included the venerable Representatives of the Queen Mothers, who for that reason were called Mothers of Panther, and the Pojitos (the Representatives of the Mothers of the kingdom's two prime ministers, Migannon and Mêwounon), who governed the domestic affairs of the Palace; they also included the royal Wives known as Poussis-Zê (Wives of Panther – "get out of the way"), from whose loins alone could issue princes capable of being designated as future rulers. These women even had to avoid contact with ordinary queens, who could pollute them. Young women of unimpeachable innocence were consecrated by special ceremonies and then commissioned into the service of the Wives of Panther, walking in front of them whenever they moved about the Palace and shaking a little bell attached to their neck as they warned any possible passersby, "Get out of the way! Get out of the way!" And that is how the name "Poussis-Zê" came to be associated with the royal Wives. The Palace also contained a number of simple queens, whose union with the Idol of the Danhomênous sufficed to cloak them in respect; furthermore, it housed the royal treasures – products of the Danhomênous' art that the kings strove to elevate to the heights of perfection and trophies of war that told the story of Danhomê victories in battle.

Each king also built a new doorway for himself to enter and leave this Palace and another one for the Queen Mother. Only one of them refrained from doing so, for he interpreted his predecessor's advice – "a son should always follow in the footsteps of his father" – as an injunction against opening his own doorway in the walls of the Palace; he insisted upon using the one that had served his noble Father.

Having left the Door of Awonnoumi, with its walls embellished by two machete-sculpted bas-reliefs, and facing Cloubousso, a monument raised by Pingla at approximately ten bamboos[1] from the Palace with stones carried from Gbowêlê in Mahi country to commemorate his victory over it, Pinglan began his

---

[1]   A bamboo is a traditional Dahomeyan measurement of length; it is roughly the equivalent of five meters. (translator's note)

2

round with praises for Houégbaja, who had instituted among the Aladahonous the practice of honoring the glory of their kings in imitation of a similar custom at the court of Awêssou, a powerful king into whose presence one entered only after having passed through the forty-one doors of his Palace, although he had been reduced to vassalage by Houégbaja:

"The indigo that has been steeping for several days can not help but dye the cloth: Houégbaja has left an indelible mark upon this kingdom! They vaunted my bravery, and my enemy blanched!"

"· ·
· ."

In several proverbial phrases, the public crier recalled the history of the Aladahonous' arrival in this part of the world: for refusing to give Daco-Donou a piece of land that he had requested and for threatening him with arrows, the local ruler Agri was enterred with his quiver in the foundation of the Palace that was built against his will and, for this very reason, called Agrigomê so that the memory of this initial victory could be preserved forever.

"Desiring to construct a residence for his successor, Houégbaja, the second king, also encountered a refusal on the part of another land-holder, Dan, when he sought to enlarge his concession. Dan suffered the same fate as Agri, whose insolence he had repeated. Houégbaja named the new Palace Danhomê to indicate that he had erected it above the last remains of Dan, who – he too – was punished for having disregarded the law of hospitality."

After having celebrated the glory of Houégbaja, who was venerated as the founder of the kingdom because he had conceived the idea that the wandering tribe should settle permanently in the area and subject its inhabitants to his rule, Panligan proclaimed in a more solemn tone of voice: "Victor over Dala, you were brave!" And with a sharp rap of his stick against the small bell of his large double bell, he marked the end of the proverbial epithets of the second king.

Walking along the walls of the Fêdê Palace, which had been constructed by Tégbéssou, Panligan extolled the merits of the third king: "The clever monkey who gambols about in the trees always reaches his goal! Acaba held firm sway over the Danhomê! The Just Man does not fear to punish the crimes of his relatives! · ·
· Victor over Yahazê, you were brave!"

Panligan dragged his feet since his voice did not finish the epithets of Acaba until he had reached Agoua – a Portal of Fêdê decorated with palm fronds and an actual powder keg that bore witness to the warlike passions of Tégbéssou, follower in the footsteps of Agaja at Gléhoué and terror of the Mahinous. This king loved to tell his people that he always kept his powder dry in order to fight the enemies of the Danhomê, a custom that the sentiment of the people translated into the following advice: "Smoker, beware when passing in front of Agoua as long as the rain has not tempered the air in this place."

In several steps, Panligan found himself beneath the walls of the part of Agrigomê that had been built by Agaja, who lived there at the beginning of

3

his regency. The fourth king of Danhomê had added a floor to signal both his intention to increase the size of Danhomê and his designs upon Gléhoué; like a bird of prey hidden in the trees, he studied that prosperous land, coveted by his people, from the top of his Palace, and he would soon swoop down upon it to conquer it with his ships, which were depicted in the bas-reliefs that embellished each side of the Door of the Palace.

Before the Door of Takin-Baya, the name of which called to mind the presumptuousness of the enemy chief whom Agaja had condemned to sweep the immense courtyard of the Grand Palace every day, Panligan recited at great length the proverbial epithets of the Great King, to whom the gratitude of his subjects had accorded the glorious title, "Agaja-the-Conqueror-of-the-Ships," because he had subdued the countries that extended from the foot of the plateau to the coast and thus enabled the Danhomê – cramped between the mountains to the North and the swamps to the South, the Coufo to the West and the Zou to the East – to breath the air of the sea and to trade with the Whites, who were distributing marvelous things in the Houéda kingdom that had been so inexorably closed to the Danhomênous until the beginning of the fourth reign.

The significance of the service he had rendered to the country was such that, far from taking offense at the cynicism with which he was elevated to Houégbaja's throne, usurped from his nephew, the fourth king boasted of it in his maxims, which the people applauded: "The tree that has not been stripped of its branches can not be placed on any hearth! Agaja laughs at all his enemies! The powerful man who requests permission to examine the property of another man beats him and takes it from him! The conqueror skillful at taking captives. . . . . Victor over Houfon of Savi, Conqueror-of-the-Ships, you were glorious!"

Circling the Palace to the left, the public crier started reciting the proverbial epithets of Agaja's successor and passed in front of the Door called "Hongboji," which was reserved for the comings and goings of the queens and guarded by the "Ahossitins," trusted servants whose mutilation eliminated any possibility that they might corrupt the virtue of the women; they had been placed under the orders of Ajaho, who, in addition to his functions as the Royal Prosecutor, served as Director of Internal Security and Public Morals in this kingdom: "The jacket placed around the neck of the buffalo can not be taken from him by force! Tégbéssou will abdicate for no one! The wellspring has pierced a hole in the rock! The exploit of Agaja's great son – the sea – is infinitely more prodigious! . . . . Victor over Zanou Houngnon, you were a great king!"

Panligan stopped in front of Patinsa, the Door of Danhomê – Houégbaja's Palace with its walls adorned by bas-reliefs, arrows, and quivers – and celebrated for a moment the courage of the sixth king: "The iron heated to redness defies the hand! Pingla the brave will confound all his enemies! The powerful axe will fell with impunity the tree in the enemy's forest. . . . ."

4

Passing between the Palace on his left and Amoussou-Coli's hut that was next to it on his right, the public crier continued his praises of Pingla until he finished them in front of the Door of Pojito Adonon – the Queen Mother of Acaba. He stopped at the foot of an apple tree[2] that shaded the Palace by this Door, which was also used for the comings and goings of the Queen Ahangbé, who was invested with a portion of the royal powers; she was the twin sister of Acaba, and custom decreed that she be accorded the same rights as her brother who had ruled in the Palace.

". . . . .

. . . . Victor over Houédanou Agbamou, you were brave!"

He quickened his pace as he crossed Ganhohi, a small market established on the flank of the Palace to supply food for the prisoners of the Palace. The Door which opened onto this market also served as an exit for the bodies of the human victims who had been sacrificed in the Palace and for other cadavres as well. To proclaim the proverbial epithets of a king on this site would be to call down misfortunes upon an august head; for that reason, Panligan confined himself to striking his double bell: kioun-go! kioun-go! kioun-go!

He began the maxims of King Agonglo in front of the Door of Pojito-Chayi (the Queen Mother of Pingla): "The scent of musk is the most pervasive! Agonglo's reign will be distinguished by great conquests! The iron bracelet that is being used will not rust! The needle cannot split wood because of its pointed end! The hoe cannot cut wood because of the breadth of its blade! The termite hill can not pretend to equal the mountain! . . . .

. . . ."

He continued his recital before the Door of Vitounsa, which served the Queen Mother of Agonglo (the Pojito Sênoumê), and then in front of the Door of Gomê, which Guézo had cut in the wall for his mother, the Pojito Agontimê. The name of this Door was only mysterious for the commoners among the Danhomênous, for it had been derived from an invocation suitable for liberating the force of a gris-gris that had been buried beneath the threshold; it reminded the princes and other dignitaries of the Pojita's sad destiny and expressed Guézo's hope of being once again reunited his mother, who had been sold to the slave-traders by the previous king.

". . . . .

. . . ."

"Victor over Ajognon of Gbowêlê, you were brave!" concluded Panligan in front of the Adanjloacodé Door, which had been built by Agonglo. The coat of arms (two pineapples and two birds) that had been carved in bas-relief on the walls to the right and to the left recalled, in the first instance, the name of this king, and, in the second, his favorite maxim: "Ordinary birds fear the nut of the raphia palm because it is so hard that it damages their beaks, but the parrot delights in it; the king, who is bravery itself, laughs at Lightning, who fills

[2] This particular tree produces a fleshy, fibrous apple containing a fairly large core formed by two husks, inside of which is a kernel. After being dried and ground up, this kernel is used to prepare a mucilaginous, stringy "caloulou" that resembles a gumbo. (author's note)

simple mortals with terror." It was through this door that Guézo had entered the Palace to overthrow the unworthy Adanzan and to install himself on the throne of Houégbaja.

The public crier had reached the immense courtyard that stretched in front of Singboji – Guézo's several-story Palace. By means of this magnificent structure, erected in emulation of the example set by Agaja, whose memory had indelibly marked the people of the region, this king had announced his resolve to enlarge the Danhomê of Houégbaja in territorial as well as moral terms and to raise it above the muck that had accumulated during the previous reign.

Gbêhonnou (the Door of Life, of the World, of the Universe, and of happiness as one desired to conceive it) had been situated beneath an overhanging second story, and its walls had been adorned with bas-reliefs of buffalos, their heads lowered and ready to attack the enemy. Facing this Door, Panligan slowed his recital and dwelled upon the epithets of Agonglo's successor: "King Guézo, the buffalo who marches through the most impenetrable forests in triumph! The worthy son of the Pineapple who laughed at the wrath of Lightning! The spool which draws to itself the strand of cotton produced by the little spindle and winds it up! He whom mockery had baptised, 'The Cardinal who can not set fire to the bush because, although his plumage suggests the color of fire, it lacks the heat.' But he proved that he is the Grass which always survives the drought. The Shark who does not fear the cayman. The warhorse who comfortably takes the bit that was too large for the steer, the king who saved Danhomê from dishonor, is indeed the Master of the Universe who will fulfill the hopes of the people! . . . .
. . . .
Victor over Glito, Chêlêti, and Logozohê, you were brave!"

Striking the large part of his double bell with a stick, Panligan signaled the end of his recital; he then flattened himself on the ground, covered his head and torso with dust, and headed back toward his hut.

Déguénon Fonfi had been performing his duties as public crier since Guézo's ascension to the throne; after each glorious feat of this reign, he added new epithets to the already numerous ones that celebrated the power and the victories of the king.

He always arose at the first crowing of the cock, and, in conformity with the injunction against speaking to any living person before reciting the praises of the kings, his initial words were the first epithet of King Houégbaja.

Unless a violent death overtook him and ripped the double bell from his hands, he would not part with it until old age had enfeebled his limbs or extinguished his voice. He was more uncertain about his end than were all the other Danhomênous. And it was always with trepidation that he picked up his bell to begin his daily round.

Before venturing outdoors at dawn, he had placed his fingers on his neck, reflecting, "once again the scimitar of the executioner is about to be raised against you . Eh! Déguénon Fonfi, your head will roll on the ground if you happen to confuse the order of the maxims!" His face had darkened at the thought that death was following him like his shadow. He had remained motionless for a moment. Emerging from his meditations, he had sighed deeply and then coughed twice, loudly as if to ward off the oppressivenes; his hand had risen instinctively to stroke his head, perhaps for the last time. . . .

He always began his recitation with apprehension, but his self-assurance soon returned at the thought that, if he could avail himself of an infallible memory, he would, as a reward for what the king regarded as loyal service, receive a wife during a solemn ceremony. He, Déguénon Fonfi, would thereby swell the number of those who had contributed to the victories that he had been charged to exalt each morning, and he would also be able to provide himself with a successor, whom he would have the joy of initiating from earliest chilhood into the duties of his profession.

He focused all his attention upon what he was reciting, drew out his words, and even slackened his pace so that the Danhomênous would not lose a single word of his epithets, or so people thought. But as for him, he knew that haste leads quickly to death.

The sound of Panligan's double bell was the signal for the king and his wives to arise, but it also betokened rest for the eunuchs, the royal guard, the preparers of gris-gris, and all the others who had stayed awake during the night to watch over the sleeping Idol of the Danhomênous and the female contingent of the Palace.

To linger on the sleeping mat in their quarters or to remain at the Panther's side after the second crowing of the cock and Panligan's round, which was the final warning to get up, would constitute a sacrilege on the part of the Royal Wives – a crime that was punished with a beating the first time, then with detention in the Palace if it recurred, and finally with incarceration at the prison of Cangbodé or even death in the case of repeated offenses that reflected a conscious intention to inflict harm upon the person of the king. The fact of the matter is that the Idol of the Danhomênous would be polluted by such an act and would have to abstain for an entire day from approaching the "Jêhos",[3] from visiting the tombs of the kings, and even from touching his gris-gris. However, any failure to perform these daily obligations toward the ancestors would result in misfortunes for the guilty person and disasters for the entire kingdom; handling a gris-gris in a state of impurity would cause it to lose its power, while depriving one's self of its protection and becoming an easy prey for the numerous enemies of the throne.

It was also a sacrilege to touch anything around one's self or to speak upon awakening – that is, before having purified one's self with ablutions of the taint

---

[3] "Jêho" literally means Room of Jewels. It is an altar which has been raised in the memory of a king and at the foot of which sacrifices are made to him. People say that the surrounding earth was kneaded with palm oil and the blood of human sacrifices mixed with gold coins and precious stones, from whence the name "Room of Jewels." (author's note)

that the night always lays upon women. For this reason, the royal Wives passed quickly and silently from their rooms to the retreat that had been prepared for them at a certain distance from their lodgings so they might perform the matinal purifying rites that they euphemistically called "the cleansing of the feet," just as they characterized the misconduct of a woman by the expression, "one's feet going astray in the bush." Hadn't such a person in fact left the safe and secure path to venture among the thorns, the snares, and the dangers of the bush?

Those women who were absolutely obliged to speak were not allowed to open their mouths, and they restricted themselves to murmuring through closed lips.

Every evening, each of the serving women concluded her day's work by fetching the water that would be available for her mistress the following morning: jugs, earthenware bowls, and small calabashes were arranged at the foot of the wall in an order recognized by their owners and representing the sequence of their arrival at the Palace.

Also for reasons of pollution, the king's footsteps never strayed into the neighborhood of the bathing rooms, which were kept apart from all lodgings and which were, in addition, reserved for the women during the period of their lunar impurity. Yet nothing prevented the king from casting a curious glance toward his wives' bathing rooms.

Waking up proved a bit difficult for the king and several of his wives this morning: an important deliberation had delayed their going to bed the night before.

As they returned from the ritual cleansing, some of the women knocked on the doors of still sleeping fellow wives. Tardiness for the morning baths was extremely rare; indeed, since puberty, the women had acquired the habit of arising from the sleeping mat at the very latest by the third crowing of the cock. Then too, didn't everyone here know that the slightest carelessness would be punished by severe penalties? Even sick wives were obliged to drag themselves to the bathing rooms. Only those unable to move were allowed to perform the purifying ablutions in their own rooms and with the aid of their fellow wives.

As soon as the bathing ritual had been completed, a few quick sweeps of the broom removed the corruption that uncleansed feet had deposited upon the floor after leaving the sleeping mat.

When the servants returned from the bathing room for young women, they proceeded to a meticulous cleaning of the lodgings and then the courtyard.

The passageway leading from the king's chamber to the mausoleum of his predecessor had quickly been cleaned by his youngest wife, who had enjoyed the honor of his bed the previous night. The king never crossed the threshold of his chamber until he was assured that he would not encounter any impurity along the way.

Certain illnesses of the king would betray the failure of his wives to observe the extremely demanding custom of daily purification. If the oracle confirmed the transgression, the perpetrator would be identified with great care. Once discovered, she would expiate her crime with a cruel death. Afterwards the chief fetishists would proceed to a full exorcism of the Palace, then of the whole capital and even, if the oracle thought it necessary, of the entire kingdom.

The water that had just summarily cleansed the bodies of the women also unleashed their tongues, so to speak. As they approached each other, they exchanged greetings, the younger ones kissing the earth and touching their foreheads to the ground at the feet of their elders; the kneeling servant women received orders from their mistresses. The queens who had been designated the night before to awaken the king and to comprise his suite during audiences with the high dignitaries in the Palace and with the courtiers at the courtyard of Singboji had taken their baths and were painstakingly adorning themselves so they might be worthy of their husband at the moment of his appearance before the people.

However, the women in whom the mothers of kings had officially been declared reincarnated as well as the Representatives of the Mothers of Migan and Mêwou, in fact all of the women who had been ordained for a religious function in the Palace (that of offering daily sacrifices to the ancestors or to the gris-gris) still observed the most profound silence. Their first words would be prayers at the foot of the mausolea, on the tombs, or in front of the gris-gris in order to request that the day which was dawning would be among the most propitious for Danhomê and its Idol.

Those who would perform the sacrifice had been selected from among the princesses who were reputed for their dignity and whose advanced age had, moreover, dulled their senses; dressed in black and with black hair coverings, they walked to the site of worship; serving women of irreproachable innocence carried offerings in baskets and calabashes: water drawn piously from Dido's sacred spring, a capsule of melegueta pepper, kola nuts, and a bottle of the white man's fine brandy as well as palm oil and the chickens or goats that were going to be offered to the gris-gris who would consume them.

Each female guardian of a tomb approached the chamber of sleep with religious fear; on her hands and knees she passed through the low doorway and crawled toward the bed that had been prepared in the middle of the room for the dead king, refraining from making any noise that might disturb the sleep of the ancestor. She adopted a very humble attitude and, rubbing the palms of her hands together after having kissed the earth and touched it with her forehead, she praised the power and glory of the dead king in endless epithets that she declaimed with a hollow, muffled intonation; then, with great ardor, she appealed for his benedictions upon the throne of Houégbaja, upon the successor who had been installed upon it, and upon all Danhomê, in the fate of which the ancestor must necessarily be interested if he desired that his name remain always upon the lips of the living and that they would honor his venerable memory in a noble way.

The eunuchs and the young virgins presented the offerings to the gris-gris.

9

Several queens, assembled in the courtyard and facing the chamber of the king, rhythmically beat the "hayé"[4] against the palm of their left hand, while one of them was singing:

Let the King be awakened!
And let him listen to the language of the "hayé"!
Let him be awakened!
And let him listen to the language of the "hayé"!
You have only the language that has been imposed upon you.[5]

The song was repeated in chorus. Seeing that the king was slow in making his appearance, the queen began to sing again:

Could you be asleep?
Could you be asleep?
The warrior must not abandon himself to the sweetness of sleep!

The choir repeated this refrain.

The Master of the Dawn showed himself on the threshold of his chamber. All his adoring wives rejoiced. They kneeled, greeted him, and asked if he had enjoyed a restful night; they expressed their hopes that the new day would bring him happiness.

The intimacy of spouses and their caresses ended with the night. When the king returned to Danhomê at the beginning of the day, he had to be treated with reverence because of the solemnity of his functions, which commenced at dawn. Although his will could brook all sorts of opposition in the intimacy of the marriage bed at night, it became absolute master with the rising of the sun.

*   *   *

The prime minister Migan Atindébacou arrived at the Palace in the escort of four men, three of whom were, like him, tall and broad shouldered; they were his assistants in his ancillary duties as judge at the court and officiant during the daily or annual sacrifices to the ancestors. Two of these assistants stood guard over a prisoner of war whose arms had been tied behind his back with his wrists bound together.

The third assistant of the sacrificing priest carried a scimitar, a raphia pouch, and a bundle of funerary mats made from the pith of raphia palm leaf fibers.

The minister's retinue stopped in the first courtyard. A member of the king's personal bodyguard, comprised of eunuchs who had been armed to defend the door leading into the courtyard of Jêho, alerted the young Amazons of the royal

---

[4]   The "hayé" is a musical instrument that consists of a narrow, long-necked gourd to which a net with fine cowries or snake vertebrae has been attached. It is used to mark the rhythm of a song. (author's note)

[5]   That is, you must not act upon your own will, but upon that of your ancestors and your council of notables. (author's note)

guard, from among whose numbers the door-keepers for the interior of the Palace were chosen.

The king came to meet his prime minister in front of the mausoleum of Agonglo. Migan prostrated himself on the ground and, covering himself with dirt, expressed his wishes for the longevity, the success in war, and the happiness of his sovereign.

The minister went back to the outer courtyard and immediately returned with his escort. He obliged the captive to kneel facing the mausoleum. His assistants flattened themselves in the dust four paces behind them.

The large blade of Migan's scimitar rent the somber veil of the dawn and fell upon the nape of the captive's neck. His head rolled three paces away. The trunk jerked erect and threw itself violently backwards unto the ground, where the body writhed, the muscles popped, and the heels beat frantically against the earth.

The king and the high priest had moved to one side.

Three or four loud death rattles, then silence and a complete lack of motion.

Migan touched the ground beside the victim's mat; then he informed the king, "the face of the dawn has been washed well; it will soon open the door to the sun – the abundance of blood augurs a felicitous day.

The sacrificial priest's aides wrapped up the cadavre, placed the victim's head in the pouch, left the Palace by the door of Ganhohi, and left to throw the body into the Ditch with which Agaja had circled the city to protect it against the invasions of the Ayonous. The head would be boiled and the flesh removed; then the skull would be added to the imposing pile that was accumlating in Migan's courtyard.

The king retired into his house of gris-gris; he washed his face with a lustral water, licked two or three powders, and took several swallows of three or four different purifying potions as he pronounced invocations calculated to activate the power of these gris-gris.

In the storehouses where provisions were kept, the stewards were arguing with the queen-cooks, who always accused them of being stingy with their allotments for the mouth of the king and those of the high dignitaries and distinguished courtisans who were still in the Courtyard of the Palace. The royal wives who had just received their daily ration never regarded it as sufficient, or they found that some of their companions, friends of the stewards, had been given more than they had.

The unhappy women threatened to complain, depending upon whether they were of common or aristocratic origins, to the Representatives of the Mothers of Migan or Mêwou.

The rare Danhomênous who strayed into the neighborhood of the Grand Palace at dawn said to themselves, upon hearing the sounds from the Palace, that Danhomê was waking up joyously and, moreover, under a favorable sign.

*   *   *

11

Shortly after the third crowing of the cock, the veil of darkness had been completely consumed, and the great velvet curtains in hues of boiling palm oil, ashes, and indigo could be seen shining over there, far away, covering the door of the house of the sun. The star of day himself arose quickly and, one would almost have said, with a cloth of crimson satin draped around him; a short while later, he abandoned it in favor of another one of dazzling gold. Nature was radiant.

The cocks of the temple, in the foliage, and on the walls of the Palace shook their fans of tail feathers and clucked, "Dowdow bow bow bow bow bow!" These senseless creatures, who were reputed to have no homes because they did not know how to build them, invoked the rain, calling out to it in their own gloomy language, "Flow, flow, now now now now now!" But in vain. Having risen with the dawn, the crows were cawing in a strange manner. Were they greeting the new day? Perhaps they were reproaching the cocks of the temple for having requested Hêviosso[6] for rain.

Three long market days had passed during which nothing had tarnished the lustre of the sun between its rising in the morning and its setting at night; not even the smallest tuft of cotton strayed across the blue inside of that enormous calebash lid that confines us to the surface of the earth.

There could no longer be any doubt about it! The long dry season had arrived! Life was going to begin again in Dan homê. . . !

But sun-filled nature failed to impart its cheerfulness to the Danhomênous who were lying in the dust of the Courtyard at the Grand Palace and waiting for the Master of the Universe.

Twenty suns could appear in the sky, and it would make no difference to them. "Avoutou"[7] was supposed to thunder forth at the Palace and its detonation to summon the answering roll of the "dogba"[8] and the chirping of the "king's birds,"[9] but it had still not sounded. For King Guézo's subjects, therefore, the world had not yet opened its door. And to be deprived of the light of the Master of the Dawn, the only star which could illuminate their life and the only one which counted for them – to be unable to rejoice in the benevolent presence amongst them of the Idol at whose feet they had come to throw themselves at the beginning of the new day – the Danhomênous became lost in a thousand speculations, which intensified their anxiety. A "soudofi"[10] confided in his neighbor: "Didn't you notice that the sacred bird which, a moment ago,

---

[6] Hêviosso was the god who sent the rain, which was conceptualized as his urine or his spittle. (author's note)

[7] "Avoutou" is an onomatopoeia for gunpowder; it referred to the shot that was fired in the forecourt of the Palace to announce the arrival of the king in the main courtyard. (author's note)

[8] The "dogba" is a sort of drum that originally came from "Houéda" country; in Danhomê it served to announce the king's appearance before the people as well as the death of a king. (author's note)

[9] Pubescent young girls from the ancient kingdom of Houéda. At the court their special cries announced the arrival of the king. (author's note)

[10] "Soudofi" literally means "one who grew up here"; it refers to captives who had been taken in early childhood and raised in Danhomê. (author's note)

shouted its "kowé! kowé!" from the wall of the Palace failed to conclude its song with the tiny laugh that is supposed to portend a joyous and favorable day? Something serious must be happening in the Palace."

A shrug of the shoulders accompanied by a pout was the only answer the talkative fellow received. A number of courtiers also observed that the bird had abruptly terminated its call and shaken its head. But the "soudofi" was the only one in the crowd to mention it. He must certainly have had "mahi" blood in his veins to be so bold.

True Danhomênous were even wary of their own shadows, as if it could go and denounce them to the authorities. Was it not well known that the most harmless observation would be reported to them after it had been magnified and distorted and that a life sentence or death always requited the act of slander, which, when it was committed against the Master of the World, was regarded as a crime.

"An illness that had afflicted the king during the night? Important news received from an enemy country? A conspiracy against Danhomê? What could possibly be the cause of such a long meeting of the council?" Several courtiers were posing these questions to themselves, and their murmurings produced an intense but indecisive buzzing in the midst of that swarm of more than a thousand Danhomênous; the echo of it even reached the ears of the princes and court dignitaries gathered around the royal couch in the reception room of the Palace.

They too had yet to see the king, but they were accustomed to waiting. They amused themselves by commenting upon the bas-reliefs in the reception room, tableaux that recounted the history of Danhomê and the victories of its kings over their domestic and foreign enemies. Anecdotes circulated about the wars of Glito, Chèlèti, and Logozohè, the first ones of this reign and all successful. People boasted about the courage of the Danhomênous and laughed uproariously at the cowardice of the enemy.

Vidaho[11] listened absent-mindedly to this talk about the glorious past of the Danhomê over which he would rule after his royal father. For two moons illness had kept him away from the court. This morning he was making his first appearance since that time and only upon the insistence of the king. His convalescence had barely begun, and his concern about not yet having seen his august father intensified his depression. He disappeared through the door that led further into the interior of the Palace in the direction of the king's lodgings, but he was stopped by the order, given to the female door-keepers, not to admit anyone; he returned to the reception room with a gloomy mien. Migan tried to re-assure him: "The calm of the king's personal bodyguard means that there is nothing to worry about as far as the health of the Master of the World is concerned. If anything were the matter, Mêwou, Déguénon-Daho[12] , and I

---

[11]   "Vidaho" literally means "Great Son." It is the title given by the people to the heir to the throne of Danhomê. This presumptive heir was not necessarily the eldest son of the king, but the choice that designated him to succeed his eminent Father ennobled him and caused him to be regarded as the first son. (author's note)

[12]   is the name which the "Déguénon-Daho ministers give the heir to the throne. (author's note)

13

would have been immediately notified by the Wives of Panther."

The bewildered look on the face of the heir to the throne indicated that he was not listening to the comforting words of the prime minister.

"The worthy son of the Pineapple who laughed at the wrath of Lightning![13] The grass which always survives the drought! . . . .
. . . ."

As the first words of these epithets burst from behind the place where furniture was stored, the courtiers rushed headlong into the courtyard and prostrated themselves in the dust.

The Master of the World was arriving. The ground resounded with footsteps.

Daclo – the female herald who walked at the head of the royal procession – soon appeared. She continued to recite the praises of the king.

The Wives of Panther entered walking backward. The first row of them raised and lowered hyena-skin fans with amulet-laden handles. The second row was comprised of women who carried a pipe, a spitoon, several white scarves, a snuff-box, and a small basket containing fine cowries; they kneeled beside the couch as their companions with the fans installed themselves at the foot of the throne.

A third group arrived; its members formed a circle, and with silk parasols that were white, crimson, or the frothy color of boiling palm oil, they created a crown above the king's head. The imposing stature of Guézo towered over his wives, who were themselves quite large.

The appearance of his august father dispelled the fears of Vidaho.

The king stretched out upon the couch, paying no attention to the prostrate dignataries in the courtyard.

Two queens loosened the girth of the large leaf-green velvet cloth that was draped around him; in this way they conferred complete freedom of movement upon his arms. They then re-arranged the cloth over his feet. The fans moved regularly up and down.

The princes and the high dignitaries rubbed the right side then the left side of their faces against the ground and smeared their foreheads with dirt; after doing this, they entreated the solicitude of the ancestors, and of the fetishes that protected the kingdom, for the king's happiness that day.

When the others had finished, Migan continued, "Danhomê of Houégbaja will continue to grow. The evil wind will never blow in its direction. All its enemies will be found and punished. This throne will always remain before us. All the previous kings will support their Representative here for the longest possible time. The reign of the Master of the Universe will surpass all those that this country has ever known. A long life, a life like that of the mountains and the sea is vouchsafed the king. . . ."

---

[13] This epithet alludes to an accident during which King Guézo's father had narrowly escaped a lightning bolt. Boasting of his extraordinary luck, the king had adopted as his name the last words of his epithet – "Sô jè dé bo agon glo" (Lightning destroyed the palm tree but was powerless against the pineapple). (author's note)

Guézo sat up. His face was solemn. With an imperious "that's enough," he arrested the prime minister's good wishes and ordered Ajaho to present Wolo, the court seer. He stared fixedly in front of himself; his right foot, resting on the other one, moved nervouosly. The dignitaries had once again sat down on the mats, their legs folded in front of them and facing the king.

The king shrugged his shoulders and, as a conclusion to his reflections, he proclaimed: "Even if the ancestors disapprove of this war, I am determined to undertake it."

Dumbfounded stares focused on him.

"A war? In what country? And for what reason? Usually it was only the council of notables that discussed the advisability of our campaigns, and it only committed the kingdom to war on the condition that the ancestors had approved of it through the voice of Destiny. Were they going to break with this wise custom today and with the one that decreed that plans for war could only be discussed in Agrigomê, that part of the Palace constructed by Agaja, whose spirit presided over our deliberations, inspired us with the best solutions to our problems, and guided us toward victory? What reasons could possibly justify such behavior?" Several princes were murmuring among themselves.

Having understood, Guézo continued: "You will all agree that it is time we avenged our friends, the white men who were massacred at Kinglo. I will make all the Mahinous pay for this crime, starting with Hounjroto, whom the report of Boya Alowé, who was born in that country, implicates in the murder of the white men. I owe my throne in part to one of them. My first three wars were undertaken to pay homage to my ancestors. The fourth ought to be dedicated to avenging the memory of our friends from across the sea, those who were massacred in such a cowardly fashion at Kinglo, in order to offer our people an example of gratitude toward our benefactors. I am even convinced that we have waited too long to perform our duty."

Among the princes, heads were shaking, pouting faces appeared, and questioning glances were raised in the direction of the dignitaries: "Did they too believe in the necessity of attacking Hounjroto?"

The princes desired to discuss the inadvisability of this war; they were free to do so. These were not cunning, hate-filled Danhomênous gathered together in this room – those who obsequiously praised the established power in public, while secretly cursing it because they were by nature jealous of all who outshined them. Nor were they among the Danhomênous who, dominated by the constant fear of being denounced for slander against their sovereign, cleverly knew how to veil their true feelings.

Those Danhomênous who had been accorded the honor of crossing the threshold of the Door of the Universe had had their eyes opened by that very fact to certain things that were necessarily hidden from the view of the masses who remained outside in the Courtyard of the Palace, and their tongues were freed.

At Singboji in the presence of the king, they had to prostrate themselves on the ground and cover their heads and shoulders with dust or wallow in the mud.

15

Inside the Palace, the customary greetings were less formal; the counsellors to the throne sat on mats and spoke to the king as if he were an equal.

The princes and the high dignitaries gathered that morning at the Palace could thus freely express their opinions about the proposed war. Their rank as prebendary dignitaries even placed them under the obligation to enlighten the kingdom with wise counsels and to exert themselves in maintaining their gris-gris in force so that it would always remain powerful, invincible, prosperous, and victorious, for they profited from a share of the spoils.

If Migan Atindébacou and Mêwou Voglossou, Gaou Déssou and Possou Linon, Ajaho and Topo, Sogan and Cangbodé, Paapa and Matonso were prepared to approve any war, if the royal chamberlain Alopé could not forget that his origins were vulgar and that it was only by special dispensation that he had acquired the right to pronounce himself in the affairs of Danhomê, if Vivênagbo could not lose sight of the fact that he was a creature of Guézo and dared not oppose him for fear of losing the king's esteem and the resultant favor of being entrusted with the powers of government when the others set out for war, if Afénou had to remember that he was the grandson of Pingla and needed to be prudent in his counsels because the sun of the sixth king had set with the death of his grandfather, the same was not true of Adoucounou, the eldest son of King Agonglo. Born of the same mother as Adanzan, the prince had not hesitated to abandon his brother and to take charge of the supporters of Guézo, at that time no more than an aspirant to the throne. Isn't it true that, having sacrificed the son of his own mother and father for the cause of one who was no more than a half-brother, Adoucounou had surely given sufficient proof of his attachment to the person of King Guézo so that no shadow of suspicion could ever be cast upon the motivation behind his counsels, even if they opposed the will of the king? And Linpéhoun? And Oundanoucou? They too were supporters and brothers of Guézo. And Tomêtin, the brother of the king by birth and by Oath of Blood? And Toffa, the first-born son of Agonglo after he had acquired Danhomê and thus the favorite child, who, moreover, was wisdom itself?

In any case, kings only find the truth to be bitter when it is served to them in front before the eyes of the people. No one sought it more than they did in the intimacy of the royal council chamber.

But, although they had been accorded the right to speak freely to the king inside the Palace, the princes and high dignitaries did not want to say anything in the presence of the queens. The suspicion that the Royal Wives were party to the decision to declare war on Hounjroto and a disdain for the weaker sex, considered incapable of reasoned judgment, silenced all tongues.

Didn't the calm expressions on the queens' faces betray them? The courtiers were convinced that they could persuade the king to renounce his plan for an expedition against Hounjroto, if he would remain alone in their midst to discuss the project. Thus, their expressions hardened to indicate to the queens that they should withdraw.

Guézo protested in their behalf: "The presence of my wives need not prevent you from freely expressing your opinion about the proposed campaign. You have not, I think, forgotten that in this Danhomê it has been prohibited for us to send the women away from our palavers ever since the directions – provided by a queen who happened, by a fortunate accident, to be present at a palaver in this Palace – enabled a king to rediscover a predecessor's tomb, all trace of which had been lost because, in those days, the Danhomênous feared that the royal sepulchres would be violated by the Ayonous, who frequently invaded Danhomê, and therefore refrained from marking the final resting place of our kings with mausolea."

The courtiers acknowledged the custom, but they persisted in remaining silent in the presence of women who, they thought, were only capable of doing good accidentally.

The seer soon arrived in the company of Ajaho. Destiny had been consulted, and it advised against the proposed campaign.

Repeatedly questioned about what it foresaw, Destiny invariably replied: "The ancestors are opposed to the war and predict defeat if they are disobeyed."

Such decisive and clearly repeated declarations, even when the questions had been posed in the most indirect manner, disturbed Guêzo enormously. He abruptly left the counsel chamber, but he forbade any courtier to cross the threshold of the Door of the Universe.

The princes opposed to the campaign thought, "that's the end of the idea of a war against Hounjroto!" They were openly rejoicing over their victory, which they believed final.

The ministers formed a group apart. The princes had dispersed themselves around the courtyard in groups of three or four, warmly confiding their thoughts to each other and supporting them with movements of their heads and arms. Only the seer had remained in the reception room, staring fixedly at the apparatus he had consulted and with a worried look on his face.

* * *

At Singboji the Danhomênous had been sitting for a long time because the signal announcing the king's arrival had still not sounded.

They told each other that an important event was in the offing. But they did not have to give it any further thought. Others assumed the responsibility of thinking for those who had only been created to execute the will of the Master of the World.

A certain Fonnou, a commoner who had been looking furtively in every direction for some time, finally screwed up his courage and removed a package from the leather pouch hanging on his left side; he at first hid it under his thigh, but a moment later he picked it up again, unwrapped it in a state of constant apprehension, and began to pick at the cotton which he removed from it in small wads.

His example was followed by other courtiers, although quite timorously at first; they picked at cotton, twisted raphia, or wove a band of straw that would serve to make a hat with a narrow lining and a broad brim – the only parasol or umbrella that the Danhomênous were authorized to use.

17

No one in the group took it upon himself to reprimand the workers. Hadn't the Master of the World enjoined his people to devote themselves to some sort of manual work during his absence in order to avoid the gossiping that inevitably led to slander?

Hands worked, while ears listened for the explosive detonation of "Avoutou," the roll of "dogba," and the chirping of the "king's birds" who would announce the Master of the World; from time to time, furtive glances were also directed toward the throne.

The sun had already straightened its darts, causing them to sting more sharply. Stomachs had been rumbling for some time; the worms were demanding their allotment. For a long time people persisted in ignoring them. But the tiny creatures soon began to gnaw at intestines. It was thus necessary to abandon one's work and forage through the pouch; the closed right hand emerged and moved toward the mouth in order to pour a handful of roasted maize into it; the people who had accompanied the chiefs were eating their meal. The chiefs themselves would eat akassa[14] and balls of fried beans. However, the Danhomênous who had come to the court with empty pouches in the hope of filling them, and their stomachs as well, with the food that the king customarily served to all the courtiers were swallowing the water that unsatisfied desire had brought to their mouths.

Their eyes, swollen with desire, rolled across the fortunate ones and then moved toward the door through which they at any moment expected to see baskets of food emerge, but still nothing appeared. . . .

Among those who were eating, no one took it upon himself to offer a mouthful to the others who had nothing to place between their teeth. Most of the latter had dozed off, and some were even chewing with empty mouths: they were eating in their dreams.

Hands made no more than ten or so trips from the pouch to the mouth. If people were so miserly to themselves with their own provisions, how could they think about their neighbors? Someone asked Abodogoué for a chunk of tobacco, and he had indignantly refused: "I should deprive myself of my own property for the benefit of a beggar so that I can descend to his level!"

Was it possible to foresee when people might be allowed to return to their own hearths?

Because the tongue had not succeeded in dislodging the food wedged between the gum and the cheek, the right index finger took charge of emptying these caches and transporting their contents back to the tongue. Why let a morsel of food go to waste when there was already less than enough?

Those who had finished eating carefully wiped their hands on their calves and the soles of their feet. An old habit inherited from the elders.

Bent double, a few of them now moved toward the earthen jugs arranged in rows to the left of the Door of Patinsa. Others finished filling their stomachs

---

[14]   "Acassa" is a maize dough wrapped in leaves; it serves the Danhomênous as a sort of bread. (author's note)

with the water that was being fetched at every moment of the day by details of common women.

Any Danhomênous who were tempted to retain the calebash of water for too long would be reminded by the club of the guardian of the water jugs that selfishness was prohibited in this place.

Once the worms had been stilled, the mind that had ceded to their imperious demands became once again obsessed with its earlier worries; the people were more and more puzzled by the absence of the king, the high dignitaries of the Palace, and the princes of his entourage.

*   *   *

By the joy that radiated from the faces of the Royal Wives when Guézo reappeared before his counsellors toward the middle of the day, the latter recognized, much to their astonishment, the imminence of the war they all believed had been renounced that morning, the former kings having disapproved of it.

Convinced that he would eventually win the consent of his ancestors by promising them numerous sacrifices, the king ordered them to be consulted again.

Destiny continued to advise against the proposed campaign; the predictions resulting from the seer's commentaries were of the most ominous nature. An agonizing silence settled over the group.

"We're saved!" thought some of the princes. "He will definitely abandon this war!"

Seated on his couch, the king stared straight in front of himself; his right foot nervously tapped the ground, and his lips moved: he was talking to himself.

Having suddenly emerged from his meditation, he exclaimed: "Not avenge the memory of our friends? By our inaction we run the risk of diluting the fear that Danhomê inspires in its neighbors; all our enemies, thinking we are afraid of attacking those vile beasts from the mountains, will be emboldened. The white men, who are, as we know, steadfast in friendship and the scourge of our enemies, will not understand our attitude. They will even blame us for complicity in the crime committed by the people of Kinglo."

Gaou, the minister of war, supported him: "The Master of the World is right to fight the Mahinous. He owes it to himself to begin with those from Hounjroto. The fact that they belong to same tribe as the foul beasts of Kinglo is reason enough to justify our actions against them. Didn't the men of old proclaim that small catfish should be made to discharge the debts of large ones? But even more legitimate reasons oblige us to begin with Hounjroto; we must avenge the memory of our friends, the white men. Three moons ago, Boya Alowé, a son of those mountains, came and assured us in this very courtyard that the inhabitants of Hounjroto bore a heavy responsibility in the assassination of our friends at Kinglo. We must first cut off the heads that inspired the crime before we think of amputating the arms that perpetrated it."

"What proof did this Mahinou offer in support of his accusation?" asked Assogbaou. "Who knows if he isn't satisfying a personal grudge by pushing us into a war with his fellow countrymen. Danhomê is the essence of wisdom; it can not rush headlong into a venture and risk its honor solely on the word of some individual."

"The white men our friends! The white men our friends!" repeated Toffa, shaking his head. Standing and with the upper part of his body leaning slightly forward, he remained pensive for a moment and then continued, looking the king straight in the eyes: "Strange friends, those on whom affection is lavished but who never offer it in return, those who, for their own profit, encourage the Danhomênous to poison themselves with alcohol and to sacrifice their lives in endless wars.

"It's time to free ourselves from the illusion that has misled us into regarding the White Bellies as friends. It is useless for us to treat them as such, for they profoundly despise all our demonstrations of friendship. Nor are they any more inclined to acknowledge the affection of the Danhomênous for them. They are only interested in people who have a commercial value or from whom some profit can be extracted. But the day these same people become useless to them, the white men will discard them just like an orange that has been squeezed dry. Even when we do succeed in gaining their friendship by means of a conciliatory word, it is never a deep or sincere friendship. There is nothing surprising in that! The difference between the white men and ourselves is great.

"Danhomênous, Mahinous, and Ayonous all have black eyes. As for the white men, theirs can be black or the color of dried leaves or the color of green leaves, like those of cats. That is undoubtedly the reason why the White Bellies do not see things from the same perspective as we do.

"How can Danhomênous, who only respect strength, ally themselves with people who are the very essence of weakness? These white men only come to Agbomê from the other side of the swamps when they are carried in hammocks, whereas a Danhomênou who has scarcely been weaned can easily cover the some twenty-three thousand five hundred bamboos[15] which separate us from the sea if the Master of the World orders him to do so. The white man's false paradise has already corrupted the black men who live like them at Gléhoué;[16] they never enter the capital unless they too are being carried in hammocks, in which they can be seen sprawling indolently. No doubt it is to save the Danhomênous from the taint they would suffer from their contact with these foul beasts from the sea that Agbé[17] becomes furious, roils the waters of the sea, and whips up a violent surf that sometimes swallows their boats or dashes them to pieces when they attempt to land on our shores.

"Do you want further proof of the white man's weakness? They can not survive without covering their bodies; no one has ever seen them going about bare-headed in the sun or walking in their bare feet. They don't raise their voices

---

[15]   Agaja invented this unit of measurement to ascertain the distance from Agbomê to the coast after the conquest of the "Houéda" kingdom. (author's note)

[16]   "Gléhoué" is the local name for the city of Ouidah, an important slave-trading port on the Slave Coast during the eighteenth and early nineteenth centuries. (author's note)

[17]   "Agbé" is the sea god or Neptune of the Danhomênous. (author's note)

20

when they speak, and they don't laugh uproariously like the Danhoménous. At night the least sound disturbs them; our drums deprive them of sleep, as they themselves admit. Nor have we ever seen them fight on the side of the Danhoménous. However, we are told that they wage war in their own country, although everything suggests that they do not face their enemies and cannot sustain close combat with sword in hand. Isn't it in such battles that strong men show their mettle?

"The white men also lack our courage. Incidentally, that is why they exercised their ingenuity to invent guns, canons, and other exploding weapons that give power to cowards by allowing them to fight from a distance, I mean at no great risk to themselves.

"People who never eat red pepper cannot be strong!

"Has the Danhomé of Houégbaja, a staunch admirer of strength and an invariably cruel master in the presence of weakness, transferred its allegiance to a new idol, and will it prostrate itself today before weakness?

"Yet if the weakness of the white men is only apparent, that is all the more reason for us to rejoice at the massacre of the three White Bellies at Kinglo and *to wish for the annihilation of all these beasts from the sea. Danhomé has not* yet renounced, as far as I know, its hatred of anything that surpasses it.

"And if the fear of becoming fodder for vultures is motivating you to seek the friendship of grave-diggers, Danhoménous, set your minds at rest. As for me, I do not perceive in the region around Danhomé any enemy whose strength is so overwhelming that we would need the white man's protection to guarantee our safety in the case of an invasion. Can anyone tell me what aid our ancestors received from these White Bellies when Danhomé was being pillaged by the Ayonous?

"Let us not nurture ourselves on illusions. We could only hope to expect their assistance if that which separates us from them were limited to the physical.

"*Danhoménous, how can you not see that these White Bellies stand for a* whole set of practices that differ from the institutions of Danhomé? What am I saying? Practices that are diametrically opposed to our manners and to our customs.

"What if we want to make our thoughts known to a distant person? We express our desires orally, and then we entrust the sceptre, which represents us, to the messenger. But the white men make marks on a piece of paper. Danhoménous don't understand it at all. For that reason, they can unwittingly transmit the order for their own execution. But what if they are afraid of what the piece of paper might contain and give it to another white man? They are treated to the following response: I am 'Agouda'[18] and don't understand what this paper says because it is written in 'Zojagué'.[19] Or: I am 'Zojagué' and do

---

[18] "Agouda" is the local name for "Portuguese", and it connotes pride and laziness. (author's note)

[19] "Zojagué" means "French" or "Frenchman" in the local language. Its origins go back to the early days of the slave trade, and it suggests the active nature of the French and their familiarity with the indigenous peoples. (author's note)

not speak 'Glinci'.[20]

"But consult Destiny. Order the name to be inscribed on a calebash shard with the point of a knife. Carry it to Aja. Show it to Ayo. Present it to Ké. Then go to Houn.[21] Everywhere you will hear it named and commented upon in the same fashion.

"It is not fitting for a Danhomênou to become friends with mysterious people. If only they wore tatoos so that their identity could be recognized quickly!

"The fact that a man can live with a single woman and allow himself to be governed by a creature with seven pairs of ribs[22] is indisputable proof of his debility. You have certainly not yet forgotten the disgusting conduct of the white man who lived for quite some time with his wife at the court of our august Father and who catered to the wishes of a woman the way a slave serves his master in Danhomê.

"All Danhomênous prostrate themselves in the dust and cover themselves with it when they greet the king. But the white men who come to this court arrogantly remain standing, like palm trees, in the presence of the Father of Life. When they make up their minds to pay homage to him, they don't even remove their hats; they content themselves with a modest nod of the head. At this very court, didn't people see one of these foul beasts from the sea extend his unclean hand toward the Idol of the Danhomênous? I wonder what these White Bellies are afraid of. That the sun might consume the goat hair that covers their skulls? Or that their head might fall to the ground?

"The king's respect for the disdainful calabashes atop their shoulders only augments their insolence toward the Idol of the Danhomênous; they openly mock our veneration for him. What Mahinou ever manifested so much disrespect for our king? Danhomênous will never understand why we are going to avenge these men of such a haughty race.

"Not only do these white men lack consideration for the reigning king; they have no respect for everything that we hold sacred: they fell trees bequeathed as fetishes by our ancestors, and to justify their sacrilege they claim that the wood of these trees is good for building.

"Our passiveness has encouraged them in their blasphemy. Not a day goes by that one of these white men doesn't kill a Panther at Gléhoué. The criminal boasts publicly about his skill. The Danhomênous who are their domestics serve as the eyes and ears of the king in the residence of these White Bellies, and they swear that these white men cover the floors of their bed rooms with the hides of Panther and even wipe the very stench of their feet upon them. Whenever we find ourselves before the corpse of a Panther that has been slain by a stray arrow or felled by old age, we mourn, we bury the sacred remains with great ceremony, and we perform propitiatory sacrifices. Do you honestly believe that

---

20   "Glinci" is the local name for "English" or "Englishman". (translator's note)

21   These are the four cardinal directions for the Danhomênous: "Aja" is the West; "Ayo" is the East; "Ké" is the North; and "Houn" is the South. (author's note)

22   According to popular belief in Danhomê, men had nine pairs of ribs and women seven. (author's note)

that alone will acquit our debt toward Agassou[23] in light of the fact that we are permitting such sacrileges to profane his venerable remains?"

He turned toward the prime minister and said: "It is also highly significant that the white men betrayed their revulsion when Migan sacrificed the victims who had been charged to inform our ancestors of the ascension to the throne of the son of 'the pineapple who laughed at the wrath of Lightning.' This revulsion resurfaces annually at our traditional festivals, which are attended by these foul beasts from the sea, and it not only reveals that they they don't have the slightest idea about life in the realm of the dead; it is also supremely insulting to the memory of our revered ancestors, who will not, I think, support us when we take up the cause of people who disapprove of our human sacrifices."

Facing the king, he continued: "I have not heard that the Mahinous wiped out all the beasts from the sea who live in Danhomê; they only killed three of them. Why don't their fellow countrymen embark upon a war to avenge them? Among themselves, these white men have never been seen to protect one another, let alone defend themselves with a sense of solidarity.

"The Danhomênous who live at Gléhoué and understand their manner of speaking report to us every thought they express. These White Bellies hardly love each other. To preserve the divisiveness that ought to benefit us as well, Yévogan[24] cleverly exploits the rivalry born in the selfishness of their hearts: he promotes some and persecutes others. The jealousies created by this policy constantly feed the hatred that exists among these slave-dealers.

"All Danhomênous present in this council today know Gléhoué. But have you ever visited the various forts in that city and noticed, as I have, the arrangement of the canons that are defending them? All the big canons of one fort are directed against the other forts.

"Were it not for the severe punishment with which the king threatens any foreigner who makes war in Danhomê, these white men would immediately fire their canons at each other; that is the extent to which they covet the slave trade.

"All the white men will certainly not applaud our expedition against Hounjroto. It could even indispose them toward us, since they dislike us already and the majority of them rejoiced at the massacre of the three foreigners.

"If these beasts from the sea loved us, would they have conspired to bring about the downfall of Danhomê?" His right hand sliced through the air like the motion of Migan executing a victim. "The proof of their animosity towards us abounds in our history. After Agaja's victory over Houfon and the destruction of Sahé, the capital of the "Houéda" kingdom that had only kept our armies at bay for seven years because it was secretly being supported by the white men, he immediately wanted to conquer Gléhoué, but the foul beasts from the sea openly defended the city. We prudently retreated and camped at a place we call

---

[23]   An ancestral totem among the Danhomênous, Agassou was conceived as a monster which was half-human and half-panther. It was the great fetish of the branch of the Aladahonous that founded the kingdom of Danhomê. (author's note)

[24]   The Danhomê Governor of Ouidah. (author's note)

'Savi'[25] – the key – where we had to wait until the following reign before we could force open the door to trade with the white men, that is to say before we could become the masters of Gléhoué. Who will ever know the number of Danhomênous who were killed in those wars? In the end we owed the victory to a ruse that was recommended to us by the ancestors.

"On the very day after our ultimate victory, those who had so obstinately opposed Danhomê's expansion to the sea abandoned their long-time protégés and came over to our side. There you have it, Danhomênous; it is for such duplicity that you want to go have yourselves killed at Hounjroto. . . ."

He paused for a moment. His peers remained silent, their mouths open. They were savoring his words. Yet his arguments appeared not to have convinced the entire court. Thus, he continued with a heightened tone of conviction in his voice: "To judge by some half-closed eyes staring into the air, I can see that the memories of most people are not sharp in regard to the past of our Danhomê. It was long ago, I agree, and like you I prefer to forget the white man's intrigues against us. But when I recall that Tégbessou and his successor pardoned them and subsequently gave ample evidence of their desire to live in harmony with the White Bellies without for one moment allaying the hatred of these creatures toward Danhomê, I cannot help but demand that we avenge ourselves upon them. Danhomênous, search in your memories and you will remember that these very white men resumed their intrigues during the reign of Pingla-the-Brave: after refusing to sell us a bronze canon, they gave it to the Ayonous. Yes, the white men whom we now overwhelm with kindness had armed our irreconcilable enemies so they could march upon the Danhomê of Houégbaja and destroy it.

"Roused to indignation by such a betrayal, the ancestors helped Pingla's soldiers capture this weapon from the Ayonous."

"That was the white man's behavior toward our fathers! Have they dealt more honestly with the sons? Was it not the white men who advised us no longer to wage war as our ancestors had done? Despite the sage opinions of a few clear-sighted people in this court people who implored us not to listen to foreigners whose treachery had been established beyond a doubt – we had the stupidity to follow the advice of those who had secretly sworn to bring about our downfall. Thus we notified the inhabitants of Chêlêti that we were preparing to attack them. It was the second war of this reign. What did it result in? Only the protection of the ancestors saved us from being vanquished. But more than two thousand Danhomênous lost their lives on the field of battle. We not only allowed this new crime against a hospitable people to go unpunished; we even resumed trading relations and renewed our friendship with the white men. Danhomênous risked their lives to ensure that these foreigners' favorite form of trade would flourish. Yet you all know, as I do, that they do not bring the same honesty to this business that we do. The king never receives exactly what he orders from them. To justify themselves, they always claim that they did not understand us. The truth is that they do not want to understand us. We are

---

[25]   A village eight kilometers from Ouidah (Gléhoué). (author's note)

in Danhomê. You will therefore agree that it is not our responsibility to learn the language of foreigners, but theirs to make the effort to understand us. We should only permit slaves to know the language of the white men so they can inform us what these beasts from the sea are thinking. On the pretext that we do not understand each other, these white men place countless obstacles in our way when we desire to obtain the things they bring into our country. What benefits has Danhomê received until now from its friendship for the white man? None!" Saying this, he suddenly released his right thumb, the nail of which had been resting on the inside of the incisor in his upper jaw, producing a sharp click.

"Take a batch of male captives to these traders, and they'll let you know with a sullen, discouraging pout that they only want female captives. Bring them women, and they no longer want anything but men. You come to sell them Ayonous, their favorite commodity because Ayonous support captivity so well? These White Bellies have you informed that they are only buying Mahinous. If you find them these stinking beasts from the mountains, you'll hear them say, 'Mahinous are stubborn. We prefer Ayonous.' I can see your annoyance. You're scowling? You haven't seen anything yet. You almost have to go down on your knees and beg your customers."

He shook his head, pursed his lips, sighed deeply, and said: "Life sometimes imposes revolting humiliations upon your sense of dignity! Beg your customers to buy the goods they need? Can these white men still claim today that they are unaware of the danger to which we expose ourselves in our wars? Danhomê of Houégbaja, your generosity has been poorly rewarded! The demands of the white man have transcended all bounds.

"Only grudgingly do they pay the insignificant tax imposed on them in return for the protection which the Master of the World accords their lives and their possessions in Danhomê. Furthermore, the future appears extremely gloomy for our great grandsons." He remained pensive for a moment, then shook his head and continued: "As a seller of slaves, you succeed by means of your entreaties in attracting the attention of one of those dealers to your batch of captives. He sorts them for you, selects from among the best of them, and then, taking them one by one, forces their lips apart, touches each of their teeth, pinches their noses, and pulls on their ears as if to see whether or not you have replaced them with clay; he blows into them (I have no idea why), prizes open their eyelids, raises their arms, bends them, and touches them all over; he examines the teeth and nostrils again, the eyes and the ears for a second time, and the whole body. Intrigued, you watch him. Other surprises are waiting for you. Now it's time for the hair. The dealer passes his hand back and forth on the top of the slave's head in order to see if you haven't blackened it with soot to camouflage the onset of an old age that would have been betrayed by greying hair. According to tradition, earlier slave-traders even licked the skin of the slaves."

He turned and spit with disgust behind himself.

"Your captives have to run, jump, make gestures, contort themselves in a thousand ways, speak loudly, laugh uproariously, and I don't know what else before the negotiations can even begin.

"Convinced of the high quality of your wares, you are already counting your magnificent profits in your head. You'll only receive them in your dreams. The crafty dealer is plumbing the depths of your heart, and he informs you with a sullen, contemptuous look: 'Only three captives out of this batch of thirty are acceptable.'

"In your naivete, you call over another dealer. But the same scenes are repeated in front of your very eyes. The white men only resort to so many ruses because they want to buy our merchandise at a ridiculously low price. And we are obliged to sell it to them, since we ourselves don't have any ships at sea. Even if we succeeded in transporting our wares to the country of the white men, an even greater disappointment would be awaiting us. Wouldn't we be dealing with the same sort of people?

"What Dahomênou ever examined the White Belly's goods with such a lack of respect? Will our great grandsons be more fortunate in their dealings with the white men? Without desiring to anticipate the future, I doubt it very much, and it is the ancestors who suggest this attitude in the following maxim: 'By the quantity and quality of the water offered to a guest at the beginning of a meal, he can form a good idea of the food his host is preparing to offer him.' But let us not worry too much about our descendants. I hope that the mice of the future will be clever enough to hold their own with the cats of their time.

"I will not approve of avenging the memory of the beasts from the sea until I have been convinced that we are going to profit from our devotion to them. From now on are they going to buy our captives at a better price and sell us their cloth, their alcohol, and their guns more cheaply? If we have such a promise from them, let us wipe out the stinking beasts of Hounjroto before the sun leaves the top of our heads."

His interrogating glance swept across his peers, who were as motionless as the pillars of the room in which they were assembled.

"No one is getting up!" he continued after a short pause. "Why? We have the right to expect reciprocity in return for our allegiance to the white men and our devotion to their cause, but this reciprocity is quite illusory.

"We left unpunished the support that these foul beasts from the sea accorded to the Houédanous of Gléhoué when we were fighting against them during the reigns of Agaja and Tégbéssou. And we were no more determined to requite the abominable treachery of these same white men when it recurred during the time of Pingla.

"Armed with the bronze cannon, the story of which I mentioned a moment ago, the Ayonous could easily have invaded Danhomê and silenced our carronades, if our ancestors had not helped us surprise our enemies and seize this formidable weapon. No doubt displeased with our friendship for these traitors, our ancestors inspired the Mahinous of Kinglo to attack the brothers of those who wished for the destruction of the Danhomê that Houégbaja had toiled to found and enlarge. And we, we of all people, want to avenge these blasphemers? No, we are not going to fight the Mahinous of Hounjroto, who replaced us at the sides of their brothers from Kinglo, because our ingratitude toward

26

the mountain people threatens to bring a series of calamities down upon the Danhomê of Houégbaja."

He fell silent, touched his forehead to the ground, and sat down. He was agitated. Muted exclamations of "it's true! it's true!" applauded his words. With a corner of his cloth he wiped his armpits, from whence pearls of sweat were running down across his ribs; then he fanned himself, cast a questioning glance at his peers, opened his mouth widely, and sucked in the air from the room to refresh a throat parched by his long speech.

The king allowed the assenters time to congratulate the speaker and then responded calmly: "Toffa is talking nonsense. His hatred for the white men makes him unjust toward them. His arguments will only convince simple-minded people. And I don't see any of them on this council. Some of the reproaches he makes against the white men are more likely to amuse serious people.

"I admit that the white men lead a different sort of life from our own, that they do not always think like we do, and that their behavior in this country has not always been worthy of praise. But would you yourselves not find it unjust if others judged the entire people of Danhomê on the basis of villainies committed by a few Danhomênous in a foreign country? Let us not therefore hate all white men. They can not all be bad. And until we have spent some time in their country, we cannot pretend to know them.

"All white men have not been drawn here by the desire for wealth; some of them have come to Danhomê out of their love for the black man and their desire to help him.

"They have their paper that allows them to be understood without speaking a word or making the slightest gesture, even at a distance. On the basis of that, Toffa concludes that they are mysterious. Is it not, on the contrary, an incontrovertible sign of their superiority over the people of Danhomê? It is often advantageous for royal messengers to remain ignorant of the messages they are carrying.

"Every country has its own customs and manners. If the white men want to criticize ours, they will, to our great shame, find much with which to find fault.

"As far as I know, the white men do not oblige Danhomênous to adopt their sort of life and become indolent.

"Toffa grows angry at the white men for not prostrating themselves to greet the king. Let us not make a crime of that. Every people has its own way of rendering homage to its sovereign. The Aladahonous do not greet their king in the same way as do the Danhomênous of our time. Have you forgotten that it was only with the reign of Houégbaja that Danhomênous, following the example set by the chief of Saclo, began to show so much respect in the homage they pay to their ruler? In his zeal to demonstrate his gratitude to the king of the Aladahonous[26] for the meals he was serving to the council, this chief of the Guédévis[27] flattened himself in the dust and covered his head, his arms, and his

---

26   "Aladahonou" is the name adopted by the tribe that Daco-Donou led to the plain of Agbomê; it signifies someone who came from Alada. (author's note)

27   The "Guédévis" were the original inhabitants of the Agbomê plain, and they extended

chest with it.

"If the white men experience a certain revulsion at the moment of a human sacrifice, we do not have to interpret that as a repudiation of our customs and a lack of respect for our ancestors. Don't some Danhomênous faint when they see the blood of the victims in whom we have entrusted messages for the dead?

"The white men mistrust each other; it's a known fact. But they have the excuse that they are not all from the same country or the same family. The spirit of back-biting and jealousy that exists among Danhomênous and even among those linked by ties of blood is more reprehensible than the rivalries that separate the white men from each other.

"The demands of the dealers at the slave markets are a function of their self-interest and an expression of their taste and judgment. To condemn the meticulous care they employ in selecting the goods of the trade is to demonstrate one's ignorance of how business is conducted.

"I believe the prince has intentionally distorted the story of the conquest of Gléhoué.

"The arms of Agaja's soldiers had allowed him to occupy a large part of that city. Only the Docomê section defended by the Agoudas remained outside his control. These white men would have been worthy of blame if they had abandoned their allies. Rather than dishonoring them, the Agoudas' fidelity is to their credit. Let us be fair. The Danhomênous only won a definitive victory, during the reign of Tégbéssou, thanks to the aid of the Glincis and the Zojagués.

"No matter how reprehensible the conduct of the white men living among us might be, we must not forget that the Danhomê of Houégbaja contracted an enormous debt of gratitude to the people of their race; their weapons helped us extend this kingdom to the sea and win our independence from the Ayonous; furthermore, their other products have made our lives easier.

"It is true that Danhomênous who respect this country's tradition, according to which a king should be designated by his predecessor, supported my efforts to regain the throne that a tyrant had usurped at my expense. But do not forget that the role the white men played in our triumph was also a large one. The wealth in cloth, alcohol, and cowries that one of them generously placed at our disposition swelled the ranks of our supporters and hastened my ascension to the throne. As for myself, I believe, in opposition to Toffa, that many good things will come to Danhomê from the white men; what they have already brought up until now is a certain guarantee of it for me. And one would have to be a person of bad faith to disagree."

Gaou, Possou, Migan, Mêwou, and all the other advocates of the expedition against Hounjroto indicated their approval of the king's speech. Nevertheless, the queens winked at him and motioned with their fingers, discretely inviting him to withdraw once more so they could prepare him to resist the assault of the arguments being formulated by the counsellors who were opposed to any action against Hounjroto or even against Kinglo.

---

hospitality to the Aladahonous. (author's note)

28

Linpéhoun didn't allow him the time to leave; he said, "the knowledge I have attained about this country's past on the basis of my dealings with the elders reveals to me the thought of the ancestors: if they persist in advising us against the Hounjroto campaign, it is because they regard it as unjust, and they only waged just wars.

"Indeed, when confronted with the proof that his hosts have only been heaping favors upon him as a means of putting him off guard so they can successfully perpetrate the crime they have been hatching against him in secret, what man would not have recourse to drastic measures? That was the justification for the murder of Wo, for after having authorised the settlement of the Aladahonous at Houahoué,[28] this chief was planning to annihilate them all in a single night. But thanks to the Blood Oath that allied him with Baguidi-Zamou, Daco-Donou (who brought us to this place) was warned about the criminal intentions of his host and forestalled him.

"Doesn't a man also have to worry about his reputation, especially if he has recently arrived in a country which is hostile toward him? When the chief of the Nagonou tribe, whom we found at Jêgbé, besmirched our honor with the gross insult of subjecting us to "Lêdahonous", those inveterate oath-breakers, it could only be restored by cleansing it in the blood of the person who had insulted us. And if the Aladahonous of the time had not punished him, we would have obliged his descendants to expiate that crime.

"Wo's successor Ayinon Pahé went to his death only because he attempted to bring about ours, seeking in that way to realize the desire of his predecessor. As a matter of fact, he decided to starve us out, and one night his men laid waste to the fields that we had obtained from Wo and planted in maize.

"What punishment was ever more well deserved than that of the king of Zapô, who captured the men we had sent to Hounsa to buy food for us?

"Never was a conquest more just than that of Tinji, the inhabitants of which refused to free the Aladahonous who had been sold to them by Acobissato.

"Threatened with famine as the result of intrigues hatched by our enemies – Ayinon-Pahé and Acobissato – we were going quite peacefully to buy our provisions at the market in Zapô. But the cowardly attack of King Aco forced us to turn back. In order to avoid starvation, we were obliged, several days later, to take up our machetes and blaze a new trail to the market: our ancestors helped us conquer Zapô.

"If Coussou-Houéton had not granted asylum to the survivors of Zapô and entertained the idea of supporting them in a war of reprisal, we would not have led our armies into his region.

"What man would not have been offended at the insolence of Agri? He refused to give us a plot of land that we needed, and he backed up his refusal with the following impudent defiance: 'This time it is in my quiver that you will find the concession you have requested.'

"The obstinacy of this petty king compelled us to erect our Palace over his

---

[28] Houahouoé, Zapô, Hounsa, and Tounji are villages near Agbomê. (author's note)

corpse and his quiver. That is how we came into the possession of Agrigomê.

"Houégbaja, unfortunately, had to confront as many intrigues as his father. Our second king was first obliged to curb the greed of Agbomêhossou, who demanded a tribute for land that had been ceded to our king. He then had to deal with the effrontery of Nagahonou Di, who had chosen to live near the spring that bore his name – Dido; on that spot he shamelessly taxed the Aladahonous and later, under a false pretext, even refused them permission to draw water. During the drought we lacked water with which to wash ourselves and to still the thirst of our new-born children. The grief of mothers, who themselves were dying of thirst and no longer had any milk in their breasts, roused the Aladahonous against Di.

"If it had not been for the sacrilege of Lansou, who abducted two of Houégbaja's wives and refused to return them, the Alahadonous would have scrupulously continued to pay him the levy he exacted from them for the use of the spring he owned at Amodi.

"When the 'aja' chief Dala laid siege to Agrigomê, the Aladahonous were not alone in being outraged at such an unjust attack. Even our fetishes sided with us and visited all sorts of illnesses upon our enemies. It was not long before the bloated aggressor saw his own body decomposing in front of his very eyes. Horrified, his men suddenly raised the siege. The Aladahonous pursued the retreating horde, and brought back to Agrigomê the putrefying head of Dala.

"If another Guédévi had not repeated the impudence of Agri, our kingdom would never have received its name of Danhomê. Having discovered that the plot of land which had been given to him for the construction of a residence for the princely heir to the throne was too small, Houégbaja asked Dan, who enjoyed sovereignty over the area, to grant him the authorisation to enlarge his concession by several feet. Such a request bears witness to the scrupulousness of Houégbaja, who did not want to make use of anything for which he had not legally obtained the right of usufruct. One can hardly understand why Dan would have taken offense at that and, forgetting the respect owed to the king of the Aladahonous, thrown the following insult into his face: 'You mason-fly who never tires of building, don't you want to relax before raising your houses in my belly?' After having responded appropriately to the criminal suggestions of this petty king, the Aladahonous wanted to devote themselves to the cultivation of the earth. But in addition to the insults of Damlopo, who reproached the founder of Danhomê for the chastisement of Dan, the intrigues of other enemies forced Houégbaja's successors to hold on to their weapons.

"By continuing to harrass the gentlest man in the world, they succeeded in embittering him. In all fairness, one cannot blame him for his excesses against those who were persecuting him. That is to say that the Ayonous' unremitting invasions of Danhomê during the reign of Houégbaja constituted the only motivation for the unconditional war which Acaba waged upon them and which his successors have been obliged to carry on endlessly.

"Then too, was it not for having repeated the crime of Acobissato that Ayizan of Tangbé, who captured some of our subjects at Tinji and sold them, was killed by one of Acaba's soldiers?

"When your neighbor enters into a Blood Oath with your enemy, you would have to be stupid not to suppose that they were uniting their forces to harm you. Once you have been alerted to such an alliance, you owe it to yourself to forestall the attack of your sworn enemies. . . . ."

A murmur swept through the group of high dignitaries.

"There you have the entire explanation behind our battles against Agloui of Gboli and Sahè,[29] who had sworn a pact of friendship with our enemy Dala.

"I just heard someone murmuring the word Aja-Savè. Danhomênous, if, in order to push the king into an unjust war, you distort the facts about which our tradition is unequivocal, you will no longer have the right to be offended by the bad faith of our enemies. Indeed, how can anyone confuse the Mahinous' eminently praiseworthy act at Kinglo with the crime perpetrated by the subjects of the king of Aja-Savè?

"Whereas those Ajanous massacred peaceable Danhomênous on their way to buy provisions in "aja" country, the Mahinous, as for them, killed, and with good reason, the vile beasts from the sea who had come to defile the "mahi" mountains.

"Each time that we fought for a just cause, the protective fetishes of Danhomê vouchsafed us victory, regardless of the superiority of the enemy's weapons, the courage of our opponents, or the respect in which a country was held by virtue of its religious nature. The conquests of Sahè and Alada are proof of that. Thanks to the protection of our fetishes and despite the fact that we were only fighting with short weapons, Danhomê ultimately prevailed over the guns and carronades of Houfon, the king of Sahè, against whom we had a number of well-founded grievances. Although our fetish Agassou is also the principal fetish of Alada, where our uncles continued to live, it was outraged at their betrayal of us when they warned the Houédanous about the war that we were preparing to undertake against them. The great fetish thus helped us conquer Alada after a short battle. Unlike us who are human, fetishes do not lend themselves to dishonorable compromises.

"Our kings of old, who never committed the least injustice during their lifetimes, also refused to second our efforts unless justice fortified our cause.

"If the 'mahi' chief had, like Têfoui of Hoji, pronounced insults against the king who ordered his sceptre to be carried before these foreigners, I am convinced that all the ancestors would rise en masse with us to crush Hounjroto, which supposedly supported the crime committed against the White Bellies at Kinglo, and we would bring back to Danhomê the head of the impudent Mahinou. Like his great grandfather Tégbéssou-Ahandé, our king could then have himself a necklace made from the teeth of the blasphemer, who would be the Têfoui of this reign. But the Mahinous of Hounjroto and Kinglo never spoke ill of the king. Nor, as far as we know, did they venture the slightest allusion to the unfortunate fate of Agontimê, the Mother of Panther.

---

[29]   Gboli and Sahè are villages on the banks of the Coufo River. (author's note)

"For waging war upon them, we therefore lack the good reasons that drove Tégbéssou to attack the inhabitants of Za eight times; after the death of the Queen-Mother Houanjéré, the people of Za let slip the following blasphemy: 'So many tears for the death of a mere woman. If the king of Danhomê has not yet buried his mother for lack of space, let him come looking for a sepulchre in our nostrils!'

"If the Mahinous had uttered a similar blasphemy, we would not only have severed their noses, as Tégbéssou did to the people of Za; we would also have ripped out their vile tongues and cut off their lips before sending them home. In this way, our other enemies would learn the penalty that is paid for slandering the venerable memory of a queen mother.

"Before our victory over Za, the local chief had compounded the blasphemy of his subjects by an unprecedented act of barbarity. The people of Za lived by stealing from others, and they had captured a woman from Danhomê. In the company of two friends, her son went to ransome his mother. The chief of Za welcomed them warmly; he seemed to regret having imprisoned the mother of such a brave young man and promised to return her to him, but first he invited them to refresh themselves before returning to Agbomê. The young men accepted. The mother came to converse with her son. At an order from the chief, the woman withdrew to eat something before getting underway. Waiting for her to return, the young men were served millet beer to dull their senses before the meal, which soon followed. Two calabashes – one filled with a meat caloulou and the other with akassa[30] – were placed in front of the three guests. They ate with a hearty appetite. The steward reappeared and asked them if they were satisfied. He feared that the "caloulou," which had been prepared in great haste, might not have been salty enough or the meat sufficiently well cooked. The young men thanked him profusely and lavished praise upon the skill of the woman who had cooked the meal. With a malicious grin, the king then said to them, "young men, go tell your fellow countrymen that the king of Za shall henceforth be known as Zanou-Houngnon (native of Za, blood tastes good); he gave to the son a 'caloulou' prepared with the flesh and blood of his captured mother, and the son ate it with relish.' He then sent away the young men, who tearfully retold the story of the odious crime to everyone in Danhomê. Moved by the orphan's misfortune, Tégbéssou undertook to avenge him. Do we have as good a motive to attack the Mahinous?

"The children of Adanzan were sold to the slave-traders in retaliation for the sacrilege committed by that tyrant, who had treated the same mother in the same fashion. That was justice! The brothers of those filthy beasts from the sea became the accomplices of Adanzan by buying the queen mother and reselling her like a common Mahinou or Nagonou; they too deserve an exemplary punishment. But I never heard that anyone ever bothered them on that account. The king justified his clemency on the basis of the friendship that bound him to Chacha Ajinacou and, supposedly, to all of this white man's fellow countrymen.

---

[30] "Caloulou" is a dish prepared with meat, fish, or vegetables and served with "acassa," a form of bread. (author's note)

"Danhomênous, our honor prohibits us from setting ourselves up as avengers of the memory of the white men massacred at Kinglo. On the contrary, it dictates that we forget for a moment our resentment against the Mahinous and the Nagonous, that we recall the white man's share of responsibility in the venerable queen mother's misfortune, and that we go to Gléhoué and annihilate all the White Bellies living there.

"Nevertheless, I would agree to defer the punishment of these filthy beasts from the sea and unleash the fury of our troops against Kinglo – not Hounjroto – if our spies had come back from there to inform us about the existence of seers whose science of prophecy and knowledge of gris-gris surpassed that of the Balibas, the same Balibas whom Tégbéssou had fought for the sole purpose of capturing their men, who were reputed for their art of predicting the future and warding off illnesses. Perhaps the Master of the World has another reason for going to war against Hounjroto than the one that has been communicated to us. Ah! If, for example, we could bring back the mountains from the "mahi" country to circle Danhomê with them and make it forever impregnable, this expedition would be justified, and any Danhomênous who disapproved should be delivered into the hands of Migan at this very instant.

"If our royal mesengers, who preceded the white men into Kinglo, had returned and told us, 'like the four kings of Alougba and that hot-headed one from Sinto Abogomê had done with respect to Pingla, the Mahinous have issued an insolent challenge to Danhomê,' and if their report had, upon verification, proved accurate, we should at this very moment follow the example of Pingla, who quickly humbled the pride of the five kings, and punish the insolence of these Mahinous. However, all our messengers affirmed that no one had bothered them; they were even showered with kindness and escorted to the first village in Danhomê for fear they might be accosted by the bandits who infest the "mahi" countryside. The accounts of our royal messengers corroborate those of our numerous spies, who have assured us that the memory of Danhomê's battles against the people of Gbowêlê is still very much alive among the stinking beasts from the "mahi" mountains. Indeed, since the terrible war that our august Father waged against these mountain people to avenge the defeats of Agaja and Tégbéssou, the word Danhomênou strikes the same fear into the hearts of this courageous people as smallpox – their most fearsome fetish. That was certainly the fear that engendered respect for the Danhomênous who accompanied the white men. Our spies, who are not in the habit of reporting our enemies' charitable feelings, found nothing to offend Danhomê among the inhabitants of Kinglo, nor among those of Hounjroto either. We therefore have incontrovertible proof of the respect in which Danhomê is held by the Mahinous.

"Ah! If someone had come to inform us, for example, that sons in their country beat their parents or abandon them in their old age, it would have been useless for these Mahinous to redouble their manifestations of respect for us; our guns and our canons would immediately remind them that the Danhomê which is ruled by the worthy son of Agonglo, who destroyed Sêguêdê for a similar reason, is an uncompromising corrector of corrupt morals.

"Carefully examining our past from the reign of Daco-Donou to that of Agonglo, I can see that all our wars have been just. When it was not the overriding self-interest of Houégbaja's Danhomê that fortified us in our expeditions against our neighbors, it was an insult to the reigning king or to the queen mother or to the memory of a former king, or it was our enemy's insolent defiance of this kingdom or the secret preparation for a war which was going to be directed against us but which we discovered in time or an aggression on the part of our enemies; it was refuge granted or assistance offered, by people we had never wronged in any way, to criminals whom Danhomê was pursuing, or the desire to avenge orphans imploring our aid, or an outrage against morality that justified our wars against Mahinous, Nagonous, Houédanous, and Wémênous. If we desire our dead to lead us to victory, let us remain faithful to the fine tradition which our ancestors have always respected and which has constituted the strength of Danhomê."

He touched his forehead to the ground and sat down.

The king raised his head and sighed deeply. Was his determination wavering?

Assogbaou believed that it was. He decided to strike and therefore supported Linpéhoun: "A campaign against Hounjroto would undermine the fear that we inspire in our neighbors, and all the more so since defeat is inevitable. They will say that Danhomê is no longer strong, that it fears the people of Kinglo, who are the true criminals, and is only attacking those of Hounjroto because they are known for being very weak. Danhomê will have seen the day when it ceases to strike terror into the hearts of its neighbors.

"Linpéhoun has just reminded us of our ancestors' insistence upon fighting only just wars and of the price our enemies have paid for insulting or harassing us.

"If we do not draw all the lessons that are to be drawn from the defeats that our justifiable anger inflicted upon these enemies, we will have cause to regret it. The king is making every effort to characterize this war as a just reprisal that is required by the honor of Danhomê, but in the eyes of our ancestors it appears to be something quite different, for they constantly advise against it.

"News about the massacre of the white men was greeted in Danhomê with unanimous shouts of approval. The country was thus of one mind with the Mahinous and would hardly be enthusiastic about an expedition against them. We will regret it if we disregard the opinion of a people who are, quite inaccurately, regarded as being totally bereft of volition or obstinately resistent to making any observation about the decrees and actions of the king. The people will not approve of this war, and seeking to impose it upon them will push them to rebel. Their anger is to be feared, as the fall of Adanzan demonstrates. The Danhomênou is skillful at concealing his ideas, and for that reason it may seem that he has no opinion about the expedition. But that does not prove he is not thinking about it all the same and that he might well refuse to fire on people with whose conduct he is in complete agreement. Do we really know what misfortunes our ancestors desire to turn aside from us by opposing this war so obstinately?

"Ah, my forefathers, this is the first time that Danhomê, which is usually so prudent, would be leading its army into a country that it had not reconnoitered in advance. Why then do we support such a large number of spies and treat them with such solicitude?

"If we are not running headlong into disaster to expiate some former crime, we are going to commit one that will sooner or later have to be expiated. Life is filled with such bizarre twists that the very sons of the people whom we now desire to avenge will be the ones who will oblige our children to expiate the crime that we, their fathers, will have committed against the Mahinous. Prudence is in the blood of the Danhomênou. He has inherited it from his ancestor the Panther. Don't our elders affirm that the feline wisely turned his back on a doe which he had been chasing and which had just plunged into the reeds of the Swamps; at that moment he is reputed to have said, 'I could lose my claws here if I follow this lowly creature!' If the blood of this prudent ancestor still flows in our veins, we will wisely follow the wild animal's example."

Tomêtin voiced his opinion: "Our ancestors are opposed to the Hounjroto campaign because they cannot permit us to forget the need to avenge the noble memory of Prince Topo-Daho and Prince Dangban, who were killed at Jigbé during the reign of Acaba, rather than taking up arms against the Mahinous of Hounjroto, who are being accused without proof of having incited the people of Kinglo to massacre the vile beasts from the sea whom we call our friends.

"If we reject the prudent advice of our ancestors, we must fear that they will abandon us during the battle; that is, in my opinion, the warning they are communicating to us through the voice of Destiny."

Among the dignitaries who supported the war, no one attempted to contradict the prince. Vivênagbo concluded from their silence that they were all convinced that the proposed campaign was an unjust one. Thus, he ventured his opinion, although still quite timidly: "It is in our best interest not to break with an old custom that people have the tendency to forget; the Danhomê of Houégbaja has never rushed precipitously into a war. It always carefully reconnoitered the country it intended to fight. Its spies gathered information about the enemy forces; they also disclosed the names of the enemy country's principal dignitaries and brought back a bundle of clothes or mats that these dignitaries had used, a tuft of their hair, clippings from their fingernails, and a handful of dirt skimmed from their spitoon or from the ground on which they had left their footprints. Because they benefitted enormously from the booty of war, these lords of the realm made gris-gris, just like we do, to assure the victory of their armies. Before engaging in armed combat with a country, Danhomê had always requested its own principal dignitaries to avail themselves of their knowledge of gris-gris in order to cast an infallible spell upon the dignitaries of the enemy kingdom. Do we know the gris-gris of Hounjroto? What objects that came from their bodies or were in contact with them have we collected? The court will agree that it would be foolhardy to go to war against this "mahi" country until we have succeeded in killing these dignitaries by the use of gris-gris, or, at the very least, in dispelling their vigilance; as long as they are alive or keeping watch over their

35

country, our defeat is certain."

He kissed the ground at the foot of the throne and sat down.

Vivênagbo's counsels were greeted with murmurs of approval, and, emboldened by his example, the old warrior Alopé took the floor; King Agonglo had always listened to his words with care. "Linpéhoun has told the truth: the Danhomê of Houégbaja has never undertaken an unjust war. But I would remind you that, even in the case of just wars, the ancestors of the Master of the World have always refused to help our armies each time the king ignored their advice to wait before going to war. In those instances, the heroism of our soldiers never overcame the resistence of our enemies.

"Indeed, as long as the ancestors felt that the war against the Houédanous of Sahé was inopportune, they did not support Agaja. Only the eighth campaign, which they did approve, was victorious.

"What city was more deserving of annihilation than Gbowêlê with its inhabitants and the criminals who had taken refuge there since the reign of Acaba? Nevertheless, when Agaja proposed to destroy this "mahi" settlement, our ancestors, who are no longer subject to the impatience of mortals, advised him to wait. Our fourth king disobeyed his predecessors. But the three expeditions he undertook failed completely to produce the effect he expected upon the attitude of these sons of the mountain.

"These Mahinous committed other crimes during the reign of Tégbéssou. Into their midst they welcomed the humpback Ahoyiwê, who was guilty of adultery. Listening only to the voice of his anger rather than to the sage advice of the ancestors who counselled him, as they had Agaja, to defer the punishment of Gbowêlê, Tégbéssou was repulsed three times in a row when he attacked the 'mahi' country.

"This king then turned and directed his attentions against the blasphemers and barbarians of Za. The ancestors were of the opinion that the time had not yet come to avenge the memory of the queen mother or that of the unfortunate woman whose flesh had been served to her son by Zanou-Hougnon. For having disdained the counsel of his ancestors, Tégbéssou had to fight against Za seven times in vain. Only the eighth campaign, which he undertook upon their advice, was successful.

"The glory of having destroyed Gbowêlê belongs to King Agonglo. But the ancestors, whose counsels were ignored at the beginning, abandoned Danhomê during the first seven campaigns. As in the conquest of Za, only the eighth campaign, which was sanctioned by the ancestors, brought us victory.

"Those are the lessons of tradition. The Master of the World owes it to himself to take advantage of them if he wants to spare his subjects a bad experience and save Danhomê from a disastrous defeat."

There was a great deal of self-assurance in his voice. Once he sat down, he cast a questioning glance at his friends, and they showed their approval with discreet nods of the head.

Oundanoucou gave his advice: "Gou, the god of arms and warfare, doesn't eat leaves, and he doesn't drink water. He only consumes meat and quenches his thirst with blood. But let us refrain from offering him the flesh and blood of innocents. Far from satisfying his appetite or slaking his thirst, that sort of food and drink increases them enormously, and they will only be stilled with the flesh and blood of the person who flung him these innocents to feed upon. Let us be forewarned, Danhomênous!"

Standing and facing Alopé, who had just opposed the plan for war, Gaou said proudly: "As a man of the people, I do not know all the traditions of this kingdom, but, in my position as first minister of war, I have become quite familiar with the history of its battles.

"In the small number of defeats suffered long ago by the armies of Danhomê, Alopé sees a punishment for disobeying the ancestors. The counsellor is hoping to succeed in turning the Master of the World aside from his resolve to crush Hounjroto by waving the spectre of these defeats before the eyes of His Majesty. Let us not distort tradition. No! The defeats which have been interpreted in such a fanciful way can actually be explained by a lack of courage or discipline on the part of the soldiers at the time. If a Danhomênou had secretly sworn to kill the warrior spirit that constitutes the strength of this people or, as I should have said, if a Danhomênou was conspiring to bring about the domination of foreigners, he could not have imagined a better bugaboo. Fortunately, there is no lack of clear-sighted and courageous people at this court.

"Alopé, what campaign was undertaken under less favorable signs than that of Abogomê? Destiny was consulted twenty times, and it invariably responded that the ancestors disapproved of that war. The prophecies of our Moslem divines seconded Destiny in discouraging us. Everything was against it. In planning the conquest of Abogomê to requite the invasion of Danhomê by Yahazê, Pingla was obeying the will of Acaba, but Acaba appeared to him in a dream and enjoined him to renounce the war.

"But Pingla owed it to himself to steal a march on Sinto, the successor of Yahazê; besides, indications of enemy preparations for war filtered back to Danhomê, and the king of Abogomê threw an insolent challenge in our faces.

"Pingla considered only the best interest of Danhomê.

"His army left Agbomê at night, determined to engage the enemy on the following morning. Just after the second crowing of the cock, a strange light illuminated the earth, even though the day star had not yet risen.

"At the very moment when our soldiers were preparing to leave their hiding places, three suns appeared in the sky. An unusual and utterly terrifying sight! The soldiers froze, as if paralyzed by this vision; their weapons fell from their hands, and they threw themselves face-down upon the ground. Those whose legs had grown stiff with fear were standing there like palm trees and shaking like leaves. The battle captains had a great deal of difficulty in reviving the courage of the troops. Then for the crowning misfortune! Scarcely arrived at the edge of the forest, the Danhomênous saw a white elephant collapse twenty paces in front of them and die, after several death rattles, in front of their very eyes. There was not the slightest trace of blood to suggest that it might have succumbed to a wound inflicted by a hunter.

"The little courage that had fortified our soldiers quickly disappeared; filled with terror, their faces turned in the direction of Danhomê, and the battle captains saw no more than the heels of their fleeing warriors. Nevertheless, the impassioned words of Gaou and Possou finally quelled the mindless panic.

"Despite the gloomy predictions that had accompanied the soldiers to war and despite the extraordinarily sinister omens they had encountered there, Abogomê was soon reduced to blood, smoke, and ashes. This fact alone should suffice to silence our hesitations today. Let us close our ears to these words of discouragement. When our hearts know no fear, our victory will be certain."

Possou, the second minister of war, supported his colleague: "Like their predecessors during the reign of Pingla, our soldiers will know how to win the war, even if lightning descends from the sky to protect the Mahinous or if their ancestors leave their tombs to fight at their sides! Let the predestined King not be intimidated by Alopé's childish spectres; let him rather keep in mind the conduct of his inscrutable grandfather and prove to all Danhomê that a superior mind, like his own, is inaccesible to the superstitions that frighten the majority of mortals."

The opinion of the two ministers of war carried the day against the sage advice of the princes. The king approved of the two warriors' words: "I have reasons to be confident in my soldiers, whose bravery will compensate for the aid of the ancestors if it is not forthcoming.

"When an old friend cheerfully extended his hand to a man who had recently been named chief, the latter greeted him with the following words: 'Buried is the familiarity of days gone by!' A final warning to my numerous counsel-givers.

"And if Alopé wants his words always to be heard, he will have to moderate his use of brandy from now on. For Danhomênous, the white man's alcohol is more pernicious than our own fermented beverages!"

The old warrior, whose scars testified to the suffering he had endured for the expansion of Danhomê, did not protest against the spitefulness with which the king had replied to his sage counsels.

All eyes turned toward Vidaho. His uncles had been convinced that he would share their opinion. But the heir to the throne persisted in remaining silent. His august Father had always advised him never to pronounce himself in the passionate debates of the court. In that way he would avoid offending influential courtiers who could cause him serious difficulties when the throne became vacant, if they wanted to avenge themselves for the wounding of their pride during a meeting of the counsel.

Fearing a new siege of arguments on the part of the princes who were opposed to the war, the king informed the counsel: "I will not offer the ancestors anything to drink until the memory of their friends has been avenged."

His statement served to warn the princes that they would be responsible for a failure to perform a sacred custom.

Until now Adouconou had not yet voiced his opinion about the war against Hounjroto. His demeanor puzzled his peers. He was not at all moved by the king's threats, which had been calculated to force the hand of the council to the throne. Finally, he broke his silence. "I don't have much confidence in the oracle. This gift from our irreconcilable enemies the Ayonous is no doubt intended to blunt our vigilance or to sow confusion in our minds. If I keep a diviner in my family, it is more to be fashionable than anything else. Let us consult our ancestors the same way the elders always did in the days of Daco-Donou, Houégbaja, and Acaba before anything was known about the oracle of the Ayonous. Let us go to the tomb of our august Father and place upon it the four cowries that will serve to question him tomorrow morning about the proposed campaign."

His advice was followed. One of the princesses empowered to present offerings to the ancestors went to offer water, melegueta pepper, kola nuts, and rum to King Agonglo, and then she implored him to pronounce his opinion clearly the next day with regard to the war plan that was dividing the court of Houégbaja. She deposited the four cowries on the tomb.

Upon a sign from the king, who was lost in thought, one of the wives who had been standing at his side knelt down, leaned over, and placed her right ear next to his mouth. The Master of the World whispered several words into it. The queen immediately touched her forehead to the ground and disappeared into the interior of the Palace. Meanwhile the queen who held the white scarf wiped the king's face and lips. The queenly messenger returned with two bottles of brandy. Daclo took them and gave them to Ajaho.

Facing his peers, the minister called them one by one and then said to them: "Here is the libation that the Father of Wealth is providing as he dismisses you." They all prostrated themselves in the dust, rubbed the palm of one hand against the other, and in an expression of gratitude prayed that the king might enjoy a long life so that he could continue to give them such excellent things. The king did not hear the last words of the court's good wishes.

As each palace dignitary left to return to his place of residence, the lines of Destiny had already become invisible in their hands.

Only the soldiers of the royal guard remained at Singboji.

Some time after the departure of the courtiers, three of the king's personal bodyguards were sent from the Palace to summon Migan, Mêwou, Gaou, and Possou. They went to Agonglo's tomb and ordered that the four cowries placed there to consult the will of the dead king be cast to the ground.

The arrangement of the cowries – an odd number of backsides – meant that the ancestor was opposed to the war.

Guézo swore the woman to silence about what she had just seen. She kneeled down, kissed the earth, and made the gesture of covering her head with dust as a sign of obedience.

"When the Master of the World and his four most important ministers have reached a decision, the voice of Danhomê has spoken; other opinions should no longer count," proclaimed the king.

The ministers joyously approved his words. As he sent them away, the king advised them not to reveal anything about their conversations to anyone.

"We would sooner allow ourselves to be hacked to bits!" swore the first minister in the name of his peers. They left the Palace through different doors.

Chapter 2

Those Behind the War

Stretched out on his mat, his left elbow resting on the pillow and his head cradled in the palm of his hand, Toffa stared fixedly in front of himself. The silence in the room was only broken by a series of "oum houm," which he occasionally punctuated with two deep exhalations.

"My master does nothing but sigh since his return from the Palace. He did not even allow the worshipful woman with the calabash to set down the dishes she was bringing for his dinner. What has happened to my lord? An illness? Where does it hurt him? Perhaps he experienced troubles at court? Did some courtier seek to damage his reputation in the eyes of the king? Let him deign to tell me. My hatred will then pursue the schemer to his grave. And it makes no difference to me if Guêzo himself was the cause of my lord's unhappiness. Let my master take consolation from his troubles by avenging himself upon me, as is usually done in this Danhomê.

"I do not think that my lord has already forgotten the incident that Yévogan Dagba recounted at the court three moons ago. A slave returned to his hut, his body battered by the blows he had received upon the orders of his master Chacha; there was anger in his heart; he grabbed his pig, which was digesting its last meal in a state of peaceful drowsiness, beat it with the utmost violence, and then said: 'My lord Chacha ordered me flogged, and no one could be found to blame him for it. I have just avenged myself upon my pig; no one will call me to account for that. Let the people and the animals that belong to us atone for the cruelties inflicted upon us at the hands of our masters.'

"I am your property, my lord, and I am prepared to suffer all the torments it might please you to practice upon me as a means of forgetting your sorrows.

. . . .

41

"Why this silence, my lord and master? Last night at this time your mouth sang tirelessly of your love, but this evening it brings forth only sighs.

"Usually when my master remains silent, at least his face speaks to me, but those eyes that I love to gaze upon seem to be fleeing from me this evening. Why this indifference? Let my lord look at me, for the sake of pity. Let him deign to smile upon me; I embrace his feet. Only a few moments ago I was rejoicing at the thought that the return of my master was imminent and that we would soon be enjoying happy moments, just like last night. I promised myself: 'Before we abandon ourselves to sleep, I will sing him a song in response to the one he sang last night!' I would like to begin. Is my lord and master listening?"

This is the manner in which Toffa's young wife, distressed by the prince's silence and sadness, was speaking to him in a beseeching voice that vibrated with sincere love. Because he remained motionless and did not seem to hear her, she became frightened and decided to go and awaken her fellow wives.

She was tall and rather stout; her color verged on the yellow of a calabash. Before the return of her husband, she had taken a bath and rubbed herself with a pomade of her own preparation; its fragrance floated in the air. A pink velvet cloth covered her breasts without, however, concealing an exuberance of development that betrayed her plebian birth, contrasting slightly with the nobility of her gestures and sentiments. Brought from the other side of the Swamps of Agbomê two dry seasons ago in the company of other young girls who had been recruited for the Palace, she stood out in the batch from which Toffa had chosen a wife, upon the orders of Guézo, on the eve of the great festival of the ancestors. Everything about her excited the admiration of the prince's friends – her stature, the charm of a glance that was shaded beneath sharply arched eyebrows amply furnished with thick lashes, the two lines that circled her neck of a well-fed antelope (a mark of great beauty!), the sweetness of her voice whether she was speaking or singing. They valued the young woman's polite and friendly manner, congratulating Toffa warmly about it and adding that so many charms signified she was a superior woman. They also endlessly praised Toffa's sagacity, for as a good judge of the human soul (which, according to one of the prince's favorite expressions, frequently manifested it in the external features of creatures with seven pairs of ribs), he had given this woman the tender name of "Doguicimi" – which means "distinguish me" – on the very day of his marriage to her, and from then on it was the only name by which she was known.

One more step and she would have been in the courtyard. With an emphatic "no", Toffa forbid her to leave the room. She obeyed, remained motionless for an instant, then came over and lay down behind him. "Come, my lord and master," she said, drawing his head toward her, "come. The night is no longer young. Come put your head on my breast, the pillow that lulls you to sleep in your moments of insomnia." He resisted. "Am I the one who offended you, author of my days? There can no longer be any doubt about it. Beat me and burden my neck and ankles with chains. Do anything you like with me. I am determined to endure everything, and I will not show the least sign of rebellion;

42

I will think myself extremely happy, if my suffering can restore my creator to his usual good humor, which is the wellspring of my life. Even Guézo would not blame you if he learned of my torments. In Danhomê only the commoner does not have the right to imprison his wife. But you, aren't you a prince? And am I not your property? You can therefore do anything you want with me."

"Calm yourself, Doguicimi," said Toffa finally, touched by his wife's affliction. "My sadness can be attributed solely to the king. At the Palace we have a man who claims to be the successor of our ancestors. Yet the moment he declares himself to be the only one who exercises authority in Danhomê, the king is setting an example of the most revolting torpor."

The prince fell silent again, sighed deeply, and then grew indignant: "Is it possible, my forefathers? Didn't the breadth of Guézo's shoulders, so admirably suited to his height, suggest that he was a man of strength? And his eyes? To think that, seeing them illuminate his virile face, we believed they could easily fathom the most hidden motives of men's actions! And that neck? So full and tall! That princely neck which clearly distinguishes Aladahonous from all the other peoples of Danhomê! That neck we thought made for cheerfully supporting the stately burden of governing Danhomê! That stout neck deceived us? My forefathers, would anyone have believed that large hands at the end of muscled arms – royal hands recognizable by their long, supple fingers with pink nails – would prove incapable of holding anything that could not be snatched from them by the feeble hands of women? And that beautiful body covered with skin the color of a calabash and so delicate that it allows the hue of his blood, the royal origins of which are beyond question, to be seen on his arms and the calves of his legs! Exuding energy and nobility, his entire appearance was attractive, so reminiscent of my august Father's majestic bearing that one could be fooled into thinking it was he; oh, irony of Destiny, does this appearance hold nothing more than weakness and cowardice? Looking at him, who would think that Guézo had not inherited the characteristics of King Agonglo? Why did we not recognize it sooner? Adanzan's successor has deceived our hopes; no one had thought that, after having eliminated the debauchery and cruelty that were a disgrace to the throne, we would install irrationality, weakness, and perfidy in their place.

"Alas, that is what governs the Danhomê of Houégbaja today now that it has fallen into the hands of women!

"Guézo only has ears for his wives, and they want a war against the Mahinous of Hounjroto.

"In defiance of very explicit warnings that the ancestors conveyed to us through the voice of the oracle about the defeat that awaits us, we are doubtless on the verge of a war for which no preparations have been made. An unprecedented event in Danhomê, a country of order, organisation, wisdom, and a prudence often carried to the point of distrust.

"The king only consulted the ancestors as a matter of formality. In fact, he told us this morning at the beginning of the council that he would disregard their advice if it opposed his wishes.

"Our former kings are the essence of wisdom, and they opposed this expedition."

"It is no doubt justified by reasons of state that have escaped the attention of the dead kings," his wife suggested.

"These Mahinous were accused of having incited their fellow tribesmen at Kinglo to massacre the two or three White Bellies who had ventured into "mahi" country to visit, or so they claimed, mountains that are not worth seeing for any particular reason.

"The foul beasts from the sea have already polluted the coast all the way to Agbomê; they now want to extend their evil influence into the interior of the country. But the Mahinous were on their guard. More shrewd than we were, they quickly saw through the plans of these stinking beasts and nipped it in the bud. What all Danhomê regards as a praiseworthy action is for Guézo a crime; the king also sees it as a slap in the face for the kingdom of Houégbaja because these white men were under the protection of the royal sceptre, and he would like to punish the Mahinous for that reason.

"The king's obstinacy in undertaking this war is incomprehensible to me.

"The forty or so princes at the council were all opposed to an expedition against Hounjroto or Kinglo. Those who lacked the courage to express their opinions discreetly applauded Agonglo's sons who advised against the proposed campaign. For a moment, we were naive enough to believe that Guézo, who owes the throne to our concerted efforts against Adanzan, could not in all decency disdain our sage advice. The oracle soon came and told us that the ancestors too disapproved of this campaign.

"Their predictions about the unfortunate outcome of the proposed war supplied all the princes with eloquent arguments in support of their opinions. I took the floor after Assogbaou and easily demonstrated the white men's hatred of Danhomê; at great length I set forth the reasons why we should be fighting these foreigners rather than the Mahinous. The king remained adamant in his determination. But it did not take us long to understand that the queens, who completely dominate this puppet, were pulling the strings. Adouconou cautioned us to distrust the oracle of the Ayonous and to place greater confidence in the old way of consulting the ancestors – the only way that had been practiced before we knew about the oracle that Jissa and Gongon brought to Danhomê from the country of our irreconcilable enemies – and upon his advice, the king ordered that everything be prepared for that consultation, which will take place tomorrow morning after the second crowing of the cock. The hope of all the counsellors who are opposed to the war hangs upon that consultation; we doubt that our ancestors will diverge from the position they have taken against the war of Hounjroto. But Guézo is quite capable of once more rejecting the advice they will be giving us through the voice of the cowries."

He remained silent for a moment and then continued: "Will we have saved our country from dishonor only to place it into the hands of base creatures with seven pairs of ribs? Those creatures who are incapable of anything noble?

"It is enough to make one weep for the ancestors! They love this kingdom, which we delight in comparing to the rock, but isn't it going to melt like shea

44

butter in the ardent and inextinguishable desire for conquests? Ah, yes, this country is running so quickly toward disaster that it will have reached it before its great grandchildren are weaned.

"To disdain the sage advice of men who are the very image of reason and fidelity while listening only to the crackbrained ideas of women! Those women who share pleasant morsels with men and turn away from them as soon as the taste of bitterness becomes noticeable! It is difficult to believe that a successor of Houégbaja could have fallen so low!

"Will the example of Ayomayi's love for Daco-Donou ever be found in this Danhomê? Despite the apparent steadfastness of her attachment to her royal husband, didn't this woman eventually abandon the ancestor who led us to this place? All women are like her. When they desire to obtain some favor from a man, they are doves, cooing a deceitful love. But if they meet with a refusal? The treachery that is smouldering in them immediately bursts out.

"Ayomayi's behavior confirms that other saying of our fathers: 'Woman is like a snail. What man could succeed in making it stick to a tree according to his will? When it is sticking there by itself, doesn't it only require a small effort to dislodge it?' Guézo is all the more reprehensible because he knows the entire tradition of Danhomê in regard to the faithlessness of women.

"Among the Danhomênous, even the commoner who possesses a bit of personal wealth remembers the lesson of the past and refuses to entrust the management of his affairs to any woman. Only Guézo has forgotten the shameful conduct of that wife of Agaja, a woman who took advantage of her position as intendant to steal treasures from the royal storehouses and send them to the Ayonous (to whom we were subject at the time) in order to bribe them to demand the recognition of her son Aguidissou as the presumptive heir to the throne in place of the young man who became King Tégbéssou.

"Ever since that crime against Danhomê, the stewardship of the royal wealth has been taken from the queens and entrusted in men placed under the close supervision of Mêwou.

"But Guézo, who owes his throne to men, no longer considers them worthy of his confidence, which he has placed, along with his keys, in the hands of his wives."

The prince was sitting up; his sadness had given way to anger. "My forefathers!" he proceded with indignation, "under the effect of what spell has Guézo forgotten that women always divert their husbands' goods toward the paternal hearth? Haven't these creatures with seven pairs of ribs been known to ruin their husbands in order to favor their lovers or even strangers?

"Just like mats, women deserve neither respect nor confidence. When new, mats serve us as something to sleep on. When worn out, they should be thrown on the dung heap.

"Only a madman would have respect for objects which never refuse to roll themselves out to serve as sleeping places alternatively for the master of the house and, in his absence, for his slaves.

"Would an authentic son of King Agonglo pay attention to the barking of bitches with seven pairs of ribs? It's inconceivable!

"Bitches created to obey the will of men, you have succeeded in subjecting a king to your whims, your goal no doubt being to hasten Vidaho's ascension to the throne for reasons that only imbeciles do not suspect; you will need to instigate but two or three wars after this one, and your desires will be fully satisfied."

"As for me," protested Doguicimi, "I think that what my lord and master has been saying about the conduct of Ayomayi is a joke among the Danhomênous. But if a royal wife actually behaved that way in the past, those like her are not numerous in the Danhomê of today. And it is not fair for my master, whose good sense is admired by all Danhomênous, to judge all women on the basis of several who conducted themselves badly."

Toffa shrugged his shoulders, spit as a sign of contempt, and turned his back on his wife. She continued: "My lord and master is pretending not to know that the number of honest women in Danhomê is legion and that, far from abandoning our fathers in times of misfortune, our mothers know how to stand by them in adversity, following the example of doves who not only fill their homes with cooings, but throw themselves upon the fire consuming the roof that shelters them in the hope of extinguishing it.

"For the master of my spirit, the snail, which readily allows itself to be plucked from the tree to which it seems solidly attached, is supposedly the symbol of our inconstancy. But the very life of this mollusk belies such a prejudiced notion; what it teaches is far more to the honor of my sex: the snail dies in its shell just like the women of Danhomê. This hut is my shell, and it will house my mortal remains unless my master has my body cast into the ditch that surrounds the city. I am not, I admit, expressing the attitude of women like Ayomayi, women who are slugs. . . .

"The prejudice that one sex only has seven pairs of ribs is equally absurd: the sex of those decapitated by Migan's scimitar can not be accurately determined by an examination of the bone pile in the Ditch. Our physical inferiority, so often denounced by men, is therefore pure fiction. If it were a reality, it would add considerable merit to both our devotion in the home and our martial valor. On the battlefield, does the heroism of women lag behind that of their masters with nine pairs of ribs?

"Assuming that we really did have fewer ribs, men's scorn for us would be turned back upon themselves, for although they are strongly built, they would lack the merit of having strong characters.

"By citing his own unhappiness, my master can not justify the gross insult he would like to pay my sex by employing the term 'bitch'. I protest in the name of all honest women. We are dogs in the sense that we are the faithful companions of masters who are not always grateful. Like our four-footed sisters who surrender all the game they capture to their masters and demand nothing in return, we content ourselves with scraps of prepared food if it pleases the man to leave any for us. Like dogs, we are the watchful guardians of the home. Indeed, we are the bitches who perpetuate the race and furnish Danhomê with

46

the soldiers who are led to the slaughter each year.

"The master of my spirit can also have confidence in my honesty; I have never even taken the feather of a chicken from his house to decorate that of my parents, whom I have, moreover, left forever. If the prosperity of any household is important to me, it is henceforth that of the prince.

"Is my master not the first man whom I ever knew in my life? He is also the only one whom I love. I have scarcely spent three dry seasons under his roof. But whatever happens, my love for him will not diminish before the end of my days. That is to say, the mat which I am for him will never be soiled by contact with another man, even if my husband should go to join his ancestors. I will also add that I would not hesitate to sacrifice myself for him whenever that might be necessary. I know that you are sceptical, my lord. But my conduct will enlighten you as time goes by, and you will certainly revise your harsh judgment."

Toffa replied disdainfully: "My conviction is so firm that your babblings about the fidelity, devotion, and integrity of women will never succeed in shaking it. Your efforts to convince me merely confirm the hypocrisy of women. You are not unaware of the blandishments showered on Vidaho by the queens who have been designated to accompany the king to the realm of the dead, for they hope to please him and thereby divert the poisoned potion from their lips. Ah, when the night of my august Father arrived, you should have seen the pitiful expressions on the faces of several queens as they resigned themselves to drinking the fatal potion after they had failed in all their efforts to evade the singular honor of serving their husband in the hereafter!"

"The sacrifice of the queens who spontaneously offered themselves and only succeeded in being buried with the royal remains after many entreaties – does it count for nothing with my lord?"

"One has to be called Guézo to be fooled by such mummeries."

"I am deeply upset by my lord and master's mood this evening. He who has always said that women are sweeter than honey now finds us to taste of gall, and he who has always regarded the king as an idol now calls Guézo the shadow of a king. Whatever indisposition my lord might have suffered during the day, let reason prevail in him, and he will quickly renounce his prejudice."

"Indisposition? Not at all! More like indignation! And it was at the court where I fought in vain against shameless queens who were advocating an unjust war; it was at the court where I became certain that the most intelligent man in Danhomê knows less about influencing the human soul than the most dull-witted woman, and it was in the presence of Guézo that I learned to despise a king without character and queens without nobility," replied Toffa in a slack voice, betraying the torpor that was overcoming him.

"Your contempt is thus only justified in the case of women like Ayomayi and the clay they shape according to the whims of the little worm in their heads. But since you want to encompass all honest women in it as well and because, in order to surround yourself with a wall of prejudice, you disparage the noble sentiments displayed by those of my sex, I will tell you about a quite recent event,

47

which, although you pretend to be unaware of it, indisputably demonstrates the devotion of which women are capable; it was the woman Yêpommê Avognondé who alerted all Danhomê with her cries and her gunshot when the sons of Adanzan came to set the Palace of Gbêcon-Hounli on fire upon the order of the tyrant himself, who had planned to burn all the Palaces in Agbomê.

"The arsonists wanted to perpetrate their crime without the knowledge of the tyrant's adversaries and then blame the fire upon Guézo's supporters, thereby hoping to abort the ascension of Agonglo's worthy son to the throne, an eventuality which they anticipated and which was, as you told me, being prepared by a conspiracy led by Tomêtin, Adouconou, and yourself. But the criminals had not counted on the woman Yêpommê Avognondé. Didn't her courageous act save your heads, which Adanzan would certainly have caused to roll as the result of an alleged sacrilege that his vassals would have sworn against you?

"Despite the danger that she herself was running, Yêpommê Avognondé calmly performed the gesture of liberation. As a reward for this heroic act, which was totally unprecedented in the history of Danhomê, a number of bitches, as you call them, have deviated from the principal function for which the Creator sent them into this world; the act of King Guézo's wife had made him aware of a new employment for members of our sex, and he created the army of women. In combat, they have always rivalled men in heroism. Amazed, the king compared the fury of these Amazons with that of buffalos.

"They are strictly forbidden the love of a man. In return, the Master of the World offers them a gun and a sabre to love and Danhomê to idolize. Don't they resign themselves to sacrificing their maternal instincts, which are very strong among the women of Danhomê, to the love of their weapons, which they jealously care for in the place of the children they are not allowed to have.

"Ah, one has to see how disciplined they are and how obedient to the orders of Danhomê, their beloved spouse, for whose power and glory they gladly give their lives.

"By their chastity and their courage on the battlefield, these Amazons have rehabilitated our sex, even if Ayomayi's misconduct, which has never been proven, could have tarnished the honor of all women.

"The wife of Daco-Donou certainly never knew true love, which is not the female's passive submission to the sensual appetites of her male; even less is it the stimulation of those appetites in the male by a few depraved females. Any man imbued with this distinction will never expect anything noble from women like Ayomayi because, in order to be capable of sacrifice, one needs to love the way I love my lord and master – to love as the Amazons love Danhomê, that is to say with pure love.

*   *   *

Toffa's head had been resting for some time on his wife's chest. Doguicimi gently caressed the hands of the prince. Her fingers passed back and forth through those of her husband, bending them slightly to the rear. She then took the prince's fingers one by one, folded them in toward his palm, and squeezed them until they cracked. Did the pain cause Toffa to essay a vague gesture of retreat? The woman at once straightened the finger and caressed the sleeping man's palm. The pain assuaged, Doguicimi released that hand and picked up the second one. She went from one hand to the other, pulling on each finger after having folded it forward.

The prince had resisted at first, but in the end he abandoned himself completely to the caresses at which the woman excelled.

After such a victory, could Doguicimi also have triumphed over Toffa's prejudice against women?

An infinitely estimable victory, if it had ever been won!

The prince had not replied to his wife's final arguments, but it is quite probable that they never reached his ear. Had he been awake, he would certainly have continued to quibble, for no one could say that he, Toffa, had ever allowed himself to be persuaded by a woman, by a creature of no importance.

Doguicimi nurtured the silence that would soothe her husband.

The terra cotta lamp that illuminated the room began to quiver lugubriously as it drank the last of the oil. The darkness gradually invading the room also filled the woman's entire being with a corresponding lethargy. Soon her right hand released Toffa's and fell heavily upon the mat; her left hand rested on her husband's chest, and she too succumbed to drowsiness. Their stomachs rose and fell in a regular rhythm, dancing to the sound of the drums that beat incessantly inside their chests. Like ivory hunting horns, their nostrils entoned a melody that accompanied the beating of the drums. The rumbling of their bowels could be heard intermittently, like the joyful outbursts of spectators who, from time to time, break into peals of laughter; the verses of their song spoke of hunger. The man had not taken any food all day, and for that reason the woman had not had the courage to eat during the evening.

Toffa awoke, for the pleasant sensation that had lulled him to sleep dissipated as soon as the woman who was giving rise to it had herself dropped off to sleep.

His pessimism and his sadness revived as well. The prince began to sigh with grief. "Woman is the very essence of deceit. When she's awake, she nevertheless pretends to be sound asleep. If she could learn your secrets, she would immediately broadcast them. Innocently, you assume that she has gone to the forest or the market or the spring whenever she is not at home. Such confidence throws you off guard, but it's perhaps better for you than a knowledge of the shameful truth. Far be it from me to shatter your illusion. Yet you need to know that the she-cat, who eagerly caresses you upon your return home and purrs her love, has just disposed of your property. . . .

"But if you shadow her all day long, she will abandon you on the sleeping mat as soon as she has succeeded in lulling you to sleep by means of her artful ruses, so that she can seek, among the slaves of your slaves, the fulfillment of her insatiable desires.

"It is to such base creatures that a king obsequiously bows his will." He shook his head, remained pensive for a moment, then swore: "By Sô![1] Let

---

[1] Abbreviation of "Heviossê" (Lightning), one of the gods in the pantheon of Danhomê.

lightening strike me if I, like this royal puppet, ever abdicate my prerogatives as a man. . . ."

These invectives fell upon a silence in which the melody of Doguicimi's breathing also disappeared after momentarily quickening its tempo and growing louder.

Toffa was haunted by other, quite vague thoughts, but because they were fleeting and did not keep him awake for long, the prince soon dozed off again.

He had scarcely fallen asleep when the conversation with his wife resumed in his dreams. She pointed out that the Supreme Being had not molded her from the mud of Ayomayi, but rather from the purest kaolin, the same as that from which her mother and the mother of her charming husband had been fashioned. For this reason Doguicimi–like these two models of virtue itself–knew nothing about the art of deception, intrigue, betrayal, prevarication, and incitement to crime. She declared that, whether she were asleep or awake, her thoughts revolved solely around Toffa, the soul of her soul and henceforth her only idol. In worshipping the one who had created her, she vowed to demonstrate the numerous virtues of the heart with which he had endowed her. Toffa protested vigorously: never for a moment had his spirit been darkened by the shadow of a doubt in regard to the nobility of Doguicimi's sentiments! Indeed, wasn't he the first man ever to have truly known her? And since their marriage, had she even once crossed the threshold of his compound? Had she spoken to another man? How then could she possibly have deceived him? Completely reassured, the woman replied: "If you turn around at the moment when you are approaching death, you will see me faithfully following in your footsteps."

The prince had no qualms about her. On the contrary, he exulted. He declared that women were excellent creatures and that Doguicimi surpassed them all. He saw himself as the only happy man in all of Danhomê, for in this woman he alone possessed the priceless treasure of love. In the midst of this beautiful dream, Toffa burst into laughter. Oh, weakness of the human spirit! The sound awakened his wife.

"If he is laughing, it is because his slumbers are filled with sweet dreams," she murmured to herself when she realized that her husband was still asleep. "May it leave a good impression on him and dispel his sadness after he wakes in the morning!"

She remained motionless for an instant, curbing even her respiratory movements out of fear that her breathing might disturb the prince's repose.

Before long, however, Doguicimi recalled Toffa's prejudice against women. Now it was her turn to judge men: "The egotism of men never struck me as forcefully as it did tonight. Men don't want to hear about the rights of creatures with seven pairs of ribs, as they call us. They are free to fill their compounds with as many wives as their wealth permits them to acquire. Even so they claim the right to sleep wherever they please and to seduce the wives of other men. Yet they cannot tolerate the thought that their example might be followed by

(author's note)

those of my sex.

"They refuse us the liberty they abuse, alleging that a woman is among the amenities which life offers men as a means of assuring their happiness and that she should submit to her master's caprices. So be it. It never even entered my mind to take possession of what I believe to be my property. But I have the right to demand that confidence be placed in me, that I be accorded more respect. Don't those egotists contend that it is in vain for them to relish savory morsels and to sip refreshing drinks or indulge freely in the pleasures of sleep, because their happiness remains incomplete until after the sexes have been united?

"In their good-humored moments, they agree that we are the thumb of hands which would, if it were ever amputated, be unsuitable for grasping any object firmly; why then do they hold us in such disdain? What ingratitude could possibly equal that of men who, thanks to us, achieve what they call the pinnacle of their happiness and then turn their backs on us, only to beseech us again a few moments later?"

A new outburst of Toffa's laughter checked the woman's bitter musings; she directed her thoughts toward her husband. She recalled the danger he would face when he accompanied the king to war; her anger then ceded to feelings of love, and she forgave the prince his harsh attacks upon women. She raged against Guézo and his wives, cursing them under her breath.

Suddenly she snapped her thumb against her second finger; she had just made a decision. She bent one leg, then stretched it out full length; she bent her other leg, dragging it noisily across the mat, and extended it in the same way. She raised her right hand and allowed it to fall upon her husband. He was so lost in slumber that he did not feel the impact.

She then summoned her courage, raised the sleeping man's head with infinite precautions, placed it on the pillow, propped herself on her elbows, and leaned toward her husband, listening to his breathing and staring at his face as if she could actually see it in the darkness. Anxiety prompted her to remain for a moment in this position, but she soon determined that there was nothing at her side but an inert body, from which all the senses had long since departed to graze elsewhere, as local belief would have it. She then arose and left the room on the tips of her toes.

. . . .
. . . .

As she reentered her husband's room, Doguicimi burst into sobs and lamented. "War. . . ? You can see war? War. . . and an end that will be. . . disastrous. . . ?"

This unwonted sound wrenched Toffa from his slumbers and caused him to sit up; it startled him. He groped around the mat, called Doguicimi, and inquired into the reason for her tears. He realized that she was no longer at his side. Still half asleep, he attempted to go outside, but only stumbled into the wall.

The woman informed him, "I am returning from the place where oracles are told. I consulted a seer about your impending departure for the war and about the sacrifices that might be able to prevent it; he saw AKANLANWINLIN.

"This oracle says that the farm-house never warns us about the war it sees in the distance;

"That the machete has come to cut down the maize which challenged it to battle;

"That the angry hammer vents its wrath upon the anvil;

"That the chattering of the magpie attracts the enemies who come to conquer his fathers' kingdom;

"That an early morning reprieve hardly brings joy to the pig;

"That strangers will come to snatch the sow and her piglets in the very field where they are looking for food;

"That the clay pipe is in danger of breaking when it falls to the ground.

"It says: the sponge enters the bathroom with joy, but leaves in tears.

"It also says: you play the hero and rely upon your own strength, but if you do not temper your ambition, you will be condemned to solitude in the evening of your life, and you will carry a cloth in your hand to dry your tears.

"It finds expression in song:

War has kidnapped the gris-gris;
War has kidnapped the creative Spirit;
War has invaded Abogomê and taken you prisoner,
Hasn't it, oh, great warrior chief?

"No doubt these prophecies of Fate largely concern the king," sighed Doguicimi. "But do they predict an unfortunate end for the monarch alone?"

"Ah, women? Women! Any man who trusts their smiles and their outpourings of love is an utter fool! After caressing me and beguiling me to sleep, this one abandoned me on the sleeping mat and went out. Now she returns and insists upon taking me for an imbecile with all this talk about some supposed augury of Destiny. And to think that this is the bitch who pledged me her love and even followed me into my dreams," exclaimed Toffa indignantly.

The woman burst into tears and collapsed on the mat. The prince turned his back on her, lit his pipe, drew on it several times, and then set it down, but the prophecy of the oracle troubled him so much that he could not fall asleep again.

"All the same, one has to admit that it's a rather strange coincidence. Doguicimi presumably came up with 'Akanlanwinlin', the same oracle that the king's seer cast this morning at court. Are the ancestors warning me as well about an impending disaster?" He heaved a sigh and then, seeking to muster his courage, concluded: "a death that strikes many people simultaneously is infinitely less odious than one which fells you alone."

*   *   *

Toffa was locked in a sound sleep when the cocks crowed for the first time.

Abruptly snatched from her slumbers by the gate-keeper, Evemon (the young girl whom Toffa had given to Doguicimi as a wedding present) tottered into the room and announced the arrival of an emissary from the king.

52

The adolescent then ushered in the messenger, who informed the prince that he had been summoned to the Palace.

Toffa did not wait for the message to be repeated.

In the council chamber he encountered Vidaho, the two prime ministers, the two chiefs of staff, all the other palace dignitaries, and several princes.

Guézo soon joined them and proclaimed: "Our ancestors appeared to me in a dream before the first crowing of the cock, and they assured me that, since yesterday was a day of truthlessness, the cowries of the oracle had completely falsified their command, which ordained a prompt punishment for Hounjroto.

"Just a moment ago, the voice of the four cowries, which had been placed on the grave of my illustrious father after yesterday's counsel, spoke to me and confirmed the will of the ancestors. Hounjroto comprises no less than three hundred villages. For the Danhomê, it is a budding rival. Who can sleep in peace when he knows that a snake is living under his roof? We owe it to ourselves to destroy any expanding kingdom in our vicinity. Hounjroto is not yet a formidable enemy: Agbomê's army will suffice for the task that has been imposed upon us.

"The ancestors promised me a quick and very profitable victory. We will be underway before sunrise; if we delay, we may lose the opportunity for a glorious victory and all the benefits that accompany it. Does the dignitary who yesterday advised us to make lengthy preparations not realize that Danhomê is filled with captured foreigners who grew up here and for whom this kingdom no longer holds any secrets? The news of our preparations for war can be spread far beyond our borders by such people. Let us beware of them! The element of surprise is the only advantage that invariably guaranteed victory for our ancestors. To surprise the enemy, one needs to decide quickly upon a plan and to execute it with dispatch. The ancestors decree the war against Hounjroto. The soldiers are armed. Let us be on our way; it would be wrong for us to delay!"

The dismay was so great that none of the princes who opposed the envisaged campaign had an opportunity to say anything.

Before retiring from the room, Guézo charged the counsellors who would accompany him during the war to make their preparations in all haste and return to the Palace by the second crowing of the cock.

Adouconou had been indisposed for the last three market days, and it had been extremely difficult for him to visit the Palace on the previous day. Both he and Vidaho were still convalescing, and neither would be able to endure the rigors of a military expedition.

Vivenagbo was to assume his role of regent as soon as the king's army had departed.

Toffa returned to his compound and hurriedly sacrificed a dozen chickens and two goats to his gris-gris. Among other things, he promised them numerous offerings if he returned safely to Danhomê.

The lamentations of his wives and children annoyed him, and even more than his desire to obey the king's injunctions, they prompted him to rush from

53

his house.

As a Danhomênou, Toffa was incapable of entertaining the idea that one could shirk the duties of war, even if one's efforts to prevent it had miscarried. He disapproved of the Hounjroto campaign because its only objective was to avenge the slain white men. Yet the warrior's blood that coursed in his veins quickly vanquished the repulsion which this unjust campaign inspired in him.

He told himself that the ominous prophecies of Destiny had nothing to do with him and that he would escape all danger: King Agonglo, his regal Father, had named him Toffa–a water lily which laughs at the drought–and Agonglo would certainly protect him.

The warriors left Agbomê at the third crowing of the cock. They pretended to be marching against a province on the other side of the Swamps. It was the wrong direction. But until the return of the expedition, the people were not supposed to know the name of the country into which the king was leading his soldiers. The army had always employed this strategem to keep the Danhomênous in ignorance and to guard against possible indiscretions.

The high dignitaries followed on horseback, surrounding the king, who was riding in a hammock carried by Adanhouindé and Ojo with the aid of two other Danhomênous.

The Amazons formed a royal guard who separated the men from about thirty queens on horseback; Topo watched over them, and he was seconded by some twenty eunuchs, who were also mounted on horses.

Approximately five hundred servants carried baskets of cloths, glass trinkets, silver and bronze jewelry, packets of the Agoudas' tobacco, demijohns of brandy, and food for the king, his wives, his court, and his personal bodyguard.

Some thirty men were burdened with voluminous bundles of mats made from the core of the veins of raphia-palm leaves.

The royal guard entoned a war song to the rhythm of the drums and the accompanying horns.

The soldiers very well knew they were going to war. That was enough, and already it was too much. Slaves or free men, they were Danhomênous above all else; that is to say, they were the things of Danhomê, and they were not only supposed to remain ignorant of the country in which they lost their lives, but to guard themselves energetically against any thought of their own destiny. Woe betide them if their faces betrayed such a preoccupation and it was confirmed to the satisfaction of Gaou and Possou during the trial by poison carried out by Tatayi, the minister of justice.

Toffa moved forward in silence. As a prince of royal blood, he was free to judge the royal order. He thought: "The mere caprice of women has caused us to set out in such a hurry for Hounjroto; and Guézo wanted to make us believe that the ancestors had ordered him to undertake this campaign. A lie is already hateful in itself. Lying is unworthy of a king. But telling a lie and attributing it to the dead is a blasphemy that will not go unpunished.

"The king dangled before our eyes the hope for a rich booty after a certain and easy victory.

"More than the wealth that we could extract from the sale of all the stinking beasts from the 'mahi' country, only one thing seems infinitely worthwhile to me; if it were only possible, as Linpéhoun facetiously suggested at the court, for us to transport all the 'mahi' mountains to our borders as a means of preventing the hatred of our enemies from ever reaching us! Ah, if that were the goal of this expedition, how I would praise the queens who inspired it! Those who decided this war are perhaps not even accompanying Guézo.

"His absence from the Palace must interest them. Delighted at having succeeded in distancing him from Agbomê, they will be smiling at other men already this evening. My departure must even have gladdened the heart of Doguicimi because I don't see her following me. Yet all last night she swore she loved me and promised to remain faithful.

"Sheer pretense, just like her wailing this morning. Once I'm absent, I no longer exist for that woman. Tonight she will be at the side of another man, swearing to him as well that he is the only one she adores in the entire world. Is her lover stupid enough to trust her? If he is, he will quickly be led to his ruin.

"On the subject of women you have infallible instincts, Toffa! When you are no longer among the living in Danhomê, a man of your discernment will be hard to find.

"Bitch with seven pairs of ribs! My foresight was accurate when I named you Doguicimi. Your name will only be remembered in Danhomê as that of the most treacherous and contemptible of women.

"And to think that there are imbeciles who believe their wives will remain faithful to their conjugal vows simply because they made them drink fetishes! They are even convinced that the unfaithful ones will die as a result of their infidelity.

"The opinion of knowledgeable people is that, no matter how many fetish potions Migan imposes on his wives when he leaves Agbomê, Mêwou will become the cock of the walk in his compound. If all women only made such a good choice!

"I would be surprised to learn that it wasn't one of my own slaves who replaced me at the sides of my wives! Don't people tell the story about a king's wife who deceived him with the most deformed man in the world – a hunchback? All women are like that queen; they abandon a rich man for a wretched one.

"Ah, women! Women! We must watch out for them! They are full of wiles.

"Doguicimi no doubt thinks I actually believed the story of her consultation with the oracle who was supposed to have informed her about the sacrifices that were calculated to exorcise my departure for the war.

"Happily for her and for that rogue of a sorcerer. . . . But I will return to Danhomê. Eh, Fadonougbo, you'll never again see your consulting beads!

"As for you, Doguicimi, you who preferred the stony ground to the soft sleeping place that the Creator prepared for you at my side, you would be more than happy if I had you killed pure and simple.

"If I cannot find torments in Danhomê proportionate to the dishonor that

55

your misconduct has heaped upon me, I will sell you to the white men and demand that, in the country where they transport their slaves, they impose the most arduous and disgusting work upon you during the day and that you will only be allowed to rest at night by cultivating the earth with a lamp attached to your foot.

"To think that there are men, let alone a king, who respond to all the caprices of women!

"Ah, if I had the power to do it, I would relieve many people of the mark of their sex, for it doesn't at all endow them with the character that should be the appanage of every man.

"I would not have worked against Adanzan if he had only emasculated that sort of Danhomênou!"

Completely absorbed in his rancor, Toffa did not notice that they had crossed Houawé. Having risen some time ago and now draped in a purple velvet cloth, the sun was leaning against the wall of his house and contemplating the warriors who pursued the red dust of the path and the hope of victory.

The army camped at Canna and did not resume its march until the day star had turned his neck; it headed in the direction of Agonlin to the East and marched all night long; the Master of the World wanted to arrive at Hounjroto by the second crowing of the cock at the very latest.

*   *   *

Vivênagbo assumed the regency. Adouconou and Vidaho came to amuse themselves at the court. . . .

The courtiers who resided at Agbomê as well as the village and regional chiefs were all present, as usual, at the Courtyard of the Grand Palace by sunrise. They prostrated themselves and covered themselves with dust before sitting down. The king was absent, it is true, but the throne of Houêgbaja was still present, and it was upheld by the regent, the heir to the throne, and the eldest son of Agonglo. The Danhomênou always conducted himself prudently, like the dormouse which, having recognized the track of a panther, respectfully kissed the ground beside it and said, according to the assurances of the elders: "If you venerate someone in his presence, respect his absence as well!"

Despite the zeal and reverence with which the people paid hommage to their masters of today, Vidaho discovered a thousand lapses in the respect due him, a sign of their disregard for His Majesty, he explained. His vassals denounced to him the courtiers who had rejoiced at his illness; they also reported to him malicious jibes of Danhomênous who claimed not to understand why the prince had failed to go and share in the perils of war.

The arms of the executioner's assistants fell pitilessly on the accused and did not lay aside their cudgels until the victims appeared to be gasping for their last breath.

The sun was still only at the height of people's ears, and already Migan's prison had taken in more boarders than it usually received in an entire day.

The Danhomênou was the very image of submission; would he become a rebel? It was simply a propitious moment for the royal heir to terrorize the people in order to impose himself upon their spirits. The Danhomênous were servile worshippers of brute force, and starting now, Vidaho wanted to show them the stuff of which he was made. As far as the informers were concerned, they were settling old grudges. But all convictions would be substantiated upon the king's return.

It was only a deferral of capital punishment. To catch the people whose heads he wanted to roll, the prince would invent crimes and solicit numerous false witnesses, who would then swear by their faith in the fetishes that these innocents had slandered the person of the king and accused him of having undertaken an unjust war. The complicity of the minister of justice had been obtained in advance. Anyone who dared refuse a favor to the future Master of the World could prepare himself to leave this life as soon as the last night of the reigning king had been celebrated.

Tired by the course of the day and completely covered with a dust that turned him purple and slightly dulled his radiance, the day star descended into the Coufo to take its customary bath.

When Vivênagbo, Vidaho, and Adouconou left the Palace, the lines of Destiny could scarcely be seen in their hands; they walked together until the Ditch of the city's fortifications came into view; their attendants maintained a respectful distance. The heir to the throne took the path to Jêgbé, where he lived; the regent and Adouconou went to Gbêcon-Hounli; they separated in front of the royal residence of King Guézo.

At the door to the city, Vidaho spoke softly into the ear of one of his attendants; the man knelt, touched his forehead to the ground, covered his head and chest with dust, and then plunged into the night.

A man overtook Vivênagbo; the two of them broke away from the group and exchanged a few confidences. After the man had left, the minister said: "The idiot who is following us doesn't have the slightest idea that he has been recognized. I can't take over Danhomê and don't, for that matter, have any further ambitions since the king's confidence raised me to the regency in his absence. My only desire is to see Guézo on the throne of Houégbaja when I wake up each morning because kings have a habit of relegating ministers from the preceding reign to subordinate roles.

"Your lordship, if one's fortunes were tied to a particular reign, one would have to be mad to plot against it, wouldn't he? Only Vidaho, who is burning with impatience to take over Danhomê, could think of having recourse to any means, even the most dishonest ones, to hasten his ascension to the throne. It is a common practice among designated successors. For that reason, Guézo is watching out for his son.

"I am the one who is keeping an eye on you, presumptuous youth, and I will inform your royal Father about your remarks and your actions! My eyes and my ears are all around you; they are present at your meals, and they share your sleeping quarters with you, although you do not suspect it," murmured the regent, his arm stretched toward Jêgbé and his hand slicing through the air like the executioner's scimitar.

As for the prince, he knew someone was spying on him, but he pretended not to know about it. He whispered into the ear of his confidant Mêhomê: "He will not always be regent over us! Someday the ancestors will surely help me engineer my august Father's loss of respect for him."

Vivênagbo allowed sleep to carry off everyone in his home; then he went to the compound of Toffa, to whom he was bound by a Blood Oath which obliged him to protect the family of his absent brother.

The regent visited all the wives of his sworn friend and encouraged them to bear with equanimity the absence of the household's chief member, assuring them they would see him again within nine days. To those who were soon expecting to become mothers, he recommended a scrupulous adherence to the regime prescribed by the doctor who was a retainer of the prince's family. He examined the sick children and advised their mothers not to disregard the orders of the doctor.

He stayed for some time with Doguicimi; then the two of them went into the room of the oracle. At a word from his illustrious visitor, the diviner emptied his consulting apparatus on the ground: all sorts and colors of grains, small bones of four-legged animals and birds of prey, assorted glass beads, shards of broken plates, shells, bells, balls, etc. . . . .

Vivênagbo installed himself on a low three-legged stool; Doguicimi sat down on a mat. She picked up a handful of cowries from a little basket, whispered several words, and then deposited them in front of the diviner, who immediately grabbed his string of eight apple-core hulls[2] by the middle and swung it forward once and backward once, muttering incantations in which the sacred names of Destiny recurred. With his other hand, he seized the two ends of his string and held it motionless for a second; his lips were moving constantly. He opened his second hand, swung the string again, stopped it as before, released it, and swung it once more; he then passed it over the cowries three times in a circular motion, laid it on top of them, and enveloped the whole thing with his hands, his lips continuing to move. He picked up the string again, swung it backward and forward three times, and then, having cast it full length upon the floor, he studied it for a moment; he then looked upward and stammered a word that no one understood. He turned over the hulls that had fallen face downward, selected a lustrous grey grain from among his paraphernalia, and touched it to each of the eight hulls on the string while asking: "Does Destiny agree?" Having set the grain aside, he poses the question this time with a cowry: "Does Destiny refuse?" Doguicimi took the two objects, rubbed them together in the palms of her hands, and then enclosed each of them in one of her fists. The diviner picked up his string again, exhorted it to tell the truth, and stretched it out on the ground. He gathered it up and cast it on the ground once again; then, having examined the arrangement of the hulls, he ordered the woman: "Open your left

_____

2   See Chapter 1, note 1. (author's note)

58

hand!" Doguicimi obeyed, laying down first the object that was in it and then the other one.

After the diviner had again touched the hulls of the string while asking the oracle a question that no one understood, her hands once more closed over the two objects. The string was cast to the ground a third time; the diviner left it there and studied it for a long time.

Vivênagbo and Doguicimi waited anxiously. Like a ram butting at some unseen enemy, Evêmon was sitting behind her mistress and desperately bobbing her head in the air; one would have guessed that she was defending herself against the sleep that was gradually taking possession of her.

The diviner shook his head; his lips formed into a slight pout. He sighed deeply, and staring fixedly at the string while suddenly opening his eyes wide as if to scrutinize something that was trying to conceal itself from him, he said emphatically: "Di bli Yêcou! Di pushed his brother Yêcou into the water, and a fish ate him."

A short silence. He once again made a wry expression, tilted his head slightly to the left, winked, and then, as if suddenly emerging from a reverie, exclaimed: "May the large jug break cleanly rather than allowing its water to ooze away; the shards of a large jug are necessarily large; the chicken does not die because it pecked on the rubbish heap. . . ."

Seeing Doguicimi's face cloud over, the minister abruptly halted the diviner's commentaries: "Let us only retain the final prediction, which takes precedence over all the others."

"The first one too ought to hold our attention, and perhaps even more than the others," responded the woman, who was determined not to let herself be duped. "Toffa is in danger, and we should not conceal the fact; far from averting disaster, a disregard for it hastens its coming and makes it worse. Let us see if we can persuade our ancestors by means of a few sacrifices to protect my lord and master!"

The diviner enumerated the propitiatory sacrifices and packed up his consulting paraphernalia.

Doguicimi led Vivênagbo toward a small room adjoining Toffa's sleeping quarters: "May His Excellency deign to visit the house of his sworn friend's gris-gris. He left so quickly that he surely failed to take with him all those which are capable of protecting him against the weapons of his enemies."

She pushed open the door, allowed her husband's friend to pass, and said: "I dare not enter. My husband has always assured me that the gris-gris would be polluted and lose their power if a woman introduced herself into this room. Evêmon is the image of innocence, and she will follow Your Excellency to light you the way. Open all the calabashes. You will easily recognize the gris-gris that could be most useful against the dangers of war."

"Toffa has everything he needs to be happy! A wife who combines a rare beauty with great virtues of heart and mind!" whispered Vivênagbo to himself as he moved toward a row of calabashes that he immediately recognized because he had similar ones at home.

"To his misfortune," observed the minister as he opened the second calabash, "Toffa forgot this gris-gris that we acquired for the price of five slaves to guarantee invulnerability against any weapon forged by the hand of man!" Holding the cover of the third calabash in his hand, the regent cried, "And this gris-gris which is more important than all the others we possess and which grants invisibility when the enemy attack us!"

He took the two gris-gris with him and promised to entrust them, and several others of his own manufacture, to a royal messenger, whom he proposed to send the next morning at the first crowing of the cock to the army's general headquarters.

The thought that her husband did not have a powerful gris-gris in his possession threw Toffa's wife into a profound state of despondency. By the time her servant girl had succeeded in calming her and she herself had fallen asleep, the moon that had been covering the calabash since the last market day was already in the middle of the sky.

Having arisen with the dawn, Doguicimi ordered the preparation of the various sacrifices prescribed by Destiny. As soon as they were ready, servants left to deposit them, according to the diviner's instructions, at crossroads, on the main streets, at Ajahimê (the central market of Agbomê), next to springs, and at the foot of large sacred trees. Other sacrifices were buried in Toffa's house. With an infusion of red sorghum husks, they dyed the left half of a little white goat and attached a bell to the neck of the animal that Destiny ordered everyone in the household to call "Enawa", a name that means, "he will return."

The diviner solemnly assured them: "The absent one will be back in his home before the dyed portion of the goat's fur has returned to its original color."

When everything had been accomplished, Evêmon, who called Doguicimi "mother", kneeled at her mistress' feet, kissed the ground, covered her forehead with dust, and said: "I dreamed that I saw the Master. You were happy at having been reunited with him again, and I was happy for you. My dreams were always realized when I was in my own country; the Master's absence will certainly not last for long."

"Implore your ancestors and the fetishes of your family to protect my husband. I will owe my happiness at seeing him again in part to you, and we will always keep you with us."

Filled with joy, the innocent child once again kissed the earth as a sign of gratitude for the assurance she had just received that she would never have to leave the shelter of this home.

Puzzled by the tinkling of his bell, Enawa began to bleat. He jumped to the right, then to the left, ran forward, and retreated, believing that he could somehow silence the little bell or get rid of it; he only succeeded in making it tinkle all the more insistently.

Doguicimi approached the goat, and as if he could understand her questions

60

and respond to them, she asked: "What do you say? Is he coming back?"

Frightened, the little animal fled to the other side of the courtyard. The woman was following it with her eyes and failed to see the kneeling messenger who had just been introduced by a servant and was saying: "The regent has received news from Headquarters. Toffa (at this word, Doguicimi stood bolt upright) sends greetings to his whole family. He instructs that his children be watched over with care and that offerings be made each morning to his gris-gris and to the protective fetishes of the kingdom."

The woman sighed: "I am prepared to quench the thirst of our idols with half the blood in my own body, if the return of my husband can only be obtained at the price of such a sacrifice!"

Chapter 3

A Danhomê Defeat

The king's camp had been set up some four hundred bamboos from Hounjroto.

Measuring almost a hundred sixty bamboos in circumference and comprised of mats that had been made from raphia palm leaf fibers, it was a vast enclosure that opened toward "mahi" country.

In the middle stood a large rectangular apatam with courtyards in the front and back. It was divided into seven rooms. The largest was about twenty paces long and occupied the entire length of the apatam; it was the council room, and it looked out over Hounjroto. The other rooms served as lodgings for the king, his queens, the royal guard, and the servants.

The casters of spells had their quarters, and there were stables for the horses in the inner courtyard. Two apatams abutted the outer wall to the right and left of the principal courtyard; one of them was reserved for the high dignitaries and the other for the eunuchs. All the rooms had been hung with velvet, the color and sheen of which would have made the sun turn pale with envy – blood red, white, the green of new foliage, ash grey, the foamy tint of boiling palm oil, the black of crows, indigo blue; moreover, these tapestries had been decorated with all shapes and sizes of mirrors.

The gris-gris that were supposed to protect the camp from enemy attack had been suspended from the ceiling, buried, or simply planted in the ground according to the instructions of those who had prepared them.

The king ordered that the valuable objects brought to Hounjroto should be distributed among all the rooms and that everything should be left open. To the dignitaries who were puzzled by these precautions, he explained: "Wherever I go in this camp, I would like to have something at hand to show the soldiers how their heroism can remind me that the Father of Wealth is eager to reward the least service to Danhomê."

"To think of heaping presents upon those who risk their lives for the Creator

63

from whom they received them!" exclaimed Migan. "People will search under this sun in vain for a comparable example of munificence. May the ancestors deign to buttress the feet of their worthy successor and thereby strengthen his hold upon the throne of Danhomê so that he can triumph over all his enemies inside and outside the kingdom!"

"All these wishes will be fulfilled! All these wishes will be fulfilled!" shouted the other ministers tumultuously.

At that very moment, the crowing of a cock echoed in the distance as if to lend additional support to Migan's prayer. It was answered by a second one, then a third somewhat closer, then another one in the distance, then others and still others from all directions and in different tones. Soon the concert was over.

During this first crowing of the cocks, everyone realized that the camp really was rather far from the nearest "mahi" village, just as Topo had assured them. The king immediately called his council together to assign a specific objective to each battle captain. Even the princes were given the command of an army division. The only ones who remained in camp with the king were the queens, the army of "buffalos" comprising the royal guard, Migan, Mêwou, Topo, Ajaho, the diviner Wolo, the doctors, the casters of spells, and the eunuchs, among whose ranks were Adanhouindé and Ojo (the king's two chief hammock-bearers) and their aides.

*   *   *

Having long since escaped the tissue of gauze that wily hands, profiting from his slumbers, had hung over the doorway of his house, the sun was rising radiantly toward the zenith. As for him, he had been able to break, like a mere spider web, the darkness and fog that the night had sent against him. But until now, nothing presaged a successful outcome for that other Source of Light, whose soldiers had been fighting since the second crowing of the cock against the mountain people of Hounjroto.

Uninterrupted volleys of gunfire seconded by periodic canon shots informed the king and his entourage that the Danhomênous were still fighting desperately against the stinking beasts. Worried at seeing the battle last beyond the deadline fixed by his hope of victory, the king finally asked the diviner seated on a mat to the right of the throne: "You still say that victory is assured?"

"Destiny has promised it, Predestined King, and since he has never deceived us in the past, we ought to have confidence in his predictions of today," replied Wolo, whose stare remained fixed upon the two rows of vertical lines he had traced with his fingers in the kaolin powder with which he had covered his consulting board.

Migan seconded this encouraging announcement: "Just a moment ago Gaou had me informed that he was delivering the decisive blow. All the routes by means of which the stinking beasts who have been spared by our guns might escape are so well guarded by Possou that we're going to capture every last 'mahi' gnat."

"The guns will soon fall silent, and the All-Powerful King will go and evaluate the magnitude of his conquest," added Mêwou, who did not want to lag behind the first minister.

The queens also expressed their confidence in a victory from which they hoped to reap a large profit because they had had the courage to confront danger in the company of the king.

However, one of them had lowered her head and half-closed her eyes, as if she were dozing. Her companions, who were dreaming of abundant spoils after a victory the Danhomênous were bound to win, asked each other in whispers: " Is it indifference or doubt?"

"As a Mahinou, she is certainly hoping in her heart for the defeat of Danhomê," insinuated one voice.

No one had noticed that the woman was listening to an inner music; her lower jaw was moving up and down against the upper one, keeping rhythm.

She suddenly broke out of her reverie and intoned a song she had just composed:

> What mania has possessed these wretched beasts of the mountain?
> Madmen, do you think you can conquer Danhomê?
> The Danhomê of Houégbaja is a rock;
> What foot can strike it without being bruised?
> The Danhomê of Houégbaja is the dazzling sun at its zenith;
> What eye can look at it without turning away?
> Only madmen could dream of defeating Danhomê,
> The sky that no glance can encompass
> And no hand can reach.
>
> Bliguédé[1] has no head. . . .
> My august and very powerful husband
> Is this ungraspable ball;
> He is also the serpent who has no paw
> And the tortoise who has no fur.

The ministers were delirious with joy: "It's true! It's true! The Danhomê of Houégbaja has always been invincible!" In contrast, the singer's companions blanched with envy.

Overcome with this infectious enthusiasm, the monarch exclaimed: "My ancestors owe me this victory, for I am avenging their friends who were assasinated in such a cowardly way upon the advice of these Mahinous."

A royal messenger arrived to announce that Possou had already captured more than eight hundred prisoners and assembled them at Soponta, the first "dassa" village that one encounters on the road from Hounjroto to Agbomê.

"Can the victory any longer be in doubt?" exulted Migan confidently.

In a frenzy of joy, the queen resumed her song with more fervor than ever:

---

[1] An imaginary monster which is a living ball with neither arms nor legs. (author's note)

What mania has possessed these wretched beasts of the mountain?
Madmen, do you think you can conquer Danhomê?
The Danhomê of Houégbaja is a rock;
What foot can strike it without being bruised?
The Danhomê of Houégbaja is the dazzling sun at its zenith;

. . . .

In her exaltation, she failed to hear the soldier who arrived like a gust of
wind and breathlessly reported: "The enemy has just halted Gaou's offensive
and captured half our soldiers; his troops are on the heels of the remnants of our
army. The Danhomênous are resisting the "mahi" counter-thrust only to give
the Master of the Universe time to break camp and get beyond the reach of these
foul beasts from the mountain."

". . . That no glance can. . . ," continued the singer as the blow of a fan
struck her on the face, forcing the next word back into her throat and awakening
her to the harsh reality. Everything was in disarray at the camp. Guézo ordered
people to take only what they wearing and what might be useful in case of an
attack.

At a loud summons from Migan, the two chief hammock-bearers and their
aides came running; in the blink of an eye, they had raised the hammock with
the king in it. With great haste they started on the way back. Helped by the
eunuchs, the queens quickly mounted their horses and disappeared. The casters
of spells continued to mutter incantations.

Adanhouindé, Ojo and their assistants believed that the gris-gris they were
wearing on their legs would shorten the way. The names of ancestors and of all
the royal family's fetishes, which were being fervently invoked, could be heard
from time to time above the rattling of weapons and the sound of feet pounding
the ground. Launched with great force from the chest, these names reached the
outside world as gasps, so relentlessly did fear tighten its grip on the throat. The
ministers walked on foot, occasionally raising the hammock to lighten the load
and to facilitate the progress of the four sturdy eunuchs who were carrying it.

The countenance of his followers revealed such widespread terror that the
king finally lost confidence in his ancestors, his fetishes, and his gris-gris.
The hammock-bearers were running as fast as they could. Neverthless, Guézo
thought they were going too slowly and shouted that he would prefer to run.
The high dignitaries dissuaded him by pointing out all the dangers it entailed.
By the time the fugitives reached the zone controlled by Danhomê, the sun
had already turned his neck; exhausted, they stopped but not without carefully
assuring themselves that nothing threatened them here.

The Mahinous did not advance past Guézo's camp. Those who had gone
beyond it were called back by the sound of a wooden flute that was used to
communicate over long distances.

Had it not been for the greed that detained them near the booty they found
at the camp, the victors would have seized a much more important prize, at least
as far as their national pride was concerned. . . .

The king demanded an account of the conduct of the battle. The soldiers who had witnessed the deaths of Gaou Dessou, Possou Linon, Afénou, Alopé, and the battle captains Chalacassou and Jajagloja came and reported the details. No one knew what had happened to the other princes.

Tomêtin and Linpéhoun were also believed to have been killed or taken prisoner, but they arrived in camp just before the royal party was to depart. The first had no information about those who were missing. Linpéhoun informed the king that Assogbaou, Toffa, and Ajéhounou had probably been captured. Displaying a large wound on his left breast, he added: "I received this wound fighting at their side. For each enemy slain, three or four others appeared from out of nowhere. The hedge of sabres raised against us soon constricted in a terrifying manner. I therefore suggested that we make ourselves invisible by having recourse to the gris-gris that could produce that effect. My comrades were not carrying any of them. I alone was able to escape the grasp of the enemy."

Guézo swore the council to the most absolute silence on the subject of this story; he then inspected the wounded. He promised rewards to those soldiers whose injuries were on the front part of their bodies: that was the proof that they had courageously faced the enemy. The bravery of Danhomênous with wounds on their sides was called into doubt. Upon their return to Agbomê, a trial by fetish would determine whether or not these injuries had been inflicted at the moment they were turning their backs upon the Mahinous. The proof of several soldiers' cowardice could be found in the wounds they had on their backs. All those who had shown their heels to the enemy were henceforth unworthy of living in freedom and under the skies of Danhomê.

The court dispatched a messenger to Vivênagbo.

The prisoners were counted: three hundred men, five hundred women of whom twenty were nursing, and about forty boys and girls between four and twelve dry seasons.

A soldier held up a head that he swore was that of the king of Hounjroto, whom he claimed to know quite well because he had lived for a long time in that country.

After a short rest, the king ordered the return to Danhomê.

The king's message reached Vivênagbo shortly after the first crowing of the cock. The regent informed Adouconou and decided to quarantine the lodgings of the princes and high dignitaries who had been lost at Hounjroto. The prince spoke out against this precaution, which he thought would throw the Danhomênous into a panic. After his advice had been rejected, he suggested, also in vain, that the heir to the throne be consulted.

This measure was quite puzzling to the families of those who were absent. Doguicimi was frightened by it: "Toffa had publicly opposed this campaign. Did he refuse to fight when he got there? I cannot believe that he would have deserted to the enemy. What could possibly be the reason for sequestering his possessions?"

The army returned to Agbomê at dawn. The injured were distributed among the battle captains, who would have their doctors attend to them.

The Courtyard of the Grand Palace was swarming with people by sunrise; the silence of the soldiers and the royal drums announced the defeat of the king's army, and many Danhomênous had come to express their sorrow to the Master of the World and to assure him they were ready to avenge the insult at this very moment if he ordered them to do so. Guêzo had let it be known that he would not appear before the people during the day, but the prime minister succeeded in convincing him to come and console his subjects, who had been deeply affected by this misfortune.

"Avoutou" exploded in the inner courtyard of the Palace; the gloomy roll of the "dogba" answered him. "Gbo! Gbo! Gbo! Oh, the Panther!" chirped a "bird of the king." Others took up the refrain in the crystalline tones of innocents: "Eh! The bird! Eh! The bird of prey! Eh! Walk majestically! Majestically! Majestically!"

The high dignitaries left the Palace and took their places by the threshold to the Door of the World, outside the bamboo-lined enclosure that was reserved for the king and his wives. The crown prince, the first minister, and Topo installed themselves to the right of the throne; the second minister and Ajaho placed themselves to the left; the princes formed a row behind them.

Several adolescent girls appeared. Their tattoos – two parallel lines on their cheeks and tiny marks like smallpox scars all over their faces – announced their "houéda" origins; they were the bird-harbingers of the king, and they continued their exhortations: "Eh! Walk majestically! Majestically! Majestically!" There was no longer any doubt. The Master of the World was coming. All the courtiers, without exception, threw themselves face downward on the ground, as if stricken with apoplexy, and smeared their faces with dust, saying: "We cover ourselves with dirt at the feet of the Predestined King. Mere mortals, we do not know how to show our gratitude to the Spirit of our spirits, one refuses to rest from the rigors of a difficult campaign until after he has brought his creatures the blessing of his presence in their midst."

The World opened its door. Following the bird-harbingers of the king, Daclo appeared and then the queens, who helped the Master of the World install himself on his throne.

The courtiers continued to cover themselves with dust and to deplore their powerlessness to demonstrate their gratitude to their Creator.

Upon a sign from the king, Daclo called Migan, who crawled toward the throne, crossed the barrier of bamboo shoots lying on the ground, then stopped and looked worriedly in the direction of the queens. They had understood and were thus already moving back to place the distance required by custom between themselves and the man. With her back turned toward the queens and her arms extended, Daclo stepped between them, thereby protecting the Royal Wives, who had gathered in one corner, from contact with a male who could have polluted them forever and caused them to fall from their exalted station.

Having reached the foot of the throne, the minister kneeled and with his body bent double and his eyes glued to the ground, he pressed his arms to his sides, placed the palms of his hands together, and touched the end of his index finger to his closed mouth.

In this extremely humble position, which the Danhomênou always adopted in the presence of his idols, Migan listened, his right ear at the height of the king's mouth. Although Danhomênous had been authorized to look at the face of the king, the Spirit of their spirits, since the reign of Tégbéssou, no mortal could do it publicly or with insolence. Filled with a reverential fear by the proximity of the great Idol of the Danhomênous, the first minister trembled. As he spoke softly into the man's ear, the king continued to tap his minister's shoulder with the tip of his right index finger, as if to push the messages, with which he was charging him, through his skin and into his spirit. When the king had finished, Migan prostrated himself, gathered up all the dust he could find, and smeared his face with it.

He returned to his station by crawling backward. The queens regained their places next to the king; the one who was holding the scarf carefully wiped the finger that had been polluted by its contact with a mortal and then the mouth and nose that had approached his ear. The queens who were waving the fans redoubled their efforts to drive away the smell of the minister. The woman in charge of the pipe lit it and placed the tube into the royal mouth.

Standing and facing the crowd that had prostrated itself in the dust, the first minister announced in a voice that always became solemn, measured, and ominous whenever he addressed the people: "Danhomênous, the bad faith of the spies, who were sent to Hounjroto by the Master of the World to gather information about the force of our enemies, delivered us into the jaws of the stinking beasts from the mountain. But thanks to the protection of our ancestors and our fetishes, these mountain people were unable to reap all the profits they might have derived from their victory. The superior intelligence of the Master of the World had devised a stratagem to which the survivors of this expedition owe their salvation.

"Knowing how much the Mahinous covet jewelry, velvet cloths, brandy, and especially the Agoudas' tobacco that they are constantly smoking, snuffing, and chewing, the King of Jewels had brought a large quantity of valuable objects to Hounjroto, and he ordered us to abandon them in the camp.

"When they arrived there after we had left, our enemies swallowed the bait, and we were able to outdistance them. The lives saved by the Master of the World are of course infinitely more precious than the treasures left behind at Hounjroto. But these possessions have not been lost forever; the sale of the sons to the slave-traders will one day bring us a hundred times as much as what the fathers took from us.

"Of all those who did not return, only Assogbaou, Ajéhounou, and Toffa were captured by the Mahinous, who no doubt surprised them among the treasures we had left behind. Despite the shameful conduct of these princes, the Master of the World vows to free them and, before appearing in the presence of King Agonglo, to avenge the memory of the soldiers killed at Hounjroto as well as that of his friends, the white men who were massacred at Kinglo. But we will not take up arms again until we are fully prepared. Therefore, be patient. Realize that another defeat would be disastrous for Danhomê: all the peoples who, until now, have been cowed by the victories of the kingdom of Houégbaja could well be emboldened by it. We will even keep all thoughts of revenge to ourselves and wait until spies more devoted to the cause of Danhomê can give us precise information about the strength of the enemy and until Chacha Ajinacou sends us the guns and ammunition that the Master of the World is going to order from him at once.

"As for the spies responsible for our defeat, they will soon be punished without mercy before the eyes of the entire court." He lay down facing the king and covered his chest with dust.

"Why stop now when there are still other princes to be done away with?" shouted Doguicimi indignantly; she was standing in the middle of the crowd about five bamboos from the throne.

Migan stood up again and gaped dumbfounded at the woman whom he did not recognize because he seldom visited Toffa's compound.

Undaunted, she continued: "Toffa and his brothers who supported you against Adanzan were in the way. And you would be unworthy of your ancestor Daco-Donou if you did not exterminate them all as a reward for having helped you obtain the throne. Your actions will only surprise those who do not know about your customary practice of erecting your houses above the corpses of your benefactors. Your kingly pride found it humiliating that the witnesses of your former misery should go on living, especially those who brought about your present happiness. Following the example set by the founder of this kingdom, you could have accused Toffa, Assogbaou, and Ajéhounou of having slandered you and plotted against your reign. You would easily have found people sufficiently devoid of scruples to testify against them.

"In that case, their bodies would at least have remained in the hands of their widows and orphans, who would have had the consolation of weeping over their graves and offering sacrifices at appropriate times. But you had them assassinated far from the country of their fathers. Convinced that the dead never leave their graves to impose quick punishment upon those who slander them, you, oh dastardly king, are seeking to exonerate yourself from the blame for your odious crime by insulting the memory of my husband, who, in contrast with other princes of Danhomê, had neither a taste for luxury nor a covetous spirit. His wives and children were the only jewels that counted for Toffa. He is an impostor who dares insinuate that this prince, forgetting the family he left behind in Danhomê, dallied near the treasures and was captured there.

"And you claim that Adanzan was disgraced because of the false accusation he ordered brought against you! May he be forever banished from the list of Danhomê kings on account of his tyrannies! You want the Danhomênous to cite your name after that of Agonglo, to call you Guézo the Powerful, and to sing

70

your praises? Nothing any longer distinguishes you from the tyrant!

"A prince deprived of your rights, you were loved for your nobility and your courage. Everyone in Danhomê remembers with joy how you interceded on behalf of Princess Sincoutin at this very court not long ago. But ever since you were carried to the Palace, where you have surrounded yourself with ignoble women, you have sunk beneath the level of a slave.

"In acts of courage, you lag far behind Adanzan. When he decided to eliminate those of his brothers who were conspiring against him and for your ascension to the throne, didn't he have the courage to declare it officially and to identify Princess Sincoutin, who was organizing your supporters? Despite the craftiness of his decision, I admire the courage of this tyrant, who had the princess lashed to a porter's rack that was going to be thrown, before the eyes of all Danhomê, from the top of the altar that had been erected for the traditional ceremony.

"He was going to add a new crime to the countless ones he had already committed, I agree. But he only bore ill will toward his adversaries. In spite of his crimes, he must be more congenial to Danhomênous than the monster who rules them today and who wants to bury, along with his benefactors, the unpleasant memory of a prince who, robbed of his right to the throne, was not long ago dragging his misery through the kingdom and begging from house to house for the support of all his peers by appealing to their respect for the custom according to which every king must be designated by his predecessor.

"Having attained your goal, you consider yourself above the human race and no longer want others to think that you were born of mortal flesh. In Danhomê, all you want is a crowd of sycophants who refer to you only with the names Predestined King, Father and Mother of His People, Master of the Dawn, Master of Life, Master of the World, and even King of the Universe.

"As the result of being adulated in this way, you develop delusions of grandeur in the end. You compare yourself to the raging buffalo who lays waste to many places, crosses the most impenetrable forests with impunity, climbs the steepest mountains, and terrifies wild animals as well as humans. Untameable buffalo, if you failed to learn wisdom from the pursuit to which the Mahinous subjected you, it will give me pleasure to see you felled far from your country by a young hunter in the near future.

"You nourish the hope of seeing your posterity rule over Danhomê forever. In expiation for its crimes, this country will fall from the summit of power to the most abject servitude. Your successor may well have the power of the lion, but in the end he too will find that there are people who can file his teeth and trim his claws until the only feline quality that remains will be his majestic gait.

"As for your grandson, he may be as ferocious as the shark. Yet he will not terrify his people and their neighbors for long; in the end, he will be chased from his country, and he will live out his miserable life far from home.

"Order my throat to be slit or have me torn to pieces at this very moment. I want to rejoin Toffa in the realm of the spirits. But, living or dead, I will plague the ancestors so much with my laments that they will decide to avenge their son

71

with your death far from Danhomê. I will be grateful to them for that."

She fell silent and, planting herself proudly in front of the throne – her hands on her hips and her left foot forward in the position of someone who was ready to fight – she looked the king straight in the eyes; for the past few moments, he had been sitting up, throwing a handful of cowries (which he took from a basket that one of his wives had given him) into the air one by one, and trying to catch them with his other hand. He was succeeding at this game, and no more than three cowries remained in the hand that was throwing them; to them he added the ones he had already caught and began the game again.

He wanted to appear not to have heard the objurgations that were falling thick and fast from the woman's lips, but besides his hands, which were rising and falling nervously, the grinding of his teeth and the rush of blood that made his eyes sparkle betrayed the anger he was struggling to hide.

The silence was so complete that the rubbing of palms and the click of the cowries knocking together could be heard within a radius of two bamboos.

Since the country of the Guédévis had become Danhomê, no one had ever heard such blasphemies.

Petrified with fear, the Danhomênous regretted having come to the court that morning, and they buried their faces as far as they could into the dust. Doguicimi's neighbors thought themselves compromised by her presence in their midst and silently implored their ancestors and their fetishes to open a crack in the earth so they might disappear into it and thereby save themselves from the storm that, having been provoked by the blasphemous woman, seemed on the verge of breaking over them. Those who were carrying gris-gris with powers of invisibility whispered the appropriate incantations to make them work, but in vain; they remained quite visible in front of the throne.

Migan pounced upon Doguicimi.

"Kill her! Kill her! Cut her to pieces! We'll offer brochettes of her flesh to all the fetishes in the kingdom!" the queens shouted to him.

This outcry dissipated the agonizing terror of the crowd, which suddenly rediscovered its voice and yelled at the executioner to incite him against the woman: "What are you waiting for, Migan? Rip out the mad woman's jaw!"

"Rip out her vile tongue as well, Migan, and give it to her to eat!" howled the rabble.

The executioner could only act upon the command of the king. Charged with anger and hatred, his gaze shifted back and forth between the throne and the head of Doguicimi. His barely restrained ire caused the arm with his executioner's scimitar to tremble. If the king ordered the punishment of the blasphemous woman, the executioner would not even have had the patience to drag his victim away from the sight of the court; contrary to custom, he would have cut off her head on the spot.

The queen who was holding the tiny basket of cowries had placed it under the monarch's hands a few moments ago and was tapping him on the wrist to indicate that it was time to pour the shells back into it. Winks of the eye, discreet touches, whispers – none of the pressures that his entourage was exercising upon

72

him had yet induced him to make the gesture that would have constituted the order to execute the blasphemous woman. Guézo's attitude brought terror back into the ranks of the courtiers.

Doguicimi was also puzzled by Migan's inaction, and she shouted disdainfully at him: "Eh! Executioner! I'm still standing! Have you suddenly become so impotent that you are unable to accord me the joy of rejoining my husband in the realm of the spirits? Give your scimitar to an aide then. But if you yourself are going to execute me, you should know that all the torments mentioned by the howling mob are no more than harmless bugaboos to me. Unless you can think of something more cruel, you will be unworthy of the ingrate who is your master!"

Despite Doguicimi's renewed insolence and the wives' insistent urgings for him to pour the cowries into the basket, Guézo nervously continued to throw the shells with one hand and catch them with the other.

His apparent indifference exasperated the Wives of Panther; they gnashed their teeth and stamped the ground in anger and impatience at the same time.

Doguicimi looked the king up and down, spat on the ground, and turned her head away.

This gesture of profound disdain moved a Wife of Panther to jump up and shout: "War came to the country where only Dossou-the-Leper had remained at home. He grew angry and said: 'Not to appear before these enemies would make them think there is not a living soul here!' She broke through the cordon of "buffalos" forming the royal guard, stepped over the bamboo that separated the people from the king and his wives, and, like a demon possessed, pounced upon the blasphemer to tear the woman apart with her own teeth, since the king seemed to be losing all his dignity while Migan was hesitating to punish Doguicimi, and no other minister had taken any initiative to avenge the Idol of the Danhomênous. The men scattered hastily to keep out of the way of the Royal Wife. People crowded confusedly together on the right, on the left, and in the middle. Blinded with anger, the queen ran into a man; pushed away, she fell upon a group.

The confusion was such that two men bumped into each other in their haste to escape and bowled over the Wife of Panther. Before she had the time to get up, Guézo ordered Migan to arrest her; then he calmly explained: "I forgive the insults of Doguicimi. They seem to be serious, yet they are nothing but words, and it has escaped no one's attention that they were expresed unconsciously insofar as they were prompted by the grief of a woman who idolizes her husband.

"As for this Wife of Panther, she is aware of the sacred nature of her position. All those who have been consecrated to it during a rigorous religious ceremony occupy the foremost place in the heart of the Master of the World as in the Palace of Houégbaja, and they have an imperative duty to avoid contact even with simple queens for fear they might be polluted by them; they can only speak to the latter through the intermediary of innocent servant girls. Whenever they move about inside the Palace, these servants walk in front of them, ringing a little bell attached to their necks and exclaiming, 'Watch out! Watch out! Make way for a venerable Wife of Panther!' so that the simple queens may move out of their way. Thusly has it always been willed by the Houégbajas. Yet in disregard for their express desires and in our scandalized presence, this Wife of Panther has just deliberately polluted herself through contact with men. To pardon a breach of tradition is to make one's self an accomplice to it. The king must vigilantly defend the integrity of traditions, and when he closes his eye upon transgressions against them, he is drawing the wrath of the ancestors down upon his head and upon the country. Therefore, I cannot overlook the crime committed by this Wife of Panther!" As he said this, Guézo poured the cowries into the basket to proclaim the fatal verdict.

In response to these words, the crowd tumultuously roared its approval as it covered itself with dirt. "That's right! That's right! A Wife of Panther must never pollute herself through contact with mortal men! Tradition is inflexible on this point. Doguicimi is more worthy of pardon than this impious queen!"

The executioner's assistants dragged the hapless queen into their master's residence, her entreaties drowned out by the jeers of the rabble.

Her unfortunate and unexpected fate was a staggering blow to her companions. So great was the general consternation that even the "birds of the king" forgot to utter the cry announcing that the Father and Mother of the People was withdrawing. When the cloud of dust raised by the courtiers who were covering themselves with dirt had subsided, the people realized that their Creator and the high dignitaries had gone back into the Palace. The Courtyard immediately became almost entirely empty.

After a short meeting of the council, the king dismissed the palace dignitaries.

On the way back to his residence with several high dignitaries, Vidaho did not conceal his indignation about the pardon that had been granted to Doguicimi and his compassion for the unfortunate queen. "When I will have acquired sway over Danhomê, I hope to be struck by lightning if I ever show such clemency for a blasphemous woman!" protested the impulsive future Master of Danhomê. He then called his ancestors to witness his resolve to avenge the memory of the innocent victim by having Doguicimi executed if she did not die before his ascension to the throne.

Bowing low, one of the first minister's servants approached the heir to the throne and spoke softly into his ear.

The prince immediately turned back the way he had come. He entered Migan's house and found him stricken with grief. More than the humiliation suffered at court, the order he had received to execute that wife of the king, his niece, distressed him.

*   *   *

Doguicimi mournfully dragged herself to Toffa's compound, many times nearly collapsing beneath the weight of her affliction. Her sobs had attracted women and children to the thresholds of their homes.

Her co-wives heard her from a distance. They hurriedly left their rooms. An outburst of wailing immediately shook the house.

74

Women, children, and slaves were weeping. "What? Is it possible? No! I can't believe it!" cried a woman who was tearing her hair. Another sprang from her room and crashed into the courtyard; she said: "Look at my life! My unhappy life! What cruel Destiny sent me into this world? When will I see the author of my days?" Still another lay prostrate in the dust, pounding the ground with the backs of her hands and moaning: "For whom did you leave me, soul of my soul, when you stayed in 'mahi' country?" Someone else had placed one hand in the palm of the other and was striking herself on the back with them, sighing: "What's left for me in this life? What's left? Where can I find death?" Princess Ponouwa exclaimed: "All I have to do is die! Die! What death will come and carry me away?"

A number of her companions repeated this lamentation.

One woman had dragged herself on her knees to the household fetish enthroned in the middle of the courtyard and was blaspheming it: "Is that the way you protected him? Have you lacked anything since his departure from Agbomê? In the past he was almost the only one who made offerings to you. During his absence, many of us made them every day. There you are, fallen from the ranks of fetishes from this day forward!"

Distressed to see their mothers, their sisters, and their older brothers weeping and rolling in the dirt, a few younger children also began to wail.

Kneeling in front of his weeping mother, a child was consoling her: "Stop, mama! Stop crying! Who has been beating you?" He lifted a fold of his mother's cloth and attempted, with his unskilled hand, to wipe her face.

Another child importuned his mother with the following refrain: "I'm hungry, mama! Stop crying, mama, and give me what's left over from the foofoo I had yesterday. I'm hungry!" Since she didn't seem to hear him, he began tapping her on the shoulder with his calabash, drenched in palm oil, and singing softly but persistently: "I'm hungry, mama! Stop crying, mama, and give me what's left over from the foofoo I had yesterday!"

A slave who had just returned from the farm huddled in a corner and, turning his back on the others, added his cries to theirs. He seemed to have been deeply affected by the misfortune of his master. His lamentations aroused the pity of a few smaller children, who gathered around him and tried to console him; they did not understand that this man was rejoicing inwardly at the disappearance of their father and saying in his incomprehensible dialect: "Ten, fifteen, twenty, and even all your princes can be annihilated! Agbomê can be razed to the ground! Little do I care! Care! Care! Care. . . !"

The litany of the slave drowned out the wailing of the women and children, who finally grew calm. Only Doguicimi continued to weep and moan. At her side, Evêmon alone might have consoled her. But the poor child herself was so overwhelmed with grief that she merely added her tears to those of her "mother".

When older sisters and brothers, upon whose consciousness the things of this world were already dawning, rejected invitations to play, the smaller children finally understood that joy was not going to show itself that day. Each of them withdrew into his mother's room.

There was no contact between calabashes and calabashes, between gourds and gourds; there was no fire in any hearth. Vivênagbo had sent five calabashes of food to the family of his sworn friend. Several women had lain down on mats; other wives of Toffa were leaning against the walls, staring into the air, and sighing between lamentations, their legs bent, their heels next to their buttocks, their arms crossed on their chest or their hands on their shoulders, their eyes red and swollen.

One would have thought Doguicimi had fallen asleep, because she was so silent and motionless beneath the cloth that covered her from her feet to her head.

Overcome with pity for Evêmon, whose tears continued to flow, the woman had decided to conceal her own tears from her, having just noticed that they intensified those of the poor child, who in turn had stopped crying so as not to disturb (she said to herself) the repose of her mother, whom she believed to be sleeping. But hidden from Evêmon's sight, the woman continued to combat the grief that was simmering inside her and threatened burst forth once again. On the verge of losing her struggle, she wiped her face and sat up. Desiring to revive her courage and renew her hope, she called, "Enawa!"

The servant girl left and returned to inform her mistress: "Enawa is lying dead in the courtyard."

"Does that mean the master will never return?" cried Doguicimi, the thought striking her like a stunning blow and throwing her violently to the ground. Her sobs reawakened the general sorrow, and new lamentations broke out.

Until evening, they would recur intermittently at the least reminder of the memory of the absent beloved.

*   *   *

At the fall of night, drowsiness lulled the entire household of Toffa to sleep, but this remedy, which so effectively heals the most painful bruises of the spirit and soothes the worst sufferings of the body, had no effect upon Doguicimi, whose sorrow rendered her impervious to the powers of this marvelous balm.

Seated on the threshold of her room, the woman sighed with grief: "Ah, my life! The unhappy life of a creature that pitiless Destiny refuses to protect against misfortune! If I had known that such an ill-starred fate awaited me in this world, I would not have come into it! A shoot brutally severed from the yam and transplanted at Agbomê, I was happy enough. Now the stake assigned to support me has broken before I could send out a tuber!"

The consolatory words of Evêmon, who was kneeling in front of her mother, poured out over Doguicimi's heart, burning with sorrow, and immediately evaporated, like drops of water falling on red-hot metal. The poor child finally lost courage as the result of her inability to comfort her mother, and she began to cry with her. Although not loud enough to disturb the sleep of the others, their sobs nevertheless dominated the thousand tiny chirpings with which the night, through the voices of crickets and other insects, surrounded the house of Toffa; thus, neither Doguicimi nor Evêmon heard anything when the main door creaked quite loudly, despite the infinite precautions that had been taken in opening it. But feeling her head grow heavy, the young girl looked behind her and saw a shadow limping toward her. Overcome by fright, she pressed against her mother and was not reassured until the shadow approached more closely and she recognized Vivênagbo, who had disguised himself as an aged royal messenger.

"Offer kola nuts to the ancestors and fetishes of your family for having thrown that unfortunate queen to the executioner and saved your neck," said Toffa's friend once he had been introduced into the room and after having assured himself that Evêmon was the only witness to their conversation. "Everyone in Danhomê knows that the poor woman's overzealousness deserved banishment at the very most, whereas only death could expiate your blasphemies. And if you for one moment have the insane arrogance to believe that your curses intimidated the king and that you can now defy him with impunity, I am telling you that you are running a greater risk than ever before. The co-wives and the uncle of the innocent victim will never forgive you her death.

"On the basis of what happened this morning, you are perhaps telling yourself that Guézo is generous? Realize that he is just as arbitrary as all his predecessors; they would pardon a crime at one moment and later demand that a mere disdainful glance, a harmless jest, or a minor offense be punished by death. My own disgrace is the reward I have received for the prudent precautions I took yesterday evening to prevent anyone from robbing the families of the princes and captains lost at Hounjroto. Each time the king leaves Agbomê, I am to go to Canna and watch over the mausolea, which, the king explained, have neither eyes nor ears and will therefore understand nothing of my alarmist actions and decrees. From now on Prince Adouconou will assume the regency in his absence. See how one's zeal is valued and realize that you will never in your life encounter this morning's good fortune a second time."

Doguicimi responded in a tone that revealed her utter contempt for death: "I have relatives and no doubt my husband as well in the realm of the dead. Far from frightening me, the thought of rejoining them fills me with joy."

"The court still hopes to see Toffa again because until now there is no proof of his death. Didn't you hear the king promise to free him? If you don't fear death for yourself, change your attitude and your way of speaking to the king for the sake of your husband because the king could avenge your insults by refusing to undertake the expedition that might free the princes who are prisoners at Hounjroto.

"It is true that the cages of hyenas and panthers have disappeared from the Palace with Adanzan, who had installed them and, until recently, threw Danhomênous to them after convicting them on trumped-up charges of high treason, but whatever you may think, Migan is not powerless. As far as I have heard, the ships are still in port at Gléhoué and still accepting slaves. Who knows whether Guézo hasn't deferred your death in the expectation of having you brutally executed before the very eyes of your husband when he returns to Agbomê? It is also possible that the king holds the prince responsible for your curses and secretly plans to eliminate him, even if Toffa protests his loyalty by publicly disavowing you."

"Your sworn friend no longer cherished the sincerety of his wives' love, and he refused to believe in it. Thus, he is not going to suffer on my account. Yet even if I were repudiated by him or sold into slavery at his behest, dishonored throughout Danhomê, or put to death by his own hands, my love for him would not diminish. I console myself in advance for all my torments with the thought that the tears of anguish I shed will have flowed over Li[2] and that my blood will have been drunk by Ogou,[3] neither of whom will be satisfied until they have quenched their thirst with royal blood and tears."

"Such an illusion could only arise in the skull of a being with seven pairs of ribs. But remember, Doguicimi, that the words, 'butcher, sell me this piece; cut it up, salt it, and add enough red pepper,' are only spoken after the pig has been slaughtered. That is to say, if the dishonor you predict for Danhomê is fated to occur, you will not be here to witness it."

"It makes no difference whether or not I disappear before the tragic end that Guézo's bad faith is calling down upon him. What is essential is that my desires be fulfilled and that this kingdom suffer the other misfortunes I am going to wish upon it before my ablutions this morning. May Danhomê be crushed and ruled by foreign masters; may Guézo's successors die far from their own country and their spirits be denied peace in the afterworld for lack of traditional burial rites; may the princes be reduced to begging their living among commoners or slaves who have become rich and powerful! Danhomê, if I can be privileged in my sepulchre to see the fall of its kings and the misery of its princes, I will rejoice!"

"The Blood Oath that binds me to you husband places me under the obligation to protect his family. But you should also know that, as a result of the fetish-potion the king has already imposed upon me a dozen times, I cannot listen to malicious remarks directed against him without informing him of them, nor can I allow him to remain ignorant of plots being hatched against him once they have come to my attention. You are placing me in an extremely embarassing position. I have forgotten all the curses you uttered tonight. But please do not repeat them again in my presence. If in spite of my advice you insist upon blaspheming Danhomê and wishing for its downfall, allow me to warn you that a diviner might survive the war he predicts, but one of the members of his family will surely die in it. Doguicimi, you are forgetting that the fall of this kingdom will also be that of Toffa's descendants."

Doguicimi immediately recognized her mistake; the expression on her face bore eloquent witness to that. The anger that had roused her against the king and caused her to become unjust suddenly melted away.

The minister continued in a more cajoling tone of voice: "Let me remind you that the king is very much preoccupied with obtaining information as soon as possible about the fate of the three princes who were lost at Hounjroto. Dry your tears then and don't any longer accuse Guézo of having eliminated his brothers in

2   "Li" is the name given to the earth, which is considered as a divinity. (author's note)
3   "Ogou" is the god of war and weapons, the "Mars" of the Danhomênous. (author's note)

'mahi' country. At a meeting of the council, he made the following declaration, which cannot be made publicly: 'Danhomê will pretend to have a great desire for peace and sincere friendship with its enemies. In that way we hope to allay their mistrust so we can prepare in complete security for the victory that will be quick to occur as soon as the ancestors have issued the order for revenge. If necessary, we will follow the strategy that worked so well under similar circumstances for our illustrious ancestor, Agaja the Conqueror.' Are you listening to me, Doguicimi? Right after the traditional celebrations, which are only two moons away, Guézo will send spies to Hounjroto. Soon Danhomê will be apprised of our enemies' military forces and their other secrets. If our spies return and inform us that there is a sleeping place worthy of a princess of Danhomê in 'mahi' country, the Master of the World will not hesitate for a moment to install one of his daughters there, and following the example of Awliponouwê at the court of the 'houéda' king Houfon, she will lay the groundwork for the victory that will bring Toffa, Ajéhounou, and Assogbaou back to Danhomê. I will bribe all the spies being sent to Hounjroto so that they will show more zeal in the search for Toffa. The tearful wife will soon have news of her beloved husband, and Vivênagbo of his never-to-be-forgotten sworn friend. But in the meantime, remain absolutely silent about your love for Toffa and conceal your resentment against Guézo. Fortunately, no one in Danhomê has the slightest idea of the Oath that binds me to the prince; it is in the shadows, and therefore in complete security, that I will be working for his liberation.

"Unless something unforeseen happens, I will not see you until three long market days have passed." Vivênagbo adjusted his disguise and walked away limping as he had come.

The night was far advanced. Aided by fatigue, drowsiness soon took hold of Doguicimi and Evêmon, spreading its salutary effects over them as well.

Migan arrived at the Palace that morning with the skull that had been brought back from Hounjroto. It had been boiled in water, and all the putrefiable parts had been removed. The first minister drew the king's attention to two kinds of horny matter on the forehead of the skull: "It is, without the shadow of a doubt, the head of the 'mahi' paramount chief. This man was chosen to rule over his fellow countrymen because of the presence of these protuberances on his skull, an incontestable sign of his great distinction, I mean to say his descendance from a four-legged animal which is supposed to be their common ancestor. Here we have the most precious trophy that was brought back from Hounjroto."

Despite the exuberant confidence of his first minister, Guézo nourished a few doubts about the importance of the person whose skull had just been presented to him.

The soldier who had brought back the head of this Mahinou came and dispelled the king's doubts by relating the circumstances under which he had killed the chief.

The king rewarded the bravery of this soldier by giving him a wife, cloths, cowries, a sabre with a velvet sash, and the command of a division. Then he ordered cloths, strings of cowries, and brandy distributed to the families of those who were missing.

They would bury a portion of these objects in their homes, specifying that they were intended for a particular absent member of the family; then they would conduct the funeral in conformity with tradition.

The dead among the missing would thereby receive their last rites and could thus be admitted into the company of their ancestors.

The entire kingdom was called upon by the voice of Panligan at Agbomê – and by those of public criers attached to governors, village headmen, and local chiefs in the provinces – to mourn in their hearts for the presumedly dead soldiers who had given their lives for Danhomê. During their morning ablutions, all women were to entreat the ancestors to aid the Danhomênous at the proper moment in freeing the captives who had remained in the hands of the Mahinous and to avenge the deaths of our soldiers at Hounjroto.

The king postponed all funeral ceremonies for the princes Ajéhounou, Assogbaou, and Toffa until he could be fully informed about their fate.

There was still hope that they might return any day, like Linpéhoun, who was believed to have been killed but then rejoined the army in the "dassa" village where the king was resting after his escape from Hounjroto.

Chapter 4

The Great Traditional Celebration

The campaign of Hounjroto, which had been justified by Guézo as an attempt to avenge the memory of the white men massacred in "mahi" country, was interpreted in a quite different way at Agbomê. Doguicimi saw in it the monarch's desire to find an opportunity for eliminating the princes who had witnessed his previous misery.

Other widows and orphans of missing princes and palace dignitaries confided in each other that, more than the punishment of the supposed accomplices of the people at Kinglo or the desire to rid himself of individuals to whom he owed his throne but whose presence had become awkward, the need to obtain victims for the next traditional celebration or captives to fill an urgent request from Chacha Ajinacou provided the most plausible explanation for the expedition that had failed, contrary to all expectations.

All of them, including Guézo himself, were in the right; if the honor of Danhomê made that campaign necessary, Doguicimi's grief excused her accusations and blasphemies, and the sorrow of the other widows and orphans justified their censures. Thus all Danhomênous who were still mourning their relatives were justifiably indignant when it became known that plans were being made for a traditional celebration scarcely two moons after their great loss. But if the Master of the World makes a decision, the people must obey. The king had explained to the lords of the kingdom that he was advancing the usual dates for the celebration in order to hasten, through public festivities, the healing that successive nights of sleep effect but slowly in wounded souls. The revenge that all Danhomê was demanding would come later.

It was the time of the waning moon. Consulted on the morning of the day of "mêjo",[1] which coincided with the market of Adogouin,[2] Destiny decreed

---

[1]   "Mejo" is the first of the nine days of "fêzan," the calandar of Danhomê. (author's note)

[2]   Adogouin was a market in the old "houéda" kingdom of Jékin, a coastal region west of Gléhoué (Ouidah); it was instituted at Canna by Pingla, the sixth king of Danhomê in memory of

that the celebration should take place on the eighth market of Zogbodo,[3] which would fall on the holiday of "bozounvodoun;"[4] twenty-nine nights thus separated them from the celebrations, which were to begin as soon as the new moon had completely covered the calabash.

Royal messengers carried the news of the planned traditional celebration, along with other confidential communications, to all the provincial governors.

The regional chiefs came to the governors' residences to learn the contents of the message received from Agbomê; they then passed word on to the village headmen, who informed the local chiefs. The good news was carried from house to house by those in charge of the census. The heads of families immediately shared it with everyone in their compounds. Two days later, the trees and the vines as well as the grass and the straw on the shores of the Zou and the Coufo learned about the forthcoming festivities in the capital from the cutting edges of machetes and the calloused hands of workmen.

One evening the royal architect Hounpatin's workers, whose role as builders caused them to be known derisively as "let the shadow pass here," arrived from Agonlin on the shore of the Zou with piles of wood, ropes of vine, and bundles of grass and straw. Hounpatin was at the head of the group. They began rethatching the roofs at the Palace on the day of "bo-savo,"[5] recommended as a holiday by Destiny. Taking oil and raphia palm fibers lashed together with rushes, they refashioned the frameworks that were so symmetrical that they looked like an enlarged honeycomb; these frameworks were then covered with a thick covering of straw. When it came time for the vestments of the royal sepulchres to be changed, the operation was entrusted to a dozen princes and dignitaries working under the supervision of Aplogan. The king himself was present at the restoration of the dwellings that housed the remains of his ancestors. With solemn faces and closed mouths, the workers paid close attention to their neighbors' gestures, studiously avoiding any noise that might disturb the sleep of the kings. The only sounds that broke the silence here were the crackings of the wood being fit and lashed tightly together and the moanings of the straw and thatch bundles as they were thrown into the air before dropping heavily onto the framework; a fine silvery palmyra palm the height of a man and with a pineapple at its foot was placed on the ridge of the house where King Agonglo was sleeping his last sleep. The tomb of Pingla sported a cutlass (symbol of the war god) and several silver trees, recalling the king's maxim: "A powerful arm cuts the tree in the enemy's forest with impunity."

On Tégbéssou's tomb a silver palm frond was standing proudly. Just as one could never oblige a palm leaf to take root, the enemies of Tégbéssou could never oblige him to obey their will.

---

the conquest of that enemy kingdom. (author's note)

[3] Zogbodo was an ancient market that the Alahadonous found on the plateau to which they migrated under the leadership of Daco-Donou at the beginning of the seventeenth century. The day of this market is devoted to the worship of fetishes. (author's note)

[4] "Bozounvodoun" was the third day of the Danhomê calendar. (author's note)

[5] "Bo-savo was the fifth day of the Danhomê calendar. (author's note)

A silver ship with its crew and the insignia of the white man's religion graced the house of Agaja's last sleep; hadn't he succeeded in triumphing over the greed of the Houédanous, who only sent to Danhomê trickles of the marvelous things brought by the white men?

Acaba loved to tell his enemies: "When the pig looks at the sun and falls into a rage, there will be no more peace that year;" thus, nothing could be more appropriate to represent the efforts of the king sleeping in this house than a silver pig.

That silver bow and quiver symbolizing the difficult beginning of the Alada-honou occupation in a hostile country marked the tomb of the founder of the realm.

A jug in which a rod was standing and at the foot of which was lying a corpse rose all silvery above the tomb of Daco-Donou and told of the brave act performed at Alada.

The task of providing new clothes for each royal cadaver followed the restoration of the roof that sheltered him. Once the sepulchre was opened, two princes descended into it with the help of a ladder and draped velvet and silk cloths over the remains of the dead king; female care-takers cleaned the chamber and replaced the bed, the sceptre, the spitoon, the sandals, the parasols, and all the other royal insignia belonging to the dead man.

Before the threshold of each sepulchre, Migan sacrificed a slave who had been kneeling between two of the executioner's assistants as the house was being repaired. The victim was being sent to inform the king buried there about the work that had been done on his tomb and about the adornment of his remains.

Because the last war had not been sucessful, Assogbapê lacked the subject for a new bas-relief at the Palace. He contented himself with restoring the colors of the older ones that had been faded by the sun and rain.

One morning the people saw the walls of Agaja's second story completely covered with webs of cowries bunched together in packets, each of which contained the skull of a victim sacrificed during the traditional celebrations that had been held during previous reigns.

Because human sacrifice had been raised to a traditional custom by Agaja, Tégbéssou had decided to honor the illustrious memory of the Conqueror-of-the-Ships by decorating his Palace with the macabre remains of messengers who had been charged with the task of informing the ancestors about the victories of Danhomê.

For the Danhomênous, the decoration of Agaja's Palace was the sign that the beginning of the great traditional celebration was near. Indeed, it was only ten days away.

One afternoon Yévogan Dagba escorted a convoy into Agbomê; many bales of cloth, bundles of parasols, and guns were lashed to the racks of the porters, who were also carrying demijohns of brandy, sacks of cowry shells, casks of tobacco, and small kegs of gunpowder.

The porters' hunched shoulders, curved backs, bulging chests, sweat-drenched bodies, and feet covered with the red dust of the highway testified that the burdens were heavy and had been carried a long distance. Nevertheless, those who arrived were walking gaily and continued to pour into the city until nightfall.

In the retinue of the Governor there were also a few Danhomênous who had been placed with the white men of Gléhoué to learn their art of cooking and serving food.

The lord chamberlain Cangbodé ordered a count of all the goods resulting from the port fees at Gléhoué, the purchases of the king, and the gifts of the trading-company managers; he then verified everything before having it placed in the storehouses.

For the past three long markets, the messengers of the farmer general Houéliji had been traveling to the smallest farms in the kingdom and transmitting to farmers the order to forward their contributions to Agbomê.

The servants of Vaokintin, suppliers of spices to the Palace, were gathering red peppers and other condiments in all parts of the country.

Mêgbémê, the chief fisherman of the coastal region, as well as Ahanlantin and Potohossou, the chief fishermen of the Zou, Coufo, and Wo Rivers, had sent word to all the fishermen in the kingdom that the king needed more fish than ever before. Those who lived too far from the capital to send fresh fish were expected to provide smoked ones.

Upon the order of Pogba, the chief huntsman of the royal family and of the people, his two assistants Agounjan and Tavi had distributed new guns, powder, and shot to all the hunters in the kingdom; they were hunting day and night, sending smoked meat to Agbomê as well as furred and feathered game that had been captured alive.

Throughout the kingdom, everyone was seeking to attract the attention of the Master of the World by offering his majesty a present worthy of him.

Sacks of grain and yams piled up in front of the Palace; gourds filled with palm oil arrived there in great quantity. The minister of agriculture Topo verified everything before taking charge of it.

The servants of Sogan enumerated the firewood stacked in the neighborhood of Ahouga.

Heavily charged porters arrived from Jija one morning; they were directed to the residence of Migan.

The goats which arrived night and day by the hundreds in Agbomê added their bleatings to the bellowings of the cattle penned at Ahouga.

Tired of walking and, what is more, having been burned by the sun that was melting his fat, a pig planted his feet in the sand and refused to advance, despite the stimulus of a whip that was stinging his flanks. The farmer who was leading it to the butchers in the Ajahito neighborhood stepped in front of it and yanked on the rope that was tied to one of the animal's forefeet; it collapsed into the dust. Its instinct having alerted it to its impending death, it was imploring in its deafening squeals: "Kill me here! Kill me now!" Overcome with the fear of death, it did not want to live any longer. They had to use a porter's rack to move it.

Night and day for the past moon in the Lègo neighborhood of Agbomê and in all the villages of Docon, the fingers of women were crushing, filtering, and kneading the clay that was being transformed into pottery of various forms and shapes and would be baked in wood or straw fires. These vessels would be used during the religious ceremonies and meals as well as for the potion the Danhomênous would be drinking at the public ceremonies.

One morning an endless line of women arrived from Docon, walking through the Ditch of Janwoun and carrying large jugs, small ones, earthen jars, and plates.

The next day Sogan, the supplier of water to the Palace, ordered Jagba, superviser of the springs at Agbomê, to increase the number of common women affected to the water-carrying detail; at the first crowing of the cock, they walked to the various springs of the region and even traveled as far as Canna and Zali in order to provide water for the inhabitants of the Palace and the foreigners who would be attracted to Agbomê by the celebrations.

Because there was not enough room at the Palace, cages of fowl began piling up at the homes of Migan, Mêwou, and several other dignitaries. At every moment of the day, there was a deafening concert of cacklings and crowings. "If only these descendants of dogs – worthy at most of being sacrificed en masse to "legba"[6] – would let people sleep at night and not awaken them before the rising of the sun, one would be grateful to them! But the night has scarcely turned his neck, and these cocks are singing their songs! Eh, you miserable creatures who tear us from our slumbers! We'll see if you can still cackle and crow at such inopportune moments in our stomachs after our teeth have reduced your necks to paste!" grumbled the women and servants for whom the first crowing of the cock was the command to begin working again; they were rubbing their eyes to chase away sleep and stretching themselves lazily. Perhaps even more than the desire to break the necks of the cocks that had awakened them too soon, the fear of being beaten for lingering on the sleeping mat caused them to leave the room in a hurry.

Those of them who were supposed to grind the grain impulsively spit twice on their hands so they could hold the pounder more firmly. And the raised wooden ram crashed heavily down upon the grain; it was replying to the dull sounds emanating from near and distant mortars. To keep their spirits high, several women were saying to themselves: "Strangers are throwing out a challenge to me! We'll see who gets tired first and who, on the day appointed by the Master of the World, gives back flour in exchange for the grains that were given to us." And "pock-lo! pock-lo!" sounded the ironwood mortar as it bounced against the side on its way up again.

At the Palace servants were drilling holes in cowries; others were placing them, twenty-five at a time, on strings that were being gathered into bundles of eight.

Zinflou and Zantan, a master weaver and a master tailor whose ancestors had come to Alada with Daco-Donou, were preparing the clothes to be worn by the king during the traditional religious ceremonies. Working inside the Palace far

---

[6] "Legba" is the spirit of evil who performs the vulgar tasks of the gods. People conciliated him with frequent sacrifices. (author's note)

85

from the indiscreet eyes of the populace, they were embellishing the material that was going to cover "Topon", a monument to be raised in the courtyard of Agrigomê.

The king's master tailor Alagbé was engaged with his assistants in making great parasols for the Master of the World.

Bent over pieces of material that had been cut out with a knife or a fingernail, another master tailor Yêmajê was making the royal breeches. His aides had acquired great skill through long years of practice, and to them he entrusted the preparation of cloths and headpieces.

The master tailors themselves were responsible for the work of their assistants, and they verified everything. Working with their own hands, they devoted several days to adorning the fringes of the parasols and the cloths intended for the use of the king.

The uniforms of the soldiers (both men and women), the fringed velvet sashes – leaf-green, indigo, blood red, the frothy color of boiling palm oil – and the cloths to be distributed to the princes, high dignitaries, and other Danhomênous were entrusted to common tailors, although they too were working under the supervision of the masters.

Seated since dawn, the master weaver Ahodi and his numerous servants did not leave their looms until night came and covered their eyes with his band of shadows. Placing their hands on their hips, they only stood up with great difficulty. Their stiff legs at first refused to unbend and support them, so they leaned for a moment against their looms. Having stood up, they now bent the upper part of their bodies backward, puffed out their chests, and yawned as if to dislocate their lower jaws; they stretched, and their joints cracked; they alone had the right to complain about being tired.

The atelier was empty in the wink of an eye. All day long, only shuttles and pedals had enjoyed the right to move about and to gossip among themselves. At nightfall they fell silent; the men were now free to exercise their jaws and tongues as they pleased before going to straighten their backs on a sleeping mat.

Jotowou produced sandals (an emblem of royalty) and leather cushions; with black, white, yellow, or green leather, he embellished the amulets that the king would wear on his neck, his wrists, his arms, and his belt. With embroidered leather, the master craftsman's assistants also adorned the baskets that would hold clothes and ornaments for the Master of the World or the presents he would be giving to the princes, the high dignitaries, and others. The master craftsman's less skilled assistants stitched purses, game bags, cartridge pouches, and other small leather objects.

At the home of the king's goldsmith, impertinent little hammers were striking enormous stone anvils, whose moans filled the neighborhood from dawn until dusk. Weary, the hammers rested. But the bellows, an unsympathetic camrade, aroused them again. And the battle recommenced. The anvil still did not move. Do you think the witnesses were interceding on its behalf? On the contrary, the red-hot metal left the fire to scorch it. Seated upon a block of wood, his feet buried in a black dust, and his body bathed in sweat, the smith, who was wearing no more than a strip of cloth passed between his legs and held up by belt of vines, worked all day long without interruption, except to swallow a few mouthfuls of food or water. It had been going on like this for several markets. But the combatants and the prompter finally exhausted themselves. Hountonji carried restored or newly created bronze, silver, and gold jewelry to the Palace.

At Hoja, Gomêcin and his assistants made copper bells for the costumes of the fetish priests and as ornaments for drums and other objects.

Agbozo chiselled or burned designs into the large calabashes for the food and drink that would be offered to high dignitaries and the white friends of the Master of the World.

Just like Assogbapê with his bas-reliefs, this artist endowed his designs with a language that was only mysterious for the commoners among the Danhomênous.

More than the fear of punishment, the privileges that the Master of the World accorded to practioners of the arts and the hope of generous rewards – gifts of fiefdoms or of slaves to cultivate their fields, hunt, fish, or weave cloth for them; appointments of doctors to care for their families; ennoblements through marriage to one of the princesses – had inspired all the artists and artisans to acquire a remarkable skill and sense of professional conscience.

Under the exalted authority of Madéou, the master drummers who lived at the Palace were teaching more than ten groups of young girls to sing the songs of the traditional celebrations. For singers who were tone deaf or slow to learn, the whip spoke often and quite loudly.

Choir directors were proceeding in the same fashion with the young men at the homes of Ajado, the chief drummer of the "dogba", and Adongbé, the master drummer who recounted the victories of the king.

Slaves whose laziness or recalcitrance had alienated their masters were brought to the court. When asked to exchange them for the "chargers"[7] that he was preparing to dispatch to the kingdom of the spirits, the king refused. His reason was explained by Migan: "Danhomênous, in our uncertainty over the fate of Ajéhounou, Assogbaou, and Toffa, who were captured at Hounjroto, we must not spare a single brother of their probable murderers if we do not want a criminal indulgence to draw upon our heads the wrath of the ancestors, who will not hesitate to destroy every roof that gives shelter to these foul sons of the mountains. All our captives from Hounjroto, including Mahinous at their mother's breasts, must die.

"Satisfaction will be given next year to all masters who are unhappy with their slaves, unless the king before then exchanges those who have been presented to him today for the batch he is soon expecting to collect and sell to Chacha Ajinacou."

"The Master of the World is right! All our captives from the last campaign should be sacrificed!" shouted the people approvingly as they poured dust over

---

[7]   The word "charger" was used to designate the horses which carried the queens and high dignitaries to the field of battle, but it also referred to the human sacrificial victims, who were secured to porters' racks for execution, because they were supposed to be as fast as race horses in transmitting messages to the realm of the dead. (author's note)

their heads.

For the past three long markets at Agbomê, Paapa had been visiting the families in which he had been told he would find pubescent young girls, and he recruited them for the Palace. In the province of Agonlin and those on the other side of the Swamps (Alada, Toli, Gléhoué, Calavi, and Godomê), the oracle, having been consulted with the greatest secrecy through the intermediary of a very reliable diviner, indicated to the head of the family what sacrifices would influence Destiny favorably toward the poor offshoot on the eve of its separation from the mother plant.

The girl who was about to leave was then led before the statues of the ancestors, who were presented offerings of water, kola nuts, melegueta pepper, a pint of brandy, and even a chicken if they demanded it.

Kneeling with her head lowered, anguish in her heart, and a flood of tears on her chest, the child listened to the prayers of the elders, who were imploring the ancestors to grant her their protection.

The women were crying; the younger sisters were saddened by this departure, which reminded them that their turn to be separated from the family would also come some day.

To console the poor victim of a despotic custom and restore her confidence, the head of the family told her after finishing his prayers: "Stop crying, my child, and don't worry about the future. The ancestors will watch over you and lead you to happiness; the banana only becomes soft when it begins to ripen. Out of this harsh separation happiness will grow."

The head of the family arrived at the Governor's residence with the young girl and said as he kissed the ground: "I am returning the ward that was entrusted to my custody so that it can be sent to the one who is Father and Mother of the People."

Each Governor hastened to send his batch off toward the capital.

The separation was painful, but the relatives had to resign themselves to it; the Danhomênou was but a mere breeding animal for the royal herd. The offspring belonged neither to the male nor to the female. The Master of the World could dispose of them as he saw fit. One could hardly blame Guézo, who was simply the heir to a tradition.

Uncertainty about the fate that awaited them once they arrived in Agbomê distressed the chicks who had been snatched from the warmth of the paternal nest. They cursed the day they had been born. One of them continually lamented: "Ah, if I had been able to foresee the miseries imposed upon me in this world, I would never have come into it!"

In the group that had left from Toli, a young girl who was the sole support of a paralyzed father, thought she could interest one of her guards in her plight; tears in her eyes, she confided in him: "My father has not seen the sky three times since the death of my mother two long dry seasons ago. He once had a quarrel with the Governor, against whom the king sided with him. . . . "

The man interrupted her curtly: "I am not the author of your days and do not want to be deafened with your complaints!"

It was a warning to the unfortunate children that they could exchange their confidences only among themselves.

Most were seeing each other for the first time. But common suffering always makes up for long acquaintanceship in terms of eliciting confidences.

One of them ventured: "I will perhaps be given to a man whose faithful service the king would like to reward. May it please Destiny (and myself) that he have me and me alone to love."

Another one, who was proud of her beauty, proclaimed: "I will be married to a prince or a high dignitary, unless the king himself decides to take me for his wife! But happiness is not guaranteed in the Palace. My aunt assured me that deviousness easily triumphs over beauty there. I will quite possibly have the honor of sharing the royal bed only once in my life. It is true that, if I become Wife of Panther, I will be living in the entourage of the king.

"But my happiness will only last as long as his reign because I will be obliged to accompany my august husband into the grave if I do not become a mother."

One young girl was more distraught than her companions; the grief at being separated from her parents was compounded by the fear of never getting married. Her features were rather masculine, and she herself was terribly ugly; she sighed: "Because it pleases the man who is known as the Father of Life, hearts made for love must become filled with hatred and arms that the Supreme Being created to carry, feed, nurse, and caress little children must devote themselves to the snuffing out of human lives. Even if she is as ugly as the backside of a long-tailed monkey, a daughter of the king will be married with pomp and ceremony to some high dignitary. And to divert women of the people from performing their duty to perpetuate the race, they never tire of citing the exploit that Yépommê Avognondé accomplished in a fit of zeal during the last reign! Do they believe that the misery inflicted upon us and the crime we are obliged to commit against Life will remain unpunished! The Supreme Being who sent us into this world will eventually take an interest in our sorry fate!"

Some of them would soon forget their sorrows, but many were to remain embittered for the rest of their lives. . . .

In distant villages, women gathered roasted maize, millet flour, mustard that had been seasoned with hot peppers and salt before being smoked, fried bean cakes, and balls of "acassa" and stuffed them into the pouches of husbands who would be accompanying their chiefs to the celebration. "Amoussou doesn't have to starve to death even if his master keeps him away from the banquets!"

Those confined to their homes by illness or for any other reason regretted being unable to take part in the festivities that the Father of Wealth was organizing in the capital.

The face of the world brightened, and the day died. Far from producing a lull in the preparations for the celebration, the absence of the sun heightened their intensity.

On the morning of "zogbodo" only three nights lay between us and the festivities.

When consulted, Destiny prescribed a number of sacrifices which would be necessary before it could guarantee unmitigated joy.

Goats, chickens, pigeons, fruit, grain, leaves, flour, palm oil, and a number of other ingredients were brought together; in large baskets, small baskets, and calabashes of all sizes the diviners then prepared the sacrifices that the servants deposited as soon as they were completed at sites designated by Destiny. Two important sacrifices had to be performed outside the city after the death of the day. Migan would preside over them.

At nightfall, the executioner and Wolo, the diviner of the royal household, left Agbomê with numerous followers by way of the Door of Dossoumoin.

The group advanced quickly and silently; the sound of their feet pounding on the ground chased off the tiny creatures, who did not leave without screeching their protests against the injustice of men, who had used the road as they pleased all day long but were now returning at a time that was reserved for the inhabitants of the bush to seek their food or frolic about. Yet those who did not move out of the way quickly enough were mercilessly crushed underfoot.

Moved by the laments of the wounded, a night hawk, whose mate was seeking insects for him by the light of the stars, tore himself away from these acts of endearment and came with a rapid swoop to intimidate the assassins; he even slapped one of them across the face with his wing.

The owls in the trees hooted at the cowards who oppressed the weak but were afraid of a night hawk.

No one among the ranks of the travelers seemed to notice either the victims or their defenders. From time to time Wola regarded the stars. As for Migan, he named the villages through which they were passing.

The Zou was not more than a thousand bamboos away. The diviner commanded them to stop. The night was late and extremely dark; the road was deserted.

The first minister motioned some of his followers to turn back the way they had come; they were going to wait about forty bamboos away.

The remaining attendants made a hedge around Migan, the diviner, and a captive.

When the bonds that held his arms behind his back were removed, the captive docilely obeyed the minister and flattened himself in the dust, his head toward "nago" country and his limbs spread out. With the blow of a large club, the sacrificial priest broke one of the victim's arms, then the other one, then one of his legs, and finally the other one. The man was a Nagonou: the anguished cries that the first blow extracted from him left no room for doubt. Migan continued to beat him on the back and on his broken limbs; then he stepped to one side. The diviner poured flour water, palm oil, and brandy over the victim; he also threw down about twenty strings of cowries, and sprinkling the entire mass with flour soaked in palm oil, he said: "All Nagonous, enemies of Danhomê, are incapable of taking up arms to fight against the kingdom of Houégbaja during our celebrations." Leaning over the victim, Migan pushed a two-cubit-long stake through the man's body to fix him firmly to the ground; striking the head of the stake with a stone, he concluded: "The Nagonous, our enemies, cannot arise and attack Danhomê."

Those who had performed the sacrifice rejoined the group that was waiting for them; they then traveled to a spot facing "mahi" country and, with a second captive, repeated the ritual that was supposed to immobilize the Mahinous as well during the celebrations at Agbomê.

They returned to the capital after the second crowing of the cock.

Two of the sacrificial priest's assistants were dispatched at sunrise to the sites of the sacrifices, and they returned to inform their master that only a few bones, scraps of intestines, a stake, scattered strings of cowries, and tracks of hyena claws marked the spots.

The minister hastened to carry to the king the news that the sacrifices had been accepted.

The council nevertheless thought it prudent to station guards on the borders; two armies were thus placed at the disposition of Houngan and Fongni, the governors of Agonlin, and of Agbolo at Jija.

The women of Canna brought the fine white sand with which the main hall of Agaja's second story would be covered; it was there that the white men announced for the next day would be staying.

The rooms were prepared, and the walls of the reception room on the first floor had been hung with enormous cloths woven locally and adorned with intricate designs.

The people had not seen their Idol for three days.

Yet before the sun had turned his head, the Master of the World left the Palace and, through the voice of Mêwou, commanded all Danhomênous to thank Migan, who had presented him with a long gold necklace and handsome parasols as well as fine cloths of velvet and silk.

The mob shouted: "Thank you, Migan! Thank you for a present that is worthy of the Master of the World! A better one could not be found!"

"Everything I have I owe to the Father of Wealth!" exclaimed the minister, covering himself with dirt and visibly delighted to see that his present had pleased the king and was now known to all Danhomê.

A commoner from the banks of the Zou approached the bamboo barrier on his hands and knees, covered his head and chest with dirt, and held out a package toward Daclo, who had come to him; he said: "The Father of Wealth has never disdained that which came from the hands of his most humble subjects. That encourages me to offer him this tinder. To gather it, I made good use of the days that were granted me by the Father of Life."

He covered himself once more with dirt and dragged himself backward toward his place. Through the voice of Migan, the king ordered him to rise, and pointing him out to the courtiers, he told them: "This man recognizes the small things that are necessary in this life. He will be useful to his master and attend to his slightest needs. I appoint him henceforth to the service of the heir to the throne."

The man joyously prostrated himself and covered himself with dirt. Vidaho offered the same expressions of gratitude to his father for the present that he valued highly. The high dignitaries, the princes, and the people added their thanks to those of their future master with shouts of: "It's true! It's true! He will be useful to his master! May the Father of Wealth be blessed for the valuable present he has given to Vidaho!"

The king gave the man one of the young girls recruited by Paapa and ordered, in addition, that he be presented with four cotton cloths and two packets of cowry strings. The young wife was supposed to increase this sum through commercial transactions so that she would be able to feed her husband.

Before nightfall the heir to the throne had obliged his new servant to drink a half-dozen fetish potions; he then entrusted him with the custody of his snuff box.

The servant kissed the ground and covered his head with his master's feet, saying: "The Master of my spirit does not need to take so many precautions before having confidence in the instrument of his will. Living in misery since my birth, I have acquired today for the first time the assurance of resting, eating, sleeping, and enjoying life with a woman at my side. From now on I have the four things that constitute happiness. I can only hope that this situation will continue until the end of my days, which I will devote faithfully to the service of my lord!"

Ajahi, the principal market at Agbomê, was at its liveliest. Because the sun had still not turned his face toward home on the other side of Coufo, buyers and sellers who had come from distant villages had not yet thought about starting back toward their compounds.

Suddenly a twin bell launched its "Kioun-go! Kioun-go!" to the four winds. Initially drowned out by by the sounds of the market, its ringing finally reached the ears of the people, and everyone quickly fell silent.

The women fell to their knees. The men flattened themselves in the dust and covered their heads with it.

The tall figures of Migan and Panligan dominated the scene. One of their attendants clasped a small raphia basket to his chest; the others surrounded a Mahinou whose arms were tied behind his back.

The group halted in front of Ayizan – the protective fetish of the market. Having remained standing beside the first minister, the public crier recited the epithets of King Guézo at great length, punctuating them with the ringing of his double bell; at the end he added: "The Predestined King has ordered that it be announced to all Danhomê that the traditional celebrations will begin tomorrow evening.

"Starting tomorrow, the Father of Wealth will distribute glass beads, cloths, and silver to his people. At this very place, feasts and libations will follow the forwarding of messages to King Agonglo.

"The King of the Universe invites his people to the feast. The festivities will last for seven days.

"Danhomênous who have heard the good news directly from the mouth of Panligan, go and pass it on to the ears of friends and allies who are not present."

With a forceful rap on the bell, he marked the end of his message and stepped aside. Migan made an offering of water and rum to the fetish. Standing in front of the Mahinou, who was on his knees and facing Ayizan, the sacrificial priest seized the victim by the hair and said: "You, go and carry this news to the land of the dead!" The scimitar swung rapidly to the left. The neatly severed head of the Mahinou spattered blood upon the fetish above which Migan was holding it.

Two servants subdued the body, bundled it up, and carried it toward the Ditch.

The sacrificial priest handed his weapon and the head to his assistants.

The twin bell of Panligan resumed its "Kioun-go! Kioun-go!" as the people in the crowd covered themselves with dirt to express their gratitude for the festivities that had just been promised to them.

The first minister went to inform the king of his people's joy at the announcement of the forthcoming feasts.

Servants returning from the market informed the family of Toffa that the traditional celebrations had officially been set for the day of Adogouin.

"Sadistic king! You organize festivities while our eyes are still wet with tears! You claim that tradition obliges you to hold these celebrations, but in vain; no one fails to recognize that you are holding them to rejoice at the loss of your brothers at Hounjroto.

"Who could possibly believe that you are unaware of the traditional custom that requires us to refrain from all festivities until after the funeral rites for a dead member of the family have been performed! May death spare me until the day of the celebration! I will know how to proclaim your ignominy to your face, even in the presence of an entire people, the unwitting accomplice to your crimes!" exclaimed Doguicimi, who found it scandalous that celebrations should be held during a period of mourning.

The woman was not the only person who was indignant at the announcement of the planned festivities. Although the heads of the families of former kings would receive all sorts of presents from the king on this occasion, they too were scandalized, especially since Guézo was breaking with rigidly prescribed traditions in regard to certain purifying and propitiatory rites that had to be performed in the holy city of Canna before he could proceed to the purification of his oracle and offer sacrifices to the ancestors. There was no good reason to justify the conduct of the king. But if even Guézo's brothers and sisters refrained from recalling him to a respect for tradition, it was hardly up to them, heads of royal families upon which the sun had set long ago, to run the risk of disgracing themselves by offering advice that might be judged offensive. The reigning family would be solely responsible to the ancestors for the breach of an uncompromising tradition.

The white men from Gléhoué and Godomê arrived before sunset; they were being carried in hammocks and followed by a large amount of baggage.

They were set down in front of the Door of the Palace of Agaja. They complained about everything, including the discomfort of the journey, and seemed to be more exhausted than the Danhomênous who had marched, sweated, and toiled for them.

The next day the sun was already rising toward his zenith, progressing at his usual speed, but the Danhomênous suspected that the daystar was slowing its pace with the intention of delaying the celebration that they were awaiting with impatience.

The booming voice of the royal drum echoed across the Courtyard of Singboji, already swarming with courtiers and filled with noise. Princesses selected from all the former royal families emerged from the Palace, singing the praises of King Agonglo. Two of King Guézo's sisters appeared. Following them, a long line of princesses (they were granddaughters of Agonglo, and their innocence had been verified in advance by the older women) passed through the courtyard. Lustrous cloths of velvet and satin descended from their chests to their feet. While still wet, a fragrant compound containing kaolin had been spread with joined fingers across their arms and busts, leaving white stripes against a black or calabash-yellow background once it had dried.

Their fingers, wrists, arms, and necks were laden with gold and silver jewelry.

On their heads they were carrying slender, long-necked vases made of gold, silver, bronze, copper, or baked red clay and adorned with the king's coat-of-arms in bas-relief.

The gold of the sun seemed to have been melted and sprayed in tiny droplets upon the metal vases and the velvet and satin cloths, intensifying their brilliance.

Staring fixedly at the ground, the members of the procession moved silently and solemnly forward, their left hands swinging freely as their right ones steadied the vases that rested upon tiny cushions of white cloth on their heads. Princesses with greying hair scurried back and forth along the line, snapping their index fingers against their thumbs and cautioning: "One should look at the ground and walk calmly!"

The group at the head of the line informed people that the women were going to draw water for an offering to King Agonglo. The praises of the king, "the Pineapple who laughed at the wrath of Lightning. . . ," poured ceaselessly from their lips.

The drums followed, rumbling. The men were singing accompanied by horns, bells, and other musical instruments. From one moment to the next curious onlookers appeared from all directions and swelled the procession.

At the spring of Dido, the young women knelt. The older princesses took the vases, filled them with water, and replaced them on the heads of the water-bearers, who remained as motionless as statues and kept their eyes fixed to the ground. Upon a signal from their elders, they started back toward the Palace as graciously as they had come. A false step that brought about a fall would indicate that the young girl had a guilty conscience. And if the fall resulted in the spilling of water or the breaking of the vessel, death alone could expiate the crime denounced by this accident.

Only the first alcarraza would be used for the offering to King Agonglo.

*   *   *

The people who had followed the procession to the Courtyard of the Palace were still discussing the costumes, the naturalness, and the beauty of the young princesses when an indiscretion on the part of the king's jester Manahin, a dwarf scarcely two cubits tall, informed them that there was another surprise in store for them.

Announced by the firing of a gun, the roll of a drum, and the chirping of the "birds", the king arrived several moments later to preside over the engagement ceremony of his eldest daughter, who resembled him from her hair to her heels.

She was kneeling on a velvet cloth outside the bamboo barrier and facing the people. Older princesses, her aunts, surrounded her.

Manahin approached the throne and, with great earnestness, declared that he would die of chagrin if he were not allowed to marry the princess. He furnished support for his words by turning three sommersaults. Everyone burst into laughter. He boasted to them: "See how hearty I am!"

With a very solemn expression on his face, he proposed, as a condition for being honored with this favor, that the suitor engage himself to perform the functions of twenty dignitaries at the court. He alone, he affirmed, was capable of such a feat, and he would immediately prove it, but he asked if he might first drink the alcohol that the princess was going to give to her fiancé.

Some of the bystanders shouted to him: "You certainly have pretensions, Manahin!"

Others jeered: "If someone doesn't tear the axe out of your hands, you'll surely cut down the 'loco'."[8]

But Mêwou thought to himself: "If that fool finds the foofoo, he will demand some caloulou." Aloud he shouted to the jester: "What madness – the ambition of a net dreaming it can catch a hippopotamus! It is true that the Houégbajas married their daughters to Danhomênous of modest circumstances, but only to those who had distinguished themselves for their skill in the arts, their courage in battle, or some other important service they had rendered for Danhomê. It is unheard of that any of our kings would ennoble someone like you by marrying him to a princess. If the daughter of a king could honorably marry a Manahin, such a favor would have been bestowed upon the first buffoon who made his appearance in this court and who rendered Tégbéssou Ahandé the service of bringing joy back into his heart after the two great catastrophes that

---

[8]   The "loco" (chlorofora excelsa) was the sacred tree of Danhomê. (author's note)

95

struck Danhomê during his reign: the firestorm that consumed Agbomê and the landslide that swallowed more than two hundred Danhomênous at the Dido spring. Because the Father of Light was downcast, one of his subjects undertook to entertain him with his clowning. The Master of the World having regained his cheerfulness, all his courtiers recovered their own. Yet the king rewarded that service more generously than it deserved when he gave the man a young female captive, cloths, and cowries as well as naming him the Manahin of the court at Agbomê. Thus you can forget your hopes, buffoon!

"Whatever you do, the princess will be in the house of Migan Atindébacou this evening. As for you, only a wood fire will help you warm your ribs!"

Guézo's face brightened with joy at these jibes. The Danhomênous were laughing so hard that tears were already running down their cheeks; they were writhing on the ground and holding their sides; they moaned: "I can't take any more. This fool will make me die laughing!"

The courtiers manifested their joy all the more loudly when they realized that their remarks and grimaces were pleasing to the king.

Manahin approached the young girl and, bowing low, addressed her imperturbably: "Adorable princess, you would certainly like to choose your own husband, and you are no doubt searching through your memory or through the prostrate crowd at your feet for the man you consider worthy of sharing your sleeping quarters with you. I am undoubtedly the one whom you would like to designate, and you can't manage to recall my name.

"My name is Mêlo – the right hand of the Father of Life," he exclaimed confidently. "Now that you know the name, don't hesitate to pronounce it aloud in order to strip the Danhomênous of the illusion they no doubt hold about becoming the delighted husband of the Master of the World's eldest daughter."

He moved backward several paces and, mimicking the voice of of a timid young girl pointing to her fiancé, quite artlessly pronounced the name "Mêlo" that he had just given himself.

He immediately replied in a male voice, "here I am!" Turning four sommersaults, he arrived within a stride of the princess, threw himself on his knees, and said in an imitation of Migan's nasal voice: "You have deigned to honor me, Princess Houétonja – The Rising Sun! I am at your feet. I will be an obedient tool in your hands. In my house you will enjoy yourself, princess, for I will let you do whatever you desire. I will be deaf in one ear and see with only one eye, and I'll stutter as well. But that is the way the husband of a princess should be. I will consider myself happy if, after receiving all those upon whom you have set your heart, you deign to accord me a small corner of the place where you sleep. Since even the high dignitaries of this kingdom cannot impose their will upon you, I am not the one who would ever harbor the thought of doing so.

"For women like you in Danhomê, and for them alone, tradition has established the right of free love. Infidelity on your part is excusable, whereas that of women from any other station in life is a crime that can even be punished by death.

"In matters of love, social standing never plays a role in determining the choice of a princess; it is more likely to result from the whims of the little worm in her head. Princess, you are free to grant your favors to your half-brother or to any other prince, to a high dignitary or a simple commoner or even to a lowly slave, who will be ennobled as a consequence.

"Because I am not savage beast, I am not thirsting for blood. Therefore, I will not be overly scrupulous; I will not demand the scarlet proof of your innocence on a white sheet, as prescribed by tradition. If even ugly girls find men to love them and to solicit their favors before marriage, what must it be like for a princess as brilliant as the rising sun! But rest assured that I will proclaim all over Danhomê that I am the first man at whom you ever smiled in your life.

"And when you have indicated your desires to me, I promise to go and find those with whom it would please you to have at your side for few moments. I know that I don't even have the right to begrudge you anything, whatever it might be. I beg you to grant me the singular honor that every Danhomênou is night and day imploring his head, his ancestors, his family fetishes, and his Destiny to bestow upon him.

"When you will have left me or when I will have died, people will always say of me: 'Manahin Mêlo had the honor of drinking Princess Houétonja's betrothal libation on the eve of the great traditional celebration that was held upon the return from Hounjroto!' That will be enough for me. I kiss the ground at your feet!" He prostrated himself and bit into the dirt, which he impetuously spewed out as fast as he took it in.

Some people were scandalized by the fool's remarks. Weaker souls feared that the babblings of Manahin might provoke a storm. . . . Neighbors who frequented the court reassured them, however, by intimating in whispers that all the remarks of a jester are pardonable.

The court could no longer contain itself; the princess herself was smiling; she finally raised her innocent gaze toward the fool and mumbled a name. Her escort leaned over her and entreated her to raise her voice. She repeated the name as softly as before. Renewed pleas from her entourage to speak more loudly. "Migan!" she exclaimed more distinctly the third time.

Far from growing angry, the king's jester, the rejected suitor, raised himself on the tips of his toes, and in a solemn, droning, comically nasal tone of voice, he echoed: "Migan! Migan!"

The people shouted the name of their immediate superior: "Migan! Migan!"

"Here I am!" replied the fiancé when his name was pronouced clearly by the king's eldest daughter; until now he had been hidden amongst his friends and relatives about five bamboos from the throne.

Through the voice of a canon that roared at the same moment, the Houégbajas in the other world took cognizance of the princess' choice and the acquiescence of the happy and fortunate suitor, who was covering himself with dirt as an expression of gratitude.

Bowing low, he made several steps toward the princess, once again flattened himself in the dust, covered himself with it, and then, still bowing, advanced toward his fiancée. There were only two strides separating them. He kneeled, resting his thighs on his calfs and heels, picked up several handfuls of dirt, and smeared them across his face and chest. Now he was crawling as he said: "Adorable princess, you deign to honor me among the people of Danhomê gathered at your feet. Today I have found the inexhaustible treasure that was predicted for me by the ancestors through the voice of the diviner when I first undertook my duties at the court. From this moment forward my life shall be beautiful. It will also be long now that it is linked with yours, and my name will be transmitted to posterity. My house has been sad, gloomy, and cold ever since it was built, but it will become gay and joyful because the light has deigned to enter it."

Turning toward the people, he shouted to them: "Before dying of chagrin, join me in thanking the Father of Wealth for his invaluable present!" He lay down again on the ground and rolled to the right and left three times across an area about one bamboo in width.

His chest erect and horribly besmirched with dirt, the kneeling fiancé happily approached his betrothed, who kept her eyes on the ground as she extended her left hand, holding a small flask of the Agoudas' rum and covered with a white handkerchief, in his direction; another white handkerchief covered the flask she was holding in her right hand.

Migan took the flask in both hands, swallowed the contents in a single draught, licked his lips, clacked his tongue, and said: "What a delightful drink! Only Princess Gandépé[9] could intoxicate one with such a nectar! Nowhere have I ever tasted its equal!"

Facing the Danhomênous, he shouted to them: "Thank for me the Father of Wealth, the Powerful Hammer that scorns no metal!"

The courtiers had not waited for the first minister's invitation to cover themselves with dirt as a sign of their gratefulness. In a forced and artificial tone, they said: "The honor accorded to Migan is reflected back on all Danhomênous!" Continuing to cover himself with dirt, the minister himself lent his support: "I am a common creature and merely deserve to be trampled underfoot like this dirt. But the Master of the World has deigned to honor me and to raise me from my lowly station. I am infinitely grateful to him for it!"

Among the people, praises were shouted and repeated at every moment for Gandépé, the name that would henceforth designate the princess who was destined to become the first minister's wife as soon as night had fallen.

The princess withdrew with her escort; she would be taken to her husband's house with about twenty servants and many other presents from her august Father.

*   *   *

The king returned to the Palace; the first minister regained his residence, quickly washed himself, changed clothes, and rejoined his peers.

---

9   "Gandépé" is the last part of the maxim, "the hammer holds no iron in contempt," and the first minister is announcing his adoption of it as the name of his fiancée. It was customary in Danhomê to give a new name to one's young wife. (author's note)

Guézo reappeared before his people. Ten pubescent girls emerged from the Palace, carrying a variety of objects in their arms as well as on their heads and shoulders; they kneeled along the bamboo barrier facing the people.

Daclo approached the two prime ministers and spoke softly to them, pointing toward the kneeling girls and a group of men who had prostrated themselves in the dust at a distance of three bamboos from the throne.

Migan and Mêwou rose and faced the people; in his nasal voice, the first minister called out, "Bognon!" There was no reply.

"Bognon!" he repeated with an even more pronounced nasal drone.

This second summons was also greeted with silence.

"Bognon!" called the minister, this time in a clipped tone that betrayed his impatience.

"An explosion can not take place without being heard!" replied a man who was hidden in the crowd about ten bamboos from the throne. Bent double, he ran forward, prostrated himself about one bamboo from the minister, and crawled up to him. Migan ordered him to rise and to let the cloth he was wearing over his breeches fall to the ground.

All eyes were focused on the three men. In the back rows of the crowd among the "lizards" who always kept their stomachs to the ground in the presence of the throne, a few audacious creatures had planted their elbows in the dirt and raised their torsos slightly in order to see better.

From the arms of one young girl, Mêwou took a cloth that had been woven in Agbomê and handed it to Migan, who covered Bognon's belt and breeches with it; over the man's upper body, he draped a sleeveless tunic that the second minister had been holding out to him, and at the man's left side he suspended a sabre attached to a sash resting upon his right shoulder; he placed a belt with a cartridge pouch around the man's waist and gave him a leather bag and a gun; he then passed a stiff metal collar with dangling glass beads around the man's neck, placed silver cuffs on his wrists, and attached silver bands to his ankles, deforming them slightly to prevent them from falling off. After having equipped him for war and dressed him in the emblems that would henceforth identify him in court ceremonies, Migan addressed him in a sententious tone of voice: "Until now you have borne the name Bognon! Under that name you have fought for Danhomê since the reign of Agonglo. You have distinguished youself by your heroism in the wars of past and present reigns. You were always at the head of the soldiers who broke through the enemy lines and entered first into the cities under siege. You have brought back to Danhomê the heads of many enemies, and you have taken many captives. Your courage has always laughed at enemy sabre thrusts and gunshots.

"The scars on your arms indicate that you have raised them frequently against the enemies of Danhomê.

"The gashes that run across your face, your chest and your stomach prove that you have never shown your heels to the enemy.

"In consideration for all your previous acts of valor, the Master of the World names you his first minister of war. From this moment forward you will be known by the name Gounada. Indeed! The god of war will one day decide which of us – we or our enemies – are in the right!"

Pointing to the stiff collar and glass beads lying on the new minister's chest and shoulders, Migan continued: "Danhomê is around your neck, and it rests in part on your shoulders as well. Be careful that it does not fall! King Houégbaja has fastened bands to your legs; chained in this way, you can no longer distance yourself from Danhomê!"

Meanwhile the men whom Daclo had pointed out earlier to the prime ministers were approaching upon a sign from Mêwou; they were carrying the musical instruments necessary for organizing a dance – drums, horns made from elephant tusks, simple bells, double bells, long-necked gourds with strings of tiny cowries or snake vertebra attached to them. A man had just brought a richly caparisoned horse. Pointing out the charger to the new minister of war, Migan resumed: "You will ride on horseback in racing to the conquest of countries that the king will designate for you. You will have no concern for wealth or provisions. You will burden yourself with nothing. You will carry no more than this leather bag, which at the most will contain three pieces of clothing – a cloth, a pair of breeches, and a tunic. At the court, you must constantly be dressed in breeches and a tunic to show that you are always ready to race to whatever place your duty may call you. You are also authorized to carry several gris-gris in this bag to protect you against enemy weapons and sudden illnesses.

"King Houégbaja is arming you with this sabre and this gun (he pointed to the weapons with which he had equipped the new minister) so that you can use them to help enlarge his Danhomê. In this cartridge pouch you will find the necessary powder and shot.

"In camp, this large parasol will shelter you while you are resting from your exertions on this chair, the height of which symbolizes that of your exalted position in Danhomê.

"These young girls will serve you to populate Danhomê with a strain of brave men. These slaves will cultivate your farms, hunt, weave, build, and conduct trade for your family. Whenever you please you will have at your disposal the cloths, cowries, jewels, and alcoholic drinks contained in these baskets.

"During the ceremonies that will be celebrated in this court, your suite of drummers and singers will be added to the numerous emblems assigned to your station in order to distinguish you from the commoners of Danhomê.

"Gaou Gounada, every time you lift your weapons to fight for the agrandizement of Danhomê of Houégbaja, Gou, the god of weapons and war, will be favorably inclined toward you. But if you betray Danhomê, he will drink your blood and eat your flesh!"

The two prime ministers and the new minister of war prostrated themselves and covered themselves with dust; all the courtiers followed their example as an expression of their gratitude for the goodness of the king who had given his armies a commander to assure them of victory.

After a short pause, the investiture ceremony for the second minister of war – Poussou Hagla (the firm quill that protects the porcupine) – took place with the same solemnity. Gaou then mounted the horse. Shouts of joy arose, drums rumbled, bells and gourds reverberated; the members of the new minister's suite began singing a song in praise of the king's munificence, and, joined by a group of warriors, they started marching around the Palace.

Poussou allowed them to cover approximately twenty bamboos and then he too jumped on his horse. Renewed applause broke out, the drums thundered, the bells clanged, and the gourds rattled in cadence. The suite of the second minister of war was swelled by the battle captains and expressed Danhomê's joy at having a new Poussou by singing a song that was full of enthusiasm.

These two ministers had been chosen from among those who comprised the court council for matters of minor importance. Unknown to them, their formal investiture had been preceded by extensive deliberations about their origins and their conduct in the face of the enemy. When the ancestors had been requested, through the voice of the oracle, to express their opinion about the choice of the court, they announced that it was acceptable to them for these warriors to command the army of Danhomê. Brought to the Palace, the two future ministers had been informed about the choice that had fallen on them and about the duties of their new positions; the king had then obliged them to drink the most formidable fetish-potions in the kingdom before taking them to his ancestors' tombs, where they swore to consecrate themselves to the glory of the Danhomê they loved.

When Guézo returned to the Palace with the princes, the high dignitaries, and the heads of the families of former kings, he presented each of them with one or two of the young girls who had been recruited by Paapa.

The soldiers who had been pointed out to the king for their brave conduct at Hounjroto were brought into the outer court, where they each received a wife, cowries, cloths, and a shoulder sash. Among the people who greeted them at the Door of the Universe, a few admired the honors bestowed upon such warriors as indicated by the green or red borders on their velvet sashes; other courtiers envied the happy fate of the soldier who would be able to start a family.

Avoutou exploded; Dogba responded to him in a solemn voice; the "birds" of the king chirped their annunciatory chorus. The people had already flattened themselves in the dust. The high dignitaries emerged from the Palace, followed by Daclo, the queens, and the king.

Announced from a distance by drums and bells, the fetishists arrived at Singboji by the road that bordered upon Agaja's second story. They had young shoots of oil-palm leaves around their waists. White and red marks made with kaolin and laterite solutions circled their eyes, ran across their cheeks and temples, and lent a terrifying aspect to their faces. Mivêdê, the chief fetishist of Zomadonou, was at the head of the procession; the venerated initiates followed him, and the common run of male and female fetishists brought up the rear; their hair had been shaved, and their torsos were bare; around their wrists and ankles they were wearing strands of delicate cowries or black grains, according to the order of the fetish to which they belonged. The chief fetishists rang their large bells in the direction of the king as a sign of respect. They paraded in front of

101

the throne several times and then gathered at the feet of Ayizan and Ajahimê; they visited the shrines of the Zomadonou, Pélou, and Ahangbé fetishes one after the other before disbanding to rejoin their respective shrines.

*   *   *

In vain, the sun clung to the mountains that were suspended above our heads – the mountains he had been scaling since early morning; he was finally precipitated into the Coufo.

"Here at last is the final night before the celebrations! But you shall see that the night, whose victory over the brightness of the day has now given her sovereignty over the earth, will also want to reign forever! When the drought persisted, the distressed Danhomênous asked their superior Migan for an explanation, and he reassured them: 'The rains may be slow in coming, but they will fall in the end!' Night, you are jealous that we are going to enjoy ourselves tomorrow, filling our stomachs and drinking our fill, but whatever you do, you will be vanquished and put to flight by the day. We will jeer at you when you leave; you can be sure of that!"

. . . .

"What! Our threats have frightened away the night? And she was getting ready to withdraw? Isn't that the second crowing of the cocks who are already wishing her a pleasant journey?"

This morning concert that gladdened the hearts of the Danhomênous was answered by a cannon shot that thundered at regular intervals throughout the day.

The drums of Ajahimê began to mutter: "We're awake! We're awake!"

No longer any doubt about it, the festivities were about to begin.

The rising sun soon succeeded in completely devouring the veil of darkness. The frenzied beating of the drums in a dozen groups at the Courtyard of Ajahimê quickly attracted the Danhomênous.

Meanwhile the king, his wives, his sisters and brothers, the high palace dignitaries, Yaya-Daho (the daughter of the king's sworn friend Chacha Ajinacou), and the royal guard had gathered before the mausoleum of Agonglo.

Guézo's sister and Chacha Ajinacou's daughter, consecrated sacrificial priestesses, were draped entirely in white. The princess presented offerings of water, kola nuts, melegueta pepper, and brandy to King Agonglo, entreating him at great length to protect Danhomê, make it powerful, ward off calamities and epidemics, favor the birth of children, maintain his worthy son on the throne of Houégbaja for a long time, bless his reign, and hasten the arrival of many white men, whose trade would enrich Danhomê.

The kola nuts, separated into lobes and cast on the ground, indicated by their configuration that the offering had been accepted by the former king. Agonglo then drank from the hands of Yaya-Daho, the daughter of a white man; she requested his protection for her fathers, who were friends of this kingdom, and implored him to grant the army of Danhomê victory over its enemies so that

102

the slave-trade, which had declined during the previous reign, might once again prosper.

Multitudes of tiny bells, which were sewn to the embroidered cloths covering a monumental altar that had surged from the ground during the night in the Courtyard of Ajahimê, invited the crowd to admire it.

There was an inextricable mass of jostling people at the base of the altar, which was, moreover, adorned with many mirrors of all sizes and shapes.

The onlookers were full of endless praise for the dimensions and the embellishment of the altar: "Under what sun could one ever find a king who performs miracles like those accomplished by the Master of the World! Yesterday evening when the day star was retiring to his sleeping quarters, there was still nothing at the place where this magnificent altar now offers itself to our admiration!"

People shoved and elbowed their way forward to obtain a closer look. Some wanted to hear the translations that a man versed in heraldric knowledge was giving of the symbolic language on the embroidered tapestries. "Do you see that enormous serpent stretched out on its back and with a house standing in the middle of it? That means: 'Dan ho meê' (in the stomach of Dan). It is the name of our country. By means of this allegory, the Master of the World recalls the founding of the kingdom of his fathers: having been obliged to punish the insolence of Dan (the Guédévi chief whose name means serpent), our second king, Houégbaja, threw his body into the foundation of a house he built and called Danhomê. The name of that house later became the name of the city that grew up around it as well as the kingdom that traces its origins to it. The sea prevents it from expanding to the South. We can only enlarge its boundaries to the East, to the West, and in the direction of 'mahi' country.

"Do you want to know the meaning of that fish which is turning away from the net? (He was pointing to the tapestry segments about which he was speaking.) That's the name of the founder of Danhomê: King Houégbaja – the fish which refuses to enter into the net. The name of the kingdom is always coupled with his.

"Look to the right," said the translator. "The ash-colored ball depicted on this section of the tapestry represents a rock. Look how the foot that knocked against it is bleeding! Danhomê is a rock. All its enemies will bruise themselves on it.

"This large crescent, with its horns pointing downward and set against a blue background, represents the sky. The hand with the fingers extended skyward has been placed beneath it to indicate that, like the sky that no hand can ever touch, the Danhomê of Houégbaja lies beyond the reach of its enemies.

"On the last side of the altar, at the very top, as you can see, there is an enormous sun, whose glory is not dimmed by a single cloud; at the bottom, here is a half-closed eye. The Master of the World is saying that the Danhomê of Houégbaja is the sun at its zenith – no eye can look directly at it!"

"Ah! That's true! That's true!" cried the amazed onlookers, who clasped their hands together and kept their eyes riveted to the altar for a long time.

After having used their heads, shoulders, elbows, and knees in a vain attempt to fight their way forward, other Danhomênous begged that a bit of room be made for them: "Until now I have only seen my face in the water where I washed it this morning and in the drink I had before coming here. Brother, let me get a little closer to the altar for a moment so that I can see my face in the mirrors that are adorning it."

The whips of the guards kept the wave of onlookers at a respectful distance from the altar.

Turned aside, their mass flowed toward the metalsmiths' neighborhood that bordered the courtyard to the West.

To the left and facing the altar in front of the shrine to the Agalé-Hounsou fetish, there was a long, open apatam that was divided into three compartments. The spectacle of the "sacrificial dogs" was edifying: ten Mahinous who had been decapitated at dawn were hanging upside down with their feet spread apart and firmly attached to a long pole suspended between two posts!

Solemnly perched upon the pole, the vultures seemed to be deliberating over problems posed by the quarry. As they awaited a solution, some of them sharpened their beaks alternatively on the feathers of their wings and the wood of the pole; others tilted their bald heads sideways and stole covetous glances toward the corpses that were already being invaded by an army of flies. The approach of men dissipated the hope, entertained by the vultures, of enjoying a fine meal. They flew off slowly, burdened with disappointment.

Flies of all colors and sizes were playing a sonorous melody around the "sacrificial dogs" who were not even wearing a simple belt. Darting from body to body, they formed circles around the blood-drenched necks or landed on the ground to drink the blood that was dripping onto it.

Others blanketed the arms, legs, and torsos of the dead bodies, watching impatiently for the moment when their satiated companions would leave. Tired of waiting, those who had not yet tasted the various dishes swooped down upon the gluttons and began to harass them. Nearly always a third pillager installed himself at the place over which the others were fighting.

"If the Father of Wealth offers ten cadavres to the flies, what lavish feasts and libations he must be reserving for his subjects during the seven days of uninterrupted celebration!" That thought filled the Danhomênous with joy.

One man proposed to a group of his friends: "Let's work up a sweat to sharpen our appetites." They followed him. At the price of a thousand jabs with their heads, shoulders, elbows, and knees, they succeeded in making their way to the enclosure that was next to the drummers and reserved for dancers; the man first walked around the enclosure, then planted himself in the center of the circle and pivoted to the left on one foot and to the right; remaining on the same spot and holding his bent arms at the height of his shoulders, he vigorously shot them forward, drew them back, and pushed his elbows behind him. These movements were frenziedly executed to the rhythm of the large drum. The muscles on his

arms and torso stood out. With a sharp rap on his instrument, the drummer sig-
nalled a pause. It was time for it. The dancer stopped, completely out of breath,
his grinning face inviting the applause of the spectators, but only his compan-
ions accorded him the charity of a few compliments. Satisfied, he stepped out
of the enclosure. A friend replaced him, but when he was finished, he found
himself alone in front of the drummers. All the spectators had run to meet the
fetishists, who were entering the courtyard en masse. Preceded by their master
Miwêdê, the male fetishists of Zomadonou[10] were in the first row; the female
fetishists followed behind their leader, who was known as the "Zomadonouci";
in the order of their importance, the Nêssouhouéhonons[11] came next and then
the fetishists of Sapata,[12] who were clucking around their leader, Michayi. The
Hêviossocis (votaries of Lightning), the Pohouncis (fetishists of Panther), and
the Mawoucis (worshippers of Mawou, the Supreme Being) brought up the rear
of the procession. The fetishists of the same order, distinguishable by their
dress and their insignia, installed themselves in the places that had been as-
signed to them and began to dance, individually at first and then in groups. The
chief fetishists remained seated beneath large parasols, the edges of which were
adorned with pieces of cloth that bore their emblems.

With expansive gestures and flattering words, a public crier announced the
arrival of the white men, the good friends of the Master of the World. They
were dressed in velvet-sleeved tunics that reached to their knees; their legs
were covered; large hats cast shadows over the hair that was falling over their
shoulders.

The celebration offered a number of Danhomênous their first opportunity to
observe white men, and they were scandalized to see that, following the Master
of the World's example, these foul beasts from the sea were wearing something
on their feet.

Among those entering the courtyard, some were phlegmatic and haughty.
One would almost have said they were trying to place a certain distance between
the ground and the solemn faces they had put on. "They are Glincis; all they
care about is money!" explained a Danhomênou from Gléhoué to a neighbor
from the banks of the Zou.

"See how active those others are!" the informant confided in a still lower
tone of voice as he pointed to a joyful group. "They're honest and energetic;
they have no qualms about approaching the Danhomênous. They would mingle
with us, shake our hands, chat familiarly with us, and even share our meals with
us, if they weren't afraid of being rebuked by the king; they are Zojagués. The
princes despise the white men on the pretext that they lack dignity. As for me,
a man of the people, I find them attractive.

---

[10]   The deified form of King Acaba and therefore a fetish of the royal family, "Zomadonou" is
the principal god of the pantheon at Agbomê. (author's note)
[11]   "Nêssouhoué" is a deified prince; "Nêssouhouéhonon" is a prince who has been deified and
is worshipped in a temple. (author's note)
[12]   "Sapata" is smallpox, which was deified because the spirits are terrified by its ravages.
(author's note)

"There's the group of Agoudas, who are called that because of their vanity and indolence. They promote the slave trade and treat their own slaves worse than domestic animals. The princes like them a good deal. People tell about one of them who was hunting with his dog and his slave when they came to the arm of a pond; the Agouda ordered the slave to lie down and make his body into a bridge. The slave got up after the master had crossed this living bridge. The dog was obliged to walk through the water and the mud. The hunter flew into a rage upon seeing that the beast had gotten its paws wet. 'Miserable slave, this will teach you to refuse to let my dog cross the arm of the pond on your back!' And bam! He shot the man. It was that evening, they tell me, as he was sipping his glass of rum that he told his fellow countrymen about his crime!"

Cries of joy greeted the arrival of jugs filled with brandy, baskets of cowries, hampers of cloths, and all sorts of food: balls of acassa; yams cooked under coals; large kettles of meat, fish, and vegetable caloulou; fried bean cakes. Legs of beef, antelope, and mutton, turkeys, ducks, guinea hens, chickens, roast or baked pigeons, large round loaves of bread, beautiful fish that had been caught in the backwaters of the Wo or brought from the coast and boiled whole, and piles of boiled shrimp excited the envy of the Danhomênous. They knew that these fine things arrayed on big platters or in copper bowls were only displayed for their admiration. The Father of Wealth was reserving them for the high dignitaries, for the white men, and for the black men who were living like them in Gléhoué and Godomê.

The principal drum at the Courtyard of Singboji boomed; the smaller drums accompanied it, bells rang, and horns intermittently injected their "van cou van" into the concert.

Attired for the festivities and surrounded by the court, the king was waiting in the "Topon" – an apatam covered with embroidered tapestries and erected in the Palace of Agrigomê upon the occasion of the traditional celebrations – for the passage of the Representative of the Queen Mother Agontimê. She soon appeared in the midst of an imposing train of pubescent girls and older women. To her right and to her left Migannon and Mêwounon were walking.

Tall, her head held high, the Queen Mother was truly distinguished. The princes and palace dignitaries affirmed that she resembled the Mother of Panther, whom she represented at the court, like a twin sister.

She was dressed in beautiful velvet and satin cloths tied above her chest and held in place by a long silk belt. Her head was covered with a white satin scarf. On her neck she wore a bundle of fine corals enwreathed by a necklace of gold. The wrinkles on her face and the muscles on her arms, which were already detaching themselves from her bones despite the long strings of glass beads wound tightly around her biceps many times, indicated that she had lived a goodly number of years. Her two emaciated hands rested on the top of a long white cane that came up to her chest; the skin on the backs of them was so thin one could almost trace the shape of the bones in her wrists and fingers.

Her entourage was full of veneration for her; some scrutinized the ground in front of her, drawing her attention to the least unevenness by snapping their index fingers against their thumbs and repeatedly saying: "May one deign to look at the ground and walk steadily!" By shouting epithets punctuated with ululations of praise made by tapping the joined fingers of one hand against their lips, others announced that the Representative of the Queen Mother Agontimê was coming.

As she passed the court to go out into the Courtyard of the Palace by the Hongbonji Door, the Mother of Panther received both the hommages of the courtiers, who kissed the ground at her feet, and the gifts of her son, who had his wife Yêpommê Avognondé present her with a thousand cowries on strings.

In the group of young girls who preceded her, some were carrying rolled mats, a seat with four human skulls decorating its four legs, a spitoon, a long silver pipe, and a variety offerings for the chief fetishists, the singers, the dancers, and the men of the people – cloths of damask, velvet, satin, and silk, bottles of alcohol, pipes, tobacco, mirrors, and strings of glass beads, all of which was openly displayed in baskets and large calabashes, heightening the admiration of the Danhomênous.

The procession advanced along the side of the Palace until it reached Ajahimê. The Queen Mother and her suite installed themselves in the first compartment of the apatam, to which they had been escorted by a servant of Mêwou.

Avoutou roared; the responding roll of Dogba and the chirping of the "birds" were drowned among the booming voices of the drums, the clanging and ringing of bells, and the songs.

The sacrificial priest's assistants left the Palace through the Door of Happiness, each of them carrying a Mahinou who was securely lashed to a porter's rack. The high dignitaries followed them; they were dressed in magnificent sleeveless velvet tunics that only they were authorized to wear in the presence of the king. A large satin cloth knotted at the waist covered the lower part of the tunic and all of their breeches; their biceps were encircled with silver bracelets, and there were silver cuffs on their wrists. The stiff metal collar with glass beads reminded them that Danhomé rested in part on their shoulders.

On their ankles they were wearing fine silver rings, symbolizing that they were also slaves of the throne of Houégbaja.

The young Amazons who comprised the royal guard were dressed in breeches; sleeveless tunics fitted closely at their waists without restricting their movements; on their heads were caps that covered their ears. A heavy velvet belt held a dagger against their left hip; they also carried a cartridge pouch and were armed with a gun.

The Royal Wives appeared in lavish dress: satin, velvet, damask, and silk cloths knotted above their breasts and falling to their heels; plugs covered with silver or gold leaf in the lobes of their ears. Their hair had been shaved, their bodies rubbed with ointments, their necks laden with gold necklaces, their wrists with bracelets, and their fingers with gold or silver rings.

The procession got underway. The sacrificial priest's assistants with their burdens moved off at the head of a long column.

Mêwou ordered the white men to advance. The Zojagués maintained the priority they had enjoyed since the beginning of their presence in the land of the Houédanous, and they went first. The high palace dignitaries and the heads of the families of former ministers walked solemnly behind the white men.

In the midst of the crowd's exuberant gaiety, the high dignitaries carried with them, like the weight of Danhomê on their neck and ankles, a constant concern for the important but peril-filled task of governance; they proceeded in the following order: Ajaho, Migan, Mêwou, Yévogan, Sogan, Topo, Paapa, Matonso, Cangbodé, Aplogan, Vidaho, and the others.

The sons, daughters, brothers, and sisters of Guézo came after the dignitaries; they were draped in brilliant satin, silk, and velvet cloths. A majestic bearing, an imperious tone of voice, heads held high – everything about them proclaims a distinction of which they are extremely jealous. The members of the families of former kings walked humbly, according to the hierarchy of their dynasty, in the shadow of the reigning branch, upon whom alone the sun was supposed to shine.

They were less sumptuously dressed, but they were resigned to their fate, even quite happy that they were not entirely prevented from enjoying life in this Danhomê that was also the work of their ancestors. The drummers followed; some of the drums were carried on the head, others were hanging over the left thigh, and still others rested on the stomach. A troop of young warriors backed up the drummers and separated them from the eunuchs with their pudgy faces and shining stomachs. Living in the Palace, they got little exercise, which was the main reason for their ample figures. They were in no particular hurry.

Composed of young Amazons whose masculine faces and determined expressions suggested that their only pleasure was to be found in powder and smoke, the royal guard was brandishing its guns and singing.

The king had left the Palace; the crown of parasols indicated his presence in the midst of his wives. He was lying in his hammock, which was being carried by Adanhouindé, Ojo, and two other hammock-bearers, their assistants. All four of them were undoubtedly eunuchs, and for this reason their presence among the Royal Wives would be tolerated.

Following the royal procession, a human wave rolled between the Door of Awonnoumi and the monument of Cloubousso, passed in front of the Door of Agoua, the Door of Agrigomê, and the Door of Patinsa; it skirted Lêto and arrived before the shrines of Zomadonou and Pélou. The king offered strings of cowries, various alcohols, pieces of fine material, pipes, and hats to the two fetishes and asked them to bless this day and to ward off any accidents that might occur during it.

The sacrificial priest's assistants crossed the Courtyard of Ajowihounsa.

A "horse" said to the man who was carrying him: "Man of Zado,[13] take me

---

[13] "Zado" was the name given to the kingdom of Danhomê by the Mahis. Zadonou (man of Zado) therefore means the same as Danhomênou. (author's note)

to your king; I would like to. . . ."

"Shut your mouth, stinking beast of the mountain," the Danhomênou interrupted.

"Your king attacked my country; he broke my calabashes and my gourds; then he sends me to my death; and you dare refuse me the right to tell him what is on my mind before I enter the realm of silence forever? Well then, I'll break you neck before your countrymen can sacrifice me!" And the Mahinou immediately began to struggle in the porter's rack.

The porter was obliged to stop. When the king was informed, he rose up in his hammock; the queens moved away. Upon a signal from the first minister, whose sturdy arm remained straight as it descended from its raised, open-palm position to a horizontal one at the level of his shoulder, his servants imposed silence on everyone; the drums and the songs suddenly stopped.

Brought before Guézo, the Mahinou gathered all that remained of his strength, and in a voice that he wanted to sound irascible but only succeeded in making pathetic, he sang:

> To the altar of sacrifice,
> A Mahinou, I am going to the altar of sacrifice!
> But am I a ram
> To be sacrificed?
> For one who does not die in childhood,
> Life reserves many misfortunes!

Migan objected: "You should be taxing your own Destiny with your laments, not the King of Jewels!"

The leader of the royal orchestra Madéou, who was unequalled in all Danhomê for his ability to improvise songs, immediately intoned a parody of the Mahinou's lament:

> To your death,
> Yes, stinking beast of the mountain, you're going to your death!
> The Master of the World will sacrifice you to his ancestors
> Like a friend sacrifices a ram
> At the burial rites of his friend.
> And if you had died in childhood,
> One of your countrymen would have replaced you!

The king's attendants were already beginning to sing this refrain. At Guézo's request, silence was imposed; he then ordered that the Mahinou should be freed and that the royal drum and all the others in his retinue should immediately pick up the rhythm of this lament, which the entire procession then sang all the way to Ayizan.

The king also offered gifts to the protective fetish of the market at Ajahi, that is to say of large gatherings, in order to obtain its favor for the court and for all Danhomênous during the celebrations that would bring them together on that spot.

All the drums paid hommage to the king in a language of long rolls, in which initiates recognized the epithets of the Master of the World.

The king installed himself in the second compartment of the apatam; it was completely hung with large velvet cloths.

The white men were in the third compartment.

They came to pay their respects at the foot of the throne.

The king uttered a few friendly words to those who were introduced to him by Yévogan as managers of trading companies.

Chacha Ajinacou had fallen ill the day before he was to have left Gléhoué and, to his great regret, was unable to come to Agbomê. His representative would convey to him the best wishes of the king and the hopes that all Danhomê cherished for the quick recovery of the greatest white man it had ever known.

The sun was at the level of the ear. "Make haste so the program for today can be completed!" ordered the king.

Daclo took the parasols, the pipes, the spitoon, the fans, and the scarf from the women and gave them to the eunuchs who would be accompanying the king to the butchery that was four bamboos from Ayizan.

The Danhomênous bought only pork that had been boiled or roasted. To the Master of the World, a special butcher would sell a sort of meat that could not be found at any market in the kingdom. The butcher who was supposed to serve the king was actually an impaled Mahinou, whose raised arm had a knife attached to the hand, as if the man were preparing to cut up his pig – another Mahinou who had been boiled and laid out on the counter in front of him.

Setting down a string of cowries on the counter, the king said: "I would like to buy some meat!"

A real butcher, who was lying prostrate behind the butcher and would replace him on this occasion, replied to the monarch by covering himself with dust: "The order will be filled! The order will be filled without delay!"

Having returned to the apatam, Guézo ordered that the "horses," which were drawn up in a line two bamboos from the throne, should be served. The sacrificial priest's assistants went through the groups of drums and imposed silence on them.

Migan was standing in front of the "horse" at the head of the line. His scimitar in one hand, he was holding two strings of cowries in the other – a viaticum for the messengers on their way to the realm of the dead.

His aides freed the right hands of the victims and served them yams that had been cooked under coals.

One Mahinou refused his portion, explaining: "My parents told me that Destiny, consulted on the third day after my birth, forbid me to eat yams. When I reached the age of reason, I received a message from the oracle, who repeated the same prohibition. When I grew older, diviners took me into the forest and initiated me to the consultation of Destiny; once again I heard repeated the injunction against eating yams. Destiny assured me of a long life as a reward for scrupulously abiding by his will.

"My ancestors, my family fetishes, and Destiny himself will testify that I have never touched a yam since I reached the age of reason.

"Destiny has broken his promise, for despite my obedience I find myself being led today toward a premature and violent death. But that does not justify me in disregarding his prohibition. If I encounter him after my death, he is more likely to be ashamed, whereas I can speak with my head held high!"

The king remained thoughtful for a moment and then said to his entourage: "Among mortals such as you are, one rarely finds such a fine example of obedience." Turning toward his queens, he asked: "Isn't it true that my people would have a great deal to gain from having this Mahinou in their midst? Let him be freed then!"

"We have much to learn from him, Predestined King!" exclaimed even the high dignitaries, feigning sincerety.

Facing the Mahinou who was now first in line, Migan, who was about to charge him with a message for the ancestors of the king, asked him in his terrifying voice: "What is your name?"

The man knew his death was irrevocable, and before the executioner's scimitar imposed an everlasting silence upon him, he wanted to show the Zadonous that he indeed belonged to the "mahi" race whose disdain for death inspired admiration even among its enemies. Overcoming his anguish and gathering all that remained of his strength, he turned toward Guézo, his eyes blazing with anger, and shouted at him: "My name is 'Quench-Your-Thirst-With-Blood'!"

The king seemed not to have heard this insolent remark. He maintained a joyful expression because he was supposed to appear serene and calm at the moment of the sacrifices to his ancestors and because he was full of confidence in Destiny, who had affirmed that no mishap would occur to disturb the celebrations. Hadn't he made all the required sacrifices? He regarded the Mahinou's quip as unimportant and convinced himself that it would not happen again. He therefore ordered that the Mahinou, to whom Migan was extending the customary viaticum, be told: "Go find my illustrious ancestors – Daco-Donou, who led the Aladahonous to this place; Acaba Yêoumê the Skillful; Agaja the Conqueror; his worthy successor Tégbéssou, who opened the eyes of the Danhomênous; Pingla the Burning Iron who could not be manipulated; my august Father, Pineapple who laughed at the wrath of Lightning; the venerable Mothers of Panther – and tell them that I will devote my reign to the aggrandizement of Danhomê. . . ."

"If those whom you have just cited are truly your ancestors," interrupted the Mahinou, "you yourself are in a better position than anyone else to find them in the realm of the dead and to render them a faithful account of your reign. As an enemy of Danhomê, I am more likely to make a false report about your reign in order to draw the ire of your ancestors down on your head. If you have me killed, it is not at all because I will carry your messages to the realm of the spirits, but because you want to comply with the barbarous customs of your country. In any case, is it possible to enter the other world and recognize individuals one has never seen in this one? Didn't your predecessor Adanzan affirm that, when the oracle transmitted the first communication on this subject and it was ignored, his own dead appeared to him many times in a dream, which he had several days before one of your criminal commemorative ceremonies, and repeated their express desire that princes be sacrificed from then on, because the messages you entrusted to strangers were never received in the land of the spirits for the simple reason that your victims did not know the former kings of Danhomê?

"I call upon the previous king to be my witness. People say that, after having usurped his throne, you exiled him somewhere in this kingdom.

"Because you want to shed innocent blood in total disregard for the wishes of your ancestors, perform your crime without trying to justify it. But I will be ashamed for you, you who consider yourself above the human race, if I ever meet you in the realm of the spirits, because, unfortunately for you, I will not close the Door to the country of the dead!"

"What you're saying is true! What you're saying is true, Mahinou! All the crimes perpetrated against innocent people in this kingdom will not remain unpunished!" applauded Doguicimi, who rose above the prostrate crowd at the foot of the throne. She continued, addressing the king: "You did not go to Togoudo to purify yourself, as the custom, which was scrupulously respected before you, requires one to do each year. How did you dare show yourself in an impure state at the tomb of Agonglo and make offerings to him? Neither he nor his predecessors approve of anything that comes from hands that have been stained with the blood of their descendants. It is undoubtedly the ancestors who are inspiring this Mahinou!"

The white men who were newly arrived in Danhomê had taken pity upon the unfortunate fate of the victim lashed into the porter's rack and upon the woman whom they took to be his grieving wife, but their companions informed them that any expression of compassion for such victims was regarded as a grave insult to the king.

Migan's assistants had already seized the woman and would have torn her apart on the spot, if Guézo had not intervened in time to order that they content themselves with imprisoning her in the first minister's compound until the end of the celebrations.

The crowd had been transfixed by the blasphemies of the "horse" and the audacity of Doguicimi, whose diatribes against the Master of the World upon his return from Hounjroto were still fresh in people's minds at the court.

"If Panther had sired this woman, her courage could not be greater than it is!" whispered Mêwou to Vivênagbo, who was seated to his right.

"The audacity of Doguicimi results only from the clemency of the king. But that will not last forever!" rectified Vidaho, who had overheard the second minister's confidential remark.

The Mahinou continued to stare Guézo straight in the eyes; then he offered his neck to Migan and, with an admirable show of impassivity, submitted to death and all the refinements of cruelty that the executioner might have devised to render the agony more painful.

Once more, events had just given the lie to the predictions of the diviners, and for that reason they were already trembling for their heads. They looked at each other surreptitiously. None of their faces expressed confidence.

The king ordered the other victims carried to the top of the altar.

Burdened with the weight of these "horses," the executioner's assistants reached the top of the altar with difficulty. And yet the imposing stature, the neck, and the sturdy shoulders of these servants bespoke strength and energy. Their loads compressed their necks. One of them confided in his neighbor: "And some of our comrades continue to claim that living beings weigh less than dead ones!"

"If these disgusting beasts of the mountain would only remain still once they've been placed on your head, we'd have less to complain about!"

Upon a signal from Mêwou, the executioner's assistants approached the edge of the altar one by one and threw their burdens to the ground below. A few remained there for a moment, unable to turn away their heads.

Other servants of the executioner had remained next to him at the base of the altar; they righted the porters' racks and placed them in front of their master.

The "horses" which fell on their heads were always picked up dead, their necks broken, their heads dangling, their skulls shattered, their faces, shoulders, chests, and backs scraped and covered with blood. The few rare victims who reached the bottom of the altar without turning over had invariably dislocated their backs. From each of them, the pain elicited a single cry, seldom a second one; the scimitar of Migan didn't give them enough time: it cut off their heads cleanly.

Here and there mouths opened and closed three or four times before remaining shut forever; tongues dangled or moved about; eyes started terrifyingly out of their sockets; more than one face was grimacing convulsively. As soon as the head was separated from the body, a few stomachs gave back the yams they had just received. One decapitated "horse" broke his bonds in a sudden fit and stood up; he opened his arms, drew them back to the sides of his body, and then fell heavily on his stomach, his whole body twitching convulsively; in the end he became calm. "He thought he was going to embrace his tormentor!" mocked a Danhomênou, delirious with joy.

Everyone hooted at the Mahinou.

The "horses" fell and continued to fall. Mêwou, whose gaze never left the base of the altar, moved his arm up and then down as a signal that the next victim should be dispatched to the sacrificial priest. Tirelessly, Migan finished them off with an unerring, sweeping motion. Blood flowed, flowed abundantly, and the sated earth wanted no more to drink. The executioner's assistants wallowed in mud compounded of blood, regurgitated yam puree, and dirt as they busily gathered up the heads and the bodies. The moans of the "horses" that had fallen head first to the ground, their efforts to lift heads that broken necks refused to support, the diligence of the servants who were constantly cleaning the site,

113

the dexterity of Migan whose sturdy arm raised his blood-dripping scimitar and cut off heads in a regular rhythm, his face and his clothes splattered with the spurting blood, his expression transfigured into the mask of Gou (the god of war), the corner of his mouth continually moving as if he were chewing a stimulant, his body sweating with fury – indeed, everything enraptured the crowd, which feasted its eyes on the spectacle.

When the last Mahinou had been decapitated, Migan handed his weapon to a servant, straightened his fingers that were cramped after having clutched the scimitar for such a long time, and stretched them one by one. At a wink of his eye, a servant who was attentive to Migan's most imperceptible gestures elbowed his way through the crowd and soon returned with about forty children, the oldest of which had not seen more than ten dry seasons. Nursing infants were strapped to the backs of the larger ones, who were also carrying bundles of straw. A few of the smallest children were crying, twisting about, and scratching their elders on the backs and arms or biting them and loudly demanding to be set down and returned to their mothers. However, others were insouciantly gnawing on a fried bean cake, a piece of yam, or a chunk of meat that had been slipped into their hands to distract them. The executioner's servants followed them, carrying large bundles of straw, packets of firewood, and coils of rope; others brutally moved the crowd back to make more room in front of the altar. The queens had surrounded Guézo and hid him from public view with their parasols as he redid his cloth and prepared himself for another ceremony.

He soon showed himself to the Danhomênous; they greeted him with shouts of joy: "When the Father of Light was hidden from us for a moment, the shadows descended to the depths of our hearts. Here we are enlightened again. Glory to the Master of Dawn, who is going to allow his people to witness a spectacle never seen under previous reigns!"

Far from deceiving Guézo, such flattery made him suspicious; he asked about what was being prepared at the foot of the altar. Mêwou told him: "Migan wants to roast groundnuts for the glorious memory of Agonglo!"

Guézo grew furiously angry and ordered the executioner to send back these innocents.

Having been pushed away from the altar, the human wave returned to fill the space. The king threw a dozen packets of cowries to the people and then motioned the high dignitaries to continue the process. Twenty baskets were emptied in a few moments. After a short pause, the King of Jewels threw out several strings of glass beads and then allowed the ministers to exhaust the contents of ten large baskets placed at their disposal. The Father of Wealth passed on to the cloths, reverted to the cowries and glass beads, and returned to the cloths.

A royal messenger having left Agbomê at the moment when the public distribution of riches began would have already covered the approximately two thousand four hundred bamboos between the capital and the village of Houawé. And yet the largess of the Father of Wealth knew no end. The crowd swarmed to the foot of the altar, much to the amusement of the white men. Even the

114

drummers had left their instruments to fight over the treasures that the King of Jewels was casting to the people. Those who succeeded in obtaining a cloth or a string of glass beads entrusted their windfall to companions remaining on the sidelines and plunged back into the crowd to try their luck again.

From a packet of two strings of cowries or glass beads, only eight or ten individual pieces of money or trinkets remained in the hands of those who fought for them.

Only rarely did anyone secure a whole cloth. Those who had secured no prize rolled their eyes enviously in the direction of those favored by fortune. During the short pauses that the king introduced into the distribution of riches to his subjects, nothing but cries of satisfaction could be heard: "From the hands of the Father of Wealth I received enough to buy a Mahinou after our next victory over that vile nation!" or else: "Today the King of Pearls has given me cloths and fine glass beads which I'll be wearing on the day I leave this world to go and serve him in the next one!"

Migan's assistants moved these men to the right. Other waves of people immediately filled the spot. In this way all Danhomênous could participate in the distribution of the treasures.

The Master of the World ordered the feasting to begin and then descended from the altar.

The sun was high overhead.

The Danhomênous shouted: "Yes, we have enough! We are already bent double under the weight of the treasures that the Father of Wealth has spread among us!"

Tables were set for the white men.

Each group of Danhomênous had soon been given calabashes of boiled cassava, fried bean cakes, acassa, and earthenware dishes filled with a caloulou made from wild game, chicken, pork, goat, or beef. At that moment the battle of the fingers began as they flew from the calabash of acassa to the dish of caloulou and then followed the road to the mouth before returning to the food and fighting over the chunks of meat which accompanied mouthfuls of acassa. Bones crunched between their teeth, tongues made a clicking sound, and hastily chewed food passed noisily into their gullets. Between two bites, people paused for a moment and inhaled a mouthful of air to calm the burning of the hot pepper; eyes filled with tears, and nostrils flowed under the effect of the spices – people wiped them with the backs of their left hands and continued to eat without interruption. It did not take long before one could see the bottoms of the dishes. The slightly crooked right index finger started in the middle of a plate, moved to the edge, and arched toward the mouth, where it would be licked clean; after several visits from the fingers, the bottoms of the dishes were dry. Libations followed. Migan's servants ran from group to group, pouring drinks into miniscule glasses. "Jogba! What a banquet and what libations!" shouted Manahin with his arms raised. "In human memory, their like is not to be found. Only the Father and Mother of His People is capable of showering his subjects with such largess. My stomach is so full it won't need another scrap of food for the next moon!"

The Danhomênous applauded him by caressing their bloated stomachs with hands that were still red with palm oil and smelled of hot peppers and the mustard in the caloulou. All of which was highly entertaining for the Master of the World and his queens. Yet more than half of those who were parading their drunkenness had only tasted the vapors of the brandy with their noses. The white men were also satisfied with the food and the service. Other dishes had followed, and there was liquor at the end of the meal.

At the time of the traditional celebrations, the Danhomênou's expression changed from what it was during the rest of the year. As if the bridle had been removed from his mouth and he was no longer obliged to flatten himself in the dust, he came and went, hurried along or walked slowly, kicked up his heels, barged about, and stretched his arms and legs. And if princes ventured to the base of the altar where the Father of Wealth was throwing cowries, cloths, and glass beads to the people, he would even contend with them for a prize.

No longer compelled to watch his words, he shouted, sang, and laughed uproariously in the presence of the king. He admitted that he was hungry, if he had not received enough to eat, and he criticized the stinginess of the ministers who had been charged by the Father of Wealth to fill the stomachs of his famished subjects. Even when he was satisfied, he chirped like the "birds" of the king: "A gift! A gift! Oh, miserly King, give me a gift! I'm insatiable! Only the Father of Wealth can satisfy me!"

His begging brightened the solemn face of the king. For that reason no one dreamed of making his criticisms into a crime: on this day he had nothing to fear from Migan's scimitar, which was busy settling accounts with the captives of war. Only two things were not permitted to him: covering his chest with a cloth and wearing sandals on his feet.

Possessed by his fetish (his only master during these festive days), the fetishist also had nothing to fear from the king. But he did have to be extremely careful in his movements, his songs, and his dances. The watchful eye of the chief fetishist was always open, and his ears as well were on the alert: a misstep, a careless remark, repeated lapses of memory in the songs or the sacred language would be cruelly punished at the shrine; the initiate's fall from grace could be pronounced and death imposed if the sacrilege were too scandalous.

Already the sun was turning his head toward his dwelling behind the Coufo.

The drums requested permission to come and thank the Father and Mother of the People; the royal drum boomed and was answered by the drums of the other groups and the fetish drums.

The chief fetishist of the "Tohossous" (Water Spirits) was Mivêdê, who came forward, followed by his assistants and his drummers. He was carrying a horse's tail; he detached himself from the group, which remained two bamboos away from the throne, and performed several leaps that culminated in bodily contortions and movements of the arms and head to the rhythms of the drums; the adepts danced after him. The chief fetishists of the other Water Spirits performed next, then the fetishists of Panther, the worshippers of Smallpox, and

116

finally those of the Supreme Being. The king retained the latter a bit longer; he was charmed by their lively dance to the cadence of two twin drums played by the same man.

The fetishists withdrew; their drums fell silent. Only the buzzing of the festive swarm could be heard. But the "kioun-go" of Panligan's double bell abruptly arrested all noise.

The songs of an obviously large choir burst forth in the distance; eyes turned toward Ahangbé's house, from whence the music was coming: a group with more than twenty rows of young girls was approaching. They advanced at a deliberate pace and maintained the rhythm of their song by tapping on the palms of their left hands with the opening of a narrow, long-necked gourd covered with a net to which fine cowries or snake vertebrae had been sewn.

They kneeled two bamboos away from the throne.

Madéou, the leader of the choir, stood up. She had a marvelous body. A leaf-green velvet cloth was tied above her breasts and descended to the tips of her feet. A batch of fine glass beads on strings circled her arms above her biceps; they were held in place by a silver bracelet with pendants. Wooden cylinders covered with gold leaf were inserted in the two holes that had been pierced in her ears and enlarged. For this reason, her ears were wide, more flared than usual, and ready to pick up the least sound. A packet of glass beads rounded her waist.

Her arms extended and her hands resting on a white wooden cane, she sang in a voice that droned and trembled. She twisted first to the right and then to the left as she sang; her song praised Guézo's majesty and munificence, the grandeur of the celebrations he was sponsoring, and the power of Danhomê since the ascension to the throne of the one whom King Agonglo had designated as his successor. A servant beat cadence for her on a single bell.

Her companions joined together in singing the chorus.

The singer stopped; at that moment, the drums resounded with the raps of the fingers and sticks of the drummers. The leader of the choir handed her baton to her assistant and came forward to dance. Her followers greeted her with lengthy applause. The fervor of their singing and shaking of gourds redoubled. Meanwhile, the leader of the chorus was getting ready to dance: with her arms raised slightly and bent, her fingers extended, and her palms facing her stomach, she made two steps to the right, returned to her starting point, and then moved left to the rhythm indicated by the beating of the drum. Standing in front of the drummers with her heels raised, her legs slightly bent, her breasts erect, her head held high, she thrust her supple elbows behind her, pointed her joined fingers downward, and, pressing her wrists to her sides, tapped the ground with the front part of her foot, first the right one and then the left, to the rhythm of the largest drum as her arms moved away from her body and came back gracefully, rhythmically, and not too quickly, like the wings of a resting butterfly; her half-closed eyes allowed one to glimpse the charm of her expression; her lips formed the shadow of a smile; one could see that she was aware of her beauty and her skill; her head turning gracefully in one direction and then the other seemed to invite the applause of the crowd, and it was not lacking. She turned her back to the drummers and performed the same movements for a few more moments, sometimes quickly, sometimes more slowly, depending upon the whims of the drum, but always with suppleness and grace, always attentive to the drum language that commanded the movements of the legs, the arms, and the head. With a single sharp rap, the drummer marked the end of the dance. At that very instant, the dancer's arms stretched forward and executed a dive.

After the leader, a number of other young women took their turns at the center of the scene. The delighted spectators applauded at great length and tapped their lips with joined fingers to punctuate their cries "Hoo! Hoo! Hoo!"

The dancers and singers flowed gracefully past the throne on the left; the drumming and singing came to an end.

A distant salvo announced Adongbé and his choir of five hundred young men dressed as if they were going to war. They arrived. Adongbé was brandishing a beautiful white horse's tail. Dressed in a pink velvet tunic and wearing a white scarf on his head, he dominated the procession by his tall stature. He was singing, "The Powers Leagued Against Aho!" to prompt the king to raise his head and look his domestic enemies straight in the eye, just as he would those from outside his realm.

I
The misfortune of this reign
Is not new to the traditions of Danhomê.
Indeed! The plots against Aho are not of today.
Neither princes nor commoners have forgotten, I think,
The struggles encountered by Houégbaja before his success
In taking this country from the Guédévis who lived here first?
Coming from Alada to this place,
Houégbaja was subjected to plots by Dan and by Dala,
Who swore they'd never allow him to settle here.
Informed of their alliance,
Houégbaja girded on his cartridge pouch and took up his gun.
Dan, the plotter, lies in the foundations of Danhomê;
Dala was killed in his turn.
Alluding to the impudence of Dan and of Dala,
The victor addressed their followers with this epithet:
"We are small in number!
But great in valor!"
The rest of the choir sang this chorus:
The high throne from which Houégbaja performed his feats
Was bestowed upon his son;
The gun that served him in battle is preserved in the Palace of Houégbaja;
The memory of his victories can never die.
He merely continued the work of his predecessor.

118

Is cowardice ever forgotten in this Danhomê?
Think about it!

II

When King Yêoummê acquired Danhomê
And wanted to enlarge it by the will of Houégbaja,
The monster Yahazê opposed him with threats.
Our king was not moved in the least:
He belted on his cartridge pouch, shouldered his gun;
After many encounters, he killed Yahazê
And adopted this glorious epithet:
He who conquered the monster and brought peace to the country!

Chorus
The high throne from which Yêoummê performed his feats
Was bestowed upon a famous Conqueror;
The gun that served him in battle is preserved in the Palace of
Houégbaja;
The memory of his victories can never die.
He merely continued the work of his predecessor.
Is cowardice ever forgotten in this Danhomê?
Think about it!

III

Dossou, "The Seller of Povê", received Danhomê
From the hands of the intrepid Yêoummê and promised to enlarge
it.
The Yorubas didn't want to see him at the head of the country.
Houfon barred his route to the sea
And thus prevented him from trading with the Ships.
Agaja, "The Seller of Povê," disdained threats and intrigues;
He girded on his cartridge pouch and grabbed his gun,
Fought against the Yorubas and, having gained their respect,
Turned his gaze toward the Kingdom of Houfon;
He conquered the country from Agrigomê to the sea,
Pursued Houfon, killed him,
And adopted this motto to celebrate his victory:
"The brave hyena puts the timorous antelope to flight!"

Chorus
The high throne from which Agaja performed his feats
Was bestowed upon his son;
The gun that served him in battle is preserved in the Palace of "The
Seller of Povê";
The memory of his victories can never die.
He merely continued the work of his predecessor.

119

Is cowardice ever forgotten in this Danhomê?
Think about it!

IV

Then came Tégbéssou's turn to guide the destiny of Danhomê,
Bestowed upon him by "The Seller of Povê."
The inhabitants of Za menaced the kingdom of Houégbaja:
"As long as I live," swore their chief Hougnon,
Whose nose was abnormally long,
"Tégbéssou will never construct a palace at Canna!"
The successor of Agaja laughed at these childish threats,
Girded on his cartridge pouch, took his gun,
Fought the people of Za, killed Hougnon, and cut off his nose,
All of which earned King Tégbéssou this glorious emblem:
"The tailor of overly long noses!"

Chorus
The high throne from which Tégbéssou performed his feats
Was bestowed upon his son;
The gun that served him in battle is preserved in the Palace of King
Tégbéssou;
The memory of his victories can never die.
He merely continued the work of his predecessor.
Is cowardice ever forgotten in this Danhomê?
Think about it!

V

When Holocé, "The Massive Rock,"
Inherited the succession of Tégbéssou,
Agbamou from the banks of the Coufo threatened to "overthrow
Danhomê
And the immovable rock on which it had just been planted."
King Pingla shrugged his shoulders and laughed at the madness of
the presumptuous man.
Enemies from the East and those from the West
Leagued together and swooped down upon Danhomê.
Holocé girded on his cartridge pouch and seized his gun.
A veritable hurricane, he ravaged Chamou,
Killed Amouo, felled Kanlan, ripped open Jinguin,
Devastated Abogomê, and slew Sinto.
The gratitude of his subjects
Accorded him this glorious title:
"He who annihilates enemies leagued against Danhomê."

Chorus
The high throne from which Holocé performed his feats

Was bestowed upon his son;
The gun that served him in battle is preserved in the
Palace of the king "stone in the water without fear of the cold";
The memory of his victories can never die.
He merely continued the work of his predecessor.
Is cowardice ever forgotten in this Danhomê?
Think about it!

VI

Hardly had he received Danhomê from the hands of Pingla,
When the king "Pineapple who laughed at the wrath of Lightning"
Was badgered by Ajognon.
The Yorubas joined with our enemy
And swore to strip Danhomê from the successor of Holocé.
All their threats were in vain:
The Pineapple who laughed at the wrath of Lightning
Fearlessly girded on his cartridge pouch, picked up his gun,
Battled the Yorubas,
Drowned them in Lake Wo,
Then turned against Ajopéou, leader of the bandits in "mahi" country,
Conquered the mountain of Gbowêlê, captured Ajognon,
And killed his acolyte Padé;
The all-powerful king slew Sêmido, the brother of Ajognon,
And captured Yênoumê, the chief of Akatagbala.
Builder of Gbêcon, "the palace of happiness,"
The Sun King who will never grow old,
When Panligan picks up his large double bell,
He will sing your victories in these words:
"The vanquisher of Ajognon,
The Pineapple who laughed at the wrath of Lightning!
Invincible king!"

Chorus
The high throne from which Agonglo performed his feats
Was bestowed upon his son;
The gun that served him in battle is preserved in the
Palace of "the Pineapple who laughed at the wrath of Lightning";
The memory of his victories can never die.
He merely continued the work of his predecessor.
Is cowardice ever forgotten in this Danhomê?
Think about it!

VII

When the worthy son of "the Pineapple who laughed at the wrath
of Lightning"

Succeeded his august father,
The deaf man mocked Danhomê,
Saying that its battle strength had run its course,
That the long furrow would henceforth be short!
He regretted that his chief warrior Vojossou was afflicted with old age
And could no longer fight;
Otherwise, he would straightaway capture Danhomênous and sell them!
Hearing of these mockeries and these taunts, the male bird
Girded on his cartridge pouch, grabbed his gun,
And led his army into the "mahi" country.
Zinsoucéfon escaped with his life by fleeing to the other side of Lake Wo;
Vojossou was captured and killed.
The all-powerful king slew the chief of Guija
And the woman Ganbajê, who had outfitted a thousand "baliba" slaves
So they could come and fight against Danhomê.
Ganbajê's brother Avajê was brought back alive to Danhomê,
Where his body was used to fertilize a long furrow
That was being ploughed by the worthy successor of "the Pineapple who laughed at the wrath of Lightning!"

Chorus
King Guézo avenged the long-standing insult to Houégbaja.
He merely continued the work of his predecessor.
Is cowardice ever forgotten in this Danhomê?
Think about it!

Adongbé the singer will conclude the history of our conquests:
Today is not the day
When the panther in pursuit of its prey will lose its claws;
Topa was lost in the war at Jigbé,[14]
Dangban was lost in the war at Jigbé,
But "the Seller of Povê" will avenge them.

Chorus
We are planning to go and fight against Hounjroto.
If Hounjroto defeats us, Gaou and Possou,
Swear that you'll not come back.
If Hounjroto can not be defeated, Migan and Mêwou,
Swear, swear that you'll remain there forever.
If King Guézo leaves for the "mahi" mountains

---

14   "Jigbé" is the city of Ouémé.

And if the country of the people with black bellies
Cannot be destroyed, Ajaho and Sogan,
Isn't it true that we'll all remain at Hounjroto?

Adongbé repeated the final stroph three times, and each time he pointed the horse's tail held in his right hand at the high dignitaries whose names he was mentioning.

With the horse's tail on his shoulder, he lowered his raised left arm, and when he pronounced the word Hounjroto for the last time, he snapped his index finger against his thumb.

The men in his choir began singing that strophe to the accompaniment to the beating drums, the horns, the bells, and the other musical instruments.

Adongbé made several feints and stopped. The crowd was delirious. With a gift of several fine cloths, packets of cowry strings, and bottles of liquor, the king rewarded this magnificent song, which, he said, deserved to be taught to future generations.

Twenty young men detached themselves from the group. Their right hands slashed through the air like sabres, rose toward the sky, then descended and pointed toward the ground, which they were pounding with their feet; they also held out their hands alternately toward the throne and in the direction of "mahi" country; the word Hounjroto rang out loudly in their song. They were singing:

When the right moment arrives,
All our dead will leave their tombs
And accompany us to Hounjroto.
If necessary, we'll raze
All the mountains that house those stinking beasts.
Let the Master of the World but give us a sign!
Let him unleash his buffalos
And let them race to the conquest of Hounjroto.
While our guns and our cannons are thundering
Against any mountain people who put up a fight,
Some of us will be lighting fires
To snuff out the old and the weak in their homes.
If the Master of the World believes these weapons too feeble
(They brandished their guns),
Let him deign to tell us so now.
Let him but give the command. We will become Lightning
And annihilate those stinking beasts of Hounjroto.
Adongbé sang once again to calm the impetuous young men:
The right moment has not yet arrived to avenge Danhomê.
The Master of the Universe remains inscrutable
But thinks nonetheless of punishing these sons of the mountains.
His attitude tells us: "Man's spit is white,
Though his body's been shaped with blood."
Let us learn to veil our hatred.

123

And when the right moment arrives,
We'll easily conquer those stinking beasts.

Advice appropriate for faint-hearted souls. As a result, it was disdained by the young warriors, the very image of martial fervor. They sang new couplets to remind Danhomênous that the honor and glory of the kingdom demanded a swift revenge and to affirm that Hounjroto would be destroyed in no time at all.

To show that they were not making idle boasts, they turned to the left; in several strides they reached a patch of thorny bushes, a vestige of those that the Aladahonous had found when they first came to the country of the Guédévis; they grabbed at the bushes. With bare hands and teeth, they each cut a thorny branch and came back toward the throne, their face and hands covered with blood and their eyes full of fury; they flourished the branches and sang:

If the Mahinous were buffalos,
We'd rip out their horns while they were still alive!

Their courage caused the spectators to dance with joy, for they no longer doubted the victory over Hounjroto; the warriors would bring back the Mahinous, even if they were covered with thorns.

Won over by this infectious enthusiasm, the king ordered that still more cloths, cowries, and alcohol be given to these young men, and he expressed his joy at having such brave wariors. "Peopled by such brave defenders, Danhomê can sleep easily!" he told them.

The daystar had already disappeared beneath the horizon. Danhomê's Father of Light was obliged to follow his example.

The royal procession formed again for the return to the Palace. The fetishists were in the lead. They regained their shrines by the time the last soldier of the royal guard had disappeared inside the Palace.

The drums in the Courtyard of Singboji and the Courtyard of Ajahimê continued to play. Their fury increased as the dusk thickened.

Danhomênous prevented from dancing during the day for fear of being ridiculed were now actively performing there and promising to confront the mockery of the spectators on the following day as long as their timidity had been lulled asleep in advance by a tiny glass of brandy.

Since daybreak, the firing of cannons had been carrying echoes of the celebrations at Agbomê into the distance.

The palace dignitaries had stopped in the reception hall.

Having removed his ceremonial attire, the Master of the Universe, who had just taken a bath, was simply draped in a cloth the color of boiling palm oil froth, and he had propped himself on his elbow as he reclined on a soft bed of mats among the Wives of Panther in the salon of his several-story house. He had complained of stiffness and pain in his arms and shoulders. The queens left him no opportunity to repeat his words; one of them immediately began to massage his back, another to knead the soles of his feet, his thighs, his arms. Gently, titillatingly their hands passed and passed again over every part of his body, driving out weariness. The king abandoned himself to these caresses and closed his eyes. Only the murmur of the fans moving slowly up and down broke the silence in the salon.

Two queens were soon following their example as they spoke softly into each other's ears. Despite the precautions they took to avoid being overheard by their companions, their whisperings pierced the silence. But the king didn't seem to be bothered by it.

Thus, one of them took heart and, to embolden her hesitant companions, said: "People who live in intimacy with the Panther must not fear him. The king is an object of dread only to those Danhomênous who never pass through the Door of the Universe and come close to the successor of Houégbaja.

"Indeed!" exclaimed one of her co-wives approvingly.

"Will that bitch be allowed to go on uttering her blasphemies forever?" asked the first one.

"And above all setting such a bad example in Danhomê?" her companion added in support.

"To beard the Master of the World so impudently all the time," ventured a new voice, "that dog must be secretly supported by some powerful individual in the kingdom!"

"Only the Master of the World's pardon of the first insult, which she addressed to him publicly after our return from the war of Hounjroto, has prompted the blasphemer to commit a second offense," rectified a Wife of Panther timidly, her head concealed behind a companion.

"No more than a tiny minority of Danhomênous sacrifice to Mawou, whereas those who heap offerings upon Legba are legion. For a people which worships power, kindness is a sign of weakness, and the weak are despised. One who realizes this feels no pity for Danhomênous who only respect you and venerate your name because you deal harshly with them."

Another Wife of Panther, disdaining the cautiousness of her fellow wives, dared rebuke Guézo himself: "The Predestined King's generosity with respect to Adanzan continues to puzzle Danhomênous who cannot understand why sacrilege lives and enjoys such solicitous treatment.

"When a few masters of slaves arrived on the eve of these celebrations and beseeched the king to deign to exchange the "horses," which he was preparing to send to his ancestors, for their slaves, whose poor attitudes had exasperated them, their request was denied, and the Master of the World justified his refusal on the basis of a decision that had been made to put all the Mahinous captured at Hounjroto to death. That decision had been greeted with shouts of joy; since then, the Danhomênous have unceasingly implored their ancestors to protect their successor on the throne of Houégbaja and to hasten the day when they would feast their eyes upon spectacles that promised to surpass those of previous reigns in extravagance. But intoxicated by a stupid song that was recited at the moment when the royal procession was moving toward Ajahimê, the Master of the World forgot his promise to his people and ordered the singer to be freed. Even then, if the king had been satisfied with this first step on the path to forgiveness and had not pardoned the Mahinou who alleged an augury of Destiny as a pretext for refusing the traditional yam offered to messengers dispatched to the realm of the spirits, Danhomê would have been subjected to neither the odious blasphemy of that 'horse' who claimed his name was 'Quench-Your-Thirst-With-Blood,' nor the scandalous interjection of Doguicimi, a true bitch!

"Has anyone every heard tell of a "horse" in previous reigns having dared to utter a word at the moment of the sacrifices or of a woman having defied the Idol of the Danhomênous?

"Every day our ears are offended by the malicious observations of the common people; they are saying that they see the king's clemency as a sign of weakness.

"Migan's scimitar must drink the blood of all our captives from Hounjroto.

"As for Doguicimi, she deserves to be tied to the mouth of a cannon and blasted into tiny pieces by the shot, unless the Master of the World, finding such a demise too quick and therefore insufficiently painful, orders that the bitch be buried alive or that the executioner's assistants trample her underfoot until she disappears beneath the ground."

"She is surely in contact with the Mahinous," suggested one queen.

Another seconded this opinion: "Ever since the Master of the World came to power, the Danhomênous have called him Guézo the Great or Guézo the Powerful. But he can believe us when we tell him that his subjects are already whispering 'Guézo the Capricious, Guézo the Coward, Guézo the Unjust!' and waiting anxiously for the day when they can throw such epithets in his face."

"Has the king forgotten that he is ruling over a people which, in the end, condemned Adanzan for his sadism and chased him from the throne?

"The Master of the World's severity toward Adanzan's sons, who were sold to the white men, and with respect to the unfortunate Wife of Panther, whose only crime was her desire to avenge the honor of the king on that day when Doguicimi heaped shame upon the Idol of the Danhomênous near the Door of Happiness – such severity contrasts sharply with his weakness for the blasphemer who is worthy of neither life nor pity.

"After going astray on the path of forgiveness at the risk of discrediting himself, why didn't the king go all the way and reprieve the Mahinou who claimed his name was 'Quench-Your-Thirst-With-Blood'?"

"The Predestined King owes it to himself, believe us, to put an end to Doguicimi's blasphemies, which are repeated at every turn.

"The audacity of that bitch will, in the end, gain the respect of the Danhomênous. Although subdued by Adanzan, the most formidable of kings in Danhomê, the people did not hesitate for a moment to demonstrate their solidarity with you the day you came to demand the liberation of Princess Sincoutin, whom the sadist wanted to have executed. Only your own audacity won over the court of Adanzan. As your popularity grew, the Danhomênous' veneration for Adanzan diminished without his even suspecting it.

"When he finally awoke, he saw you as Master of Danhomê.

"We weep to see the Master of the World close his eyes upon the past, an infallible guide for anyone who desires to triumph over the dangers of life. It's unheard of! A man who owes his ascension to the throne to his own audacity fails to recognize its importance today!"

These words set the keynote for the other queens. They all pretended to have been weeping over their august husband's lack of concern, which was, they lamented, diligently undermining his reign.

Some of them wiped their eyes with the backs of their hands; others passed a section of their cloths over their faces. Yêpommê Avognondé alone remained silent.

Guézo did not appear to have been affected either by his wives' arguments or by their tears.

He sat up and indignantly replied to them: "You must all be conspiring to bring Danhomê to a hasty end since, to attain your goal, you can find nothing better than the crimes to which you would like to incite me.

"In all good conscience, how can you reproach me for the pardon granted to Adanzan? Don't you realize the calamities that would be unleashed upon this kingdom if the blood of a prince or, even worse, the blood of a king, whose person is sacred, were to be shed on its soil? A country which killed its king would, from the very moment of the crime, be infected with a kind of leprosy, and while still alive, it would be condemned to watch its own decomposition. Luckily the misfortune of such a sacrilege would not be incurable. However, the only remedy capable of returning the country to health would be to designate as my successor a son of the poor victim of such momentary madness. Do you really want the tyrant's family to regain the throne?

"Even the simple overthrow of a king calls down severe punishments upon the head of his adversary if it has not been motivated by the superior interest of the kingdom. I was so convinced of this that, despite the tyrant's injustice toward me, I had resolved not to create any difficulty for him during his reign. Didn't I reject Jossou's offer to help me acquire Danhomê after I had been slandered by Adanzan, who had one of his lieges accuse me of murder?

"But the tyrant's sadism and debauchery was dishonoring the throne of Houégbaja; his scandalous plan to sacrifice princes during our traditional celebrations ran counter to our beliefs and stirred the people to revolt; the sacrilege of his sons, who wanted to set the Palace of Houégbaja on fire, raised the indignation of all Danhomênou to a fever pitch. Soon rumors of the Ayonous' preparations for a war against this kingdom reached Agbomê. Under these circumstances, I saw myself obliged to seize the throne in order to save the country of my fathers from disaster.

"During my reign, Adanzan will not be disturbed in his retreat at Damê. As

127

long as he does not plot against the man whom Agonglo designated to succeed him on the throne of Houégbaja, the fallen king will enjoy all the happiness that is assured to any loyal subject of the Master of the World.

"I would not even have sent his sons away from Danhomê, if I had not feared that their presence among us might attract the wrath of the ancestors upon our heads.

"The pardons I granted this morning to the Mahinou who recited a song full of wisdom and to his fellow countryman who, knowing he was about to die, nevertheless refused to violate a prohibition imposed upon him by Destiny – these pardons testify both to my intention that the Danhomê of Houégbaja become known as a country where wisdom is cherished, no matter who expresses it, and to my desire to see my people acquire the virtues of constancy and loyalty.

"As for the Mahinou who said his name was 'Quench-Your-Thirst-With-Blood', his blasphemy is inconsistent with our conception of the continuity of life in the realm of the Spirits. To pardon him would have been to accept his heresy and to admit to all Danhomê the futility of our human sacrifices.

"Doguicimi, that thorn in your side, offended no one but me, and I have many reasons to pardon her. But your companion, whom I had executed upon my return from Hounjroto, had polluted herself through contact with men and thereby violated, as you very well know, this country's inexorable laws about the sacredness of the Wives of Panther. I explained to all Danhomê that a failure to punish this sacrilege would make me an accomplice to it and would, as a result, draw down upon my head, and upon the country as well, the wrath of the ancestors who placed me on this throne. Because I punished the sacrilege of your companion with death, you want the head of Doguicimi to roll too? I will not follow your suggestions. He who is implacable is not far from being inhuman. If I allow myself to be pushed into committing a crime, how will I be any different from Adanzan?

"If it is true that a man has two more pairs of ribs than a woman, I do not think it necessarily follows that he has more courage than members of the opposite sex. The little worm in your head begins to turn? That's the end of your usual sweetness, calm, and Level-headedness! You become more dreadful than the Panther whose little one has just been ravished from her. Disaster for any innocent person who wanders into your proximity.

"Men know that woman is like Legba, who, without consulting the will or opinion of any divinity, acts upon all sorts of whims that pass through his head. You cannot have already forgotten the shot that your companion Yêpommê Avognondé fired upon the followers of Adanzan when they were invading the Palace of Gbêcon-Hounli. Who advised her to do it? On the basis of this act of heroism, unprecedented until then in the history of Danhomê, I had the idea of creating an army of women; before that time, did anyone in Danhomê suspect that so much valor was lying dormant beneath those breasts that were believed to be swollen solely with tenderness? What Danhomênou could have guessed that you would fight during wartime with a courage that even our enemies extol? You women were only seen as keepers of the hearth, obliged to submit to your husbands' every demand and then to nurse and raise your children, but you proved to be veritable furies on the battlefield, and for that reason I bestowed the name "buffalos" on you. In certain respects, you are superior to men without realizing it."

He remained silent for a moment, then continued: "At the time of Agaja, we saw Aguidissou's mother's love of her son propel her into a crime against Danhomê. During the reign of Adanzan, a love of duty prompted another woman (he smiled at Yêpommê Avognondé) to shoot one of the tyrant's followers. Ever since her act revealed your courage to me, a love of Danhomê has driven women in the army of the buffalos to their deaths. Today, a love of her husband drove Doguicimi to blasphemy. Like a fire that reduces to ashes the basket that contains it, love instantaneously transforms those whom it possesses into unrecognizable forms and drives them to commit thoughtless acts. Having experienced the fervor of love, I cannot be too harsh in judging those crimes to which it incites people.

"Neither the hyena and leopard cages installed by Adanzan nor the scimitar of his executioner Migan Donouvo intimidated Agontimê, the Mother of Panther, who protested vehemently against the usurpation of her son's throne. The tyrant had no peace until the day he sent my venerable mother far from Danhomê. If she had remained a few days more in this country, she would certainly have committed a crime to avenge the unhappy circumstances imposed upon her son. Her hatred for Adanzan must still be alive, even if she is happy in her exile.

"In memory of Agontimê, Mother of Panther, I am therefore determined to forget Doguicimi's insults."

A Wife of Panther responded to him: "There are insults that one cannot pardon without falling from one's throne. The Predestined King no longer concerns himself with his dignity. But please let him not desecrate the hallowed memory of Agontimê, Mother of Panther, by making an outrageous comparison between her legitimate protests and the blasphemies of an ingrate, who at most deserves to be given to a slave, since it was not the Master of the World's wish that she dedicate herself to celibacy in the army of buffalos."

The king replied, still calm and emphasizing certain words: "Doguicimi surpasses all of you in courage."

All the royal wives turned their eyes toward Yêpommê Avognondé, who had lowered her head.

"And if I had given her to a slave, I would have taken her back the very day of my return from Hounjroto. You are losing your time trying to influence me against her and waving in front of me the spectre of a popular revolution that you want to make into a terrible bugaboo in hopes of having her head. You should rather be lamenting with me the loss I suffered in giving this woman to Toffa, and let me tell you that I know the Danhomênous better than you do. Although I always see them lying face downward in front of the throne and covering themselves with dust in my presence, I know it would be a serious mistake to allow myself to be seduced by all these signs of obeisance into thinking that my subjects are completely harmless. But if there are vipers among them, there are also a large number of snakes.

"The Danhomênou is firmly convinced that he is no more than a thing and that, as a consequence, he has neither life nor liberty, because he belongs body and soul to his sovereign, whom he calls his Father and Mother, the Master of the World, the Star of the Day, and I don't know what else!

"This Danhomênou who obstinately refuses to look or to listen for fear of being called as a witness in a trial, this Danhomênou who never wants to discuss the act of the king, this Danhomênou who distrusts his own father and mother because he is convinced they would betray him to the superior authorities for the least crime or word of slander, this Danhomênou who (listen well to my words!) scrupulously guards himself against all negative thoughts in regard to the king, this Danhomênou whose profound veneration for the king – his idol – is known to me, this Danhomênou who swears oaths on the name of the king or invokes it in case of danger, this extraordinarily servile Danhomênou is not the one who would dare criticize my acts or see my magnanimity as a sign of weakness and therefore conspire against my reign. Even Smallpox and Lightning, the most awesome fetishes in this country, do not inspire as much fear in these people as their sovereign does.

"When I was merely a claimant to the throne, my generosity toward the Danhomênous earned me their confidence, and they showed me their souls. For that reason I am convinced that I know them better than anyone else in this kingdom. What I am saying about them can never be denied. Why do you want me to doubt the loyalty, the fidelity, and the devotion of this people after they have given me so many proofs to the contrary? People who gladly rush to their deaths at a simple sign from their king deserve my complete confidence!

"These people worship power, as you have so appropriately said, but knowing that their king is power itself, they never look him straight in the face. More than that, in the absence of the king the Danhomênou adopts the prudent attitude of the dormouse, who upon recognizing the tracks of Panther's claws respectfully kisses the ground next to them and says: 'If you respect people in their presence, respect them also in their absence!'

"No, these people who cover themselves with dirt in front of my mere sceptre and accord it the same honors as my person are not people who would ever dare rise in rebellion against their king."

One of the Wives of Panther objected: "The Master of the World is forgetting that Adanzan too was the very image of terror and that he too was the object of profound veneration on the part of the Danhomênous. That did not prevent them from cutting him down just as they would have done to a banana tree that no longer bore fruit."

"That's true! That's true!" murmured her companions approvingly.

"You exaggerate the force of these people, who never take any initiative. You are of good faith, I realize that. But the truth is that the only revolts against royal authority ever mentioned in Danhomê are those undertaken by princes; that is to say that the fall of Adanzan was not brought about by the people but by the princes. Until now they are not displeased with me.

"Don't they realize that I am the one to whom they owe the privilege of exchanging the course, home-made raphia cloths, which the tyrant obliged them to wear even on solemn occasions at court, for the beautiful materials brought by the white men?

"If this were my only claim on their gratitude, they could easily forget it. But in addition to the revocation of that tyrannical decree that very much undermined their princely dignity without their being able to utter a word of complaint, they owe me the life they presently enjoy. Ah, if that sadist had reigned for another dry season, how many princes would he not have eliminated during the traditional celebrations! My intervention on behalf of Princess Sicoutin merely postponed the tyrant's plans. Only my ascension to the throne aborted them completely.

"The death of Doguicimi that you are requesting could well cost me the respect of the princes and the veneration of my subjects as well.

"Indeed, this woman who dares attack the king, the very image of power, herself incarnates courage and audacity, the highest virtues in the eyes of the people. Ordering the execution of Doguicimi would signify that the most cherished virtues of our ancestors are no longer recognized during my reign. Danhomê would have experienced the day we ceased worshipping the power, courage, and audacity that created it.

"Therefore, if you have not sworn to bring about the death of this country, don't repeat your criminal advice any longer in my hearing.

He became lost in thought, then continued with a deep sigh: "Every Danhomênou who loves this country should be concerned at this moment with discovering a way to halt the Mahinous' impudence, which could be repeated tomorrow and which is capable in the long run of sullying the prestige of Danhomê."

He waited for a moment. No one in his entourage had any advice to give.

"Since you can't lend me the assistance I need in putting an end to a situation that gives increasing cause for alarm, you can withdraw," he said with anger in his voice.

The harsh words of the king severely wounded the evil spirit of jealousy in the Wives of Panther but could not entirely vanquish it. With terrifying vigor, it arose once again.

"Who could have believed that the Idol of the Danhomênous would allow himself to be defied so insolently by a mere child?" asked a queen who left the group as a sign of disdain for what she called the passivity of the king of Danhomê.

"What about me? Didn't I make the tyrant turn pale more than once at this very court?" countered Guézo.

The queen retraced her steps and retorted: "But the prince never uttered a blasphemy, although everything gave him the right to do so — the circumstances of his intervention and his position as the legitimate heir to a throne that had been usurped from him. Simply because you might have given a member of your family a well-deserved slap in the face, would that be a justification for suffering the same insult from the hand of the lowest of your slaves? He who remains silent beneath a tree runs the risk of receiving the droppings of birds on his head, as the elders say. By that they mean that one should not always remain impassive in the presence of those who spew out insults."

Still calm, the king responded to her: "To remain impassive in the face of an insult is to disdain it and to show by such an attitude that it does not affect you. Pardoning it when it does affect you is to prove that you are superior to the person who has insulted you. If only his mind is perceptive, he will be overcome with remorse and repent. You must also realize that those who are weaker than we are often make us pay our debts to those who are stronger. If I forgive Doguicimi her tirades, it is, as I told you before, out of gratitude to Yêpommê Avognondé, whose shot at the tyrant's followers raised the alarm about the sacrilege taking place in Danhomê and earned her her freedom from the sadist; it is also out of gratitude for the heroism of all the Amazons who sacrifice their beauty, their maternal instincts, and their hope-filled lives to the aggrandizement of Danhomê, and it is, finally, in memory of my august Mother's protests against the usurpation of my throne."

After having swept his gaze over all the queens, Guézo continued with a greater indignation in his voice: "It is astonishing that women can be filled with so much gall. Your advice to govern ruthlessly, ruthlessly and pitilessly, can only lead me to the loss of my throne. You can withdraw. Notify the worshippers of the calabashes that they can wait on me and inform the palace dignitaries that they will be introduced next for a meeting of the council."

The Wives of Panther went away full of shame but also more filled with hatred than ever.

One of them expressed the opinion that their defeat was due to the silence of Yêpommê Avognondé, who had not joined in their protests.

A second queen advised: "A clever ruse would be a better instrument than persuasion for attaining the goal we have in mind. Didn't we prevail upon him to undertake the war of Hounjroto, despite the opposition of Tomêtin, Adouconou, Toffa, and other princes who have a great deal of influence at the court? We'll merely veil our hatred without letting it expire."

A third supported her: "We shall be able to bring about the fall of that impertinent woman! Confronted with the proof that all Doguicimi's expressions of love for Toffa are pure affectation, the Master of the World will no longer hesitate to order the execution of a woman against whom we will easily obtain damning testimony. We will also demonstrate to all Danhomê that it is the prerogative of the Royal Wives alone to love with an incorruptible love and to drink the poisoned potion in order to accompany their husband into the realm of the spirits; wives of princes, high dignitaries, and common people lack the courage to make such a sacrifice.

"Indeed, if the conduct of Doguicimi convinced the Danhomênous that this bitch was not inferior to us in nobility, devotion, and courage, that would be our greatest humiliation!"

Before separating and returning to their individual living quarters, they swore once again that, if they could not have the head of Doguicimi, they would devote themselves actively to ruining her reputation in all Danhomê.

Jealousy has this characteristic trait: it knows how to reconcile rivalries and enroll them in the service of a common cause, even though it will rekindle them with the same passion as before once the goal has been reached. Despite the veiled hatred that existed between the Wives of Panther and the ordinary Queens, the former, who were infatuated with their own privileges and usually placed a great distance between themselves and the co-wives whom they mockingly called "the doubtful ones," lowered themselves and made peace with the latter to plot the fall of Doguicimi. . . .

Free to go everywhere in the Palace of Houégbaja and even to frequent the small market at Ganhohi without being escorted by servants, the queens of the second rank met with servants (emissaries of people from outside) and gathered information that they peddled about the Palace. They also transmitted messages for people who were strangers to the Palace.

The servant queens filled the salon. Charged with satisfying the stomach of the king and called "worshippers of calabashes" on account of the complete confidence placed in them, these queens brought in a number of calabashes that were very large and irreproachably clean. They arranged them on a mat stretched out at the foot of the royal bed and then kneeled down.

One queen walked on her knees toward the king, carrying her calabash in her hands. She put down her burden and removed the cover: in it were a folded white scarf and three medium-sized calabashes, two of which were filled with water. The woman placed the empty calabash beneath the hands of the king, who was holding out his arms; she picked up one calabash of water, swallowed three mouthfuls of the liquid it contained, and then carefully washed the king's hands, rinsing them with water from the second calabash after having drunk several mouthfuls of it as before; finally she dried his hands with the white scarf and retreated.

In the order of their respective ranks, her companions were already enumerating the dishes and the drinks that had been brought to serve the mouth of the king. A queen who had remained in the background continued to recite a list of the dishes that remained in the hands of the cooks.

Upon an almost inaudible word from the king, a servant whose eyes were glued to the king's lips ordered the fourth worshipper of calabashes to come forward. The woman whose dish His Majesty had deigned to select obeyed with a show of joy. She removed the cover from her calabash, took out a hollow dish containing boiled maize; next to it she placed a tiny calabash filled with plump palm nuts.

The queen who carried the calabash of drinks was on his right, and two others were on his left; one of them was holding a white scarf.

The king looked at the dishes without daring to touch them. The worshipper asked for water, carefully washed her hands, and ate two mouthfuls of maize to show that the food could be eaten without danger. The king still did not move. The worshipper brought to the top that which had been covered and took another two bites. The king still refused to touch the plate.

"The Father of Wealth undoubtedly does not want what the worshipper is offering him!" suggested a queen.

The other servant queens immediately began once again to enumerate the dishes they had brought and to laud the flavor of them. The fixity of the king caused the queen to tremble with fear; she cast worried, interrogatory glances to the right and to the left in hopes of discovering what crime she might have committed. But her companions were equally puzzled by the attitude of the king. Then her face suddenly brightened; she believed she knew what it was. She said to herself: "He distributed cowries and cloths at Ajahimê. He was complaining of fatigue and stiffness; he would no doubt like to be fed!"

She took a small portion of maize and lifted it toward the king's mouth. Another queen was already calling out: "The light of day is extinguished! The light of day is extinguished!" Except for the queen who was serving him, all the others lowered their heads and closed their eyes. As a demi-god, the king was not believed to be subject to the common needs of other mortals; thus, no eye was permitted to watch him perform acts such as eating or drinking. Only a few rare individuals in Danhomê could claim to have seen the king putting food in his mouth.

The worshipper of calabashes on the left placed her cupped hands within reach of the king so he could spit out any hard parts that might be found in the food or anything that might remain after he had chewed it.

An emphatic "no" uttered by the king caused heads to rise and questioning glances, more worried than ever, to be cast in his direction. He did not make them wait long for his response: "Fried bean cakes, you are not what you appear to be on the surface. . . ."

"Who, us?" protested the queens, striking themselves on their chests. "Oh, why can't people recognize a person's innocence by simply examining the depths of her stomach, just as a quick glance allows one to ascertain whether or not a calabash is clean? For if that were the case, we would have our stomachs slit open so our lord and master could see that we are not harboring any criminal feelings."

The king did not listen to these protests of loyalty and sincerity but rather continued: "While pretending to worship me, you are all plotting to bring about my downfall."

"By Agonglo, we swear we are innocent!"

"Where then are the kings' skulls that were brought back from Glito, Sêlêchi, Logozohê, and Hounjroto? Those kings had all the good things of the earth. But they were brutally deprived of their possessions by the wars we conducted against them. You are not unaware of the fact that they will only refrain from avenging themselves and inflicting a violent and premature death upon me, if their skulls are present at all my meals and around my bed when I am enjoying the pleasures of life among my wives.

"Preoccupied with the idea of bringing about the fall of Doguicimi, you forget the most important duties of your position. Shun hatred! People who cede place to it in their hearts are driven to harm even those whom they idolize, although that is not what they desire."

The queens offered a profusion of excuses, in which was apparent a quite sincere regret at having failed in their duty, albeit unintentionally. One of them had disappeared a moment ago, and she returned with a calabash containing the four heads of enemy chiefs. She arranged them in front of the king.

The worshipper of calabashes whose dish had been requested by the king placed four handfuls of maize in a miniscule calabash; she added some palm nuts and deposited the dish in front of the skulls.

"The light of day is extinguished! The light of day is extinguished!" proclaimed one of the queens. All heads bowed once again.

A moment later, two soft dry coughs could be heard. The worshipper who had brought the drinks stood up at once and removed the covers from her calabashes. The king indicated what he wanted by making a slight gesture; with a wooden rod, the servant queen stirred the beverage that had been made from pounded millet paste dissolved in water. She poured a swallow of the liquid into the hollow of her left hand, drank it, then poured two more swallows on the ground before the skulls of the enemy chiefs, and lifted the drink toward the lips of the king.

Satisfied, Guézo removed his mouth from the calabash and ordered that the food be cleared away. The queen who had been holding her hands together to catch whatever the king might spit out now individually licked the royal fingers that had dipped into the boiled maize. Meanwhile, the co-wife who was holding the scarf wiped the king's lips. The woman carrying the water washed his hands. The skulls were replaced in the calabash, and the worshippers left the room.

The palace dignitaries were ushered in for the council meeting that would decide the program for the following day's celebration.

Lêguêdê took the floor first and reported to the court about the information his secret police had gathered, among the Danhomênous and among the Foreigners on the other side of the Swamps, in regard to the impression that the celebration and the events of the day had made upon them.

Murmurs of reproach for the pardon granted to Doguicimi passed across several lips. Guézo responded with a shrug of his shoulders.

The first minister said: "A few days before the beginning of these celebrations, the Danhomênous were promised that they would see all of our captives from Hounjroto perish. The sacrifice that I called the 'roasting of groundnuts' was appropriate, I thought, only with the youngest 'mahi' children and only in honor of Agonglo. The Master of the Universe prohibited me from carrying out this sacrifice, which would have provided the people with an amusing spectacle of an entirely new kind. The King of Jewels perhaps wants to reserve it for Pingla?"

Guézo was lost in reflection; he seemed preoccupied with more important matters. In the end, his silence convinced the court that he disapproved of this sacrifice. To prevent Migan from returning to the attack and proposing another murder that the Master of the World would certainly accept in order not to offend his first minister, Mêwou informed the council that the young princesses had gone to the spring during the afternoon.

The king gave orders for the next day's celebration that would be held in honor of King Pingla and the Queen Mother Sênoumê. He then advised the court of his apprehensions about the Mahinous' impudence, which could be repeated at that time.

The counsellors consulted each other with their eyes but had no solution to propose. They were all embarassed, except Migan, who said calmly: "The generosity of the King of Jewels extended even to the flies, who sounded their trumpets in thanksgiving all day long, once they themselves had been satisfied. This generosity, which is without precedent in Danhomê, has also been accorded to the hyenas, who are in the Ditch howling long "ouhou-ou-ou's" to express their gratitude to the Father of Wealth for having filled their lairs with corpses.

"In their own ways, wild beasts and insects know how to demonstrate their gratefulness toward the Master of the World. We, his human subjects whom he has granted the greatest capacity for creative thinking and upon whom he has bestowed favors at every instant of our lives, we would be extremely ungrateful if we did not attempt to remedy a situation that is becoming worrisome." He looked around; all heads were lowered.

"Where are the dignitaries who contrived to untie what Migan had tied up?" the prime minister asked with his characteristic savagery, as his gaze fixed upon Mêwou, whom he inwardly accused of having jealously brought about the miscarriage of the new "roasting of groundnuts" sacrifice he had devised.

No one uttered a word. He triumphed. "All right then!" he continued solemnly, "Migan Atindébacou will show all Danhomê tomorrow that the confidence with which the Master of the World honors his first minister is not misplaced!" He prostrated himself and kissed the floor. His colleagues followed his example, despite the resentment that was simmering in them against the egotist who did not want anyone to be regarded as his equal.

The king's face brightened. Before dismissing the dignitaries, he ordered his devoted minister to keep close watch over Doguicimi.

The anger that had been smoldering in him ever since Doguicimi's new blasphemy and the fiasco of his plan for the "roasting of the groundnuts" suddenly exploded over the heads of his assistants: they should have cut her to pieces or strangled her before the Master of the World had time to announce that he was pardoning her. Their lethargy constituted a betrayal that would be punished by the club this time, but if it repeated itself, the scimitar would impose a harsher expiation. The sycophants who had been trained to proclaim the magnificence of the celebration, the munificence of the king, and the felicity of his people had played their role well at the beginning: they had skillfully inspired the crowd to sing the glory of the monarch. But they had soon lost all sense of proportion: their excesses had caused the new sacrifice, their master's own project, to be aborted. If only the servants charged with bringing the children to the altar had arrived more quickly, the sacrifice would have already started before the king even knew about it.

All the guilty individuals were bound securely and beaten with the utmost brutality.

Other people might have begged their masters for mercy. But on the part of Migan's servants, the least moan would have been interpreted as sheer poltroonery, and it would have redoubled the ardor of those who were persecuting them. The victims of the beating gritted their teeth, but their eyes remained dry.

When they were freed, they immediately returned to their places among the ranks of their companions, and no further mention was made of the punishment.

The drums continued to play at Ajahimê as groups of four or five relayed each other. The cannons roared at regular intervals. By the third crowing of the cock, the crowd of onlookers was already swarming around the altar and the drummers, looking for the cowries and glass beads which had come loose from their strings during the previous day's distribution and which were now covered by a thick layer of fine Canna sand that had been spread across the surface of the courtyard.

A few rare individuals ventured in the direction of the "hanging dogs."[15] The time had come for the vultures to take possession of the quarry. The first arrivals installed themselves between the legs of the victims; they whetted their appetites with morsels they found beneath their claws. One of them leaned over opened a grotesquely distended stomach with a slash of his beak. The slit widened. Tightly compressed intestines spewed out. A second slash of the beak released their excess gas and other contents, to the great joy of the flies. Other vultures followed the example of the first one. The Danhomênous avoided any place that was downwind of the cadavres but prudently refrained from any expression of repugnance, which could have gotten them into trouble.

The flies were also buzzing noisily around the butcher and the pig laid out on the counter in front of him. The people addressed a chorus of jeers to the butcher, who was allowing himself to be eaten, just like his merchandise, by the flies and the worms.

The sun rose to the level of the ear.

The baskets of food that followed the jugs of brandy, the small baskets of cowries, the hampers of cloths, and the entry of the Foreigners from the other side of the Swamps announced the arrival of the king. The festivities were about to begin again!

"What a happy life during the reign of the generous Father of Wealth!" The "horses" arrived, as always, firmly lashed to porters' racks. The royal drum boomed. The Representative of the Mother of Panther Sênoumê was at the head of the procession. The princes and high dignitaries appeared in the same order as they had on the previous day.

---

[15] The "hanging dogs" were human victims who had been crucified by their feet. (author's note)

The members of the families of former kings had changed clothes, but they remained less magnificently dressed than the brothers, sisters, wives, and sons of Guézo, although Pingla's descendants were more impressively adorned than the others.

Mêwou had objects, animals, and people arranged in their proper places. Migan imposed silence on all the drums. His assistants freed one hand of each "horse" and served them the traditional yam. Some ate their portion; others deposited it on the ground.

In his powerlessness to break his bonds, the lead "horse" threw his yam in Migan's face and spit in his direction, shouting: "People like you claim that you owe your ignoble position as executioner to your strength and courage. If your king would allow me to measure my force against yours, I swear I would break you in two like a twig, even if your body is made of iron."

The sacrificial priest seemed not to have heard this insolent challenge. From a small raphia bag held by his aides, he pulled out a little device made of two polished sticks; the larger measured a full span in length and was pointed at one end; the other end was firmly attached cross-wise to the middle of the smaller stick, the ends of which each sported a strong piece of string. The long stick was wrapped with raphia from the junction with the smaller stick to about a fingerlength from the point. Aided by his assistants, who bound the "horse's" hand again and held open his mouth by means of a wooden wedge, Migan placed the middle branch of his apparatus inside it, pulled the two strings backward, and tied them around the man's neck.

His mouth wide open and his eyes starting from their sockets, the Mahinou, who felt the device pressing down against his tongue and penetrating his gullet, struggled to get rid of it; he stretched his neck, shook his head, and tilted it to the rear but quickly straightened it again when pricked by the stick in his throat. Spittle dribbled from his mouth and ran over his chest. His desperate movements increased his torment and delighted the rabble.

"You have nothing more to say, Mahinou? Have you by any chance swallowed your tongue?" mocked the sacrificial priest.

That was like a signal to the common people: "Mahinou, have you swallowed your tongue?" they howled.

Confident in his invention, Migan allowed the "horse's" torments to last a bit longer. His radiant gaze shifted from the victim to the throne, inviting praise; then it wandered across the mob. But the Danhomênous were more inclined to address their applause to the Master of the World, whose superior intelligence alone was capable of inventing this muzzle to put a definite end to the impudence of the Mahinous.

The sacrificial priest planted himself in front of the "horse" and asked him his name three times. The victim's only response was the froth that slobbered from his mouth. Triumphant, Migan then threw himself on the Mahinou with the joy of a savage beast which, having brought down his prey, is about to drink its blood: "Well then, stinking beast from Hounjroto," cried the executioner, "go tell your fellow countryman who claims his name is 'Quench-Your-Thirst-With-

Blood' that, if the Mahinou has heart, the Danhomê is far from lacking it and even supplements it with an infinite amount of intelligence."

His scimitar fell upon the Mahinou and cleanly severed his head.

The amazed Danhomênous continued to praise the ingenuity of the king. . .

In no time at all, Migan's servants muzzled all the "horses" with the aid of "choke-pears", whose application was being witnessed for the first time in Danhomê.

Guézo triumphantly ascended the altar, and the sacrifice began. The king subsequently showered his subjects with cloths, cowries, and glass beads, over which people fought as eagerly and fiercely as they had the day before. Feasts and libations followed. Dances concluded the program on this second day of the celebrations.

The memory of King Tégbéssou and his wife Pojito Chayi was honored the following day. Then it was the turn of Agaja and the Queen Mother Adonon. On the fifth day, they celebrated the memory of Acaba and his mother Pojito Apatêwou; then Houégbaja was honored. The festivities concluded with a celebration in memory of Daco-Donou.

The further they went back into the past, the less splendor was displayed.

*   *   *

The day after the festivities, there was a meeting at Agrigomê of the great royal council that was composed of all the palace dignitaries, the brothers of Guézo, the heads of the families of former kings, Governors of provinces, regional chiefs, the heads of all organized services in the kingdom (such as water and hunting), the chief diviners, the doctors of the king, and all other Danhomênous who had distinguished themselves by their courage or their wisdom. Several new faces could also be seen there: those of soldiers who, having conducted themselves bravely since the first war of this reign, had earned the right to express their opinions in the government of the Danhomê to which they had given proof of their loyalty.

The council first settled the question of what gifts to offer the white men as souvenirs of their stay in Agbomê.

Then the king asked: "Isn't it true that someone who receives interesting news from a distant relative should share it with his friends?"

Everyone nodded their approval.

Pointing to a red clay alcarraza resting upon a solidly made little pillow, he told the counsellors: "Our cousin Dê from Hoghonou[16] informs me that the Ayonous, his neighbors to the East, are threatening to impose the old tribute upon Danhomê again and that the Wémênous[17] have promised to support them. Our cousin sent us these objects from Alada and communicated the following

---

[16] "Hoghonou" was a city in the kingdom of Porto-Novo. Têagbanlin, the founder of this kingdom, was the brother of Daco-Donou, the founder of Danhomê. (author's note)

[17] The "Wémênous" are inhabitants of the region called Wémê (Ouémé) after the large river that runs through it. (author's note)

message to us: 'Here is the little pillow that Agassou and Ajahouto[18] made together.' Let us watch over this symbol of conscientious worksmanship so that it shall be preserved in perfect condition.

"Here is the thin-necked alcarraza that Agassou and Ajahouto molded from clay. Never can two fingers enter it at the same time. As long as the descendants of Agassou and Ajahouto live in perfect harmony around these two objects, no enemy can conquer them."

He threw the little pillow into the air and allowed it to fall on the ground. A counsellor picked it up and gave it back to him. The king examined the object and proclaimed in a joyous tone of voice: "The little pillow of Agassou and Ajahouto did not come apart.

"It will serve us by cheerfully bearing the heavy burdens that our ancestors have bequeathed us."

Trying in vain to pass two fingers through the narrow neck of the alcarraza, he concluded: "Two fingers can not enter the alcarraza of Agassou and Agahouto at the same time. We will therefore not be divided by conflicting interests."

Everyone nodded approvingly once more.

His head lowered beneath the weight of his concerns, the king asked after a long silence: "What enemies should be feared by the Danhomê of Houégbaja?"

Migan assured him: "The Wémênous have been held in check since the reign of Agaja and no longer seem to pose any real threat. But the Ayonous of whom Dê was speaking are not our only enemies. The Mahinous, too, dream of dominating Danhomê so they might freely go and buy liquor and tobacco from the white man."

"If madness drives the Ayonous and Mahinous to attack Danhomê someday, they will be skewered on the end of my spear of Alada." Saying this, a standing Aplogan gripped his spear in both hands and made a thrust as if to combat enemies from the East as well as those from the "mahi" country to the North.

"And what will they have done with Gaou Gounada before having the audacity to attack Danhomê?" asked the first minister of war. "The time is past when Danhomê worried about eventual attacks from enemies. The god of war would certainly favor us in our struggles with the Ayonous. Isn't it more for themselves that our cousins from Hogbonou are afraid of an invasion by the Ayonous? The situation demands our continuing vigilance."

Possou Hagla did not wish to lag behind his fellow warrior; he said: "My soldiers and I are to the kingdom of Houégbaja what quills are to the porcupine. The fool who tries to seize that animal will not do so with impunity. Likewise Danhomê is no easy prey. And if its enemies succeed in vanquishing it while I am still alive, I ask to be tied to a stake where the soldiers of Houégbaja can pass by one at a time and cut off a piece of my flesh to be thrown to the dogs. As for what remains of my carcass, let it be fed to the caymans of the Zou."

The king confidently declared: "The time is indeed past when this kingdom was invaded every year by the Ayonous. Danhomê is today the scourge of its

---

[18] "Ajahouto" is a deified ancestor of the Aladahonous; he is worshipped by the descendants of Têagbanlin. (author's note)

former oppressors. Their blustering as reported to us by Dê should not disturb us overly much. But have all our domestic enemies been reduced to impotence?"

Linpéhoun assured him: "Adanzan was the only significant enemy inside the country. I don't think the fallen tyrant poses any serious danger today; Danhomênous prefer light to darkness, and they will not turn their backs on the Day Star in favor of a king who has been thrust into the shadows."

"That's true! That's true!" chorused the other counsellors approvingly. "The Danhomênous know that happiness can only be found in the hands of the never-aging son of the Sun!"

"Danhomê's security is perfectly assured with regard to its enemies!" proclaimed the king, whose face had taken on a happier expression. "Let us move on to other things. The council is not unaware of its obligation to be frank with me. I would like to hear its opinion of my rule. What does it find that is reprehensible?"

Mêwou spoke first: "None of the reproaches merited by the previous reign can be legitimately directed against yours. The king is not distant; he does not abandon himself to the pleasures of living in the Palace among his wives; he is not the one who fears the sun and the rain; he is not the one who supports the Danhomênou in his indolence; he is not unjust and cruel; he does not disregard the well-being of his people or the health and prosperity of the country,

"During rainy periods as during the hottest parts of the year, the Master of the World appears before his people; only meetings of the council or ceremonies within the Palace prevent you from coming to the threshold of the Door of the Universe. You discovered the energies lying dormant in the bodies of women, and you knew how to exploit it in creating the army of the Amazons. Danhomê is also in your debt for the standing army of men. The soldiers are treated well. Every year the Danhomênous engage in expeditions to avenge insults inflicted upon our ancestors, our friends, and our sense of propriety. Your reign is very gentle for the people, and your justice is like that of a father. What a difference from the reign of terror you overthrew!

"Every year you give money, cloths, bottles of alcohol, birds, goats, pigs, cattle, and even slaves as offerings to the principal fetishes of the kingdom so they will favor wives becoming mothers without complications; in this way Danhomê will have a large population. You also ask the fetishes to assure that sea voyages will take place without shipwreck and that Lègba will refrain from igniting fires or bloody battles in Danhomê. Well received and well protected during this reign, the white men do not conceal their joy at seeing their affairs prosper; Danhomê too has grown more wealthy. Life has become pleasant for the Danhomênous. Can't they freely acquire the good things the white men have brought, and don't they make use of these things as they see fit? It was far different during the previous reign when irksome regulations caused the white men to leave our country and led to the decline of the slave trade."

The court manifested its approval.

"In my opinion," said Houngan, Governor of the Province of Agonlin, "the king undertakes his wars a bit too hastily. That is the sole reason for our defeats.

Barely four years have passed since you acquired Danhomê. You have already undertaken four wars, that is to say one each year. If our defeats continue, they will discourage the country and embolden its enemies. The Ayonous are easier to fight than the Mahinous, because they are less protected by the mountains and especially because they have grown flabby as a result of the soft lives they lead; let us therefore turn against them."

Yévogan objected: "But the white men who carry on the slave trade prefer Mahinous over Ayonous!"

"Let them come and capture them themselves, if they can!" exclaimed Gaou. The assassination of three of their fellow countrymen at Kinglo offers them sufficient proof that the Mahinous are not the easy prey they were assumed to be."

"Danhomê cannot tolerate a powerful nation on its borders. All our efforts should therefore be deployed to weaken the 'mahi' countries," advised Possou.

Dêmênou diverted the course of the discussion when he expressed his opinion: "If our victories are the symbol of Danhomê's power in the eyes of its enemies, the kindness of the king threatens to destroy all respect for that power among the Danhomênous. Has anyone ever heard tell that Houégbaja punished odious blasphemies with a mere imprisonment? All Danhomê knows that they can only be expiated by death. I do not understand the king's weakness for Doguicimi."

The king had been expecting severe criticism from the royal council on the subject of his attitude toward the blasphemer, and he had prepared his defense.

"Danhomê worships courage. That woman is courage incarnate. To eliminate her would mean that we disdain a virtue that enabled us to create this kingdom and then to enlarge and fortify it.

"Doguicimi's outbursts are excusable in light of her anguish at having lost a husband she idolized."

Migan turned to his peers and looked interrogatingly at them: "Doesn't the king's indulgence foster a thousand invidious conjectures that reflect poorly on Houégbaja? Isn't that your opinion, Danhomênous?"

He received no more than a mute murmur of approbation.

"The mockeries provoked by our kindness would be nothing compared to the hatred that our cruelty might engender," the king responded.

The majority lined up on his side of the question.

Dêmênou did not consider himself beaten: "The king could have acted differently," he insisted once more. "Publicly condemning Doguicimi to death, for example, and then sending her into exile at Afomayi.[19] By the time Toffa returned to the country, the Danhomênous would already have forgotten the death sentence imposed on his wife, and she could have rejoined the prince in the greatest secrecy.

"The Master of the World's apparent harshness toward Doguicimi would guarantee that the people remain in fear of their sovereign."

---

[19]   "Afomayi" literally means "there where feet do not go;" it refers to a place of exile for princes and other high dignitaries whose crimes do not deserve the death penalty. (author's note)

142

"You are advising me to prefer hypocrisy over honesty!" retorted the indignant king.

A tumult of protests broke out and drowned his voice. He stopped speaking and only continued after order had been reestablished: "I cannot bring myself to be cruel. This people has suffered enough from tyranny. The Houégbajas have always sought to surpass their predecessors in something. As for me, I want to surpass them all in kindness. Only those people who have never fallen into error will disapprove of my resolve."

His gaze fell upon Vivênagbo. The former regent understood the allusion; he smiled. His voice was dominant among those of the counsellors who expressed their approval of the king.

Mêwou changed the subject of the discussion: "It seems to me that the king is concealing some illness from us. What is he suffering from? He is no longer his usual self; his collar-bones are showing, and his lower jaw is gaunt. Where does the Master of the World feel pain? Does he sleep well? His doctors are probably neglecting the treatments they should be giving him."

Migan consulted the doctors with a glance, but they vehemently proclaimed their zeal.

The king intervened: "I do not suffer from anything that can be treated by doctors. By itself, the sorrow I feel at seeing three of my brothers in 'mahi' captivity kills my appetite, disturbs my sleep, and depresses me."

Linpéhoun grumbled in reply: "The king is wrong to worry about such a trifle. The Houégbajas have entrusted Danhomê to you, and neglecting it because three brothers were lost at Hounjroto is likely to upset them!"

Guézo promised to change; he then informed himself about whether or not the number of births had increased since the last meeting of the great council, whether there were more foreigners in the country than before, whether fewer women were dying in childbirth, whether there had been any epidemics or unusually high mortality rates among men, women, older people, or children, whether the diviners were being reasonable in terms of the sacrifices they imposed upon people after having consulted Destiny, whether the doctors who cared for the people were charging them excessive fees, whether much precipitation had fallen in various parts of the kingdom during the last rainy season, whether the harvests had been good, whether the morale of the soldiers was high, whether the number of deaths in the army had increased or diminished, whether there had been many desertions (and if so what the cause of them had been), and whether or not his counsellors had any desires to express. He requested that they inform him honestly about the mood of the people.

In his position as Governor of a province that contributed greatly to the wealth of Danhomê, Yévogan was the first to take the floor: "The white men are becoming more and more demanding in their selection of the slaves Chacha is offering them; as a pretext for paying ridiculously low prices for the only merchandise they buy from us, they allege difficulties in the resale of such goods. Yet at the same time they are requesting a reduction in the tariffs imposed upon the import of cloth, alcohol, tobacco, iron, weapons of war, and ammunition."

"Nothing will be reduced!" Migan interrupted in a surly tone of voice. "The conditions set for them by the king of Danhomê are less restrictive than those imposed by Houfon upon the white men who do business in the 'houéda' kingdom. Don't these Foreigners know that the tariffs the king collects from them are expended solely to guarantee the safety of Danhomê, to assure that epidemics do not run rampant, and to foster the growth of the population as well as the prosperity of commerce?"

"Migan does not know the white men as well as Yévogan and I do," broke in Mêwou, the immediate superior of the Governor of Gléhoué. "I suggest that the reduction requested by our friends be granted. But in order not to lose in the process, the king shall require that they sell us their goods at a better price and that they agree to buy all the slaves we offer them. Two moons from now we will raise the tariff on alcohol and tobacco."

The king was of the opinion that he should do nothing until after having spoken with Chacha, who would come up to Agbomê as soon as he was well.

"I am requesting a hundred slaves to cultivate land near Alada," said Aplogan. "The produce will be equally divided between the throne and myself."

"The allotments proposed by the Governor of Alada are unreasonable," objected Houéliji, the head of the agriculture section. "Doesn't the Governor realize that the king has many mouths to feed? In addition to the people at the Palace, there are soldiers who, as long as they are well nourished, will always assure us of victory. In an imperative tone of voice, the dignitary settled the point: "The king should have the right to two of every three storage bins. Does Aplogan agree?"

The Governor nodded affirmatively, but he muttered about Houéliji's zealousness.

When Segan was consulted about the number of available slaves, he leaned toward Bapé, his chief assistant, and then, facing the throne, informed the council: "More than three thousand slaves are waiting for the Master of the World to make use of their hands."

Aplogan would receive his serfs. Joyously he kissed the ground as an expression of his gratitude.

"What good does it do to dream about the prosperity of Danhomê, an increase in its population, and the abundance of food if we only produce and reproduce for the benefit of the enemy?" asked Houngan. "The council must also consider Danhomê's security. I cannot emphasize this point too much. Allow me to distance myself from the premature confidence of the council. I sent nearly a thousand used guns to Agbomê. In return, I only received five hundred, and they were badly used. During the council that followed last year's celebrations, I asked for a thousand soldiers, and it was only two markets ago that I received four hundred of them. The Ayonous are restless, as Dê has indicated. Fongni confided in me that the Wémênous are no less so. I will not be responsible if you continue to skimp on your expenditures for the security of Danhomê."

Questioning glances passed alternately from Gaou to Possou.

The first minister of war did not let people wait long for his reply: "The

144

plan for an expedition against the Mahinous and that alone had delayed the sending of troops to Houngan. Their numbers had been reduced because the permanent council estimated that the army at the disposition of Houngan and Fongni was sufficient to hold in check our enemies to the East. Our cousin Dê, whom they would encounter on their march toward Agbomê, could give us ample warning. And we would have enough time to send reinforcements to the two battle captains who are guarding our eastern borders."

It was decided that Houngan and Fongni would leave Agbomê with five hundred well-equipped soldiers.

"Since the last meeting of the great council, I have supplied the throne with thirty thousand sacks of smoked game from all my provinces," Pogba informed the council. "I received no more than a thousand guns and a thousand small kegs of powder. Furthermore, the king has done nothing to diminish the dangers of the hunt; nearly three hundred Danhomênous have been devoured by wild animals this year; exactly ninety-six guns have exploded in the hands of their owners and killed them; two hundred hunters have injured their feet during their excursions through the forest; more than half of them died of their wounds. People have been stingy in putting together the offerings we leave in the forests so that the guardian spirits there will protect hunters from all accidents."

The last criticism was addressed to the king. He responded to it with some intensity: "I provided more offerings than were necessary to muzzle the savage beasts. As for accidents that have been caused by guns and wild animals, they cannot be imputed to the negligence of the king. Who knows whether these victims might not have betrayed a sworn friendship and were merely expiating their broken oaths? Our sacrifices are only supposed to benefit those who are innocent of sacrilege.

"A prohibition against footwear has been imposed upon the common people in Danhomê, but it does not apply to hunters. Some need only to exercise moderation in loading their charges of powder, others to protect their feet with a sturdy pair of sandals and to watch where they are going; in that way, accidents like those mentioned by Pogla would no longer have to be lamented in the future."

"The chief hunter has no doubt anticipated my criticism; our soldiers would have starved to death if we relied solely upon him to provide them with food. Fortunately, the king's herds of cattle supplied us with the meat we needed," said Gaou in support of the king.

Pogba's chief assistant Agoujan suggested: "The hunters' precautions alone will never suffice. It is absolutely necessary to double the offerings made to the protective spirits of the forest in order to incline them favorably toward human beings."

Mêgbémê, the chief fisherman of the coastal regions, took up the argument: "People have not only been stingy in their offerings to the forest, but also in those for the rivers. During previous reigns they never engulfed as many travelers as we are lamenting today, nor have they ever refused with such obstinacy to deliver up the fish they shelter in their depths: bow-nets, draw nets, seines, and baited hooks frequently return to the surface of the water without the tiniest fish.

"You will never know the difficulties we overcame and the privations we endured to furnish Agbomê with the two thousand baskets of fish and dried shrimp it received. Rivers overflowed their banks in many places and forced the nearby inhabitants to flee; at night floods carried away those who were too obstinate to leave; canoes sank with their cargoes, their crews, and their passengers. Caymans devoured more than a hundred Danhomênous. I only know of a single remedy for these misfortunes: increase the offerings!"

"The problems of the fisheries and the damages caused by floods were no less severe on the banks of the Zou, the Hlan, the Coufo, and the Wo," reported Ahanlanho and Potohossou, the two chief fishermen for the rivers bordering on the region of Agbomê, in support of Mêgbémê's point.

The council decided to augment the offerings to the waters and the forests to appease the anger of the spirits who inhabited them.

Facing the chief fishermen, Jagba, the head of the water service chuckled: "Divert the surplus water of your rivers and streams to Agbomê, and you will earn the gratitude of the Danhomênous. Our springs dried up during a good part of the year. My servants were obliged to go as far as Zado in search of water with which to supply the Palace, the residences of the high dignitaries, and the soldiers on a regular basis. This year the drought was so severe that the thirsty cattle attacked people returning from the water detail, broke open their clay jars, and drank the water that spilled on the ground.

"Danhomê is sufficiently powerful today that it no longer need fear an enemy invasion, and that was the only consideration that prevented our ancestors from drilling wells."

His opinion was not shared by others.

Vaokinto, the chief supplier of red pepper, requested that this spice be cultivated in all the provinces. His assistants had visited more than a hundred farms without being able to fill five sacks. The forty servants sent to Gléhoué four moons ago had returned to Agbomê with a single sack of peppers. Yévogan had told them that the mouths of Gléhoué had as much right to red peppers as those of Agbomê.

"Can one imagine soldiers who are spirited and victorious without having eaten adequately spiced caloulous? For once our irreconcilable enemies the Ayonous are right, since they say that red pepper is the appropriate remedy for anyone who wants to live a long time.

"Yévogan does not, I believe, desire our soldiers to grow soft and the court to disappear in the near future.

The Governor of Gléhoué protested energetically against the statements and attitudes attributed to him, and he explained that, if Vaokinto's servants only found a single sack of peppers in his province, it was because they arrived after the harvest.

Supported by Gaou and Possou, Vaokinto prevailed, and Gléhoué was charged with furnishing two hundred sacks of peppers each year.

All the counsellors who had wishes to express were accorded the opportunity to express them. The council listened to everything, discussed at great length, accepted what they considered useful, and rejected what seemed to them contrary to the best interest of Danhomê or simply inappropriate.

Exaggerated claims were invariably brought back within the bounds of truth by Ajaho's commentaries.

The heir to the throne observed a strict silence and hung on every word of the discussion.

Orders were given to satisfy reasonable requests.

Houngan and Fongni were given renewed assurances that they would be leaving Agbomê with weapons and soldiers as well as rewards (wives, money, cloths, and sashes) for those assistants to whom the two battle captains had called attention for their zealousness and good counsel.

Mêwou received money, cloths, and alcohol that he would send to Cacalacoun. The principal customs officer would pass all these presents on to Avrékéténon, the chief fetishist of Avrékété, who would proceed to make all the necessary sacrifices to protect the boatmen who crossed the bar.

The minister entrusted Yévogan with cloths, liquor, money, two head of cattle, and two young female captives of recognized purity for Hounon. The pontiff of the fetishists at Gléhoué would exorcise the entire city; he would then cross the bar on the back of a steer, go out far from the coast, and marry the two young virgins to the fetish Hou, presenting him with gifts that had been prepared at the court. This important fetish would henceforth be favorably inclined toward the affairs of the white men who had brought wonderful things, including the instruments of Danhomê's victories.

The king insisted upon passing out a few souvenirs to the new counsellors. He gave them money, cloths, fringed sashes, bottles of the white man's alcohol, and wives. The soldier who had brought back the head of the "mahi" chief was admitted to the council for the first time. Because he regarded the wife who had been given to him as ugly and unworthy of his valor, he kissed the ground at the foot of the throne and said: "My heroic act deserves more than the baboon given to me in return for the trophy I brought back from Hounjroto, all the more so because this young girl is my first wife!"

"You have spoken the truth," declared the king with approval. "Let him be given a second wife, additional cloths, and more cowries."

Covering himself with dirt as an expression of his gratitude, the new counsellor exclaimed: "If Hounjroto has ten chiefs, I vow to bring back all their heads the next time we engage in a campaign against that country. If I do not fulfill my promise, let me be cut to pieces and my flesh be fed to the dogs of Danhomê!"

Banquets followed the meeting of the council. By the time the palace dignitaries left, the sun had already climbed overhead.

The crowd of princes and common people who had gathered in the Courtyard of the Great Palace were wide-eyed with envy as they stared at the dignitaries. They pointed their fingers toward those whom the Father of Wealth had just showered with presents.

Soldiers were proudly carrying sabres attached to fringed velvet sashes on their hips. Those who had received wives in addition to this distinctive emblem of their courage on the battlefield were holding the wrists of these young girls tightly in a pincer-like, iron grip and hurrying toward their homes, a smile on their lips and joy in their hearts.

Migan informed the people that the Predestined King would reappear as soon as the sun, whose arrows had just begun to rain straight down, would have turned his head. For the courtiers, this announcement constituted an order not to leave the Courtyard. All those who desired to retreat behind the hedge to satisfy whatever needs they might have would do their utmost to return quickly.

*   *   *

The sun had turned his face toward his dwelling place behind Coufo and was already moving in that direction.

Soon the high walls of the Palace and Guézo's second story were blocking the view of the day star. Shadows covered nearly all of the Great Courtyard where the swarm of courtiers was buzzing and milling about.

Migan's servants arrived with the white men's chairs and arranged them to the left of the throne. Twelve lavishly dressed, pubescent girls appeared. Each was carrying a large basket. They set down their burdens and kneeled behind them. Other servants came and placed next to each basket a demijohn of brandy and a raphia sack with bulging contours that proclaimed it was not empty.

Avoutou roared. Dogba replied. The "birds of the king" sang: "Eh, the bird! Eh, the bird of prey. . . !"

The king arrived. The Danhomênous threw themselves face down in the dust and covered their heads with it as they expressed their best wishes for the health, longevity, and power of the Master of the World so that he could continue to offer his subjects such magnificent festivities.

Yévogan showed the white men to their places. The dust that had been raised was suffocating them, and more than one of them was burying his nose in his handkerchief. One of them, who was quite familiar with the customs of the court and the sensibilities of the monarch, discreetly advised them to put away their handkerchiefs.

Upon a sign from Daclo, Migan crossed the bamboo barrier and crawled on his hands and knees toward the king. The queens moved aside. With outstretched arms, Daclo as usual protected them from the polluting touch of mortals.

Returning toward the white men, the minister conveyed the king's message to them; an interpreter was standing beside them. He translated: "The King of the Universe hopes that you, his friends from beyond the Swamps, have enjoyed yourselves during these festivities and that you are satisfied with your stay in Agbomê.

148

"He sends you back to your concerns with the promise that he will favor the expansion of the slave trade.

"The Father of Wealth desires to leave you with a souvenir of these celebrations. To each of you for your own personal use, he is giving a demijohn of brandy and a sack of cowries so that you can acquire other souvenirs from Agbomê. He is bestowing upon you as well a cloth woven in Danhomê and a young female captive who will sweep your house and bring you water. Each of your porters has been given a bottle of brandy.

"Chacha Ajinacou, the great friend of the Master of the World, will receive his gifts from the hands of Yévogan. The King of the Universe grants you permission to depart from Agbomê as early as tomorrow. He has commanded Yévogan to watch over you during your journey. A procession of Danhomênous with drummers in the lead will accompany you as far as the edge of the Swamps."

The minister returned to the foot of the throne, prostrated himself, and covered his head with dust; he reported: "The message of the Father of Wealth has been faithfully transmitted to his friends!"

Standing up, the white men bowed toward the throne; the candid smiles on their faces bespoke their joy; with their open palms facing downward, their outstretched arms moved up and down three or four times as if they were fanning the throne; the friends of the king were thanking him for his generosity.

The Danhomênous acclaimed the munificence of the Father of Wealth, who was also a Providence for bachelors. . . .

The king went back into the Palace, followed by the high dignitaries; the white men returned to their lodgings. For the king, the joy manifested by his friends was due to the presents and, above all, to the promise they had just received. But the confidences exchanged among these foreigners and overheard by the interpreter, who immediately reported them to the king, soon disabused him: "These foreigners are in a hurry to leave Agbomê, where they have been deafened by so much noise and where their hearts have been wrenched by so many horrors. They would risk going mad, they affirmed, if they had to stay until the next market. One of them said these exact words: 'Last night my sleep was interrupted by the cries of the sacrificial victims who were reproaching me for having abetted – by my silence, by my indulgence for their murderers, and by my very presence at these festivities – the crime that was perpetrated against them!'"

The next morning the monumental altar in the Courtyard of Ajahimê had disappeared just as it had emerged from nowhere on the eve of the celebrations.

The Courtyard where the festivities had taken place was invaded by an army of urchins, their bodies so dusty they seemed to have been disinterred that very morning, their bloated bellies shining, and their legs so skinny they seemed incapable of supporting such a heavy burden. With their hands and feet they were sifting the sand in search of the glass beads and cowries buried there.

Stronger boys suddenly appeared, bowled over the smaller ones, pummeled them, and tore the found objects out of the feeble hands that were holding them up. Devious ones asked to see the lucky find and then appropriated it for themselves. Fists flew in children's faces; the weaker ones resorted to their teeth and their screams to protect their possessions; a few older ones intervened, and others turned their backs.

Among the ranks of the sacrificial "dogs," flesh was hanging from bones and turning to liquid. Nests of worms fell to the ground, much to the delight of the lizards who snapped them up.

The flies were also picking through the leftovers. They buzzed with indignation at the children who were disturbing their quarry.

Male and female fetishists from all the shrines had returned to their homes and had thus taken off the ceremonial attire and the symbols they wore during religious rites. The narrow, woven raphia band that circled their heads above the ears as well as the two strings of fine cowries or black grains that were wound around their biceps, their wrists, and their ankles signified that they were still partially possessed by the fetish and therefore in a sacred state. For that matter, they continued to speak in the language of the fetishes. Floods of them spread through the whole city and into the smallest market places. As they returned to normal life, these fetishists were renewing their acquaintance with the profane world and profiting from public veneration by gathering supplies of food and cowries in little baskets that they were relearning how to use. The male and female worshippers of Sapata excited laughter by their licentious remarks.

*   *   *

Among all the high dignitaries who came to the Palace on the day after the departure of the white men, only the heir to the throne was retained for a discussion with his august Father.

They retired to the privacy of the room where Agonglo had slept his last sleep. Guézo installed himself on the bed that had been prepared for the dead king's repose. Vidaho sat down on a mat that was spread out at the foot of the bed. His legs crossed, his arms pressed against the sides of his body, his head lowered, the young prince listened in this humble position to the advice that he knew was being heard by his grandfather.

After a moment of reflection, Guézo said to his heir: "You have been chosen to govern this people, of whom you have seen all types during these past few days as they assembled for the celebrations that take place around my throne.

"These celebrations were strewn with incidents that are regrettable for the common run of mortals but infinitely rich in instruction for superior beings like us.

"For people who are supposed to know only the awe-inspiring side of many things in this country, Danhomê is a sacred sphere that must remain hidden from the eyes of the Danhomênous and be passed on from one king to the next as they succeed each other on the throne of Houégbaja.

150

"In reality, Danhomê is no more than a profound knowledge of the very complex and mysterious soul of the Danhomênous.

"This knowledge can only be acquired by the prince who has probed the depths of the past, the customs, and the institutions of this kingdom.

"I will not wait much longer to conduct you there because death arrives at the moment we least expect it.

"It is true that Destiny has predicted a long life for me. But his predictions have so often been proved wrong by events that I have finally lost confidence in him. When I recall, moreover, that this oracle has come to us from the country of the Yoruba, an irreconcilable enemy of Danhomê, I ask myself whether these Yorubas didn't very cleverly give us the oracle, which they claim to be both wisdom itself and an infallible means of predicting the future, in order to inspire us with a confidence that will allay our vigilance.

"Therefore, a knowledge of human nature will be a more reliable guide than the oracle in the governance of this country, if you can supplement that knowledge with the teachings of the tradition bestowed upon us by the ancestors whom you have been chosen to replace on the throne of Danhomê, and if you do not lose sight of the prudent advice of your august Father.

"Danhomê is like a large earthenware jug that, although riddled with tiny holes, was bequethed to us by Houégbaja with the express order that we pass it on to our successor without spilling a single drop.

"Every king who desires to conserve this sacred trust intact must protect his people, foster the prosperity of their families, and earn the veneration of his subjects; it is on these conditions that he will assemble a sufficiently large number of Danhomênous around the jug to plug all the holes with their fingers and thereby prevent any water from escaping and emptying the container.

"My predecessors always based their royal authority upon impressive processions and the privileges of wearing sandals on their feet, being carried in a hammock, and sheltering themselves with parasols.

"Accustomed to submission, the Danhomênou will hasten at any moment to execute promptly the orders of his sovereign.

"Being the Master, the king must have a proud, indolent bearing and make stately gestures; activity is a sign of servitude, just as impatience is a sign of weakness.

"Realize, however, that these external trappings and affectations will be worth nothing, unless they are complemented by virtues of the heart and intellect – the only virtues capable of elevating you above common Danhomênous and giving you a true sense of dignity.

"Respect wisdom even if the person embodying it is from a low station in life. Does someone condemn you for that? Invoke the example of your august Father: he pardoned the Mahinou who reminded us, in the song he sang on the first day of the celebration, that life is full of misfortunes for those who do not die in childhood.

"This wise man was telling the truth! Did Adanzan and his sons foresee their Fate? Do I myself know what Destiny holds in store for me?

151

"Anyone who reflects upon the unfortunate ends suffered by this kingdom's great figures, those whose dignity was thought to have removed them forever from the sphere of human miseries, will become wise and treat the humble with kindness.

"Examine the songs that are popular with the common people. Songs are the best weapons of the weak. Having neither knife nor club to avenge the injustice inflicted upon him and lacking access to the court, where he might lodge his complaints, the man of the people first takes consolation in songs and then uses them to obtain justice. For a king, popular songs are thus an important source of information about the mood of his subjects, and for everyone they represent a valuable source of knowledge about the past.

"The Danhomênou changes his opinions more quickly than a chameleon changes colors. Wherever you encounter an honest man, shower him with favors. If you can, elevate him to the highest positions. In that way, you will surely succeed in inculcating the masses with the constancy of the Mahinou who refused to violate the prohibition of Destiny.

"After having experienced a Danhomê that tyranized over princes and commoners without distinction, a Danhomê that disdained wisdom and purity, a Danhomê that abandoned itself to debauchery while encouraging hypocrisy and obsequiousness, I would like to see a Danhomê that is just, good, fair, and solicitous of promoting virtue. Continue in my tradition, and you will have amply honored my memory.

"To those who desire to incite you to crimes and tell you that 'Danhomê was created by force and can only live, prosper, and grow larger through the use of force,' you should reply: 'Force was indeed necessary to deal with the savages whom our ancestors encountered shortly after their arrival in this region. Such a weapon is useless against subjects who have given proof of their loyalty.'

"If you need to resort in certain cases to force, you should not exclude considerations of humanity and justice. Do not act in such a way that posterity will associate you with Adanzan in its curses. On the contrary, conduct yourself in such a manner that people will bless your name as they do those of Houégbaja and Agaja.

"Do not accede to the will of the rabble. There is nothing noble about it. It is characterized only by ignorance, folly, and cruelty. And it is totally lacking in courage. When it does arise among such people, they become insolent. But in normal times, the rabble is a contemptible coward. As a benefactor, it is too demanding for those who are in its debt. For this reason, I have always refused to be in its debt for anything. It was detached from Adanzan as easily as a snail is detached from a tree on which it is resting. The rabble would have killed the tyrant if the princes had not energetically opposed it. Do you remember Doguicimi's first tirade against the throne at a moment when the news of her husband's disappearance had momentarily deranged her mind? At first the rabble was petrified. But the indignation of a Wife of Panther must have suddenly instilled it with courage. It rediscovered its voice and called for a torture heretofore unknown in this kingdom. Its cruelty precipitated it into folly:

it proposed that the blasphemer's lower jaw be ripped out and that she be given her tongue to eat. Believing that it was saying something sensible, it bombarded me for a long time with its inanities. Yet how can you make people eat anything if they no longer have jaws? Intoxicated with their folly, the rabble obstinately insisted upon calling for this torture as if it were a real possibility.

"Refrain from committing the least injustice.

"Always tell yourself that there is no such thing as a little tyranny.

"See how quick the human mind is to distort the truth. It is no longer Adanzan who usurped my throne. But I am the one who is regarded as the usurper. The Mahinou who claimed he was called 'Quench-Your-Thirst-With-Blood' was merely echoing the rumor that had no doubt traveled discreetly from Danhomê to the 'mahi' country. Expect your best actions to be misinterpreted. But far from taking offense at the injustice of men and dealing harshly with them, you should persevere in the path of goodness and justice. Slander will never harm you as much as the evil you do yourself.

"Departing from the tradition which decrees that all princes should be prevented from holding positions of responsibility in this kingdom, I have entrusted several of them with such positions in return for their loyalty and devotion at the time of my struggle against Adanzan. Deal tactfully with the sensitivities of the princes and the important personages of the kingdom. They are very jealous of their privileges. But do not seek to outdo your august Father in generosity. Limit yourself rather to the usual gifts: wives, slaves, fiefs, cowries, the white man's alcohol, and cloths. Prudently keep the princes away from positions of authority in your government. Bestow complete confidence only on common people and captives who have grown up in Danhomê and whose loyalty is incorruptible. If you want to avoid serious problems, never lose sight of the following maxim: 'Just as dampness bloats a seed and causes it to rot, positions of responsibility swell princes with a stupid pride that causes them to revolt against royal authority, as witness the conduct of Topa and Aguidissou at Alada.'[20]

"When you are obliged to deal harshly with the princes, do not listen to your anger or to your retinue, no matter how odious their crimes might have been. Do not forget that the blood of a prince must never be shed upon this soil. Be content with exiling princes convicted of crimes to Afomayi. If you are implacable, you will soon become inhuman.

"In the eyes of Foreigners and even Danhomênous who only judge by appearances, the king is the image of power. Yet I do not have all the authority I am reputed to have in this kingdom. Imprisoned in tradition, obsessed with customs from which I must not stray by a single step, and petitioned by those

---

[20] "Topa" and "Aguidissou" were sons of Agaja, the fourth king of Danhomê, and therefore brothers of Tégbéssou, the fifth king. Aguidissou's mother had plotted unsuccessfully with the Ayonous to have her son placed on the throne instead of Tégbéssou. Aguidissou himself later revolted against the authority of his brother the king at Alada. For having severely criticized the harsh suppression of that revolt by the king, Topa was cursed by his brother Tégbéssou. (author's note)

in my entourage, I am, most of the time, no more than an instrument in a multitude of hands that are invisible to the people, who attribute many so-called royal acts to me, although in reality they have been conceived and executed by my secret Masters. The king is perhaps the person with the least freedom in this entire kingdom, and yet he is at the same time the most unhappy, because he is obliged to walk in the ruts of tradition and submit to the will of the court at the very moment when he is expected to maintain the dignity of being in command; he must often permit action to take place in front of his eyes, even when his conscience disapproves of them. As far as the people are concerned, orders that are carried out emanate solely from the person whom they, in their naiveté, regard as sovereign and call the Master of the World.

"It is not with joy in my heart that I order human sacrifices. Agaja is great. But the important contributions he made to this kingdom have been tarnished in my eyes by the human sacrifice that he instituted as a customary practice.

"You should know that it is only under pressure that I commemorate each year the crucifying that began under Tégbéssou's rule. Yet if I attempted to suppress these horrors, my standing would immediately fall in the eyes of the people because this sadism has become a part of their customs. I believe I will have done enough during my reign by refusing to allow other horrors to be added to these sacrifices, as Migan would like to do. If I had not intervened in time, this sadist would have offered the Danhomênous a spectacle unprecedented in the traditions of this country – a spectacle that he with joy in his heart called the "roasting of the groundnuts" – and he would have done it in my name. He did not think of the indignation that would inevitably have revolted the proud sensibilities that graced Danhomê with the artisans of its power and greatness. I Guézo would have bequeathed an ignoble example to history!

"The kings of this country never want to lag behind their predecesors. I can already see what you would have striven to add to the abomination that Migan was going to commit in my name if I had not stopped him in time.

"To honor my memory, try to surpass me in virtue, if you can, and avoid actions that will cause your name to be cursed as it is passed on to posterity.

"Never allow yourself to be pushed into a war against the white men. Their friendship has always been profitable for Danhomê and in particular for your august Father, who owes his throne in part to one of them. Remember that your grandfather so esteemed the manners of these white men that he enticed a household of them to his court, and they initiated him into the customs of their country. Make friends among the white men who are living in this kingdom. There are more than enough means at your disposal to acquire their friendship. But the Blood Oath is the most certain. Attach these friends to your person by according them privileges. In small part out of gratitude but largely in response the the needs of my policies, I named Chacha Ajinacou a viceroy of Gléhoué. Ever since I came into possession of this kingdom, Yévogan's task has been reduced to serving as the eyes and ears of Danhomê in our coastal province. Yes, Yévogan is merely an observer because prudence requires that every king have a secret police that accurately informs him of everything, down to the most insignificant yawns of his subjects and the foreigners living in his country.

"Be particularly solicitous toward the sons of Chacha. Whatever crimes they may commit, treat them with clemency. The Blood Oath that binds me to the Father imposes obligations upon my successor to safeguard the sons.

"When you have disagreements with the white men, invite them to a palaver at Agbomê. In that way you will be better able to assess their mood. Never trust the reports of an intermediary; he can sow discord between you and the white men and diminish you in their esteem.

"The white men now living in Danhomê are honest and good. I would like to hope that the sons will be worthy of their fathers.

"Danhomênous live exclusively in the present, whereas the white men are constantly dreaming of the future. In this regard they are superior to us. Chacha Ajinacou foresaw that the slave trade would fall into disrepute, and he found a new source of revenue for Danhomê in the cultivation of our palm groves. I have been much preoccupied with this idea lately, and I would like to share it with you.

"Lend your protection to Foreigners when they are honest; they import the experiences of another people into the country where they settle.

"Certain Danhomênous are interested in the elimination of a few individuals, and they will condemn your magnanimity or hold you up to ridicule if you resist their attempts to incite you against the innocent. Always remind them of the pardon your august Father accorded Adanzan and Doguicimi.

"What arguments have the Royal Wives not adduced to obtain that woman's head!

"It is true that the wife of Toffa has made herself guilty of reprehensible aberrations of language. But her curses – my tragic end, the enslavement of my successor, my death far from the Danhomê of Houégbaja, and who knows what else – are no more than impassioned outbursts during moments of confusion brought on by her sorrow at having lost her husband. When I will have brought back her husband to her, she will surely repent. For that matter, I have never worried about my own death. I do not see what catastrophe might shorten my life. The knife of a Danhomênou? People's minds in this country are too submissive ever to conceive of such a crime. The shot of a soldier overcome by a fit of raging madness? Could I forestall such an end if it is part of my fate? Die on the battlefield? But that would be glorious! It is true that, according to the ideas of the Danhomênous and their enemies, this sort of death is dishonorable for a king because it would be intepreted as the expiation for some offense against a sworn friendship. But a prince should free his mind of the commonplace ideas of the people.

"I will therefore not acquiesce to the demands of the Wives of Panther. A king must protect those of his subjects whose criticisms reveal to him what is reprehensible in his government, just like a mirror alerts us to our physical imperfections. Our ancestors were right when they affirmed that the monarch who does not tolerate criticism will show himself in public with spots on his clothes.

"In my haste to relieve the suffering of the families and griefstricken wives who could find no consolation for the loss of those who did not return from Hounjroto, I failed to perform the purificatory rite that is supposed to absolve a king for offenses committed against his ancestors, for the death of presumably innocent individuals he had executed on the basis of false accusations or in a fit of anger, and for injustices perpetrated upon the living as well as upon his own person. This purification ceremony protects the king against illnesses and misfortunes that are regarded as an expiation for the violation of traditional custom or as a punishment for his crimes; it also predisposes the ancestors to support him for a long time and to assure his happiness on the throne of Houégbaja.

"The sycophantic courtiers did not dare remind me of this omission, but Doguicimi had the courage to shout it in my face.

"The failure to observe this religious rite explains the incidents that somewhat tarnished the brilliance of our celebrations.

"We were also defeated in the war of Hounjroto for not having listened to the ancestors and for having violated the custom concerning a declaration of war.

"The barbarity of the tortures being proposed as the only possible means of assuring the expiation of Doguicimi's blasphemies made me suspicious, and I soon discovered the reason for the hatred that the queens and Migan bear this unfortunate woman. Neither they nor he were in any way implicated, as they would have me believe, in the curses that Toffa's wife addressed to me on two separate occasions. They pursue her with their hatred solely because she surpasses them in virtue; she is a treasure of love and marital fidelity, a truly martial soul who by herself would have done more to adorn my Palace than all the women whom I have brought together there and whose only reason for living seems to reside in a desire to plot schemes against an honest woman."

He paused, became contemplative for a moment, and then continued energetically, as if replying to some inner question: "Yes! Doguicimi was worthy only of the Master of the World or his heir. I was lacking in perceptiveness when I married her to Toffa. You cannot imagine the depth of my regret at having suffered such a loss.

"Eliminating that woman would be to tell all Danhomê that the high cult of the virtues she embodies – courage and fidelity – has been forever abolished in this kingdom.

"Danhomênous are not fools. That is to say, they recognize, as I do, the exemplary qualities of Doguicimi. But since the important people of this kingdom never suffer their neighbors to surpass them by a hair, ministers and queens are conspiring the death of that woman.

"In the bottom of the hearts of all the high dignitaries whom you see lying prostrate in front of your august Father there simmers the hatred of knowing they are not my equal. Do not doubt it for a moment.

"Migan is the most influential of my ministers, and he governs Danhomê with me, but he is secretly jealous of Vivênagbo, to whom I entrust the regency

156

during expeditions that rarely last more than three long markets.

"The man of the people who presented me with tinder two days before the beginning of our celebrations has but a single desire – not to lag behind my other subjects.

"The Danhomênous never look down, always up, and they all want to bring others down to their level. It is from the country itself that they acquire this attitude; isn't Danhomê always jealous of any power that is not its own?

"Having clearly understood the base instinct that motivates their relentless attacks on Doguicimi, who is the very incarnation of the highest virtues of our race, I pardon her all her abuse. I will have her freed this very evening."

He paused to listen to an objection from his son. But with a nod of the head and a smile that brightened his face, the prince approved of his august Father's decision.

Then the king proceeded: "It will not be enough for you to resist the instigation of the rabble to commit crimes against honest people whom Destiny has raised above the lizards. Following my example, strive as well to cure your people of their morbid tendency to bring everything down to their level, for it paralyzes the best intentions and hobbles the rise of the Danhomênous.

"Ah, why do these people, despite their intelligence, fail to realize that any attempt to equal their superior by raising themselves to his level is infinitely profitable, whereas the country suffers when they undermine him to bring him down to a lower level! The Danhomênous would make rapid progress on the road to perfection if they could understand that they should strive to reach the level of excellence rather than reducing it to their level."

The heir to the throne touched his forehead to the ground and kissed the floor at the feet of his royal Father: "Since the ennoblement of this people's soul is no less dear to the hearts of our ancestors than is the aggrandizement of Danhomê, my life shall be consecrated to the attainment of these two goals. From now on, the image of Danhomê will also be etched in my mind – a jug riddled with holes but containing water that must be passed on intact to my successor. To be certain of retaining this allegory, I will have it carved in bas-relief at my Palace.

"Following my august Father's example, I pardon Doguicimi for her diatribes against me, and I will henceforth take her under my protection."

Satisfied with his heir's promise to continue in the tradition of his father (that is, to be magnanimous, just, and kind), Guézo dismissed him with assurances that he enjoyed the king's benediction as well as those of his ancestors.

Chapter 5

From Hate to Love

More than the insight he had been accorded into the soul of the Dan-homênous, more than the advice he had received about how to govern Danhomê and render glorious hommage to the memory of his ancestors in order to reign for a long time, and more than the counsel he had been given about how to conduct himself vis-a-vis the white men in the hope of gaining their friendship, the discovery of Doguicimi as as treasure of valour greatly preoccupied the thoughts of the heir to the throne.

He had been counted among those who were secretly plotting the fall of the wife of Toffa. But whereas the other enemies of Doguicimi were motivated by vulgar emotions like jealousy and vengefulness, he was angry at her for having attacked everything he held sacred – the ancestors, the throne of Houégbaja, the reigning king, in short Danhomê itself. His august Father, who ought to be the first to take offense at Doguicimi's blasphemy, had just revealed to him that it was a sign of courage and that to punish the woman would be to proclaim that Danhomê henceforth disdains this highest virtue of the race.

The king had unwittingly cast into this passionate, receptive soul the seed of a love that would grow despite the young prince's efforts to stifle it, for his conscience represented all its dangers to him.

From the day he made his discovery, Vidaho knew that the throne of Houégbaja was not the only thing he lacked to make his happiness complete: not a single woman in his large harem was comparable to the wife of Toffa. He felt very much humiliated by this realization.

Many times a day the image of Doguicimi appeared to his mind's eye, triggering a pleasant sensation that ran through his body and spread across his face. He saw the woman standing, sometimes as she was on the morning of Guézo's return from the war of Hounjroto, sometimes in the stance she had adopted on the first day of the traditional celebrations; he heard her, at the court as in the Courtyard of Ajahimê, flinging her blasphemies, which transfixed the people, into the face of the Idol of the Danhomênous. Her curses no longer made him indignant; quite the contrary, he was charmed by them. He said to himself: "She is courage personified. No doubt at all that she must have been fathered by a prince from Danhomê; only a person whose body is steeped in the blood of our ancestor Agassou (the Panther) could have had the audacity of that woman. Her captivating appearance, the clear and engaging tone of her voice, her refined manners, her confident courage, everything about her betrays her noble origins. She is of the same phalanx as the queen Yêpommê Avognondé, who fired on the followers of Adanzan when they invaded the Palace to pillage it before lighting the fire. In Doguicimi alone are united all the various virtues that are usually scattered among a hundred women. Whoever has the good fortune to possess her could desire nothing more. That's the secret behind the constant joy that radiated from Toffa's face; it's also the explanation for the great wisdom that characterized him. One could only benefit from being with this woman: in moments of weakness, one would draw energy, courage, and perseverence from this woman's presence, as well as the wisdom necessary to govern people who only worship a man capable of imposing himself upon them by his great virtue. The sons Doguicimi bore to a king would unite all the qualities needed to acquire Danhomê and to enlarge it through conquest. In this kingdom, the king or his heir should have a monopoly over all the best things. And if it occurs that these things happen to be in the hands of the Danhomênous, they should be stripped of them to the benefit of the persons of rank for whom they are appropriate. Those who resist should be eliminated without mercy.

Quite frequently, when our spirits are troubled, we find peace in sleep. But if you are under the spell, the strong spell of love, sleep intensifies your anguish rather than alleviating it. Thus, even when the newly smitten lover was asleep, he was often dreaming about the woman of his desire. Sometimes he was abruptly torn from his slumbers; besieged by thoughts of Doguicimi, his troubled mind would then keep him awake until dawn. The prince engaged in imaginary dialogues with the woman and, in the end, convinced himself that she shared his love and was even pursuing him with her entreaties, imploring him to marry her.

For the past moon, only his body was present at the councils of the court. Upon returning to his residence, he stretched out on his bed and abandoned himself to his dreams, henceforth his only source of joy. Even when surrounded by his wives, he escaped from them in his thoughts; his mind carried him toward the home of Toffa, and his gaze focused upon something that was invisible for his entourage; he was delighting in the imaginary presence of that woman with her mellifluous name and stately bearing, with her charming face and bewitching courage. He stared admiringly at her and told her with a smile that she was destined to become the Wife of Panther. He assured her: "Doguicimi, from now on you alone will enjoy the rights of my bed. You are enough for me. My other wives will become your servants!"

He didn't know how that thought surfaced, but like a needle, it pricked the conscience of the old prince sleeping inside him and incited it to rebellion.

Violently jerked from his reveries, Vidaho asked himself: "How can I – heir to a tradition that values opulence, prestige, authority, and power over a full harem and a large family – even think of being satisfied with a single woman, the sign of poverty and a base condition?"

The intoxication that his love for Doguicimi had produced in him during the past two moons evaporated immediately. Reason became dominant. He thrust his hand vigorously in front of him as if to push away a terrifying spectre. With a forceful, "never in my life!" he rebuffed a person whom he alone could see and hear. Aloud he continued his line of thought: "In all decency, I cannot take Toffa's wife from him. What would the sons of Agonglo think of such an abduction? Toffa is a prince of the royal blood. He is loved by his brothers, and since his misfortune, the affection of the royal family and the veneration of the common people for him have increased. Bound by the solidarity of his brothers and sisters, who had supported him against the tyrant and helped him regain his throne, my august Father himself would never take my side against them!"

He withdrew into himself, and then, sighing profoundly, he continued: "If only one could be certain of Toffa's death at Hounjroto, the entire family would find it quite normal for his wife to remarry Vidaho. But the whole country is hoping that the prince will return to Danhomê because Destiny caused him to be named Toffa at his birth, signifying that, like the waterlily which always triumphs over the drought, he will never perish in a war. If only he were a simple Danhomênou! Even if he were a high dignitary, he could be sent away from Danhomê and his wife could be given to me. The king could cloak this exile under the guise of an appointment to a new and more prestigious position. But would Toffa consent to exchange his favorite jewel for the position of viceroy in Gléhoué?"

The indignation that the abduction of Toffa's wife by the heir to the throne would undoubtedly arouse among the peers of the unfortunate, captive prince emerged clearly in the love-struck Vidaho's imagination. His desire vanished instantly, calming his aroused senses. His eyes half closed, he became meditative for a moment, then shook his head as if something horrible had just presented itself to his mind.

Standing up, he shook his cloth with several grand flourishes before going out into the courtyard; similarly, his mind shook the grasp of a criminal love: "No!" he said to himself forcefully. "I must not allow anyone to suspect my love for Doguicimi! Have I not more than once committed myself to punishing her blasphemies once I have taken possession of Danhomê?

"The Danhomênous would no longer have confidence in their future master if he were to break his word. Even if they forget the prince's promise to deal harshly with the blasphemer, my own memory of it will be painfully etched in my mind. And how could I explain my change of mind to Migan? The first minister is vindictive, and his influence on my august Father is great!

"At Ké, at Houn, at Aja, and at Ayo, everyone knows that I am the one who will reign over Danhomê after my august Father. They would learn tomorrow that I had been stripped of my right to the throne? I would see the flour and my

161

hand would fall short of the foofoo? My only crime would have been my love for Doguicimi? My name would become proverbial to designate one who scorns a precious object in favor of a trifle? When rebuked by others, Danhomênous would seek to justify such conduct: "Vidaho Badohoun sacrificed his throne to conquer Doguicimi!" Prefer a woman to the throne of Danhomê with all its riches and honors? Destiny is cruel enough to avenge such folly by ripping out the very tongue of anyone who could even think of perpetrating it. He would not be the one responsible for my fall; on the contrary, I would be regarded as the architect of my own unhappiness. And I would not be surprised if Doguicimi, in a moment of idiotic pride characteristic of beings with seven pairs of ribs, said to me: "Look at what a humiliating situation you've created for me!"

In most men such a gloomy presentiment of the future would have sufficed to annihilate a love so prejudicial to their moral and material well being.

But Doguicimi was the idol, and Vidaho was the one who idolized her.

Doguicimi, a woman of great distinction and the incarnation of courage – the highest possible virtue in the eyes of the Danhomênous!

Vidaho, the heir presumptive who had been raised with the assumption that the king and his heir should enjoy a monopoly of the best things in Danhomê!

The prince leaned against the wall to prevent himself from falling. He sighed: "Ah, the miserable life of a prince obsessed by a desire he can not satisfy at his leisure!"

His head tilted to the left as if he were straining to overhear some confidence, his lips taut, and with a blank expression on his face – everything indicated that he was once again plunged in contemplation. His secret interlocutor reminded him of a fact. His face beaming, the prince exclaimed: "But could Migan himself speak out? Would he dare advocate my downfall? Isn't he also guilty of a serious transgression against the authority of his sovereign? One good deed deserves another. If the minister tries to harm me in the eyes of my Father, he will lose his scimitar. . . ."

After a brief pause to reflect, he continued: "It is true that Migan might seek to exonerate himself of his felony by accusing me. But I will have not the slightest difficulty in proving my innocence.

"If the king decides to determine the truth by having me submit to an ordeal by poison, what priest in this Danhomê would dare declare Vidaho guilty?"

This thought comforted him. Other fleeting thoughts crossed his mind – inadmissible thoughts that were immediately driven away by more honest ones: "Ah, no! It shall never be said that I sullied my name to marry a woman!" he blurted out, stamping the ground with his right foot.

An ephemeral triumph for the prince's reason! Passion soon made a violent comeback, its momentary respite having merely allowed it to recover its full force. Because he slept little at night, the love-struck prince began to grow weak, and he could no longer pass the entire day at the Palace.

Love forbidden is love ardently desired! All the prince's efforts to drive the persistent image of Doguicimi from his mind were in vain. Vain too was the family loyalty that demanded respect for Doguicimi! Vain as well the dictates of honor that obligated the prince to fulfill his promise to punish the blasphemer! Hadn't she already become the mistress of his soul? More than vain was, for several days, the nightmare of the first minister and the political argument which ordained that Vidaho safeguard his position by doing what Migan wanted him to do.

Only the satisfaction of the prince's desire would extinguish the fire that was burning inside him.

In moments when his mind regained a bit of his former lucidity, he endlessly asked himself: "What powder did Doguicimi smuggle into my food to possess me in this way? It's stronger than I am!"

Indeed, as strong as his hatred against the blasphemer had been, just so powerful did his love become for one who had been revealed as a treasure of valor. He did not understand how a love for Doguicimi could replace the hatred which had previously filled his heart. He no longer took pleasure in food prepared by hands that were not those he now desired to see offering him his meals.

More and more, he avoided the society of his wives and grew melancholy, irritable, even bad tempered. It was not long before his appearance began to reflect the langour of his soul and the effects of prolonged fasting. The first part of his body to be affected was his face, which soon betrayed his state of mind: it became bony with hollowed cheeks, a gaunt and elongated lower jaw, sunken eyes, and more prominent brow ridges. His collar bones could be seen on the upper part of his body, and one could easily count his ribs. His emaciated neck could scarcely support his head, which was constantly falling on his chest beneath the weight of his melancholy reflections.

His wives did not succeed in discovering the reason behind this mysterious wasting away.

Nevertheless, they did their utmost to restore the prince's happiness and his strength. They knew the torments that awaited them if the trial by ordeal proved that they were responsible for their husband's listlessness.

The moon before the previous one had been waning when the king revealed the soul of the Danhomênous to his heir. The present moon had been covering the calabash for two days. On a night when even the slaves were taking pleasure in life at the sides of their wives, Vidaho, who was already partial master of the people, animals, and things of Danhomê, remained awake, his mind tormented by the thought of Doguicimi. "It's stronger than I am!" he repeated endlessly. Then, shrugging his shoulders, he exclaimed: "Bah, the squirrel who is dying because he overindulged in the fruits of the palm tree can console himself in these terms: 'Dying of indigestion is better than starving to death!'"

From that moment on, his faint-heartedness disappeared. "The indignation of my uncles and aunts, the anger of my august Father, the possible loss of my honor, the eventual plots of Migan to deprive me of my right to the throne are all mere spectres!" he said to himself, having decided to conquer Doguicimi, even if it meant his disgrace.

163

He convinced himself that, as the future master of Danhomê, he had only to express his desire and the woman would humbly submit to him and even render thanks to Destiny for having awarded her such a rich prize.

Those of the prince's wives who had sufficient seniority in his household to express their opinions freely discussed the situation with each other and, through the intermediary of a servant who alerted a Wife of Panther in the Palace, notified the king about the changes that had occurred in the tastes and habits of the heir to the throne and about his melancholy, which the combined efforts of all his wives had failed to dissipate.

The king too had observed the irregularities in his heir's appearances at court, his repeated lapses of attention during meetings of the council, and his emaciated condition as well, but he didn't attach much importance to them.

He consulted with Migan and Mêwou. It would be quite humiliating for the throne of Houégbaja if people outside the Palace learned that Vidaho was susceptible to the evil effects of a gris-gris! What king in this world had supported as many gris-gris men and doctors reputed for the depth of their knowledge as had Guézo!

When consulted, Destiny proclaimed: "The tree grows young again during the season of renewal!"

The king and his two principal ministers inferred from this response that the prince's wives no longer knew how to make him take pleasure in life. The council decided to increase the size of Vidaho's harem. Each Wife of Panther was invited to present a pubescent young girl selected from among the most beautiful of her servants.

But when Destiny was consulted, he declared that the spirits of only twenty of these young girls were in harmony with that of Vidaho.

The king obliged them to drink a fetish-potion to assure that they would love, honor, and remain loyal to the man who was going to become their husband that very evening. The prince's aunts urged them to make every effort to please their new husband, to divert him so the joy he had lost would return.

The young wives so artfully multiplied their caresses that Vidaho momentarily regained his gaiety. But this remedy, which the court believed infallible, was a mere palliative.

Discouraged, Guézo resolved to allow the uninterrupted course of nights and days to effect the cure that his parental solicitude had been unable to produce in his heir. Yet he was inwardly preoccupied with seeking among his numerous children for a new successor in case the situation should grow worse.

Only common Danhomênous married women without inquiring into the compatibility of their spirits. Vidaho owed it to himself to consult Destiny on the subject of his love for Doguicimi. In this way he would learn how to triumph over the enmities that such a marriage was sure to provoke. He decided to purify his oracle in advance.

Informed of the rite that was about to take place at the home of his heir, the king ordered his Steward to place the necessary alcohol, cloths, cowries, goats, and chickens at the disposal of the prince.

All night long the princely residence, redolent with the aroma of the white man's liquor, echoed with sacred songs, shouts of joy, and the most flattering compliments being paid the prince by his courtiers.

Of all the wishes for his happiness, he was most pleased by the one expressed by his sister Noucounzin, who said: "Destiny will bow before the will of the prince. A simple desire on the part of Vidaho would cause even a bird living in Aja or Ayo to come and land within reach of the prince's hand!"

The love-struck prince thought to himself: "The princess is undoubtedly alluding to the conquest of Doguicimi. How did Noucounzin find out about my love for Toffa's wife? I have confided this secret in no one! If I have been betrayed, it can only have been by love itself, which the elders define quite accurately as 'a fire that, if it doesn't consume what is covering it, will at least heat it and thereby make its presence known.' No act of treason to be feared on the part of the princess. Moreover, she is quite obliging and very clever."

When approached the next morning, the oracle affirmed that Doguicimi's spirit was in harmony with that of the prince and guaranteed the success of the enterprise. The diviner immediately proceeded to perform all the prescribed propitiatory sacrifices.

Filled with the hope of possessing the woman of his desire and reassured about his right to the throne, the prince was completely transformed from that moment on.

No more long periods of solitude and melancholy! No more sighs! No more gloomy expressions with absent stares! This newfound cheerfulness revived the appetite which restores a person's strength.

Nevertheless, the king, the court, and the prince's harem still retained a few doubts about a definitive return to health on the part of the future master of Danhomê.

*   *   *

Two days after the end of the traditional celebrations, life had returned to normal in Danhomê. The memory of the soldiers lost at Hounjroto grew more and more faint in the thoughts of those who remained. In the houses where the families' dead were commemorated, "assens"[1] served as surrogates for those who were absent; children had been born to most of them.

But these absent members of the family would never be completely forgotten. If the birth of children, who were (as Destiny assured many families) the reincarnation of the dead, did not keep the memory of the missing ones sufficiently alive, they themselves would know how to revive these memories between the annual traditional celebrations by periodically disturbing the sleep, the calm, or the affairs of the living.

---

[1] "Assens" are miniscule parasols that symbolize the dead person; near the house where the "assens" are on display, victims were sacrificed in their honor. (author's note)

165

As for widows who had remarried other members of the family or who had, on orders from the king, been remarried to soldiers without families, the slightest quarrel with their new husbands or some caprice with which their husbands did not wish to comply frequently brought the dead man's name to their lips.

The homes of the three missing princes also echoed with the cries of new-born children.

But their wives had not yet been granted the authorization to remarry.

Only Princess Ponouwa, a blood sister whom Toffa had stolen from her first husband, had openly continued to carry on her affair with another brother as she awaited the opportune moment to abandon him in favor of a third man in a highly responsible position.

Any king who, by suppressing the rights of a free love that had become an accepted aristocratic practice, attempted to prevent a princess from enjoying life this way in the kingdom of her fathers would immediately have made himself unpopular.

Doguicimi herself only endured life in the hope of seeing her husband once again. Having arisen before dawn, she invoked at great length the protection of kings from the spirit world, entreating them to protect their son Toffa and imploring them to bring him back to Danhomê even if it were only out of pity for her.

Her kola nuts, her melegueta peppers, her bottles of palm oil and brandy were always the first to arrive at the fetish shrines on the days offerings were to be made. Her servants invariably brought a single wish with them: "The prompt return of their master to his hearth!"

Through the voice of the oracle or that of the guardian priest, the fetishes often demanded sacrifices of goats and chickens so that the missing person might, as they assured, be brought back safely.

Doguicimi had once had as many as twenty baskets of valuable cloths, but she no longer possessed more than five; she had also stripped herself of all her jewelry to acquire objects that might be offered to the fetishes. She even sold two slaves given to her by Toffa during the first year of their marriage. All the money she collected was spent on sacrifices.

When Evêmon advised her one day to moderate her expenditures, she replied: "I owe this wealth to Toffa and therefore desire to sacrifice it for his deliverance! If my resources give out before his return, my strength will procure others for me, and I will use them for his ransome."

She spent her mornings washing the children whose care had been neglected by their mothers; later she served them the leftover foofoo that she had reheated in the caloulou.

In the middle of the day, her lodgings, which served as a meeting place for the younger children, echoed with their babblings and bursts of laughter punctuated with occasional tears.

The ancestors had not yet accorded Doguicimi the privilege of becoming a mother, but she proved to be an exemplary mama to all her husband's many children. She consoled some by replacing a mouthful of foofoo or a piece of meat that had been snatched from the hands of the weaker by the stronger. Others she scolded for teasing the smaller children. And when she was obliged to deal harshly with one of them, her left hand quickly pressed to her bosom the child her right hand had just punished. Her reprimands were so filled with tenderness that the admonished children soon forgot their annoyance and promised to be good.

More than one of them fell asleep, cheeks still swollen with food. The woman washed their hands, stretched them out on a mat, and covered them with a cloth. A few infants refused to go to bed. Evêmon and other servants, who followed her example, quickly added a cloth to the one they were wearing, and with a turn of the hand, the little master was solidly attached to a woman's back. Her hands stretched behind her to support her precious burden, the impromptu little mother walked around the room for a long time, rocking the capricious little one and reciting a song to put him to sleep.

Only when some of the children had grown drowsy and others had gone outside to play after their stomachs had been satisfied could Doguicimi enjoy a momentary liberation from the care she lavished on these adorable children, who in her eyes stood for her dear husband, in memory of whom she called them: "My Spirit!"

If the resemblance between the son and his Father was particularly striking, the woman embellished the term of endearment: "Master of My Spirit!"

At night each child retired to its mother's lodgings. Then Doguicimi dismissed her servants. She was invariably overtaken by sleep in the midst of her thoughts about Toffa as she continued to weep and lament.

Vivênagbo, who had previously been so assiduous in his concern for the wives and children of his sworn friend, no longer brought his words of encouragement to the house of Toffa.

But every day the king sent someone to gather information about the families of his brothers who had been missing since Hounjroto; he inquired about their needs, informed himself about whether the serfs were supplying them regularly with grain, wood, oil, and spices, and determined if the hunters were providing them with game. Every third moon, he had cloths distributed to them.

Doguicimi would have preferred that the king had troubled himself more about the captive princes at Hounjroto, since their families in Agbomê were in no danger. For this reason the woman always received Guézo's messenger coldly and grew indignant at her co-wives who lost themselves in expressions of gratitude to the king each time his envoy paid them a visit.

*   *   *

Although assumed by Doguicimi to be supremely indifferent to the unfortunate fate of his brothers who were being held captive at Hounjroto, Guézo was more preoccupied than ever with them. For that matter, on one of the very nights the woman spent in the company of Evêmon, evoking the memory of her absent husband, imploring the ancestors to bring back Toffa, and beseching them to punish the man she held responsible for the disappearance of the prince, Guézo was in council with his ministers, his brothers, and his heir.

The king had imparted to them his intention of dispatching a spy mission to Hounjroto. Vidaho did not share his august Father's opinion, and he did not hesitate to express his opinion: "If we don't have any better reasons for sending our troops into the 'mahi' country, let us rather unleash their fury against the Ayonous. Avenging the honor of our venerable ancestors, who were insulted by our enemies to the East, seems more imperative to me than avenging the memory of Toffa, Assogbaou, and Ajéhounou."

Migan agreed with the heir to the throne. For different reasons that neither of them dared to acknowledge, both of them were opposed to the idea of a war that might deliver the three illustrious prisoners.

Guézo retorted: "Since when has the infiltration of enemy territory by spies meant the immediate outbreak of hostilities? Don't you realize that our emissaries need to remain undetected over there in order to gather precise information about the fate of the three princes and the military strength of our enemies? We will not even contemplate a campaign against the Mahinous unless the superiority of our forces is evident and our victory certain."

Mêwou, Gaou, and Possou supported the king's opinion.

Thus it was decided that a spy would be sent to Hounjroto.

At the next morning's meeting of the council, Ajaho proposed Zanbounou as the only person in Danhomê capable of successfully carrying out an espionage assignment in "mahi" country. During the last war he had served as a liaison between Vivênagbo and the king.

When Destiny was consulted, he affirmed that the choice was a good one. Zanbounou was instructed with his mission and then compelled to drink a fetish-potion that would punish him summarily in case of betrayal. Accompanied by his counsellors, the king subsequently went to his ancestors' mausolea, where he made offerings of water and rum for the success of a mission that he was placing under the sign of their protection.

Casters of spells brought gris-gris, explaining their effects and the proper way of handling them. The spy was also given a hundred strands of glass beads and as many of coral, a porter's load of tobacco, a demijohn of brandy, velvet and satin cloths, a large white cloth two arms' lengths wide, and swatches of blue, black, grey, green, and yellow cloth, each of which measured approximately three by five spans. Three men were placed under his command. The king promised them generous rewards if they succeeded in their mission.

Born in Acaraounpa,[2] Zanbounou was very familiar with Hounjroto, although it was a traditional enemy of his own people. But he intended to pass as a slave-trader who was coming from the other side of the Swamps to replenish his stocks.

At the end of the session during which he was instructed with his mission, he was told by Migan and the two ministers of war: "Report to us in particular the

---

[2] "Acaraounpa" is a "mahi" region. (author's note)

Mahinous' insults addressed against the king and against Danhomê!" Zanbounou had understood the watchword.

He started on the road to Hounjroto at the third crowing of the cock and was already inventing insults in case he didn't overhear any in "mahi" country.

*　　　　　*　　　　　*

The sun was radiant that morning, and Nature smiled as a result. The joy spread by the day star communicated itself imperceptibly to people and animals as well.

Only Doguicimi wished no part of a joy in which her husband could not participate. She shut herself in his room. Leaning against the wall and facing the sleeping place that was still made up as if the master of the house had never budged from Agbomê, she wallowed in the tears that the memory of her last night in this room with the prince prompted her to shed and the tears that welled up in her at the thought of the privations he was undoubtedly suffering in Hounjroto.

A servant appeared and announced a visit by Princess Noucounzin.

Doguicimi washed her face and joined her guest in the reception room. Evêmon soon came into the room with a calabash of cool water, kneeled before the princess, and presented it to her after having drunk a mouthful that she had poured into the hollow of her left hand.

Noucounzin took the calabash, poured several drops of water on the ground for the dead, wetted her lips, and said as she set down the calabash: "I was almost afraid to approach you, Doguicimi, for I didn't know what sort of welcome you would accord to a friend who has not been here twice since your misfortune!"

"Charming princess, one cannot reasonably expect friends to stick to you as closely as your shadow during times of adversity."

"And to friends whose constant attentions are in no way profitable, one should prefer those whose visits, although rare, offer your wounded soul the consolation that will comfort it," the princess hastened to complete her thought.

Doguicimi agreed with a smile that was seconded by a nod of the head.

The princess owed it to herself to exploit this initial success as quickly as possible; feigning a tone of compassion, she asked: "Do you at least have any news of the missing prince?"

"Alas, only Destiny and the fetishes sustain my hope of his return."

"You ought to see several important people in the kingdom. They could certainly give you more precise information, and they might even be able to work secretly toward the liberation of Toffa.

"The drought-stricken palm of Alada observed to the parrot of Alada that winged folk only visit trees with leaves. Princess, do the missing and the unfortunate have friends or protectors in this Danhomê?" sighed Doguicimi, whose face darkened at the thought that her husband had been abandoned even by his sworn friends.

"What about the King, the Father and Mother of His People! What about the heir to the throne, who is goodness personified?" asked the princess with a honeyed tone in her voice and an engaging smile on her lips.

"Those who have the most to gain by the disappearance of my husband? Charming princess, it is not with jests that one soothes the pain of people who are suffering," retorted Toffa's wife bitterly.

Shocked, Noucounzin straightened abruptly as if she had just been pricked in the back. "I can see you don't know that you owe your own liberation to Vidaho. It would be in your best interest to seek the prince's help. The king, who has designated him for the throne, trusts him with secrets that even Migan and Mêwou are not privileged to share. My brother would willingly do you a favor."

"You are telling me, princess, that His Royal Highness would condescend to help me recover my husband?" Doguicimi asked sceptically.

"Certainly! Vidaho is the friend of the unfortunate; he sympathized a great deal with your sorrow. And if he had not been held back by the fear of seeing his offer rebuffed, you would have forgotten your misfortune several moons ago," Noucounzin assured her.

"May all the ancestors buttress the life of the generous prince with health and happiness and prepare him for a long reign!" interjected Doguicimi, whose face brightened at this good news.

"My dear friend, you can regard the prince's aid as assured. Your happiness depends only on yourself," concluded the princess, who then mentioned a religious rite requiring her presence at Houawé[3] as a pretext for taking leave from the mistress of the house. In reality she merely wanted to pass on to Vidaho as quickly as possible the assurance she had just received that his conquest of the desired woman would be but a matter of days.

"Charming princess, I will not refrain from any sacrifice to get back my husband. I will tell him upon his return that you were the intermediary who enabled me to approach the heir to the throne and to persuade that prince to help bring him back from captivity!" exclaimed Doguicimi, whom a fit of joy had thrust to her knees at the feet of the woman who had rekindled her hope of seeing her missing husband once again.

She succeeded in detaining her visitor for a moment as she spoke glowingly about Toffa, noble prince, gentle husband, good father. Noucounzin continued to insist that Vidaho was the only person who could be useful to Doguicimi in her sorrow. They parted with joy in their hearts. Each of them believed in the depths of her heart that her own cherished idea had triumphed.

*   *   *

After Noucounzin had reported the success of her mission to Doguicimi, the heir to the throne vacillated between doubt and confidence. "Is it possible? Can it be true? Maybe I'm dreaming? It can't be anything but an illusion!" He

---

3 "Houawé" is a village about twelve kilometers from the capital. (author's note)

felt himself for a moment and then continued: "Didn't Destiny assure me that I would conquer this woman if I made the required sacrifices? And didn't I make them with all the recommended care and generosity? I would certainly be justified in expecting this success. . . . But is it possible?"

When he began to study the significance of his victory, he was once again besieged with doubts. He could scarcely believe that he would finally enter Toffa's house at the invitation of Doguicimi, that he would be able to approach this woman at leisure, this woman who combines a peerless beauty with a rare courage, this woman who surpasses all others and for the possession of whom, as he admitted to his confidante in his fits of passion, he would willingly renouce his right to the throne if his royal Father obliged him to choose between Doguicimi and Danhomê.

The news that his sister Noucounzin's adroitness had opened the door to Toffa's house for him today and would make him master of Doguicimi's heart tomorrow cured Vidaho of the languor that had afflicted him for several moons. It did not take long for the people of his entourage to notice the change.

Regretfully he agreed to postpone his visit until the evening on the advice of his sister, who reminded him that it would be imprudent for a personage of his rank to enter Toffa's house in the middle of the day without being on duty, that is to say without his customary retinue.

His impatience made the day seem unusually long to him. He felt frustrated that the sun could not, like the Danhomênous, be submitted to his will.

Still but partially shrouded by the gloomy veil that night was just beginning spread over the earth, the prince arrived magnificently dressed at Toffa's house. He was a bit disappointed, for he expected to be received in the intimacy of the woman's room and with expressions of joy.

Doguicimi offered him a chair in the reception room, then touched her forehead to the ground and kissed it as she recited the formulaic greeting for a royal prince: "I humbly request news of the princely residence." She sat down on a mat two paces away from the prince as he was replying: "The princely Palace continues to be in an excellent state!"

With a sign, the visitor demanded that Evêmon leave the room. The servant withdrew, but very attentive to her mistress's least winks, she returned to a place very close to the prince without his suspecting it. His bare chest erect and visible through the casual folds of his cloth, his left fist resting on his hip, Vidaho was adopting the jaunty pose characteristic of the princes of Danhomê and offering, for the woman's admiration, a glimpse of his admirable body with skin the color of fine, sun-baked brick against which the beautiful blue cords on his arms stood out impressively. He had carefully rubbed his body with an ointment that, he was convinced, would inspire love in the heart of the desired person. His face beaming and his eyes slightly reddened by the leaf extract that had been squeezed into them a few moments before in order to increase their intensity and vanquish all resistence on the part of anyone upon whom his gaze happened to focus, the prince swaggered in his own way before the woman he had desired for several moons; he repeated to himself the incantations of the gris-gris that were supposed to force Doguicimi's love.

He smiled at the thought that the only obstacle between himself and victory had just been eliminated. He had convinced himself that he could easily exploit his position in the kingdom to seduce Doguicimi. "In this Danhomê, anyone blessed with reason and unimpaired senses could hardly remain impervious to the prince's great distinction adorned, moreover, with the bloom of a youth that was maintained by meticulous daily treatments."

Doguicimi observed to herself that Vidaho very much resembled Toffa, and the thought disturbed her a great deal.

Unable to endure the flame cast at her by the ardently passionate princely gaze, the woman lowered her head. The drumming inside her became more intense; she was suddenly stricken with a headache.

She whom all Danhomê secretly admired for her courage was overcome with an incomprehensible fear as she pulled nervously on a straw from her mat.

The prince prided himself on his knowledge of women, for he had all sorts of them in his own residence, and he thought he could see the depths of Doguicimi's soul as one can see the bottom of a calabash through clear water. For the love-struck prince, the woman's confusion signified that she had been caught in his net. He once again repeated the incantation of one of his numerous gris-gris and then broke the silence in a cajoling voice: "Look at me, my spirit! I am only here at your behest. And with me comes the joy that has not visited this house in many moons!"

"May His Highness deign to speak. I am listening," stammered Doguicimi, whose stare remained fixed on the mat, eloquently expressing her troubled state of mind.

"You have never received news of your missing husband. The spies I convinced my august Father to send secretly to Hounjroto have returned and informed us that the vigilance of the Mahinous is never relaxed even for a instant; for that reason, the king does not at this moment want to undertake the war of revenge that I have proposed. Not before my reign will you see the liberation of our soldiers who were taken prisoner at Hounjroto."

The lie that the prince had just uttered immediately showed on his face; his voice lacked assurance. But Toffa's wife was too overwrought to recognize the signs that betrayed her visitor.

"And His Highness will be worthy of his ancestors!" she said, venturing to accord him a timid glance in which Vidaho thought he could read her love.

"But who knows whether or not the three most important prisoners will still be alive when we engage in another war?"

"The death of Toffa will not sadden me as much as his captivity."

"All the more so since I will soon make you forget him. In all Danhomê and overshadowed only by the royal Palace, my residence enjoys the privilege of housing the best things and all the pleasures appropriate for a woman of your

172

distinction. Doguicimi, you have cried enough over your absent husband. Smile now at the happiness I am bringing you."

"My sole happiness resides in his return, noble prince."

"And if Toffa is no longer of this world, it will indeed be necessary for you to seek happiness under another roof."

"Next to him alone," Doguicimi corrected him abruptly.

"Happiness can only be found here below," rejoined the prince with assurance.

"I would like to believe it because it is Vidaho who says it and thereby proclaims the futility of all the human sacrifices that the king has performed each year in memory of his ancestors," Doguicimi retorted.

"Ah, no!" the heir to the throne protested energetically, caught in his own trap. "As in this world, kings enjoy perpetual happiness in the realm of the spirits, and their subjects must suffer, if necessary, to preserve it for them."

"To a dying soldier, Agaja gave weapons of war. 'Has the Creator refused me rest even in the city of the dead!' exclaimed the soldier indignantly. If, after all the suffering my husband has endured in 'mahi' country, Destiny persists in being cruel toward him and depriving him of happiness in the realm of the dead, that would be one more reason for me to join him as quickly as possible in order to alleviate his sorrows. But he conducted himself so honestly in Danhomê and served the country of his Fathers so loyally that I am convinced his ancestors will welcome him with open arms to the familial Palace, whether he dies here or in captivity at Hounjroto where he went to fight for the honor of this kingdom. And I want to be at his side so that I can continue to idolize him and take pleasure in life."

"Our position in this world is retained in the world of the spirits," explained Vidaho, uneasily attempting to extricate himself from his trap. "If you were a porter here below, you would carry your miseries with you into the realm of the spirits; if you were a commoner in this world, you would not stop working in the city of the dead; if you were Mother of Panther or King, you would continue to be worshipped in the other world, where the happiness reserved for kings and queen mothers alone will be reserved for you. This much is certain; our ancestors have repeatedly assured us of it in dreams and oracles. For this reason, anyone who respects himself should seek to acquire the best possible position in this world to guarantee his happiness in the next one. Doguicimi, you have made an indelible impression on me ever since the day of your first attack upon the Master of the World after his return from Hounjroto. You repeated your curses on the first day of our recent celebrations. You surpass all the women of Danhomê in beauty, wisdom, and audacity. Because you incarnate the force that Danhomê idolizes, you have vanquished me. Henceforth I want to worship you alone and to be the only one to do so.

"You will be Wife of Panther, Doguicimi. All my wealth will be at your disposal. Celebrations will often be held in your honor. You will be happy because, like the sea, the queen of waters, your voice alone will command in my Palace; you will have no rivals. In my residence, you will shine like the sun during the day and like the moon in a cloudless sky at night. After having brightened my days and my nights, you will be accorded the singular honor of accompanying me to the realm of the spirits, where our happiness will continue when the ancestors will have called us to them."

"No mortal can alter the work of Destiny. If I was born to be unhappy, raising me to the most exalted position in this country would be in vain: my inexorable fate would continue to torment me. It would be madness to deceive myself into thinking that it could be otherwise. Besides, I believe nothing could be better for me than it is in Toffa's house. In his dwelling I am also the sea, whose roar drowns those of the wildest rivers; here too I am radiant like the sun during the day and like the moon at night. No matter how many co-wives I have, they are not clouds that are capable of obscuring my light. No, Your Highness, I could not have a better life in any palace. . . ."

Her voice was muffled in sobs.

"You claim to be happy, Doguicimi, but your tears reveal the mourning in your soul. I want to put an end to your sorrow. Are you sure that Toffa really loved you and that he loves you still, that he is thinking about you now and that, when he returns to Danhomê, he will still be the passionate husband you knew in the past? I can see that you don't know about the hideous mutilation the Mahinous have practiced on him," said the prince in a compassionate tone of voice as he leaned toward the woman to dry her tears.

Jumping back with a start to avoid Vidaho's touch, the wife of Toffa retorted: "Toffa forget Doguicimi! It is not by seeking to implant this doubt in my mind that anyone will ever succeed in taking me from him! Even if all his limbs have been amputated, I will never stop loving him provided that his heart returns to me as pure and noble as I have always known it!"

The prince saw the impending storm that was brewing. He did not forget that he had come to this house in the greatest secrecy and that it would be extremely imprudent for him to advertise his visit. He didn't insist any further. But he told himself that his defeat was not permanent. To brace his courage, he thought to himself: "Women are the same everywhere. The hypocrisy in their hearts is such that, when they are in the presence of something they like, they will pretend at first to be displeased with it. The one who rejects my suit today will humbly submit to all my demands tomorrow, as long as I persevere a bit!" Since his failure seemed temporary in his eyes, it did not affect him at all. By dint of repeating that Destiny and his gris-gris would in the end enable him to possess this treasure of love and valor that his father had revealed to him, he became supremely confident.

Remaining alone in the room, Doguicimi thought to confound the the crown prince's innuendos and bear witness to her husband's unwavering love for her by singing this song that he had sung to her two days before his departure for the war:

What star in the skies shines like the sun?
At night what star casts as much light as the moon?

There are many animals in the bush.
But are any more imposing than the elephant?
Which beast is more lithe than the Panther?
Which bird attains the height of the ostriche?
Which shall ever equal the peacock's beauty?
There are many waters.
But which possesses the size and roar of the sea?
Doguicimi, you are the incomparable star
That brightens my house by day;
You are also the moon whose light
Eclipses that of all the other stars,
Soothing me to sleep at night
And filling me with gentle dreams.
You are my only favorite
Because you alone combine feline suppleness
With the elephant's majesty and the stature of the ostrich.
A peacock with feathers!
The rarest of birds beneath the skies of Danhomê,
Sent into this kingdom by the Creator
To adorn my house and my house alone,
To delight no one but me,
You should take pride in the wealth of your plumage.
Like the ocean whose irrepressible roar
Drowns the murmur of all other waters,
Doguicimi, you alone are the voice in my house,
And you alone have a right to my heart.
For like the sea that brought us the white men
With the wonders they bring in their ships,
You give rise to the breeze that revives me at nightfall,
You soothe away my tiredness with your caresses,
And you carry off to distant exile the dark thoughts
That sometimes assault my soul!

As if speaking to some invisible interlocutor, she said aloud: "That's how my never-to-be-forgotten husband, the man who is now being slandered, sang his love to me! Convinced that any woman can be easily seduced, Vidaho dangled wealth, honor, and everything he calls happiness in front of my eyes. But Toffa is the only jewel that counts for me. And even if I had to wear a course raphia cloth to be with him after his return from Hounjroto, I would never cease loving this noble prince, whose life was spent here without luxury, without obscene pleasures, without covetousness, and without thought of crime.

"Because Vidaho has been attracted by my beauty fused with my courage, may Sapata disfigure me, may Dan[4] twist me and give me a humpback, and

---

[4] "Dan" is the snake worshipped as a fetish in its ordinary form as well as in the guise of the rainbow, the wind, and fits of epilepsy. (author's note)

may my ancestors make me ugly to frighten away the prince who haunts me with a unrequited love.

"Ah, if I could only be certain that Toffa has a wife to soften the rigors of his captivity, I would give thanks to my ancestors, and I would depart from this world without regret to go and await the prince in the city of the dead. That's the only way I can escape Vidaho's importunities. But there is nothing to indicate that 'mahi' chiefs are as generous as our kings, who often heap favors upon war captives."

Her eyes grew damp at the thought of the privations and sufferings her husband was probably being obliged to endure at Hounjroto.

With the back of her hand she wiped her tears, but others came even more numerous to replace them. Suddenly she burst into sobs.

When calm had finally reestablished itself in her soul, Doguicimi remained silent for a moment. Emerging from her reflections, she said to herself: "The oppressed and weak who have neither cutlass nor club with which to avenge themselves can always find consolation in song!" As if obeying an order from a higher source, she began to sing this elegy that she herself had composed:

I
The master of this house,
The light of this house,
Left it many long moons ago.
When will I have the joy
Of seeing his noble face again?
Destiny and the fetishes say "He shall return!"
But he fails to appear.
I don't even see him in dreams.
Can he be angry with me?
For what reason then?

Chorus
Oh, if I could only have prooof
That he's no longer alive,
I'd join him at once!
But if he were dead,
Wouldn't he have appeared to me. . . ?

II
I'm in no way envious
Of wives who enjoy life
At the sides of their husbands.
I only envy the fate of birds:
If I had wings like theirs,
I'd have joined my husband in "mahi" land.
I'd like to be Hêviosso

And reduce Hounjroto to ashes,
Though I'd spare Toffa, Assogbaou, Ajéhounou,
And the other prisoners of the Mahinous.

Chorus
Oh, if I could only have proof
That he's no longer alive,
I'd join him at once!
But if he were dead,
Wouldn't he have appeared to me. . . ?

III If I could become Sapata,
I'd decimate the beasts of the mountain,
Sparing only the three princes
And the other prisoners of the Mahinous.
Oh, if I were the sea to whom he compared me,
I'd flood all of "mahi" land.
Only Toffa, Assogbaou, Ajéhounou, and the others would be saved.
If I could be Ayidohouédo,[5]
I'd swallow the princes and other captives at Hounjroto
And spew them out whole in Danhomê.

Chorus
Oh, if I could only have proof
That he's no longer alive,
I'd join him at once!
But if he were dead,
Wouldn't he have appeared to me. . . ?

This song revived Doguicimi's memories of Toffa, and tears welled up in her eyes again. By the time they had dried up and the woman could fall asleep, the night was already far advanced.

As for Vidaho, he was thinking that another man had become absolute ruler in the heart of the woman he coveted. But the prince did not despair of conquering this woman, about whom he dreamed even in the middle of the day, and he began to refer to her only with the expression: "Treasure of love and valor!"

*   *   *

Noucounzin too refused to believe in a definitive failure, which would have been extremely damaging to her reputation as a skillful diplomat. Thus she returned to the charge two market days later; she was accompanied by three of her sisters, who had been made privy to the secret.

Doguicimi suspected it was not for nothing that the four of them came together. She was cautious in her choice of words, while at the same time

---

5   "Ayidohouédo" is the rainbow; it is regarded as a fetish and worshipped. (author's note)

177

refraining from any gesture that would allow them to realize she recognized their motives.

The conversation was initially kept alive with an assortment of trifles. Noucounzin grew impatient with the inconsequentiality of their talk, which she found boring; she offered to tell an anecdote. Curious, all eyes turned toward her.

She coughed three times and then, with a smile addressed solely to Doguicimi, recounted the story of the farmer who visited his friend with the intention of borrowing a velvet cloth for the fast-approaching day of a family celebration. "The friend was eating. Invited to place his hand into the same dish from which the master of the house was serving himself, the farmer did not have to be asked a second time. Meanwhile, another man showed up. Asked to share the two friends' meal, he thanked his host and announced that he had come to make a more urgent request: he wanted to borrow his friend's handsome velvet cloth so he could attend the festivities being planned by his in-laws. The fellow who had preceded him to the house declared: 'That's the same cloth for which I've come!' But the master of the house contradicted him: 'No, my friend, you came to eat. Please continue!' The cloth was loaned to the second visitor."

The story-teller herself was the first to burst into laughter. Douguicimi laughed at the gluttony of the first visitor.

Noucounzin's sisters understood the lesson.

"My sister's anecdote reminds me of the discussion we had on the way here," one of them said. "Let Doguicimi be the judge! She will surely be of my opinion; her eyes are too beautiful to be bad at seeing." Pointing to her hostess' cloth and then to the cloth worn by one of her sisters, she asked: "Which does Doguicimi prefer – this local material or that velvet?"

The judge indicated her preference for the material from Danhomê, adding that its firmness was the hallmark of durability. Noucounzin appeared to be scandalized by what she called a lack of critical judgment.

"All Danhomê vaunts the beauty of your eyes, Doguicimi, but could it be that they are not as good as they are beautiful?" she inquired with a smile on her lips. "How can you disdain this velvet, the sheen of which makes the sun at its zenith blanch with envy, in favor of that somewhat vulgar material? Why persist in rejecting the beautiful in favor of the ugly. Doguicimi, is your sagacity overrated?"

"I am then in the habit of making bad judgments?" asked Doguicimi, smiling.

One of her visitors responded with an anecdote about the Mahinou who, having mislaid his tobacco pouch, refused the pipe that a companion politely offered him; being unable to satisfy a desire that had become a necessity, he died during the night.

Doguicimi laughed at the improbability of the anecdote. The story-teller objected that it was true to life. But no one was fooled.

Noucounzin deemed all the rhetorical circumlocutions, with which they had until now cloaked their intentions, to be quite useless; she addressed the wife of Toffa: "Did you not reject Vidaho, the very image of honor and happiness? You have just been reminded in a friendly way that your eyes are too beautiful for

178

them to be bad at seeing. I am rather inclined to believe that you knowingly scorn the happiness that is being offered to you. One who closes her eyes to happiness today runs the risk of opening them on unhappiness tomorrow. Doguicimi, realize that only your union with the heir to the throne will immortalize your name."

"When she wants to do so, a woman can always find room in her heart for the love of several men," opined one of the other princesses.

"Certainly!" exclaimed another in support. "One can love the uncle and the nephew at the same time."

"You have sufficiently honored your husband's memory. Your attitude by itself condemns your co-wives to widowhood. It's time for you to free yourself from that," advised still another.

"Put an end to your tears, Doguicimi. Toffa is not the only prince who was lost at Hounjroto. Follow the example set by the wives of Assogbaou and Ajéhounou; they long ago found ways to console themselves. Let us, his nieces, weep for him. As a woman of the people, you are no more than a bird that landed accidently upon this tree!" argued one of the princesses in a tone of voice that was filled with disdain.

"Birds can not be prohibited from grieving over the fall of a plane tree, even though it seems to delight the other trees of the forest!" retorted Doguicimi with dignity. Looking into the eyes of the woman who had just spoken so harshly to her, she continued: "Birds. . . , do birds have any more secure place of rest and refuge than the thick foliage and high branches of a tree? Don't they feed upon its fruit? Don't their songs become melodious among its boughs? Princess, it is unjust to criticize the bird who remains inconsolable after the fall of the giant plane tree, when this bird is not the parrot of Alada, who turns his back on the tree that has lost its leaves."

Noucounzin inwardly reproached the blunder of her sister, who was on the verge of ruining everything. Smiling, she said: "If you were to remarry another man at this time, nobody would have anything to say about it. People would not criticize you unless you made a choice that was unworthy of you. Vidaho alone is appropriate for you. He is big, handsome, rich, powerful, and heir to the throne. Your remarriage to him would make sense to people, and they would easily forgive you. But if you do not want to wear this string of coral as a necklace, nothing would prevent you from belting it around your waist, where it would remain hidden from public view!"

One of her sisters seconded her suggestion: "When a woman, even if she is the wife of Migan or Mêwou, grants her favors to a prince, no one should speak to the king about it. And if this prince happens to be Vidaho, that's all the more reason to shroud his affairs in the greatest secrecy."

"If you are obsessed by the fear of a premature and dishonorable death because your husband made you drink a fetish-potion to preserve your marital fidelity, reassure yourself, Doguicimi. From the pontiff of this kingdom's fetishists, Vidaho will obtain a compound that can counteract the effect of all the fetish-potions you might have swallowed!" another one affirmed.

179

"Perhaps you secretly desire that the ancestors and the fetishes of your family shall liberate you from a love for Toffa that lays siege to your heart in spite of yourself? The heir to the throne will find a philtre that is infallible in its power to rid you of the love that is harassing you," suggested a princess.

Until now Toffa's wife had been smiling as her gaze wandered over her visitors, who had been stringing together praises of their brother, but she scowled at the mention of this vile proposition.

Noucounzin, who had not yet noticed Doguicimi's rising anger, petitioned her for the last time: "Don't reject our blood, Doguicimi. You are forgetting that Vidaho is a royal prince."

These words signified to her the profound disdain the princesses felt toward her husband, and she exploded: "Toffa is also a full-blooded prince. Moreover, he was the first son born to Agonglo after that king ascended to the throne of Houégbaja. Toffa thus has all the qualifications for ruling over this country. And if he had cared to dispute Guézo's right to the throne when the Danhomênous, tired of Adanzan's debauchery and sadism, were secretly looking for a successor, my husband could very easily have acquired this kingdom and to the great joy of the Danhomênous.

"You should also know that I have absolutely no need to leave my name to posterity. In any case, I would hope that my love for Toffa could provide me with the means to do so. For nothing in the world will I ever prostitute my soul, which was created for the sole purpose of containing my love for Toffa.

"My co-wives do not have to follow my example if a separation lasting several moons is enough to destroy in them the memory of their missing husband. As for me, that separation has merely served to intensify my love for the noble prince, the beautiful coral that so handsomely adorns the black jewel that I am.

"A woman of the people, I was raised with the idea of never prostituting myself, even if Destiny had made me the wife of a slave, because all the ancestors would rise up against the woman who dishonored the family by her conduct. Were I unhappy in this household, I would still have to stay here until the end of my days, maintaining the purity and fidelity of any wife worthy of the name.

"More than any fetish-potion, which, for that matter, he never dreamed of imposing on me, the education I received from my family and the dignity of a woman who respects herself constitute strong armor that protects me from the passions of men.

"Even if I were a princess, I would never take advantage of the free love that has been accorded to you by custom. To love a single man would have sufficed for me. No spells, no promises, nothing can alienate me from Toffa."

Such biting words would have fatally wounded the self-esteem of others. But the princesses were not affected by them. One of them returned to the charge: "Doguicimi, do you pretend to be wiser than those who affirm that the woman who has only known a single man in her life will be disgraced in the realm of the dead?"

"Words from the mouths of corrupt people. Such ideas open the door to adultery," answered the scandalized Doguicimi.

With these words, she dismissed her visitors on the pretext that she had to prepare a meal for the children, and the princesses withdrew shamefacedly.

On the way back, one of them expressed her opinion: "I find it hard to believe that any woman could preserve her integrity to such a point. If we look more closely, we will see that another man has already replaced the absent one in the heart of this woman who thought it necessary to lecture us on marital fidelity and that her allegedly all-consuming love for Toffa is no more than a sham. The successful master of her heart undoubtedly had recourse to a powerful philtre. For no woman could resist Vidaho's handsome features and high rank if she had not been placed under a spell by another man."

This observation suggested an idea to Noucounzin.

Her diligence in Doguicimi's presence had enabled her to collect several pinches of dirt from the ground on which Toffa's wife had just walked, and they would allow a gris-gris man to call the spirit of the desired woman and to imprison it in an alcarraza with a narrow throat.

The gris-gris man assured her that Doguicimi would come of her own free will and offer herself to Vidaho within three days, at the very latest, of the time when the gris-gris was prepared.

The prince waited an entire moon in anticipation of Doguicimi's arrival, but that only exacerbated his desire. On the advice of his sister, he ordered all sorts of compounds to be prepared with his spittle, his fingernail clippings, his blood, and the powder of a bitter kola nut that, recovered the day after he had swallowed it whole, was cut up, dried in the sun, and mashed.

From that day forward, Noucounzin repeatedly offered Doguicimi food and alcohol into which Vidaho, who defrayed the cost of these gifts, had mixed his various philtres.

When the compounds that were supposed to conquer the heart of Toffa's wife had been exhausted, the prince told himself that he needed do nothing more than show himself before Doguicimi and she would docilely follow him like a dog following its master.

Noucounzin too was convinced of it. Hadn't she observed a few changes during the last three moons in the woman whom she no longer called anything but "the one in whose breast I shall be reincarnated" or, in other words, her sister-in-law. In fact, the name Vidaho, which had previously left her indifferent if not indignant, was now pleasing to her ears.

This good news delighted the prince, and on the day Noucounzin passed it on to him, it earned her a great show of grateful affection.

The next day the princess arrived at Toffa's house under the cover of darkness; she was followed by five servants carrying numerous calabashes and heavily laden baskets.

When she was alone with Doguicimi, the princess displayed velvet and satin cloths, strings of coral and vari-colored glass beads, silver bracelets with pendants, and two gold necklaces: "The heir to the throne has charged me to deposit these cloths and these jewels at the feet of the Idol, to whom he henceforth desires to sacrifice everything, as a token of his resolve to spend the rest of his life worshipping the incarnation of beauty and courage that has just been revealed to him."

Doguicimi was unable to utter a word or make even the slightest gesture. For the princess, this meant she had been struck with amazement. She rushed away in a hurry, overjoyed at having succeeded in her mission, because she had feared she would be shown to the door with her servants and their loads. She didn't even hear the woman who was calling after her.

"Burn these objects! I don't even want to see their ashes! Go and throw into the Ditch those that fire will not destroy!" Doguicimi ordered Evêmon as soon as the servant had rejoined her after the departure of the princess.

Ignorant of the truth about the fate of the gifts he had just offered to the woman he coveted, the prince exulted, for he saw a victory in the acceptance of the tokens of his love.

The next night brought him to the house of Toffa; he arrived there as usual, superbly dressed and cheerful. Convinced that he would be bringing Doguicimi back to Jêgbé with him, he had, as he was leaving his residence, given explicit orders to his wives about the reception they should accord the woman, the song they should sing for her, and the joy they should manifest at realizing she would henceforth be among their number in enjoying life at the sides of the heir to the throne.

Doguicimi was extremely troubled by this unexpected visit. But she recovered her composure by the time the prince had the opportunity to speak to her in a voice that he made sweet as honey: "See how everything is cold, gloomy, and sad in this place. By insisting upon living in darkness and remaining in a house of misfortune, you are growing pale, Doguicimi; you are becoming taciturn, you who are the essence of gaiety. Let us go to my residence which radiates with joy. Let us go and partake of the happiness that the ancestors cached there for me and for a woman of your distinction."

"Prince, why pursue me with a love I cannot share? Why not allow me to weep for my unfortunate husband in peace and to mourn in the suspicion that he lives no more? Why seek to prostitute me? In what way am I different from the women who live in the Palace of Jêgbé?" asked Doguicimi timidly as she continued to stare at her mat.

Unruffled, the lovestruck prince answered her: "Doguicimi, you are beautiful by virtue of those qualities that our Fathers have always sought and worshipped – audacity and a disdain for death. These qualities are remarkable in a being with seven pairs of ribs, and they make you attractive to all Danhomênous. My royal Father himself is full of admiration for you. He told me that you are a treasure of love and valor fitting for him alone and that he very much regretted having given you to Toffa. He literally said: 'Everything that is beautiful in this kingdom should belong to the king or to Vidaho.'

"The Master of the World can not take you from your husband, his brother who helped him regain his throne, but it would make him happy to know that what had escaped him was caught in the nets of the son whom he has designated to succeed him. As for me, I owe nothing to your husband. I can take you from him.

"I am Vidaho, and I possess all that is needed to assure your happiness.

"Without you my residence is like a body without a head.

"I'm telling you again, our union is desired by the Master of the World. It would also enable me to protect you from the hatred secretly borne you by the queens since the day when my august Father told them you surpass them all in virtue.

"I will soon be Master of Danhomê. The people of this nation worship power, and to govern them I will need a forceful person at my side. You alone are the incarnation of power in Danhomê.

"You shall dictate all my acts. I will reign over Danhomê, but I will abdicate all my powers to you. You, my beloved Wife of Panther, shall be the one who governs Danhomê.

"Your audacity is without precedent in this country. The tree can be known by the fruit it bears. The child of you loins will inherit, I am sure, your courage – the courage that has amazed all Danhomê. To the first son born of our love we shall bequeath the throne of Houégbaja.

"Our names will always be linked together in the songs of Adongbé and other singers, in the epithets that Panligan will recite every morning, in the oaths sworn by the people, and in the prayers they address each day to their ancestors to solicit their support for the throne of Houégbaja upon which we shall have been installed.

"After having been adored and obeyed by your royal husband and honored by his subjects, you will continue to be venerated by all Danhomê when you enter the realm of the dead. Wife of Panther who became Mother of Panther, you will have your own mausoleum next to mine.

"I call all my ancestors to witness my promise to make you happy! Believe me. Happiness awaits you at Jêgbé. Come with me."

"Vidaho owes a great deal to my husband. The king admits that Toffa helped him regain the throne. Didn't that make it possible for His Highness to become heir to the throne? Even if it could be shown that Vidaho owes nothing to Toffa, I myself owe him my fidelity.

"The promises of the heir to the throne would only turn the head of an ambitious woman. Vidaho knows very well that he cannot violate a strict traditional custom for my sake: the only women who can be consecrated Wives of Panther are the forty one young girls received by the heir to the throne from the hands of the king, his Father, when he publicly designated him as his successor; and these forty one young girls gave proof of their virginity on the very day of their marriage. It is also among the sons born to these forty one Wives of Panther that the Master of the World must choose his successor. However, I am already a wife," said Doguicimi without lifting her eyes from the mat.

183

"Love regards nothing as impossible, Doguicimi, because it can accomplish anything, make everything seem easy. With the complicity of the diviners to the throne, I will find reasons for deviating from the customary rules of succession for the kings of Danhomê. Do you understand me, Doguicimi? Believe me."

Remaining calm, she answered him: "How do you expect me to understand you, prince? I comprehend nothing in the language of the passion that is consuming you. Nor can I believe in it, for it is an illusion. Your persistence succeeds only in increasing a love for Toffa that already fills me to overflowing. Even if I were assured of indulgence on the part of my ancestors and family fetishes, despite the dishonor my shameful conduct would cast upon them, how do you expect me to greet Toffa upon his return, Toffa to whom I have sworn absolute fidelity? The elders are wisdom itself, and they say: 'It is the fear of being disgraced that causes the day to fade and the night to vanish.' A person without shame debases himself by descending to the level of the dogs. . . ."

"Since the fear of his return poses an obstacle to the flowering of our love, I will simply allow the prince to die in captivity, or I will eliminate him if he returns to Danhomê in spite of us. I am Vidaho. Everything is permitted to me in this kingdom over which I already reign in part."

"Me?" exploded Doguicimi, striking her chest with her left fist. "Me? Me plot against the liberation of Toffa? Agree to his death so I could marry his murderer? You miserable wretch, how dare you think of such a crime while I am still alive? How dare you speak of it with joy in your heart? I am telling you again, I owe absolute fidelity to Toffa. And the more I recall that I am his wife, the more I despise you, prince, you and all your wealth, your rank, and your handsome features, which count for nothing with me." She had stood up, a furious expression on her face, and was facing the prince, who had also risen and was preparing to leave in the fear of provoking a scandal that could be harmful to him; the terrifying spectre of Migan appeared to Vidaho, who realized that the first minister could damage his standing in the eyes of the king in order to avenge the prince's betrayal.

He wanted to leave, but his wounded pride bridled. Forgetting his situation, he retorted angrily: "Danhomê belongs to me and all Danhomênous along with it. The king, my august Father, desires that everyone in this nation be subject to me, as indicated by the name 'Jêgbé' that he gave to the Palace he ordered built for the heir to the throne, for it means, 'the human tongue does not refuse the taste of salt.' You should know, Doguicimi, because you pretend to have forgotten it, that I am the salt for the princes as for the common people. If Toffa were here, he himself would deliver you into my hands, and he would cover himself with dirt at my feet as a sign of gratitude if I accepted you."

"Toffa too is a prince," countered the woman.

"But his power was extinguished with the king, his Father. And custom obliges your Toffa to pay hommage to me, under penalty of death. If he refused to offer you to me upon his return to Danhomê, I myself could offer you his skull to clean before joining it with yours and burying both of them in my bathing room, where they would be soaked with the impurities that the water washes from my body every morning and evening."

"The heir to the throne can break the customary law that expressly forbids him from spilling the blood of a prince on this soil. But the criminal would be deceived if he hoped to enjoy the pleasure of wringing the least moan from us. Under the threat of death the ram responds to his murderer: 'Only my tail will fail me. But my executioner shall be making a serious mistake if, seeing it move, he concludes that I was afraid.' No, prince, the tears that might flow from my eyes would not mean that I fear death," continued Doguicimi energetically after a brief pause. "The sadist can also subject our remains to all sorts of abominations. What difference does it make to us! What creature has ever troubled himself over his corpse after life has gone out of it?"

"Your defiant boasts have no affect at all on me. Don't forget that the wares of the merchant who greedily raises their prices in a troubled market will have them taken away from him without a purse having been opened. Whatever I cannot obtain for the asking will be brought to my house upon the orders of my royal Father if I express even a momentary desire for it; I will in any case be your master. But watch out, Doguicimi. I will not accord you the honor of my bed. Ah, no! You will be given to the ugliest of my slaves. Then, when he will have grown weary of you, I will have you cut into pieces and fed to my dogs."

"The slave of the slave of His Highness will have no more than my dead body to defile. Regarding the prince's threats to have my mortal remains butchered and served to his dogs, I can only laugh at them."

She burst into laughter. She regained her composure. Her calm was an eloquent expression of her disdain for the torments with which the rejected suitor was menacing her.

"I love you, Doguicimi. But you push me away with disdain. Do you have any doubt that I can avenge, and in very cruel ways too, the affront you have inflicted upon me?" said Vidaho in a bittersweet tone of voice.

"Where has anyone ever heard tell of a head that withdrew into a body at the threat of being severed from it? For that matter, Toffa is worth my remaining faithful to him at the cost of enduring any torment that Vidaho's rancor might imagine."

His pride deeply offended, the prince, filled with rage, moved toward the door. Suddenly he wheeled and retraced his steps. He indeed belonged to the race of Panther, who slinks away after having been hit by a bullet, if his wound has not immobilised him, but who always returns a moment later to the place where he was attacked so that he can take his revenge – at least that is what the ancestors say. "Doguicimi, your ears remain deaf to my pleas!" he shouted to the woman. "Be careful; otherwise, Migan's scimitar will quickly deposit your head at the foot of my Father's throne!"

His new threats were greeted with silence. He left, still muttering words that the woman did not understand at all. In the street, he gnawed on his lips with anger. Overly enamored of his own handsome appearance, his fortune, his high rank, and the efficacy of his gris-gris, supposedly infallible in their power to dazzle, seduce, and conquer Doguicimi, he could not believe the defeat that had been inflicted upon his confidence with all the brutality of a hawk pouncing upon its prey, the defeat that had so cruelly wounded his royal prince's pride.

He, the future Master of Danhomê before whom all things were obliged to prostrate themselves, he to whom all things owed submission and obeisance, he had been humiliated and reduced to the level of a common Danhomênou – a thing.

This thought succeeded in discouraging him. Rather than walking, he dragged himself along, vowing that he would send someone to abduct Doguicimi before dawn.

He had posted a servant beneath a tree along the road and left him with the order to go quickly to his residence and announce his return; when he saw the man pass him and run on ahead, he recalled that his entire harem knew about his love for Doguicimi, that he had made all his wives jealous by praising the woman's extraordinary virtues, and that only the fear of punishment held them in check. He was afraid of the mockery that would greet the news of his failure. He stopped, looked to the right and to the left, and then exclaimed to himself: "I can't bear to endure the humiliation!" He plunged into the thick underbrush on his left.

The brambles demonstrated with considerable cruelty that they had never differentiated between princely flesh and that of commoners. Painfully he took three steps, flailing about in vain with his arms to blaze a trail for himself. The thorns that tore at his limbs and his clothes almost put out one of his eyes and did bring him to the realization that no power on this earth fails to encounter opposition and that it is folly to be stubborn. His feet and his arms were smarting with scratches. The pain restored him to reason, which had momentarily left him. He returned to the road, leaving several threads from his beautiful satin cloth to the thorns. Bowing under the weight of his defeat, he moved in the direction of his residence. Beware anyone who might happen to express feelings of joy. The rejected lover would certainly discharge his anger upon such a person. He promised himself that his first act after acquiring Danhomê would be to order the execution of the gris-gris man who had made a fool of him.

Everything was silent at Jêgbé, the wives of the heir to the throne having been informed that he was returning alone.

Noucounzin came to meet him about a hundred paces from the Palace and exhorted him to have courage and confidence, assuring him: "That which will be enjoyed for a long time is not acquired without disappointments and difficulties!"

Her words brought back a touch of courage to the heart of the embittered lover and a bit of cheerfulness to his face. The caresses of his wives, who pretended to be devastated and prayed aloud that the ancestors might grant the wishes of his princely heart, eventually succeeded in calming him and putting him to sleep.

Once the prince had left, Evêmon came out of the corner where she had been hiding. Kneeling in front of her mistress, she ingenuously reported to her about the fear she had felt and her intention to call for help at one moment. She added: "It does no good to be Vidaho: a snail cannot, I think, be obliged to attach itself firmly to a tree!"

Emerging from her meditations, Doguicimi informed the poor child: "A misfortune is hanging over our heads, my daughter. I don't want to hide it from you any longer. I had a foreboding of it on the very day when the prince first entered this house. I fear this misfortune less for myself than for you who have barely left your mother's womb. In this kingdom that is so blind to all sense of humanity and justice, it is, alas, customary to extend the responsibility for a crime committed by the head of the household to everything in the house, down to the calabashes and the gourds. But may it please Destiny and yourself that you be spared the hatred of the prince!"

Extremely worried, she paused briefly and then continued: "Ah, my forefathers! Beauty is a cause of trouble for women in this Danhomê, this country of passion, selfishness, and crime! All the women in whom I shall be reincarnated will be horribly ugly so they can enjoy peace."

"The beauty of my mother is not her only quality that seduces men. They are also attracted by her rare courage and her great shrewdness."

"You are right, my daughter. Life is incomprehensible. If you're a coward, even the ends of ropes take pleasure in swaying like snakes and frightening you. And if you're courageous? There will be no rest for you in this kingdom where everyone worships power."

"I have always shared in my mother's joy. Why would I allow her to remain alone today and drink the calabash of bitterness that Destiny is imposing upon her?" said the brave child as she kissed the ground that had been moistened with the tears she was trying in vain to hold back.

"Under such circumstances, our ancestors always took recourse in the science of the diviners. Tomorrow we shall see if we can tease a scrap of light from Destiny to illuminate the future, which seems quite somber to me now!"

Chapter 6

Conditions for the Liberation of Toffa

The thin crescent moon had first appeared in the West at the end of an "ajahi" day and then grown larger each night until it had finally covered the calabash and become completely round as it left its house in the East, where it had been transported two markets ago. It was the third moon that people had seen since Zanbounou's departure for Hounjroto, and, until the present, neither the spy nor any of the men in his company had returned.

Yet the Master of the World had ordered the leader of the mission to send one of his assistants back to Danhomê before the death of the second moon in case their stay in Hounjroto needed to be prolonged further.

The court was beginning to worry, not about the fate of the spy but rather about his loyalty.

The only warrant of it they had was the fact that Zanbounou had served as a liaison between the regent and the army's headquarters during the war of Hounjroto.

Questioning glances were directed toward Ajaho, who had recommended Zanbounou as being capable of performing an espionage mission in "mahi" country.

The minister was not at all concerned. He said: "Didn't the ancestors affirm that the Mahinou was the perfect person for the very important mission that was about to be entrusted to him? Would they have deceived their descendants? I cannot believe that."

When Destiny was consulted about the fate of the mission, he made an ambiguous declaration. On the basis of it, the king concluded that they should abandon all hope of ever again seeing Zanbounou, who had undoubtedly betrayed Danhomê.

"Or who perhaps was killed at Hounjroto," several counsellors suggested.

The court decided to send another spy into "mahi" country, despite the opposition of Ajaho, who did not believe Zanbounou was a traitor.

189

The very night of this decision brought the spy back to Danhomê. The high dignitaries were hastily summoned to hear his report.

He informed the court that he had planted all the gris-gris with which the king had supplied him. Those that were supposed to sow discord among the important people in "mahi" country so they would never agree upon the measures to be adopted in forestalling the revenge of Danhomê had been buried according to the instructions of the casters of spells. To large trees throughout enemy territory he had firmly attached gris-gris that would, whenever they were shaken by the wind, create dissension at Hounjroto or, as the gris-gris men had claimed, cause epidemics to break out and sorely try the population before the king again led his army in that direction. Zanbounou had seen about ten of the Amazons who had been captured by the Mahinous. They had promised him their help in burying the gris-gris he had brought from Danhomê in the houses of the "mahi" chiefs, whose wives they had become, and even in introducing them into the food and drink of these stinking beasts. He displayed fingernail clippings, hair, fragments of mats, and scraps of cloths that he swore had been taken from the bodies of the four regents of Hounjroto or had at least come in contact with them. On the floor he then spread out the white cloth he had received just before he left on his mission; swatches of variously colored and bizarrely shaped material had been sewn to it. Kneeling by the edge of this cloth and speaking to the counsellors who were leaning over it, he guided them through the villages that surrounded Hounjroto and were represented here by round grey patches, the size of which was proportionate to their importance. Pointing to the forests – irregularly shaped but invariably green pieces of material – he provided some information: "This one is reputed to be the haunt of wild animals. In all of Hounjroto not more than three hunters are known to have had the courage to set foot there. This other forest is protected by a formidable Ayidohouêdo – the Rainbow fetish. According to popular belief, one can enter it, but no one ever leaves. I myself have traveled across it in all directions: it is almost impenetrable. It is swarming with boas and savage beasts. Thirty thousand people could live for many moons in these forests without their presence being suspected by the inhabitants of the city."

Larger pieces of grey material depicted the mountains. The one closest to the city was Soponouta. The grey ribbons that started at the villages and outlying farms and wound their way toward the center represented paths. Following Zanbounou, his little band had taken one of them, and it led them into the city. The houses of the four new chiefs occupied the center. Next to the dwelling of Cotovi, the oldest and therefore the most influential of the chiefs, the spy pointed to a small circle, the prison of Toffa, Assogbaou, and Ajéhounou. Facing the king, he informed him in a voice filled with confidence: "The Blood Oath I had sworn with an important man in Hounjroto (he is in my debt for return of the peace that had fled his house after his ardor had been quenched) proved extremely beneficial for my purposes. I have his word that I will be allowed to see the three princes during my next trip to Hounjroto." After a pause, he added: "Most of the Danhomênous captured by the Mahinous were sold to the white men who run the slave-trade in Tê-Agbanli."

"And Dê, our cousin at Hogbonou, didn't lift a finger to redeem these unfortunate sons of the country and send them back to Danhomê!" shouted an indignant prince.

"Did he even try to inform us about it? He must be secretly rejoicing over our misfortune," another seconded him.

"And to think that he continued to seek our support for the already existing union between Agassou and Ajahouto! We may allow our cousins' collusion with the enemy to go unpunished, but our descendants will know how to deal with them," asserted Vidaho.

The king sighed: "Let us not be angry with anyone but implacable Destiny, who has been dogging our heels.

Zanbounou concluded his report: "The people of Mopa take an exaggerated pride in the aid they provided the king after his defeat at Hounjroto. All sorts of anecdotes offensive to the honor of the Houégbajas are making the rounds there."

Adipéto was the fetish priest in attendace at the court that day, and he administered the ordeal to determine whether or not the spy had spoken truthfully. As usual a cock took the place of Zanbounou and swallowed the poison. When he was released, he rose up on his legs, flapped his wings against each other three times, swelled his neck, craned it, and with a loud "cockadoodle doo" proclaimed the good faith of the spy.

The counsellors were delighted with the success of the mission and congratulated Zanbounou on it. The king ordered that he be given a wife, cloths, and two packets of cowry strings, adding that the next moon should find him back in Hounjroto.

One of the queens who was present at the meeting of the council whispered in her neighbor's ear: "Isn't that spy from your country? He has a mahi accent."

"He's my cousin. We were captured in the same war and grew up in Danhomê. As for him, he has never been able to rid himself of the accent from our place. He paid me a visit at the Door of Ganhohi on the eve of his departure for Hounjroto and will not fail to come and see me now that he is back."

Zanbounou was supposed to be placed under surveillance at Ajaho's residence. But Vidaho had expressed the opinion that the conscientiousness with which the spy had accomplished his mission was an undeniable proof of his loyalty toward Danhomê and that he ought therefore to be trusted and left at liberty; no one among the ranks of the princes and high dignitaries dared to argue with him.

Joyously, Zanbounou crossed the Courtyard of the Palace, his new wife following him and carrying the other presents from the king.

Ever since a time that had begun three market days ago, the spy regularly left his house at nightfall only to return at the first crowing of the cock. His absences during the day were rare and very short.

Having left at the break of day, Fadonougbo, the diviner in Toffa's household, did not return until the shadows of dusk had covered the lines of Destiny in people's hands with its somber veil. He came to inform Doguicimi how the commentaries he had made upon the oracle during an important ceremonial consultation of Destiny, to which he had been invited along with a number of other eminent diviners, had attracted the attention of a man who had taken him aside and asked him to explain another oracle. "Having told him of an impending journey or one that had already been taken, I learned from him that he had recently returned from mahi country and was going to return there very soon.

"He is coming to see me again because he is certain," he told me enthusiastically, "of finally having found a divinier whose science of the future can illuminate his way, helping him to succeed in his mission while avoiding the traps that the wariness of the Mahinous might lay for him.

"This man is no doubt spying on Hounjroto and must keep his mission very secret. But nothing can be hidden from diviners like us. I will skillfully draw out of him everything he has been able to learn about the absent beloved. And if he didn't bring back any news of the Master from his first journey, I will succeed in persuading him to undertake an investigation for us when he returns."

Zanbounou actually came the following morning to consult "Fadonougbo, who is unequalled in all Danhomê for clairvoyance," as the spy repeatedly said in approaching Toffa's diviner.

Introduced to Doguicimi, he confided in her: "I have just come back from Hounjroto; I saw the prison where the three princes are being held and spoke with their guards, to whom I even sold a span of tobacco. I was promised that I would be allowed to meet Toffa, Assogbaou, and Ajéhounou during my next trip."

His hesitations, the oath of secrecy he had initially imposed upon his hosts, the voice that he lowered, and the anxious glances that he cast to the left and to the right to assure himself that there were no witnesses to their conversation – everything about the man inspired great confidence in Toffa's wife.

"You say that you will have the pleasure of seeing him!" exclaimed Doguicimi, striking her chest with the palms of both hands after a sudden joy had propelled her out of her chair. She approached the spy and suggested to him: "I will disguise myself as a man and follow you on your next trip."

"Not only do I not choose my own traveling companions, but there are several among them who watch my every word and every move to report back on them to Ajaho when we return to Danhomê. Spies find themselves in an unfortunate situation. They are mistrusted even by those who make use their services!" explained Zanbounou with a tone of regret in his voice at being unable to offer the woman the happiness of going to see her dear husband."

"Ah, if only my eyes, ripped from their sockets and entrusted to you, could go to look upon him and report back to me, I would give them to you this very instant! But since you are going there without me, tell him that only the thought that he is still alive and the hope that he will return to Danhomê are keeping me alive.

"Tell him as well that children were born to him as soon as the second moon after his departure for the war and that those who could not even sit up while he was still in Danhomê are now beginning to walk and to talk. In their ignorance of the misfortune that has overtaken them, they fill the house with a joy they share only with themselves. Tell him that his wives weep for him every day and make offerings to his ancestors and to all the fetishes in the kingdom in the hope that they will facilitate his escape. As he awaits the glorious day of his return, which I so ardently desire, let him deign to think of me and to appear frequently in my dreams. As a result of not having seen him, I let my hair and my fingernails grow long."

It was with great difficulty that Zanbounou succeeded in taking leave of Doguicimi to go into the room of the oracle with Fadonougbo.

The sacrifices prescribed by Destiny brought the spy back to the diviner the next morning, to the great joy of Toffa's wife, who never tired of questioning him about Hounjroto and burdening him with messages for the noble prince. She showed him all the children who had been born since the disappearance of their father and exhorted him not to forget their names.

Zanbounou left Agbomê five days after his first visit to Toffa's house. This time the king gave him six men loaded with an assortment of goods chosen according to the tastes of the Mahinous as identified with the help of information provided by the spy himself: the Agoudas's rum and tobacco, velvet and satin cloths, glass beads, mirrors, pipes, etc. . . .

When she heard about the departure of the second espionage mission for Hounjroto, Doguicimi invoked the ancestors of Toffa at great length to assure Zanbounou's success. Until the spy returned, she would offer sacrifices to the fetishes on the days devoted to their worship so that they might protect him and guide him safely to Toffa.

Every morning before cleaning her teeth with a polished wooden stick, she promised the protective fetishes of the kingdom that, if Toffa returned, they would receive goats paid for with her fortune and sacrificed by the prince himself.

*   *   *

By the first crowing of the cock Zanbounou, having already passed through the last village that separated him from Hounjroto, had arrived in the great forest where, according to the beliefs of the Mahinous, Ayidohouêdo had his abode. They were some eight hundred bamboos from the city. The spy gave instructions to two of his assistants, who immediately left for Hounjroto, which the Mahinous themselves call Hounjrogonji.

Led by an occasional guide to the shrine of Sapata, one of the country's protective fetishes, the two Danhomênous passed for brothers from Gbowêlê who had just been instructed by the powerful fetish, which spoke through the voice of the oracle, to perform a sacrifice that would enable them to find their

193

elder brother Bossa, who had left for Zado many dry seasons ago and from whom they had heard nothing since that time. Their offering consisted of a goat, a cock, a chicken, a sack of beans, a calabash of maize flour, two bottles of palm oil, and as many of the Agoudas's rum, and they promised to multiply these gifts if the missing brother returned home.

The chief fetishist presented the offering to the fetish and entreated it to bring Bossa back to the house of his fathers. The two strangers, the adepts of the cult, and the personnel of the shrine were all kneeling and facing the house of the idol as they lent support to the prayers of the sacrificial priest. Over all the idols grouped together in the structure he poured the palm oil which had been offered by the strangers but which contained ingredients that were incompatible with Sapata. The goat and the fowl were then sacrificed.

Fires were already burning in four fireplaces, each of which had been constructed with three large stones and was amply supplied with wood.

The sacrificial priest opened the bottles of rum. Among the assistants, cheekfuls of chewing tobacco were already being depleted, and everyone was impulsively spitting to the side without paying any attention to his neighbor's feet. They all gazed longingly at the bottles and swallowed the saliva that a still unsatisfied desire brought to their mouths.

Most Mahinous didn't offer anything more than millet beer. These people from Gbowêlê must really be in contact with the Zadonous. It was no doubt the missing brother who had brought this delectable and extremely rare white man's drink from there. One was certainly justified in missing that sort of absent relative.

A few drops of rum were poured over the idols. The miniscule calabash that was used on such rare occasions was filled and passed around among those who were present. The most advanced initiates received two swallows; the bottles were soon lying on their sides. A sudden warmth raced from the mouth to the bowels. Tongues clicked noisily. An old man who had received his portion dipped his finger into it and allowed the drops to fall on the ground; it was the ancestors' share that he was offering them. He swallowed the liquor, then closed his eyes, squeezed his nostrils between his two little fingers, and plugged his ears with his thumbs. He remained in this position for a moment. In this way, he thought, neither the warmth that had passed from his mouth to his bowels nor the aroma of this delightful drink would find a way out of his body, and he would be able to enjoy them at his leisure. The warmth rose back into his head; from whence it came he did not know. He opened his eyes; they were red. He released his nostrils and unplugged his ears. "After my death, I'll be reincarnated in the land of the white men! They alone know how to make delicious things!" the old fellow exclaimed.

Warmed by the drink that, although it never makes the bottle drunk, acts quite differently on mortals, tongues were loosened. People didn't listen much, but they talked a great deal and very loudly. One old chap had already fallen asleep, leaning against the house of the fetish and snoring. His peers mocked his lack of virility.

Tapping his throat, one Mahinou declared: "From time to time we need the warmth these cunning white men know how to put in bottles, for it rejuvenates the old men!"

Leaning toward the two strangers, another one assured them: "Brothers, your lost relative will soon return to the hearth, and we will be happy to see all three of you again at this shrine."

An old woman fetishist began singing a sacred song. Someone asked her from whom she had received the order or the suggestion to do so.

"From the white man's delectable beverage of course, since women seem to understand its language better than you men!" retorted the old woman, her eyes sparkling.

Her reply sparked an outburst of laughter.

The singer began her song again. The assistants intoned the refrain in chorus. They accompanied themselves by beating their hands simultaneously against their chests and their thighs. People started to dance. One could get tired that way. Several paces away from the dancers the smell of the meat, which was already being removed from the pots to prepare the foofoo, had just announced that the food would soon be served.

The cock and the chicken had been done for a long time. The stews made with their bullion were already getting cold in their large calabashes.

Two beans pressed together between the thumb and the index finger were reduced to a paste; they were sufficiently cooked, but there was still a bit too much water. But by the time the pot with the foofoo was placed on the ground, all the water in the beans had evaporated.

"A few more sacred songs and a few new dance steps, time enough for all the dishes to be well cooked!" suggested an adept of the cult.

"I've already sweated out all my rum!" shouted an old man.

Explosions of laughter applauded his remark.

"If you pray well for the prompt return of our brother, you will once again enjoy the white man's delectable beverage," advised one of the two strangers.

Songs and dances started again but less fervently than before. Large, steaming calabashes soon arrived; they were filled with beans that had been sprinkled with oil. Four more large calabashes followed with stew made from boiled goat and chicken meat. Two mouthfuls of each dish were deposited on the great fetish, on all the idols surrounding it, and then on all the idols of the shrine. The fetishists crouched in groups of six or seven around the calabashes from which the different dishes were being served. When all the assistants had eaten their fill, two calabashes of leftovers were taken to the shrine's main courtyard, where songs and the clapping of hands that announced the celebration of an important rite had attracted a crowd of children and passersby.

Before bidding the two brothers farewell, the fetishists once again assured them that the great fetish of the Mahinous would protect their relative and bring him back home before the harvest of the yams.

When they returned to the forest, the two spies were given new missions to

195

accomplish in another part of the country, while Zanbounou, followed by his other assistants, made his way to the city.

Already the next day he took advantage of his old friendships to travel to all the villages and farms near Hounjrogonji with the help of guides furnished by his sworn friends.

*   *   *

Two moons later, having disposed of all his gris-gris and judging himself sufficiently well informed, Zanbounou left "mahi" country and returned to give an account of his second mission.

The ordeal by poison was administered to determine the truthfulness of the spy, and it once again pronounced itself in his favor.

Migan asked if it might not be possible to engage in an expedition before the next moon. The two ministers of war saw no obstacles to such a plan. But the king thought differently: "A third mission is needed so that bewitched oil and alcohol can be spread over all the 'mahi' fetishes and thereby make certain that Hounjroto will be protected by none of its fetishes."

The council sided with his words of wisdom.

At the suggestion of Vidaho, the king again rewarded the spies with more than they had hoped to receive.

The next day Zanbounou went with his assistants to thank the prince, who took him aside and spoke at great length with him.

Zanbounou's visit that evening at Toffa's house brought with it an unexpected joy.

"I cannot tell a lie. I did not see the prince. But with these ears (the spy pulled on their lobes), I heard his deep voice. He was talking with his brothers, and I picked up these words: 'Who in Danhomê cares about the fate of those who are missing?' I immediately wanted to cry out that the Master of the World, their own wives and children, all Danhomê, and especially you, Doguicimi, were hoping for their swift release and that I had come to Hounjroto for the second time to effect that very purpose. I was prevented from doing so by my guide, who placed his broad hands across my mouth just in time. The man led me away from there and severely censured me, pointing out that a single word from me would have betrayed me irrevocably and resulted in not only my death and his but also those of the three prisoners who would be obliged to expiate my imprudence.

"The Mahinou whose protection enabled me to approach so closely to the three princes is the eldest son of the 'mahi' king who was killed in the last war.

"His Father had only been chosen to reign because he had two sorts of horns on his forehead, a sign of great wisdom, as Destiny affirmed.

"Since the death of this king, whose decapitated body was found in front of his palace after the retreat of the Danhomênous, the ancestors and the fetishes have designated four regents from among the important men of the kingdom – all of them related to the dead man – and notified his sons that the condition upon which one of them can succeed to the throne is the recovery, in advance,

196

of their father's skull, which should always be at the side of his successor before any important decision can be made.

"The pretender to the throne promised to have me taken to the illustrious prisoners if I can obtain the skull of his Father for him.

"The young prince to whom I am bound by a sworn friendship even committed himself to facilitate the escape of the most interesting of the three prisoners.

"I was careful not to report a word of this conversation at the court because the king had assigned me a very specific mission when I left Danhomê: to evaluate the enemy's military strength, to ascertain the Mahinous' intentions toward Danhomê, and to distribute the gris-gris that are supposed to afflict the population of Hounjroto with hardships and to sow discord among the regents. The Master of the World is only concerned with the conquest of the 'mahi' country as a means to his own glory, not because he desires to liberate his unfortunate brothers, as you believe.

"Doguicimi, it depends upon you alone to facilitate a meeting for me with your husband, to hasten the moment when you will see the idol of your heart once again. Obtain the skull in question for me as quickly as you can. The king may well order me to return to Hounjroto before the next 'ajahi,' which is only four days away. It seems he is only waiting for the return of the royal messenger who has been dispatched to Alada before furnishing me with a new supply of gris-gris and sending me on my way to 'mahi' country. During my next visit here you must give me the skull and any commissions you might have for the prisoner. Take advantage of the friendships your noble husband did not fail to make among the high dignitaries of this kingdom, and try to obtain the skull as soon as this evening!"

When Zanbounou had left the reception room, Doguicimi remained lost in thought. Her faithful servant had already been standing beside her for a few moments. Evêmon had seen the spy enter the house, and she suspected that he had come back from Hounjroto, but she did not know what news he had brought about the missing prince. "Nothing serious!" she thought. But why was her "mother" so sad and silent? The young child respected her mistress's meditations.

Doguicimi sighed deeply, shook her head, and said: "If I can believe this Mahinou, there is a skull in the Palace, and for my husband to be freed, it only needs to be returned to Hounjroto. How could I succeed in stealing this macabre trophy? Who would help me in this most dangerous of undertakings? The queens? I shouldn't even think about them. They have sworn to bring about my downfall, as the heir to the throne assured me. Vidaho is also not the one who would help me because this skull would allow me to be reunited with Toffa, and no one seems more interested in keeping my husband at Hounjroto than the future Master of Danhomê." She plunged back into her meditations, and as she reemerged from them, she said to herself: "I know that he would quickly agree to obtain this skull for me if I would only consent to renounce my honesty. Ah, what a miserable life is mine!"

A new silence reigned, intermittently broken by the woman's sighs. She finally regained her sleeping place and extinguished the small oil lamp so as to abandon herself more completely to her thoughts.

When sleep did overtake her shortly before the first crowing of the cock, she had still not found an honorable solution to her dilemma. But to give herself courage, she had told herself: "Only that will occur which Destiny has ordained! I will go straight to my goal."

The next day Evêmon left at the behest of her "mother" to summon Princess Noucounzin.

At Doguicimi's request that she arrange a meeting for her with Vidaho, the princess replied that she did not see how she could possibly convince the noble prince, who had been so grievously mortified the last time, to return beneath this roof.

"You were neither flexible nor shrewd, Doguicimi," she added, staring into the air. "It is difficult for me to understand it on the part of a Danhomênou with your reputation. I really do not know how I can approach the prince and pronounce your name in his presence. You know little about a prince from Danhomê. The person who suffers from an abscess is the one who should run after the possessor of a knife, as the elders say. Vidaho would no doubt receive you at Jêgbé."

Toffa's wife reminded her that custom forbid her to make such a visit.

Noucounzin left without insisting further on a visit to Jêgbé by Doguicimi but also without giving any assurances that the heir to the throne would come to Toffa's house.

Nevertheless, Doguicimi awaited the prince's visit until after the middle of the night. Her eyes on the alert and her ears pricked in the direction of the portal, she took a simple sound as the creaking of a door being opened, a shadow as the illustrious visitor for whom she was waiting, and the desire of her heart for reality. Hope deceived was reborn a moment later only to fade away and be reborn again.

The next day one of Noucounzin's servants came to inform Doguicimi that Vidaho had been detained at the Palace all day and all night for an important meeting of the council and that his sister had been unable to reach him.

The following night brought the heir to the throne back to Toffa's house. When he knew the substance of the matter, he exaggerated the difficulties and potentially serious consequences of the favor she was asking him. Only the queens could obtain the skull for him, but he didn't see where he could communicate with them to obtain what Doguicimi desired. If he succeeded and if the king noticed the disappearance of this war trophy, Vidaho would certainly be denounced by someone. Jealous of his choice as the heir presumptive, his brothers would have an easy time destroying his right to the throne by accusing him of high treason or by portraying him as a man subject to the whims of beings with seven pairs of ribs and therefore incapable of reigning over Danhomê, which needs a forceful king.

He would like to be useful to the woman who had rejected him, but he could not assure her that he would be able to obtain the skull of the mahi king for her.

Any other woman would have thrown herself at the feet of her powerful admirer and attempted, in a fit of tears, to move him to pity so as to extract from his tender heart the definite promise that he would bring her the "mahi" king's skull. But Doguicimi was in control of herself, and she disdained devious methods. She would go to work more rationally and on more fertile ground. She looked the prince straight in the eye and asked him: "Ah, the heir to the throne really doesn't have all the power he boasted of having in this kingdom?"

The wound that this barb inflicted upon his princely pride caused him to stiffen haughtily; with a gentle smile on his lips, he promised to do everything necessary to please the woman whom he adored, even though she despised him.

He left, filled with the joy that is aroused by the hope of a victory – the conquest of a desired woman. But if, in the absence of such a conquest, he could prove that the woman who claimed to love her husband so much had been guilty of adultery, he would immediately bring the evidence of Doguicimi's infidelity to the attention of the court and have her sentenced to death before the return of her husband in order to set an example for other wives.

Doguicimi had also foreseen all the difficulties surrounding the favor she was going to ask of the heir to the throne, and she feared the serious consequences they would face if they were ever betrayed. She was astonished that Vidaho consented so quickly to obtain for her the skull that would help bring about Toffa's return to Danhomê. And she lost herself in conjectures about the possible motivations of the prince: "He perhaps knows that Toffa is dead, and he has convinced himself that he will easily conquer me after having done me this favor? Or is it that I am indebted to Destiny, as supported by my ancestors and family fetishes, for Vidaho's failure to make the performance of this service contingent upon the condition I feared most.

Despite the assurances the prince had given her, she doubted from time to time that he would actually do her such a favor. She even considered the possibility of a simultaneous betrayal by Vidaho and Zanbounou. But she was completely reassured the next evening by a visit from Noucounzin. The princess brought the skull and informed Doguicimi that the heir to the throne had been detained at the Palace by a council meeting that had been taking place since that morning and that he regretted being unable to come in person; nevertheless, he renewed his promise to do anything he could to assure the happiness of the woman who persisted in refusing to share his love.

At the third crowing of the cock Zanbounou arrived at Toffa's house; he informed Doguicimi that during the previous night the council had decided to send a new espionage mission and that he had been told about it just a few moments ago; he would leave before nightfall. He took the skull and left, promising to return with Toffa.

In actual fact he did leave Agbomê that very day. His absence only lasted two moons.

The importance of the information he brought back was such that, soon after the council had heard Zanbounou's report, the king dispatched royal messengers to the Governors of the provinces beyond the Swamps.

During the night the spy went to Toffa's house. Doguicimi did not even think of offering him a place to sit and water to drink before asking him: "He did not come back with you? Did you at least get to see him? Is he going to remain in captivity for a long time?"

Zanbounou replied as he held out a packet to her: "He gave me this gris-gris, which guarantees invulnerability against all weapons, to serve as a royal messenger's baton in the eyes of his favorite wife, proving clearly that I had the pleasure of seeing him and passing on all the messages with which I was charged. He assured me that you would recognize the gris-gris because you yourself had it sent to him with the help of Vivênagbo on the eve of the battle at Hounjroto. He recommends that you tell no one about the information he will be imparting to you through me."

Pressing the gris-gris to her chest, the woman danced with joy. When Evêmon heard her, she ran into the room. Doguicimi ordered a second oil lamp to be lit so that she could gaze upon the eyes that had experienced the happiness of seeing those of her husband.

Examining the traveler's face as if she could see Toffa's image imprinted on it, she queried him: "You saw him? You saw him with these eyes? And he gave you this gris-gris? You told him that I'm wearing my hair and fingernails long out of grief at not having seen him for such a long time? Ah, if my absence wouldn't be noticed, I would go with you to Hounjroto!"

"Toffa is also burning with impatience to see his favorite wife again. A prince of Danhomê, especially if he is the brother of Guézo, is not made to live the life of a captive in 'mahi' country, where he will find none of the good things Danhomê has acquired from the white men for the happiness of high dignitaries and members of the royal family."

"But didn't the son of the king of Hounjroto promise you that he'd facilitate my husband's escape?"

"I would have brought Toffa and Assogbaou back to Danhomê, if the Master of the World had expressed for a single moment the desire to see his brothers again. Even more than the services I have rendered this kingdom at the risk of my own life, the Blood Oath that binds me to the king reassures me with regard to Guézo, who would certainly pardon my overzealousness. But the talk I overheard during the council meetings at court proves that the queens and palace dignitaries have sworn that Toffa will never see Danhomê again. Without a doubt they would make me pay for the deliverance of your husband with my life."

"Surely Vivênagbo cannot be counted among the noble prince's enemies, and he is a powerful patron. Toffa was already well liked by the Danhomênous, and his sufferings in captivity have heightened their affection for him. Once he returns to Danhomê, he will be venerated, and if you are under his protection, you will have nothing to fear, not even for the least hair on your head."

"As far as Vivênagbo's commitment to Toffa and his family is concerned, he is only performing the duties of loyalty, protection, and devotion that the Blood Oath imposes, under penalty of terrible punishments, upon those who are

200

bound by it. Without having contracted such a pact with the king, I would never have agreed to go and place my life in danger by spying on Hounjroto. I also owe the success of my many missions into 'mahi' country to this practice. As long as I have not entered into a sworn friendship with you, I will not undertake anything for the salvation of your husband. Only the Blood Oath would offer me a certain guarantee that Toffa, once he had returned here with my help, could never dream of rewarding my services by having me killed, since it is customary for princes of Danhomê to eliminate their benefactors. Don't you know that the pride of these princes is always offended by the memory that they do not owe their fortunes solely to their own efforts, their merit, or their high birth? Wasn't Toffa among the princes who, at the risk of their own lives, supported their brother against the tyrant and made him King Guézo? What was your husband's reward? He saw himself sent to Hounjroto, where a group of soldiers, acting upon an order that had been transmitted to them with the utmost secrecy, delivered him up to the enemy. Toffa's exact words were these: 'I was betrayed by Danhomênous themselves. I was supplied with gris-gris that were infallible in warding off bullets and knives. But I didn't have any gris-gris that could protect me against cabals organized by my own brother and totally unsuspected by me. I was wounded in such a way that I am justified in saying, like the tortoise who was hit in the neck by an arrow during the war: A member of my own race who knew my vulnerable spot was undoubtedly the one who shot this arrow at me!'

"Doguicimi, I cannot be too mistrustful of the princes. If your husband were saved by me, he would not fail to plot my downfall. I doubt that his pride could bear the thought that he, a son of Agonglo, would have owed his salvation to a man of my race, which your princes scornfully refer to as the 'stinking beasts from the mountains!' I don't know how many dry seasons I have been rubbing shoulders with the Lêdahonous, who are not at all insulted by their reputation as oath-breakers. I owe it to myself to demand a foolproof guarantee. Doguicimi alone seems to offer one because she is a woman of the people. I will liberate Toffa as soon as the Blood Oath links me with his favorite wife. This is the practice to which Guézo owes the recovery of the throne that Agonglo had bequeathed to him. In the same way Doguicimi will be reunited with her husband, who has been missing for many moons. After the return of the prince, we will renew the pact together; that is how I can be certain that Toffa will remain absolutely silent about the details of his escape from Hounjroto."

"You do not know the man. He is a prince, it is true, but all Danhomênous who have ever rendered him the slightest service have had nothing but praise for the way he expresses his gratitude."

"He will not continue being grateful forever! And if he were still here, people would already be mourning his benefactors! You will not convince me that the old blood of Daco-Donou will never rise in this prince. Unless he is not of the same race! I am determined not to lift a finger for the liberation of Toffa until the Blood Oath binds me to his favorite wife, the only person who could oblige him to spare my life when he might want to take it in return for my devoted service, following the example of his ancestors, whom you yourself have upbraided in public."

"What offer of assistance would I reject if I had the assurance it would help me deliver my husband from his captivity!" said Doguicimi in a resigned tone of voice.

"Tomorrow I will bring the necessary objects for the rite we will perform far from any indiscreet glances; we will crouch down facing each other in the same state as we were when the Creator sent us into this world; we will dig a small hole and surround it with symbolic designs; in a human skull that serves me for this purpose we will prepare the oath-potion we shall drink after each of us has allowed several drops of blood to flow into it and sworn the oaths of truthfulness, loyalty, and devotion. We shall thus have each other's blood in our bodies. In the end we will show each other that there is nothing we can refuse to a 'brother' or a 'sister' of the pact. I will then attempt to deliver Toffa. If I have to pay for his salvation with my life, I will die without regret! The thought that will console me in my final moments is the knowledge that my blood continues to flow in the body of a Danhomênou woman who will surely protect my family."

"After this pact, I will no longer belong entirely to Toffa."

"His return will make you happy. One only enjoys happiness that has been bought at a high price."

"One should only give to others what belongs to one's self. I no longer belong to myself since the day when the king gave me to the Master of this house. I cannot dispose of other people's things without prior permission, and I do not know in what terms I would dare speak to my husband about it."

"Would you need a drowning person's permission to save him? For that matter, nothing obliges you to disclose to your husband the cost of the sacrifices you made to bring him back to Danhomê. In his presence we will even refrain from any remark or familiar gesture that might betray our relationship. Even if he suspected it, would he blame his wife for it? Is Doguicimi not aware of how little respect the Danhomênou has for his women and how little importance he attaches to their infidelities? I saw Toffa (he touched his right eye with the index finger of his right hand). He entrusted me with secrets that allow me to assure you that he would not hesitate to sacrifice everything he owns, including his wives, to regain his freedom."

"I am his property; he can therefore sacrifice me whenever it is in his interest to do so. I will never complain in such a case. But far from reassuring me, the precautions you urge upon me are very upsetting. Moreover, for me to reject your proposal, all I need to know is the state in which you require me to present myself in front of the oath-swearing hole. If Toffa's deliverance can only be bought at the price of my dishonor, let him die in captivity. The nobility of the prince's soul is such that he will approve of my decision when we see each other again in the city of the dead." She looked the spy straight in the eye and then addressed him with indignation: "No, Mahinou! The woman who rejects the propositions of a horse-trader will not accept those of his stable-boy. You should also realize that the mouth which has been accorded the honor of sharing the meals of a panther will never stray toward the leftovers fed to a dog." She reinforced this insult by spitting and turning away.

"If I die before dawn, the deep wound that your pride has just inflicted upon my self-esteem will have been the only cause. One can see that the return of your husband is not really important to you. If you didn't already know it, be apprised that the beast from the mountain who is standing in front of you and whom you despise so much is the very person who made possible the escape of Ajéhounou, believed by all Danhomê to have been killed at Hounjroto." Swelling with pride, he continued: "The prince returned last night in the company of Zanbounou, who will never divulge the name of the person or the nature of the sacrifices responsible for the happiness of Ajéhounou's family at being reunited with him."

The spy left, humiliated and frightened at the same time. Who would have believed that he who had succeeded in much more difficult missions at Hounjroto could have failed so miserably today?

He thought: "When a woman grants you her favors, the betrayal seldom occurs consciously by itself. If she rejects your proposal? You have to fear she will denounce you. I knew in advance that, if Doguicimi ever began talking about my attempt to seduce her, no one would admit that I had been sent to that house with the specific mission of helping to conquer this woman or of bringing about her downfall if she persisted in closing her eyes to the prospect of happiness. Overcome with pity for her, I had decided to remain silent about the favors she might accord me and to divert the blow of Migan's scimitar, which was hanging over her neck. Her disdain for me frees me from any pity I might have felt for her; all I have to do now is devote my efforts to bringing her down. Zanbounou, you still have to face the anger of the love-struck prince who was counting on you to satisfy his passions or to avenge him if that proved impossible!"

Doguicimi was far from suspecting all the intrigues that had precipitated Zanbounou into her life; she only knew that the nation of spies was profoundly malicious, and she feared that Zanbounou's rancor would turn against Toffa in his captivity.

"Don't you agree, Evêmon, that we must not purchase the Master's liberation at the cost of our own dishonor?" she asked now that she was alone with her servant.

"My mother is right. Nevertheless, let her deign to recall the prophecies of Destiny: 'Something good will be given to us at the hands of a foreigner.' Since Zanbounou's umbilical cord was not buried in this country, he is undoubtedly the foreigner about whom the oracle was speaking. Wouldn't it be imprudent to reject him completely?"

"Destiny actually did give us this advice. But what honest woman could accept this man's infamous proposal? Ah, that other stinking beast from the mountain was telling the truth when he sang his song at the last traditional ceremony: 'Life reserves misfortunes for one who does not die in childhood!' Doguicimi refused the heir to the throne, who offered to marry her officially and promised to elevate her to the rank of queen mother; would this same Doguicimi dishonor herself with a slave? I can't do it! If I had only heard that Toffa was no longer alive! I would immediately join him!"

"We must defer to the wisdom of Destiny when our own honorable efforts to overcome a bad situation have failed. Recourse to extreme solutions is often a sign of cowardice.

"Ever since my mistress urged me to pray for the Master's return and promised never to send me away from her if my prayers were answered, I have not ceased to invoke, morning and evening, the protection of my fetishes and my ancestors on behalf of the missing prince. The thought that my happiness depends on his return causes me to redouble the fervor of the pleas I address to my Creator. But I am prepared to sacrifice this prospect of happiness for that of my mother, who remains inconsolable at the loss of her husband. People don't go on foot when they have a good mount. . . ."

A profound sigh was the only response to the sisterly affection that spoke in the voice of this child, who continued: "I am part of the wedding basket presented to you by the prince at the moment of your marriage. To bring back the Master, you have sold your cloths and your jewels to purchase the offerings that have been made to the fetishes. Nothing prevents you from disposing of me in the same way. Am I not your property just as much as the objects of which you have deprived yourself? My mistress very well knows that people don't pick up filth with their hands if they have a hoe."

"Prostitute you, my daughter? I would die before I decided to do that!"

"No marriage could be more in conformity with custom than mine with Zanbounou, and no one would blame you for it. Isn't it permitted by tradition? Thus, you don't even need the king's authorization to act."

"That's true," sighed Doguicimi. "But the wretch only wants me. Yet you are very pretty! And I don't believe any man in Danhomê is capable of resisting your charm for long."

"I can't promise anything if the Mahinou is merely obeying a specific command from someone else. But if passion alone is motivating his desire for my mistress, I will know how to please this man and make him accept me in your place. Your honor will be saved. Once I have conquered Zanbounou, I shall have no difficulty at all in imposing my will on him and accompanying him on his next trip to Hounjroto. I will see the Master and tell him of your suffering.

"My mother, if the Master's return depends upon no more than my union with this Mahinou, we will soon see him again."

"But he's a capricious person and could reject you."

There was a long silence. Her forehead resting in her left palm, Doguicimi remained for a moment in the same position. When she raised her head, her face was bathed with tears. She sighed: "Oh, Destiny has been cruel to me!

Is anyone in all Danhomê more unhappy than Doguicimi? What malice on the part of all the men who so mercilessly exploit the misfortune of a poor woman!

"One of them dangles in front of my eyes the supposed happiness he is preparing for me in his Palace. When I turned a deaf ear to his protestations of love and his pleas that I accept him as my husband, he resorted to threats, believing he could intimidate me and seduce me in that way.

"Now another man proposes a disgusting transaction as his price for freeing my husband from his captivity in 'mahi' country. And to think that somewhere there is a Creator who unconcernedly watches this misfortune occuring to the most innocent of his creatures!

"At least the Mahinou can do something to bring about the noble prince's return. He saw Toffa! I am quite familiar with the gris-gris he brought back from Hounjroto, and it obviously proves that! Zanbounou assured me that it would be just as easy for him to free my husband as it had been for him to bring back Ajéhounou, who everyone thought was dead! But what a vile condition this unscrupulous spy placed upon his help in liberating my husband! Toffa loved me; I can have no doubt of that. I was his favorite among all the wives who lived with him in Danhomê. I shared his joy; when he was worried, his gaze invariably turned toward me; he always followed my advice and accorded all the favors or kindnesses I ever requested for his servants or some one of his wives. He believed in my fidelity. His harsh judgment of all women on the eve of his departure for Hounjroto was a mere outburst of pique; moreover, his anger was justified by the behavior of the queens.

"Although his misfortune may have resulted from the whims of the king's wives, Toffa must nonetheless continue to venerate women, as he was fond of saying, in memory of his good mother.

"It would be odious to deliberately deceive the confidence this man has placed in me! Trying to justify such an act by claiming that I desired to save him would never exonerate me from my guilt."

She fell back into her meditations, which she soon continued aloud as she shook her head: "Prostitute myself? Condoning in Toffa's house the sort of behavior that my mother never allowed beneath my father's roof? Doguicimi would sooner die than accept such a disgrace!" she asserted forcefully. "Life is already too painful for me! Much too long I have been plagued by the thought that my noble husband is suffering privation and humiliation at Hounjroto at the very time when I am living in abundance at Agbomê! Prostitute myself?" she asked herself again in an indignant tone of voice. "Ah, my ancestors! Why don't you put an end to my sufferings, which have already lasted for so many moons? What unsuspected offense are you obliging me to expiate? How could the shame they are urging upon me be an expiation? Destiny conceals many secrets from us simple mortals, but my mind refuses to admit that such infamy could serve to expiate crimes committed in some former life!"

Warm tears flowed abundantly across her cheeks and bathed her chest, even though she was clenching her teeth and biting her lips to prevent her sorrow from surfacing.

Chapter 7

A Conspiracy

Evêmon's innocence found expression in the fullness of her bosom, the firmness of her breasts, and the frankness of her eyes, and it admirably complemented her graceful form.

The princes who encountered her in public silently congratulated the fortunate father of such a rare jewel before addressing a few compliments to the young girl herself. Flattered, she occasionally replied with her innocent smile.

Doguicimi herself was fond of saying that the Creator had fashioned her and the child with clay dug from the same pit, because the physical as well as the moral resemblance between them was so great. It is true that Evêmon had not yet offered any proof of her courage. But Doguicimi could have no doubts about her, assuring herself that every heart filled with love was capable of commitment, which never occurs without the courage that this child certainly possessed in a latent state.

Ajéhounou had actually returned to Danhomê with the help of Zanbounou. His liberation had given new hope to the families of the other two princes still held captive at Hounjroto, and it had confirmed Doguicimi's opinion that the spy could contribute significantly to the freeing of her husband.

Bowing to Evêmon's entreaties and after having consulted Destiny, who had declared the young girl's spirit to be in harmony with that of Zanbounou, Doguicimi resigned herself to give her to the Mahinou in marriage. But the wedding would not be celebrated until after the return of Toffa.

One night she sent for the spy, who did not have to be begged to come back. On the way there, he told himself that she was no doubt summoning him to apologize for the insult she had inflicted on him and to accept as a token of

207

reconciliation the pact he had proposed. At that thought, his resentment faded away.

During all the moons he had been coming to Toffa's house, he had always been received by Doguicimi in the company of her servant, but the latter had never seemed to exist for him. For that reason, he had never noticed Evêmon's beauty until that night. At first he was sceptical when Doguicimi informed him that she was intending to give the young girl to him from that moment on.

Finally convinced by the tone of sincerety in the woman's voice, he swore a passionate oath to do everything in his power to bring Toffa back to his family as quickly as possible. But his joy was soon tempered by a fear that became obsessive in his mind. Hadn't he promised to obtain proof of the woman's infidelity? Having been shown out of Toffa's house one moon ago, he had been called back tonight to be engaged to Doguicimi's young servant. He was not consumed with any particular passion for the unfortunate woman, and by himself he would never have thought of the idea of seducing her. But his love for Evêmon was deep and sincere.

He made himself no illusions about the punishment with which he would be obliged to expiate such an alliance, which would be viewed as a betrayal, but in the end he didn't worry too much about it, telling himself that an old monkey like him from "mahi" country would know how to escape a Zadonou's trap unless Destiny had decided that he should perish in it.

His love for the young girl completely displaced the fear in his heart of the revenge that his powerful patron at the court might exact from him. He now spent all his leisure time under Toffa's roof; the time he was obliged to spend away from his new idol seemed very dismal to him. He begged that his formal union with the beautiful servant might be moved ahead so that she could accompany him during his next mission to Hounjroto. In this way he hoped to convince Doguicimi to reverse her decision not to allow him to marry Evêmon until after the return of Toffa. No chance! His unacknowledged plan had been to run away while there was still time and thus protect his head from the threat of Migan's scimitar. He was angry at first but eventually resigned himself to what he called his sad fate. Meanwhile, he continued to look for a way out in case his betrayal was discovered.

He had formerly entered Toffa's house only in disguise and never until night had enveloped him with veils so dark that the best eye could not have seen through them, but now he cast aside all precautions and no longer seemed to be worried about anything.

When he arrived at Toffa's house around dusk, he didn't leave until the middle of the night. If he came with the dawn, he didn't dream of returning to his own hut until the sun had risen overhead.

It did not take long for his comings and goings to attract the attention of Doguicimi's co-wives. The first two or three women who noticed him had refrained from making any observations about his visits.

But is it possible for women, and especially jealous co-wives, to hold their tongues for long under such circumstances? Within three market days the entire house knew about the man's visits, but not everyone knew him.

Women who encountered the visitor by accident quickly turned away their heads or bent down as if to clean their heels of the bird droppings that were soiling them.

No one wanted to look the man in the face for fear of being accused of having made observations about him, because people suspected that he was not entering the house with such audacity on his own account.

Mothers never tired of secretly advising their children to avoid all contact with the visitor and to refrain from making any comments about him: "Be blind in one eye, be deaf in one ear, and stutter if the need arises. What if you encounter him in spite of yourself? Quickly turn your blind eye in his direction. What if you hear comments about his visits and about the behavior of someone whose name I don't have to mention? Immediately turn your bad ear toward the gossipers. If it should happen that, in spite of your precautions, you overhear a few remarks about the woman and her accomplice, show that you are a stutterer and that it is impossible to drag an intelligible word out of you. Even better, I beg you to forbid yourself any reflection upon the behavior of anyone, whoever it might be, in this house. You never know what can happen!"

Nevertheless, women who were on intimate terms with one another confidentially exchanged the scraps of information that had come to their attention, but they invariably concluded their conversations by recommending to each other that they hold these fact in the greatest confidence.

The injunction against seeing and speaking merely intensified the curiosity of those who did not yet know the person now identified solely as the "Consoler."

Todoté, a child who had scarcely been weaned, fled one morning at the approach of the man and took refuge in her mother's cloth, crying: "Mama, mama, he's come back, the man you told me so much. . . ."

His mother placed the palm of her hand over his unwittingly indiscreet mouth, asking him: "You want bring about your mother's ruin, Todoté?" Several resounding slaps on the backside forced the child's babblings back into his throat.

The women who did not yet know the "Consoler" had been precipitated out of their lodgings by his alarms. Pretending to be occupied in talking with their co-wives, they spied on him without appearing to do so. His arrivals and departures had already been taking place for two moons when Princess Ponouwa happened to visit her former companions, whom she had not seen ever since she left the compound.

She visited all the lodgings, beginning with that of Houwanon, Toffa's first wife, and ending with that of Doguicimi.

She came back to Houwanon with whom she had been on the most intimate terms. In a few moments, the place was full: everyone had come to listen to the princess, who would report the news of the city and could no doubt shed light on the mystery that so intrigued her former companions, who themselves had not crossed the threshold of this compound since the disappearance of their husband.

Besieged with questions, Ponouwa satisfied everyone's curiosity to the best of her ability to do so.

Standing pressed against each other, they were chattering away without listening to each other; the last ones to arrive were vainly trying to approach the princess so they might hear what she was saying. Some of the women were listening, their pipes in their mouths, puzzled expressions on their faces, hands resting on their hips.

Bursts of laughter and exclamations of doubt, astonishment, and joy intermittently punctuated the news reported by Ponouwa.

Finally she asked them: "Do you think your mats will be soiled by contact with me?"

Stretching out the mats, the mistress of the dwelling protested: "It is not contact with you that would soil whatever there might be in this house. The excitement produced by the news you have brought so distracted me that I forgot my duties as host."

They sat down: some with their busts facing forward and one hand planted on the ground; others leaning against the wall, their legs stretched out one on top of the other or bent, with thighs resting upon feet and heels pressed against buttocks.

"Is there perchance anyone among you who has already forgotten the noble prince?" queried Ponouwa, whose gaze wandered over the group to seek out the guilty one.

"Then the wind that passes through here doesn't carry with it the echo of what is happening in Toffa's house?" mumbled a woman who lowered her head and pretended to be looking for something in a fold of her cloth.

"There is something new here then, dear friend?" asked an intrigued Ponouwa, who turned to face her neighbor.

The woman next to her replied: "Princess, you will not learn from my mouth, the mouth of Fajo, that the mouse has the iron."

"The most extraordinary things are happening here then!" exclaimed the princess, more and more intrigued.

All the women looked questioningly at each other and then burst into laughter. All of which piqued the curiosity of Ponouwa.

Passing her arm around the neck of her neighbor on the right side, she drew the woman toward herself, saying: "Dear friend, show that you can be more confiding than our companions, who make everything into a mystery!"

"The princess knows very well that every Danhomênou should be blind in one eye, deaf in one ear, and mute or at least afflicted with a stammer," timidly replied the woman Ponouwa had addressed.

"As for me," said the mistress of the place, "I cannot hide anything from the princess who was my confidante for such a long time. The only good eye that I have sees men entering and leaving at all moments of the day and night. Who is sending them here? What are they coming to do? I have never inquired into the matter."

210

"There have really been too many comings and goings of men in this house since the master's disappearance!" exclaimed a woman who had been inspired with courage by the audacity of her co-wife.

"And to think that she was the one who put on such an show the morning of the master's departure for the war and railed against the king upon his return from Hounjroto and during the traditional celebrations!" added another indignantly.

"And yet she was his favorite. Moreover, she passed herself off as the most faithful, the most loving, the most noble," Houwanon said disdainfully.

Ponouwa was visibly interested. She expressed her indignation sometimes with a movement of the head or a gesture, sometimes with a word, and she promised her former companions to avenge their unrequited love and devotion.

Her promises kindled their spitefulness. A sense of absolute solidarity soon established itself among these worshippers of hate; now each rivalled with her neighbors to see who could be the first to discharge the gall that had been filling their bowels for seasons and seasons.

"Do you believe she still thinks about the master?" asked one of them.

"It's nearly to the point where she's already wishing for him to die in captivity!"

"The return of the master would in fact impose a certain restraint upon her. I don't see how she could ever succeed in controlling her passions. It is just as impossible for a depraved creature to return to the innocent state of her youth as it is for a river to flow back to its source."

A burst of approving laughter greeted this sally.

Only Dagnondé did not laugh. Her protests interrupted the slanderous talk: "You're exaggerating! I don't think she has fallen that low. How can anyone believe that Doguicimi would wish for the death of our husband so she could give free rein to some imagined perversion? You're mistaking your dreams for reality!"

"You have doubts about it?" asked one of her companions, vexed at having been contradicted. "You have doubts about it? Why then does she send her servants to the fetishes with offerings every five days? You don't believe me? I see casters of spells marching through her lodgings night and day; what can they be doing there? You will no longer have any doubts about the criminal intentions of that bitch, whose conduct is a disgrace to us all, when I tell you that her gris-gris men, who are well versed in the arts of black magic, threw a needle, which to them represented our husband, into the sea far from shore after having conducted ceremonies during which they pronouced the name Toffa many times. He is not supposed to return to Danhomê unless the waves wash the needle up on shore. There is little hope that a needle cast into the sea will ever return to solid ground!"

Behind the woman who had just denounced the gris-gris that had allegedly been prepared to keep Toffa in Hounjroto, another voice supported the accusation: "Someone told me that a whole live cow with its legs tied firmly together was drowned at sea far from land. The sorcerers claimed that the beast represented our husband. Toffa was supposed to return home if the animal reached shore while still alive. You know as well as I do that the sharks quickly devoured the windfall! The carcass alone might perhaps have been cast up on shore. And that's not certain! It was Doguicimi's friends who had this gris-gris prepared."

Another co-wife went even further: "You know all about the spells being cast into the sea at Gléhoué. But you haven't the slightest idea about what is happening under the prince's very roof. His enemies have become the friends of his favorite, and to prevent the master from returning, they have driven stakes into the ground beneath this house – stakes with leaves, animal skins, and red parrot feathers tied to them and all smeared with the blood of sacrificial victims."

The neighbor on Houwanon's right also grew indignant: "In Danhomê the voice of the first wife is second only to that of the master; it commands all the others and organizes certain domestic affairs. When the prince married the woman whom we call our 'mother,' he named her Houwanon, a word that means 'let all other waters make way for the majestic sea!' By means of this name Toffa glorified his first wife and signified that he found no woman in all Danhomê comparable to her. Today the daughter of a bitch has succeeded through the use of magic spells in supplanting Houwanon in the affections of the master. Believe me!"

"It's true," sighed Houwanon, who could not resign herself to her disgrace.

"We have to excuse Dagnondé," suggested one of the women, "she has not been in this house long enough to recognize the extent of Doguicimi's perversity. Danhomênous are advised to be blind in one eye but not in both because they should see certain things and report them to the Master of the World. Yes, the king wants us to be deaf but only in one ear because we have a moral obligation to collect the unfriendly remarks made about his government by some of his subjects so that we can inform him of them. Danhomênous should only be mute with regard to some of the Master of the World's actions and those of his heir. As for me, I regularly collect information from one of Doguicimi's servants. That's how I learned that the men she brought here were burying gris-gris, which they claim represent the master, in the courtyard and in the master's sleeping room. If I have any doubt – listen well, Dagnondé – if I have any doubt, it is not about Doguicimi's crimes (they are all too evident), it is rather about the master's return, for I never heard of anyone coming to life again after he had been buried. . . ."

There was a profound silence. In the meantime, heads were bobbing up and down as if they were being gently rocked by the observations that continued to occur to them. Deep sighs responded to long inhalations. All faces expressed a pained surprise after the revelations of this co-wife, whose lodgings were so close to those of Doguicimi that she could easily spy upon the most insignificant gestures of Toffa's favorite and overhear her conversations. In fact, she was the woman who had alerted the rest of the household to the visits that Doguicimi was receiving.

Her neighbor on the left finally broke the silence: "As far as I am concerned, it was her friends who were interested in our husband's disappearance, and they alone convinced the king to bring him to Hounjroto. Once there, they undoubtedly procured the help of the soldiers to get rid of the prince. Only Dagnondé, the mother of twins and a woman whose entrails are pure, could doubt the evidence and display such an excessive indulgence."

"It is cowardly to attack a companion who is not present. Anyone with heart should defend her, especially when she is convinced that the absent person is being slandered. If attitudes were being attributed to any of you in my presence, and if I had never known you to express such attitudes, I would be equally prepared to defend you. It is unreasonable to base one's opinion upon the mere contentions of interested informers. You have doubts about Doguicimi's conduct! But that's not sufficient grounds for you to invent so many crimes and shameless accusations against our companion."

"Be careful, friends! Mother panther is looking out for her cub!" a co-wife shouted with irony in her voice.

"Dagnondé, it is your right to rise to the defense of your benefactor, just as it is ours to judge the woman whose conduct reflects discredit upon us," Fajo retorted brutally.

"Anyone who wants to defend Doguicimi can do so. No one can prohibit me from making observations about a bitch's daughter toward whom the son of Agonglo was more respectful and attentive a short while ago than he was toward me, Princess Ponouwa, in whom the eldest daughter of Gangnihêssou[1] has been reincarnated, she who was the very image of wisdom and who, in another reincarnation during the reign of Agaja, contributed through the shrewdness of her commitment to the conquest of the 'houéda' kingdom. If all my former companions have forgotten the scene Toffa made the day I ventured an innocent jest about that bitch's affectations, I myself remember quite well how the prince beat me and humiliated me in public. That was the reason, moreover, why I left this compound after the army returned from Hounjroto. The aggressor is always quick to forget the injury he has inflicted, but as for the victim, he retains his scar, the painful memory of the insult.

"The moment of my revenge has arrived! I will never belie my name of Ponouwa, which means: 'No beast insults the Panther with impunity.'"

"And you will be perfectly justified in hastening the punishment of Doguicimi, who fed our husband who knows what powder to make him lose interest completely in the rest of us," said Fajo, who was overjoyed with Ponouwa's resolve.

"If she had limited herself to the distinguished individual I first saw at her place, no one could blame her much," said one woman who glanced furtively at Dagnondé.

"Kind friend," ironically added another in support, her gaze resting upon the face of the woman who had been defending Doguicimi, "I will inform you, since you don't seem to realize it, that the most disgusting little creatures strut along the path that was blazed through the forest by the elephant.

---

[1] "Gangnihêssou" was the son of Dogbagri and the brother of Daco-Donou, at whose side he fought to establish the Aladahonous on the plain of Agbomê. (author's note)

"Upon the master's return, none of this will prevent her from posing as the most faithful among us, whereas she has actually led the life of a princess in his absence," Fajo said indignantly.

The chorus of laughter that greeted this quip drowned out the protests of Ponouwa: "I'm a princess. It is true that I have the right to free love, but I don't abuse it, and I am far from being a pervert like that vulgar daughter of a bitch."

Because the assembly continued to laugh, Ponouwa got up, redid her cloth, and began to leave. But her companions prevented her from going and reassured her of their respect for her: "We lived with you for a long time, Ponouwa. You are the most honest princess in this kingdom. You know that our hearts don't approve of what our mouths are saying most of the time!"

Dagnondé burst out laughing. Her body contorted with sudden fit of hilarity, she fell backwards onto a neighbor, who pushed her away, proclaiming self-righteously: "I'm not the friend of a fellow wife who fans the flames of a quarrel."

But Dagnondé continued to laugh even more uproariously than before. Wiping away the tears that welled up in her eyes, she explained: "Doguicimi's flesh has whetted appetites. But since she wasn't enough to satisfy them, the hyenas are now feeding upon each other."

She was once again overcome with laughter.

A voice from the group declared: "Princess, don't pay any attention to the antics of Dagnondé. She laughs at the very moment when everyone else is crying; she alone speaks ill of a companion whose virtues are on the lips of the entire household."

"Have you ever reflected on the meaning of that bitch's name?" asked the mistress of the house, her suddenly beaming face announcing a discovery that would alleviate the embarassing situation created by the unwitting insult that had been inflicted upon the princess. Houwanon knew that, if Ponouwa left with ruffled feelings, their hatred would never be appeased. She explained: "Doguicimi means 'distinguish me, cite me as an example!' Why do you expect anyone with such a significant name not to behave in ways that justifiably arouse our indignation? It's absolutely necessary for this bitch to distinguish herself from us in some important characteristic. It's necessary for her to surpass us in lying, treachery, guile, and servility so that honest women like us can look their husbands in the eye and tell them in response to their distrust: 'You should regard yourselves as happy to be in the possession of wives who are not at all like Doguicimi, the personification of depravity and hypocrisy!' You see, dear companions, it's the name that has influenced this daughter of a bitch. I have no intention of trying to excuse her actions. But I would like to point out to you that this predestined name supplies honest women with arguments to counter the ingratitude and distrust of husbands who are insufficiently generous in rewarding the fidelity of their wives."

"In my opinion Doguicimi's misconduct is more of a disgrace to our entire sex," exclaimed another of Toffa's wives. "In fact, men who recognize that woman's affectations for what they are will no longer have any confidence in us. Don't men already have the tendency to generalize on the basis of a few isolated cases? From now on it will be in vain for a woman to give her husband proof of her sincere love; the man will always be distrustful and reply with justification: 'As long as you are standing in front of me, you swear love and fidelity. But all I have to do is turn my back and you are lavishing your affections on another man!'"

"You're telling the truth!" said one of her co-wives approvingly. "Ah, what a corrupt life that bitch is leading!"

Another completed her thought: "Doguicimi is a disgrace to all women. She's not the one who is going to abide by the suggestion that was made, according to the male sense of humor, by a soldier to his wife as he was leaving for war: 'If anything is going to touch you during my absence, let it be no more than water and your own hand!'"

Her companions broke into laughter, writhing with mirth and falling all over each other; tears streamed from their eyes. Holding her sides, one of them exclaimed, "I can't take any more! I can't take any more!" but she erupted in laughter again.

A voice shouted: "If that gibe reached the ears of this bitch, she would be thunderstruck!"

"The straw of a mat is soon flattened by the use to which it is put. Women are like mats. Look how Doguicimi is wasting away. She'll soon be witnessing the disintegration of her own body. Haven't you noticed that she is already speaking through her nose? That's the sum of the profits she has earned in the business to which she has so energetically devoted herself since the night after the prince's departure for the war."

"Chi!" a companion seated near the door spat disgustedly. "Fortunately my mouth has never touched her calabash!"

"The infection could only strike me though the intermediary of my pigheaded sons," sighed another. "Since three markets ago they have abandoned my house for hers. They find that the wanton woman is a better cook than I am, and now it's rare for them to show up in my place. It's in vain that I threaten them, beat them, confiscate the leftovers they bring back, or hide their calabashes; they continue to frequent the woman."

"And mine as well! Children are like ants; they're attracted in large numbers by sweets. The spells that succeeded in alienating the husband from his other wives have now been called upon to separate the sons from their mothers," declared Houwanon.

"That's true! Last night when I warned my Todoté against the food he had been eating in that bitch's hut, the simple child replied: 'All right, mama! And if she insists that I share in the meals she is offering to my other brothers and sisters, I'll tell her I can't disobey my mother, who forbade me to eat them.' You can imagine that I explained to him how he couldn't find a better way if he wanted to bring about his poor mama's ruin."

"Anyone who watches this traitor showering the children with so much care can't help but notice her hatred for them!"

Another voice added: "To love children sincerely, one needs to have carried them for nine moons in one's womb, to have experienced the pains of childbirth, and to have suffered all sorts of anguish next to the mats of these frail creatures when they have been stricken with illness. And you expect that anyone who has not endured such sufferings can love children? Believe me, she is only enticing them with the intention of making their mothers weep for them someday soon."

Dagnondé could not suppress the desire to laugh that continued to seethe in her.

All eyes instinctively turned toward the princess. The imprudent words that had just been spoken left a painful impression on everyone present.

"I too have never had any children," protested Ponouwa, "but that doesn't make me love them any less."

To pacify her, her companions sang the praises of her sincere affection for children. One of them recalled her memory of the princess' grief when such and such a companion's child had suffered a fit of convulsions. Another remembered the beautiful cloth she had given Todoté for his first bed, and the infusions that, prepared according to her instructions, had succeeded in curing children after all the doctors' medicines had failed and when their own mothers no longer expected to see them live. This was all that was needed to reassure Ponouwa.

To fully convince the princess about the sincerity of her companions' feelings in regard to her, Houwanon finally declared: "In light of all the proofs you have given us of your affection for our children, who among us would dare to place you in the same category as that harlot who is prostituting such an innocent child as Evêmon?"

Dagnondé uttered an exclamation of doubt.

"You don't believe me?" cried Houwanon, annoyed. "These ears (she pointed to her ear lobes) nevertheless heard that debauched female telling the innocent child: 'You will replace me! I don't know many men who are capable of resisting your charms.' And if you still have any doubts, Dagnondé, I can even be more precise and name the man to whom she has married the child."

"You are still confusing your imaginary ideas with reality! Evêmon is still living under this roof. This very morning Fajo asked her to split a log for her, and she can bear witness to that," Dagnondé informed the slanderers.

Ponouwa was no longer listening; in a triumphant tone of voice, she announced: "In this Danhomê only the king, who is master of all, has the right to dispose of a Danhomênou. Does Doguicimi by any chance consider Evêmon as her slave?

"That bitch's daughter still believes she can do whatever she pleases, just as in the days when she was under Toffa's protection. She will soon learn that Evêmon was born as free as she was. As long as I'm alive, none of the crimes of that bitch's daughter will remain unpunished. Her protectors will die with her if they don't abandon her quickly enough!"

"Our Destinies and our hearts support you, Ponouwa, in your efforts to make certain that this pervert and schemer will be punished!" chorused Doguicimi's co-wives.

"Since you seem determined to denounce a crime of high treason, you will need precise information; Evêmon is now housed in the dwelling of a Mahinou named Zanbounou," said Houwanon, glancing contemptuously at Dagnondé, who paid no attention to this expression of disdain.

"My, but our first wife is well informed!" one of Toffa's young wives exclaimed with a smile. "If I hadn't experienced the coldness that has existed between you and this bitch's daughter since the day she supplanted wives and children in the master's heart, I would think you were her confidante. I'll wager that her best friend (the woman pointed toward Dagnondé with her outstretched lips) is not as well informed about the actions of the chaste. . . ."

A child's cry interrupted her speech and prompted all eyes to turn toward the door. A woman who believed she recognized her son's voice rushed in the direction of the cry; her two hands were folded across her chest and holding the flabby breasts that pounded against her ribs. She soon returned to her companions and told them with a smile: "It was only Hêdagbe and Jiglocé fighting over a handful of foofoo in the house of the digger wasp.[2] When Hêdagbe lost out, he threw his calabash at his brother's head. They soon had recourse to teeth, and that's how the tears came about."

The thread of the conversation had been suddenly broken by a child's sob, and it proved difficult to resume it. Everything that was said seemed uninteresting. Ponouwa stayed a while longer, time enough to draw several puffs on the pipe that Houwanon handed her and to swallow several mouthfuls of water; then she arose and wiped her palms across her buttocks as a sign that she was taking leave of her companions.

The room was soon empty. All the women accompanied the princess to the portal of the compound, their jealousy-filled hearts having already incited her against Doguicimi, whose only crime resided in her beauty, her shrewdness, her noble bearing, her courage, her love for her husband, and the preference he manifested for her.

Before leaving Ponouwa, Houwanon whispered in her ear: "I think you've got enough information to convince the king that Doguicimi was not satisfied with blasphemies but has proceeded to the most reprehensible acts. I will send my faithful servant to you when I learn anything more."

The sun was already offering the people a view of the beautiful scarlet cloth he habitually wore as he descended behind the Coufo, where he passed the night.

The women dispersed; following the sun's example, they shut themselves in their houses to prepare the evening meal.

---

[2] According to popular belief in Danhomê the digger wasp was sterile. But because it has highly developped maternal instincts, it steals the larva of other wasps and treats them with motherly affection and care. This belief was the source of the offensive comparison between the digger wasp and a woman who had not experienced the joy of becoming a mother but who nevertheless loves children a great deal. (author's note)

Several of them met again after dinner and exchanged confidences before abandoning themselves to sleep. . . .

Chapter 8

The Torments of an Innocent

Two market days. . . ! Four market days. . . ! One moon. . . ! Ponouwa no longer returned to Toffa's compound, and nothing more was heard from her. Humble and inconsolable, Doguicimi went on living as usual. Zanbounou's visits became less frequent.

The jealousy of Toffa's other wives brought them together several times a day at Houwanon's hut, and although they found Doguicimi more arrogant than ever, they were already losing hope of ever seeing her punished for what they called her crime; they advanced a thousand conjectures to explain the princess's inactivity. Ponouwa no longer inspired many of them with confidence; some even regretted having been too frank with their former companion; others told themselves that she was no doubt busy consolidating a new love and that she wouldn't even think about her promise to avenge her co-wives until she had grown bored with her fresh conquest.

On this particular morning of "zogbodo," the entire inside wall of the immense calabash cover that imprisons us on the surface of the earth was veiled with ash-colored cloths so thick that the rays of the sun failed to penetrate them: all of Nature was sad and gloomy; the long dry season was coming to an end; dull rumblings in the distance and other premonitory signs of the rainy season no longer left any doubt that Hêviosso was preparing to water the ground generously, as only he could do, to the great joy of plants, animals, and people in whom life had been dormant for the past three moons. Saturated with humidity, the cool air penetrated to your bones.

During the night, Doguicimi's sleep had been troubled by frightening nightmares, and she was still lying down in her room.

Since three long markets ago, the woman, who was always the last to retire, had arisen before the second crowing of the cock. Her faithful Evêmon had been worrying about her in vain. She thus felt gratified to see her mistress lingering on her sleeping mat that morning.

219

It was the day designated for the worship of fetishes in the kingdom. The previous evening Doguicimi had prepared offerings for Hêviosso and Sapata, who had assured her once again through the voice of the oracle that they would soon bring the prince back to Danhomê. She had not forgotten the Agalé-Hounsou fetish, which had promised her victory over all her enemies and protection for Toffa if she would offer him forty-one servings of food and have a beautiful velvet cloth draped over him.

Evêmon had already entered her mistress' room twice without daring to disturb her.

As she entered for the third time, Doguicimi stretched, showed her face, and called, "Evêmon!" Kneeling at the foot of the sleeping mat, the young girl kissed the ground, asked whether her mother had slept peacefully, and informed her that everything was ready for her bath; she then reminded her about the offerings that were to be made to the fetishes that morning.

She immediately departed with her first load for the shrine of Sapata. Doguicimi's gaze followed her to the portal of the compound. "Poor child! May the Creator bring back the prince quickly, if only out of pity for you!" she exclaimed after sighing deeply.

Leaning against the wall, she was thinking: "Misfortune has been pursuing me for one season after another, tormenting my heart like a hawk greedily tightening his grip on his prey. Despite the nobility of my sentiments and countless proofs of my love for him, my husband wronged me on the eve of his departure for the war by lumping me together with women like Ayomayi. He is a captive at Hounjroto, but his spirit, which must return frequently to this house, cannot be unaware of all that I am suffering in order to remain faithful to him. If his spirit does not come here to inform itself, the master will surely discover upon his return to Danhomê, even though Doguicimi herself might be dead by that time, how his favorite wife steadfastly avoided any action that would blemish her character. But if he is not fated to return to Danhomê until after Doguicimi is already under the ground, I am ready to rejoin my ancestors on this very day. . . ."

Evêmon's return roused the woman from her melancholy reflections. The young girl gave an account of her mission: the fetish had accepted the offerings from the first cast of the kola nuts and renewed its assurances that the master would soon be home.

"May its predictions be fulfilled!" muttered the woman in a voice tinged with doubt.

"My mother has no faith? As for me who actually heard the fervent promises pronounced in the name of the fetish, I am convinced that our happiness cannot be postponed for long!"

Doguicimi carefully refrained from disabusing her of her illusions. Seeing her walk away with a load of offerings for the Hêviosso fetish, she told herself: "At her age one is full of hope. If that weren't the case, it would be disheartening. Personally, I have many reasons for being sceptical, just like the blind man who replied to those who informed him that his son had killed an antilope: 'I won't believe it until I have touched the animal's horns!' He knew his son's lack of courage and skill."

When Evêmon returned to fetch the third calabash of offerings, she found her mistress stretched out on the sleeping mat. Thinking she was asleep, the young girl picked up her final load and started to leave on the tips of her toes; Doguicimi called her back. She came over to her mistress and repeated the encouraging promises of the fetish.

"Oun houm!" exclaimed the woman, whose gaze revealed the emptiness she felt.

She sighed again, then asked for something to drink.

"It's too cold to drink cool water. My mother has not yet eaten anything. I shall prepare her some foofoo?"

Doguicimi wanted nothing but water. She then went into the reception room where she hoped to find a bit more heat despite the absence of the sun.

When the servant's return was delayed, her mistress sought for explanations: "Could the chief fetishist be absent? That would be unusual on a day set aside for the worship of fetishes. The crowd of people who came to offer sacrifices must have obliged Evêmon to wait her turn."

The latter explanation calmed her mind. The woman lay down again on her mat. She was soon overtaken by sleep. When she awoke, the sun was already overhead. She called Evêmon. Zokindé, another servant whom Evêmon had instructed to remain close to their mistress during her absence, came and told her that Evêmon had not yet returned.

Doguicimi began to worry.

The kneeling servant inquired: "What does our mother desire? Should a meal be prepared for her? It would be ready in an instant; the water is already boiling. . . . Why is our mother so sad, and why does she only answer me with sighs. . . ? Evêmon must have gone by way of Ajahimê. I will try to find her."

Doguicimi nodded her assent, and the girl left immediately.

Seeing her walk away, she mused to herself: "The well-meaning child was asking about the cause of my sadness! Could I really define it? I feel a sort of apprehensiveness without being able to explain it in words. I am vaguely uneasy, just like the hunter who, preparing himself to encounter the savage beasts, wanted to know: 'Am I missing anything?' Yet nothing is threatening me. Unless my sadness is a presentiment of some misfortune? But isn't it more likely that it is the effect of the nightmares that troubled my sleep all night long? Perhaps, too, it is the sadness of Nature that has spread to my very soul? Ah, Spirit of Creation, how do you expect to be revered by the creature whom you have abandoned to herself in the depth of distress!"

The final word had scarcely died upon her lips when six of Migan's servants erupted into the room.

"He will have only my corpse to defile!" Doguicimi shouted. Standing up, she buried her right hand in the folds of her cloth just below her stomach. When she brought it out, it was empty, and biting her index finger, she cried: "I'm undone! The beast has taken me!" In two jumps she was in her sleeping room, but she only had time to lift her pillow and pick up a small flask. At that very moment, one of Migan's servants, having followed her into the room, grabbed her around the waist. Another snatched the flask from her, examined it, and exclaimed: "It's mercury! It's mercury!"

Since the night when Vidaho had made veiled threats of abducting her, Doguicimi had kept this white man's poison by her side, although it was forbidden, under penalty of death, for any Danhomênou to be in possession of it. At night the woman placed the little flask beneath her pillow, and in the morning she never crossed the threshold of her house without having first concealed the poison in the folds of her cloth.

The Creator whom she thought indifferent toward her was actually protecting her. Indeed, it could have been none other than he who, not wanting her to end her life in a pathetic manner, had slipped forgetfulness into her mind at the moment she left her room that morning, and it was he who later prevented her from remembering the poison despite her efforts to recall it.

The woman's cries attracted only the children and a few servants.

They wept to see their kindly mother struggling in the grip of strong men. One urchin suggested: "Let's throw rocks at them!" And clods of dirt, and calabashes, and sticks of wood, and anything else their feeble hands could lift and send flying in the direction of those evil men who were beating up their beloved mama.

Todoté was more bold than any of them, and he bit one of the men in the calf. Hêdagbé tried to follow his example, but he was brutally shaken off and left with his feet in the air, sobbing, cursing, threatening. . . .

Alerted by one of their companions who was secretly watching Doguicimi's arrest, mothers came and led their children away by the hand. The recalcitrant ones stretched themselves out on the ground, assuming that their mothers would hardly be so cruel as to drag them across the dirt, but they were soon brought to their feet by a few resounding spanks. "Faster, you son of a dog! Faster!" These curses shouted by angry mothers could be heard above the sobs of the children and the servants led by Zokindé, who had turned around and come back when she saw Migan's servants insolently entering her master's house.

Three men loaded Doguicimi on their shoulders; one of them passed his mighty arms around her feminine heels, another immobilized her arms and held them tightly pressed against her thighs, and a third grabbed her by the shoulders. She turned her head and caught the last one's ear between her teeth; he cried out in pain. With a slap across the face, one of the other men in the group forced Doguicimi to let go and then placed his large hand across her mouth.

They set her down five paces from the throne. The Courtyard of the Great Palace was filled with the noise of the lizard people, whose great numbers indicated that an important event was about to take place.

The high dignitaries left the Palace, followed by the heads of the former royal families. One of Migan's servants who had been sent to Toffa's house gave the first minister an account of their mission.

Avoutou thundered, dogba replied with its muffled roll, the "birds of the king" began to chirp behind the Door of the Universe. Daclo appeared; dressed for a solemn occasion, the flood of queens surrounded the throne and obscured it from view. . . . The parasol-carriers brought up the rear, encircling the king. The people smeared their heads and upper bodies with dirt as they expressed their wishes for the health, the long life, and the victorious success of their Creator.

Doguicimi was on her knees in front of the throne. The Wives of Panther were staring at her. They could barely contain the joy with which their victory had filled them. A few of them, however, did not deviate from the prudent attitude they had adopted ever since the day when an untimely zeal had cost one of their companions her life after the return from the war of Hounjroto.

Doguicimi asked herself: "Can the Master of the World have sent for me in order to marry me to the royal prince? Why then the brutality of Migan's servants? The king is perhaps intending to give me to the lowest slave in this kingdom? It could also be that my husband Toffa, having returned to Danhomê and heard about my diatribes against the king, was overcome with zeal and wants to torture me with his own hands? Ah, such a fate would be far more pleasant to me!"

The sight of Zanbounou being led by another of Migan's servants revealed the truth to Doguicimi. The spy's arms above his elbows were firmly pinioned behind his back. His collar bones and ribs were bloody, his shoulders raised and pushed forward, his biceps rounded, the skin on his arms taut, his eyes starting out of their sockets and red with pain. Pearls of sweat formed on his forehead, his temples, and his sides. He complained that the rope was biting into his flesh. He moaned and occasionally proclaimed: "I'm innocent! I'm innocent!"

Zanbounou was indeed suffering. He was begging Migan and the heir to the throne for mercy. His palor and panting breath betrayed the fear that was haunting him. . . .

The administration of justice was always carried out far from the throne by the high dignitaries. The king ordered that this custom be disregarded.

The first minister's wink, which went unperceived only by those courtiers who were distracted by the Mahinou's grimaces, caused the latter to begin talking: "Eternal King who sees into the depths of my bowels, here is the architect of my downfall (he extended his lips outward and pointed with them toward Doguicimi, who had been placed to his left), and it was a terrifying dream that brought me together with her.

"In my sleep, I saw myself being cut to pieces. The following morning I went in search of a diviner. Fadonougbo was recommended to me for his clairvoyance. This woman arrived in the oracle's reception room at the moment of the consultation. I didn't even look in her direction. When I returned to my hut, I was astonished to receive the visit of two young girls carrying large calabashes that contained dishes worthy only of a princely palate. These children had been sent by Doguicimi. The white man's liquor followed on the third day. Two market days later she offered me velvet and satin cloths. I asked myself what could possibly justify such generosity toward me on the part of such a distinguished woman who was not related to me in any way. I had not reached the end of my surprises. One night Doguicimi arrived at my house and declared her love for me. . . ."

He was interrupted by the exclamations that arose from the mob.

"Roused to indignation," he continued with as much effrontery as ever, "I categorically rejected the vile proposal of this emissary from Lègba and chased her from my home, but in vain.

"She swore she would hold our relationship in the greatest secrecy, and as a pledge of her discretion she offered to contract a Blood Oath with me. I tried to protect myself from this daughter of temptation, explaining to her that, as a slave, I was not permitted to have relations with a prince's wife and that I would never for anything in the world violate the Master of the World's very explicit prohibition against any of his subjects entering into sworn friendships. When the wiles she employed to entice me into evil left me cold at her side, she set one of her servants at my heels. How persistent was that girl, who had undoubtedly been given lessons by her mistress! No matter which way I turned to avoid her, I was always running into her. By day she pestered me with her entreaties, and by night she laid siege to my slumbers.

"I asked Destiny for an effective way to rid myself of this temptress. The oracle declared that an intrigante would make me a proposition. I knew that the woman in question was the one I had been trying for a long time to avoid, and I vainly exhausted my modest resources in offering sacrifices that were supposed to keep that daughter of Lègba out of my hair. All the solicitations addressed to me by this woman had but a single purpose, which I only discovered much later. During the visit this temptress paid me two days later, she gave me a human skull and told me: 'Mahinou, I would like to help you return to your parents, from whom you have been separated since childhood. I will only ask you for one thing in return. I know that your fellow countrymen are conducting sacrifices to the ancestors and to the fetishes of your land in the hope of obtaining their aid in recovering this skull, which is that of their king who was killed in the last war, and which has since then been in the Master of the World's possession. On my behalf you will offer it to them in exchange for Toffa. But we must first contract a Blood Oath that will assure me of your good faith.'

"When this infamous proposal reached my ears, I solicited all our former kings for help and beseeched them to divert the misfortune that this Lègba was intent upon bringing down on my head; I said to the temptress: 'Having been captured before the age of reason, I don't know the country of my birth, nor do I even want to know it. From now on I am only interested in the grandeur and prosperity of Danhomê. For nothing in the world will I ever betray this generous country that has nurtured and educated me and continues to give me abundant proof of its goodness.'"

He ventured a furtive glance toward Doguicimi; she didn't even appear to be listening to him, although she hadn't been fooled at all. The woman's attitude heightened the audacity of the spy, who cynically asked her: "Can you dare deny all this and your other slanders against the Master of the World as well?"

Doguicimi looked him up and down, then turned her head away.

Emboldened by the woman's silence and the court's interest in his deposition, Zanbounou continued: "This Lègba still continued to send her servant to my house with calabashes of food, in which she had undoubtedly mixed magic potions, as she had been doing for a long time, to paralyze my will and make me as submissive to her as a dog to its master."

He began once again to complain that the rope was eating into his arms, and he begged his guards to loosen it.

"My agents will have no difficulty shedding more light upon many points in Zanbounou's deposition," affirmed Lêguêdê, the head of the king's secret police.

"Let them not waste any time!" Migan grumbled as he shook his large head.

"Has a woman as perverse as Doguicimi ever been seen in this Danhomê of Houégbaja?" asked Sogan.

"And to think that it is barely six dry seasons ago that she was wallowing in grief and railing against the king at the announcement of her husband's disappearance!" Topa added in support.

Lêguêdê returned to the charge: "She has already buried the memory of Toffa. And when she gave Zanbounou the skull we brought back from Hounjroto so he might return it to the Mahinous, I doubt she was doing it for the prince's sake."

Migan grew indignant: "To assure the man's silence, she dared revive a practice that kings have strictly forbidden their subjects! The King of Spirits can exercise clemency if Doguicimi simply bribed a man who was in the service of Danhomê or if she merely violated one of the king's decrees. But she went beyond her rights as Evêmon's guardian when she married the young girl to Zanbounou.

"The Predestined King owes it to himself to follow the example of his predecessors who, ever since the reign of Houégbaja, have punished princes as well as common people with death for having disposed of a Danhomênou as if he were a simple slave. All Danhomê knows Doguicimi's hatred for the Master of the World, and it is a fact that she has been carrying a flask of mercury on her person since our return from Hounjroto." He displayed the poison that had been confiscated from the accused. He continued: "We can now understand her persistence in seeking to gain entry to the court! But the ancestors are watching over the Master of the World. They alone denounced the criminal and prevented her from approaching the King and perpetrating her heinous crime."

"I've never heard of this poison and don't even want to see it," proclaimed one Danhomênou, who nevertheless glanced furtively in the direction of the throne.

"That's enough to convince the Master of the World that Doguicimi, not satisfied with blasphemies, has proceeded to acts and is therefore no longer worthy of pardon," exulted a queen joyfully.

Vivênagbo intervened: "Zanbounou has placed on display a web of insubstantial accusations in which a number of gaps are visible. This man does not suspect the extent to which the court is concerned with justice. Some of the Mahinou's accusations can be verified, and among them is his contention that Doguicimi had possession of the war trophy brought back from Hounjroto. If it is not to be found in the hands of Houégbaja, the Master of the World ought to take precautions. And if it can be proved that Toffa's wife gave the mahi chief's skull to Zanbounou, we must unravel the complicities that enabled the woman to obtain this precious trophy. As far as I know, she herself does not enter the Palace. The trial by poison will help us discover the truth that the accuser and the accused continue to conceal in the hope of abusing the judges' good faith.

"The Predestined King will deal harshly with the guilty parties, regardless of their rank. His people have faith in his justice." He covered himself with dirt.

He had spoken in a clear, measured tone of voice.

An impressive silence reigned around the king and among the ranks of the high dignitaries. Hostile glances were cast in the direction of the former regent. The heir to the throne was worried.

Invited to defend herself against the accusations of the Mahinou, Doguicimi replied calmly: "I would like to drink the trial poison myself!"

"You will not have the peaceful death you desire!" retorted one of Migan's servants.

The trial by poison had originally come from Ajalouma in Mawou-Bagbo country north of Dassa, where the Nagonous went every year in a procession on a pilgrimage to the Creator; there they underwent a mysterious trial by poison to demonstrate that they were not guilty of any crime and had not even harbored any criminal thoughts. Only people with a clear conscience returned safely from the pilgrimage.

The use of this trial by poison had been introduced by Tégbéssou so that justice, too often distorted by the deformations of truth contained in the denials of the accused and the lies of the accusers, could be administered in an enlightened fashion.

This institution had heightened the veneration of honest Danhomênous for their king, who indeed had many other claims as well upon his people's gratitude. As the man who continued the work of Agaja, he had completed the conquest of Gléhoué, which was considered so important by the Danhomênous because it offered a profitable outlet for their warlike activities and an opportunity to channel toward Agbomê the wonders being distributed among the Houédanous by the white men; in contrast to his predecessors, he had opened the eyes of the Danhomênous by allowing them to look upon his august face; he had also introduced the cults of neighboring peoples' protective fetishes in Danhomê, and that had attracted their benedictions upon the kingdom of Houégbaja.

226

The trial poison was prepared from the bark of two different trees – one male, the other female.

The king of Danhomê supplied himself with it through the intermediary of the king of Dassa, who dispatched his royal messengers to the country of the trial by poison. In the name of his god, Bagbanon (the Priest of Mawou-Bagbo) presented the bark he always gathered at night to the King of Dassa's emissaries.

Those who carried this marvelous bark were forbidden to have or to consume any palm oil during their journey.

Designated to probe the conscience of the Danhomênous, the Priest of the trial by poison was expressly forbidden from entertaining any relations with them, and for that reason he was kept under strict surveillance at Canna, where he and all the other principal chief fetishists were obliged to live.

He only came to Agbomê on zogbodo days, which were devoted to the worship of fetishes in Danhomê. He shut himself up in the residence of the king's prosecutor Ajaho, under whose surveillance he proceeded to prepare the trial by poison.

Servants whom he had initiated into this practice were assigned to the provincial Governors, who had been ordered to utilize their services in simple police matters, the only ones that fell within their jurisdiction.

Ajaho spent the day of zogbodo in his residence and only appeared at court to report the results of a trial by poison.

If there was any doubt about the accused person's guilt, the king would order the procedure to be administered again.

Two of the executioner's assistants got ready to take Doguicimi and Zanbounou to the home of Ajaho.

The king's hand with its raised index finger moved in a circular motion and then fell to indicate that he was intending to make certain that justice was scrupulously carried out with regard to the accused.

Muffled whispers arose within the king's immediate circle, although they could not be heard beyond the bamboo barrier: the Royal Wives were meekly protesting against the violation of a custom dictating that the trial by poison should be administered far from the court.

The king paid no attention at all to these protests.

At a sign from the first minister, one of his servants began walking in the direction of the Royal Prosecutor's residence.

The minister soon arrived, followed by Baba Tatayi, the Priest of the trial by poison and an individual whom many people only knew by name.

Dressed in a flowing white boubou, he was wearing two long strings of black grains interspersed with fine white cowries, one slung across each shoulder. A bundle of raphia that had been twisted and dyed red served him as a necklace. His head was swathed in a red-dyed scarf. His wrists and ankles were wreathed with strings of cowries interspersed with black grains.

In his left hand he was holding a phial made from a gourd and in the left an assen crowned by a skull-cap sewn with tiny cowries. His dress and his symbols lent him a mysterious and terrifying air.

He knelt down, kissed the earth, sprinkled a narrow band of it on his arms, and made a gesture as if to cover his chest with it.

In the meantime, his servants had quickly spread out a raphia-palm leaf-fiber mat and set down a large flat stone, a round one the size of a fist, a pouch with swollen sides that indicated it was quite full, a small jug of water, a cage filled with roosters, and a three-legged stool that had been carved from a single piece of wood; they then paid hommage to the Master of the World with all the customary obeisances, from which Baba Tatayi was exempt on account of the sacred aura surrounding his person as High Priest.

The Royal Prosecutor and the Priest of the trial by poison were informed of the serious accusations that Zanbounou had made against Doguicimi.

Seated in front of the assen, which had been stuck in the ground and represented Mawou, the Creator, who clearly saw into the hearts of his creatures and revealed, by means of the trial by poison, the crimes they were unwilling to admit, the Priest had the throne and the high dignitaries on his left, Doguicimi and her accuser two paces in front of him, and, on his left, the crowd of courtiers lying prostrate in the dust.

He placed the gourd-phial on a miniscule cushion at the base of the assen and poured out the contents of his bag on the mat to his right – fine cowries and seeds from the native sapodilla tree; he then crushed two pieces of bark (one male, one female, and both the size of the tip of a person's little finger) on the large stone, mumbling invocations known to him alone. They were quickly reduced to a red powder.

Gbêgoudo, one of Ajaho's servants, was kneeling within reach of the Priest's hands; ready to fulfill his function (which consisted of presenting the poison, the cock of the accuser, and then the cock of the accused), he was using his hands and knees to immobilize the first cock, lying on its side and facing the Priest. The bird's neck was being held vertical between the middle and ring fingers of his left hand, its head tilted slightly backward and its jaws held open by the thumb and the index finger.

Zanbounou never stopped protesting: "I have not testified falsely!"

The mixture that was poured into the gourd-phial foamed up as soon as water was added.

"I never lied in my life!" the accuser repeated, grinding his teeth, writhing with pain, and begging in vain for someone to loosen the ropes that were biting into his arms.

Just as his denials, his agitated movements, and the expression of cunning on his face betrayed his duplicity and revealed his guilt, Doguicimi's silence, her calm, and the peacefulness of her expression proclaimed her innocence.

"Zanbounou! Zanbounou! Zanbounou!" Ajaho called three times in a voice that invariably rent the heart of the guilty. The spy immediately lowered his head. One would almost have thought that he had a telltale sign on his forehead and did not want the Priest of the trial by poison or the Royal Prosecutor to see it. His heart was beating frantically; he was overcome with a violent headache.

Two tears flowed from his pain-reddened eyes. His body was wracked with shivers that he attempted in vain to curb; not a single dignitary could ignore the fact that he was afraid. Fear caused the lizard people lying face down in front of the throne to flatten themselves even more into the dirt.

The Royal Prosecutor continued: "You accuse Doguicimi, who is here present, of having asked you to betray Danhomê and to participate in the revival of a practice that has been prohibited by the Master of the World; you furthermore accuse her of having offered you her young servant in return for the requested service when you, as you claim, refused to entertain culpable relations with her! You are going to undergo trial by poison!

"You will not be held responsible today for any false accusation you may have made previously against anyone, no matter who it might be!"

The Priest touched the cock's head with a cowry that he then presented to the assen and threw to the side. In this way the spirit of the trial by poison took cognizance of the absolution that had just been granted to the accuser. One of the Priest's servants placed the little shell back into the pouch.

"The fact of having failed to perform sacrifices decreed by Destiny will in no way influence the trial you are about to undergo!" As before, the Priest duly registered this pronouncement with the spirit of the trial.

"Past failures to fulfill promises of offerings to fetishes will in no way influence the trial you are undergoing today!" The Priest solemnly executed the usual movements.

"The misfortunes that the whims of Lègba are preparing in the greatest secrecy to unleash upon you will not be taken into consideration here!" Another cowry was cast to the side after having been applied to the head of the cock and presented to the spirit of the trial by poison.

"None of your previous crimes, committed against your neighbors or the ancestors and unsuspected by us, will influence your trial today!"

More and more confident, Zanbounou gradually raised his head.

The Royal Prosecutor now spoke in accented rhythms: "You will only be declared guilty if the specific accusations you have lodged against Doguicimi, who is here present, are false!"

The Priest then touched the head of the cock with a sapodilla seed and threw it on the ground at the base of the assen next to the gourd-phial containing the trial-poison.

The accuser lowered his head; in a quavering voice he proclaimed: "I am not guilty! I have never accused anyone falsely!"

Gbêgoudo approached the cock. Zanbounou could not suppress the shiver of anxiety that once more wracked his body. To bolster his courage, he wanted repeat "that he didn't accuse people falsely," but fear tightened its grip on his throat, and when he finally succeeded in speaking, his voice cracked pitifully.

From the second hole that had been fashioned on the top of the gourd-phial, the Priest poured the mixture into the throat of the cock, which was immediately released.

The bird shook its head and, with a loud "ko-ay," vomited up most of the potion. Three times in a row it flapped its wings together across the top of its back; it then swelled its neck, rose to its full height, and let forth a resounding "cock-a-doodle-doo!" which the court greeted with the cry: "Your cock survived the terrible trial! You have told the truth, Zanbouonou!"

Startled, the cock shrieked, "koko-ay! koko-ay! koko-ay!" and tried to fly away.

One of the Priest's servants caught it and immobilized it by placing his knee on its feet.

The pain incited the bird to protest anew: "Koko-ay! Koko-ay!"

"Proclaim your innoncence! Proclaim it as loud as you can! You have every right to do so! Your victory over the terrible trial by poison is the conclusive proof of Doguicimi's guilt!" the mob shouted tumultuously.

Zanbounou could not believe his eyes. The calloused palm of one of Migan's servants fell upon him to remind him of his duty to cover himself with dirt as an expression of gratitude toward the Master of the World, who had deigned to offer him this opportunity to prove that he had not testified falsely.

The Wives of Panther rejoiced. They were finally triumphing over that bitch's daughter by the name of Doguicimi.

The Priest glanced inquiringly toward the throne. The king expected that the defendant would be granted the same opportunity, which was always extended to anyone accused of a serious crime before this court, to vindicate herself with regard to the crimes imputed to her by the spy. Zanbounou's face once again clouded over; the joy of the queens was suddenly dampened. The Priest set about preparing the mixture for Doguicimi's cock.

The two pieces of bark proved hard to grind, forming an almost glutinous paste. A bad sign! Several high dignitaries shook their heads sadly.

Confidence was reborn among Doguicimi's enemies.

Nevertheless, the defendant remained impassive.

Ajaho tried in vain to elicit from her the usual denial of the accused, "I am not guilty!" Pressed about the matter, she replied drily: "My innonence is so evident that I have no need to proclaim it!"

The Royal Prosecutor then said solemnly: "Doguicimi! Doguicimi! Doguicimi! If the person present here is not you but one of your namesakes, let the spirit of the trial by poison state it clearly!" The Priest took cognizance of the will of Ajaho.

The Royal Prosecutor listed all the absolutions that had been anticipated in advance, and the Priest successively gave official notice of them to Destiny.

"But if you are the very person who committed the crimes denounced by Zanbounou and abhorred by all Danhomê," said Ajaho, "let the trial by poison reveal it immediately!"

The Priest touched the cock's head with the sapodilla seed and placed it at the foot of the assen.

Lying on its side with its claws and wings pinned to the ground by Gbêg-oudo's feet, Doguicimi's cock twisted and turned.

The Priest administered the trial poison to it according to the usual ritual. . . .

When released, the bird wanted to stand up but collapsed awkwardly on the ground; it attempted to get up – its legs refused to support it, its talons furrowed the earth, it struggled for a moment, and spread its wings as if it wanted to take flight; its yellowish green eyes were starting from their sockets as life was departing from them; its comb was ruddy, a sign of asphyxiation, and the neck it was striving to hold straight flopped backward in despair; its lower jaw flapped open and shut; since its nostrils no longer sufficed, the bird sought to draw in the life-giving air through its throat, but in vain. . . .

The court jeered Doguicimi, whose guilt had just been amply proven by the death throes of the cock who represented her.

This band of lizards was, to be sure, too deeply immersed in dirt to have noticed the different thickness of the barks ground together for the two trials or the different treatments accorded to the cock of the accuser and the cock of the accused. But it had not escaped Doguicimi's vigilant eye that the quantities of the two barks chosen for her was so disproportionate that the death of the cock was inevitable and, furthermore, that the legs of her cock had been so brutally yanked backward that it would have been astonishing if they had not been dislocated at the knee; its neck had been pulled and so firmly choked during the entire time when the extraordinarily long preparation of the trial potion was taking place that the bird must have been asphyxiated. As a crowning blow, the Priest's assistant had dislocated the bird's vertebral column with a skillful turn of the wrist at the very moment when the Priest himself was about to pour the mixture down the gullet of the cock.

The king too had seen everything. But he didn't want to mention it, for the slightest hint of malfeasance would immediately destroy his subjects' faith in the infallibility of the trial by poison that was supposed to inspire royal justice.

For the mob then, Doguicimi had been convicted of four crimes: bribing a spy in the service of Danhomê, treason toward the kingdom, prostituting a child entrusted to her care, and, most odious of all, the attempt to poison the sacred person of the one to whom all Danhomênous were indebted for the life and happiness they enjoyed.

Although in agreement about the crimes, the court could not decide upon the appropriate punishments for expiating them.

Someone in the crowd suggested: "Let her be burned alive!" Another proposed: "Let her be crushed to death!"

"Send her to the army of evil-doers that enrolls wanton women like her!" shouted the mob boisterously, already covering itself with dust as a sign of gratitude, for they believed the king would undoubtedly accede to this demand. But they were interrupted by a voice emanating from the ranks of the high dignitaries: "She would be too happy there! The frog who's been thrown out

231

of the house and over the hedge lands in the swamp and finds himself in the element of paradise for those of his sort!"

"She should be empaled in the Courtyard of Ajahimê than! It's the only torture that'll instill virtue in those, like her, who frequent our markets!" interjected a voice from the crowd.

"Her secret supporters could find nothing better to spare her the lingering agony she deserves!" said Migan in a surly tone.

"Let's cut her up while she's still alive!" one of the executioner's aides suggested.

"Let's bury her alive in a hole filled with ants!" recommended another.

One of Ajaho's servants urged: "Let her be skinned alive and then obliged to take a bath in a sauce of hot peppers!"

A servant of Migan went him one better: "Before the despicable criminal expires, she should be made to eat chunks of her own flesh in front of the eyes of the court, and she should be made to drink her own urine mixed with the mercury that was found on her!"

Doguicimi remained unperturbed in the midst of this mob that was proposing all sorts of atrocities as ways for her to expiate her alleged crimes.

The king, who had until then been lying on his couch, suddenly sat up; he ordered the tohubohu of horrors being suggested by the screaming rabble to be cut short.

"Let us leave such torments for our sister kingdoms," he said calmly. "A flogging will suffice to punish the crimes of this woman, who will subsequently learn wisdom during a long stay in Cangbodé's prison."

"It would be impossible to find a more just punishment!" the crowd concurred as it covered itself with dust.

Several Wives of Panther were whispering to each other: "Why send her to the prison reserved for the female personnel of the Palace instead of imprisoning her at Ajaho's residence? The Master of the World is confusing a bitch's daughter and a criminal with the rest of us who are the very essence of purity!"

Migan wanted to drag Doguicimi out of the king's sight. But since Guézo had ordered her to be beaten in his presence, the executioner grudgingly bound her wrists and lashed her legs from the soles of her feet to her thighs. Then he brought her arms down to her feet, pinioned her four limbs together, and passed a stick one arm's length between the trunk and the extremities of the firmly trussed victim.

With a loud slap that sent a shiver through the lizard crowd, Migan turned Doguicimi over and planted his left foot on the stick in order to keep her lying on her left side and facing the throne. From a bundle he selected a gnarled switch two cubits long and tapering from the size of a thumb at its base to the size of a little finger at the other end. This switch had been soaked in hot pepper sauce for half a day. A sweeping movement of the arm, and the switch fell upon the woman's back. The arm rose again and then fell once more. At first slow and measured, his movements soon became rapid and frenetic. The uninterrupted shrieks of the switch furiously cleaving the air and the clicking of the iron and silver bracelets that covered his arms told those who were too timid to look in the direction of the throne that the executioner was continuing to strike. But the woman herself was so silent that they believed she had already been killed by the first blow.

A few bolder spectators ventured furtive glances toward the executioner; Doguicimi was writhing with pain. Her skin was abraded away, and when the switch landed on an open wound, blood spurted out; flesh and pieces of skin were ripped away and followed the switch into the air.

The Royal Wives secretly rejoiced, convinced that Doguicimi could not survive such torment, but they prudently refrained from uttering a word. . . .

Among the ranks of the high dignitaries, two men sitting face to face stared at the ground during Doguicimi's agony. They raised their heads from time to time. Their eyes met, and both of them seemed to be giving the other the following password: "Let us sympathize with her in silence!" They were indeed suffering, and a great deal too, but each for a different reason.

One of them desired to arise and, at the risk of his own life, save that of his sworn friend's wife. But an inner voice told him: "You could not imagine a more certain means of hastening her death. One can work effectively in the shadows on behalf of a protégé."

He followed his own prudent advice. . . .

The other was asking himself if he shouldn't prostrate himself in front of the throne and denounce to the whole court the invidious schemes devised in connivence with Migan, Zanbounou the spy, and a few Royal Wives to disgrace Doguicimi and bring about her execution.

This high dignitary would have liked to admit the base sentiments that had incited them to heap on Doguicimi's head all the lies recited by Zanbounou; he would have said that one of them did not forgive the woman for the death sentence imposed on his niece, that he himself, the heir to the throne, was avenging the love that the faithful wife of Toffa refused to share with him, that the stinking beast from the mountain was making the woman expiate her disdain for him, that other accomplices had been motivated by jealousy, and that the queens could not admit that the mere wife of a prince could surpass them in virtue.

But the consequences of such a confession appeared extremely serious to him. He would not move. Nevertheless, he was consumed with remorse. If he had decided to punish the woman who was guilty of having despised him, he had not expected to carry his revenge as far as her death. In love and having failed in his efforts to make her love him in return, he had hoped to exploit the cabal being hatched against her as an opportunity to convince her that marrying him was the only way to save her own head from the threat of Migan's scimitar. But he looked on with horror as the executioner deployed all his efforts to kill the woman with the blows of his switch. He promised himself to make amends for all the harm done to Doguicimi's reputation and for the torture to which she had been subjected.

The flogging proceeded. The crown prince prostrated himself on the ground, covered himself with dirt, and left for Jêgbé under the pretext of a sudden illness.

The executioner continued to deliver his blows savagely, methodically; the victim's entire left side was nothing more than blood and open wounds; Migan pulled on the stick to turn her over. When his efforts proved futile, he thought she was intent upon resisting him. He therefore slapped her four times with his calloused hands that were laden with copper and wrought iron rings. Blood flowed from the woman's mouth and nose. The executioner paid no attention to it. He grabbed the inert package by the arms and turned her onto her left side, selected a new switch, and set to work again.

The impudent woman, who had escaped him twice in the past, was now in his hands. He had not been given permission to kill her with a single slash of the scimitar at the moment of her initial blasphemies, which she had repeated on the first day of the great traditional celebration. Today he was hoping to fulfill his desire with blows of the switch. But first he would draw a word of entreaty or, at least, a groan of pain from Doguicimi. "Yes, she will cry out to all Danhomê that Migan Atindébacou is the scourge of his enemies and that he could make a wooden statue weep by beating it! She'll shout it to the sky! She'll shout it to the sky!" At that thought, the energy of the executioner was redoubled. But only the clicking of his bracelets and the whistling of the switch as it moved through the air broke the silence that reigned over the crowd, suddenly struck dumb with fear.

The body of the man administering the punishment was bathed in sweat. "He will not release Doguicimi until she has begged for mercy. He has always got the better of Mahinous, although they were obstinate! It will never be said in this Danhomê that a mere being with seven pairs of ribs held the savagery of Migan Atindébacou at bay. That would be a great dishonor for him. He wouldn't survive it!" And the switch wore itself out violently on the woman's back.

The king had understood what Migan wanted to do. The impassivity of Doguicimi, whose body was being lacerated by this unchecked fury, had earned her the pity of the court as well as the admiration of several high dignitaries. With a gesture Guézo stayed the arm of the executioner.

This time the rabble, who just a moment before had been demanding the death of Doguicimi, put itself in the place of the unfortunate woman, who had fainted long ago, and with the greatest sincerety implored the ancestors to bless the most merciful king.

Migan prostrated himself at the foot of the throne and, although vexed by his defeat, joined in the wishes the court was expressing for the power, happiness, and long life of the monarch. Meanwhile, his aides were untying Doguicimi. Judging by the icy pallor of her hands and feet, they believed her dead and decided to throw her body into the Ditch. As they lifted her body, they saw her bloodshot eyes flash in the depths of the sockets of a face horribly swollen by the blows that had been inflicted on it.

Life had not wholly departed from this body then? They tried to make her stand on her legs, but she collapsed, lamenting: "These tortures lasted too long! It would be better to finish me off!" She fainted again. They loaded her on to their shoulders. They were the same men who had arrested her. As executioner's assistants, they performed tasks that had long ago closed their hearts to any feelings of pity for their fellow human beings, but not their sense of admiration for acts of courage. Only the fear of being denounced to their master by a companion in a fit of zeal prompted them to remain prudently silent.

Doguicimi was confined in the filthiest cell of Cangbodé's prison.

In Danhomê only the king had the right to punish anyone with imprisonment or death. To punish certain minor transgressions on the part of queens or female servants who deserved only a few days of detention, he had created two prisons in the Palace and placed them under the supervision of its two first women, Migannon and Mêwounon.

At Migan's residence there was a prison for the common people. Mêwou presided over the one for princes and princesses. Ajaho's gaol held the men guilty of having committed adultery with an Amazon. The smallest of the four was that of Cangbodé, and it was reserved for the female personnel of the Palace. Its entire periphery did not exceed three hundred bamboos.

The Lêguêdês, or inspectors of the royal police, paid unannounced visits to these places of detention and reported to the king about the results of their interviews with the prisoners on the subject of the treatment they were receiving.

Did a high dignitary or a prince need to be imprisoned in perpetuity for a crime that did not deserve the death penalty? The king gave him a wife.

Any escape from the prison of Cangbodé was rendered particularly difficult by the size of the surrounding walls, which were more than one bamboo high, and by the vigilance of the guards who lived in huts all around the walls; for this reason, it was called "Héjannan-mon-nou" (only the winged folk will see it).

On the inside three walls divided the compound into four courtyards; the lodgings of the chief director were in the first one; in the second and third courtyards, dungeons had been built for groups of female prisoners and cells for single individuals. The back courtyard contained only isolated cells for prisoners sentenced to solitary confinement.

Chains attached to stakes that were firmly planted in the ground behind the latter passed through the lower part of the cell walls and culminated in an iron collar that the warders ironically called "the collar that distinguishes virtuous people."

Throughout, the ceiling was high, and the massive door was made of iron-wood, the hardest substance in all Danhomê.

A variety of crimes brought people to this prison. Some of them were known only to the king; the most serious ones required that the prisoner be locked up in one of the cells in the back courtyard, the iron collar around her neck and leg irons on her ankles; she would remain seated with her back against the wall, although when the tension on the chain was relaxed, its additional length allowed her to get up and stretch her legs a bit in her cell.

Anyone who ended up here had no hope of deliverance.

Had Cangbodé secretly received the fatal command with regard to a prisoner? She would then be placed in solitary confinement.

The chief director's principal assistant Pêli would pass behind her cell and yank forcefully on the chain to break the neck of the unfortunate woman, who would suffer a long, agonizing death.

Feigning grief, the director would come to inform the court that the prisoner had "spoiled the iron." Her body would then be removed under the cover of night and buried in the greatest secrecy.

Had it been decided that, instead of this brutal end, only a natural death should free the prisoner from her chains? She could spend season after season in this cell, where she would be tormented by hunger, thirst, vermin, lice, and blood-sucking larva.

Attracted by the smell of the small jar that served as a chamberpot, which the warders purposely did not empty for many days, swarms of flies entered the cell by means of the hole through which the chain had been passed.

How long had such a Royal Wife been imprisoned here? Suffering and privation erased every memory from her mind. Extended isolation also caused her to lose almost all vestiges of human speech. For that reason, it was with great difficulty that any precise information, or even four consecutive intelligible sentences, could be drawn from her. The notches carved by the warders each day with their knives almost entirely covered the long stick that had been driven into the ground in front of her cell, and they could easily satisfy our curiosity if we had the patience to count them. But her general condition leaves no doubt that she has been imprisoned here since the previous reign. And her crime must have been extremely serious for Guézo not to have pardoned her upon his ascension to the throne!

The scraps of cloth with which she had wrapped the iron collar and the leg irons to alleviate the rubbing were black with filth, and the rag that served as the sole article of clothing on her body was red with the dust in which she was lying.

Accustomed to the darkness of her cell, her eyes could no longer tolerate the sunlight that flooded the room whenever anyone opened the door. Tangled, dusty hair covered the nape of her neck; her aspect was skeletal as collar bones, shoulder blades, ribs, vertebral column, and hip bones protruded beneath a dry, caked skin; her fingers were withered and her nails disproportionately long; the backs of these fingernails were blackened with her own blood, which had bloated the lice she was constantly crushing with them, and the other side was caked with the filth she scratched from her body – the only two distractions she had.

Her arms and legs had atrophied; as the result of prolonged deprivation, the miserable woman was consuming her own muscles after having lived off her fat. A single meal a day could not sustain a human being, especially when it consisted of no more than two balls of akassa and a caloulou, on the surface of which a vague drop of palm oil was floating and whole peppers were dancing in the company of indefinable vegetables.

It was not without serious cause that one ended up here, especially during the reign of Guézo, who was the very image of justice and mercy. No pity for this prisoner then! Any efforts her parents might secretly undertake to procure the indulgence of her jailers would encounter the obstacle of rigorous orders promulgated by the king.

Who then would be willing to run the risk of disgrace by taking an interest in a prisoner of that category.

The privations and torments of a life in such foul air could not help but shorten the days alloted to us by Destiny when he sent us into this world, even if they were many in number.

Conditions were less harsh in the cells of the third courtyard, where the prisoners, free of neck and ankle chains, still nourished the hope of being liberated on the day when it occurred to the Master of the World to think about them.

Simple misdemeanors led to imprisonment in the second courtyard, where the prisoners were obliged to drill holes in cowries and place them on strings. Advantage was also taken of the skills developed by those with special talents: basket-makers, weavers of sacks, and spinners of raphia palm fibers found distraction from their boredom and temporary surcease from their sorrow in the exercise of their professions. They were given water with which to wash themselves and allowed visits from relatives of the same sex, who could bring them food to supplement the austere diet of the prison.

When queens were reinstated at the Palace upon the recommendation of Pojito, Migannon, or Mêwounon after an incarceration lasting several market days or several moons, they remained chastened for a long time.

But none of the Wives of Panther whom the Master of the World had felt constrained to imprison in Cangbodé's compound would ever again enjoy the right of sharing the royal bed: the fall of a monkey romping through the trees disgraces him forever. . . .

The sun had returned to his home behind Coufo; night was now shrouding the earth with its somber veils.

When she regained consciousness, Doguicimi realized she was lying flat on her face; her entire body was sore – her back, her sides, her thighs, and her arms were smarting. She felt an intense pain in her ears. It seemed as if invisible hands were still beating her head against the wall or piercing her skin with needles.

She tried to move one of her hands behind her, but sharp spasms in her arm and side caused her to abandon the effort. What was the burning sensation on her back? That dull ache in her limbs and her head? Because she could not move she thought she was tied to the ground. What had happened? Everything was confused in her mind! Where was she? The darkness was so profound that she could make out nothing at all.

With a supreme effort, she directed her hand toward the burning sensation on her side. Her fingers gathered up a pasty substance, but when she brought it to her nose at the cost of countless difficulties and almost unbearable pain, she couldn't recognize it by its odor.

A fleeting glimmer of hope passed through her mind. She felt the ground around her, looking for the servant who, she believed, would be at her side. Her movements revived her pain and caused her wounds to begin bleeding again; she remained still and made an enormous mental effort to recollect her memories; more and more she became conscious of her situation and of the place in which she found herself. A nauseating stench revolted her. She turned her head. The odour persisted. She blocked her nostrils with her upper lip. Painful itches that she tried to scratch made her aware of blood-sucking larva on her stomach and thighs. She who was the very essence of fastidiousness, she who had such a horror of flies that she not only refused to leave anything lying about her house that might attract them but also insisted that all brooms must be washed after having come in contact with anything coveted by these disgusting insects, she who could not bear the thought of being bitten by blood-sucking parasites, she had been precipitated into garbage pit where bloated flies were trumpeting their joy as they sought out our leftover foods and beverages, on which they vomited the surplus from their abdomens; she had been thrown into a muck compounded of urine, vomit, and other undefinable substances where the larva deposited by the flies were swarming! Nausea revolted her heart.

The torments endured at the court were infinitely more bearable for her than life in this filthy prison.

The thought that her body had been lacerated and was now at the mercy of blood-sucking larva intensified her horror of the place.

At that very moment several dull moans emanated from the other end of the cell. They frightened her. The words that followed were muffled and incoherent, but they reassured her somewhat; she was not alone. She pricked up her ears but could only grasp the following words: "Mercy. . . . Mercy. . . . Feet are burning. . . . can lie. . . . die . . . . rather die. . . ." The final words had been pronounced very feebly; then the moans began again.

Incapable of recognizing the voice, Doguicimi thought: "Sister in misery, you who are delirious, I do not know who you are or what crime you are expiating. Perhaps you are, like me, an innocent victim of their cruelty? May your ancestors, and mine, and those of all their previous victims exact punishment on our common persecutors. . . ."

The laments that resumed on the other side of the cell, more confused than ever, interrupted Doguicimi's train of thought; she listened again and, puzzled, asked herself: "I have the feeling that I've heard that voice before somewhere! But I can't recognize it. . . ."

Cries followed the moans: "Water! Water! The thirst is killing me!"

Doguicimi collected all that remained of her strength, rose to her knees, placed her hands on the ground, and sought to drag herself to the sufferer in the hope of offering her some consolation in lieu of the water she was requesting.
. . .

She collapsed before having moved her leg. Her pain was aggravated by the fall, and her wounds started bleeding worse than before.

Her thoughts focused on Toffa. Since the noble prince's disappearance, her memory of him had become the only refuge the poor woman's mind had found in the midst of all her afflictions and her only prop in the battles she had been obliged to wage against those who wanted to turn her aside from the path of virtue.

Doguicimi henceforth assimilated the memory of her faithful servant to that of Toffa: "As for him, he is a prisoner at Hounjroto and cannot come to save me from this place. Those brutes are surely keeping Evêmon under guard, and that is what has prevented her from coming to me. . . ."

The creaking of the door aroused her from her meditations. By the light of the earthenware lamp carried by a man who was being followed by four others, she saw the group move toward her mysterious companion in misery; they were bringing her the news of her liberation. They thought she was dead, but she had only fainted.

"Poor child! What crime brought you here and in such a state?" whispered one of the men.

The jailer who had admitted her lowered his voice and confided in them: "She is supposedly the servant of a woman who has serious accusations hanging over her head. They were expecting to obtain damaging testimony against the accused, but since the girl refused to talk, Migan entrusted her to his servants with the order to extract her secret from her. They set to work with fire and cudgels, but all in vain."

"The first minister acted without informing the Master of the World, who ordered the unfortunate child's release as soon as he heard about it a few moments ago," one of the royal messengers explained.

Another exclaimed sadly: "Oh, model servant! Devotion and courage incarnate! May your ancestors henceforth allow you to experience better days among them in return for your fidelity! If you were a member of my family, I would never tire of singing your virtues!"

"An end to your prattling! They brought her to me half dead. Take her away before she gasps her last breath!" grumbled the chief warder, who had just arrived. The royal messengers knelt down and touched the dying child's hands and feet. "But it's a dead body that we're taking away!" one of them said.

"She only died when she was in your hands!" the chief warder replied. "It's up to you to explain it at the court."

A royal messenger passed his arms under those of the young prisoner and picked her up; another one took her by the feet and they left.

They had spoken so softly that Doguicimi, rendered almost entirely deaf by the blows she had received, had been unable to comprehend anything of what they had been saying.

The door creaked again a moment later.

A prisoner came to help Doguicimi go out to the veranda and receive a visit. "The king perhaps?" thought Toffa's wife. "He is known to pay unannounced visits to the prisons at night to determine whether or not all the prisoners have been formally sentenced. He also questions them about the way they are being treated. That is how he informs himself about individuals to whom he can grant pardons." Doguicimi promised herself that she would explain to the king the motivations behind her actions and the way in which her thoughts and actions had been distorted, magnified, and misinterpreted with the intention of harming her.

On the veranda she found herself in the presence of the crown prince, who started in horror at the sight of her hideously swollen, ugly face. Her head had been so violently rubbed into the ground that the scalp had peeled away on the right and on the left; the cheeks and temples were scraped and swollen. A large bruise protruded from her forehead; her ears were puffy and her lips inordinately swollen. Sunken in their sockets, her bloodshot eyes could not bear the light from the little lamp.

In that horribly deformed face Vidaho had difficulty recognizing the beautiful countenance over which he had been sighing for so many seasons.

He was tormented with remorse. Toffa's wife interpreted the prince's sadness more as the compassion that suffering invariably provokes in any sensitive soul.

The love-struck prince finally mastered his emotion; before Doguicimi had the chance to resist him, he removed the cloth that she had draped around herself. Bringing his lamp closer, the prince saw that the woman's entire back was filled with open wounds that continued to bleed despite the akassa with which they had been covered to protect them against fly bites and promote healing. Doguicimi thought that only Evêmon could have lavished such affectionate and tender care on her before she had been transported to this prison.

Covering her with the cloth again, the prince said in a wheedling tone of voice: "The whole court was amazed by your impassivity, which held Migan's fury at bay. Devastated at being unable to stop the executioner's arm, I left the court as an expression of protest against the tortures being inflicted on you. My august Father understood my gesture and ordered them stopped before I had even turned my back.

"I wanted to get to the bottom of the crimes that had been imputed to you. In this way I learned that Zanbounou had been bribed to seduce you. Several persons in the king's entourage wanted to see you convicted of criminal mis-

240

conduct with the Mahinou. Having failed in that enterprise, they fabricated the accusations that brought you here. Your secret enemies were also the ones who gave Zanbounou the idea of asking you for the skull of the king of Hounjroto. They were not unaware that you were under my protection, and they secretly planned to compromise me in a crime of high treason. They renounced their scheme at the last moment because the consequences of their accusation seemed to menace themselves. The Royal Wives were the first to fear for their own heads, for suspicions would first of all be directed toward them, and they did handle the macabre war trophy many times each day. They have certainly taken the skull back from the Mahinou and returned it to its proper place. At least you didn't tell that stinking beast from the mountain that you obtained the skull from the heir to the throne?

"In the belief that this war trophy had been sent to Hounjroto, I lived in the fear that my august Father would notice its disappearance, and I offered sacrifices to my ancestors so they might protect me against a denunciation that could lose me my right to the throne.

"The Danhomênou is inherently distrustful. But disdaining the most elementary precautions, you placed your confidence in that disgusting beast who had been brought back from Gbowêlê.

"You showed a lack of perceptiveness, Doguicimi. It is true that, when someone confidently promises a sick person the cure for which he has been waiting impatiently, he will not hesitate to make any sacrifice to obtain it. In this Danhomê, I alone know how much you suffer as the result of Toffa's disappearance, and I alone can console you. . . .

"Unfortunately, the court believed Zanbounou's accusations. My august Father would have liked to have treated you leniently again. But there was that flask of mercury! It wasn't that the Master of the World lent credence to his first minister's explanation in regard to your criminal intentions with regard to the sacred person of the king. If he had not dealt harshly with you today, the slaves of our slaves would have acquired this deadly poison tomorrow, and that would have been the end of the masters in the Danhomê of Houégbaja.

"Don't forget that Migan never lays down his weapons and that your present torments are no more than gentle caresses in comparison with what is still to come.

"The first minister has persuaded the king to order an investigation into the source of the poison that was confiscated from you.

"Migan is the sworn friend of Cangbodé. I'm afraid that he might consent to your murder, which would later be presented as a natural death. If your life didn't appear to me to be in danger as long as you remain in this prison, I would gladly let you stay here until the day when my august Father would deign to answer my prayers and pardon you. Believe me, your enemies are at this very moment hatching conspiracies that will cause your head to roll. You will tell me that death does not frighten you. That's possible. But aren't you also a bit concerned about your honor? Zanbounou's accusations have so besmirched it that only your marriage to me can cleanse you of the disgrace that has been heaped upon you.

"I will make you a Wife of Panther, and, from that moment on, there will not be the slightest doubt about your honesty in the minds of the people. With the help of the ancestors, you will become Mother of Panther. That will increase the Danhomênous' veneration of you.

"You will leave this revolting prison tonight. Let us go to Jêgbé, where happiness awaits you. My august Father will suspect nothing of your abduction."

After Vidaho's speech, Doguicimi appeared sceptical and replied: "Only the tomb confines mortal beings without any hope of escape!" The love-struck prince then proceded in a cajoling tone of voice: "You don't believe me? You don't believe me, Doguicimi? I will inform my august Father of your liberation, and he will not condemn me for it, because it is one of the privileges that accrues to my station as a royal prince." He cast a glance in all directions. Having assured himself that there were no witnesses to their conversation, he leaned toward the woman and whispered in her ear: "You would believe me, Doguicimi, if I showed you that the impetuous Wife of Panther – the one who attacked you in a blind fit of rage at the moment of your blasphemies after the return from the war of Hounjroto and whom the king ordered to be executed because she had polluted herself through contact with men – is living safely in my Palace. Exercising my right as Vidaho and at the request of her uncle, the Migan, I granted a reprieve to that queen, who is the sole support of her widowed, invalid mother. The king knows nothing about it. I am prepared to free you in the same way as that royal wife.

"Cangbodé could announce your death this very night. But you would continue to live – for me alone – at Jêgbé. If necessary, we'll find a corpse to present at the court.

"As soon as the king has joined his ancestors and I have become Master of Danhomê, I will inform the court that I am exercising clemency and pardoning you on the occasion of my accession to the throne. You will then make your appearance in the Courtyard of the Palace and ask the people to join you in supplicating me to accept you as the servant of my favorite wife. You will insist even if I pretend to despize you. You know the Danhomênous. They will applaud you and cover themselves with dust as an expression of gratitude for my concession."

Doguicimi begged him to postpone the abduction until she had completely recovered, alleging (to inspire Vidaho's confidence in her) that she was not unaware of the danger hanging over her head and that she herself would, a few days later, have requested the prince to take her under his roof, if he himself had not come to offer her his protection.

Joyfully the prince assured her: "You will see your faithful Evêmon again; she is the incarnation of loyalty, and this very night she will receive the reward of her affection for you. Despite the tortures by means of which they hoped to extract information from that child about your conduct since the disappearance of Toffa, she invariably replied: 'My mother is virtue itself. Neither by word nor deed has she ever done anything capable of corrupting a child.' Her courage, coupled with her frankness, seduced my august Father, who decided to make her a Wife of Panther this very evening. From now on Evêmon will be happy. For my part, I am bringing you your happiness. I want you both to enjoy days of happiness at my side. You as soon as you are recovered, and Evêmon when I will have acquired Danhomê. In the meantime, I will give orders for Zokindé to join you before the first crowing of the cock. . . ."

The prince was interrupted by the arrival of a guard who brought Doguicimi's dinner. He asked what dishes were contained in the calabash that Cangbodé's servant was presenting to the woman.

The man answered him churlishly: "So, along with the unprecedented permission to communicate with the prisoner, you were entrusted with the task of inspecting our work in this prison? If your eyes don't give you enough information, put your tongue to work."

"And what if I ordered that impudent wretch, in case he refuses to obey, should put out his eyes and cut off his tongue at this very moment so that I might be the last person whom he would ever see or to whom he would ever address such insolences?" inquired Vidaho in an irritated tone of voice as he arose and stared his interlocutor in the face.

Having recognized him, the warder threw himself face down on the ground, and scraping the soil with his fingernails to gather it up and cover his body with it, he implored the prince, in the name of all the Houégbajas, to spare his life and make him the slave of his slaves.

The woman cast a beseeching glance toward the heir to the throne. She never suspected the complicity that existed between the prince and the guard. Having understood her meaning, Vidaho smiled at Doguicimi to indicate that he was pardoning the warder's insolence as a tribute to the woman he idolized.

But Cangbodé's servant continued: "Royal prince, it is antilope, highly seasoned. We prepared it according to Migan's instructions."

Drawing the calabash toward her, Doguicimi said: "The executioner wants to achieve at all costs what was denied to the strength of his arms today. Well then, I accept my death!"

"I will preserve these foul dishes and make use of them to send your tormentor to the city of the dead once I have acquired Danhomê!" exclaimed Vidaho as he tore the calabash from her hands; he gave it back to the warder with the express order to go and wait for him in the courtyard.

Getting ready to leave, Vidaho repeated to Doguicimi: "It was your own fault that you ended up in this place. You scorned the prince who loved you with a sincere love, and you confided in your enemies, in a despicable Mahinou who was like fried bean cakes in his dealings with you, for they too have a different color on the inside than the one they show to the outside world.

"Believe me, my beloved Doguicimi, it was the spy who, in collusion with your co-wives and a princess, a former wife of Toffa, betrayed you through the intermediary of the queens."

The prince feigned a profound sincerity and failed to mention his own rather substantial responsibility for the unfortunate woman's torments.

Some people successfully conceal their ignominy beneath a facade of honesty for their entire lives. That was true of Vidaho.

He took leave of the woman with the promise he would return the following night; he then spent a few moments in private conversation with Cangbodé. The prince, who never suspected the blood oath that bound the prison director to Toffa, sought to deceive him into thinking that he was the missing prince's sworn friend, who in that capacity was taking an interest in Doguicimi and would protect her against all her enemies; he would even like to take her out of this prison in order to guarantee her safety until the day of her husband's liberation.

Upon his return to his Palace, he sent Doguicimi a calabash with several kinds of food, a basket filled with cloths, and a dozen mats. When the prince's messengers returned, they described for him the prisoner's joy and the prayers she addressed to the Houégbajas for the benediction of the future Master of Danhomê.

Hope revived in Vidaho and intensified his passion for Doguicimi.

The desired woman whom one has not yet had in one's possession always seems superior to all those in one's immediate surroundings, but this was not the only reason the prince felt drawn toward Doguicimi. According to the king's own words, she was the incarnation of courage. Her assaults upon the Master of the World (the very image of terror!), her impassiveness that had frustrated the unbridled fury of Migan (who prided himself upon always drawing tears or cries of entreaty from anyone who fell into his clutches), the woman's disdain for the luxuries that seduced the average Danhomênou, her resistence to temptation, the strength of her soul – everything indicated that Toffa's wife was indeed superior to most women in this Danhomê.

Ever since his conversation with Toffa's wife at the prison, the prince often repeated to himself: "More than once I have seen the flour without being able to touch the dough with my hand! Before three market days have passed, I will seize the happiness that for me resides solely in the possession of Doguicimi, this treasure of courage, which is the highest of virtues in the eyes of the Danhomênous!" Many times he had actually seen the realization of his happiness, but only in his dreams. Everything had vanished as soon as he awoke or entered the house of Toffa, and his disappointment merely heightened his passion.

He persuaded himself that his power had inspired the woman with admiration, that she had become convinced of the danger hanging over her at the prison and regarded Jêgbé as the only place she could be sure of finding salvation, and that, having been moved by the visit he had paid her and the many proofs he had given her of his love, Doguicimi would soon consent to marry him. In the depth of his heart he promised himself he would generously reward all the Danhomênous who had contributed to framing the accusation that, by precipitating Doguicimi into prison, had brought him closer to her today and undoubtedly placed him on the path that would lead to the realization of his desires.

These reflections vouchsafed him the peaceful sleep he had no longer enjoyed since the day when his august Father had revealed to him Doguicimi's superiority over all the women in the kingdom and thus unwittingly aroused in him the love he felt for her.

Doguicimi had regained her cell within a few moments of the prince's departure, and the door had closed behind her.

Cangbodé had ordered that all the heir to the throne's presents be taken from the woman.

The thought that she was profoundly alone in the darkness of the cell now frightened the woman. She reflected: "Why do they persist in locking me up when they know perfectly well that I am too weak to stand up and attempt an escape? Even if I were in good shape, I would still need the complicity of the guards to get out of this prison. And what Danhomênou would dare compromise himself in such an affair, knowing that he could pay for such complicity with his life. . . .!

"They can't have imprisoned me again for the simple pleasure of torturing me! In the hope of beguiling the prince's love, didn't I tell him that I would now prefer the enjoyment of life at his side above the prospect of death? He obviously didn't believe me since I didn't agree to follow him to Jêgbé. Discouraged by the failure of his efforts, he has perhaps stationed a man with iron hands in this dark hole and given him the task of strangling me as a punishment for my obstinacy in refusing to share his love? Death? But death has never terrified Doguicimi!" The woman promised herself she would not resist the murderer.

"But if some scoundrel had been given the order to dishonor me instead!" she exclaimed to herself.

Such a fate sent a shudder up her spine. Wasn't it for having wanted to preserve herself from any taint that she had been brought to this prison after being tarred with insults and lacerated by Migan's switch? She reproached herself for not having followed the heir to the throne. A doubt infiltrated her mind. Season after season she had been suffering because of her love for Toffa, but did he really love her, and was he still thinking about her? She recalled the prince's harsh judgment of women on the eve of his departure for Hounjroto. Even if, in spite of that ill-tempered outburst, his love for her was sincere, what obligations did she have toward him after all? No child for him! And, furthermore, he had never caused her to drink a fetish-potion! Moreover, no fetish-potion forces one to remain married to a single husband all one's life or punishes one for abandoning her husband! Adultery alone has been strictly prohibited to wives. Doguicimi would have no punishment to fear on the part of the authorities unless she married a man of inferior station after abandoning Toffa. The princesses had assured her that no one would blame Vidaho for appropriating the wife of any man in this kingdom.

As for Vidaho, he loved her; she could have no doubt of that. Season after season he had tirelessly multiplied the proofs of his love for her. He had vowed to make her a Wife of Panther. She had also received the promise that she would become Mother of Panther if she could give birth to a son. In this way her memory would be honored forever. She had the assurance of happiness in this world and in the next one. What more could a woman desire in this Danhomê, where women were regarded as inferior beings necessarily subject to all the whims of their masters and without the slightest hope of reward?

What she had to fear, especially at this moment, was the anger of the prince who, if he were rejected again, could very well avenge himself cruelly on her. Then again, Doguicimi had no proof that her husband, once he returned to Danhomê, would not sacrifice her to please the heir to the throne. The king could also order his sister-in-law to be abducted and taken to the Palace of his successor, even before Toffa's return to Danhomê.

Vidaho had sworn he would give her to the slaves of his slaves and allow them to defile her! In all justice, she could not accuse Destiny of having led her to this prison. She told herself that her torments could only be ascribed to her own obstinacy in repudiating the happiness promised by the heir to the throne.

For a moment, her mind remained devoid of thought; then she plunged even deeper into her meditations. When she emerged, she exclaimed aloud, as if replying to someone who had asked her a question: "A 'yes' and I could have deflected this dishonor from myself. But a 'yes' would have implied free choice. And contact with a royal prince would not have been any less dishonorable for the wife of Toffa. Whereas if I succumb to violence, I remain beyond the reproach of my husband's fetishes and his ancestors. . . ."

She had found a way out of her dilemma! She who had resolved to convince her husband that she was not made of the same clay as Ayomayi and that she would always hold herself above any hint of pollution, she was now asking herself what might prevent her from obtaining her liberty by means of the most regular of marriages. But an inner voice immediately reminded her of her last conversation with her husband. She had told him that some wives were capable of remaining faithful indefinitely. He hadn't wanted to believe it. Wouldn't her fall merely confirm Toffa's prejudice against the women whom he called snails, bitches, and who knows what else?

He would not fail to say: "Wasn't I right, Doguicimi? Before marrying another man, did you wait until my death had been confirmed by a war of revenge against Hounjroto?"

She shook her head and concluded: "Having resisted temptation since morning, I would have succumbed in the evening – that is to say, on the verge of triumph? No! My sufferings honor me more than would my marriage to Vidaho!"

This thought restored her completely to Toffa. The idea of a possible taint caused her to tremble. Her head became hot, and she fell victim to a violent headache. It seemed to her as if calloused hands with ring-laden fingers had once again begun to rain blows upon her ears, so loud was the throbbing in them and so intense the shooting pains that occurred there. With a supreme effort, she lay down on one side, drew her thighs up to her chest and her heels to her buttocks, as if she wanted to confine and thereby quickly extinguish the fire of the fever that was burning in her. The thought that a man could come at any moment to carry out a fatal order deepened her trance.

Soon the first crowing of the cock sounded. "It'll undoubtedly take place at the second crowing of the cock," she thought. Overcome with anguish at the thought of the pollution that would be imposed upon her by a man, she heard a body fall to the floor of the room. "King Guézo, save me!" she exclaimed, panic-stricken. As if squeezed by invisible hands of iron, her throat allowed her to emit no more than a feeble cry, to which a plaintive meow replied. A cat had been chasing a rat across the roof beams and fallen through the rectangular hole that had been cut in the ceiling.

This fright caused the prisoner's heart to beat violently and increased the fever that did not diminish until the second crowing of the cock. Doguicimi finally dozed off. In her sleep she rolled over on her back.

Intense pains immediately awakened her.

Not the slightest complaint had been drawn from her yesterday by the most atrocious torments, but she was weeping and moaning this morning as the two female prisoners, into whose care Cangbodé had confided her, passed warm compresses over her pain-wracked body and dressed her wounds. She referred to it as her supreme torture, and when it was over, she was installed in a clean hut with a pounded earth floor that had been glazed with dried cow dung.

The sun was in the midst of his course toward a position directly overhead, and Doguicimi was still moaning; it would be like that all day long at the least movement of her arms and legs.

About mid-day three young girls arrived at the prison with voluminous calabashes containing a variety of dishes and the white man's alcohol.

Cangbodé doubted that a sworn friendship actually bound Toffa to the crown prince. His missing friend had never spoken to him about it, although it would not have been in his interest to conceal a blood oath with such a high-ranking person. The prison director sensed something quite different, but he refrained from questioning the woman on the subject. He recalled the secrets his sworn friend Vivênagbo had confided in him. . . . He would contrive to serve Doguicimi's meals before the arrival of Vidaho's messengers; he would also make certain that she did not make use of anything the prince gave her to keep. That was the only way in his power to shield her from the attraction that would not fail to be aroused in her by the love potions that the prince was undoubtedly mixing into the food and drink being offered to the desired woman. Hadn't the trial to which he had subjected the prince's first presents to Doguicimi yesterday evening been conclusive in determining whether or not they had been adulterated?

He would leave the woman in ignorance of all the efforts he was making to counter the spells prepared by the prince. Let misfortune befall all those who trust those of her sex! What Danhomênou failed to recognize that the two pairs of ribs that women lacked in comparison to the stronger sex deprived them of masculine virtues like discretion, loyalty, level-headedness, and nobility?

People were now seeing the second moon since the imprisonment of Doguicimi.

By means of a personal police that even his ministers did not know about, the king knew everything concerning the life of this women since the disappearance of her husband, and he had decided to protect her without seeming to do so. For that matter, didn't the blood oath that linked him with Toffa place him under an obligation to do precisely that? He had his reasons for preferring to send Doguicimi to Cangbodé's prison; during the previous reign, this Danhomênou was the director of the prison where the tyrant had confined his creditor, the slave-trader who was to become Chacha Ajinacou. Bound by a blood oath to the prince who was contesting the usurper's right to the throne of Houégbaja, Cangbodé agreed to facilitate the escape of the white prisoner in whom the pretender to the throne was interested. When Guézo came into the possession of Danhomê, the devotion of this high dignitary was recompensed with the honor of being named director of the prison reserved for the personnel of the Palace. The king was not unaware that Cangbodé was also the sworn friend of Toffa.

Esteeming that this prison would shelter Doguicimi more effectively than the roof of Toffa's house from the persistence of a lover, whom he did not want to rebuke publicly, and from the hatred of her enemies, the king did not want to free her. He had secretly enjoined the prison director to care for her and advised him not to let her be approached by anyone except those queens whose good will toward her had been verified by him.

Sworn friendship alone would have provided sufficient reason for the director to soften the prison stay of a missing "brother's" wife, but in this case it was reinforced by the imperative under which the king's order had placed him. Cangbodé no longer needed to conceal his solicitude for Doguicimi. But he was mistrustful and kept her in the dark about the reasons behind his protection of her.

For the past four days the king had been holding council meetings that lasted until the first crowing of the cock. The crown prince no longer showed himself at the prison. Doguicimi was puzzled. Finally she lost courage and became depressed.

Since the ill-starred campaign of Hounjroto, she had heard speak of two expeditions against Gbêjêwin and Gbaji,[1] but there was no longer any question

---

[1]   Gbêjêwin was an outlying settlement of the Kingdom of Porto-Novo; Gbaji is in mahi country. (author's note)

of waging a war of revenge to liberate the captive princes at Hounjroto. Should that lead one to conclude that the court had learned of the death of the two illustrious prisoners? And what about the messages sent by Toffa? And the gris-gris that Zanbounou had brought back from Hounjroto as proof that the prince was still alive? Doguicimi had reason to doubt that her husband was dead, but she was also determined to precede him into the land of the spirits.

She continued to be obsessed with the idea of dishonor. She told herself that it was certainly her ancestors who had inspired her with forebodings of a misfortune like this. Dishonor would befall her either through Vidaho or through one of his slaves, as he had threatened; the order would perhaps even be given by Toffa in his desire to please the king or the heir to the throne? She would not wait around for such a disgrace to occur! Only let her strength be restored; she would climb to the top of the prison wall and throw herself head-first into the abyss! That was the only way she saw to escape dishonor at the moment when Vidaho, tired of having been played for a fool, would decide to avenge himself in the manner he had described to her.

As for the illustrious lover, he regretted the length of the council meetings that deprived him of the pleasure of seeing the adored woman as often as he would have liked, especially since he was convinced that she could no longer elude his grasp.

Yet the excellent news he received regularly about Doguicimi's health and her sentiments toward him were not enough for him. He was burning with impatience to go and hear from her own lips the assurance that she shared his passion. For this reason, he hurried to her side on the first evening when the tiredness of the king left him free. He found her extremely depressed, and that grieved him. On her forehead a single bruise remained, and it was much smaller than it had been; the swellings on her cheeks, lips, and ears had completely disappeared.

Despite the lampblack she smeared across her cheeks and temples every day, they had not yet regained their original color. If it had not been for these blemishes and for her eyes, which remained bloodshot in the corners, Doguicimi's face would already have recovered its seductive charm. On her back two wounds were not yet completely healed. Daily applications of lampblack were beginning to obliterate the striations that the switch had scored on her delicate skin. Puzzled by the profound depression of the woman he adored, the prince inquired whether she was regularly receiving all the food he sent her. The woman replied affirmatively with a nod of the head, which she raised and lowered; between two sighs, she informed him that she was treated with respect and solicitude. Vidaho was still not satisfied. He was convinced that Doguicimi was concealing some sorrow from him, and he desired to be fully informed about the reason for her sadness.

Assailed with questions, she claimed that her depression resulted from an insomnia that had been caused by the shooting pains she still felt in her ears and on the lower part of her back.

This explanation did not completely still Vidaho's curiosity. When he requested more precise details about the pain she was still experiencing, the heir to the throne received only the most evasive replies. The secret sorrows that a desired woman confides in the man who loves her reveal to him that his feelings are shared. It became clear to Vidaho that he was not yet the master of Doguicimi's heart. He promised on his next visit to bring his doctor, whose treatments would put an end to all the woman's malaises.

His left elbow on his thigh, his forearm straight, his jaw resting between his forefinger and his thumb, and his right fist placed firmly on his right hip, the love-struck prince winked at her with one eye and, with the other, sought to detect on the woman's face the secret he was certain she was hiding from him. Powerless to discover it, he spoke to her cajolingly about her imminent liberation and the happiness that was awaiting her at Jêgbé.

Her eyes were filled with a doubt that also manifested itself in a deep sigh as she raised her glance toward him, then let them fall.

"You don't believe me, Doguicimi? Nevertheless, it's true. I call upon my ancestors to bear me witness!" he exclaimed in a persuasive tone of voice.

Another sigh answered his assertions. Doguicimi plunged back into her meditations. The prince continued to bombard her with the fiery darts of his questioning glances. His lips were moving; he was repeating to himself the invocations that were supposed to activate the gris-gris that would enable him to conquer the woman.

Forgetting that she was in the presence of the prince, she spoke aloud, unwittingly betraying the resolution she had promised herself never to reveal to him: "One who has decided to leave this life has no right to make plans for the future!"

Convinced that all women, even those who appear very attached to their husbands or quite determined never to allow themselves to be dishonored, can be seduced and that those who remain indifferent to the first signs of a man's love, unmoved by his physical attractiveness, high birth, or power, and deaf to his entreaties or the language of magnificent presents, will be unable to resist the spells embodied in love potions, Vidaho had employed one approach after another in his attempt to conquer Doguicimi.

But for this honest woman, no beauty or power could ever surpass those of Toffa; neither beautiful promises nor the most splendid presents were capable of dazzling her to the point of diverting her from the path of virtue. The education she had received in her family had fashioned her soul, as she herself was fond of saying, into a strong defense against any attempted seduction. Love potions should have no effect upon an honest character, even when the fetishist believes wholeheartedly in them, because it the world would be in a hopeless state if virtue could be corrupted so easily.

The prince had been a bit slow in grasping such truths. But he did not consider himself defeated.

He had discovered Doguicimi's weak point – the desire for motherhood, a desire common to all the women of Danhomê and the most frequent cause for the fall of some – and he had undertaken to exploit it skillfully. One day he had insinuated that she was not yet a mother because her spirit was not in harmony with that of Toffa, and he had passionately promised that he was certain to give her that supreme joy. But she had replied to him that she was not duped by his words: "Procreation is not an act of human will! And it is wrong to consider our sterility as a disgrace. Such an attitude seems to originate with men who are hostile to the honesty of women. For that matter, it is not so long ago that I married Toffa. As long as the night has not yet fallen, it is unreasonable to mock the ill fortune of a market woman. . . ."

At times when his passion flagged and his mind regained all its lucidity, the love-struck prince reproached himself for his less than candid methods. "It's truly unfortunate that a crown prince should be reduced to such mean and humiliating measures!"

One day when Doguicimi had brusquely sent him away from Toffa's compound, he had said to himself as he left: "She's rejecting me! I will show her that, when a heart swollen with love is disdained, it can become filled with hatred and exact a cruel vengeance!"

Then he had begun to plot against her. His schemes had not made him master of the woman's heart, but they had landed her in Cangbodé's prison. She remained within his zone of action, and he still nourished the hope of ultimately vanquishing her resistence. But now the thought of suicide haunted him.

He pretended not to have heard what she had said, but to himself he reflected: "She doesn't want to live any longer! I, Vidaho, will successfully keep her alive in spite of herself. Just a few days more and I will lay siege to her with the gris-gris that the Ajanou I sent for should be preparing for me!"

He then reflected upon the best way to divert the woman from her criminal project. "Wouldn't it be better to tell Doguicimi the secret he had resolved to conceal from her?" He had actually said to himself that, if the woman discovered how a war of revenge was being planned for this rainy season, she would no longer want to become the wife of the future Master of Danhomê, because she would be hoping that the war might bring about Toffa's return. Now he convinced himself that only a knowledge of the court's recent decisions could deter Doguicimi from acting upon her idea of suicide. As if desiring to communicate a simple piece of advice that would only be in the interest of Toffa's wife, he confided in her: "In your place, I would not commit such an act of folly when Danhomê is about to undertake a war of revenge against Hounjroto.

"When the ancestors were queried five days ago about the timeliness of such a war, all of them promised us victory. Gaou and Possou gave reassuring accounts of the army at Agbomê and in the surrounding villages. A royal messenger was dispatched yesterday to the Governors of the provinces beyond the Swamps. He will see Adamou at Apê, Agbota at Houégbo, Ato at Atogon, Danwin at Donou, Aplogan at Alada, Lansou at Azowê, Ajara at Toli, Aponi at Savi, Yévogan and Chacha at Gléhoué, and Nibomê at Godomê; upon his return we will be informed of the battle strength of our provincial contingents. We will assemble the strongest army in the world, and we will attack on the day that the ancestors, consulted through the intermediary of the oracle, will have deemed favorable for our campaign against Hounjroto. The entire mahi country will be destroyed in a short time, and the two illustrious prisoners will once again see the calabashes and the gourds they left behind in Danhomê many seasons ago."

He had hit the mark. The upper part of Doguicimi's body straightened, and a gentle smile brightened her face. She implored the Houégbajas to accord their blessings to their worthy successor on the throne of Danhomê. She rejoiced as if Toffa were already back in Agbomê; she saw herself at his side, telling him of her trials and listening to her husband, who was recounting the misery and privations he had suffered during his long captivity. She did not conceal from Vidaho the fact that she now had a compelling reason to continue living.

The prince left her, overjoyed at having succeeded in sowing the seed of a hope that would fortify and sustain her faltering spirit. In this way he was certain Doguicimi would remain alive until the arrival of the Ajanou for whom he was waiting.

After returning to the company of the two prisoners who had been assigned to her service, Toffa's wife acquainted them with her impending happiness.

All day long Doguicimi never tired of asking them: "He'll soon be back in Danhomê, won't he?" As if the prince's return depended only on the two prisoners and they had given her assurances he would be brought back as soon as possible!

One of them advised her to temper her joy: "Happiness has often been seen to elude the grasp of hands that seem to be holding it securely. The most steadfast courage is always overwhelmed by the disillusionment that follows. The happiness you enjoy most is that which comes upon you unawares." Wisdom itself was speaking in the words of Doguicimi's companion in unhappiness, but Toffa's wife continued nonetheless to believe that her husband would surely see Danhomê again before the next moon.

After the fall of night, joy kept the woman awake, and it was only subdued by sleep toward the first crowing of the cock. She arose before dawn, mocking the sinister predictions that Toffa's enemies had been making not very long ago. Vidaho too numbered among the prophets of ill omen. Doguicimi's desire outstripped reality; she saw all of them confounded by her husband's return. Her thoughts also focused on Evêmon: "It appears the brave child is happy at the side of the king! It will soon be my turn to be happy in the presence of my beloved husband!" she told herself.

During the day, a servant acting on Vidaho's behalf brought Doguicimi the news that she would quite probably be liberated before the sun was overhead on the day of the second "ajahi."

"There's no more doubt," exclaimed the woman! "The contingents from the other side of the Swamps arrived during the night! Esteeming his army strong enough to conquer Hounjroto without difficulty, the worthy successor of

Agonglo has decided upon a war of revenge. The soldiers will probably leave Agbomê at daybreak. The Master of the World is going to order my release because he will want Toffa to find his harem complete!"

When night came, it found her filled with joy. In the hope of receiving a visit from the heir to the throne, she stayed awake for a long time, but she was obliged to go to bed disappointed.

On the day scheduled for her release, every rattling of the gate caused her to move her head forward and open her eyes wide to catch a glimpse of the messenger who would be carrying the good news for which she was waiting impatiently.

The messenger still did not come; Doguicimi began to worry. She told herself that something strange must be happening. Could the ancestors have postponed the day of departure for the war? They perhaps advised against the expedition at the last moment? No one in the prison had received any news from the outside and could not, as a consequence, confirm or deny her conjectures.

In the men's prison she might have found a diviner who would have agreed to consult Destiny in secret for her. The science of the future was virtually unknown among the women of Danhomê. Doguicimi's anxiety increased with the waning day. The comforting words of the two prisoners assigned to her service could not reassure her.

*   *   *

Night had already taken complete possession of the earth. Informed of the arrival of Ama, Yévogan's official messenger, Mêwou immediately had him brought in. After having kissed the ground and touched his forehead to it as a mark of the Governor of Gléhoué's respect for the second minister, his immediate superior, the kneeling messenger said: "The day before yesterday as the sun was descending, two look-outs, who had been assigned to their observation posts at the top of tall trees by Ganpê, the chief watchman of the coast to the West, perceived a ship approaching under full sail. They immediately informed their superior, who reported it at that very moment to Dognon; Woton was told about it by his aide. The principal customs officer hastened to give an account of it to Cacalacoun, the chief of the village of Zoungboji, and he dispatched his emissary to the Governor of the province. The ship arrived that same evening in the harbor at Gléhoué but was unable to unload anything. Yévogan immediately sent me to carry the news to the court." After a brief pause, he added: "The captain certainly sent his sceptre ashore yesterday morning. The traditional reception ceremony undoubtedly took place during the day." He once again kissed the ground.

Ever since he had begun carrying to Agbomê the news of ship arrivals at the harbor of our maritime province, Ama had never transmitted such laconic and imprecise messages.

Having left Gléhoué at nightfall, he had covered almost three thousand four hundred bamboos at one stretch before stopping at Toli in the residence of Ajara, the Governor of that province. He had started out again at the second crowing of the cock. As he walked, he ate the roasted maize that constituted the only food ever consumed by official messengers while on duty; he only stopped once during the day to drink some water.

When he arrived at Agbomê, dusk was already blotting out the lines that Destiny had engraved in people's hands. It would not have been possible for him to have come more quickly. According to popular belief, he was supposed to have a gris-gris that shortened his route. His superiors themselves eventually lent credence to this belief, for he actually did travel the twenty-three thousand five hundred bamboos between Gléhoué and Agbomê in less than two days, whereas other messengers had difficulty covering the distance in three days. He was exhausted, and Mêwou therefore thought that the messenger's fatigue was solely responsible for his lapses of memory. The minister would allow him time to remember what might have eluded his recall in the message Yévogan had charged him to deliver at the court; Ama was thus not be introduced at the Palace until the next morning, for the night that rested his physical fatigue would certainly refresh his mind at the same time. However, the messenger so energetically defended the faithfulness of his memory that Mêwou was obliged to bring him to Mêwounon. She too was astonished at the extraordinary terseness of the message that had been sent from Gléhoué. With serious reservations, she carried the news to the king, who expressed the desire to hear it from the lips of Ama himself. The royal council was hurriedly called together to listen to the words of the messenger; he was then submitted to a trial by poison. In that way one could be certain he had not omitted anything from the message entrusted to him. The king nevertheless ordered Ama to be placed under house arrest at the second minister's residence, and he did not conceal his annoyance at having received excessively brief or obscure messages from Gléhoué for some time now.

Migan imputed the tepidness of the Governor's zeal to a lack of forcefulness on the part of Mêwou, who was charged with the oversight of that province. The first minister concluded his harangue with the following sinister prophecy: "If we don't open our eyes, Gléhoué will soon escape from us! I have the feeling that misfortune will enter Danhomê through that poorly guarded door. Since Yévogan continues to neglect the duties with which he is charged, only his removal from office can forestall the danger that his carelessness causes to hang over the throne of Houégbaja."

All eyes turned questioningly toward the second minister.

He was not at all disturbed by his colleague's attack. On the contrary, he replied calmly: "I was the first to notice and draw attention to the lack of precision in the news that has been arriving from Gléhoué for some time. I reported the cause of it to the court: Yévogan's influence has diminished considerably in our maritime province as the result of the Chacha Ajinacou's investiture as viceroy. Yévogan always informs us faithfully, like our own eyes and ears, about the mood and the least acts of the Danhomênous at Gléhoué. Only, now that the Administration of the city has passed into the hands of Chacha, the conduct and the attitudes of the white men remain hidden from us.

"Dêmênou is the head of the Master of the World's personal police at Gléhoué and a man who can not be suspected of bias in favor of Yévogan since he was chosen from the family of Dassou, sworn enemies of the Yévogans, who supplanted them in the city, and Dêmênou (you will agree with me) always reported to this court that the Governor has made laudatory efforts to assure that nothing about the lives of the people and animals in our maritime province remains hidden from us.

"The fragmentary information that reaches us about the white men of Gléhoué is due to the initiative of our Representative, who has placed servants in the households of these foul beasts from the sea.

"The facts reported by Yévogan have always been confirmed by an investigation conducted without the Governor's knowledge by Dêmênou.

"I proposed the only possible cure for this situation, which I have never ceased to deplore, and that is the complete restitution of Yévogan in his powers as Governor. In this council, Migan alone opposed my idea, claiming that the Master of the World could not in all decency withdraw the privileges he had granted his 'brother' according to the terms of the pact. How can the first minister now attribute to me the brevity of the reports received from Gléhoué and our complete ignorance of the lives of the white men living in that province? I will not be so cruel as to recall the response of Migan himself to my warnings: 'Happiness nearly always follows unhapiness. If the former necessarily enters by the same door as the latter, we can do no more than resign ourselves to it!' Who was the one who spoke these words?

"I performed my duty to the utmost. I have sounded the alarm more than once in Danhomê about the danger that the investiture of Chacha as viceroy at Gléhoué poses for the kingdom of Houégbaja! I demand to be submitted to trial by poison if there are any doubts about my administration."

He struck his forehead to the ground and cast a severe glance in the direction of Migan, who had lowered his head.

Ajaho was of the same opinion as Mêwou; since Chacha's elevation at Gléhoué, the secret police of the third minister had experienced great difficulty in comprehending the behavior of the white men.

The other dignitaries and all the princes concurred with Mêwou.

In the depth of his heart, Migan himself agreed that his colleague was conscientiously fulfilling his duties as overseer of the Administration at Gléhoué.

Vidaho alone remained silent. Having been kept regularly informed about the behavior of Chacha Ajinacou, the protector of his fellow white men, by Yévogan's confidential reports to him, he would have liked to express his opinion, but he recalled his august Father's advice: "Refrain from taking sides in empassioned discussions at the court." The heir to the throne also did not want to let it become apparent that he had been concerning himself in the affairs of Gléhoué without the knowledge of his royal Father. But he vowed to himself that he would put an end to all this disorder that Chacha's investiture had introduced into the Administration of Gléhoué. . . .

After having resorted to gris-gris and then to intrigues in a series of vain attempts to resume possession of his rights, a large part of which had passed into the hands of Chacha, Yévogan now counted only upon the future Master of Danhomê to help him recover his former authority in the province that had been ruled by Yévogans since the fifth reign.

The Governor promised himself he would fabricate crimes to bring about the irrevocable fall of the man whose investiture had resulted in his own virtual eclipse. Since Guézo's ascension to the throne, hadn't he been reduced to the undignified role of spy and collector of tariffs and anchorage fees in the maritime province?

The council decided to send a messenger who would inform Yévogan about the court's concern that the Governor was no longer serving as the watchful eyes and ears of Agbomê at Gléhoué.

A second messenger sent to Agbomê by Yévogan on the day after Ama's departure for the capital arrived on the evening of the third day.

The king was in council. When Mêwou was informed, he alerted Mêwounon, who came and spoke softly into the ear of the Master of the World. She left the room and returned a moment later with a sceptre that the king received with both hands clasped together. He placed it across his legs. Covering himself with dirt, the messenger said: "At the sight of the ship which appeared on the horizon five days ago, the principal watchman Ganpê hastened to inform Woton, who ordered the king's flag to be hoisted. The next day, the chief customs officer could not obtain timely information concerning the ship's nationality and its cargo. The canoes that Woton dispatched toward the ship and those launched by the crew were unable to cross the bar, which had been suddenly embroiled in turbulence by the mad fury of the sea, until the sun had risen overhead.

"Alerted to the state of the bar, Cacalacoun had to dispatch a cursory report with the official messenger who normally carried to the Governor a paper containing the information which the ship's captain had sent ashore. That explains Ama's lack of precise details, upon his arrival at the court, about the ship that is moored in the harbor at Gléhoué. When a calmer sea permitted communications to be established with the ship, Cacalacoun had the Governor informed that the vessel belonged to the Glincis. The captain declared that he was not carrying guns, ammunition, alcohol, cloth, jewelry, pipes, or anything else that Danhomê usually purchasede from the white men. Nor was this ship coming in search of slaves. They were only carrying about twenty white men who claimed they had been entrusted with a mission to the Predestined King. For this reason, they hastened to send their sceptre to Yévogan so that it could be carried to the court."

The messenger continued to cover himself with dirt.

The Governor, suspecting that the king would demand an explanation for the brevity of his first message, had quite spontaneously hastened to justify himself. His second messenger had met the messenger sent from Agbomê in the midst of the Swamps.

The court did not accept Yévogan's explanation until after the trial by poison had confirmed his sincerety. However, the news that the newly arrived white men were Ambassadors merely served to heighten the king's misgivings.

Ama was sent to Gléhoué with the following message for the Governor: "Inquire as discreetly as possible into the purpose of the mission that has come from the white man's country, inform the court about it in great detail, and await orders before sending the white men on to Agbomê."

On the way the messenger passed another envoy coming from Gléhoué. Puzzled by the mysterious demeanor of the new arrivals, Yévogan had not waited for the court's order to attempt to discover their secret.

The white men wanted to go up to Agbomê on the very next day after they landed. The Governor dissuaded them because the custom was to wait, before traveling to the capital, for the return of the sceptre that the foreigners had sent there in advance of their arrival. To violate this custom would be to show a lack of respect for the throne and to run the risk of being refused an audience.

Yévogan's third messenger gave the court an account of the reception accorded to the white men: "At the very instant when Cacalacoun's messenger brought information about the ship that had arrived the previous night, Yévogan instructed two dignitaries from his Palace to announce the arrival of the Glincis's ship in the harbor at Gléhoué to Chacha first of all, then at the Fort of the Glincis, and finally to the other commercial agents in the city. From each of the agents the Governor's messengers received the customary presents – two bottles of brandy and several strings of cowries.

"In the morning the entire city was invited by the voice of the town crier to gather at Agoli[2] as soon as the sun was directly overhead in order to accompany the Governor to Zoungboji, where he would receive, with all the customary honors, the Master of the World's friends who had been brought by the ship that had arrived the previous day.

"Knowing the importance attached to such receptions by the Father of Life, all the high dignitaries and a large part of the population of Gléhoué were at the designated spot by the time the sun had passed the level of the ear.

"The details of the ceremony had been arranged in conjunction with Chacha and the Commander of the Fort of the Glincis, who paid for the expenses of the reception.

"Preceded by drums and surrounded by dignitaries, some of whom rode horseback, Chacha and Yévogan, who were also mounted on horses, traveled at the head of the procession. The white men from all the Forts in the city followed in hammocks. The local chiefs came after them, then the heads of households, the servants who were accompanying their masters, and, finally, the crowd of spectators. They proceeded along the road to the beach. Cacalacoun, Woton, Dognon, Ganpê, their principal assistants, and all the men placed under their orders received the procession on the outskirts of Zoungboji and conducted them to the foot of the tree where receptions are held.

"Salvoes from the ship's canons had already been saluting the Vice-Roy and

---

[2]   Agoli is the Residence of the Governor of Gléhoué (Ouidah). (author's note)

the Governor of Gléhoué for some time as the captain and the Ambassadors came to meet them in an apatam that had been erected at the foot of the tree.

"Many bottles of the white man's alcohol were spread out on a large table, offering themselves to the covetous glances of the Danhomênous.

"After the formal introductions had been made, the Commander of the Fort of the Glincis ordered drinks to be poured for the white men and the dignitaries seated around a table. Then the feasting began. The local chiefs and the heads of households were served on mats. Meanwhile, the people were singing and dancing. Afterwards, they fought over the scraps.

"When the sun had turned his head, it occurred to Yévogan to do the same, and he accompanied the new arrivals to the Fort of the Glincis.

"The white men did not conceal their joy at having received a warm welcome. Yévogan explained to them: 'In conformity with our customs, Gléhoué has merely poured water on the ground for the Master of the World's guests. Only the Father of Wealth is capable of receiving his friends with true splendor.'

"The other white men returned to their establishments. Chacha regained his Palace at Singboji. Yévogan went to Agaja near Zobê, where he gave thanks to Lègba for having declared a truce in his willful ways on this day of festivities and for having spared us from misfortune.

"Upon his return to Agoli, the Governor dismissed the dignitaries and the chiefs in his retinue; he then dispatched me to Agbomê. He was to call a meeting of the council for that night."

The messenger had finished; he covered himself with dirt.

Once he had left, Migan, the implacable adversary of Yévogan, asserted mockingly: "Yévogan was in a great hurry to inform the court of the reception he accorded the white men, as if that were the only thing that concerns the Master of the World. He who should be the watchful eye of Houégbaja at Gléhoué no longer observes anything but that which he enjoys; he has sacrificed the interest of Danhomê to his own pleasure. To exonerate himself for the inadequacy of the information he provided to Agbomê, he invented the story of the bar that was supposedly overwhelmed all of a sudden by some mad fury of a turbulence!"

Mêwou proposed that his subordinate and the messenger be subjected to the trial fetish.

Their truthfulness was demonstrated by the sprightliness of the cock, which showed no effect at all of the poison it had been obliged to swallow. Nevertheless, the first minister prevailed upon the assembly to have the messenger detained at Mêwou's compound, for Danhomê must always be watchful and conduct serious investigations to verify even those reports that have been confirmed by the trial fetish.

At Gléhoué the new arrivals were rejoicing over the magnificent reception that had been reserved for them – a token of the success that would, they hoped, crown the mission to be carried out at the court of the King of Danhomê.

Their baggage followed them ashore the next morning.

Dêmênou's police were busier than ever. Day and night Ajaho received messengers from the policeman at Gléhoué, and he visited the king without the knowledge of all the other dignitaries.

The cocks had already ended their second concert of cock-a-doodle-doos, and the council of the throne was still in the meeting that had followed the session with the messenger who had arrived from Gléhoué during the previous evening.

During the course of this meeting, a doorkeeper entered and whispered a few words in Ajaho's ear. The king understood. A moment later he interrupted the meeting under a false pretext; the high dignitaries were clustered in groups according to the opinions they held, and they ardently continued their debate.

Having left the Palace through the Door of the Universe, Ajaho had reentered it through the Door of Patinsa so that he could converse with the king far from any witnesses.

The news that had been brought by Dêmênou's messenger corroborated the reports that Yévogan had been making to the court for the past three market days.

The council went back into session. Migan, the two ministers of war, and two or three princes shared the same opinion in opposition to the other consellors.

Gaou argued: "Danhomênou, when a white man offers you a slip knot into which your little finger can barely pass and you naively put it there, you will immediately be caught in an inextricable noose, and that's the end of your freedom!"

Possou seconded him: "We should never have abandoned the prudent attitude adopted by the kings of Sahé toward these foul beasts from the sea and allowed them to drill wells and freely sell their merchandise to all Danhomênous. Look at the ingratitude with which they are now repaying the confidence we placed in them!"

The heir to the throne emerged from his silence: "Isn't it true that wisdom sometimes resides in the mind of a fool? A number of Danhomênous greeted the words of Cingbé the fool with mockery, when, seeing those foul beasts from the sea arrive in Agbomê at the time of one of our traditional celebrations, he exclaimed: 'Danhomênous, if you are the ones who invited these white men, you should know that you have brought misfortune to Danhomê. And if they have come of their own accord, you should also know that misfortune is paying a visit to the kingdom of Houébaja!'

"What many Danhomênous dismissed at that time as the jesting of a fool was actually a prophecy that is being realized today in an extremely cruel fashion for Danhomê.

"The white man's dream of dominating Danhomê does not date from yesterday. In fact, tradition tells us that, when one of our Governors refused to accede to their whims, he was removed from his post by Tégbéssou, whose good faith these beasts from the sea had succeeded in abusing. That was the beginning of the disgrace of Dassou, Danhomê's first Representative in our maritime province and a man whom the white men regarded as insufficiently docile. This chief was a victim of his own loyalty and vigor.

"Tégbéssou's court did not understand the white men's secret plan, and it sacrificed this faithful son of Danhomê to the malice of this kingdom's enemies. Let us not repeat the error of a past reign!"

The king did not approve of this counsel; he objected: "So much caution is but a sign of weakness. Today Danhomê is strong enough to have nothing to fear from these dealers."

Because the court could not agree upon the reception to be accorded the new arrivals whom they were anticipating, Guézo proposed to consult the Representatives of Mothers of Panther from previous reigns as well as Migannon, Mêwounon, the heads of the families of former kings, and indeed all Danhomênous who enjoyed a reputation for great wisdom or keen intelligence.

In a sententious tone of voice, Migan interjected: "When Awliponouwê lost his horse, he went to look for it in a chicken cage, as if such a container could hold his noble charger. Panic never accomplished anything intelligent. If the court does not care to follow my initial advice, it should recognize that we will never succeed in eradicating the repulsion felt by these stinking beasts from the sea at the sight of our human sacrifices, or in persuading them to appreciate all our customs, or in converting them to the worship of our fetishes, unless of course we soak all of them in indigo, as was done to one of these White-Bellies for several days in a row during the last reign!"

Guézo's face clouded over at the mention of the tortures experienced in the tyrant's prisons by his sworn friend, the one whom he considered the noblest of all white men. The opinion expressed by Migan on the first day of these council meetings was reintroduced into the discussion and approved by the majority of the counsellors: the king owed it to himself to adopt a forceful attitude toward all the White-Bellies who carried on trade in his kingdom and to forestall their ancestors from ever thinking of demanding Danhomê to commit suicide.

The court contented itself with consulting the ancestors through the intermediary of the oracle. Their opinion agreed with that of Migan, Gaou, Possou, and others.

The king was obliged to accept his council's proposal with regret, although he secretly nourished the hope of finding at the last moment a means of according his guests an amiable reception, as his friendship for a man of their race and the great kindliness of his own nature inclined him to do.

A Danhomênou carried the sceptre of the new arrivals back to Gléhoué. He had also been entrusted with secret orders for the regional chiefs and the Governors of the provinces through which he was traveling.

At Agbomê the court actively engaged in preparations for the reception of the announced Ambassadors.

Bapê dispatched about twenty of his servants to the slave camps that had been scattered around the outskirts of the capital and placed under his jurisdiction.

The two ministers of war reviewed the soldiers from the Hoja barracks and then equipped them with new weapons.

Mêwou ordered the cleaning of the Palace of Agrigromê, where visiting white men were housed when they came to Agbomê.

One afternoon farmers arrived with loads of yams and various grains, large bellied gourds of palm oil, bundles of firewood, cattle, goats, pigs, and cages of chickens.

Hunters brought the game that had been caught in nets, clubbed to death, and brought down with gunshots or arrows.

Agbomê was as animated as on the eve of a traditional celebration.

The people assured themselves that a pleasant surprise was in store for them, but it was only on the next day, the day of Ajahi, that they were invited by the voice of Panligan to the reception that the Master of the Universe was planning for the white men who, having been sent on a mission to his majesty, were scheduled to arrive shortly. Their joy attained a fevered pitch at the thought that their love of pleasure was about to be offered a new opportunity for feasting, drinking, and dancing. All Danhomênous promised themselves to profit handsomely from the festivities being organized to honor the friends of the king, unless illness or service outside the capital prevented them from doing so.

When the news of the white men's impending arrival reached Doguicimi, she began to curse these intruders, whose visit was going to delay the war of revenge against Hounjroto. She asked herself why the deadly Serpent, which, according to the elders, lived in the depths of the sea, had not swallowed these foul beasts who were the cause of her unhappiness. If he had disdained them, why hadn't Agbé engulfed them? She did not understand the fetish's indulgence for these wretched creatures.

She plunged momentarily into a state of meditation, but she soon shook her head and continued her line of thought: "Perhaps I'm making a mistake. Is it possible that these white men are by any chance related to those who were massacred at Hounjroto? Having grown impatient at the delay in mounting a campaign of revenge against the assassins of their brothers, they are no doubt bringing us weapons, formidable weapons that are certain to avenge their fellow white men and free our prisoners! According to Vidaho, the king was waiting for the return of a royal messenger before engaging in war, and he was no doubt sent to bring back these white men, who will insist upon directing the operations against Hounjroto themselves. In that case, victory is assured! May our fetishes hasten the arrival of these white men then!"

This idea acquired substance in Doguicimi's mind. She convinced herself that it constituted the only purpose of the mission that was expected in Agbomê. For a long time she invoked the protection of Danhomê's fetishes for these foreigners.

During the night she dreamed that white soldiers with many weapons had arrived to help the king conquer Hounjroto. This dream filled her with joy for the entire following day.

The king's messenger had arrived at Gléhoué on the afternoon of the day after his departure from Agbomê.

Yévogan alleged a minor illness, which prevented him from arranging the Ambassadors' transportation to the capital, as a pretext for postponing their departure until the next ajahi that was three days away.

In reality he merely wanted them to be preceded by the messenger he had just sent to Agbomê with the latest information that had been communicated to him by the servants at the Fort of the Glincis; they had sworn by the fetishes to have heard everything from the very mouths of the white men during the course of a midday meal at which alcohol had flowed freely. He gave new orders for the service at dinner and instructed the servant-spies in the manner of speaking to the new arrivals, the attitude to adopt in their presence, and the sentiments to be feigned. He promised to draw the Master of the World's attention to all those who brought back valuable information.

Chacha intervened to expedite the Ambassadors' immediate departure for Agbomê, but his efforts were in vain.

"You dare not think of undertaking such a journey on your own. The authorities would not assume responsibility for any accident that might occur. And accidents seem to lurking at every step taken by the foolhardy traveler in this mysterious land," the Commader of the Fort of the Glincis explained to his impatient fellow countrymen.

On the day scheduled for their departure, the Ambassadors got underway at the second crowing of the cock. Yévogan's official messenger walked at the head of the group, carrying a long baton in his hand. Chacha Ajincou's messenger followed; at the head of the Ambassadors was the Commander of the Fort of the Glincis, the man who would introduce the mission to the court. Ten interpreters were spread through the group; they all spoke the language of the Zojagués as well as those of the Agoudas and the Glincis, but they had, with the greatest secrecy, been enjoined against allowing the white men to suspect that they knew any other language than the one spoken by the new arrivals. The rest of the Danhomênous (about two hundred servants, cooks, porters, and additional hammock-bearers) brought up the rear. Orders had been given not to hurry.

In each village along the way, the chief scrupulously followed the instructions he had received from Agbomê; some acted with dispatch, whereas others were excedingly slow in furnishing what was requested of them by the travelers. All chiefs scrutinized the white men's words and gestures to gather information that was forwarded to the capital before the foreigners were sent on their way again.

The leader of their escort contrived a thousand excuses for not proceeding quickly. When the Ambassadors became insistant, he bowed to their will, but the porters and hammock-bearers, having been forewarned by a discreet wink or some other sign that had been agreed upon in advance, immediately came to his aid; they claimed to be exhausted, complained about the heat of the sun, and called for someone to relieve them; others dallied behind, and it was necessary to wait for them because, as the official messengers explained, there were thieves in the area. From time to time they also stopped to distribute the customary glass of brandy to these toiling men, who claimed to draw all their strength from it. A number of them staggered afterwards, pretending to be drunk and threatening to turn everything upside down. They frequently had to pitch camp for a while.

The Danhomênous played their roles so often and so well that they didn't reach Alada until the end of the day. The newly arrived white men were traveling in hammocks for the first time, and they found them uncomfortable; the stifling heat of Danhomê drained their energy and exhausted them. They were a pitiful sight. The Commander of the Fort was an old veteran whose long years under the hot sun of Danhomê had baked his leathery skin and hardened his character, and he wanted to stay overnight at Atogan. After a long palaver, the leader of the escort was obliged to accede to the desire of the white man, who believed he had achieved his goal by threatening to complain to the court about the recalcitrance of the escort. At the moment when the loads were being lifted again, it became apparent that about ten of them remained without porters to carry them. One of their companions explained: "They prefer to go into the bush now rather than having to request permission along the way when the need becomes urgent." The group was forced to wait for them because Aplogan had only found a few ulcer-ridden urchins as possible replacements. "They couldn't find a better way to make fun of people!" grumbled a young Ambassador.

The man who was going to introduce them at court calmed the impetuous fellow by informing him that the country took pleasure in torturing those for whom time passed slowly. "The secret of succeeding with the natives," he confided in his fellow countrymen, "is never to become impatient. Life," he added, "does not use the same means to move all people forward; some are incited by the prick of a needle, whereas others are handled with velvet gloves. Only when these people become aware of the new necessities of life will they acquire the same conception of time that we have."

What threats rained upon the laggards when they returned! To hear the leader of the escort one would have thought they were going to be skinned alive upon their arrival at Agbomê for having delayed the journey of the king's friends. . . .

At a bend in the path about a hundred bamboos from the village, the official messenger at the head of the procession suddenly stopped; their route was barred by two enormous pythons, one behind the other. On his knees the man begged them to allow the Master of the World's friends to pass.

The head of one of the snakes was turned to the side.

"He is warning us about a dangerous encounter and ordering us to go back the way we came!" the Danhomênou explained to the white men.

The frightened voice of the second official messenger verified the accuracy of his interpretation: "The great fetish is wisdom itself, and to disobey it would be to go irrevocably toward one's own death!"

Several loads had already been placed on the ground, and their porters were sitting beside them, their little head pads in their hands. One of them declared: "Only a hoe could uproot me from this place!"

Those who were carrying heavier loads had already gone back.

The official messengers rushed to place themselves in front of them, facing the coast.

The Commander of the Fort intervened with his fellow countrymen just in time to prevent them from shooting the troublesome snakes.

The Ambassadors had to return and make camp at Alada.

"Danhomê is such a puzzling, mysterious land!" grumbled a young Ambassador. "The nature, the people, the animals, and everything else is so aggressively hostile to strangers.

"First of all the climate draws all the blood from your body; the heat turns your skin to leather, curls your hair, and then stikes you mad if you go about without a hat.

"Thunderstorms here are outrageously violent.

"The natives are mysterious. One seldom finds an honest face among them. Men and women, children and old people, all are conspiring to bring about the ruin of strangers.

"During the day the flies attack you. At night the swamps send you not only their stench but also an army of mosquitoes that sting you with their poison darts.

"Besides their suffocating fumes, the plants that invade all the paths impede your steps, lacerate your hands and feet, scratch your face raw, and even threaten to put out one of your eyes.

"The earth opens up at your feet, and you don't know how it happens. Stones take pleasure in moving about and maliciously placing themselves in your way so that you will fall.

"How difficult it is for a stranger to triumph over the treachery of the elements, the little beasts, and the people of this land!"

The Commander replied that the young man was forming his opinions on the basis of a tenderfoot's preconceived notions and that he would at least partially modify his harsh judgments after having spent a few months in the country.

At the third crowing of the cock, the official messengers informed the Ambassadors that the porters and hammock-bearers, whom they finally succeeded in awakening, had refused to leave their mats on the pretext that they were too tired.

When the time came to take up the loads, it was noticed that four people were missing. Aplogan declared his inability to replace them: "It is the season for working in the fields; since a few days ago the people of the town have moved out to the countryside," he explained to the travelers. They waited a long time for the missing porters. Because they didn't return, the Governor of Alada finally provided them with replacements.

Without appearing to do so, one of the interpreters was spying on an Ambassador as he took out his writing stick and scribbled mysterious black marks on white leaves. "Ah, if I could only spirit them away from him," thought the Danhomênou, "what a reward it would earn me from the Father of Wealth!"

The sun had already reached the height of the ear by the time the travelers were able to get underway again. They made a brief pause at Houégbo for lunch. The Governor of the place proved extremely amiable and diligent, to the great surprise of the white men; they were planning to spend the night with Adamou at Apê on the edge of the Swamps.

To allay their impatience, the Commander of the Fort explained to the new arrivals that it would be foolhardy to venture into the swampy region at night, especially since it was infested with wild beasts who came there looking for food.

The next day the Danhomênous deliberately wandered about in the Swamps, for they were hardly ignorant of all the good routes through the area. When they finally emerged, the sun was already turning his head toward his dwelling place; according to popular belief, he had been in such a hurry to return home that he had broken the jar of palm oil he always carried with him. The western sky was completely covered with it and had therefore turned red. The foreigners were enraptured by this spectacle, which left the natives quite indifferent.

The official messenger and leader of the escort informed the Ambassadors that they would be spending the night with Jêmêkê at Agrimê.

This order had come from Agbomê, and it had been transmitted to him at Apê. To reassure the foreigners, he explained that they would be on their way by the third crowing of the cock and that, unless something unexpected happened, they would see the tops of the plane trees before the arrows of the sun came straight down from above. The Ambassadors resigned themselves to their guide's every whim.

When they reached Adanwé, the sun had already risen directly overhead. Porters and hammock-bearers lay down their loads under the pretext of being tired. In reality, they were obeying a secret order.

An emissary who had been awaiting their arrival in the village left for Agbomê at once.

The thunder of a carronade being fired in the capital arrived as a muffled echo in Adanwé. Chacha's messenger winked at his companion, who immediately bent his big toe downward to indicate that he too had understood. A moment later they gave the signal to depart.

Soon the wind that was blowing in their direction brought with it the sound of drums beating in the capital. They were approaching Agbomê. The clamor of singing reached them, confusedly at first but then more distinctly.

The white men's faces brightened with a sudden joy when they realized that the king of Danhomê had organized festivities for the occasion of their arrival. They instantly forgot the difficulties of their journey, which had been quite eventful.

Hammock-bearers and porters hurried so they could go and take part in the festivities. The earth reverberated to the pounding of their feet that were shod with the red laterite dust of the road. A cloud of dust remained in the air for a long time after they had passed. They arrived within sight of the Door of Dossoumoin. Curious individuals had crowded together by this principal entry to the capital. The new arrivals crossed the Ditch, but they were unable to advance through this impenetrable swarm. The guide's repeated shouts, "Watch out! Watch out!" were drowned in the din of horns, large and small bells, drums, and the oaths and songs of the joyful crowd. Different groups of drums had been installed all along the path that led to the Courtyard of the Grand Palace.

The leader of the escort had vain recourse to his baton in attempting to blaze a trail through the crowd. The long line of newly arrived travelers broke into fragments, knocked about by eddies of the mob that penetrated their ranks. The procession halted, to the great dissatisfaction of the porters and hammock-bearers with their stiff necks, bent backs, distended chests, and sweat-covered torsos. Was it really curiosity that produced this swarming, or were the idle masses obeying orders?

After having attempted to effect an exit with the aid of his baton, the guide admitted defeat. The Commander of the Fort came and offered him his assistance, but he too pushed and shoved the dancers in vain. Suddenly the official messenger's face brightened; he had found a solution. "I remind the Dan-homênous of the respect owed to all white friends of the Master of the World!" he shouted, brandishing his baton once again.

"The friends of the king! The friends of the king!" Passed from mouth to mouth, these words instantly opened a path through the crowd. The new arrivals could contemplate at their leisure the groups of dancers that they pointed out to each other.

The noisiest one was comprised of Amazons who were equipped as if they were about to go to war. They charged up to fifty paces toward their imagined enemies. In ten leaps they were back in front of the drummers; their right arms cut through the air like sabres in a composite movement; they turned their backs on the drummers, again swooped down upon the enemy, and then returned to their point of departure, singing loudly all the time.

Facing the new arrivals and holding their right arms straight forward at the height of their shoulders, their hands open, palms downward, they executed the motion of cleanly cutting through anyone who might oppose their arm movements. . . .

Fearing that they had not been understood, they took out their sabres and flourished them menacingly. They sheathed these weapons, picked up their guns, wheeled around, and fired upon their imaginary enemies. . . .

At the same time they were inciting themselves to battle with refrains sung in deep male voices.

The leader of the escort did not wait to be asked before explaining that these were Amazons, an innovation of this reign.

The chorus of their song went as follows:

266

We were created to defend
Danhomê, this pot of honey,
Object of desire.
Can a country of such great courage
Abandon its wealth to strangers?
As long as we're alive, anyone who tries
To impose his will on it must be mad.

Overcome by the enthusiasm of the Amazons, the Danhomênous accompanying the white men went even further: "Danhomê is the sun whose brilliance is unequaled in the universe and shall never be eclipsed! Let these words be repeated by all its enemies!"

An Ambassador shook his head.

"Anyone who knows these people realizes that these are not empty boasts!" explained the Commander of the Fort and the man who was going to introduce the mission at court.

The porters and hammock-bearers grumbled that their loads were getting heavy; the official messenger at the head of the procession started forward again, and the Ambassadors were deposited in the Great Courtyard of the Palace.

Their frail hands disappeared into the large, calloused, sweat-covered palms that squeezed them to the point of bruising them against the heavy iron and twisted copper rings that circled the black fingers. Esteeming that the squeezing of hands in such vice-like grips did not sufficiently impress these foreigners, whom they were receiving in the name of the king, with the strength of Danhomê (which could not be intimidated by anything), Migan, Mêwou, and Ajaho shook their arms as if to dislocate them, while the feigned sincerity of their smiles dissimulated their true feelings toward these white men.

The first minister asked the new arrivals about the fortunes of their king, their queen, the royal family, and the court; he inquiried whether their sea voyage had not been too tiring and concluded by assuming that the friends of the Master of the Universe had received all the honors due them at Gléhoué and in all the other provinces through which they had traveled.

The Commander of the Fort hastened to begin speaking so as to avoid a possible blunder on the part of his fellow countrymen; he replied that the royal household of the Glincis was doing quite well; the king had heard a great deal about Danhomê; although he deeply regretted that the affairs of his kingdom did not afford him the leisure to come and personally make the acquaintance of Agonglo's successor, he was delegating his ministers to undertake the journey; the latter had been received in a manner that exceeded their expectations at Gléhoué and in the smallest villages along the road to Agbomê; the Danhomênous understood very well how to pay their respects to the Ambassadors of a monarch who was the friend of their sovereign.

The visitors were invited to follow Mêwou, who showed them to their lodgings.

"Chi!" the first minister spat as he curled his upper lip toward his nose and

267

walked away, saying: "It's unpleasant to be in the path of a wind coming from the direction of these foul beasts from the sea. Their odor disgusts you even at a distance of two bamboos. It stinks like leather that has been left in water. It has a fetid smell. That's undoubtedly the reason they use so much perfume! Look at those villainous cat's eyes! And the Predestined King assures us that these white men see further with them than we do. . . . He was no doubt fooled by the length of the noses that disfigure their faces. The comportment of Zanou Hougnon proves that the length of one's nose is hardly a sign of intelligence. The proposal that the long-nosed beasts from the sea are coming to make at the court of Danhomê confirms it. Forty-one Danhomênous together don't have as much hair on their bodies as their leader, whose furry chest looks like that of a gorilla from our forests. How can you expect creatures whose heads are covered with goat's fuzz instead of hair that curls back on itself like ours not to have truncated, oversimplified ideas? To foster the illusion that great ideas are hatching in their skulls, they wear false hair that falls over their shoulders and back when they come to the court. But Danhomênous with good sense don't place any faith in such things."

Having descended from the second story where he had observed the arrival of the white men without their suspecting his presence so close to them, the king ordered that the Danhomênous in their party be brought to him one by one.

To each of them Migan gruffly repeated the following refrain: "Danhomênou, you are not unaware of your duty to be loyal to the Master of the World! Remember that the Predestined King generously rewards services rendered to the throne of Houégbaja by his subjects and that Migan Atindébacou punishes disloyalty with the greatest rigor!"

The man called upon all the ancestors of the king to bear witness that he was determined to tell the truth.

The first minister then ordered him to give an account of the trip; at the end, he invariably asked if anything else of interest to Danhomê had been heard, seen, or done during the course of their journey.

One Danhomênou informed the court: "To gain time, the white men wanted at all costs to press on through Alada and make camp at Atogon. Aplogan insisted upon detaining them so that the official messenger he had dispatched to Agbomê shortly after our arrival could set out before they did. We had to resort to a subterfuge that Yévogan had devised in advance. Just before our departure the Governor had in fact equipped us with two enormous pythons. I ran ahead and placed them across our path, and the leader of the escort announced that he could not proceed one step further because the fetishes were against it. The white men were obliged to leave the hammocks and follow their guide back the way they had come, all the more so because the hammock-bearers, who were in on the ruse, threatened to dump them on the ground if they didn't act quickly and allow them to turn the hammocks around. Several white men even shouldered their rifles and would have fired at the two fetishes if the Commander of the Fort had not intervened."

Another Danhomênou told the court that a white man had drawn a number of signs on white leaves during the journey. The priest of the trial by poison had been in Agbomê since the second crowing of the cock, and he verified each statement with a trial that unequivocally confirmed it.

Meanwhile the Ambassadors, who had finished unpacking their bags, washing, and donning formal attire for the reception, were waiting for the king to deign to have them introduced for the audience he had scheduled for the very day of their arrival.

Mêwou, the chief of protocol at the court of Danhomê, finally came to take them to the reception room just behind Agaja's several-story addition to the Palace.

Laid out from East to West, this annex was a good hundred feet long and thirty feet wide; it received light from the north, in which direction it opened onto a vast courtyard that had been covered with a rug of white sand from Canna; supported by pillars that were five spans wide and spaced twenty feet apart, the framing for the roof was so symmetrical that it could have been mistaken for an enlarged honeycomb; all the pillars were decorated with bas-reliefs; the curiosity of the Ambassadors was fully satisfied by the interpreters' explanations of them. "On this ship one of your people is depicted brandishing the venerated symbol of your religion; it portrays the conquest of the houéda kingdom by our fourth king Agaja and the official opening of commercial relations between Danhomê and the white men. . . ."

To the East as to the West and on the side facing toward the sea, the reception room was enclosed by walls that had been plastered and then whitened with kaolin. A door had been opened in the west wall, and it linked the annex with the section of the Palace that had been the first construction of the present reign. On that side, a thirty by thirty foot surface of the reception room had been raised a cubit and a half. The walls of this section were draped in dark red velvet; swaths of leaf-green velvet formed a ceiling over the throne – that is to say, a sofa covered by a satin cloth the color of boiling palm-oil froth. Tablecloths of leaf-green velvet also covered the large tables that had been pushed together and occupied the length of the reception room for nearly sixty feet. Around the edge of this composite table were arranged as many of the white man's overstuffed armchairs as there were Ambassadors and interpreters. The ground had been covered with large cloths of local manufacture.

About thirty richly dressed young women pulled back the chairs from the table, pushed them back behind the Ambassadors, and, with a gracious gesture accompanied by an innocent smile, invited the men to sit down. The leader of the mission occupied the head of the table, facing the throne; the Commander of the Fort was on his right, his first secretary and an interpreter from his retinue on his left. Mêwou placed the interpreters between the other members of the mission.

The white men could not conceal their surprise; they had not expected to find so much comfort and luxury at the court of the kings of Danhomê, who had been described in some travelers' accounts as crouching semi-naked on rudimentary mats in the midst of the most disgusting filth.

An interpreter explained to a white man sitting on his right: "One of your people and his wife were living at the court of Agonglo, and they initiated the late king to the manners of your country. Following the example of his august Father, the worthy successor of Agonglo received advice and the objects you are admiring from Chacha Ajinacou, his 'brother' by the Oath."

The Ambassador confided to the ear of the interpreter: "These black men who possess a superior talent for assimilation and understanding would develop more quickly than any other people in Africa, if they placed themselves under the tutelage of an honest nation, like that of the Glincis for example!"

The arrival of the ministers and Vidaho, who installed themselves around the base of the throne, immediately brought all conversations to a halt.

Avoutou exploded; dogba responded with the solemn roll reserved for days of important palavers; the "birds of the king" began to chirp. Their song precipitated the courtiers to the ground with their faces pointing downward; tumultuously and with the usual gesture of covering themselves with dust, they expressed their wishes for the health, longevity, and power of the king.

The fully armed Amazons arrived, beating the ground with their feet as if they were angry; they formed a line in front of the throne and kneeled down facing the newly arrived guests. Then the wives of the king entered, following Daclo and arranging themselves around the throne.

Guézo appeared, impressive beneath the crown of parasols that his Wives held raised above his head; his tall stature dominated his entourage. His face betrayed a certain sadness, as if he were consumed with remorse for having done violence to his conscience.

The king stretched out on his sofa and pretended not to notice the presence of his guests in the reception room.

The queens kneeled; the fans began to wave, and the keeper of the spitoon raised it to the royal lips, which one of her companions immediately wiped with a white handkerchief. The keeper of the pipe offered it; the king refused with a nod of the head. Twice he coughed slightly as if to relieve a tightness in his chest; the Royal Wives said: "Gently! Very gently!" Meanwhile the high dignitaries were coughing loudly to indicate that it was better for simple mortals like them to be discommoded rather than their Creator.

Mêwou kept an attentive eye on the throne. Lost in meditation, the king was no longer thinking about the gesture he had agreed to make. The silence was impressive. The chief of protocol broke it. Addressing himself to the leader of the mission, he smiled and declared: "The Master of the Universe is ready to listen to the emissaries from the chief of the Glincis."

The Ambassadors approached the throne in two rows and, bowing deeply, deposited at his majesty's feet the tribute which the king of the Glincis had entrusted to them for the king of the Danhomênous.

Guézo put on a forced smile, which Migan interpreted in his solemn voice: "The King of the Universe accepts this tribute from the king of the Glincis."

Outside, the drums were beating wildly, accompanied by the unflagging "von koon von" of the horns and the clanging of the single and double bells. The songs and joyful shouts of the mob mingled with the music and penetrated as far as the reception room that sheltered the guests of the king. The intermittent thunder of carronades announced to the world that Agbomê was in the midst of a celebration.

The leader of the mission began his speech in a voice that betrayed his emotion. "We have been charged," he said, "to communicate to His Majesty the desiderata of our king, who is giving expression to the wishes of all the powers of Europe.

"Among the traditions of Danhomê are customs that contravene the rights of all men to life and liberty, namely the odious practice of human sacrifice and the iniquitous one of slavery.

"Every year you undertake wars so flagrantly unjust that you make every effort to legitimize your massacres and overcome your shame by alluding to an imaginary insult or some attack suffered in the distant past, but your efforts are in vain. It is clear to everyone that your victims' only crime was their weakness and that the only real motive for your wars is the desire to take captives for the slave trade and the human sacrifices.

"They tell of a small tribe that was terrified by the crimes of your ancestors, who were considerably indebted to it when they first came to this area; the members of this tribe only found salvation by fleeing to the North. Incorrigible oath-breakers, you sacrifice your honor to your three principal goals: the enlargement of your kingdom, the taking of captives, and the pillaging of entire tribes.

"It is a cowardly act of murder, and not war, to mount an attack against the unarmed, the aged, the sick, the infirm, pregnant women, young children, and, in short, anyone whose vulnerability should oblige the strong to respect and protect them.

"The act of forcibly depriving others of the fruits of their labors is called pillage.

"It is also a heinous crime to infringe upon the liberty of others.

"Anyone who has the courage to defend his right to life, liberty, and the usufruct of his property is assassinated without mercy. Does this mean that people will be spared if they allow themselves to be captured when surprise and terror have granted you the victory?

"Those who were not killed in the battle to defend their liberty and their property have a chance to remain alive only if they are strong or have a commercial or aesthetic value.

"You separate husband and wife; you snatch children from their parents; by murdering mothers and fathers, you deprive childhood of its natural guardians; in short, you destroy the family, which is sacred to all peoples.

"Young girls uprooted from their homes swell the harem of the king, or they are awarded to princes and commoners whom he desires to repay for sevices rendered or to overwhelm with friendship for their cleverness, their flattery, or their barbarity during massacres – what your people call courage.

"A number of other young girls are condemned to celibacy in your armies.

271

"Men are reduced to slaves who perform the most arduous or disgusting work for masters who consider manual labor as dishonorable for people of high birth.

"Regardless of their age or sex and depending upon the whims of the despot who requires it, some captives are armed against the very country that gave birth to them, nourished them, and raised them – that is to say, against their fathers and mothers.

"A substantial number of captives are sold like cattle. The profits extracted from this infamous trade enables you to obtain guns, ammunition, cloth, alcohol, and other of the white man's fine things.

"As for the slaves whose strength has been sapped by old age, illness, or infirmity, do you accord them the leisure and the care they deserve after long years of faithful service? Once they have become useless, they are dismissed as laggards and declared unfit to live. It is with the blood of these unfortunate victims that you knead the clay of the mausoleums that you erect in memory of queen mothers and former kings.

"If it could, the day would cease to dawn over Danhomê because its appearance triggers the death of innocent victims whose blood, you claim, serves to wash the face of the heavens before the appearance of the day star, a word the people also use to designate the king in this country. When a king utters his last sigh, a slave is sacrificed before the threshold of his death chamber for the sole purpose of reddening the nail of the king's right big toe with the victim's blood. After that, a large number of queens who never experienced the joy of motherhood are obliged to drink a poison beverage; they are then interred with the royal remains. In the sepulchre you entomb a living man whose only crime was to be a dwarf. He is given a lighted lamp. As if it were a glorious title, the kings of this country boast about such a sadistic act in the following maxim: 'When death shall have struck him, a dwarf holding a lamp will go before him to light his way to the city of the spirits.' Each year the commemoration of previous reigns occasions a bloodbath involving other victims who, you say, are charged with messages for the ancestors. One king of Danhomê, we are told, did not believe that his messages for the other world could be delivered by strangers who, not having known his ancestors in this world, would be unable to find them in the next one.

"When such news reached us in Europe, we were naive enough to believe that such a doubt would certainly put an end to these odious sacrifices in Danhomê. However, the king soon decreed that princes would henceforth be sacrificed with the captives of war in order to introduce them to his ancestors in the realm of the dead. Then we understood that, in citing the pretext of a doubt about the transmission of his messages, the sadist was merely looking for an opportunity to eliminate a few relatives whom he found irksome in attempting to carry out his policies. But the selfless courage of the present king, who was then a pretender to the throne of Danhomê, saved both the princess, who, as the first victim selected, had already been lashed into a porter's rack and was on the verge of being sacrificed, and a number of princes over whom the same threat was hanging.

"Why did such a decision arouse the royal family to indignation? Do you have a right to life that the men you are sacrificing do not have? More than the Mahinous and the Nagonous, who ought to claim the honor of carrying messages to former kings? The descendants themselves of these kings! Why then relinquish into the hands of such despised captives that which should be the unique privilege of princes who reserve so many rights for themselves in this Danhomê? Everything suggests that they are convinced neither of the necessity of the messages entrusted to these captives, nor of the possibility that such messages might actually arrive at their destination. It is therefore time to put an end a monstruous error that, we believe, must have originated in a moment of madness. Princes fear death, and they love life and its pleasures. Let them recognize that all men have the same horror of death, that they experience the same desire to enjoy life, and that they have a sacred right to do so.

"Man is born free, and it is an injustice to reduce him to slavery; human life is sacred, and it is a heinous crime to extinguish it without legitimate reason.

"Your human sacrifices are crimes, and they will certainly be expiated by all those who have perpetrated them.

"The futility of your human sacrifices does not even escape the intelligent people of this kingdom.

"It is for these reasons that all the nations of Europe, with our own in the lead, desire that you pledge your solemn word to undertake no more wars, to discontinue the horrible practice of human sacrifice, to terminate your involvement in the infamous slave trade, and to emancipate all those slaves presently living in Danhomê.

"From now on, make your justice more equitable and humane; in this kingdom, it appears that a common man is never right when he is in conflict with a prince or a high dignitary and that you cut off people's hands, if not their heads, for a trifle. You do not respect an orphan's right to his inheritance, and, for crimes that are often imaginary, you deprive simple farmers of the land they have cultivated with the sweat of the brows. No longer close the borders of your kingdom to foreigners; let your subjects freely purchase the white man's merchandise and make use of it without being harassed.

"From now on, direct the zeal of your arms toward the cultivation of your fields; there is nothing dishonorable in that, no matter what your princes may think. Your land is marvelously fertile, and Nature is infinitely lenient toward you; your climate is not as rigorous as that of Europe; the soil of your country bears produce that is unknown in our part of the world. Plants introduced to Danhomê by men of our race grow extremely well here and add to the country's wealth. It is time to stop depending on the slave trade and to look for new sources of revenue. You will certainly find them because you lack neither intelligence nor determination.

"We bring you the experience of a nearly two-thousand-year-old nation that is still powerful and prosperous because its sovereigns are the very image of justice and kindliness; its institutions are the incarnation of wisdom and its customs the embodiment of purity. As for the kingdom of Danhomê – created by force and the breaking of oaths, enlarged through expropriation, fortified by terror and arbitrariness, and enriched through pillage – it will not only be unable to last, but it will come to a miserable end someday soon. It will only have a good chance for survival if it abandons the path of evil in time and makes amends for its past crimes.

"When a repentant Danhomê regains its prosperity, it will have to facilitate trade, especially with the Glincis, decrease the taxes that are imposed on them, allow them to circulate freely throughout the kingdom, show greater respect for them, accord them precedence over other white men at the court of Agbomê, and give preference to their merchandise."

Despite his efforts to remain calm, Guézo did not succeed in concealing from his retinue the distressing impression that the blasphemies of the scarcely diplomatic Ambassador had made on him.

Fearing that a decision different from the one they had agreed upon in advance might be introduced by the king, Migan turned at once toward the Ambassadors and informed them: "It is the custom in Danhomê not to respond to the desiderata of visitors until after having offered them some refreshment."

The Ambassadors regained their places around the table.

Mêwou left, followed by the young girls who had lined up against the wall.

They returned, carrying copper, bronze, and silver trays filled with bottles of the white man's alcohol, glasses, and gold or silver ewers containing fresh water.

While some of them were placing the glassses in front of the Ambassadors, others were opening the liquor bottles, from which still others began to serve according to the preferences of the white men, whom they addressed with engaging smiles as they held up several bottles at the same time.

Although very nervous, these young girls, who were the essence of innocence, acquitted themselves quite skillfully of the task they were performing for the first time in their lives. Some of them laughed secretly at the awkwardness of two or three companions who almost tipped over the glasses. Far from being annoyed, the latter quietly promised to do better the next day. . . .

A servant circled the table, surveying all the glasses with a glance and assuring herself they were all full. She left the room. The long procession of servants filed out gracefully after her, leaving behind them the fragrance of both the pomade with which they had anointed their bodies and the white paste applied to their necks and busts that attracted admiring stares from several attachés seated across the room, where discrete proddings of their neighbors' elbows broke the spell and recalled them to the necessity of drinking to the health of the king.

The faces of all the young girls, even those of the young princesses, beamed in the pride of seeing eyes bulging with desire fixed upon them and in the hope as well of being able to remember, in the evening of their lives, how they had been singled out for their beauty and how they had been chosen for the honor of serving refreshments for an important mission from the white man's country.

They were radiant in their reflections. The thought that it was customary to offer a young girl to each white man who came to the court at Agbomê made some of them happy but saddened those who were dissatisfied with the appearance of the white men behind whom they had been placed. . . .

The men's thirst was so acute that nearly all the glasses returned empty from their lips. A few of the Ambassadors regretted that the servants were no longer there to refill their glasses. "They have no doubt gone in search of food," an interpreter whispered into the ear of an Ambassador.

The secretaries of the mission were already preparing to record the king's declaration in order to submit it at once to the signature of the court.

Outside, songs and drums suddenly fell silent. The vague buzzing that ensued there was hardly loud enough to disturb the impressive silence that reigned here.

The Ambassadors had turned toward the throne and anxiously awaited the moment when the king of Danhomê, in his name and in that of his successors, was going to renounce the wars, the slavery, and the human sacrifice that were condemned by the law of human rights, the validity of which they had just, they thought, convinced the king and his court.

At a sign from Guézo, the keeper of the spitoon approached him. Her neighbor then wiped the royal lips. The queens kissed the ground at the foot of the throne in an expression of gratitude for the honor that the King of the Spirit had just vouchsafed them in allowing them to touch his venerable lips.

The king emitted two mute huum-huums to which the ranks of the courtiers replied with a chorus of deafening coughs; meanwhile, the queens were saying: "Gently! Very gently!"

Was the king getting ready to speak? It was as if all eyes were focused on his lips. The coughs had scarcely died away when male servants dashed into the room and lined the table with the trays that had been used to carry in the drinks for the Ambassadors, but they now contained the heads of those naive young girls who had just poured their drinks with so much charm and who had received smiles from some of them, compliments on a youth and beauty that reflected innocence. On all the severed heads, faces still retained the appearance of life, eloquently revealing what had been the imploring expressions of these innocent victims at the moment of their execution. Here, eyes are full of anguish, and abundant tears are welling forth to beg for mercy. A bit further away, they are red and haggard; on other faces, eyelids are struggling in vain to open so that eyes can look for one last time upon the things that are going to cease to exist for them. Still further, three, four, five, many bleeding tongues are dangling, nearly severed by jaws that snapped forcibly shut on them. Several lips move convulsively, brows become furrowed, and grimaces appear. A mouth opens, the tongue emerges, moves about, goes back inside, and reemerges; the child continues to cry. She can no longer be heard, but she is understood; she is proclaiming her innocence, her right to life, and imploring pity for her youth. Having failed to move the executioner, who was only listening to the savage fury in his heart, she is beginning with all her might to call upon her ancestors and fetishes to exact vengeance on Danhomê – the expression on her face leaves no room for doubt. In one tray, the abrupt opening of the lower jaw overturns a head; a thin spurt of blood rises in the air and falls back on the table cloth.

One Ambassador fainted with a shrill cry; others turned aside, thrusting out their arms in the direction of the heads and agitatedly moving their hands, which they had stiffened as if to push the spectacle away.

Migan, whose departure had earlier gone unnoticed, boisterously reentered the room, his large, blood-drenched scimitar grasped firmly in his hand. His face with its blazing eyes, dilated nostrils, and protruding jaws was, like his clothes, completely smeared with blood and had assumed the fury of an enraged gorilla charging, foam at the mouth and teeth flashing with menace.

A few of the mission's attachés trembled; others threw themselves against their neighbors and knocked them over. Crazed with terror, one of them ran to the end of the reception room. Two or three hid under the table.

Facing the leader of their mission, the executioner told him with a sardonic smile: "You well-dressed men, you are demanding that Danhomê tie its hands so it can become an easy prey for its enemies, that this kingdom raise slaves to the rank of their free-born masters, that the King of the Universe no longer honor his ancestors with human sacrifice; that is to say, you want him to draw misfortune down upon his head by abandoning a custom that dates back six reigns and that has until now enjoyed the approval of all our ancestors?

"You desire Danhomê to bring about its own ruin by renouncing the slave trade and to allow foreigners to travel freely through the country, sowing illness and chaos among the people?

"The Predestined King had initially decided to send you yourselves to carry your desiderata to his ancestors. At the last moment, he preferred to replace you with these young girls who listened most attentively to your speeches. If the Master of the World's ancestors approve your proposals, they will not fail to send these messengers back to let you know. Wait for them then!"

The leader of the mission was unable to utter a single word, so tightly was his throat held in the grip of anguish. With an expansive gesture, the triumphant executioner placed his scimitar across the heads in the two trays at the middle of the table, then walked over and prostrated himself at the foot of the throne. The king withdrew. The princes and princesses who were gathered in the courtyard heaped sarcastic comments upon these beasts from the sea who had been reduced to such a pitiful state by fear. Someone in the crowd mockingly asked: "Was it really the fate of our victims that brought these White-Bellies to Danhomê? Wasn't it rather because they lack the courage to witness the shedding of blood that they came to advise us to abandon war, slavery, and human sacrifice?"

"What use do they expect us to put the swords, guns, carronades, and powder that they send to Danhomê?" seconded a prince.

"Swords to fight the gnats, guns to bring down the fruits from the trees, carronades to serve us as benches during our palavers and as pillows during our siestas, powder no doubt for us to lick!" sneered a princess.

Informed of what had just occurred, the mob outside the Palace lauded the intelligence of the king and jeered the panic-stricken fear of the beasts from the sea. Drums and canons joined the courtiers in their praises for the king and their sarcastic observations with regard to the Ambassadors.

Before three days had passed, all Danhomênous, including infants at their mothers' breasts, would learn of the witty response that the Master of the World had made to the Glincis, who had come to ask the Danhomê of Houégbaja to commit suicide. Tradition would preserve the story to sustain a mistrust of the Glincis, sworn enemies of Danhomê, for generations to come.

Guézo refused to accept the presents from the king of the Glincis. The mission obtained permission to leave for Gléhoué as soon as the following morning. "We have to get away as quickly as possible from this kingdom, which is so steeped in crime that it revolts against any thought of human decency!" explained the leader of the mission to those of his colleagues who would have liked to rest for a day in Agbomê.

Silk, velvet, damask, satin, parasols, head-dresses, shoes, silk flags with the colors of the Glincis' country, gold and silver jewelry, expensive liquor, and other valuable objects were hurriedly repacked. Before closing the lid on the statues and paintings that had been executed at the behest of his sovereign by the great artists of his kingdom, the leader of the mission contemplated them, sadly shaking his head and then sighing: "The waggish Lord Chimmery was unquestionably right when, after I had shown him these masterpieces just before our departure, he foresaw our debacle and advised me to have the artists inscribe their works: 'A dream that will be realized when this country is no longer an island. . . .'"

The interpreters were summoned to the Palace, where they received new instructions for the return journey.

Royal messengers carried new orders at top speed to all the regional chiefs and provincial Governors.

The night was noisier than the day: the cannon thundered intermittently, and the drums beat with frenzy to the tireless accompaniment of horns, rattles, large bells and small ones; the crowd screamed songs of triumph that had been composed for the occasion. This tohubohu would continue until the departure of the white men.

Surrounded by his wives and the rest of the court in full ceremonial dress, the king received the farewell visit of the Ambassadors in the Courtyard of the Palace at the moment when the sun was rising to the height of the ear. In a cavernous voice that he injected with terror, Mêwou enjoined the escort to watch carefully over the good friends of the Master of the World.

Guézo was lying on his sofa. Silent and morose, his head cradled in his left palm, his elbow planted in the pillow, he gazed after them for a long time as they moved into the distance, seated in their hammocks, their busts leaning forward, their feet dangling; it was obvious that they were cowed. They had already disappeared behind the nété[3] and palm trees, but the king was still following them in his thoughts, speaking to them: "My august Father was also preoccupied with a desire to temper the customs of this people. With that goal in mind, he invited a white man and his wife to the court; he believed that their presence here would help him considerably in overcoming the bloody traditions of Danhomê. Your two compatriots instructed the court in the good manners of your country. When I was able to take possession of Danhomê, I too dreamed of realizing my royal Father's dream as quickly as possible. I only engage in just wars. You find that our surprise attacks against our enemies are cowardly. Didn't I lead this country to the brink of disaster at the beginning of my reign because I followed the advice given by one of you about declarations of war?

"You vehemently reproach me for trading in slaves! But didn't you – the Agoudas, the Glincis, and the Zojagués – introduce the idea and develop a taste for it in this country? Weren't you the ones who constantly armed Danhomê against the small neighboring tribes and encouraged the slave trade by the very transactions that you now consider so infamous? I did not wait for your advice to oblige my heir to promise that, when he acquires Danhomê, he will turn his attention toward the exploitation of the land, in which he will discover a new and honest source of wealth for his people.

"Well before the arrival of your mission, I was also looking for a means to curtail human sacrifice. But I ran into insurmountable difficulties; our human sacrifices trace their origins to our belief in the afterlife, and they are deeply embedded in our way of life. In this Danhomê, the king who attempts to eliminate them all at once will pay with his life for what would be regarded as a sacrilege.

"In contrast to my ancestors, who always sought to surpass their predecessors in conquests, ostentation, and even horror, I myself would like to be greater than them only in magnanimity. Did I hesitate to disapprove publicly of Migan when he wanted to institute, during my reign, a children's sacrifice that he called "the roasting of ground nuts for my ancestors?"

"I did not eliminate human sacrifices, but I considerably decreased the number of them by fostering the slave trade as an alternative; the majority of our captives are thereby kept alive, for which they ought to be infinitely grateful, no matter how far away they might be transported or how arduous the work imposed upon them might be.

"I have only had several hands cut off so that people will respect the property of others. By beheading a few individuals, I am surely protecting the masses.

"It is to protect the physical and moral health of my subjects against disease and subversive ideas that I have set rigorous limits on the freedom of foreigners to travel among them. It is to prevent my people from developing a taste for

---

3   The nété (Parkia biglobosa) is a tree, the seed of which is used to prepare native mustard.

luxuries and great vices that I have restricted the sale of your wares in my country.

"Ever since one of my predecessors decided that the property acquired by a poor man should be respected, Danhomênous have always enjoyed the fruits of their labor. Only the lazy are expropriated for the benefit of the more industrious. Orphans have no patron more solicitous than I am. The people bless my reign, in which they see the advent of justice tempered with fairness and benevolence.

"You will never know the joy I felt at the announcement of your mission! In fact, thanks to you, I was hoping finally to have found a substantial enough argument to convince my people to diminish the number of our human sacrifices. But your ignorance of the Danhomênous' soul caused you to mount a brutal attack against their most hallowed feelings, which you mortally offended. In me as in my subjects, you aroused the fearsome Danhomênou whom I was very discreetly attempting to stifle a little at a time. I was determined to give a favorable reception to your proposals, about which Yévogan had informed me down to the last detail within two days of your arrival on shore. But you imprudently confided your secrets to the inhabitants of Gléhoué, and they were reported to Agbomê, where they enabled my ministers' plan to carry the day, and it was not a humane one. Why did you tell my subjects in the maritime province that the reign of liberty was going to be definitively established for them, that the tears they had shed on account of the miserable situation reserved for them in this kingdom would at once be dried, that their subjugation would soon be no longer but a faint memory, and that, in the shadow of your flag, which would be floating above Danhomê in a few days, they would henceforth enjoy the fruits of their toil, be treated in the same fashion as the princes, and see a new respect accorded to their families? Why did you show them that painting, which they say is highly insulting to the throne? On a vast canvas dominated by your flag, you had depicted Danhomênous whose chains or bonds were being removed by two or three of your countrymen beneath the gaze of an impotent monarch cowering apprehensively in a corner, where he was obliged to witness the liberation of those whom you called the prisoners of his despotism. Why did you also bring that statue in which you had portrayed a white man holding back the scimitar that the executioner had raised and was about to let fall on the neck of a victim lashed to a porter's rack? You are not, however, lacking in perceptiveness! Yet how can it be that your king didn't recognize how all this would be offensive to Danhomê and especially humiliating for the self-esteem of Migan, the avenging arm of the Houégbajas? This is what prompted him to imagine the bloody response, for which I quite grudgingly gave my approval.

"Ignoring the true author of these new crimes, you attribute them to me, and my people praises me for them as if they were the mark of great wisdom. . . .

"While proposing to the council of the throne the response that was accorded you, my first minister declared that it was the most eloquent proof we could offer to show that no foreigners, not even the white men to whom we owe the weapons that forged our power, can ever hold back his arm, which is that of Danhomê itself.

"At heart, his peers don't like him because they are predisposed against him by the base spirit of rivalry that is common to all my people and invariably causes them to denigrate even the best ideas expressed in council for the simple reason that these ideas had been advanced by someone else; nevertheless, Migan succeeded in persuading the entire court to accept his point of view. Under other circumstances his colleagues would have rejected his proposals. But everyone had been offended by your attitude at Gléhoué.

"The Danhomênous do not understand you! On the contrary, they find you inconsistent. That is one of the reasons for the rigor with which my ministers opposed your untimely zeal.

"Indeed, wasn't it to avenge your countrymen, who were massacred in mahi territory, that I decided to wage war against the inhabitants of Hounjroto who were responsible for the crime committed by those of Kinglo? Who more than you should desire the destruction of the mahi country? If you have already forgotten your dead so soon, Danhomê, as for it, still remembers Toffa, Assogbaou, Afénou. Gaou Déssou, Possou Linon, Alopé, Chalacassou, and Jajagoloja; it still remembers the thousands of sons who sacrificed their lives to avenge three of your people. The fathers and mothers, widows and orphans of this kingdom are still mourning the loss of their leaders at Hounjroto, and Danhomê does not understand how you can demand that we throw down our arms before having avenged its dead and your own, before having liberated the princes who are prisoners in mahi country.

"The indiscretion of the inhabitants of Gléhoué revealed to you many things that should remain hidden even from the Danhomênous themselves; how then can you be unaware of this nation's profound veneration for its dead, and do you believe it could leave unpunished the insults that have been inflicted upon them, especially when these dead are kings?

"You will never know what you owe to my august protection. At the first word of your blasphemies, my executioner would have made your heads roll in the dust if you had not been the guests of his sovereign, who still remembers that he owes his throne in part to a 'brother' of your race.

"It was extremely difficult for me to save your heads. I was unsuccessful in my opposition to the will of the council of the throne insofar as the young girls selected to serve your refreshments were concerned. You should realize that, had it not been for my friendship toward your race, this people, whose religious sentiments you so grossly insulted, would surely have drowned you at the side of your ship under the very eyes of your fellow couontrymen still on board, that is, if they had not already knocked you over the head during the journey or thrown your bodies into the Swamps.

"Trusting outward appearances, you think the kings of this country are all-powerful. The council of the throne alone decides everything at the Palace, often against the will of the king, who must indeed submit to the will of this council and follow the ruts of tradition. As far as the people are concerned, the order that is executed before their eyes emanates exclusively from the man whom they, in their naiveté, regard as Sovereign and call the Master of the World.

"You are taking away a bad impression of a king who is good, just, merciful, and sparing of human blood! Perhaps it is my fault. . . ."

He heaved a profound sigh.

The Ambassadors had long ago passed through the Door of Dossoumoin. They were going away in silence, vexed by their failure and especially by the fact that, having come with the intention of healing a wound, they had merely succeeded in aggravating it.

The interpreters scrupulously followed the instructions received before their departure from Agbomê: avoid all idle chatter and keep their ears wide open so as not to lose a single word of the confidences exchanged among these white men, who were leaving the court of Agbomê unhappy and disappointed.

Breaking the silence, the leader of the mission uttered the following prayer to console himself and his compatriots: "May the Almighty, who knows how to make the blood of a single innocent man blossom into the salvation of all humanity, bequeath a martyr's halo to yesterday's innocent victims and redeem, by means of their deaths, the freedom and happiness of an entire people groaning under the tyranny of a dynasty!"

Guézo's sadness did not escape his court. The first minister suspected that the king was tormented by remorse; he feared that the monarch might try to rebel against the council's suggestion, recall the Ambassadors, and submit to their will in apprehension of a war against their country. Desiring to assure the king that, as long as a single Danhomênou remained alive, the beasts from the sea would never subjugate the Danhomê of Houégbaja, Migan turned toward the people and informed them: "Danhomênous, nothing but the Predestined King's determination not to see you fall beneath the domination of the Ayonous and the Mahinous, who dream of enslaving you, obliged him to reject the proposals of the Glincis, who were demanding that Houégbaja bind his hands at the very moment when his irreconcilable enemies are arming themselves to attack him. Even if all the beasts from the sea were to invade Danhomê with their guns in their hands, isn't it true that you would stand up to them as you have always done in the face of all your enemies who have ever ventured into the kingdom of Houégbaja?"

The male voice of Gaou replied in the name of the crowd that was lying prostrate in the dust: "Let the Master of the World set his mind at rest! The Spirit of Creation continues to protect the Danhomê of Houégbaja! He desires to shelter it from the envy he knows its prosperity will inspire in others. Look at these hills that separate us from mahi country, at the River Zou located between us and the Ayonous, at the Coufo, a veritable trench between the backward Ajanous and the Danhomênous, and at the ocean that places such a great distance between us and these filthy beasts from the sea, who are leaving, that it takes them many moons to cross it, an ocean that always flies into a rage to prevent the stinking beasts it harbors from coming ashore along our coast! Only a few days ago did the reason for the existence of the Swamps between Agbomê and the coast become clear to me! Our royal messengers, who only enter them with trepidation, have always wished that the Master of the World would drain and fill them. Agassou alone could have fashioned these Swamps. Having foreseen our settlement in the land of the Guédévis and desiring that we should live there in freedom and prosperity, safe from the pollution of these foul beasts from the sea, the great fetish of our ancestors created these Swamps and entrusted the custody of them to the vigilance of mosquitoes and wild animals that do not bother the Master of the World's subjects but fill our enemies with terror. Also, only those Danhomênous whose steps are guided by the ancestors can cross these marshlands without incident.

"The white men who are not escorted by us get lost there and sink into the quicksand, if they are not devoured by panthers.

"I therefore do not believe that these beasts from the sea, who, once they have left their lair and arrived in Gléhoué, have never walked more than two hundred bamboos on foot, these beasts who are always seen lounging in hammocks and who could never reach Agbomê except for us who provide them with this means of transportation, without which they could not get past Savi – I do not believe, Danhomênous, that these feeble beasts from the sea can conquer the Danhomê of Houégbaja, which is, at the same time, the block of granite against which feet bruise themselves, the sky that cannot be reached with the hand, and the midday sun whose splendor is too radiant for any human eye to behold. But if they think themselves capable of defeating us, let them try!"

Possou supported the words of his colleague: "When the sound of the fish folk's preparations for a war against the cayman broke over the den of this aquatic reptile, he joyously exclaimed: 'May the fetishes deign to bring these foolish creatures here! In this race, only the fastest will find salvation by fleeing!' Yes, Danhomênous, our best interest will be served if madness one day moves these vile beasts from the sea to wage war on the Danhomê of Houégbaja! We will strangle them with our bare hands and finish them off with our teeth if the guns and carronades that come to us from their country refuse to fire on them!

"If, therefore, the Master of the World's sadness stems only from any doubts he may have about the resolve of his subjects, let him be confident: for the joy of their Creator, the Danhomênous are prepared to sacrice the life they have received from him!"

He covered himself with dirt.

"Gaou and Possou have told the truth! They have told the truth!" the people shouted tumultuously as they covered themselves with dirt.

The king sighed once more and shook his head in an expression of doubt. Then he withdrew.

"The Master of the World is reassured!" thought Migan, overjoyed at having been the only one, along with the two ministers of war, to have found a remedy for the king's sadness.

In reality, Guézo was more worried than ever. The future seemed very gloomy to him.

During a council that was held a few moments later, Migan concluded the expression of his views in these terms: "The Danhomê that undertook to punish the people of Hounjroto, the instigators of the massacre at Kinglo, has been poorly rewarded by the countrymen of the white men who were killed there. We must watch out for them! The lengthy discourse delivered by the leader of these beasts from the sea indicates that there is nothing they do not know about our past and our most secret customs. We must discover the Danhomênous who laid Danhomê open to the sacreligious eyes of these wretched beasts from the sea."

Adouconou indignantly added: "Toffa was absolutely right. Nothing noble can be expected of these vile beasts from the sea!"

The king had once again plunged into his meditations: "Chacha Ajinacou's behavior toward the tyrant as well as other incidents routinely reported from Gléhoué demonstrate that, in contrast to the Danhomênous, white men are perseverent and tenacious. They must have reflected long and hard before doing what they did yesterday, and they have certainly envisioned forceful measures against Danhomê in case, as was probable, their diplomatic effort should fail.

"People don't speak that way unless they have already decided upon repression!

"If my reign is destined to witness the white man's domination over Danhomê, how will it be judged by the secret supporters of the tyrant who was overthrown for my sake? Guézo, upon whom the people are counting to enlarge the kingdom and render it invincible forever – will Guézo see this country enslaved by the white man during his reign? Until now my name has been blessed; will it be cursed henceforth like that of Adanzan? What if the Danhomênous refused to judge the conduct of their king? And what about our ancestors?

"Did they entrust Danhomê to me because they know that I am not the tiny child from the top of whose head the hawk can steal fried bean cakes with impunity?" He shook his head and sighed, then authorised his councillors to go and rest until the next day.

Since the evening when the news of the white men's arrival at Gléhoué had arrived in Agbomê, the palace dignitaries had often held council meetings until the first crowing of the cock and returned to the Palace at dawn.

During the day, the king only appeared for a short time in front of the people so as not to throw them into a panic over the health of their Creator.

The drums had fallen silent again.

Vidaho was detained for a conversation with his royal Father, as was customary after every important event.

The king only opened his heart to the person whom he had chosen to succeed him on the throne of Houégbaja. The sole witness of these confidential talks, which raised the royal prince considerably in the eyes of his brothers, was the dead king on whose tomb they took place.

Among other observations, Guézo confided his fears for the future of the kingdom to his heir: "When a white man succeeds in poking his little finger beneath a heavy load, he eventually lifts it up, thanks to his perseverence; it is largely through the efforts of Chacha, who wanted to avenge himself for the tortures of Adanzan, that I was able to overthrow the tyrant. This proves that white men hold their grudges tenaciously. Even if mountains rose up and barred the route in front of them, their march toward the enemy would not be halted. Today they dream of holding sway over Danhomê. Our ancestors will never endure such an affront. I have made my decision on this subject."

He became silent for a moment, sighed, and then continued, emphasizing his every word: "If the white men are obliged to wait until your reign before attempting to impose their will on Danhomê, command your people to poison all the waters of the kingdom with the most deadly plants of the region so that the white men and the Danhomênous will both die when they drink from them; in that way there will no longer be either masters or slaves!"

Calling his ancestors to witness, the heir to the throne vowed that the white men would never take Danhomê from him without bloodshed.

When he left the Palace, the sun was already climbing overhead.

He did not wish to wait until nightfall, as prudence might have suggested, before visiting Doguicimi. To stifle the fear that was settling into his mind, he assured himself: "It will be as if I am entering the prison to carry out a mission. Why should I even worry about it so much? This kingdom belongs partly to me. No Danhomênou who suspected the attentions I have been paying Toffa's wife would ever have the audacity to breathe a word to anyone!" On the way, he convinced himself that the desired woman was not unaware that all the favors she enjoyed in her prison were solely due to the intercession of the prince who idolized her. Thus, in return, she could not fail to accede to the wishes of the man whose love for her had prevented her enemies from getting rid of her on the very night of her imprisonment.

"She no doubt remembers that I vowed to make her happy. My protection has assured her of staying alive for season after season, and it guarantees the happiness that awaits her at my side in this world and in the next one after my ancestors have called me to them."

He was full of confidence and his face was beaming as he approached Doguicimi. The woman received him with less coolness than usual. With a smile in which he saw his ultimate victory, she even told him: "The four market days of the prince's absence seemed like four dry seasons to me."

In a voice that his love tinged with cajolery, the prince replied that their separation had been much more painful for him and that his absence had resulted from the interminable councils held at the court to achieve consensus on the reception to be accorded the white men who had been sent on a mission to his august Father.

As if the desires of her heart had already been realized, she joyfully asked: "Isn't it true that they brought soldiers and guns to exterminate all the stinking beasts from Hounjroto and to free our prisoners? Will the Master of the World continue to delay the sending of an expedition now that he is assured of the white man's support?"

"Get rid of your illusions, Doguicimi, and from now on turn your disdain upon these beasts from the sea, whose demands have roused all Danhomê to indignation; they came to prohibit us from undertaking further conquests, from holding slaves, and from continuing our human sacrifices. If the court followed their advice, Danhomê would have to abandon warfare and devote itself to the cultivation of the land; we would have to deprive princes of the privileges they hold by right of birth and to respect slaves rather than living from their work and the profits made by selling them; we would have to support the indolence of some farmers and protect all sorts of criminals; and what is even more odious, Danhomê would have to cease adding, by means of human sacrifice, to the retinue of the ancestors in the city of the dead.

"Forewarned about the white men's mission by Yévogan and Dêmênou, the court consulted the ancestors one by one through the intermediary of the oracle and were informed by each of them that the secret goal of these foul beasts from the sea was domination over Danhomê.

"My august Father," he continued in a jocular tone of voice, "first offered them refreshments in conformity with our custom, which decrees that strangers should always be welcomed in this manner before the object of their visit is addressed; then, in the same trays that had been used to bring in their drinks, the Father of Life had them served with the heads of the young girls who had waited on them, girls who had been selected from among the captives taken during our last war against Gbaji."

"Oh, the innocent victims!" cried Doguicimi, who trembled at the news of this horrible event. The prince appeared to have heard nothing and continued in the same vein: "Shortly thereafter, Migan entered and told those vile beasts from the sea that, if the ancestors were in wholehearted agreement with their opinion (that is to say, if they disapproved of our conquests, our slavery, and our human sacrifice), they would immediately send these young messengers back to tell us that.

"The faint-heartedness of these White-Bellies never appeared so clearly to us as it did yesterday: more than one of them fainted; one did throw himself into the arms of a traveling companion, beseeching him to save him; another ran panic-stricken to hide at the other end of the reception room, and a number of them hid under the table.

"The Master of the World only spared them so they could go and tell their king that the Danhomê over which Guézo rules will never submit to the will of the beasts from the sea.

"At this moment, the Ambassadors must be in the vicinity of Ayivêji at the edge of the Swamps. There is no doubt that they are still reflecting on Danhomê's power, which dazzled their eyes during their brief stay in the capital.

"All the Danhomênous in the escort of these foul beasts from the sea will return to the court, where they will give an account of what they heard, saw, and did during the return journey to Gléhoué.

"Yévogan himself and Dêmênou, the leader of the secret police at Gléhoué, will come up to Agbomê after these Ambassadors have boarded their ship again.

"Chacha Ajinacou will also come to inform us about the strength of these

285

Glincis. At the same time, the 'brother' of the king will be receiving a sizable shipment of guns and ammunition.

"The Master of the World has decided not to leave Agbomê until the necessary time has passed for these foul beasts to regain their lair, prepare for war, and return with an army to fight against Danhomê. Since one never knows what is being hatched in those skulls covered with goat fuzz, it is prudent to be on the alert. At the moment then, other things are more important than the conquest of Hounjroto; the very survival of Danhomê is being threatened by the greed of the Glincis.

"The selfishness and cupidity of these slave-holders are proverbial, and they have been suddenly converted into abolitionists?

"They'll never make me believe it! The intelligence of the princes of Danhomê, for whom the duplicity of the Glincis holds no mysteries, soon exposed the real motivation behind this new-found benevolence, which is just as self-interested as that of the blacksmith, who, having lost the strength in his arms, immediately began to condemn the manufacture of the white man's guns and bullets, supposedly dishonorable means of taking human lives.

"Chacha Ajinacou has informed us that, as the result of a war against subjects who revolted against their demands, the Glincis had just lost the country where they sold the majority of the slaves they bought here.

"Since this major market was closed to them forever, they swore to bring down the other nations who are still profiting from the slave trade, and by offering magnificent gifts, they were hoping to enlist the Master of the World's support in their conspiracy against those who continue to be favored by Destiny. But a king of this country is too noble to play the game of these rogues, who cunningly pretend to be overcome with pity for the fate of the inhabitants of those countries where we wage war to feed the slave trade! Would they come here to demand that we call a halt to our wars if our traditional celebrations consumed all our captives or only left a small number for our own needs?

"See how grateful these filthy beasts from the sea are toward Danhomê for having sacrificed the lives of more than a thousand of it sons in order to avenge the three White-Bellies massacred near Kinglo at the instigation of the inhabitants of Hounjroto!"

Doguicimi had collapsed against the wall. The news of Toffa's death in captivity would not have been a greater blow to her. She stared straight ahead in a daze and no longer heard anything of the refrain that Vidaho had resumed in his wheedling voice about the happiness he had prepared for her at his side. Her eyes clouded over; large tears were soon rolling across her cheeks and unto her chest.

The prince asked her if he was the cause of her grief.

When she didn't respond, he begged her to forgive the injury he had unwittingly inflicted on her.

Controlling her emotion, she informed him in a muffled tone of voice: "The royal prince has nothing to do with my affliction. If it depended only on him, I would have been happy a long time ago. But human hands can not weave our happiness; it comes to us from Destiny, and when Destiny did not bestow it upon us before our arrival in this world, we are obliged to drag our misery around with us as long as we are here. 'The light of the firefly is predestined,' say the elders, and with good reason."

The lover said to himself: "She realizes that I passionately desire her happiness, but she doubts that happiness is the work of human hands!" He reassured her to the best of his ability and did not leave her until he thought she had agreed that mortal beings could indeed bring about our happiness and that the heir to the throne of Danhomê was well situated to assure the happiness of Doguicimi.

On the way back to his residence, he thought: "She is finally caught in the nets I set for her such a long time ago! Having tasted neither the food nor the alcohol I sent her while she was still under Toffa's roof, she could not be seduced. Unaware of that, I had approached her in the belief that she was vanquished, but I was shown to the door.

"Here I am now, my goals realized because she is living solely from food which is prepared by Noucounzin and into which I have sprinkled love philtres. Of all those I used, the only one that seemed effective was the one made from the bitter kola nut that was swallowed one evening, found intact the next morning, dried in the sun for several days, and reduced to a powder together with a parrot's red tail feather that had been smeared with my blood. The reputation of the Ajanous as skillful casters of spells is well deserved! I will never again separate myself from the one who has just compounded the irresistable philtre that would have compelled Doguicimi to throw herself at my feet and beg me to marry her, if it were not for the modesty that no spell could ever succeed in vanquishing among the women of Danhomê. . . ."

*   *   *

In her thoughts Doguicimi overtook the white men who were fleeing Agbomê, the capital of horrors.

Her disdain burst over these contemptible wretches: "Stinking beasts whose presence in Danhomê was only tolerated out of an inexcusable complaisance, you want to meddle in the affairs of this kingdom and even impose your will upon it? You want Danhomê to disarm itself in front of its enemies, who are becoming more and more threatening, and you want the slave to give orders in his master's house, while the master is reduced to poverty? The secret desire of your hearts, which are filled with hatred for this kingdom, is that the ancestors will abandon it because people have ceased to honor their memories as ordained by tradition. The Mahinous were certainly right to have forbidden you access to their mountains!

"Your initiatives are finally going to open the eyes of the king, who is full of good will toward you.

"Inflexible matrons in regard to the innocence of young girls, but have you preserved your own? Don't you wage war in your country? It is out of place for a corrupt person to preach virtue. Your hypocrisy is nauseating to widows and orphans, although they loathe the war that brought about their unhappiness. Your own share of responsibility for the Danhomênous' warlike passions is large.

"When they first arrived on this plateau, the Agassouvis imposed respect on a small tribe hostile to their settlement, but they only used clubs, slingshots, arrows, and spears that were sustained by enormous courage and the loudness of their voices. Since these weapons did not appear sufficiently powerful to you, you replaced them first with guns, then with canons; later, you incited the Agassouvis to attack their neighbors so they could take captives and sell them to you.

"Tradition reports that, at the beginning of your settlement in the land of the Houédanous, you asked Agbangla, one of their kings, for young men whom you could instruct in the use of guns and canons in order to prepare them for hunting other men. But since your original friends lacked martial courage and didn't provide you with enough slaves, you were delighted to have discovered the Danhomênous. You did not hesitate to abandon your friends and, what was even more odious, sacrifice them as soon as Agaja entered into battle against them.

"Encouraged by your indifference, his successor Tégbéssou went to Gléhoué and massacred your first friends under your very eyes. Overcome with remorse, you sought to justify your betrayal by accusing them of indolence, drunkenness, and disloyalty.

"That Commander of the Fort of the Agoudas was certainly a member of your race, and tradition has preserved his memory in a way that reflects little honor upon it. From his camp at Savi, where he held, as he said, the key to Gléhoué, Tégbéssou planned to complete the conquest of his predecessor. But Amoua, chief of the Docomê section, was committed to you; at the head of his men, whom he had gained to your cause, he was at your side, defending the unconquered part of Gléhoué. Having learned that only the presence of this man gave heart to the Houédanous grouped around you and thereby delayed the victory of the Danhomênous, our king proposed an alliance to him and succeeded in inspiring him with enough confidence to attract him to Savi. Amoua only went to the king's camp on your advice. The men of your friend's retinue soon returned to inform the Commander of the Fort of the Agoudas that their chief had been detained as a prisoner. Even today Danhomênous jeer at the faint-heartedness of your compatriot, who came to the king's camp and trembled when Tégbéssou presented him with the head of Amoua as a token of his hospitality.

"When the king came to finish the conquest begun by his father, did you protect your friends at Docomê? The day when the Houédanous, who had re-volted against the Danhomênous, triumphantly paraded their defeated and bound enemies through the streets of Gléhoué, you liberated the Danhomênous and supported them in their offensive against the Houédanous because you feared that the definitive victory of your old friends would bring about a decline in the slave trade, which had expanded vigorously under the King of Danhomê's administration."

"You're wrong!" interrupted a voice coming from behind her. It belonged to one of the prisoners assigned to the service of Toffa's wife. Having seen the prince depart, Cangbodé's lodger had hastened to rejoin Doguicimi and hear the news that the heir to the throne had brought her. "My childhood was spent at Gléhoué in the company of an old aunt who loved to tell me about the brilliant past of the former houéda kingdom.

"The evidence of tradition in regard to the definitive conquest of Gléhoué by Tégbéssou is more favorable to the white men. As my aunt told me the story, Agaja's victory had allowed the Danhomênous to establish commercial relations with the dealers at Gléhoué. But the Houédanous still controlled a part of the city that remained under the protection of the white men's carronades. Around the Forts, bloody battles frequently broke out over trifling matters between the original inhabitants and the invaders. During one of these battles, the Houédanous, who had been in contact with the white men for a long time and were skilled in the handling of knives, routed the Danhomênous despite their courage. The victors proclaimed their success throughout the city, pushing before them the moaning Danhomênous who were tied together with a rope. They passed in front of the Fort of the Glincis. The Commander and his lady came out to look at them, visibly exultant over the triumph of their old friends. Drunk with victory and undoubtedly also with the brandy to which the white men had accustomed him, Foli, one of the houéda chiefs, fired on the two white people, whom he claimed to find intrusive; his shot mortally wounded the woman.

"This was the crime that unleashed the Glincis' and the Zojagués's carronades against the Houédanous and turned the tide of victory in favor of the Danhomênous."

"If the event occurred as you reported it," retorted Doguicimi, "the Houédanous's crime certainly deserved to be punished. But in their hearts the white men must have been delighted with the outcome. Didn't it give them the opportunity, for which they had long been secretly yearning, to help the Danhomênous become masters of the city so they could revive the slave trade from the doldrums into which it had sunk? Beginning at that time and armed by the white men for the express purpose of hunting other human beings, the Danhomênous ravaged many regions to take captives and sell them at Gléhoué. In vain our kings raised taxes and subsequently multiplied their harassments of the people, but the white men, who had already sacrificed to their own self-interest the friendship that had linked them with the Houédanous since time immemorial, also abdicated their dignity to fully satisfy their greed. For them, the essential concern was finding slaves to trade at the cost of any humiliation! The goods they bought at ridiculously low prices in Danhomê must have yielded enormous profits. Don't people also contend that their kings pay these dealers substantial bonuses by the head for each slave imported into their countries? They tell how these slaves work day and night for their masters and how it is forbidden for slaves to adopt the religion of the white men so that the latter would not be obliged to treat them like brothers, as their Mawou desires.

"These kings favored the slave trade by all possible means; how could they change their orientation so abruptly and revolt against the business to which

289

their country owes its wealth? The behavior of the Glincis today can only be explained by their loss of control over the slave market, a loss they want to inflict on everyone else of their race as well. The ideals they pretend to extoll are thus highly suspect. But is it really their king who sends them to the Master of the World? If the chief of the Glincis truly wanted Danhomê to put an end to its wars, he would find within his own country the means of doing so, and he would not have to send his Ambassadors to insult the memory of our ancestors and to provoke the death of innocent children by their lack of diplomacy.

"The majority of the firearms sold in Danhomê come from the country of the Glincis, we are told.

"These white men have merely to prohibit the export of these tools of war, while pledging, all of them, never again to send their ships to our shores for the purpose of taking on slaves.

"But even if they made such a resolution, some of them would continue to engage clandestinely in the slave trade. They have developed too much of a taste for it to give it up completely!

"I also doubt that the words of the Ambassadors will bring about the elimination of human sacrifice or that the Glincis will succeed in eradicating this practice from the customs of Danhomê.

"See how pitifully they capitulated yesterday! And if they by some chance decide to demand reparations, they will not hesitate to make their claims in monetary terms; that's the nature of people obsessed with an unbridled desire for wealth.

"These Glincis' love of money has always caused them to break the promises they have made to their best friends.

"These white men will never be the ones who agree spontaneously to the dissolution of their protectorate when their subjects have developed sufficiently stand on their own. The only things they will be seen undertaking for the welfare of their subjects are those that will not impede the enrichment of their masters.

"Indeed, I have little confidence in demands for the abolition of the slave trade when they are proclaimed by the Glincis, whose greed and disdain for Danhomênous are well known.

"I would be no less surprised at the emancipation of slaves on the part of those white men whose arrogant indolence has earned them the name Agoudas. They delight in idleness and would never take the initiative in introducing such a measure because the slave trade furnishes them with men who toil and sweat so that they, the masters, can lounge about in sensual pleasure.

"Only the rule of the Zojagués could bring about what the Glincis came here to demand — peace for the small tribes around Danhomê, freedom for the humble, and the reform of brutal customs. The Zojagués are forceful; they have compassion for the humble. Tradition preserves the memory of their cordial relations with the Houédanous from the time of their earliest settlement at Gléhoué — that is to say, long before the emigration of the Agassouvis to 'ayizo'[4] coun-

---

4   The ayizo country was the region around Alada that was inhabited by the Ayizo people. (author's note)

try. The Zojagués of today hardly seem different from their ancestors. It is true that the people of Gléhoué have reported several incidents of cruelty on the part of certain Zojagués, but the majority of them are, fortunately, quite decent. These white Danhomênous will certainly succeed where the flegmatic and distant Glincis have failed and where no one pays any attention to those incorrigible slave-holders, the lazy Agoudas.

"Zojagués! (Doguicimi saw them in her mind) If Destiny ever makes you masters of this Danhomê, as I desire with all my heart, let it be for the greatest good of this people. Danhomênous may have little material wealth to offer, but despite the appearance of savagery and mental backwardness, they possess marvelous intellectual and spiritual gifts that their ancestors have cultivated throughout the ages – a lively understanding, the desire to improve, respect for authority and discipline, concern for the well-being of the entire society, family solidarity, courage, personal dignity, fidelity toward friends, scrupulous honesty, a sense of justice, and a deep religious feeling.

"Be careful not to destroy these noble sentiments in them unless you want to transform these snake people into vipers and thereby undermine your rule. Keep alive their faith: that is what gave rise to order and discipline in this Danhomê. Attack only the inhuman aspects of their religious beliefs. Never allow them to see examples of scepticism or amorality, much less atheism, for that would cause them to lose confidence in you.

"Before the arrival of the white men in this country, our ancestors' desires, like their needs, had been very modest. Your society imposed a new sort of life on our grandfathers, while elevating money and material well-being to the top of their preoccupations, which had until then been exclusively moral in nature. This sufficed to deceive them into believing that honesty and personal dignity are humiliating if one is poor. Their taste for lucre was no longer to know any limits; it soon introduced the basest instincts into their hearts – ostentatiousness, greed, covetousness, jealousy, and selfishness, all of which resulted in the endless wars, slavery, and human sacrifice against which the men of your race are campaigning today. Combat the materialistic attitude that your coming, the white man's coming, introduced into the minds of these people.

"It would be a serious mistake to assume, on the basis of the Danhomênous's overt expressions of veneration for their kings and all others who are their superiors and on the basis of their submission to the will of their sovereigns, that they are docile and that, as the successors of these kings, you will inherit their rights and can, as a result, treat them like things, make them work without pay, execute them when they complain, close your ears to their charges when they demand justice, and oblige them to respect you by the use of terror: the wrath of the humble will be dreadful.

"Our kings acquire our veneration not, as appearances might suggest, through despotism, but rather through the sacred character with which their persons have been invested by the religious ceremonies they perform every day and every year in order to purify themselves, through the idea that they are representatives of the ancestors, and through their own exalted qualities of heart and mind.

"They are not as arbitrary as they are thought to be; they have always respected the possessions their subjects have acquired as a result of their work. They revise their judgments as soon as they are shown where they went wrong, making appropriate restitution to individuals or families unjustly despoiled of their possessions. They always punish the corruption of village or provincial authorities, and they never tolerate atrocities against the humble, such as the one committed at Gléhoué by the white man who allegedly killed his slave, whose only crime was not having allowed his master's dog to cross the arm of a pond on his back. It is to protect the humble that our kings forbid imprisonments in the homes of individuals and reserve to themselves the right to inflict the death penalty.

"Do not hesitate to remove from office and deal harshly with any chiefs who might be tempted to disregard every man's right to life, liberty, and the enjoyment of the fruits of his labor, a right that the men of your race have just solemnly proclaimed; your failure to act under such circumstances will discredit you in the eyes of the people because they will then consider you to be in league with their oppressors.

"Watch closely to make certain that your people retain their dignity in this country. You should know that hundreds of thousands of eyes are upon them, scrutinizing their every act, and that Danhomênous comment upon these acts, compare them, and conclude that behavior, which might hardly be reprehensible and pass unnoticed in your country, can for a number of reasons become an enormous scandal here and threaten to discredit an entire race, which we would like to idolize for its inventive genius and its cordiality. Indeed, those among you who do not conduct yourselves in this country with the exemplary self-discipline that one has the right to expect of them will be doubly guilty: guilty toward their own race for the discredit brought upon it by their behavior and guilty toward a nation which, like a younger brother, expects his elders to set a good example.

"In the absence then of a sacred aura that might cloak your leaders with respect, let them always uphold high moral standards in this country. I cannot insist too much on this point.

"Be honest in your dealings with the Danhomênous, logical in your actions, and clear as well as firm in any orders you might have to give them.

"Whenever you are obliged to deal harshly with them in the interest of the society at large, let your decisions be inspired by justice, and let a sense of humanity constantly govern any sanctions you might apply; like a leaf that the wind moves in spite of itself, the Danhomênou is unconsciously buffeted at every moment by a whole set of ancestral customs and therefore deserves to be treated with a good deal of indulgence. As you wait for him to develop a new consciousness of life according to your conceptions, be for him the Mother and the Father whom he always, and despite appearances to the contrary, sees in his Sovereign; goodness has a more powerful hold over his heart than tyranny, which he never mistakes for moral or physical superiority; whereas he admires the former, he eventually revolts against the latter, as the fall of Adanzan and the enthronement of Guézo demonstrates.

"The use of force to terrorize people's minds will produce an opposite effect. Filling the prisons with so-called trouble-makers and exiling them from the land of their fathers will only increase their bitterness and create popular sympathy for them; that is to say, it will confront your government with a whole army of uncompromising enemies who will be all the more dangerous because they will be close to the masses and exercise a powerful effect over them while posing as victims of the hatred of white men who oppose progress for the people of this country. From the fact that a few individuals allow themselves to be bullied without protesting, it would, I repeat, be a mistake to conclude that the masses are docile and can be oppressed with impunity. The revolt of a timid person who has been pushed into a corner is always dangerous! If you want to be understood and loved rather than hated, you should not speak to the color of these people's skin, but to their intelligence, which is receptive, and to their hearts, which are sensitive and impressionable.

"One cause of dissatisfaction might arise from a failure to make distinctions among Danhomênous and to cultivate an unjustified distrust toward the descendants of the ruling families. The responsible duties performed by the ancestors invariably mark the character of their descendants with nobility, and it would be a serious mistake to subordinate them to the former servants of their families under the pretext of effecting justice, or even, because birth is no longer supposed to determine social rank, to place them on equal footing with the descendants of men who have always played an insignificant role. The loyalty of members of the former ruling families toward the authority in power is indefectible. I am not saying that it is impossible to find men of value among former servants and that their merits should go unrecognized, nor am I contending that respect should be lavished upon the sons of the former masters when it has been shown that they are unworthy of their forebears.

"Give frequent consideration to the miseries of the people, not to mock them, but to remedy them and offer consolation. It was by such commiseration that our kings conquered the affection of their subjects.

"The Danhomênous learn quickly because their ancestors endowed them with a yearning for progress. Nowhere will you find a more disciplined and receptive intelligence than theirs. Look at what they have assimilated from your white man's civilization since they first entered into contact with it. Teach your language to the Danhomênous if you want them to understand and appreciate you, for the fertile union of souls is to be sought in a common language. You will quickly make yourself unpopular if you impede their progress and oppose their legitimate aspirations on the pretext that they are moving too quickly. It would be serious mistake to conclude from their atavistic servility that they are unable to reach great heights. Tributaries of the Ayonous when they first settled on this plateau and later prevented from trading with the white men for many years by the Houédanous, the Danhomênous eventually emancipated themselves from their former masters and even subjected them to their rule.

"Trust those who stand out from the mass and resemble you in their thoughts and in their way of life; they will help you communicate with their more backward brothers. Your disdain for the latter will always open wounds of the heart that are difficult to heal.

"The taxes that you pay to do business in Danhomê are insignificant in comparison with the profits that you realize in the slave trade. When it becomes your turn to collect these fees, do not impose ruinous exactions upon the Danhomênous and take all the fruits of their toil from them. If you do not want to make your government an objerct of abhorrence, avoid making them pay for the right to urinate, to spit, to gaze upon the sky, to walk in an upright position, to move about in the land of their fathers, to lie down on a mat, to sleep, to sell the produce of their fields or the work of their hands, to bury their dead, to celebrate their funerals, to laugh, to sing, or to organize their inoffensive dances.

"A veritable apiary, Danhomê will only allow substantial profits to be drawn from its honey by the man whose greed has not misled him into harassing the industrious bees.

"Decisively curb the covetousness that threatens to ruin this people and to discredit your administration.

"Don't deprive the Danhomênous of their fathers' land and transform them into common laborers under the false pretext that they don't know how to cultivate the soil and in the fear that, being intelligent, they might acquire money and power, enabling them to regain their independence rapidly; such expropriations would create a major source of difficulties for you because subversive ideas take hold more easily among itinerant laborers than among men who are attached to the farming of their ancestral lands.

"War, slavery, and human sacrifice should be eliminated from the customs of these people. But other institutions reflect honor on them and should be preserved in your interest as well as in that of the Danhomênous themselves.

"Zojagués, listen well, if you foster the native virtues that reside in the hearts of these people and enlighten their minds, if you only send to Danhomê those of your sons who can represent you with dignity, the spectre of revolt will never be seen here!"

"The uprising of Danhomênous against the masters you are wishing upon them is a chimera, just like the dream of the mahi slave who saw himself being carried toward his native mountains in a hammock by two princes from Danhomê, where he was receiving his daily rations!" interrupted Doguicimi's companion, who had been listening very attentively to the counsels she had been giving to the Zojagués about the governance of this country.

"It's perhaps not as unrealisable as you think, sister of my unhappiness!"

"The Danhomênous would need a great spiritual strength and a sense of solidarity that they are far from possessing. Moreover, suspecting the possibilities of these people, the white men would make short work of annihilating their will and sowing discord among them by favoring some and persecuting others. Witness what these beasts from the sea have made of that beautiful race of Houédanous."

294

"Let's not push things so far," Doguicimi protested.

"Isn't it true that Awliponouwê used alcohol to pave the way to victory over Sahé for the armies of Danhomê? And don't the white men continue to drown our country in this poison so admirably suited to bastardize and bestialize our race?"

Doguicimi was obliged to agree. After a moment of reflection, she declared: "As for me, I see the possibility of a lasting union between the two races; all we need is for the Zojagués to understand their duties of protection toward the Danhomênous and for the Danhomênous to show evidence of their loyalty. . . ."

The conversation of the two prisoners was brought to an end by the visit of Cangbodé, who was making his rounds after four long market days of absence to assure himself that all his lodgers were present.

Left to herself, Doguicimi cursed the white men. She no longer made any distinctions among them. She no longer had any preferences; she only saw the vile beasts from the sea who were the cause of her unhappiness; she found them inconsistent, ungrateful. Her rancor was intensified by the thought that the initiative of the Ambassadors was going to delay the planned expedition to liberate her husband, a prisoner of the Mahinous.

Chapter 9

The War of Revenge Against Hounjroto

Yévogan and Chacha reassured Agbomê with regard to the Ambassadors' sentiments. Dêmênou's report arrived to confirm the information that the Governor of Gléhoué and the king's "brother" by oath had provided: "At the end of the farewell banquet that the white men of Gléhoué had held for them, the leader of the mission had acknowledged his failure and declared that he would advise their sovereign to allow the passage of time to disarm the Danhomênous and improve them."

Nevertheless, Guézo still remained somewhat mistrustful.

One morning Gaou suggested that they go to war without delay. Adouconou was of the opposite opinion. Fearing a possible attack on the part of the white men, the prince proposed they not leave Danhomê before the beasts from the sea would have had time to go back to their lair and return with instructions for war.

Possou overcame the court's hesitations with the following arguments: "Inaction soon inspires people's hearts and arms with cowardice and allows them to grow unaccustomed to war. Even without major expeditions against distant enemies, a few small campaigns would inure our soldiers to the hardships of war and hold all our enemies in check. Our standing army of men and women, an innovation of this reign, was not, as far as I know, created for the pleasure of staging parades. How can the Master of the World be expected to justify himself in front of his ancestors for his failure to fulfill the promise he made them, when he took possession of Danhomê, to undertake a war every year to avenge the outrages committed in the past by the Mahinous, the Nagonous, or the Ayonous?

"The seventh year of Guézo's reign thus witnessed the conquest of Sêssêgnigo in mahi country; the end of the eighth year was marked by the joy of our victory over Dassa-Lêmon; Ajassê[1] was destroyed in the middle of the ninth year;

---

[1] Ajassê was also in mahi country. (author's note)

the campaign against Doïza, also in mahi country, was undertaken the following year, and it too was successful; it was then that the king deified his son Guéchangon and created Zahohinnou for the worship of this new god he had given to the Danhomênous."

These victories gladdened the hearts of the people and gradually effaced from their minds the memory of the defeat they had suffered at Hounjroto and the humiliation of knowing that two of the king's brothers were being held prisoner there, but they also heightened the rancor of Doguicimi, who was indignant because the king failed to understand that the conquest of Hounjroto and the liberation of Toffa and Assogbaou would do him greater honor than his battles against small harmless tribes, while earning Danhomê the protection of its dead kings far more effectively than the worship of the most obscure deified princes could ever do.

Doguicimi was determined never to cede to an illicit love, although Vidaho still nourished the hope of overcoming the resistence of Toffa's faithful wife, although he had become a bit more prudent in his visits, which had become the subject of gossip; yet despite the assurances he had given himself, he was haunted by a certain anxiety.

At the beginning of the eleventh year of his reign, Guézo decided to go to war against Hounjroto before anyone caught sight of the new moon that would emerge upon the death of the present one, which was already covering the calabash.

One morning he informed the council of the throne in assembly at Agrigomê: "It is time to go and conquer Hounjroto. The espionage missions we have sent there report that Toffa and Assogbaou only endure their captivity because they are sustained by the hope of being liberated.

"Since they have not seen us return during the first three years after our defeat, the Mahinous are convinced that we have abandoned our desire for revenge.

"Our first campaign failed largely because it was undertaken during the dry season; at that time of the year all the Mahinous had loaded their guns for hunting.

"This time we will attack during the rainy season; the growth of the new foliage is complete, and the forests can hide us for many days as we lie in wait for the opportunity to take our enemies by surprise. Circumstances will be favorable; at this time of the year, the Mahinous are working in their fields. Even when handled with the greatest skill and courage, farming implements are incapable of holding their own against our guns and canons."

The oracle informed the court that the ancestors did not support Migan and Vidaho, who alone advised them to temporize.

Many diviners were asked to interpret the same oracle and to conceal nothing of the predictions it had made, even if they were unfavorable. Although consulted separately, they all foresaw victory.

The first minister had to acquiesce in the opinion of his peers, but not without offering a final piece of advice: "The Master of the World should refrain from participating in this campaign, despite the fact that it seems to have been endorsed by the ancestors. His soldiers will bring back the victory to Agbomê."

Gaou took upon himself to respond on behalf of the king: "Ever since Agaja was wounded on the field of battle, his successors no longer followed their troops into combat. But the tyrant changed the order of things. The only courtiers who can counsel idleness on the part of the king are those who cherish the secret desire to see Danhomênous reviling him and alleging to anyone who will listen that, as far as courage is concerned, he lags far behind the man who was overthrown in his favor. If the king decides upon this war, he must participate in it. In the case that our forces are victorious, there will be no glory in it for him unless he has shared in the dangers confronted by our soldiers. Moreover, what would be better than his presence to inspire our combatants with courage if they had just wavered under the vigorous onslaught of the enemy?"

Vidaho ventured a last word of advice: "Although the oracle is predicting victory, we have to anticipate the recurrence of what happened the first time at Hounjroto. My opinion is that the Master of the World should leave the task of punishing the stinking beasts from Hounjroto to his successor. Between now and then, the Mahinous' suspicions will have been completely dispelled."

The memory of the dangers Guézo had run during the first Hounjroto campaign were invoked by his heir to talk him into renouncing the the proposed war, but they left him utterly indifferent. He answered his counsellors sharply: "My ancestors will support us in the struggle because the motivation behind the new expedition is far more noble than the one that called us to arms against Hounjroto seven dry seasons ago. Indeed, the support accorded to Agaja by the Houégbajas under very similar circumstances will not be lacking in our case. Aren't we going to avenge Toffa and Assogbaou, who are the Topo-Daho and Dangban of this reign?

"The misfortune of the wild beast who lost his claws while chasing a doe is not anything new.

"I am going to Hounjroto, and if I do not succeed in conquering it, I will not return." He fell silent, gazed at the ceiling, and continued his reflections to himself. A moment later he shrugged his shoulders and said: "If it is not your destiny to perish at war, you can be thrown into the midst of the battle with your hands and feet tied, and you will return home, every hair on your head still intact. But since no one can foresee everything that Destiny holds in store for us, I am going to take steps for the case that I might not come back. The greatest misfortune for Danhomê would be the loss of its king and the heir to the throne in the same war. Therefore, Vidaho will not leave Agbomê."

The proposal to go to war was adopted. The counsellors were not to let any hint of it come to light. They swore themselves to secrecy, calling upon the ancestors of the king to vouch for their discretion.

Five days were devoted to the sacrifices that had been prescribed by the diviners and were intended to guarantee victory to the Danhomênous. All the ancestors received offerings with the request to protect the army of Danhomê. The king offered sacrifices to all the fetishes of Agbomê; he then sent Yévogan seven head of cattle to be sacrificed to Danhomê's seven major protective fetishes, which were worshipped in the maritime province: Dangbé (the python signifying wisdom), Hou (the sea that brings the white men and their wonders), Mawou (God, the Creator), Daguélé-Houéci (smallpox, the terror of criminals), Li (the land that generously nourishes people, plants, and animals), Zo (fire, the peerless destroyer), and Aladhouin (the Panther as Agassou, the common ancestor of the conquerors). In the name of the Master of the World, the Governor promised each of them two head of cattle if Danhomê proved victorious over its enemies.

Along with other secret instructions, messengers carried to all the Governors of provinces the order to make offerings of brandy, chickens, and goats to the principal fetishes of their regions and to request their support for the victory of Danhomê's armed forces.

Having left their villages on the night following the morning when the war drums had echoed in even the most remote corners of the kingdom and assembled them in the huts of their commanders, the soldiers of many brigades from beyond the Swamps had been camped at Canna for two days. The army of the most important chief fetishists from the provinces was also waiting there for the orders of the king.

At Agbomé, Gaou and Possou spent their mornings closeted with their brigade leaders at Agrigomê, studying the cloth that Zanbounou had brought back from his first espionage mission to Hounjroto; fifty chief warriors were crouching over the cloth, their eyes wide open and their attention focused on the matter at hand. The spy's fingers and, following their lead, the imagination of the onlookers strolled through the maze of mahi paths that were indicated by long, narrow bands of ash-grey cloth the color of the soil in this country of granite; then they explored all parts of the forests, represented by bizarrely shaped pieces of green cloth; they counted the giants in the forests; they scaled the grey hills that were marked by triangular pieces of ash-colored cloth as Zanbounou pointed out the steepest sections and the routes that led safely to the top; they traveled through the villages and farms of Hounjroto and located all the most important buildings, whose round ashen-colored walls were symbolized by rectangular patches no larger than the first joint of a little finger and topped by those funnel-shaped pieces.

The conscientious guide did not forget the wells that the mountain people had dug on the plain and those they had found on the ridges of the hills; these had been marked by tiny pieces of cloth in the shape of the gourds used by the Mahinous to carry water to their houses. After having traveled through the

300

three hundred and thirty one villages and farms of the country, they were now reconnoitering the immediate surroundings of Hounjroto; they walked around the capital and counted the entries; they passed through the main one, crossed the city, left by another gate, and then returned by way of a third one; they were so diligent that they knew all the entries to the city in no time at all. They paused in front of the houses of the country's four regents – Cotovi, Ajahini, Agougni, and Boussa-Ahêli.

Their misgivings had been put to rest a long time ago; Zanbounou and his followers took advantage of the situation to explore their houses at leisure without arousing their suspicions about the identity of the men who were being introduced into their homes by captives taken during the last war the Danhomênous had waged against them. They say that a stranger with large eyes never sees things in a country as clearly as a native inhabitant with small ones! The Danhomênous in Zanbounou's party could argue that this was a false assertion and boast that Hounjroto no longer held any secrets from them, for they would soon demonstrate that they knew all the enemy's weak points as well as all the exits and passageways in the residences of their chiefs and in the huts where the two princes were being held prisoner by the Mahinous.

Gaou then guided their steps across mahi country on the living canvass.

After him, Possou retraced the same itinerary, his companions following him with open ears and eyes attentive to everything.

During this time the "Ahossitins" (eunuchs) were walking about among the counsellors and the pillars of the reception room, their vigilant gaze continually scrutinizing the tops of the pillars and the framework of the roof, as well as the walls, in search of any lizard imprudent enough to approach the counsellors; if one were sighted, upraised clubs would immediately descend upon it and execute the death sentence upon the traitorous creature who had come to collect state secrets with the intention of betraying them. As all the diviners agreed, this was the cause that lie behind the widely deplored divulgence of important secrets in the kingdom of Danhomê, the loyalty and discretion of the counsellors themselves being above suspicion.

Considering that the knowledge the brigade leaders had just acquired of mahi country was sufficient, the two ministers of war now assigned each of them a site to be occupied at the beginning of the siege and an objective to be attained as soon as the army launched its attack.

Zanbounou and his assistants were confined to Migan's residence; they would not leave it except to follow the king to war under a watchful escort.

All the battalions camped at Agbomê and Canna were reviewed in minute detail by the two military leaders. Several kegs of gunpowder were expended to make certain that all the guns and the forty-four canons they expected to take with them were firing properly.

The army of doctors as well as that of various diviners and casters of spells were actively concerned with completing their stocks of gris-gris and the objects from which to make more of them if necessary; they were also gathering together the ingredients for the sacrifices that would be offered during the campaign. At the waning of the day, as at dawn, a messenger was sent to the ancestors with the request to apprize their successor on the throne of Houégbaja in clear terms, either through the voice of the oracle or in a dream, if they had changed their opinion with regard to the projected war, or if they foresaw any causes for defeat that remained unsuspected by the living.

The king still did not receive a counter-order from the ancestors in his dreams; consulted several times during the day, the oracle invariably continued to affirm that the ancestors would support the Danhomênous. Small bags of shot manufactured with iron brought from Gléhoué were sent each day to Possou and Gaou by Ajomou, the master blacksmith from the Dozoémê section of the city; Ton, the chief of the blacksmiths in the Tongbonou and Ajahito neighborhoods; and Agbanlin, the master blacksmith at Dossoumingbonou; these balls of shot were half as large as the top of a man's forefinger.

*   *   *

At the close of the council meeting held on that morning of "adogouin," the king passed through the Door of Takinbaya and appeared before the people, who had been assembled in front of Agrigomê by the discreet instructions of Migan's emissaries. The Master of the World was dressed in his war costume. As he approached, he stamped angrily on the ground. He was no longer accompanied by his following of queens or his usual crown of parasols. A cloth that passed under his right arm pit was knotted on his left shoulder above his war tunic, thereby allowing him complete freedom in the use of his arms. On the outside of it he had belted his cartridge pouch; his head was covered with a sort of two-sided hood that concealed his ears beneath a chin strap that was attached to the the back and held it in place when the head was exposed. This headpiece had been dyed red, and like the rest of his apparel, it sported gris-gris suitable for preventing the head, that sacred and eminently rational part of the human body, from being hit by enemy weapons.

A gun on his left shoulder and holding a buffalo horn filled with gunpowder in his right hand, the king delivered a long invocation in a powerful, staccato voice, concluding with words calculated to activate the gris-gris. The people understood that the buffalo was going to fall upon an enemy country to sow death and devastation there. In the end he called Possa, Migan's principal assistant, and gave him the powder horn.

Facing Amagnanlankan, the dignitary passed him the powder.

On his knees, the latter called Gaou and Possou. The people, as usual, lent their tumultuous support. The two ministers of war came running from the other side of the Courtyard; they kissed the ground, covered themselves with dirt, and sat up on their knees, their upper bodies stiff.

Amagnankanlan covered their heads with a scarf that had been dyed red, belted them with cartridge pouches, gave each of them a gun, and then held out the powder horn to them, saying: "Houégbaja commands you to avenge its offended honor!" Each grabbed the horn with one hand and said: "I am holding it!"

The king, who had continued to invoke his gris-gris, interrupted to explain to his two ministers of war: "I am giving you powder with which to conquer the country that dared look direrctly at Danhomê, the sun at its zenith!"

That was the signal to the people that the war was about to begin. But their thoughts became lost in a thousand conjectures, in which were mingled the names of the Ayonous, the Mahinous, and the beasts from the sea. They didn't know exactly what to believe. The length of the invocations and the vigor of the king's voice told them only that Danhomê was preparing to engage powerful enemies in battle.

The king went back into the Palace.

The next day "Aflémougan"[2] started tinkling at the break of day.

The warriors and the non-combatants gathered in the Courtyard of Singboji.

The sun was climbing toward the height of the ear. The court left the Palace through the Door of Takinbaya. Drums, bells, and horns singers cast music into the air, and singers added refrains that were calculated to bolster the courage of the most timorous.

The royal procession got underway, headed toward Zassa, the Palace of Pingla on the outskirts of Agbomê, circled it, and then departed for the Palace that Agaja had built at Hoja. From this small occasional residence, the royal procession eventually wended its way to Pêtêgnonpa, where a large enclosure had been erected for the court the night before by the servants of Hounpatin.

The enormous Courtyard that stretched out in front of it was swarming with Danhomênous over an area more than two hundred bamboos long on every side.

Avoutou, dogba, and the "birds of the king" announced the appearance of the king with their respective detonation, beating, and chirping. The people laying prostrate in the dust at a distance of three bamboos from the barrier were already covering themselves with dust and tumultuously addressing wishes to their Creator for a long reign free from troubles, when Migan's solemn voice imposed silence on the mob with a powerful, "Danhomênou, that's enough!" The king's face was sombre and anxious.

With a very discreet sign, he motioned the first minister to approach and whispered into his ear.

Standing and facing the people, the spokesman for the Master of the World said: "Danhomênous, ever since Topo-Daho and Dangban, descendants of Houégbaja, died at Wémê during the reign of Acaba. each of our kings has been under the obligation to conquer at least one city in Wémê to honor the remembrance of these two princes. Because we failed to avenge their memory rather than that of the white men killed at Kinglo, we did not receive the support of the ancestors during the war against Hounjroto, as they themselves informed the Master of the World upon his return from that expedition. Although he now has the support

---

[2] "Aflémougan" was small double bell that was sounded to order the people to assemble in the Great Courtyard of the Palace. (author's note)

of his ancestors, who have assured him of their protection in the battle against the Wémênous, the Predestined King hesitates to take up his arms. He fears that his soldiers will prove no more courageous than those who followed him to Hounjroto!"

He fashioned such an expression of anxiety on his face and injected such a tinge of sorrow into his voice that the people were moved to solicitude for their Sovereign.

Roused from his place by the indignation he felt against the cowardly soldiers of the first campaign against Hounjroto, a colossus, who had until now remained hidden among the prostrate crowd at the foot of the throne, took four large strides and stopped within a half-bamboo of the barrier. He covered himself with dirt. Standing and facing the throne, he said: "Let the Master of the World be reassured! An army comprised of creatures as large as me can not be defeated on any field of battle. If these Wémênous feel secure on the other side of their river because the first rains have swollen its waters, those of them who are spared from our clubs will abandon their illusions as soon as our ropes begin to cut into their arms and the points of our swords prod them toward Danhomê! Danhomênous do not know how to swim, that's understood! But is anything impossible for a man of strong will? If ordered to do so by the Master of the World, I and my brothers in the army of the giants will at this very instant cast our bodies into the river and make them into a living bridge over which our Creator can pass on his way to go and conquer Wémê!" His arms raised to the height of his shoulders and bent so that his clenched fists were facing each other in front of his chest, he had bowed slightly and stiffened his torso; his muscles rippled.

"If we grow weak," he continued, "may the Master of the World have us cut into pieces and our flesh fed to the caymans of the river!" He lay face down on the ground and covered himself with dust.

The Danhomênous were enraptured as they watched this colossus return to his place, his eyes gleaming. Courage and confidence emanated from his entire being.

Another soldier followed him; he too spoke in the name of his comrades: "When my army finds itself in the presence of these Wémênous, it will capture them and kill those who resist."

Danhomênous leaving for war still felt repugnance at the thought of a third eventuality, their own death, which was nevertheless quite possible.

A third soldier approached. He was a stocky man with muscled arms and bulging calves; stomping on the ground and striking his stomach with the flat side of his sword, he said: "If we return to Danhomê without victory, let the Master of the World have us beaten this way on the stomach until the blood begins to flow!" A murmur of admiration greeted this demonstration of strength and desire to conquer. The soldier was from Toffo's contingent; flattered, he rejoined the delegation of his brothers in arms; one of them whispered to him: "You promised too much from us. Are you forgetting that the Danhomênous have good memories and that victory does not hinge solely upon our will?"

Other warriors followed, then still others; from every mouth came nothing but promises to conquer, promises made in the name of their units in the army. Up to twenty of them appeared. The Danhomênous lying flat on the ground rejoiced: "With such a formidable army, victory is inevitable!"

That was not yet the end! Adouconou arose; introducing about ten soldiers, he announced: "The princes, from the descendants of Daco-Donou to those of my august Father, "The Pineapple who laughed at the Wrath of Lightning," have gotten together and equipped a thousand warriors chosen exclusively from the royal family.

"If the men of the people insist upon going to avenge Topo-Daho and Dangban, the princes who are their peers would consider themselves dishonored if they remained behind; they would therefore like to march at the head of the army and share in the dangers of the war against the killers of their brothers."

The king did not conceal his joy at this surprise that had been prepared for him by the princes. The people also rejoiced at it.

A soldier jumped on to the scene apparently from nowhere. Thick-set, head shaved, cheek bones and lower lip protruding, a masculine face – nothing about her revealed to the Danhomênous at first glance that she was a being with seven pairs of ribs. She was wearing a pair of breeches known as "pigs' ears" because small patches of material shaped in the form of this carnivore's ear had been sewn to them behind the knee. A large handkerchief folded in half and knotted in the back covered her chest, flattening her breasts and giving her figure a virile appearance; a sleeveless vest and a cartridge pouch belted across it contributed to this impression. A sort of hood that was split in the front and back and had pointed edges on either side was covering the holes that had been pierced in the lobes of her ears and then enlarged; they could have betrayed the weaker sex.

Her left hand was on her hip, her thumb pressing against her lower back and the other four fingers spread across her abdomen, her eyes sparkling; she said her name was Ganwoumê, and she spoke in a male voice, accenting her words with powerful blows that echoed through her chest as she struck it with the bundle of the five fingers on her left hand. For herself and all her sisters in arms, who, according to her, had nothing but contempt for the torments some of the soldiers proposed as punishments in the case of defeat, she promised: "If we are not victorious, let Migan tie us one by one to the mouths of the Master of the World's carronades and fire them so that nothing will remain of us!" As if to demonstrate that she was not joking, she threw her gun into the air and caught it between her jaws, which clamped over it like pincers; she walked back and forth, her hands on her hips, as she paraded the weapon in front of the admiring eyes of the crowd. Someone remarked that she belonged to the army of "Egbélémacou" (Let me not survive defeat!).

The king smiled, full of confidence. The Danhomênous were delirious with joy: "You are braver than a man! You have offered a glimpse of your unit's will to conquer! A handful of Amazons with your courage would suffice to defeat all the countries that are hostile to Danhomê!"

Guézo ordered that she be given a cloth and ten strings of cowries; he then announced that she would, from that moment on, be adjutant to the brigade leader in the woman's army, promising her additional rewards upon their return from the war if her conduct under fire proved consistent with her words.

Standing up and facing the people, who were lying face-down on the ground, as well as the two kneeling ministers of war, the king declared: "I want the enemy king, his favorite wife, his eldest son, his first minister, his principal diviner, and the pontiff of the fetishists in his kingdom to be brought back to me alive!"

At every mention of a person whom the king desired to have captured alive, Gaou noted his sovereign's wishes in these terms: "The war will spare him!"

Assured of victory by his soldiers' solemn vows to defeat the enemy, the king instructed them: "I want you to bring back, intact and without destroying it, a plant that accidentally happens to be mixed among the straw and might be uprooted along with it![3] I also want your weapons to spare the infirm, the weak, the sick, pregnant women or those in the labors of childbirth, old people, children, and, in short, anyone who is not armed to fight against you!"

Sogan reinforced the king's order: "Let all warriors hear and scrupulously abide by the strict recommendations that were passed at the first secret council meeting during which this war was decided upon; they will be repeated on this day when gunpowder alone will have the right to speak."

Migan informed the people that the Master of the World was encouraged by his soldiers' promises to vanquish the enemy and had decided to go to war immediately. He would entrust the Danhomênous to the ancestors and to the protective fetishes of the kingdom.

In passing, the first minister reminded everyone of the inexhaustible treasure that was awaiting all those who followed the king into the dangers of battle and contributed to avenging the memory of the princes Topo-Daho and Dangban.

He concluded by insisting upon the duty of the people who would remain behind in Danhomê; every morning and every evening they should implore the ancestors to grant victory to the Master of the World's army.

As far as the people were concerned, they were unaware of the preparations that the court had been making in the greatest secrecy for many years, and they were convinced that the war had just been decided, that the king was only going to fight the Wéménous, and that the attack would begin that very day.

This was not yet the case at all!

Reassured about victory and about the combatants' attitudes toward those whose condition or infirmity placed them at great physical disadvantage and ought to be respected, the king joyfully started back toward Agbomê.

The war was no longer mentioned in public for three market days. People were asking themselves if the planned campaign had not been abandoned at the last moment.

Meanwhile, the wives of high dignitaries, princes of the blood, and heads of the royal families were receiving grain or dried meat and preparing millet flour,

---

[3]   By means of this expression, one refers to a foreigner who had not entered the country with the intention of lending it his support. (author's note)

fried bean cakes, roasted maize, hard akassa, fried fish, and other dishes that would last for several market days without spoiling.

The battle captains reviewed the soldiers of Agbomê and Canna and had armaments and accessories for about twenty shots distributed among them – a gun, a cartridge pouch, an antelope-skin bag, a gourd with granular powder, another with finely ground powder, four handfuls of shot, three flints, a ball of wadding the size of a man's head, a club called a "mapo" (stick of fury), a new sort of sword that had been invented during this reign and was therefore called the "sword of Aligo," and a leather rain shade to protect the breech of the gun from rain.

Each soldier had received ten joints of roasted maize for food and, to drink, a gourd of water no larger than a cow's bladder.

To these supplies, the king had added a locally manufactured cloth that the soldiers had folded lengthwise and tied around their waists. They understood, without needing to have it explained to them, that this cloth would serve them as a shroud in case an enemy weapon should fell them forever on the field of battle and if their brothers in arms had the opportunity to accord them a burial that might preserve their bodies from the decapitation that was customary in these wars.

The soldiers were not authorized to supplement their equipment except with gris-gris that could render them invulnerable to enemy weapons or arrest sudden attacks of illness during the campaign.

*   *   *

The diviners who consulted the oracle with strings of apple core hulls and those who used palm nuts to make Destiny speak were once again called upon to query the ancestors, who affirmed that they were abiding by their promise to guide the Danhomênous to victory.

The Muslim diviners also gave the same assurances after having examined at great length the lines that had been traced on a carpet of white Canna sand spread out in front of them.

They could now march without fear upon the enemy. The army left Agbomê as night was falling. The fetishists came first, invoking their fetishes for the success of the army; the soldiers and the court followed in silence. Zanbounou and his assistants had been tied up and placed under heavy escort. It would be unfortunate for them if the army fell into an ambush! That would constitute proof of their betrayal, and it could only be expiated by death. Porters from Agonli were laden with supplies of food and munitions of war; besides those that had been distributed among the soldiers, they were carrying enough to conquer four countries. The court had food for one moon. Adouconou, the regent at Agbomê, would resupply them if necessary.

Noucounzin came to inform Doguicimi that Vidaho had convinced his august

Father to undertake a war of revenge against Hounjroto and that the soldiers were already on their way to Canna, where they would pick up the army units that had been summoned from the provinces beyond the Swamps and were presently stationed in the sacred city. The princess concluded her string of revelations with the admonition not to let anything come to light. For a long time, Toffa's wife prayed the kingdom's fetishes and all the dead kings to bestow success upon the army of Danhomê. She also requested their benedictions for the reign of Guézo. She repented the harshness of her attacks upon the king, whose ancestors saw into the depths of her heart and, as she said to herself, knew that only the unfortunate fate of her husband, one of their sons, had incited her to utter blasphemies against Guézo. She vowed to make offerings to the ancestors as soon as Toffa returned and thereby calm the anger of those she had offended by her curses against Danhomê, whose life, power, and prosperity were so close to their hearts.

All night long the ground reverberated with the tread of the departing soldiers. By the third crowing of the cock, the army was encamped in a forest; it would not be leaving until the following night. Another thousand bamboos, and it would be on foreign soil. The soldiers still did not know which tribe they were going to fight.

During the day the two ministers of war and the battle captains huddled over Zanbounou's cloth map, locating once more the villages, the farms, the forests, the hills, and all the other points of interest around Hounjroto.

Consulted from one moment to the next, Destiny continued to assure them of victory; the court did not fail to perform any of the sacrifices he prescribed to bring it about more quickly.

The army got underway as the day was expiring and soon arrived in the region of the mountains; the soldiers received the order to put on their sandals. The entire "dassa" country was sleeping in the hills and had not the slightest suspicion that the army of Danhomê was passing in the plain below.

Zanbounou assured them that the first crowing of the cock was coming from Mopa. The court held a meeting of the council. Opinions were quite divided over the course of action to be adopted in attacking this mahi country.

When Destiny was consulted, he declared: "The egg that is not brooded will never hatch!" The evidence was clear. The army followed the sage advice, believed to have been found in this declaration, and advanced with great deliberation. They would know when they returned!

The soldiers were then told they were going to liberate Toffa and Assogbaou. By the second crowing of the cock they had reached the region of Hounjroto. Zanbounou asserted that Hounjrogonji, the capital, was no more than some two thousand bamboos away. The army could make camp at this distance from the city, and the king could set up his headquarters here, for Destiny, having been consulted and reconsulted many times, invariably announced that the ancestors were certain no danger would threaten the spot from which the handful of dirt presented to the oracle had been taken.

As a measure of prudence, relays of horses and hammocks with soldiers had

308

been stationed in each border village of Danhomê. Infinite precautions were taken to assure the Master of the World's safety in this place.

Moreover, he was full of confidence because he had armed himself with Achocoun and Jantra, two powerful gris-gris that would make him invisible if he were attacked by the enemy.

The battle captains and their armies took up their positions in the forests or on the hills assigned to them by the two ministers of war. Members of the Dangbénon and Houécinon families[4] as well as the doctors had been spread out among the different units of the army. The worshippers of Python would remove the sacred snakes that might be encountered in the forest, making offerings to them and supplicating their favor on behalf of the army; when they returned from the war, they would bring these fetishes back to the great Temple at Gléhoué.

The presence of the worshippers of Smallpox in their midst was very reassuring to the soldiers. This deadly fetish often lent support to the enemy and decimated the entire army before a single shot could be fired.

The chief fetishists knew how to mollify him as soon as he had aimed his arrows at a few of the soldiers.

Chief fetishists from the other cults had been equipped for purely formal reasons; their duties here consisted of invoking the protection of fetishes for the armies of Danhomê; in the case of a victory they would assume responsibility for taking the fetishes of the conquered country back to Danhomê so they could henceforth protect the kingdom of Houégbaja; novices captured in the shrines would also be brought back to Danhomê, where they would complete their initiations.

In each brigade ten soldiers disguised as itinerant traders assured the liaison between headquarters and the various army units; they were carrying the traditional porters' racks with an assortment of the white man's wares – brandy, tobacco, pipes, glass beads, mirrors, and cloths of velvet, satin, and damask as well as other items.

The man who had been singled out by Zanbounou as his most trustworthy assistant, and in whom the oracle informed them they could have confidence, was entrusted with the mission of going to Hounjroto in his usual guise as an itinerant trader and observing once again the Danhomênous being held captive in the residence of the four regents.

The Mahinous who encountered these traveling merchants along the paths to their farms declared that, if it were not for these brave Zadonous who exposed themselves to all sorts of dangers in order to resupply Hounjroto with the white man's goods, the people of the mountains would be utterly bereft of these fine things in their lives. They complimented them. With alacrity and a smile, the flattered traders offered their wares for sale, boasting of their quality and requesting information about nearby farms and populous villages. Everywhere people wanted to buy gunpowder. Feigning regret, they claimed they didn't

---

[4] Dangbénon was the chief fetishist of Dangbé (the Python), which had originally been worshipped only by the Houédas. Houécinon was the chief fetishist of Daglé-Houéci (Smallpox). (author's note)

have any and added: "It seems the white men are fighting a war in their own country and using up a great deal of powder; they're no longer supplying it to Danhomê." The traveling merchants promised to bring powder on their next trip.

"Their goods are certainly cheap!" several Mahinous confided to their companions. "They've just arrived in this country and aren't yet as greedy as those who have been here before!"

"You'll see, it won't be long until they've been corrupted by the old ones, who'll teach them a lesson or two. In the meantime, let's take advantage of the situation!" replied those to whom these confidences were addressed.

The Danhomênous continued to pretend that they understood nothing of the conversation.

People bought a chunk of tobacco and then obligingly pointed out villages where families were making preparations for a fetish or marriage ceremony and had been seeking such and such an article for a long time.

The traders thanked them, then joyfully hoisted their burdens.

The Mahinous went on their way without suspecting anything. At a turning of the path about two hundred bamboos away they would be taken captive and gagged by soldiers who were following in the wake of these so-called merchants. Mahinous who resisted were bludgeoned to death on the spot.

Escorted to the army's headquarters and interrogated in great detail by Ajaho, the prisoners who willingly provided the information that was requested of them were spared and dispatched to Danhomê; they traveled only at night, still gagged, bound, and placed under heavy escort. As for the obstinate ones, their throats were slit, and the gris-gris were bathed in their blood.

The liaison staff made a great show of activity.

Solicitude was lavished on diviners, doctors, and sorcerers. Weren't people convinced that victory depended, in part, on their science?

The first delivered long commentaries on the oracle resulting from their consultations; they subsequently proceeded to offer propitiatory sacrifices.

Guided by their profound knowledge of the properties of plants, the doctors would fight vigorously against any disease that might break out.

From the sorcerers' lips welled forth the appropriate incantations for activating the gris-gris that were supposed to keep all danger away from the king, his entourage, and the army, while allaying the enemies' suspicions.

Taking posts smeared with blood and pounding on them to drive them into the ground as they murmured the appropriate incantations, the two sorcerers entrusted with this task were certain they were burying in mahi soil all consciousness of the danger closing in on the country.

Other sorcerers kept vigil close to four small wooden statues to which they had given the names of the four regents of Hounjroto: Cotovi, Ajahini, Agougni, and Bossa-Ahêli.

These little statues were lying on mats and enveloped in cloths; they were like new-borns, for whom the role of mother was being filled by the four women sitting next to them, women of the people who had given birth on the eve of the king's departure for the war and whose babies had been entrusted to other women who had also recently given birth.

They offered their milk-swollen breasts to the statuettes, inviting them to suckle and then fall asleep. They rocked them gently, called them by their names, and interspersed their caresses with incantations dictated to them by the sorcerers and calculated to activate the gris-gris; an overwhelming torpor would thus flow into the minds of the four regents of Hounjroto; as if they had returned to infancy, they would be incapable of volition.

Great excitement among the creatures of the forests! They had all suddenly abandoned their homes in the face of a human invasion and were running toward the neighboring hills to seek refuge there, but they encountered their frightened hosts descending toward the plain; they too were fleeing the invasion.

The forest of Ayidohouêdo was seldom trod by human feet, and it would no doubt offer a secure hiding place! Yet wild beasts barely penetrated its borders before they retraced their steps, growling. Men even there! Men everywhere! They didn't shoot at the animals. They didn't even throw the smallest stone at them. They didn't set traps to catch them. But man was still the irreconcilable enemy of their species, and it was to shield themselves against him that they had invoked the protection of Aziza, the guardian spirit of the forest.

Once he had eaten his fill of the animals' flesh, man continued to torment them by beating on the skins from which they constructed their drums. Remaining where they were meant certain death and torture after death! Leaving the region of Hounjroto for someplace else would be the wisest thing to do! But where to go? Who knows if the hills and forests there might not also be occupied by the enemies of four-footed folk?

Panic-stricken antelopes, wart-hogs, and buffalos swept through the city. A doe who had been separated from her fawn by the invasion was filling the woods with her laments. She heard a reply and rushed in that direction; it was other fawns calling for their mothers.

The reptile folk had found salvation in the mass exodus; it poured into the city, where the straw of the roofs, the cracks in the walls of huts, the drainage ditches, the large rocks, the large vases placed under the edges of the roofs to collect rain water, and even the tiniest crannies offered them refuge from the danger.

The snakes and lizards who were betrayed by their inordinate length or girth or by the frightened shrieks of the chickens were beaten to death by the inhabitants of the huts.

After having wandered from one forest to another in the futile search for asylum, the wild birds were reduced to coming and nesting in the trees of the city, which soon filled with their tumultuous chirping; they also darkened the sky with their nervous flights. Others had left Hounjroto for safer skies. In nests abandoned by their parents, baby birds were cheeping endlessly. A few mothers appeared momentarily and then fled.

Their instinct having alerted them to an imminent feast, the vultures refused to go away. As they awaited a more copious meal, they assuaged their hunger with the bodies of dead snakes and other reptiles.

The tiniest beasts, even the insects, rushed away from the bush in fear; in the grass, the weakest of them were crushed underfoot by the invaders.

Mahinous who strayed into the forest to look for medicinal plants, firewood, and construction materials were captured; at Guézo's camp they suffered the same fate as their fellow tribesmen who had been taken prisoner as they were returning home from their farms or going out to their fields.

More energetically than ever, the Danhomênous completed their knowledge of the country by taking advantage of a passivity their gris-gris induced in the minds of the Mahinous.

In each brigade, look-outs posted at the tops of giant trees in the forest provided their superiors with detailed information.

Their directions allowed the impromptu merchants to shoulder their burdens and hasten to their encounters with Mahinous heading toward the city or the farms; they also permitted the soldiers designated for this purpose to proceed with the capture of these groups of enemies.

The information gathered at the different observation posts was dutifully transmitted to Gaou and Possou, who informed the king of it.

It was morning on the third day of the siege. Members of the liaison staff had just informed the court that the men's stools were still plentiful, soft, and yellow; they had thus not yet broken out the provisions of roasted maize. "Despite orders to the contrary, many soldiers must have left Agbomê with akassa and fried meat," remarked Migan. The king shrugged his shoulders. The diviner resumed his commentaries on the oracle after having been obliged to interrupt them while the court listened to the messengers from the brigade leaders.

As day was lapsing into darkness, the entire liaison staff carried this message to the various units of the army: "The ancestors appeared to the Master of the World in a dream during a short siesta they imposed on him at noon today; they assured him of victory only on the condition that the attack be delayed. It is absolutely forbidden to speak, to break the smallest twig, or to move from your station unless you receive orders from your superior. Avoid anything that might reveal the presence of the army of Danhomê in this country. Let the lookouts keep their eyes open and discover as much as they can about Hounjroto. Half the soldiers are authorized to take turns with the other half in keeping watch during the night."

The ancestors had spoken; their Representative in this world had transmitted their will to the soldiers. Who could dare disobey?

The groups that had left the forest to carry out an order regained their positions as silently as they had departed.

Two days after this message, military leaders traveled through the forests, inquiring into the condition and needs of the troops, while examining the ground more attentively than ever. Having completed their rounds, they communicated to the king that they had found nothing in the forests but hard, black turds that were, moreover, quite scarce; the soldiers had exhausted their akassa and fried meat and were now eating only the roasted maize that had been distributed to them before the departure from Agbomê.

The next day when the sun was rising overhead, members of the liaison staff came to inform Gaou and Possou that, by having asked several soldiers to give them something to drink under the pretext of being very thirsty, the battle captains had confirmed that most of the gourds of water were now empty. No more than a handful of maize remained in a few pouches.

The court considered it wise not to wait until hunger had eroded the strength of the soldiers' arms before launching them into battle against the enemy.

The Danhomênou who had been sent to Hounjroto the previous day had returned to headquarters during the night after having successfully completed his mission.

The council ordered the attack for the following night at the first crowing of the cock. The oracle declared that the ancestors approved of the court's decision.

The following message was communicated to all parts of the army: "The Master of the World has just learned that the soldiers' supplies of food and water are nearly exhausted. At headquarters too, people have seen the bottoms of sacks and gourds since yesterday. But Hounjroto is overflowing with everything that is lacking to the Danhomênous.

"The Master of the World orders the attack on this country to take place at the first crowing of the cock. The ancestors have assured the army of their protection and of victory!"

The instructions for the conduct of the war and the objectives assigned to each unit were repeated to the brigade leaders.

*   *   *

Weary of constantly anticipating the enemy for the first two years following the bloody defeat that had been inflicted upon them, mahi vigilence had relaxed considerably by the third long rainy season and become utterly dormant after the sixth one. Thus, at the beginning of this long rainy season – the eighth since that unjust aggression on the part of the Danhomênous had failed so abysmally – all Hounjroto had, as usual, abandoned the city for the fields, where this agricultural people was completely absorbed in tilling the soil and sowing seeds. A few rare individuals had brought their guns with them in case a wild animal might stray into the fields in plain daylight. But even they had only enough powder for three or four shots.

In the city as well as in the villages, one met only old people, women in the throes of childbirth, young girls, sick people, invalids, and children.

That afternoon a group of young people were chatting idly at the foot of a plane tree that stood majestically erect near the principal gate to the city, its massive branches shading the Courtyard for a distance of six bamboos.

Having returned from the bush, where he had gone to deposit the sacrifices prescribed by the oracle that had been consulted during the morning, Dêê was walking toward the tree.

His wrinkled skin was already loosening its hold on his flaccid muscles, revealing his advanced age.

Successive captivities at Agbomê, Gléhoué, and Hogbonou and then, after his escape from his last master, repeated journeys between Hounjroto and the country of the Zadonous in his capacity as an itinerant trader had contributed to the weakening of his body, yet they had also, in contrast, sharpened his mind, which remained vigorous and penetrating.

He was fond of saying that, in spite of his age, he could reach Agbomê in two days, were it not for the enormous gourd he was carrying. In this way, on the days when millet beer had put him in good humor, he poked fun at the infirmity with which he was afflicted and which remained but partially concealed beneath an apron that fell below his knees.

The young people were discussing the recent disappearances of men and women, disappearances that were extremely puzzling to the Mahinous.

Farmers who had left their farms and gone to the city with the promise to return to work the following day had not been seen at Hounjroto, nor had they reappeared at their farms. Those who had left the city to go to the farms were still being awaited there. Worried, their families had consulted the oracle without discovering anything in particular.

According to some of the young people, the missing individuals had no doubt been devoured by wild animals. Others imputed these disappearances to the presence of the robbers who infested the mahi country.

"But the robbers only steal children to go and sell them to the Zadonous! Now then, there are older people among the missing. Furthermore, the gluttony of wild animals would have had to grow beyond all proportions for them not to have spared a single person in a group of three or four Mahinous whom they were attacking! Would they eat everything down to the clothes of their prey? That would be strange!" objected someone in the group.

"Dêê always has an answer for everything," opined one of the young people. "He will no doubt be able to clear up the mystery which has been troubling people at Hounjroto and about which the oracle itself has remained vague."

All eyes turned toward the old man. Someone handed him a tiny gourd and suggested: "Start out by taking a good pinch of snuff, Dêê; it'll revive your memory. But have mercy on us and tell us only about the disappearances, for that's what we're interested in. Spare us your endless memories about the country of the Zadonous."

314

"Dêê will also have a wad of tobacco to chew, especially if he proves concise," assured one of the others.

"And precise at the same time!" added a voice from the back of the group.

Leaning over as if to examine his toes, another young man grumbled: "What truth do you expect from such senility?"

The old man seemed not to have heard this insolent remark.

He tapped the little gourd against his stick three times, opened it, and poured a pinch on the nail of his left thumb, which was completely encircled by the forefinger that he had bent around the outside edge of it. He moved the pinch up to one nostril, closed the other one with his right thumb, and breathed deeply. He remained stunned for a moment, his upper lip slightly raised as if he were about to sneeze. Coming to himself again, he said: "I will not reply to your idiocies until after another large pinch. Who knows whether or not I'll be able to take one tomorrow!" He helped himself to a second dose.

Two powerful sneezes followed his momentary daze and propelled the excess snuff from his nostrils; his entire body was jolted with a fit of shivering; his eyes were watering; his nose was running. "Young man, you can boast that you have no equal in this country when it comes to preparing a pinch!" he said in acknowledgment of his gratitude as he handed the gourd back to its obliging owner. "You said it, young men," he now declared to the onlookers, whose eyes were glued to his lips, "robbers only abduct children, and wild beasts don't eat the clothes of their prey. What you don't know is that every time our great fetish "Ayidohouédo" kidnaps a person, he immediately alerts the relatives through the voice of the oracle, and as soon as the cult is established in the family, the prisoner is freed. You yourselves realize that the oracle, which is ordinarily very precise, proved unusually vague when consulted about the fate of the missing individuals. None of the explanations that have up til now been given for these disappearances are satisfying to the mind. But there remains another one that is quite probable, although no one has yet envisaged it: these disappearances are the harbingers of great misfortunes. . . ."

Someone interrupted him: "Dêê is in the evening of his life. It's not surprising that he sees everything in gloomy colors. My opinion is that all these decrepit old bodies ought to be relegated to a hill, which they would only descend in time to fall into their graves, dug for them at the foot of the hill."

The old man disdained to notice this new insolence and calmly proceeded: "Yes, misfortunes are menacing Hounjrogonji, and it will not be long before they strike. These incidents of wild animals in the city are sure signs of an impending disaster. The regents should have consulted the oracle this very day to discover the exact thoughts of our ancestors and the protective fetish of the country. The negligence of those governing us can only be the result of gris-gris that the Zadonous have certainly prepared to allay our suspicions. Common Mahinous are putting themselves in the regents' place and worrying about the country's security.

"This rash of mysterious disappearances is only meaningless to simple minds.

"I wore my first loin cloth at Gbowêlê, my mother's home and a place to

315

which the Zadonous brought war during the reign of Agonglo, their seventh king. I fought at the sides of my maternal uncles. Taken prisoner, I was sold at Gléhoué after a long stretch in Agbomê. Less than a year later, my master disposed of me, along with a batch of twenty-five other mahi and nago catives, to a white trader who had come from Hogbonou to lay in a supply of slaves. Having landed up in the kingdom of Tê-Agbanlin, I soon acquired the confidence of my new master, who, hoping to drive any idea of escape out of my head and to assure himself of my fidelity, promised he would always keep me at the head of his cadre of domestic servants. I succeeded in escaping the night before the loading of the slaves on the beach at Hogbonou, for I had heard that this master was in the habit of drawing upon his cadre of servants to fill gaps in the cargoes he was sending to his customers. Ayidohouédo watched over me and guided my steps back to Houjrogonji, the land of my father. Since that time I have returned, I don't know how many times, to Gléhoué and even to Hogbonou in order to resupply the Mahinous with the white man's goods. These eyes have seen many things, just as these ears have gathered great quantities of information. That is to say, I know the Zadonous' military tactics extremely well. When these sons of dogs attack a country, they stay off the roads and even the paths, or they only appear on them at night. If necessary, they will lie in ambush for seven or eight days in the forest, preparing gris-gris and offering sacrifices to beguile the vigilance of the country's leaders while waiting for the most favorable moment to seize their prey. Anyone who leaves the city without suspecting the danger that surrounds him as well as those who return to their farms or enter the forests for any reason whatsoever are siezed and gagged before they can utter a sound. All those who try to defend themselves are beaten to death, dragged into the forest, and buried. The Zadonous deliver to their king those who, preferring slavery over death, allow themselves to be captured.

"I have good reasons for believing that this is the entire story behind the disappearances that have thrown the people into a turmoil for the past few days. Those shrill whistling sounds that can be heard from time to time during the day are warnings, given to us by Ayidohouédo, about the misfortune that is hanging over our heads. As much as these omens, the incident of the wild animals at Houjrogonji and the remarkable irruption in the city of birds and insects from the bush – don't they tell you anything? What other four-legged creature can dislodge the most powerful forest-dwellers from their lairs – the elephants, lions, and panthers that have been seen on the outskirts of Hounjrogonji?

"See how the crickets, locusts, and cicadas are rushing to the city. Listen to them; they've been chirping tirelessly since this morning. The cawing of the crows has become more ominous than ever during the last few days – doesn't it tell you anything either?

"Have the magpies been chattering so much for nothing the past three days?

"In normal times, are eagles, pelicans, parrots, and the other winged hosts from the great forests to be seen in the city?

"Why are owls and other birds of ill omen defying the light of day and mothers' curses to come and roost in our houses? Tell me what boas and vipers are seeking under the rocks and water jugs in our houses. Bush fires are not burning anywhere; on the contrary, the forest has regained all its greenery. As far as I can see, only the invasion of their retreats by men (and it could only be the Zadonous) offers a plausible explanation for the exodus of these creatures from the woods.

"Believe me, everything points to a cunningly prepared misfortune that is rapidly closing in on us. It has always been this way. But only the wise men understand their language.

"Without a care in the world, you have been enjoying yourselves for the last four days. A great amusement offers itself as an outlet for your youthful energies: you spend your days killing rabbits and bush rats. Your younger brothers, who can't yet hunt little animals, set traps for them. The littlest ones exhaust themselves capturing beetles and butterflies. Little Bossa, the son of my neighbor Bossou, gave me something to think about this morning. Chasing after a baby bird that was fleeing the invasion and had just collapsed in the courtyard, its wings fluttering, the child shouted: 'I'll capture you before they capture me!' His mother Boyivi burst into laughter at these words, which were no more than childish babble to her. I was unable to convince this woman that children are fetishes and that the truth to guide our steps often emerges from their mouths rather than our own, polluted as they are by slander, smut, and lies. The innocence of children must know more secrets than the longest meditations of the mature mind.

"However, that's not the case with you. You who pretend to have explanations for everything, you are no doubt going to find the motivation for the bush-dwellers' exodus in the wetness of the season. Your youthful love of life is revolted by the discovery of the hint of a shadow. Unfortunately, that doesn't prevent the clouds from gathering in our skies.

"Believe me, the storm is ready to break. Do you see that milliped coming toward us? (He was pointing at one of the insects that had been present in abundance since the beginning of the rains.) Misfortune is like him in certain ways; you can only make it impossible for the milliped to walk by breaking all his legs; similarly, we have to take a thousand precautions against the misfortune that threatens us and is, in contrast to the milliped, approaching at great speed.

"Once the gun has been fired, it's impossible to prevent the shot from leaving the barrel by placing your hand in front of it."

Dêê fell silent; his stare plumbed the sky, and his expression darkened.

Emerging from his meditations, he nodded his head and heaved a deep sigh.

In response to the old man's wisdom, the same young man countered with these insolent words: "If the diviner who predicts the war escapes unscathed, one of his relatives will surely perish in it!"

One of his neighbors added even more disrepectfully: "Life is gay for us and, moreover, full of promise. Let's not tolerate a deluded old man casting gloom over it with his pessimism and ruining it for us with his melancholy omens!"

The old man continued to accept such insolence with calm: "Will young people then increasingly disdain the instruction of the elders, through whom wisdom and experience speak? The misfortune that has been hanging over Hounjrogonji for eight dry seasons has descended and is now closing in on us without anyone here even suspecting it; this misfortune is attributable to people like you. Our country was enjoying friendly relations with Danhomê, and this had encouraged Guézo to ask us to allow his friends, the white men, to visit our region after they had traveled through Kinglo. We had acceded to his request, and five elders, of whom I was one, had offered themselves to guide these foreigners through the country. But several young men from Hounjrogonji went and stirred up the Kinglonous against the new arrivals, claiming that they were responsible for the endless wars waged against mahi territories by the Zadonous to acquire captives who were highly prized by these white men for their durability as farm laborers. These young agitators advised them to smash the white men's heads as if they were vipers. Following these criminal suggestions, the Kinglonous took advantage of the King of Danhomê's friends and killed them in their sleep.

"All Hounjrogonji was indignant at this crime. The council of the court quite spontaneously agreed to deliver the guilty individuals from here to the Zadonous. They refused our offers and used the pretext of the massacre of their friends to invade Hounjrogonji in the intention of subordinating it to their rule. However, no one is more jealous of his independence than a son of the mountains. The people of Hounjrogonji rose en masse to face the invaders and repel them.

"But for years we were unable to sleep without keeping one ear open.

"The Zadonous are returning at the very moment when we no longer expect them. They are surely laying in ambush somewhere. That's their usual strategy. I wish I were wrong! But if my predictions prove accurate, I will die without regrets. I'm through with buying and selling in this huge marketplace called the world; I have enjoyed life enough! Nothing interests me any longer. If the Zadonous do not deign to kill me here, I will certainly not reach Danhomê alive. Nevertheless, I don't want to be selfish. I feel sorry for you, young eagles who have not yet left your nests! The herders who are coming to take you by surprise will exact a cruel revenge on you for the injury your fathers inflicted on them.

"I'm telling you again – these feet have trod upon the soil of I don't know how many foreign countries (he pointed to his feet with their twisted little toes, beak-like nails, and skin that had been swollen by gnat stings and creviced by the roughness of the terrain); everywhere I encountered only young people who respected both the customs of their tribe and the elders who were the faithful guardians of them. One has to ascend into the mahi hills to find arrogant young people who push insolence to the point of irreverence.

"More than once I have already heard young hotheads asserting that the elders are shackles placed on their legs.

"You want to move quickly, forgetting, on the one hand, that you will never transcend the earth and, on the other, that haste invariably precedes a fall. If you no longer remember your own experience, take a look at what is still happening to your younger brothers who are in a hurry to free themselves from the hands

318

that support them as they learn to walk; they always fall. Only by listening to advice and words of encouragement from adults will those just starting in life ever succeed in finding their way without endangering themselves.

"Arrogant young people, you who are proposing to eliminate the old age you find so useless and vexing, if you want to break definitively with the elders, why don't you begin by draining from your body all the old blood that they set flowing there and that links you with all those who came before you in this world. Don't keep any trace of the things that have been marked by the memory of them. Stop speaking the language they taught you; create a new one to express your sentiments, which you will also have to reinvent. Don't walk in the same way the elders do. It's old fashioned and degrading for you. Devise a new way of moving about.

"Destroy all their handiwork that might profit you in any way: demolish houses, burn clothes and harvests, break the tools they passed on to you; make new implements without modeling them on those of the elders; abandon all the work techniques you learned from them. Outmoded, they are unworthy of you who are so full of ardor and creative intelligence. Don't work any of the fields that they watered with their own sweat to give you something to eat; clear new land, and bring it under cultivation.

"Level these hills that they have inhabited for such a long time; turn upside down all the lands that have been polluted by their feet.

"This sun is also old! It burned a long time for them! This moon gave light to their nights; extinguish them!

"Perhaps all that seems difficult to you?

"You were weak and poor when you came into this world, and to the elders who preceded you, you owe the clothes and shelter that protected you from the cold as well as the food and care that kept you alive.

"You will agree that the memory of all the pains they took for your benefit is humiliating. In the face of all these humiliations, you have only one option: die and reincarnate yourselves as adults. You will have to return to this world accompanied by everything that is absolutely essential so that you can dispense with the elders and all the things they contributed to your childhood.

"Once you have accomplished these miracles, and only then, will you have the right to despise the elders!

"Ah, you do not know what the world would be without us, the essence of wisdom? Well then, my children, listen to this song that I learned in the kingdom of Tê-Agbanlin, where it was addressed to people like you, telling them of a past event that is full of instruction."

The young Mahinou who took pleasure in contradicting Dêê objected: "But you old men are the ones who bear responsibility for the war that the Zadonous brought to Hounjrogonji. Desiring to purchase peace at the price of several young people's lives, you merely succeeded in whetting the appetite of the warlike passions of people whose unquenchable thirst for blood proves that they really are descendants of the Panther whom they claim as a common ancestor.

"For the Zadonous, who were already dreaming of conquering the Mahinous, that was clear evidence of your weakness. Yet everyone knows that they never attack anyone stronger than they are. Without your untimely zeal, therefore, the idea to come and disturb Hounjrogonji would never have occurred to them."

The audience became more compressed and grew very attentive. It wasn't that they believed the old man's auguries, but the attraction of a song about the Mahinous was irresistible, and wasn't Dêê getting ready to perform one of them that he had brought back from the kingdom of Tê-Agbanlin?

The old fellow informed the young men that his nostrils were calling for a bit of warmth.

The audience became impatient; nevertheless, Dêê unhurriedly took a pinch with which to stimulate his memory.

Emerging from his daze, he explained to his entourage: "It's already been several days since the little worms in my head received a pinch."

He gently pressed his nostrils together with the thumb and forefinger of his left hand and blew his nose loudly. Then he shook his hand rapibly back and forth, wiped his fingers on his thigh, and said: "It's not the right moment for songs. Perhaps I won't be able to sing them tomorrow? Let's do it as long as there is still time, Dêê son of Agonsavi!"

He beat the rhythm on his stick, which knocked against the rings on his fingers.

I

Youth who find old men troublesome
And would like to be quickly rid of them,
Listen to this song,
And don't forget the lesson it teaches:
The day after he first put on shoes,[5]
Dê-Messê[6] summoned the young people to a palaver.
Not one was absent. But all grey heads
Had been disdainfully excluded:
"I'm not the king of old men;
I want none of that decrepitude around me,"
Said the king to the youths lying before his throne.
"See how most of them are bent double;
They're already on their way to the grave.
When they've reached such a state, how do you expect
Them to judge properly the things of this world,
To which they hardly belong any longer?
When their words and their acts betray their senility,
And you make them aware of it,
They protest, pretending to be a sacred repository
Of experience and wisdom.

---

[5] In the kingdom of Porto-Novo, this expression refers to the enthronement of a king because he was the only one authorized to wear shoes, an emblem of royal authority. (author's note)

[6] Dê-Messê was the fifth king of Porto-Novo. (author's note)

Of folly, more likely, wouldn't you agree, my friends?
Believe me, before life and strength
Have decided to leave their worn-out bodies,
Reason has already fled long ago.
And yet this decrepitude shamelessly
Claims a supposedly sacred right
To demand our respect
And a place of honor at our assemblies,
To interrupt our speeches, to humiliate us,
And to dismiss our best thoughts as hare-brained ideas.
What good can we hope to find in senile minds?
Their advice leads only to laxity
And can but result in our misfortune.
Thus to govern this country.
I'll depend only on the youth.
They're its true strength:
The neighbors' greed is held in check
Because this kingdom has the good fortune
To have thousands of young men,
Whose courage alone can assure victory over its enemies.
If the old were no more than useless,
We could tolerate them while waiting
For the ancestors and protective fetishes
Of this kingdom to rid us of them!
But they corrupt to a large extent.
Being in the bleak evening of life,
They instill pessimism, born of their chill,
Into the soul of youth
To extinguish its ardor
Or to quell, at the very least, its passionate fury.
Yes, youth, the flame
That constitutes the pride of this kingdom,
Might be extinguished by the chill of old age,
Which is nothing less than water!
Fire cannot extend its sway
When confined by dampness.
Thus the health of us young people
And the best interest of the kingdom
Requires all our old parents to be put away!
I no longer have mine,
That you know very well. . . !"
The king left his audience
No time to reflect,
But rather made their heads swim with barrels of brandy
That were emptied in minutes.

Then he sent them away with the following words:
"Go, dear friends, and without delay
Eliminate the decripitude that disgraces our homes,
Paralyzes, what is more, the best initiatives,
And will by its very presence amongst us
Surely hasten the end of this kingdom.
As soon as you return home, use all possible means
To rid this land of parasites,
Which are, I repeat, a danger for you."

II

The young men returned home,
Their heads still warm with the heady brew
And the no less heady speech of the king.
Clubs, axes, hoes, stones, and machetes,
Intent on breaking them for ever and ever,
Fell upon the respectable repositories of wisdom,
Where, despite what the royal fanatic might have said,
Youth finds the light that guides them through life
And draws the strength that allows them to triumph
Over the misfortunes of this world.
Other old people were entombed alive
In abandoned wells.
These feeble bodies begged for mercy,
Implored in vain that they be allowed to go hide
Their decrepitude beneath other skies,
Since it seemed to offend the youth.
Breaking with ancestral customs,
Highly respected until their time,
The young people gave no thought to providing a grave
For the bodies of their victims;
They were piled high in fortification ditches
To the great joy of all necrophogous beasts,
Whose numbers promptly grew in the realm.
Hyenas filled the nights with their "oo-oo-hoo-oo!"
Vultures perched in great numbers on rooftops and trees.
The very next day an army of flies invaded the ditches.
Their music blended with the cries of gratitude
Addressed to Dê-Messê by the hyenas and vultures
For the great feast he was offering them;
Nauseous odors of decaying corpses
Rose from the ditches and moved toward the Palace,
Informing the king that his counsel had been followed.
Gbêtohocouê, the leader of the youth in the realm,
Came and said to his comrades

To justify his lateness for the meeting that morning,
"I beheaded my father.
For fear he might come back to life,
I cut him up, then buried a few pieces;
I threw parts in the water and burned the rest.
In truth, I'd been disgusted with him for a long time
And was secretly seeking a chance to be rid of him."
He told his story with a show of sincerety;
The blood that stained his clothes
Lent some credence to his words.

III
Our youthful assassins went to the Palace.
"Sire," they said after praising the wisdom of the king
And offering their wishes for his happiness and power,
"We executed your orders;
Purged of its fatal decrepitude, your kingdom
Is henceforth assured of long life."
How could they forget
That whatever lasts must of course grow old?
Didn't the fools reflect
That if everything destined to age
Is, in this kingdom, condemned to death
As useless, troublesome, and even harmful,
Whereas in reality most things improve with age,
The unhappy fate of older people
Would be reserved tomorrow for the executioner of today?
Delighted with his success,
The king ordered that barrels of brandy be opened.
At their leisure, the young criminals drowned
Their remorse in the white man's liquor
And then passed on to the feasting.
During the dance that followed,
They emptied another hundred kegs of strong alcohol.
Songs of joy rose to the sky,
Sustained by the drunkenness of all.

IV
Back in their homes,
Stinking and sweating of alcohol,
They mistreated their wives,
Their brothers, and their sisters who were
Still mourning their old parents, beaten to death.
The children who came to console their mothers
Were thrown violently aside by the assassins.
To protect these feeble beings, there were no more

Arms with white hairs,
That, under similar circumstances,
Rediscovered enough strength
To halt youthful anger at once
And all the tyrannies it fosters.
The roof no longer had a supporting beam;
A thunderstorm drenched it abundantly.
The house collapsed, its walls eroded by the torrent;
The family no longer had its protector,
And it was already beset with misfortunes.
All passions could be given free rein;
There were no more grey heads to respect!
Hadn't the young people broken the sacred vessels?

V

Dê-Messê allowed two market days to pass,
While his emissaries traveled throughout the realm;
They returned and informed the king
That all grey heads had indeed been eliminated.
A new palaver brought everyone to the Palace.
"My cousin, a king always victorious at war,
Sent me, on the occasion of my accession to the throne,
Ten enemy chiefs captured in a recent campaign
And asked me to sacrifice them on my predecessor's tomb.
I'd like to show this cousin that,
If his subjects have the virtues of war,
Mine possess a high degree of inventiveness.
Find me a present then to surpass
The one I just received."
The king waited and waited.
His gaze examined the soul of his court.
"Have rats gnawed the livers[7] of these lowly lizards?"
He exploded, full of disdain
For the prostrate crowd at the foot of his throne.
The banality of everything the young men proposed
Merely insensed him the more.
He railed against the poverty of their minds
And decreed they should remedy this flaw by themselves
Or his Migan would do so and diligently too.
More than one of them secretly wished
The earth would open and offer him a place to hide.
Heads turned anxiously to the right and the left,
Already seeking a refuge from the executioner's sword.

---

[7] In Danhomê, the liver is the seat of intelligence according to popular belief. A slow-witted person is regarded as one whose liver has been gnawed by a rat. (author's note)

Having discerned his subjects' terror in their tremors,
The king lowered his head, closed his eyes, and mused.
Emerging from his thoughts, he cried, "I got it myself!
My cousin is repairing the altars of his predecessors
In preparation for the next commemorative ceremonies.
I'll send him two hundred bundles of wood for building,
Five hundred bundles of thatch and as many of straw,
And three thousand coiled strands of red clay.
The day after tomorrow then, each of you will bring me
A hundred armspans of this cord, half as thick as your little finger.
I want it flexible, I want it strong.
Later we'll see about the wood, thatch, and straw."
"Sire," said the young men in voices tinged with fear,
"It will be done according to your wishes!"

VI
The whole country was soon filled with the sound of hoes
Furrowing the ground, breaking the clods,
And the songs of women preparing the workers' meals,
And the joyful shouts of children drawing water.
It was up to everyone to outdo his companion.
The clay was kneaded before the sun's darts came straight down
from above.
It was piled in heaps. Judging it sufficiently drained,
They decided the next day to draw it into strands.
Seated next to a pile, each worker placed
A handful of clay on his thigh.
His hand flattened it,
Then rolled it back and forth many times
As he drew it into a rope.
But he'd scarcely made a strand two fingerlengths long,
When it split apart. He put it back together.
With a bit of skill, he succeeded in making a span.
He wanted to test its strength:
A section remained in each hand.
"It's because the mixture is too thin!"
He added some sand,
Then set to work again,
But was no more successful in making strands of clay.
"Now the mixture is too thick!"
He recalled how, while braiding cords on their thighs,
The elders used to spit impetuously into their palms.
He followed their example, and his hand came into play.
The work failed to progress.
Soon discouragement, like an inner fire,

325

Dried up his throat.
His hand plunged into a calabash of water,
Passed across his thigh, and passed again.
The rope always broke before being drawn for a span.
He thinned the mixture with water.
It became slimy and sticky
And impossible to work.
He lost heart.
He ran to his neighbor to see if he'd been successful.
He too was embarassed and was coming for advice.
Sitting side by side at the foot of a clay pile,
The two friends united their efforts, but all in vain.
He rapped himself on the head.
His wit found no solution to suggest.
He lost patience.
Curses and stamping feet showed they were annoyed and discour-
aged.

VII

The young men chose to admit their failure to the king:
"Without the help of experienced people,
We were unable, Sire, to execute your orders,"
They stammered to Dê-Messê.
The king waxed furious:
"If in five days you've not brought me the desired rope,
The sixth dawn will inevitably witness your death!"
Gbêtohocouê fearfully glanced about.
Many of his companions had already fainted.
Back in their huts,
They did what they could,
But were unable to make two spans
Of "clay rope that is flexible and strong."
The king's threat returned constantly to haunt them.
Tears flowed.
They felt very unhappy
And bitterly lamented their old parents,
Who, if they were still alive,
Would certainly have found the answer to the riddle.
They asked each other,
If anyone hadn't had the idea
To hide his old father someplace or other
Where everyone might go and consult him at once.
But not a single old man, it seems, had been spared
During the massacre decreed by the king.
They sought in vain for a man who'd learned the oracle,

Hoping that the ancestors, consulted by this means,
Would take pity on their unhappy descendants
And deign to show them the way out of their dilemma.
They remained at the foot of their mounds of clay
Long after the sun had set;
Sleep overtook them, granting surcease from sorrow.

VIII

Gbêtohocouê did not fall asleep.
He alone had rebelled against
The heady speech of Dê-Messê
On the day when the king had counseled the extirpation
Of all grey heads in his kingdom.
In a neighboring country the young man had hidden
His old father Ayiwou,
The only relative he had in the world.
Gbêtohocouê went to the old man's side
And told him in tears
Of the death threat hanging over the young men's heads.
The old man laughed about it for a while:
"Ah!" he said finally, "if you had followed your comrades' example,
Your lack of skill in carrying out the king's orders
Would have given him the opportunity to eliminate
Those of you he found in the way
Of his ambitions.
Return with confidence to your hearth.
You still have, you say, four days
In which to give the strands to the king?
We have plenty of time then.
Come see me again tomorrow night
In the company of a few of your comrades;
I will reveal to you the quite infallible secret
Of drawing clay into ropes.

IX

The following night the delegation of young men gathered
At the refuge of the old man, who said to them:
"Ayiwou[8] is my name.
At the birth of your comrade here,
I named him Gbêtohocouê.[9]
My children, I learned from our elders
That the mind of man is
What makes him superior to other creatures,

---

[8] "Ayiwou" is a Danhomê name signifying "it is by means of intelligence." (author's note)
[9] "Gbêtohocouê" is another name from Danhomê; it complements the previous one and means,
"man has merit." (author's note)

And that we draw wisdom
From the advice of our old parents
To complete it later with our own experience.
Dê-Messê doesn't lack common sense,
And he knows very well that the wisdom of old men
Opposes the whims of youth.
Isn't he himself young too?
The elders he found troublesome,
Because they constantly reminded him when he was prince
To respect the customs he'd like to break at will.
Your ignorance of the past and the customs of our land
Proved favorable to his ambitions.
It was, you can be sure, to dominate you more easily
That the despot called for the death of your parents.
Fortunately for you, wisdom
Has not been utterly destroyed in our kingdom.
For that, you can thank your comrade Gbêtohocouê,
Who had the idea to find this sanctuary
For a former counselor of King Houdé,
The predecessor of Dê-Messê.
Intimately familiar with tradition in my fathers' land,
I more than once opposed
The caprices of the late king.
To my son I'll give the recipe
For rope made of clay,
And he'll do the work you all need to have done."
He motioned to the youth, who approached on his knees
And placed his ear next to the old man's mouth.
. . . .
Gbêtohocouê's face beamed with joy;
He now knew the secret so fervently sought.
"Return to the king.
My son will attend to making for you
The required lengths of clay rope.
Go in complete confidence to find the despot;
Not a hair on your head will be touched,"
Said the old man, wisdom incarnate, as they left.
But neither his words of encouragement,
Nor the joy shining in his son's face
Completely reassured the young men.

X
Many preferred to live out their lives elsewhere.
A small number of those who returned to the kingdom
Went to the Palace the next morning.

328

"They wouldn't have the courage to come empty-handed,
If they didn't have something inside their heads!"
Thought the king as he saw them coming with smiles on their faces.
They flattened themselves in the dust
And wished happiness upon the royal household,
Then, looking the king in the eye, Gbêtohocouê said:
"We are ready to execute His Majesty's command.
The king has, it appears, a length of clay rope
That he succeeded in braiding
When he was still heir to the throne.
This cord, a true marvel
That reveals the inventive genius of our revered Master,
Is still pliable and strong, although dry.
We undertake, my comrades and I, to stretch it
And furnish to the king, defender of youth,
A long enough cord
To link the opposite sides
Of the enormous calabash cover
That confines us on this earth."
He kissed the earth; his comrades followed his example
While at the same time pressing
Their right forefinger against their left little finger
And snapping it into the palm of their hand.
"There are still old men in my kingdom!
Bring them to me at once!"
Ordered Dê-Messê, amazed at the young men's wise reply.
Gbêtohocouê answered him:
"Sire, on your orders we got rid of them all."
The queens intervened to exonerate their husband:
"You can not hold the king responsible for your crimes.
Did he put weapons in your hands?
Your haste to kill your old parents
Proves that you yourselves had also been seeking
For a long time to rid yourselves of them!"

"Young Mahinous, you have not yet committed, it is true, the crime of those mentioned in the song. But you already despise the elders, who are treasures of wisdom, prudence, experience, and clear-sightedness.

"Poor flies, the tarantula who has been lying in wait for you a long time is now approaching stealthily under the cover of your indifference. You will decide too late to overcome her fascination. She will surely gobble you down," said the old man bitterly.

He again requested the gourd with the snuff, served himself, and, before moving away, gave the pensive young men a final warning: "The sun's coming back to sleep behind the hills. It's time for Mahinous to open their eyes and keep watch more attentively than ever. We'll continue the song tomorrow if the Zadonous accord us the leisure of doing so."

The chirping of the insects and the gloomy laments of the evening birds were the only response to the wisdom that spoke in this old man's voice.

He went to the residence of Cotovi, the first of the four regents of Hounjroto. He found him in council with the other four chiefs. None of them were as old as he was.

"You have been brought together here at this moment only by the ancestors, who desire you to listen to me and promptly make a decision for the salvation of the country," he told them as he sat down on the gourd-chair that Cotovi indicated to him in the corner of the room.

He laid out the purpose of his visit. He had touched upon the subject with the second regent the previous day.

Here too he received the reply that, like him, everyone had noticed the unusual movement of bush creatures and even those from the deep forests toward the city, but that one shouldn't be overly concerned about it.

Dêê insisted: "The sun returned to its sleeping quarters a moment ago. Nature is spreading her dark veil across the earth and inviting all creatures to rest after the example of the day star.

"And yet the crickets, who normally retire before the other grass-dwellers, are far from wanting to take their rest. There are many of them in this room. They had to cross three other rooms to get here. You have not yet lit your lamps; therefore, you can't say they have been attracted by the light. Look at them jumping around! Listen to their chirping! It can only mean they are warning us: 'Watch out, Mahinous. Don't sleep or you will be crushed by your enemies! If you are unable to arm yourselves, follow the example of the animals from the bush. While there is still time, flee the invasion!'

"We will regret not having listened to this prudent advice.

"Yes, the war that hung over Hounjrogonji for eight dry seasons has been crouching in our forests for the past several days. It is slyly advancing under the cover of night and our own insouciance, and it will surprise us in our sleep."

Cotovi answered him brusquely: "Dêê runs the risk of sowing panic in people's minds. Let him listen to his reason rather than to the chirping of crickets who are greeting the night because it permits them to indulge in their frolics. War exists only in the deluded mind of this old man. War is inflicted on men by others of their kind; animals too must suffer invasion on the part of their fellow creatures. If that isn't the sole reason for the flood of tiny beasts who are troubling Dêê, they must then be fleeing from some epidemic, for their instinct will have told them that they would find asylum among us who are not subject to the calamity that afflicts them."

"Isn't it more reasonable to believe that they are coming rather to warn us about an impending catastrophe? If it had been possible for them to do so, the plants themselves would have left their native soil to come and shake us out of our lethargy," the old man insisted again.

"Something else is on our minds at this moment; we ascertained this morning that an important trophy from the last war has disappeared, and we are considering the best way to conduct an investigation. Dêê will be welcome if he can give us useful information about the escape route of the thief!" proclaimed Cotovi.

"My opinion? My opinion?" asked the old man. He fell silent, stared the four chiefs straight in the eye for a moment, then shook his head and continued: "This trophy, which you have failed to identify in precise terms, has certainly not flown away. I would be astonished if it is not already in the hands of the Zadonous after having been abducted from here!"

At a discreet sign from one of his assistants, Cotovi invited Dêê to drown his worries in the millet beer that could be found a few steps away in a gourd toward which he was motioning. The old man only accepted it out of deference to the chiefs. As he poured several drops of the beverage on the ground, he said: "May the ancestors and the tutelary fetishes of Hounjrogonji guide us safely to the day of tomorrow!" Having taken a drink, he wiped his lips with the back of his left hand and continued: "May the ancestors and the fetishes preserve you for a long time among us so that you can offer us such delicious beer again!"

"The gourd is empty!" exclaimed one of Cotovi's servants who had dashed into the room and was moving the vessel back and forth next to the old man's ear.

This servant was a Danhomênou who had been a prisoner since the war against Hounjroto; intrigued by the arrival of the other regents just a few moments before that of Dêê, he was listening at the door of the mahi chief, whose complete confidence he had succeeded in winning by virtue of his crafty manner, and inwardly cursing this stinking beast who had just raised the alarm of war in the presence of his fellow tribesmen. Fearing that the old man, seduced by the beer, might remain in the reception room for a long time and eventually triumph over the scepticism of the regents, who did not want to believe in the war that was threatening them, the slave had come to tear the gourd out of his hands at the very moment when he was preparing to serve himself again. This abrupt intervention by a Danhomênou would have sufficed to awaken other minds to the danger that was hanging over the country.

The old man picked up his stick again and started home, grieving to see that even the chiefs, who were nevertheless not children, could reject the prudent advice that his unerring knowledge of the Danhomênous' war strategy was dictating to the people of his country.

The four regents thanked the servant for having gotten rid of this evil omen for them.

As he left, he mused to himself: "That young people don't want to believe in the misfortune about to befall their country because a desire to enjoy life takes precedence over everything else in their eyes – this is excusable. But chiefs? Why this blindness among men of another age? Doesn't it prove that the Zadonous have not remained idle since their last defeat? Their spies must have lived among us for a long time without our knowledge, and in mahi soil they must have buried the gris-gris that have destroyed all consciousness of danger in us and paralyzed our resolve to fortify the country. Our enemies have also no doubt succeeded in obtaining the complicity of our fetishes, which are no longer protecting Hounjrogonji!

"The death that does not threaten you alone is so much more bearable!" he concluded to bolster his courage.

*   *   *

The soldiers carefully anointed their bodies with palm oil that had been skimmed from their gris-gris before they left for war. They were now sure that enemy swords would become dull if they struck them and that enemy shot would slide across them. They also ate several grains of melegueta pepper and then spat them out on other gris-gris, entreating them to grant invisibility when the enemy attacked. A chicken or a goat, depending on the state of the soldier's fortune, was promised as an offering of gratitude if one returned safely to Danhomê.

The darkness was complete. The look-outs of each army unit descended from their stations to inform their chiefs that the last lamp had been extinguished in Hounjroto. Everyone was also sleeping in the surrounding villages and farms.

The look-outs climbed back to their observation posts. The soldiers moved out of the forests. The entire army of the princes encircled the residence of Chief Cotovi; a brigade split into three groups and surrounded the houses of the other regents. Under the cover of night the invading cordons constricted around the villages and the smallest farms. The order had been given to capture the entire male population. People would only be killed when absolutely necessary and then as little as possible with guns; the club, the newly invented sword, and the sabre were to be the weapons of choice. The signal for the attack would come, as always, from general headquarters; it was to be a gunshot that the Mahinous would think had been fired at wild game by one of their fellow countrymen.

Assogbaou was not sleeping. The regular snoring of his guards told him they had dozed off. He left the room in a great hurry, clasping a package tightly between his arm and his left side. He crossed the ring of soldiers who had laid siege to Cotovi's residence. They surrounded him, their clubs, swords, and sabres raised high. He was taken at once to the main gate of the city, where he met the Danhomênou who had visited him the previous day with the aid of a fellow captive and without the knowledge of the Mahinous. Scrupulously abiding by the instructions the prince had given him, Zanbounou's assistant had been at the appointed spot since night fall.

At General Headquarters, Assogbaou told the story of his travails during the long captivity and described the murder of Toffa; the useful information he provided was immediately brought to the attention of the princes' army that was surrounding Cotovi's residence.

As the first chorus of cock crowings echoed through Hounjroto and the outlying villages and farms, it was answered by the agreed-upon signal from

General Headquarters, and then frenzied shouts arose here, there, further away, still further away, and finally everywhere: "Fire! Fire! Mahinous, fire!"

Suddenly awakened but their eyes still heavy with sleep, they bumped into the wall two or three times before they found the way out. They were cursing everything as they opened the door: "Listen to the yelling of these women and old men! They always know how to scream when their carelessness has set the house on fire. Look into it, and you'll discover that a single hut is burning and that the accident was caused by a woman who forgot to put out the fire in her hearth or by one of those old men who are in the habit of calling upon fire every night to provide the warmth their bodies have lost. And these bitches are screaming as if all Hounjrogonji were on fire!"

Once outside in the light of the courtyard, they heard the crackling of the straw and thatch of roofs that were still green; they saw the red tongues of flame rising, falling, reappearing, licking the roofs, and consuming neighboring huts that were crowned with a thick cloud of pink smoke; and they realized that the danger was greater than they had thought. Crazed with fear, the cattle broke their bonds and, with deafening bellows, ran to seek refuge in the distance. The goats struggled in vain to free themselves from the ropes that kept them close to stakes that had been driven into the ground; because the pig sties had also caught fire, the pigs too were grunting and squeeling in fright. The dogs were barking, barking endlessly; they ran toward the enemy, whose presence their keen sense of smell had detected, and then retreated in fear before advancing a short way again, barking all the while.

The birds who had fled the bush and the forests to seek asylum in the city were circling above the blaze and uttering plaintive cries; they had thought themselves safe, but misfortune had pursued them even here.

Worried pigeons were flying around the fire, beating their wings in the belief that this might help extinguish it; in their impatience to control the conflagration, they threw themselves into it: "It would be a sign of ingratitude on our part to survive the master of the house's misfortune when he has fed us for years!" they thought.

The panic-stricken inhabitants of the burning houses rushed outside without even thinking of their clothes; they ran toward the jar of water lined up beneath the edge of the roof.

Gunfire greeted all those who attempted to put out the fire. It was then the Mahinous understood they were being attacked. But their guns were still inside the huts. Surely no one who entered this fiery furnace in an attempt to get his weapons would ever come out alive. Thus everyone sought salvation in flight. Whichever way they went, they fell into the hands of the enemy. In no time at all, the captives were bound hand and foot.

The army of incendiaries set to work with a method: they only set the houses on fire. When the straw torches they were using had been consumed, they hurriedly made other ones with straw from the mahi houses.

Several mothers were violently grabbing their breasts and stamping their feet on the ground as they implored anyone to please save their children, who were still asleep in the burning houses. In tears, one of them approached a group of men. They were enemy soldiers; without saying a word, they seized the unfortunate woman, bound her, and sent her back toward their camp.

Another mahi woman had just carried two children from a hut and was returning to save the third. The roof collapsed. She fell, her upper body inside the house and her feet outside.

The Mahinous who understood the situation before they had been subdued were clutching at the soldiers and snatching their fingers between their teeth. Other Mahinous were looking for the enemy's vulnerable parts. Only the aid of their companions in arms saved the lives of the soldiers who were grappling with the beasts from the mountains.

In the houses, gourds filled with gunpowder for hunting exploded, and loaded guns went off.

The confusion was so great that there were not more than a hundred shots fired on the part of the Mahinous, and yet each family had at least two guns.

People who slept soundly, children, the infirm, and the sick died in their houses, suffocated or burned to death.

Because the order had been given to alert General Headquarters to all acts of bravery performed by Danhomênous, the brigade leaders decided to dispatch the soldiers themselves to relate their heroic deeds to the king as soon as they had done them.

One soldier found a Mahinou fast asleep; he rolled him up in a mat, hoisted him on to his shoulder, and carried him to General Headquarters. The sleeper did not awaken until he had been placed on his feet.

The court warmly congratulated the warrior. The king promised him an advancement in the army upon their return from the war. The soldier lay face down on the ground, covered himself with dust, and returned to the conflagration, his courage heightened in anticipation of the honors awaiting him in Danhomê.

The court then witnessed the arrival of a young Amazon who was prodding a Mahinou, his hands tied behind his back and limping, in front of her with the point of her sword. She explained: "This stinking beast from the mountain was being chased when he tried to flee through a hedge. My sword of Aligo didn't give him the time; it sliced through his calf."

She delivered her prisoner to Gaou and disappeared; she didn't even hear the court's congratulations for her courage and skill. The first minister of war apprised his colleagues that this particular Amazon was under fire for the first time.

The king informed himself about her name and origins and ordered that she be presented to him after the victory.

Another Amazon arrived. It was Ganwoumê. She was carrying a mammoth Mahinou armed with a gun. She said: "In a hut I surprised a diviner who had spread out the oracle at his feet and was insisting that Hounjroto would emerge victorious from its struggle with Danhomê and that the man who had come to consult him would return from battle without a scratch. The latter shouted: 'Then I'll crush the Danhomênous like rats!'

"With a single shot, I shut up the old imposter. I spared his companion so that he could come here himself and repeat his insolence."

"You're a man! You're a man!" exulted the court, marvelling at Ganwoumê, who was flattered but covered herself with dust to indicate that she, a simple subject of the Master of the World, was merely doing her duty.

The king ordered that these acts of heroism, which could inspire new vigor in the hearts of those whose courage was faltering, be communicated to the troops as soon as they were reported to the court.

From their observation posts, the look-outs gauged the progress of the fire and reported what they saw to General Headquarters.

By the second crowing of the cock, thick pink clouds of smoke had replaced the tongues of flame nearly everywhere. The cries of pain that arose from the wounded reached the ears of the king, informing him that the enemy had been taken by surprise this time and that Hounjroto had been defeated.

An emissary was dispatched to Adouconou, the regent at Agbomê.

Before dawn, not a single able-bodied Mahinou remained in Hounjroto or the outlying settlements unless he had been tied into a column of prisoners.

The day finally came. The sun was veiling his face with dark, thick clouds. Was he himself horrified at the spectacle of flames, smoke, blood, and agony in the Hounjroto that the king was surveying with a satisfied look from the vantage point of his hammock?

Guézo was surrounded by the royal guard and the high dignitaries. At his right Assogbaou was standing. The Danhomênous who had been prisoners at Hounjroto since Danhomê's initial defeat were serving as guides for the royal procession.

Someone pointed to a toddler who was crying next to a dead body and tapping it on the stomach with his little hands in the vain attempt to awaken the woman who had no doubt been his mother. Further on a group of children, some standing, some sitting, were weeping and calling for their mothers in the middle of a pile of pottery and calabash shards.

The king ordered that all these orphans be gathered together and consoled with fried meat and a few chunks of yams that had been cooked under hot coals.

In the courtyards, at the base of houses, and in various spots, there were bodies of men and women with a head split open, a shoulder severed, a chest smashed, a back roasted, or a stomach spilling out its contents. From everywhere emanated the moans of the wounded who still had some breath in their bodies. Only the bust or the lower half of the bodies allowed one to identify the sex of the cadavers here. Others had been completely charred; their arms and legs curled up, the fat in their bodies made them look at first glance like pigs or sheep. The corpses of children whose heads had been crushed or whose intestines were lying between their legs added to the horror of a scene that provoked the victors to mockery.

The still standing, smoke-blackened walls seemed sad without their roofwork crowns, which had collapsed; smoke continued to rise slowly from them. In some places, the air was heavy with the smell of burning flesh. From time to time, detonations sounded inside the houses: the last gourds of gunpowder for hunting were exploding, and the last loaded guns were firing. The conquerors resumed their tour after a brief fit of emotion. As they rounded the residence of Cotovi, it was rocked by a powerful explosion. The court decided not to continue its promenade.

Gaou ordered the army units that had until now remained out of action to sack the city, the surrounding villages, and even the smallest farms, while at the same time finishing off the worst of the wounded.

Following the directions given by two Danhomênous who had been prisoners at Hounjroto, a detail of soldiers dug holes in the ground at more than ten spots around the outside of Cotovi's residence.

Other fresh troops razed all the walls.

The battle captains came and reported to Gaou and Possou that there was no longer a living soul in Hounjroto, nor was there a single head of cattle, a chicken, a granary, or a storage bin.

Zanbounou and his assistants had been freed.

Information provided by Assogbaou, the spies, and the other Danhomênous who had been held captive at Hounjroto permitted the identification of the four regents, all of whom had been captured and none of whom had received the slightest injury.

Despite the rope cutting into his arms and provoking cries of pain, a Mahinou grew indignant at one of the soldiers who was itemizing the booty: "Don't mix up the animals. The first ones belong to Cossêvi; the others that you're bringing are mine!" He was ordered to keep quiet.

"Keep quiet when I see you confusing my possessions with those of a neighbor! You must be crazy, Zadonou!"

"Since you are about to have the choke pear administered to you or to be loaded on a ship at Gléhoué, it won't be long before you learn that you no longer own anything on this earth!" the soldier retorted.

"All the same those were my things. And they were not the spoils of pillage. If you strip me of them, you can be sure that your. . . ."

A resounding slap forced the final words back down his throat, but only for a moment. Collecting all his strength at a moment when no one expected to hear anything more from him, he yelled: "Your descendants won't benefit from them!"

The Danhomênou answered him gruffly: "Should misfortune befall them, you won't be the one who lives to see it!"

"What difference does that make!" shot back the Mahinou.

A soldier advised his comrade not to continue talking with this stinking beast from the mountain.

The inventory completed, they came to give an accounting to the king; they also told him about the protests of the captive.

Guézo withdrew in the company of Migan, Mêwou, and the two ministers of war. Sorcerers gave him powders to be licked; they then made barely noticeable incisions on his chest and in the middle of his back, rubbed other powders into them, crushed between their palms some leaves that were known to them alone, moistened them slightly, squeezed them, and allowed the juice to drip into his eyes; finally, they attached protective gris-gris to his wrists and ankles and gave him others to wear on his belt, refreshing his memory about the incantatory phrases he had to repeat to himself in releasing their power.

Assured of being sufficiently protected against any evil spell, the king ordered his soldiers to bring in Cotovi, the chief regent of Hounjroto and the man whose capture meant more to him than all the booty carried off from this country.

At the sight of the mahi chief hobbling forward with tiny steps (his legs had been fettered, his arms tied behind his back) and wearing around his neck an iron collar that was attached to a chain held by his guards, Guézo flew into a feigned rage against his ministers, reproaching them with having contravened his order not to inflict suffering upon the mahi king, but rather to show him all the respect due a person of his rank.

Freeing the prisoner, Migan promised to find and to punish the soldiers who failed to comply with the Master of the World's instructions regarding the deference with which the person of Cotovi was be treated.

The king continued: "I want even our enemies to do justice to King of the Universe for the depth of his gratitude."

Looking the mahi chief straight in the eyes as he had him offered a seat in front of his own, he said to him in a cajoling tone of voice: "Let the great mahi chief not be astonished at my solicitude for him. I will never be able to repay the favor he did for my brother Assogbaou, for whom I have a singular affection and who informed me that he owes the good fortune of having been found alive to the protection of the first regent of Hounjroto.

"If I had known sooner that a man of your dignity could be found in Hounjroto, I would have tried to contract a Blood Oath with you in the name of our two countries instead of waging war against you. In a few days we can do it anyway for the future.

"I would be happy to learn that no member of your family had been lost in the battle. I gave the order that your palace should be surrounded and that no shots were to be fired at its inhabitants.

"The commanders of my armies have assured me that my orders were followed. I am already having your wives and children separated from the other captives."

"I should have done more for Assogbaou, and I now regret having been obliged to deal harshly with his brother Toffa," replied the Mahinou, placed off guard by the tone of sincerety in Guézo's speech.

"I know Toffa. Even in Danhomê, he made himself obnoxious as the result of his pride. He wanted to impose his will on everyone under the pretext that he was the first son born to King Agonglo, my august Father, after he had taken possession of Danhomê.

"Just as this prince was bloated with pride, he was lacking in courage. I have just learned that he was weeping like a young girl on the day of the battle and that he was fleeing in front of your soldiers when he fell into the hands of a group of Mahinous who were not even armed."

"Toffa is no longer of this world, but his spirit is certainly present among us, and I should not slander him. You could not find a braver warrior than this prince. I can still see him raging against the mahi soldiers. I found myself at the head of a unit that had attacked the one he was commanding. We were more than a hundred against twenty or so on your side. Having exhausted his gunpowder, he drew his sword and rushed toward us. Six Danhomênous were following him; soon he was the only one left standing in front of the Mahinous. He wielded his weapon with such dexterity that not one of his thrusts or slashes missed its mark. It was something to see how our guns refused to fire at him, and how the shots from those that did went sliding over the surface of his body, when they didn't come back and hit us; hearing our companions screaming with pain as they doubled over, their hands seeking to hold back intestines that were spilling out, and seeing shoulders hacked off, arms dangling, chests gashed, and heads split open, our ranks were overcome with panic, while the battle rage of the prince grew stronger. We were in front of the main gate of the city. The battle took place at the foot of the sacred tree, which remained red for three rainy seasons with the blood that was spilled on it that day. It still bears the scar of the sabre slash that Toffa was aiming at one of my soldiers when it went astray and struck it. Anyone who can revive the simple receptivity of the ancients and decipher the language of the trees when the wind is rustling their leaves would be seized with horror and admiration at the same time by the tale that our sacred tree, much better than men, could tell about the prince's bravery, which it witnessed at first hand.

"My men were already showing their heels when I called out to them: 'Mahinous, my brothers, we've been saved! The god of war has come to our aid! The Zadonou has been disarmed!'

"They regained their courage, turned to face the enemy, and saw that the Zadonou was struggling in vain to free the sabre that, having been swung with great violence, remained deeply embedded in the trunk of the tree.

"Seeing himself embattled, he released his sabre, picked up his gun again, and still slew a few more of our men.

"A Mahinou succeeded in grabbing hold of him; I seized him by the feet; other countrymen lent us a hand, and we subdued him, but not without a struggle.

"In the hope that he would agree to prepare for me the gris-gris that rendered him invulnerable to our weapons, I restrained all the raised arms that were about to fall upon him.

"We subsequently captured all the other Danhomênous who had been hit by our gunfire but were only slightly wounded. Assogbaou was among them.

"Informed about the prisoners' social rank after the defeat of the Danhomênous, I reserved the two princes for myself."

"Instead of subjecting them to the rigors endured by the other captives, I employed them only in caring for my horses.

"Assogbaou adapted quickly to his new way of life; Toffa was intractable. Often we had to put him in irons.

"He didn't enjoy himself except in the company of my brother Gbéjiga, a savage being like himself. But their alliance fluctuated according to the whims of their extremely temperamental spirits."

"My entire family was genuinely afflicted by the prickly character of the prince, upon whom we nevertheless lavished our cares in the hope of calming him.

"One afternoon I heard loud cries coming from the side of the residence occupied by the two princes. Frightened women and children were running in all directions. I learned that Toffa had, with a single knife thrust, fatally wounded my brother Gbéjiga, who had been sleeping beside him without suspecting anything.

"Some servants had already subdued the murderer, who was threatening to kill other people."

He hesitated. Fear gripped him by the throat.

Dominating his emotion, Guézo told him: "In your situation, who could possibly have remained calm? I understand you and forgive you. Finish your story then!"

The captive resumed, his voice muffled and his eyes glued to the ground: "That very morning Gbéjiga had been imploring me to send his friend back to Danhomê. He had suggested to me that we could tell the Mahinous later he had escaped. My brother had only a few gasps of breath left. The mocking laugh of his murderer transformed my sorrow into anger. I would be unable to say exactly what happened next. I only remember having seen the servants carrying away Toffa's inert body a few moments later."

Guézo gritted his teeth so fiercely that he succeeded in stifling the cry of pain that the story of Toffa's death had been about to provoke in him. He clenched his toes and tightened his grip on the head of his cane in order to curb his emotion. His eyes grew moist. He turned his head aside to prevent anyone from seeing them, wiped his cheeks with a rapid motion, and dried his eyes.

The Mahinou continued without the slightest suspicion: "The day after the murder of Gbéjiga, the other three chiefs informed me of the Mahinous' desire to have Assogbaou executed. I had the people called together; our palaver lasted for an entire market day. I told the Mahinous that this prince had done nothing to merit such a punishment, that he had even been the first to express his indignation at his brother's crime, and that I vouched for his good character.

"I had a great deal of difficulty convincing my fellow countrymen to abandon their idea.

"My colleagues then proposed that Assogbaou be tatooed in the manner of the Nagonous. They told themselves that the prince's pride would never allow him to accept this mark of slavery, and they were hoping to use his refusal as a pretext for reaching their goal by other means.

"I secretly warned the prisoner and advised him to submit to the whims of his new masters without a struggle, that being the only way he could save himself.

"The next day in front of all the people, a Mahinou incised him with scarifications from the nape of his neck to the small of his back, from his chest to his abdomen, from his shoulders to the back of his hands. He did it so sadistically that I felt obliged to intervene at the sight of the patient's suffering. My fellow countrymen then accused me of having known about Toffa's crime in advance. They even claimed that, if I was protecting Assogbaou, it was because I wanted to arm him as well and thereby rid myself of relatives I found troublesome.

"All their slanders left me cold. I myself dressed his wounds.

"I kept Toffa's skull. I would be happy to give it back to you, if it had not disappeared yesterday morning. Only many moons later did I think about his body. When I asked for it, my servants could no longer remember where they had buried it."

From the very mouth of Toffa's murderer, Guézo had obtained information that agreed in part with that provided by Assogbaou, a fellow captive, and he admonished him not to say anything to any other Danhomênou, seeking to reassure him completely by adding: "I was thinking that, after we return to Agbomê, I could send all the prisoners back to Hounjroto and put you in charge of them. Because your countrymen seem to reproach you for your protection of Assogbaou, they are not going to be the ones who come back here with you. I will conquer another mahi kingdom, and all the captives from there will be reunited to live and work in peace under your rule and protected by the friendship of Danhomê.

"From now on I want to guarantee your safety against a possible revenge on the part of Danhomênous who might learn of Toffa's death from the idle chatter of the Mahinous. I am therefore placing you in the midst of my royal guard, that is to say, in my own retinue."

Cotovi thanked him for his solicitousness. When the king rejoined the court, the sun was already rising overhead.

Guézo was stricken with remorse for the less than honest means he had employed to gain the mahi chief's confidence. The first minister told him that such scruples were unnecessary when dealing with a stinking beast from the mountain.

Gaou and Possou called the assembly of the troops.

Migan went to the sorcerers and had them present him with the gris-gris that delighted in human blood; he placed choke-pears in the mouths of the three other regents of Hounjroto, beheaded them in Cotovi's presence, bathed all the king's gris-gris in their blood, arranged their heads on a copper tray, covered them with a cloth that had been dyed red, then came and deposited the tray in front of Guézo, who was sitting on the throne of war.

The Master of the World placed his left foot on top of the three heads; at the same moment, dogba, brought to life under the drummer's rapidly beating

340

fingers, solemnly notified everyone that Hounjroto had been conquered and that the order had been given to set out for Danhomê.

All sorts of drums, horns, large bells, and small ones answered dogba; war songs broke out among the ranks of the soldiers. The carronades added their thunder to the din and broadcast in all directions the news of Danhomê's victory over the stinking beasts of Hounjroto.

Five army units moved off and took the lead; the booty – people, animals, and things – followed under the escort of ten other army units. Some Mahinous were leading animals, others were laden with various objects; each of them wore a rope belt attached to that of his neighbor, from whence the name "people of the rope" had been given to the captives. Women were carrying children who had been strapped to their backs with two gnarled strips of tree bark. The larger one held the child's legs and buttocks firmly against the woman's lower back and was tied across her abdomen; the other one, as wide as a person's hand and knotted on the mother's chest, passed just beneath her armpits and those of the child.

Children too big to be carried in this manner but not strong enough to walk the great distance that separated them from Hounjroto were traveling on the shoulders of the men.

The high dignitaries, the queens, the servants, the royal guard, and Guézo followed; the remaining army units brought up the rear.

They made camp in sight of Mopa. Consulted after a brief meeting of the council, the oracle announced that the ancestors approved all the Danhomênous' plans. The living booty was sent ahead to stay at Soponta, the first dassa village. The animals were tethered to shrubs in the bush.

Great precautions were taken with regard to the captives, both men and women: they were seated with their legs outstretched and tied together around the ankles and across the instep; their arms were also bound at the wrists, and all four members were firmly attached to a stake that had been driven into the earth in front of their feet. A second stake had been set in the ground so that their stomachs were resting on it. Trussed up in this way, they could not have escaped, even if they had not been guarded; indeed, it was impossible for them to bend their legs, to lean forward, or to reach their ankles with their hands in making any attempt to free their feet from the hobbles that immobilized them.

The order was given to surround Mopa and begin firing. Overwhelmed with panic, these Mahinous fled in all directions. They couldn't go far. The carronades positioned in the forest, in the valley, or on the neighboring hillsides permanently felled those who had escaped the guns and were coming to seek asylum there.

Before the sun had turned his head, all the survivors of Mopa were moaning in rope fetters; the worst of the wounded helplessly watched the sacking of the village.

The Master of the World was satisfied! The destruction of Mopa was also the end of a painful memory for the king, whose life had been saved by its inhabitants at the time of his defeat during the first campaign against Hounjroto.

341

Hadn't Danhomê's spies reported that these foul beasts from the mountains were taking pride in the favor they did for the king?

"Not one captive from Mopa will remain in the land of the black man!" declared Migan. The court accepted his proposal.

Twice victorious during the course of a single expedition, Guézo ordered that the news of his triumphs be immediately carried back to Danhomê. The army quickly crossed dassa country, skirting the base of its forty-one hills; for the moment they paid no heed to other mahi kingdoms. But ever since the echo of the Danhomênous' carronades had reached them, people everywhere had been cowering apprehensively in the forest, under rocks, or huddling in caves burrowed into the sides and tops of the hills.

"Hey, Zadonous, is this the state in which we're going to enter Danhomê?" The voice of an old Mahinou, visibly afflicted with an infirmity, was posing the question to a soldier.

"Curious beasts these mountain-dwellers! Surrounded by his countrymen's anguish, this one is only worrying about hiding the gourd that dangles below his knees!" exclaimed the Danhomênou.

The prisoner of war's remark was reported to the king, who laughed and requested that the man be presented to him. All the queens had turned aside their eyes.

One of the Danhomênous, a former captive in Cotovi's residence, recognized him: "But it's Dêê! The stinking beast who sounded the alarm of war in front of the four regents yesterday!"

"Wasn't I telling the truth?" asked the old man calmly.

The king ordered the beasts from the mountains who had large cloths to share them with their fellow prisoners.

Dêê received half a cloth and used it to stabilize his gourd and make it less of an impediment.

*   *   *

Everyone, with the exception of Doguicimi, was sleeping in Agbomê. She found the campaign too long and, as a result, fell victim to a host of imaginary fears: "The first expedition against Hounjroto didn't last this long. It is true that the elders, the very essence of wisdom, affirm that the woman who dallies at the spring always brings back clear water. Will the Danhomênous have been victorious this time?" She hoped so. She even anticipated that Hounjroto had been conquered and that Toffa's return to the hearth could not be far off. But from time to time she was haunted by a vague apprehension. An inner voice warned her against deluding herself too much. Doubt even infiltrated her spirit, and a great sadness ensued.

She had not seen Evêmon since the day when the brave child had left to carry offerings to the fetishes. Vidaho had assured her that her former servant was living happily at the side of the king. But why had she never thought of sending her a message or undertaken some initiative to free her? What conclusion was to be drawn from that? It is true that the Danhomênou is only a friend of the present moment, of wealth, and of power. But she had been a second mother to Evêmon, who had vowed more than once to die for her – could Evêmon have forgotten her once she became a queen?

Doguicimi thought it more likely that only some misfortune could explain the poor child's silence. Memories crowded into her mind. Fleeting and imprecise, they gave her no information.

Her thoughts then shifted to her husband. She said to herself that everything Zanbounou had told her could not have been false. He had certainly seen Toffa, and it was undoubtedly from him that the spy had obtained the gris-gris he had brought back to Danhomê as proof that the prince was still alive. She was very familiar with that gris-gris; Vivênagbo had taken it from Toffa's sanctuary with the promise to get it to him on the night of the prince's departure for the first campaign against Hounjroto.

The thought of Toffa's return comforted her. To herself she said: "When he returns to Danhomê and learns how I publicly defied those who were slandering him and how I defended his noble memory, when he becomes aware of the sacrifices I offered to the fetishes to obtain their protection for him and of the struggles I waged against the royal prince who was seeking to take me from him and against the spy who wanted to dishonor me, when I recount to him the intrigues hatched in vain by the queens with the connivance of Vidaho and Zanbonou, whom I had spurned, to bring about my downfall, and when I tell him about the tortures that their serious accusations succeeded in having inflicted upon me, there is no doubt but that his prejudice against women will be vanquished and that he will believe in the genuineness of our love!" The joy she experienced at this thought was short-lived.

The inner voice of a moment ago made itself heard once again: "Doguicimi, it would perhaps be best for you to abandon your illusions." Her mind vacillated between the hope of finding her happiness again at Toffa's side and the presentiment of some great misfortune. "Who can assure me they won't try to kill my husband's affection for me with their slanders?

"But if the prince's common sense enables him to see through the wiles of his favorite wife's enemies, won't they exert pressure on him, alleging some imaginary reason of state to demand that he throw Doguicimi to the dogs, who, with fangs bared, have been waiting eight dry seasons for this prey?

"In this Danhomê, people are convinced that the executioner's hand strikes only the guilty. To save their own heads, friends and relatives invariably proclaim their indignation and denounce you.

"Although virtuous, I would be slandered and disgraced? If I had a child, he at least would not abandon me? A child is his mother's incorruptible friend, the one in whom she confides her innermost thoughts, the one who consoles her and remains faithful throughout her trials, the one who never allies himself with her tormentor. The woman who has never experienced the happiness of being a mother is indeed to be pitied!"

The realization that there was no one to sympathize with her afflictions brought tears to Doguicimi's eyes.

When she had recovered her composure, she assured herself that she would be able to remain as steadfast in misfortune as she had been in the face of temptations dangled in front of her by the heir to the throne and the spy. Her enemies would never have the satisfaction of extracting a word of complaint or supplication from her. The executioner would be deceiving himself if he thought the tears that flowed in a moment of torment marked a victory over her. One's eyes might succumb to weakness, but as far as the soul was concerned, it would always remain constant.

The woman eventually fell asleep. Pleasant dreams brightened her slumbers. She saw herself in front of her husband's reception room. There were many visitors, and they were noisy. A man was coming toward her. She recognized him; she ran toward him and threw herself at his feet: "Since when has the creator of my days been here then? Why did he not let me know? I am ashamed to present myself to him in this condition. How my lord and master has grown younger! How handsome he is!"

This exclamation awakened Zokindé, who had been sleeping at the woman's feet. "My mother is speaking to me?" asked the servant, rubbing her eyes with the backs of her fingers to chase away the drowsiness that had closed them.

The young girl's question yanked Doguicimi from her slumbers. She nervously moved her hands in all directions as if she wanted to catch hold of someone who was eluding her grasp.

Seeing that she was still stretched out on her mat, she began feeling the floor to her right and left.

When she awoke to the harsh reality, her disappointment drew a sigh from her: "I dreamed that my husband had come back; he had filled out handsomely and was advancing proudly toward me. But when I wake up, he's no longer there. When are these tortures going to cease – these tortures that Destiny, in his cruelty toward the helpless plaything I have become in his hands, has been inflicting on me ever since the disappearance of the prince?" She broke into tears.

"His spirit has already returned home; the master himself will certainly come back soon!" Zokindé said to console her mistress.

"Maybe the child is right," thought Doguicimi. "Hasn't it happened to me before – to think about somebody, only to see that person arrive a few moments later? The elders also assure us that, when a person traveling in a foreign land is about to return home, his spirit nearly always precedes him. But why didn't I think of that right away?" the woman asked herself. She was ashamed of her tears. "Toffa has no doubt already set out for Agbomê!" she concluded to herself.

Beguiled by this hope, she fell back into such a deep sleep that Adouconou, who entered the prison at the second crowing of the cock, was obliged to rap very sharply on her mat a number of times in order to arouse her. He informed her of the Danhomê victory over Hounjroto and of the order he had received to release her before the Master of the World's return to Agbomê.

344

The regent added that this message had reached him shortly after the first crowing of the cock.

"No more doubt about it! My husband has been saved! That's the reason the king can no longer keep me in prison!" thought Doguicimi as Adouconou led her back to Toffa's house in conformity with the king's command.

Her co-wives surrounded her. They filled the house with joy and immediately began to clean the prince's lodgings. At the break of day servants went to the Acodéjêgoto section of town to gather cow dung with which to glaze the floor of his sleeping chamber and his reception room.

Other servants were washing the prince's cloths, which had been stored in baskets since his disappearance. All the jugs were filled with the fine water from Amodi. The prince would take a bath, and his wives would anoint his body with a pomade that take away the stench of the mahi country. Doguicimi was also thinking about a good purgative and her husband's favorite dishes. She called, "Evêmon!" Zokindé appeared with a smile on her face. Taking cognizance of her mistake, the woman mused: "It's true, Evêmon has become a queen! The brave child! If only she's happy! I too am going to be happy at the side of my idol, and no later than than dawn tomorrow! The innocent child and I have suffered a great deal, and we deserve to enjoy life from now on!"

On her knees, Zokindé reminded her that she was still awaiting her mistress' orders. The servant then learned that she should obtain some finely ground maize flour for the master's first meal.

Already that night Doguicimi wanted to give her body all the beauty treatments it had not received during the last eight dry seasons. "In that way," she told herself, "my entire time can be devoted to Toffa during the day!"

Her confidante Dagnondé offered to shave her head by the light of a lamp.

"They only shave dead people's heads at night, Dagnondé. Do you think I'm dead or about to die, my dear friend? I know that a co-wife has always been viewed as a rival in Danhomê. But you, I don't suppose you can be wishing for my death?"

Dagnondé protested her affection for Doguicimi, the model companion. For her part, Doguicimi reaffirmed her sentiments for her friend.

After all her dreams and the cruel disappointments that nearly always followed, it was now time for reality – that is to say, a happiness that would last forever because, having enjoyed this life in Toffa's company, Doguicimi would continue to experience happiness in the realm of the dead, still at his side. As she said to herself, she had triumphed over all her enemies and should no longer feel the slightest bitterness.

The joy of the adults even communicated itself to the children born within nine moons of the prince's disappearance. They all wanted to see the papa whom they had never known.

Such was the swarm of children in Doguicimi's room that it would have been difficult to find a spot to place one's foot there. Their joy at being reunited with her was great. Several times the young woman had to interrupt what she was doing in order to answer the endless questions posed by those whom she called Little Masters of her spirit.

"Isn't it true that I threw my calabash at the head of one of those bad men on the day they came to beat you here?"

"Yes, my savior!" replied the woman.

"As for me, I bit one of them in the foot," boasted Todoté joyously.

"Thank you, my protector!"

"My mother came and dragged me away at the very moment when I was going to throw water on them," claimed a third.

"You, you didn't do anything that day," Hêdagbé reproached Bognon, a stern expression on his face.

"He was even laughing," seconded Todoté.

"He won't share in our meals any longer, now that you're back. I have told him so many times since you've been gone," Bossouhê decided.

The banished urchin grew angry, and his fist flew toward the back of the boy who had condemned him. The latter hit back. Teeth came into play. Sobs once again distracted her from what she was doing. She blamed the stronger and consoled the weaker.

"You aren't going to share what papa brings back from his trip for us?" said the victim of the quick-tempered Bossouhê, wiping his face.

"Me, I often came to sleep here during your absence. My mother took me away," Mêtodê informed her.

Drowsiness alone put an end, one by one, to the chattering of these "Little Masters" and increasingly restored her to her preoccupations.

Adouconou had not notified Vidaho until after he had taken Toffa's wife back to her husband's compound, and for that reason the heir to the throne developed a lively resentment against the regent.

The love-struck prince could have exploited the opportunity, which had just presented itself, to overcome the resistence of the woman he adored.

When he had last seen her on the day after the king's departure for the war, he had been convinced that, if he succeeded in obtaining her freedom, he could conquer her once and for all.

Doguicimi had expected to be pardoned before the beginning of the Houn-jroto campaign, but she had been sorely disappointed. She seemed to count only on Vidaho to regain her liberty. If he had been the one to come and take her from the prison, the woman would have believed she owed her deliverance to him. Thus, swayed both by the power of the future master of Danhomê and by his love for her, Doguicimi would not have hesitated to marry him. Vidaho knew that only the highest patronage protected Doguicimi and put her out of the reach of his love.

Hadn't Cangbodé, usually so tractable in the face of all the royal prince's demands, refused to cooperate in an abduction of the prisoner?

The director of the prison was also avenging his friend Vivênagbo, whose disgrace had been brought about by the prince.

As for Adouconou, he had nothing to hold against the heir to the throne. What aberrant motive could a prince possibly have to league himself with common Danhomênous against another prince? The eldest of Agonglo's sons could not say that he was protecting Toffa's interests. All Danhomê knew that Adouconou did not have particularly tender feelings toward his younger brother.

"I'll persuade my august Father to withdraw from you the regency, which you have used against me, and to give it to one of my trusted friends.

"We'll also settle accounts and quite well too, once I've taken possession of Danhomê!" threatened Vidaho, whose right hand sliced through the air in the direction of Adouconou's compound.

The Slave Chain

Chapter 10

A Danhomê Victory

Shortly before the third crowing of the cock, the echo of a muffled boom from a carronade reached Agbomê. At first it was thought to be a clap of thunder. A second followed, a bit more distinctly, then others at irregular intervals. The roofs of the houses trembled, the wooden frameworks creaked.

Awakened by these rumblings, the city assumed that the fury of the Master of the World's troops was being unleashed against the Wémênous.

But as these rumblings grew louder and louder, they puzzled the Danhomênous. "Could the enemy have pushed the king's army back to the Zou?" they asked worriedly. They assembled in courtyards and listened attentively. Three more reports were heard from the carronades; then it was calm for a moment. Suddenly a wind passing over the city brought with it a faint echo of drums. "The Master of the World has probably triumphed over those Wémênous?" Stillness reigned for a few instants that seemed interminable to the Danhomênous who continued to listen attentively.

Soon the booming of the drums could be clearly heard, and the carronades resumed their accompaniment. "But they're announcing a victory!" proclaimed a voice.

The still confused echo of songs wafted once again through the air. "There's no longer any doubt! The army is returning in triumph!"

At dawn, the songs grew louder, but people could not yet make out the words.

Having arisen earlier than usual as if he wanted to celebrate the victory of Danhomê, the sun had donned a cloth of the purest coral hue; the entire eastern sky was draped in pink velvet. The sun soon abandoned his initial crimson robe in favor of another that was blindingly bright in its profuse blending of so much silver and gold. One would have said it was to obtain a better vantage point from which to observe the return of the victorious army that the day star quickly climbed to the top of the highest of those white mountains outlined against the immense calabash cover that envelopes us, its inner walls now seemingly hung with a cloth that had just been removed from a vat of indigo dye. Tempered by the azure of the sky, the dazzling gold and silver of the sun admirably embellished the natural surroundings.

From time to time, wispy tufts of cotton held by invisible hands passed across the face of the sun, wiping it clean and then drifting off to pile up on the other side of our maritime provinces. The crest of these gigantic mountains with their fantastical shapes remained a brilliant white, although they were dark at the base. If a storm was brewing, it would break out far, far from here, beyond the sea, so that the sky of Danhomê would stay serene and clear for this entire day.

The soldiers must not be very far away; their songs could now be heard quite clearly. But they weren't coming from the direction of Houawê; they seemed to be emanating from somewhere near Mougnon.[1] "Had the Master of the World gone to fight against the Mahinous then?"

Soon the plunder of war flooding through the Door of Doussoumoin and covering the Great Courtyard of the Palace left no more room for doubt.

A delirious joy overwhelmed the Danhomênous; they went out to meet their Creator.

The column of prisoners, all of whom were wearing collars made from the young shoots of oil-palm leaves, was more than five hundred bamboos long.

The soldiers were singing:

> Guézo the buffalo fell upon Hounjroto and crushed the stinking beasts
> Who believed themselves safe from his fury
> Behind the mountains where they had chosen to live.
> Look at them on the rope!
> On their necks they're wearing
> A mark of surrender to the Master of the World.
> They're offering all their wealth to Danhomê;
> They're even bringing trees uprooted from their land.
> Not a span of wall was left standing by the Conqueror.
> He no longer wants any being who eats salt to live at Hounjroto.
> The king also conquered Mopa to punish the betrayal
> Of the other stinking beasts,
> Until now disdained by the armies of Danhomê.
> They wanted to warn their countrymen at Hounjroto of our arrival.
> But the ancestors of the king betrayed their envoy.
> He was captured, and the gris-gris drank his blood.
> The army is returning, drunk with glory.
> The sun that rises in the sky
> Can't be regarded directly without danger to the eyes;
> So too is the Danhomê of Guézo.

---

[1] "Mougnon" is a village about ten kilometers from Agbomê. (author's note)

The rash fools who touch the fire
That is Danhomê will burn themselves.
The stinking beasts of Hounjroto and Mopa
Have just learned this to their sorrow. . . .

Lying in his ceremonial hammock, Guézo circled the Great Palace seven times with his procession of drums. He finally passed through the Door of the World, went straight to his father's tomb, and paid tribute to him for his dual victory.

*   *   *

Having been distracted from her preparations a few moments before, Doguicimi was plunged in meditation.

The booming of the drums and the echo of the songs informed her of the victorious army's return to Agbomê and propelled her out of her chair; she dropped the glass beads she had been stringing. Her pearl, the one of immeasurable value, was coming! Nothing else mattered to her! She was even annoyed at having dallied with such trifles at a time when the carronades, drums, and songs had been announcing since the third crowing of the cock that her lord and master was returning triumphant from his long captivity.

As she got ready to go with her co-wives to the Great Courtyard of the Palace so they could escort the prince back to the house he had left eight dry seasons ago, Doguicimi recited this song that she had just composed to greet the master:

I
They told me you'd never see Danhomê again.
I confidently replied:
"The water lily doesn't live under water
But rather on the surface;
So Toffa will return to the land of his fathers."

Chorus
Wasn't I right?
Now you're back, master!
I rejoice and bid you welcome!

II
They answered me back:
"But the water lily that's held to the bottom
Does not see the surface again!"
Then I asked them: "What about oil?
Can it be held down, even in the depths of the sea?"

Chorus
Wasn't I right?

Now you're back, master!
I rejoice and bid you welcome!

III
Your detractors continued: "Like fire that burns oil
And leaves not a cinder behind,
The hatred of the Mahis has consumed Toffa utterly!"
My soul remained steadfast
Amidst the tortures they inflicted on it.

Chorus
Wasn't I right?
Now you're back, master!
I rejoice and bid you welcome!

IV
But the imposters returned to the charge:
"If the fly now and then escapes the web of a spider,
Never does the strength of man prevail over the tomb!
Let's not worry too much about the memory of our dead!
Let us enjoy life with the living!"
I replied as confident as ever:
"Like the sun that devours a web of morning fog
And climbs radiantly into the sky,
The prince will come back to Danhomê.
He's the water lily who always triumphs over drought.

In the swarming crowd, Doguicimi worked her way further forward than her co-wives.

Announced by Avoutou, dogba, and the chirping of his "birds" and preceded by his ministers, the king soon emerged from the Palace. The common people and the palace dignitaries threw themselves face downward in the dust and covered themselves with it as they tumultuously greeted the king and manifested the wish that the reign of the worthy son of "Pineapple Who Laughed at the Wrath of Lightning" might be long and know only victories.

Migan, who followed the king's gestures closely, raised himself slightly on his left elbow; lifting his right arm backwards before lowering it into the dirt twice, his enormous open palm facing the ground, he imposed silence on the mob and the drums, supporting his hand signal with an imperious, "That is enough, Danhomênous!"

The red curtain of dust that had been raised between the people and the king soon fell; Doguicimi planted her elbows on the ground and lifted the upper part of her body; she craned her neck to the right and the left, examining the rows of prostrate dignitaries at the foot of the throne. Powerless to discern their identities, she stared at the queens one by one. She did not perceive Evêmon among them either. "Yet Vidaho assured me," she thought, "that the Master of

352

the World, seduced by her courage, had made her a Wife of Panther. If he was telling the truth, Evêmon would not fail to accompany the king to the Door of the World. Each time kings appear before the people, it is customary for them to surround themselves with their most beautiful wives. Isn't Evêmon a jewel of the rarest kind? How could Guézo have tired of her so quickly?"

The memory of the groans Doguicimi had heard several paces away in the prison of Cangbodé came back to her. A flash of insight resolved the mystery of her first night as a prisoner: wasn't it Evêmon who had been dying at her side as she herself lay there in complete ignorance? The heir to the throne must have spoken to her about the young girl's marriage to the king with the intention of consoling her and perhaps of overcoming her resistence as well.

An inner voice told her she had just discovered the truth and that it was futile to seek her devoted servant among the Royal Wives.

Doguicimi's gaze then returned to the high dignitaries.

A man arose. At first no one among the ranks of the people recognized him; he was tatooed after the fashion of the Ayonous, and he was gaunt; it was Assogbaou. His tall stature had grown stooped under the weight of misery during his captivity; his hair had turned white.

In a nearly inaudible voice that was tinged with a mahi accent, he declared: "During our first campaign against Hounjroto, the Mahinous attacked Toffa's army, in which I was fighting. The enemy had five times as many men as we did. His gunpowder exhausted, Toffa grabbed his sword and fell upon the attackers; we followed him. A wretched shot passed through my right thigh and placed me out of commission. Around Toffa, the Danhomênous were falling one by one. Soon he was alone in front of the enemy. He wrecked such havoc that they were suddenly overcome with panic. But at the very moment when they were showing their heels, the prince was betrayed by his weapon; it missed a fleeing soldier and buried itself in the trunk of the tree under which we had been fighting. Their strength bolstered by the disarming of this fury, the Mahinous subdued him, but not before he had crushed several heads with his gun and opened several stomachs with his sword of Aligo. The enemy surveyed our ranks and gathered up the wounded. Toffa had not received the slightest injury.

"In the hope of discovering the secret of the gris-gris that had made my brother invulnerable to mahi weapons, Cotovi, the brother of the king who was supposed to have been killed in that war, appropriated him along with another batch of captives, and I was among them. This Mahinou also kept a large part of the booty that had been captured in our camp after the departure of the king. Entreaties, ruses, threats, nothing enabled the mahi chief to overcome the scorn of Toffa, who was determined not to prepare any of his gris-gris for the vile beast from the mountain.

"Gbéjiga, Cotovi's younger brother, then vowed to triumph over Toffa's obstinacy and, with this idea in mind, devised all sorts of tortures to extract the prince's secret from him.

"We pretended to be outraged by Toffa's attitude. We let it be understood that we could convince him to satisfy our masters' wishes. We gained the confidence of these beasts from the mountains; they allowed us to visit our brother, and we secretly fed him on the days when our tyrants withheld food from him.

"Driven to rebellion by the tortures of Gbéjiga, who had been humiliated by his failure, Toffa fatally wounded him one afternoon.

"We were brought to the dying man's side by the alarums of the wives and children. Three Mahinous subdued Toffa, whom they had disarmed with great difficulty. Cotovi arrived; without even asking about the circumstances of the slaying, he fell upon the prince and slit his throat.

"All Danhomênous were instantly placed in irons.

"The mahi chief forced me to be tattooed. He claimed this was his way of warning me that Toffa's fate would also be mine if I so much as touched a chicken in his courtyard. We only saved our own necks through guile; we pretended to be mourning the chief's relative, whereas in reality we were bereaved by the death of our brother.

"Freed from our bonds after five moons, we would have escaped from Hounjrogonji if the interest of Danhomê had not required our presence in the midst of these stinking beasts, for we wanted to understand them better and study their country so we could give exact information to the spies we were convinced the Master of the World would not fail to send to Hounjrogonji before returning with his army to carry out a war of revenge.

"All our efforts to discover Toffa's burial place were in vain. Nothing was found as the result of excavations undertaken by the Master of the World's soldiers in accordance with coordinates provided by Mahinous whose confidence we had managed to gain.

"Cotovi gave a false account of his crime to the king, thereby hoping to exonerate himself. The Master of the World had three mahi chiefs executed and brought Toffa's murderer back alive."

Doguicimi clenched her teeth and her fists, pressed her arms against her chest, and struggled to curb the passion that her tears betrayed.

Assogbaou's story of the noble prince's tragic fate drew exclamations of sympathy from the people, and to console them, he added with a tone of pride in his voice: "Oh, irony of Destiny! Toffa's name means 'Water Lily Who Defies the Drought,' and everyone thought he would prevail over the Mahinous, but he succumbed to them. Fortunately, all of him has not remained at Hounjrogonji. The Houégbajas helped one of our companions in misfortune to procure the prince's skull two days before the outbreak of the war that was to deliver us. I have given this skull to the Master of the World. Every time the stinking beasts of Hounjrogonji gathered around a gourd of millet beer at Cotovi's residence, he displayed Toffa's skull and boasted of being sole possessor of the most valuable trophy from the war against the Zadonous. This skull passed from hand to hand as everyone present heaped blasphemous taunts upon it. Once the strong drink had loosened their tongues, a flood of insults was directed against Danhomê. Each Mahinou vowed that he too would acquire the skull of a prince from Danhomê the next time the Zadonous attacked Hounjrogonji. The second mahi chief was fond of adding: 'But I'm going to transform this trophy into a cup for the days when sacrifices are offered to the ancestors!'"

The prince fell silent, overcome with emotion. He prostrated himself and covered himself with dirt.

At a sign from the king, Migan had approached the throne a few moments earlier; he came back toward the people and announced: "Danhomênous, the day after tomorrow the Predestined King invites all of you to the courtyard that extends from the base of Gbêcon-Hounli and must be crossed when going from here to the second Palace of the King."

"My market day in this world has come to an end! Joyfully I depart for the land of the dead in the knowledge I will be telling Toffa that justice has been done to his memory, which had been slandered upon the return from the first campaign against Hounjroto!" sighed Doguicimi as she kissed the earth and withdrew.

"Go put a rope around your neck and hang yourself if that's what you want to do!" grumbled one of the Royal Wives.

Doguicimi's co-wives were also lamenting between sobs: "There's nothing left for us to do but join her!"

The queens were more sympathetic toward them.

The king and the dignitaries went back into the Palace. The royal council decided, among other things, that the captives would be distributed among the ministers' residences. Cotovi alone was entrusted to the watchfulness of Migan.

There were no more than two hundred wounded, most of them burned by the fire, and they would be treated by the doctors assigned to the residences of the two ministers of war.

Already that evening Topo's emissaries were fanning out through the smallest villages in the vicinity of Agbomê; they went as far as Jija, ruled over by Agbolo, and Agonlin, where Fonghi and Hougnan governed; afterwards, they scoured the farms on the banks of the Coufo and the Swamps to the South.

*   *   *

During the council, which he found longer than usual, the heir to the throne listened distractedly with one ear to the deliberations of the court.

Upon returning to his residence, he shut himself up alone for a moment. A messenger had been dispatched to Princess Noucounzin, but she did not arrive until after the sun had turned his head.

She and her brother secluded themselves far from any sound.

When they emerged, the night was already enveloping the earth with her somber veil.

When he saw her leave, the prince was rejoicing in the thought that he was finally going to marry Doguicimi, who was now free. He told himself that the decision the woman made this morning could hardly be irrevocable.

Having heard Doguicimi's remarks at the court, Noucounzin had stopped to see her before meeting with the heir to the throne, and didn't she inform him that the woman had not taken her life, as her words this morning seemed to imply she would? The princess had also reported that Toffa's widows, orphans, and menial sevants were wallowing in grief but that Doguicimi appeared almost unaffected by her husband's misfortune.

"She has certainly realized that life is good and that it is folly to leave it before having enjoyed it fully," the love-struck prince assured himself.

With the exception of Doguicimi, Toffa's entire family was indeed expressing its sorrow openly.

Noucounzin found the prince's favorite wife in the reception room; she was sitting on the bare ground, her back against the wall, her bloodshot eyes staring into space, her eyelids puffy, tears rolling across her chest.

The princess took her aside and sang to her in the name of the heir to the throne:

I

Dry your tears, Doguicimi!
To see you so sad, wouldn't people think
That all Danhomê had been destroyed?
You have no reason
To wallow in your grief this way.

II

Dry your tears, Doguicimi,
And let me teach you
That our tears,
Far from assuaging Destiny,
Merely set him against us the more.

III

Neither your brave father, nor your venerable mother,
In whom you might have confided your sorrows,
Are here to comfort you.
Dry your tears then, Doguicimi,
And accept my condolences.

IV

Grieved to see you in mourning,
I come to dry your tears,
For you've not the good fortune
To have a child who can tell you:
"Mama dear, don't cry!"

V

Dry your tears, Doguicimi!
Calm yourself
And learn that consolation

Is not the only good
That comes to us from our descendants.

VI

If you leave a child behind you,
Doguicimi, your sweet name
Will be preserved for posterity:
The highest reward for pains of childbirth
For cares and agonies of motherhood.

VII

And it's a woman's duty
To seek this joy.
Dry your tears then!
Doguicimi dear, the moment has come for you
To share in the happiness of this world!

VIII

Take advantage of the situation
Being offered to you; enjoy life
And leave a living memory behind
In this Danhomê.
Everything gives you the right, my idol!

IX

But if you're determined to join Toffa,
Wait at least til my august Father
Has fulfilled the promises,
Made to the ancestors this morning,
To immortalize the conquest of Hounjroto!

X

Wait and see everything
Before going to inform Toffa.
Dry your tears then,
Come and enjoy life for a moment
At my side, Doguicimi dear!

The widow marshalled enough strength to gain control over her emotions
and to respond to Vidaho's envoy: "I thank the prince for his condolences. But
let him deign to realize that not all nets cast into the waters emerge with fish in
them. And there can be no humiliation for the fishing gear when such ill fortune
occurs. It's not my fault if I'm not a mother. Were my husband a slave, I'd
still follow him to the other world: a new kettle can not impart as good a taste
to the food as an old one can. My happiness is more certain in the realm of the
dead than here on earth!"

"Doguicimi will regret that she was so stubborn in turning her back on happiness."

"If I could appear to you in a dream, princess, I would prove to you that Vidaho does not enjoy a monopoly on happiness in this Danhomê."

Noucounzin did not want to hear any more.

On her way back to the royal prince's residence, she inwardly condemned her brother's obstinacy: "Why don't some men realize that you can't make a snail attach itself to a tree? Women are like these creatures."

Despite his sister's discouraging words, the suitor did not consider himself beaten; his youth, his fortune, his position as the future Master of Danhomê, faith in the efficacy of his gris-gris, everything rekindled his hope of someday triumphing over the resistence of the woman he desired.

Doguicimi's heart was burning with such love for Toffa that all Vidaho's words of consolation and promises of future happiness evaporated there like drops of water on red-hot iron. She thought to herself: "Having children is the happiness to which, it is true, all the women of Danhomê aspire. But to contend that only our offspring can transmit our names to posterity is to overlook the resources of the beautiful soul that the ancestors have fashioned for us. The future Master of this kingdom has been blinded only by his passion, which leads his mind astray and causes him to talk nonsense."

Doguicimi then called to mind the prince's constant attentions to her during the past eight long dry seasons, his schemes to seduce her from the path of virtue, and the proposals of marriage he had just reiterated. From now on she was free. No one could therefore have any objection to her union with the royal prince. Even in the city of the dead, she could meet Toffa with her head held high. To the man who called her fidelity and that of all other women into question, to him she would have been faithful, for she had never consented to dishonor herself by remarrying as long as there was still hope of seeing him return to Danhomê. All that was true! But she was determined never to attach her name to that of another man. No, she was not, as Toffa thought, the mat that could serve as a bed for many different men. The noble prince's ancestors did not bring him back alive. But at least they enabled his skull to be recovered. May they be blessed for that! She also owed thanks to the gods. If the education received from her family and the love she felt for Toffa had permitted her to resist the seductive proposals of the royal prince and the spy, only the protection of the fetishes and her family's ancestors enabled her to triumph over the traps laid for her by the vengefulness and jealousy of those who were interested in bringing about her downfall – for her, there could be no doubt about it.

Not many days after his capture, Toffa had fallen victim to Cotovi's knife. Yet for eight long dry seasons in Danhomê, his young wife, unaware of her freedom, courageously defended her honor as a married woman. Between men and women there shall always exist an intense struggle: men are very selfish and would like to live by a single law – the passive submission of the other sex to their sensual appetites, whereas those who are the object of male desire have as a dominant passion the need to retain their purity. The only women who will triumph are those whose families respected virtue and were neither polluted by a taste for the vanities of this world nor mired in the poverty that often make the weaker sex an easy prey for the passions lurking in wait for it.

Doguicimi was impatient to go and convince Toffa that she was not fashioned from the clay of Ayomayi.

*　　　　　　*　　　　　　*

When the king's orders were transmitted to a family by Topo's servants, its members immediately began to assemble packloads of the current market goods in which they happened to specialize: food supplies, spices, drinking water, domestic animals, birds, live game, smoked meat, oil, raw cotton, skeins of cotton thread for weaving, pottery, medicinal plants, religious objects, farming implements, mats, and the remains of birds and animals from the bush for the gris- gris or the sacrifices ordained by the oracle. The market of Ajahi was scheduled to take place the next day, and many people decided not to go there with the articles they had prepared for that purpose.

Ordinarily buyers and sellers were so tightly packed together at the Ajahi market that a calabash thrown into their midst would not find a place to land on the ground, but now there were empty spots to be seen.

At the end of the day, even those who had exhausted their stocks of merchandise opted to stay in Agbomê; some went to spend the night in the outlying villages of the capital so the sun might find them at the appointed place when he arose the next morning.

In villages nearly four thousand bamboos away, loads had already been placed on people's heads by the first crowing of the cock.

Arriving from Jija, Docon, Zassa, Canna, Agonlin, and the edge of the Swamp, men, women, and adolescents streamed into the capital as early as dawn through the Door of Towoun, the Door of the Ditch of Janwoun, the one known as the Door of Lepers, and finally through the enormous Door of Dossoumoin.

No one wanted to miss the Master of the World's palaver.

Migan's assistants had been entrusted with the task of maintaining order, and they assigned the new arrivals to spots that had been cleaned two days previously.

People sat down next to their loads. They lost themselves in conjectures. They only knew that the king had returned in victory from Hounjroto! Those who thought they knew why the people of Agbomê and the surrounding area had been summoned were prudently holding their tongues with regard to their own opinions: "Speak and you'll see what difficulties you bring down on yourself! Someone will soon inform against you, and your words will be blown out of proportion, if not distorted. The authorities will ask you to prove what you've been saying, then they'll force you to inform against the person from whom you got your information. They'll never want to admit that you could have guessed the king's intention. For ministers who are always in a zealous mood, you must have been maligning the Master of the World in the company of a friend or relative whose name you are refusing to divulge. Your whole family will be subjected to the fetish of the trial by poison. Your guilt will have been decided in advance; your good faith will never be acknowledged. You will disappear, while your calabashes and gourds are being forwarded to Agbomê! That's how it was during the last reign. This one promises to be lenient on the people. But be careful at first. Keep your tongue still if you want to drink the water of life as long as possible," admonished the fearful souls who had not forgotten the rigor with which the authorities had punished people accused of slander, when their only crime had been committed, more often than not, in the imagination of those who had informed against them.

Nevertheless, the swarm of spectators was buzzing noisily. In the ranks of these thousands of Danhomênous surrounding a circular courtyard about thirty bamboos in diameter, one heard mostly *"fon,"* but a "fon" that was not the same everywhere; interlarded with *"nago"* words when spoken by people from the other side of the Zou or Jija and its vicinity, it was also alloyed with *"aja"* expressions among the smaller tribes from the East.

Having brushed away the web of darkness that had been spun across the threshold of his dwelling, the sun was showing himself off in all the splendor of his satin cloths – scarlet in the center, the color of boiling palm-oil froth on one edge, ash-gray and indigo blue on the other.

All eyes suddenly turned in the direction of the Courtyard of Singboji, where bellowing, bleating, or grunting animals and barking dogs were being dragged toward the assembly by men; the women were heavily laden, some carrying porters' racks, others large baskets.

They were accompanied by an escort of soldiers. The clubs of Migan's servants cleared a path for them through the wave of Danhomênous surging toward the Courtyard. The Mahinous were herded into a circular space bounded by stalks of bamboo; the area allocated to the birds was next to that of the animals; they were followed by foodstuffs, hand-wrought articles, medicinal plants, and all sorts of ingredients for the preparation of gris-gris and sacrifices to the ancestors.

A spot six bamboos long and five bamboos wide had been kept empty at the center.

"I thought so!" exclaimed a Danhomênou, whose face suddenly beamed with a broad smile. Inquisitive glances turned in his direction. Prudently, he closed his mouth, surveyed the curious bystanders, then looked skyward, a bemused expression on his face.

A cannon shot reverberated through the air. The principal drum, the secondary drums, the little bells, the large ones, and the horns replied in chorus. Songs accompanied them. The Master of the World was coming.

Young servant girls were drawling, "look out! look out!" as they shook the little bells attached to their necks. In their wake, the wave of Royal Wives billowed into the gap; they installed themselves around the throne, which had been placed on a large cloth of crimson velvet. The drums appeared; they were beating more frenziedly than ever. The royal guard was reciting a war song.

The king was arriving. The Danhomênous threw themselves face down on the ground and covered themselves with dust to express their appreciation to the "Sun who illuminates their days" with the gaiety that his presence sheds over them.

Furtive glances were cast in the direction of the king, who was stretched out in his hammock, a long silver pipe in his mouth.

The palace dignitaries brought up the rear. Three times the procession circled the people, animals, and objects that had been brought back from Hounjroto. The king pretended to ignore their presence and focused his gaze instead on the Danhomênous.

When ordered to do so by Migan's servants, the captives began to cover themselves with dust. The king finally had himself set down inside the enclosure. The families of Toffa, Afénou, Alopé, Gaou Dessou, Possou Linon, Chalacassou, and Jajagoloja, all of whom had been lost at Hounjroto, were gathered to the right of the throne; the high dignitaries had lined up on the left.

The king was standing. He ordered the parasols to be closed; his wives were kneeling and so was the royal guard amidst a forest of guns about ten paces from the throne.

The king handed his cane, the white handkerchief used to hold it, his pipe, and his head-dress to the queens; he took off his cloth and his sandals.

The Danhomênous stared dumbfoundedly at him. He was wearing velvet breeches the color of the foam on top of boiling palm oil.

On his limbs, cords could be seen standing out against his skin, the color of a dry calabash. It almost seemed as if their extensions on the backs of his broad hands were actually moving.

Before the fifth reign, Danhomênous never saw their kings' faces, which were concealed behind strings of glass beads because these monarchs were demi-gods whose countenances were covered with sacred tattoos.

Tégbéssou had decided differently, and by doing so he had opened the eyes of the people to what had previously been shrouded in great mystery.

The gratitude of the Danhomênous had bestowed the glorious title of Civilizer upon this king.

But never had their idol appeared before them in simple dress.

Guézo stood even higher in the esteem of his subjects both because he permitted common mortals to gaze at their leisure upon the creator in all the intimacy he was revealing to them on this day, and because his tall stature and solid frame were without equal in all Danhomê.

Murmurs expressing gratitude and admiration at the same time ran through the crowd.

Guézo was truly handsome! One had the impression that there was an enormous store of pent-up energy in this giant's body.

The king took several steps forward. His breeches were rather baggy, allowing his legs complete freedom of movement.

The royal guard stepped aside; one man remained on his knees. With a powerful, "Come, Mahinou!" Guézo invited him to approach. Cotovi was the only Hounjroto chief who had been spared by Migan's sabre on the day when the victorious army of Danhomê had broken camp to return home; he now stood up apprehensively. His height and bulk were no less impressive than those of Guézo, but he was not as strong-limbed as the idol of the Danhomênous. His shoulder blades and ribs were visible beneath his black, wrinkled skin, which was peppered with tiny scars (where he had been stung by the gnats that infested the mahi country) and completely covered with the dust in which he had been sleeping since his departure from Hounjroto. He was obviously in a weakened condition. Either he had been deprived of food since his capture, or his mind, obsessed night and day with a presentiment of disaster, had taken away his appetite entirely. The diarrhea from which he had suffered the day after his capture also contributed to his weakness.

He wanted to come forward; his breeches, made of local fabric, were tight and impeded his movements.

The Danhomênous would have looked in vain to find any weapon in the king's possession.

Holding out his arms toward the Mahinou, Guézo challenged him: "Let us fight!" Cotovi did not move.

"What's this!" shouted a scandalized Migan. He leaped into the enclosure, his right hand grasping the handle of his scimitar and ready to draw it in an instant. He placed himself between the king and the prisoner of war, then asked: "The Predestined King measure himself against this vile Mahinou? The humblest of the Master of the World's subjects would never agree to pollute himself through bodily contact with this filthy beast from the mountain! May His Majesty deign to entrust this task to my sabre, which I can purify afterwards!"

The king enjoined his first minister to return to his place. He obeyed, much against his will.

"Come on! Let us fight!" repeated Guézo.

Cotovi pressed his elbows against his sides, crossed his forearms in front of his chest, and bent his upper body slightly forward in the humble pose of a servant in the presence of his master.

"Come on! Let us fight, my friend!" insisted Guézo with an engaging smile. He forced his left hand between the Mahinou's arm and his right side; with his other hand, he lifted his adversary's left arm and said: "Let us fight for a few moments! We fought against each other as long as we didn't know one another. Now that we find ourselves in each other's presence, a little fight can put an end to our quarrel!"

Cotovi had still not made up his mind to fight against the man who had vanquished his country.

Guézo had already adopted a fighting stance, feet firmly planted on the ground, upper body leaning forward, chin pressing down on the opponent's left shoulder, arms encircling his trunk, and interlocking fingers joined across his back.

Still unsure of himself, the Mahinou placed his head on the king's left shoulder and attempted to enfold his adversary in his arms, although he could not do

362

it easily because his arms passed on top of Guézo's and slipped at the slightest tightening of his grip, for the king had anointed his body with palm-oil scraped from his gris-gris.

The mahi spectators were filled with anxiety.

Guézo had given so many proofs of his strength that his victory over the Mahinou was not subject to the slightest doubt among the Danhomênous. When he was still but a pretender to the throne, hadn't he on two occasions saved his sister Sicoutin from the claws of the tyrant, who had ordered her bound hand and foot to a porter's rack that one of Migan's servants was about to throw from the top of an altar to sacrifice her?

Since his ascension to the throne, he had also demonstrated that he was not a common mortal who grew soft under the influence of earthly pleasures. Two moons before his departure for the last war, people had rushed to Gbêcon-Hounli to tell him that a mad bull had been terrorizing the city and was coming in the direction of the Palace. Guézo waited for the animal on the edge of the road near the foot of a baobab tree, despite his courtiers' attempts to dissuade him by pointing out all the dangers of such a position. Soon the beast arrived; his anger mounted at the sight of a man defying him; he charged the Master of the World, who grabbed him by the horns and instantly broke his neck in plain sight of the Danhomênous, who were trembling with fear. The beast sank to the ground, his eyes starting out of their sockets, his tongue dangling, his mouth foaming. To the awe-struck crowd the king said: "Only a rampaging buffalo could cross the city with impunity. Cattle can only do so in the countries of cowards."

Guézo tries to throw his adversary to the ground. Cotovi resists; he plants his feet as firmly as possible in the dust.

The king draws the Mahinou to him and squeezes his chest in a vice- grip, then stands up, towers over his opponent, and seeks to bend him in half. The pain causes Cotovi to stiffen; he marshals what strength and concentration he has left to avoid being thrown to the ground by surprise. The two combatants twist about and put forth great efforts, one to conquer, the other to defend himself. The earth reverberates with the stamping of their feet; their muscles tauten and stand out distinctly. Their joints crack; sweat pours over their sides and around their necks. Their breathing grows labored. Since victory does not come quickly, anxiety overtakes the Danhomênous. Among the ranks of the Mahinous, hearts are ablaze with ardent hopes. The vanquished know they are facing certain death, but before then they would like to see their chief throw the king of the Zadonous for a fall.

Guézo slides his arms down to the Mahinou's hips, grips them tightly, lifts his adversary at the moment when he is least expecting it, and throws him violently to the ground. The pain draws a cry from the defeated man. The hearts of his countrymen fall. One of them charges the wrestlers. Migan stops him short with a slash of the sabre. Guézo is straddling Cotovi, his eyes blazing with fury. His knees are pressing his adversary's shoulders to the ground; he grabs the man's head and twists his neck. The vertebral column snaps. The Mahinou's eyes bulge from their sockets; his body quivers; his heels are beating the ground with redoubled intensity; his hands succeed in freeing themselves and make a final convulsive attempt to gain a hold. His fingers clutch at the victor's thighs, but they hardly present a danger: his fingernails had been cut back to the flesh.

Triumphantly Guézo proclaims: "Beast from the mountain, go and tell my ancestors that their worthy successor is the brush fire that chases the bird from its nest; tell them that Hounjroto has been utterly devoured and that today is the day when Cotovi has truly avenged Gbêjiga!"

The Danhomênous were delirious with joy. A few Mahinous had lowered their heads; others were stamping on the ground in anger – the defeat of their chief humiliated them even more than the conquest of their country.

The victor stood up. With a single blow of his weighty sabre, Migan cut off Cotovi's head; he picked it up by the hair and paraded it past the joyous Danhomênous. The Mahinou's bloody tongue dangled back and forth, caught in the pincer-like grip of his jaws. The muscles of his face were contorted into a grimace. The Danhomênous were boundless in their praises for the king who had just avenged his brother Toffa in a glorious fashion. Two of the executioner's sevants came and hoisted the cadaver on to a gibbet at the Door of Dossoumoin.

Guézo had already rejoined his wives, who formed a hedge around him with their own persons; some wiped his neck and his sides, while others were bathing his hands and knees; they then draped a satin cloth over him and gave him back his sandals and his head-piece. He stretched out on his sofa; the guardian of the royal snuffbox placed a pipe in his mouth and lit it, as his retinue continued to celebrate his courage.

Orders were given for the Mahinous to spread out the items that had been brought to be sold. The market came to life. Soldiers passed in front of the makeshift merchants, asking the price of some article, depositing one or two strings of cowries on the ground or in a money basket, and taking away the object; meanwhile, the Mahinous withdrew into a disdainful silence.

A volley of sarcastic comments burst from the crowd. As their only response, a few of the vanquished stared fixedly at the Zadonous and spit on the ground. His voice filled with disdain, one of them said: "What are you celebrating about? About the fact that goats were born to you from eggs that were brooded by chickens? It's no miracle to conquer people by surprise or underhanded tricks."

The sham market took place under the satisfied patronage of the court.

At a sign from Migan, who had just been informed by Topo that the Mahinous had exhausted their stocks of merchandise, the first minister's servants walked through the market, imposing silence everywhere.

A man dug a hole about one span wide at the spot where the king had pinned the mahi chief to the ground. His whole arm disappeared into the hole.

Four of Migan's assistants brought forward a young Mahinou; they fitted him with a choke-pear, knelt him down, forced him to place his elbows on the ground, and held him firmly. Two other assistants pushed a six-cubit long stake into his rectum. The victim uttered but a single cry, and even it was stifled by the contraption that filled his mouth and immobilized his tongue.

The torturers raised the stake sharply, planted it in the hole, and packed dirt around the base of it. The crowd danced with joy at the sight of the empaled Mahinou moving his arms and legs convulsively; his eyes starting from their sockets, he opened and closed his mouth as if he were speaking. His body was shaken by a final violent contraction; his arms and legs shot out, stiffened for an instant, then fell limp. One end of a stick was shoved into his side and the other into his wrist to hold his arm aloft. In his hand they attached the pole with this dynasty's flag – a rectangular piece of material the color of boiling palm oil and bearing a buffalo cut from red cloth in the center. A mouse was tied to the foot of the stake in front of the Mahinou.

Migan had invented this torture, and he informed the delirious crowd: "During a consultation, the oracle assured this stinking beast from Hounjroto that the Danhomênous would be defeated and that he himself would return from the war without the slightest scratch. The Mahinou then vowed to massacre Danhomênous like rats. Let's see if he succeeds in killing this mouse!" Raising his eyes toward the flag, the executioner laughed with a sneer: "But the only thing this beast succeeds in holding up is the flag of Aligo! It thus proclaims the Master of the World's victory over Cotovi and offers a brilliant rebuttal to his oracle!

"Danhomênous shall replace the Mahinous and sell their merchandise.

"The mahi country has been transported to Agbomê, where it will become a market that has been named Hounjroto by the Master of the World and will henceforth be held here on the day after each Ajahi. By this, the Predestined King means to announce that, like a market, Hounjroto will no longer be inhabited. Even the fetishes have abandoned the mahi country that has just been defeated. Rituals conducted during the past two days have made them favorable to Danhomê, and they will be appropriate for sellers in this market, which they will protect from all sorts of dangers. From now on the trees brought back from Hounjroto will provide shade for sellers here and in all the principal markets of Danhomê, even as far away as Zobê[2] at Gléhoué.

"As soon as the sun has turned his head, all Danhomênous should gather in the Courtyard of Gbêcon-Hounli."

Covering themselves with dust, the people expressed their appreciation for the new proof that the Master of the World had just given them of his solicitude for the well-being of his subjects.

The actual market began. Among the crowd of buyers, Topo's emissaries were the most active; on the king's behalf, they acquired cattle, birds, smoked meat, large jugs, kettles, earthenware plates, lamps, millet, maize, and other food supplies.

---

[2]   "Zobê" is a market at Ouidah (Gléhoué); it dates back to the time of the first European settlement in this city, and, according to tradition, it was created on the site of a former firing range. (author's note)

The sun had already turned his head toward the dwelling built for him on the other side of the Coufo. A cannon shot resounded in the Courtyard of Gbêcon-Hounli and brought the people streaming there from the market. Bamboo stalks lying on the ground marked a boundary the people knew they must not cross. Mahinous (both men and women) emerged from the Palace leading cattle, goats, and pigs and carrying cages of fowl, sacks of grain, gourds of palm-oil, baskets of food, demijohns of brandy, large empty jugs, kettles, plates made from baked clay, strings of cowries, hampers filled with cloths, new guns, two barrels of shot, twenty of gunpowder, wadding, a cartridge pouch, and a sabre attached to a red velvet shoulder strap. It was all arranged to the right of the throne. To the left the drums were beating frenetically.

A member of the palace guard approached a spot four paces from the royal sofa and deposited a three-cubit-high package wrapped in a crimson velvet cloth on another velvet cloth so dazzlingly white it would have made the sun pale with jealousy.

The high dignitaries and the families of the ministers and princes who had been lost at Hounjroto arrived with Assogbaou in the lead. The royal guard followed, and then the Wives of Panther in ceremonial attire flowed by. The king installed himself on the throne. Mêwou unwrapped the package at which the puzzled crowd had been staring. It was a throne fashioned of white wood and supported by four skulls. Three cubits high, a span and a half wide, it easily measured a span and a finger joint deep. On the bottom, the four sides were serrated and adorned with elaborate fretwork. On the top, six small columns a bit more than a span tall supported the seat, which flared outward. The highest of the seven thrones that symbolized the seven preceding reigns of record was not half as tall as the one being presented to the conqueror of Hounjroto. None of them were as richly ornamented as his was, nor could any of them boast an equally glorious origin.

"The Master of the World has truly distinguished himself from his predecessors," said the Danhomênous, whose eyes remained fixed on the majestic throne.

Houndo, the master sculptor of the royal household, had lavished all his skill and intelligence on the construction of this chair. Flattered by the images contrived by the artist, the king had rewarded him generously.

The solemn voice of the first minister had just put an end to the people's adulatory comments, and facing the Danhomênous, he told them: "The Mahinous of Hounjroto have been harshly punished for their share in the responsibility for the murder of the white men, our friends.

"In this kingdom no one has ever cited the example of a prince who was avenged in as heroic a fashion as Toffa was this morning. The beasts from the mountains committed sacrilege against the remains of a noble son of Agonglo. Cotovi and the three other chiefs of Hounjroto responsible for this blasphemy will expiate it in perpetuity, for it is their skulls that support the throne of this reign."

Pointing to the throne that was displayed for the admiration of the Danhomênous, he continued: "The six columns you see there are hammers; the seat they support is an anvil. The hammers represent the past reigns up to and including that of Pingla. By this, the victor over Cotovi means to say: 'The hammer has its own weight, to be sure. But as for the worthy son of Agonglo, he is an anvil, and he vows that his deeds will surpass those of all the kings who preceded his august Father in this Danhomê.'"

The Danhomênous praised the appropriateness of the allegory and tumultuously proclaimed that the desires of this reign would be fulfilled.

Migan imposed silence on the crowd, then called Zanbounou. He rushed forward with his assistants; they were all equipped like soldiers. People could not be allowed to suspect that they were spies in the service of Danhomê. The chief spy received two nubile young girls selected from among the captives of Hounjroto. One of them was carrying a basket filled with cloths; the other was burdened with a basket of cowries. Every Danhomênou who had accompanied him, sharing in the adversities of the journey or the dangers of an espionage mission, was given a young wife and a basket of cloths and cowries.

When they got up, they were no longer recognizable under the dust with which they had covered themselves as a sign of their gratitude for the munificence of the king. Their hearts full of joy, they departed with their wives.

These women would have to resign themselves to living with the principal architects of their country's destruction.

All the soldiers who had distinguished themselves for bravery at Hounjroto came forward to be recompensed according to the significance of their exploits: a captive for one, a cloth for another, a string of cowries for a third. They invariably thanked the king by covering themselves with dust before withdrawing.

The young Amazon who had slashed the calf of the Mahinou fleeing through a hedge and her sister-in-arms Ganwoumê, who had killed a diviner and then captured the man who was consulting him (the one who had been empaled that morning), were too effulgent with the warlike virtue worshipped by Danhomê not to take their place from now on among the Wives of Panther, although the marriage ceremonies were postponed until the after the period of mourning being observed by the court.

At a sign from the second minister, Assogbaou prostrated himself on the spot that had just been vacated by the soldiers.

The king ordered him to be presented with ten young female captives, selected from among the most beautiful ones, to serve him.

Covering himself with dirt, the prince replied: "Won't these daughters from the mountains become filled with their own importance if they are admitted into my harem? I prefer to sell them, but only to the Father of Wealth. Let him deign to pay me what they are worth – just barely a little glass of brandy."

The court laughed at the prince's contempt for the Mahinous.

A steward arrived and handed him a glass filled with the white man's alcohol.

Assogbaou emptied it at a single draught in plain sight of the captives, then turned to them and said: "The entire profit from your sale can only pay for a little glass of brandy. You really are worthless beasts!"

He again covered himself with dirt as an expression of his gratitude for the king's generosity.

Mêwou motioned Toffa's family to come forward.

The king had been speaking in Migan's ear for a while; now the first minister faced the people and informed them: "King Houégbaja will provide a magnificent funeral for Toffa. The ten captives who have just been sold to the Father of Wealth by Assogbaou will be added to these twenty (he pointed his finger toward a batch of young female war prisoners who were kneeling to the left of the throne). It will be upon their dead bodies that Toffa's skull will rest. The burial will be conducted before the first crowing of the cock.

The velvet and silk cloths, the breeches, and the headpieces contained in these ten baskets are being offered to the prince by Houégbaja. Ten demijohns of brandy, ten baskets of cowries, ten guns, as well as barrels of powder and shot will be buried with him. The cowries will enable him to repay the disembodied souls in the city of the dead for pointing out the route he must follow to be reunited with his ancestors, before whom he will appear in the company of an armed guard.

"Toffa experienced a glorious death! For this reason we should not overly sad. His funeral celebrations will last for two long market days, and the drums in this area shall beat uninterruptedly for the entire time. People shall sing the prince's heroism day and night. Five head of cattle, ten goats, and as many pigs will be sacrificed each day. Danhomênous will eat and drink until they are full.

"At each rising and setting of the sun, a Mahinou will be dispatched to tell the ancestors about the funeral celebrations of the preceding night or day.

"The blood of Mahinous will be used to knead the clay of the mausoleum that shall be built over the prince's grave after the celebrations. Glass beads and corals will be added to that clay, and rum bought with profits from the sale of mahi captives to Chacha Ajinacou since the return from the war will be poured into it."

The members of Toffa's family covered themselves with dirt as an expression of their gratitude.

A murmur of approval ran through the crowd.

*   *   *

Doguicimi approached the throne and took up a position in front of Toffa's eldest child. She kneeled down, kissed the ground, gathered up a bit of sand, rubbed it against her forehead three times, kissed the ground again, and sat up straight. She displayed none of the blind rage that had animated her against the king upon his return from the first war of Hounjroto or on the first day of the traditional celebrations following the campaign that had caused her unhappiness.

Judging by certain movements of her face and body, one could nevertheless sense that she was struggling to maintain control over the grief betrayed by the tears she wiped away in a rapid gesture with the back of her hand. She wanted to speak, but twice she opened her mouth in vain; her throat was constricted with emotion.

With a supreme effort, she said in a muffled voice: "I committed a blasphemy when the Master of the World returned from Hounjroto without my husband. I defied the king once again on the first day of the celebrations held after the return from the war in which my husband was lost; my crime deserved to be punished by death. But having no doubt understood that my vituperations were motivated solely by my grief, the king, who is truly the Father and the Mother of his subjects, did not deal harshly with the blasphemer whose head was being persistently called for by the outraged courtiers. Brought before the court a short time later and charged with odious crimes of high treason that could only be expiated by death, I saw myself subjected to a punishment that proved to be a defeat for my detractors. The all-merciful king undertook a second war against Hounjroto to liberate my husband, whom he thought to be still alive. But the noble prince had been killed a long time ago by a beast from the mountain.

"I sincerely regret my unjustified attacks against the king.

"I am convinced that the Houégbajas who hear me today will grant a long and glorious reign to their successor for having brought the skull of Toffa back to the land of his fathers.

"But I doubt that they approve of entombing the prince's remains with the cadavres of these foul beasts from the mountains. These venerable remains were initially defiled at Hounjroto, and if this taint enters his sepulchre with him, it will not fail to accompany him to the city of the dead and disgrace the prince in the eyes of his ancestors.

"May the Predestined King deign to be satisfied with smearing the blood of these Mahinous on his gris-gris and ordering that their bodies be discarded as fodder for the hyenas and vultures or hung from all the doors of the city just like the 'dogs' that are sacrificed to the fetishes.

"Before his departure for the war, my husband could only fall asleep when his head was resting on my chest.

"I implore the Master of the World to accord me the favor of allowing me to be buried with the skull of the noble prince; in the sepulchre my body will replace his, which remained at Hounjroto."

She kissed the ground and wiped dirt across her forehead three times.

The Royal Wives blanched with mortification. One of them whispered in her neighbor's ear: "This daughter of a bitch wants to follow her husband in death? By offering to make a noble gesture, which should be the sole prerogative of queens like us, she is trying to efface the painful memory that her disgraceful behavior has left in the minds of others. When people came to inform a blind man that his son had killed an antelope, the sceptical invalid retorted: 'I won't believe this piece of news until I have touched the animal's horns.' She's deceiving herself if she thinks death is as gentle as the king whom she affronted on three occasions without risking very much!"

369

Guézo went back into the Palace; the council of the throne arranged the details of the prince's funeral celebrations and then, before the burial of Toffa, ordered the carrying out of a ritual that was supposed to assuage the anger of Gou, the god of war and weapons – in other words, to prevent him from spilling the blood of other members of the royal family.

Mêwou carried Toffa's skull to the prince's family along with everything else the king had offered for the burial and the funeral celebrations.

The grave was dug in the middle of the spacious courtyard that spread out behind the prince's reception room. The sound of the hoes still biting briskly into the earth and breaking off bulky clods of it was eclipsed by the funeral laments being sung by a group of grave-diggers who had remained near the edge of the burial pit and were accompanying themselves by beating their hands against their chests and thighs and shaking rattles and bells. The dirt removed from the grave had been piled about ten bamboos away.

The chief grave-digger Dopêgan supervised the work and stimulated the ardor of his assistants with copious glassfuls of brandy.

All the members of the household were weeping. Widows and orphans were rolling in the dust. The men kept their grief under control. Several children were sitting beside their mothers and consoling them. Many of them were surprised that the *caloulous* had not been heated since morning, that hearths, water jugs, kettles, and mortars for pounding foo-foo were in complete disarray, and that even the large rocks used for grinding grain had been removed from their usual places.

Doguicimi acknowledged that Cotovi's death had avenged that of Toffa. But she reflected to herself that the destruction of Hounjroto, the creation of a new market, the torments of the Mahinou who was empaled at the site of this market to expiate his insolence, and finally the construction of a throne supported by four enemy skulls redounded solely to the glory of the king. She would have wanted the memory of Toffa's captivity, and the sacrifice he made of his life, to be preserved in this country, and she regretted being a mere woman who had no means at her disposal of immortalizing her husband's name.

That was the reason she was crying, although less audibly than her co- wives and Toffa's orphans.

A single thought comforted her in her afflictions: the Master of the World had not opposed her request to be buried with the skull of her husband.

At nightfall, the dead man's friends and relatives sent to the family the gifts that would be interred with the prince's skull.

*   *   *

Funerary drums, stone crocks over the top of which a buffalo-hide fan had been stretched, resounded mournfully in more than ten groups located in the Courtyard of Gbêcon-Hounli, in front of Toffa's house, and near the site of his interment.

Funeral laments were sung continuously to provide a bit of solace for afflicted hearts by reminding them that this world is a transitory dwelling and that the land of the dead is an enormous house where we must all return to live forever alongside the ancestors of the tribe.

The night was far advanced. A group comprised of Vidaho, Migan, Dopêgan, the princes, and the friends of the dead man had gathered in the reception room, where Assogbaou never tired of recounting the miseries of their captivity.

A gravedigger approached them, kneeled down next to Dopêgan, and whispered a few words in his ear.

The chief gravedigger went up to Mêwou; the two of them remained absorbed in private conversation for a moment.

The second minister leaned toward Migan and the heir to the throne; they spoke in hushed tones, then Mêwou walked over to Toffa's room, where the widows and some of the orphans had assembled. The minister returned and informed his colleagues that everything was ready. The high dignitaries surrounded the sepulchre. Soon Toffa's children and servants arrived, followed by the prince's wives, their bodies besmeared with dirt, one arm swinging freely, the other folded across the chest with the hand on the opposite shoulder.

The order was given for the drums and singers to remain silent for a short while.

The gravediggers brought forward the gifts being offered by the king for the interment. Dopêgan had the cloths, breeches, and headpieces unwrapped; he then announced to everyone present: "King Houégbaja is offering these clothes for the interment of Toffa!" One of his assistants removed a narrow strip of material from each cloth and made a small tear in the breeches and headpieces. The chief gravedigger then called out the other gifts: weapons (guns, a sword with a fringed shoulder strap), war supplies, the prince's sleeping mat, a tripod made of white wood, the necessities of a smoker (a silver pipe, a leather snuff box containing chopped tobacco, tinder, and flint), and baskets of cowries; after ordering one of the ten demijohns arranged in front of him to be uncorked, he sipped its contents, clacked his tongue, and proclaimed with an unavoidable grimace: "It's strong stuff!"

He went on to the gifts from the high dignitaries of the court and those from the princes, then concluded with those from the dead man's widows, orphans, and servants – farmers, hunters, and weavers. He ordered all the presents carried down into the sepulchre.

The gravediggers came back to report that everything had been arranged; Dopêgan went to check. Vivênagbo wanted to see the resting place that had been prepared for the final sleep of his sworn friend. His tall figure disappeared into a shaft two cubits in diameter and descended to the bottom of it on a ladder that was eight cubits high; on his knees he passed through a side corridor two armlengths long. A second ladder brought him to the bottom of the sepulchre, which measured a good bamboo and a half wide and two bamboos long. Despite his height, his hands could not reach within an armlength of the ceiling. At the foot of one of the longer walls and facing the entry, there was a small mound of earth; a cubit and a half high, four cubits wide, and at least six cubits long, it constituted a bed that had been elevated even more by a thick layer of mats and velvet cloths. The wall on this side, like those to the right and the left, had been hung with cloths of white velvet. Little triangular niches had been excavated in the last wall, which was entirely bare, and they held the four lamps that illuminated the sepulchre.

The baskets of cloths and cowries, the barrels of powder and shot, and the demijohns of brandy had been arranged in rows to the right and the left; the guns had been hung on the walls and the snuff box placed at the foot of the bed.

Vivênagbo returned and informed his colleagues that Toffa truly did have a viaticum and a resting place worthy of him.

Vidaho, Migan, Mêwou, Dopêgan, four of his assistants, and the prince's oldest son went to the room where Doguicimi was staying.

The time of the interment was approaching. The grief of the prince's family burst forth once again. Some pounded the floor with their feet as they wept. Others rolled on the ground, lamenting: "I'll never see him again in this world!" "I'll never hear his voice again!" "Master, is it true that your gaze will only appear to me in dreams from now on?" One widow threw herself violently on the ground and moaned: "What death will strike me at this very instant to take me from this world and convey me to his side?"

Drying her eyes, a princess, who had been moved to tears by these truly distressing lamentations, declared: "A woman who has never gone through this ordeal can not understand your grief! During the last dry season, I too yearned for the death that would bring me closer to my husband!"

All at once, a voice was heard singing; its fullness overpowered the lamentations:

> When you know that the smallest insects
> Escaped the conflagration
> Which consumed the forest
> And that only the lordly elephant died there,
> How can you not pity him?
> What an unhappy fate was his!
> His death is sad and humiliating too!
> Listen to the laments that sorrow inspires
> In the wives and children of the noble prince!
> Poor little birds! The fire
> That devoured the giant plane tree
> Took your refuge from you, forever.
> You have good reason to lament!
> Weeping is more than a widow's and orphan's right;
> It's a moral obligation for them.
> Thus no one can blame those of you
> Who want to look for asylum somewhere else!
> No one can decently reproach a created being
> For wanting to be reunited with his Creator.
> Toffa's now resting along with his ancestors.

He must need my attentions in the city of the dead.
Knowing that, I can not agree
To remain in this world and enjoy its pleasures.

It was Doguicimi who was singing. On top of three velvet cloths that formed a fold around her waist, she was wearing a larger, brilliantly white satin one that fell to her heels and was held to her body by an equally white velvet belt tied above her breasts. Pendants dangling from silver bracelets tinkled on her arms and wrists.

Her ears were enlarged by beautiful white wooden cylinders that had been passed through holes in each lobe.

As she passed by, the scent of the pomade with which she had anointed her body hovered in the air, mingling with the odor of a compound which she had spread across her neck and chest and which, when it dried, left white spots that were highlighted against the calabash- yellow background of her skin. Her hair had been shaved, her fingernails cut.

Doguicimi had taken infinite pains to adorn herself, for she did not want her husband to feel ashamed when she appeared before him in the city of the dead. She was walking at a deliberate pace, pressing a packet wrapped in white satin against her chest – the skull of Toffa.

Someone preparing to sacrifice a goat to a fetish as an expression of gratitude for a wish that had been granted could not have been more serene.

But wasn't she going to sacrifice her life with all its youthfulness and beauty and promise of future happiness?

Why then this joy that everything about her seemed to exude? Many people were puzzled by it. Vidaho explained it to himself in his own way: "Toffa completely dominated Doguicimi by mixing irresistible love potions in her food and drink. As a result, my own were powerless to divert her glance and her affections in my direction and to detain her in this world!"

The royal prince had difficulty concealing his disappointment at the fact that this woman, who did not have her equal in all Danhomê, was eluding his grasp.

She reached the edge of the grave.

"Are you abandoning me? Without you, what will happen to me?"

Doguicimi looked back. It was Zokindé whose laments she had heard. The poor child continued: "Mother, dear mother, into whose care are you confiding me?"

Two large tears welled from Doguicimi's eyes and fell upon the skull she was pressing to her chest.

Dopêgan held out to her the little flask of poison that the queens took under such circumstances and that he was offering her for the second time. The woman pushed it away, announcing: "I want to be buried alive with the skull of the noble prince!" These words stunned all those who were present.

The heir to the throne reflected to himself: "People have seen the Wives of Panther agree to follow the king to the city of the dead, but in advance they always drank rum mixed with mercury, and no more than their dead bodies were interred with the royal remains. In the entire history of Danhomnê, has anyone ever heard tell of a queen who agreed to face the agonies of death in her husband's tomb? Only dwarves have ever been buried alive in the royal sepulchres. And all the strength of Dopêgan and his assistants was necessary to oblige these monstrous creatures to accept their fate!" No one there believed the woman capable of persisting to the end.

"We'll soon be jeering at her!" mocked a gravedigger.

Hearing this taunt, the love-struck prince was filled with hope; he said to himself: "Doguicimi doesn't want to take the poison. She won't die quickly then. It is undoubtedly to keep her alive and to help me overcome her resistence that the Houégbajas inspired her with the idea of refusing the poisoned beverage!" He ordered the woman's wishes to be respected but added that he would consult his august Father before the tomb was sealed over her.

The two first ministers followed him.

On his way to the Palace, the royal prince was thinking: "The king is probably unaware of the passion that has been tormenting the heir to the throne ever since the morning when he took his son, whom he was preparing for the governance of this country, to the tomb of Agonglo to reveal the soul of the Danhomênous to him and inadvertantly provoked in him a love for Doguicimi.

"If the Master of the World happened to discover the desire of his heir, could he fail to satisfy it now that Toffa's death has freed his wife of her obligations to him?"

The preceding afternoon Vidaho had attempted to decline the honor of presiding over the interment of Toffa's skull on the pretext that he was suffering from ill health. In reality, he didn't want to see Doguicimi die in front of his very eyes while he remained powerless to seize her from the grip of death once the traditional potion, which was used by the Wives of Panther designated to accompany the king to the realm of the spirits, had begun to take effect.

He now realized that, by insisting upon imposing what he considered to be a difficult task on the son, his august Father was unconsciously obeying an unsuspected directive from the ancestors, who, having taken pity on their successor, had secretly decided to satisfy his desire.

Outside the drums had begun beating again; the songs had resumed more empassioned than ever. Cannons thundered. Great shouts of joy soon greeted the arrival of stone jugs filled with brandy.

Before leaving, Vidaho had suggested to Mêwou's servants that they serve the dancers and spectators something to drink. He wanted the Danhomênous to demonstrate, through their expressions of joy, that life was good and that it would be folly to leave it before having fully enjoyed it.

The moon was adding its illumination to that of the lamps placed on top of bamboo stakes driven into the ground at the Courtyard of Gbêcon-Hounli, around Toffa's house, and in his courtyard. Attracted by the booming of the drums, Danhomênous were streaming into the area from the most distant neighborhoods; there was not the slightest danger in remaining away from home that night, for the Master of the World had commanded the people to attend his brother's interment in great numbers, and he himself had promised to remain in the Courtyard of the Palace until after the second crowing of the cock.

When he was informed of the resolve expressed by Toffa's wife, the king exclaimed: "Only common mortals can be surprised by that!" Turning to his wives, he continued: "Didn't I tell you that the soul slumbering in this child's body knows no equal except for that of my never-to-be-forgotten mother?"

Just as oil poured on a dying fire restores the flames to life, the king's renewed eulogies to the courage of Doguicimi rekindled both the resentment of the queens and the ardor of the passion that had been smouldering in the soul of the heir to the throne ever since his royal Father had revealed to him the virtues of Toffa's wife.

The promises Vidaho had made to assure Doguicimi's happiness first in this world and then in the next, the love potions he had mixed into the food and drink that had been offered to her, the threats to punish this woman who disdained him, and finally the schemes to conquer her by utilizing the services of Zanbounou – nothing had succeeded for the prince in his attempt to induce her to share his love. He was angry at himself for having taken detours that had not brought him any closer to his desired goal. He recalled the anxiety of the king when he was seeking a cure for the listlessness of his heir, who had been wasting away after the traditional celebrations following the defeat of the Danhomênous at Hounjroto. At the time, the love-struck prince had been planning to have someone drop a hint to the king that the possession of Doguicimi was the only remedy that could cure the illness from which the royal prince was suffering. The only thing that had prevented Vidaho from approaching the king's most intimate counsellors with such an idea was what he knew about the character of his august Father, who never gave precedence to his paternal sentiments over the duties of his office, the imperatives of the blood oath, or the obligations of gratitude. The spectre of Migan's vengeance had also haunted the prince's spirit for a short while, but it quickly dissipated when he recalled that the first minister was indebted to the heir to the throne.

Fear of the king's censure had caused the prince to reject his trusted friends' advice that he abduct Doguicimi from Toffa's compound. The consequences of a scandal seemed unbearable to him; he would be risking much more than his right to the throne, for he could be thrown into prison.

But from now on Doguicimi was free. Vidaho convinced himself that, if he told the king of his love for her, the Master of the World, deeply concerned for the well-being of his heir, would not hesitate to give him the desired woman; the mahi bodies could then be spread out in Toffa's sepulchre to provide a suitable resting place for the prince's skull, as had been decided initially by the council of the throne.

Among the ranks of the high dignitaries, voices would be raised, advising the court to consult the oracle. Taken into the future Master of the World's confidence, Wolo could argue that Toffa opposed the sacrifice Doguicimi wanted to make of her life and that he would only accept his first wife as the bearer of his skull into the realm of death.

The king was sitting up, his left elbow resting on his thigh, his chin between his thumb and his forefinger, his eyes half closed.

Interpreting the older man's pose as a sign of fatigue, the heir to the throne feared that his august Father might suddenly decide to go and lie down. He told himself he had to anticipate the king's decision and that, if he made himself very humble, his request would certainly be granted. He gathered up what dirt he could find so as to cover his head and chest with it before speaking. Abruptly snatched from his meditations by the tributes of his heir and thinking that the prince and the two first ministers were getting ready to return to Toffa's compound, the king said to them: "You say that Doguicimi has asked to be buried alive with her husband's skull? She is obviously fulfilling a pledge she made to the deceased. To prevent someone from discharging a vow of this kind is tantamount to bringing the dead man's anger down upon our heads. Make certain then that everything is done according to this woman's wishes and before the first crowing of the cock!"

The prince covered himself with dirt as a sign of obedience to the orders of the king.

He thought: "The king has spoken the truth! To bring Doguicimi back to life would be to offend Toffa and also perhaps the ancestors whom I will someday replace at the head of this kingdom!"

The hapless lover had to resign himself to going and observing the burial of both his love and the procession of dreams that had been accompanying his unrequited passion for the past eight dry seasons.

On the way back to Toffa's compound, he confided in the two ministers: "The Master of the World is right! Let's be careful not to disobey the wishes of our dead."

Mêwou completed his thought: "For if they are generous when we bow to their will, they can also be relentless if we disobey them!"

"That's true! Quite true!" said the prince approvingly after heaving a deep sigh.

Scarcely had the heir to the throne and the two first ministers turned their backs to go and inform the king of Doguicimi's intention, when she herself descended precipitately into the grave.

Lying upon the pallet prepared for her husband, she placed her hands over the skull that rested on her chest.

Having vainly beseeched her to climb back to the surface before Vidaho and the two ministers returned, Dopêgan ordered his men to extinguish the lamps in the sepulchre and added: "You will see her again in a moment, even if she has to carry a boulder on her chest. What woman could possibly endure the horror of darkness in the tomb?"

The gravedigger who carried out his superior's order urged Doguicimi to climb out of the pit before she was engulfed in utter darkness.

The woman did not move. Fearing that the gravediggers might return under cover of the descending gloom to snatch the prince's skull from her, she had placed it beneath the mat and covered it with her body, determined to sink her teeth into the throat of anyone who might dispute her possession of it. Upon the return of the three high dignitaries, a second gravedigger was sent to relight the lamps, and when he saw her in that position, he thought she had died after swallowing some fatal potion she had secretly brought with her; he shook her.

"What is it?" she asked, anger quivering in her voice and flashing in her eyes.

"I am bringing you light!" replied the gravedigger anxiously.

He reported this exchange to Dopêgan, who whispered the following advice into his ear: "Learn to stammer!"

The drums redoubled their fury; from time to time the drummers gulped down a small glass of rum to heighten their ardor. The memory of the singers was inexhaustible; the royal prince's emissaries passed among them and murmured a few words into their ears. Songs describing the heat, the darkness, and indeed all the horrors of the grave now rapidly succeeded one another on their lips; these funeral laments alternated with those that celebrated the sweetness of life on this earth, as if a dead man could, at the very moment of his interment, be inspired with the desire to begin breathing again so that he too could experience the joy of life among people who were expressing their happiness in songs, dances, and shouts of delight.

They scrupulously avoided funeral dirges that celebrated the delights of the afterworld and songs which conceded that we all live in an alien country for the duration of our existence in this world or that our final resting place is always the city of the dead. Around the sepulchre, nothing at all was heard that might offer a modicum of solace to the souls of friends and relatives devastated by this painful separation, nothing that might give courage to a person who was preparing to meet death.

Three gravediggers brought down the prince's divination apparatus, the last objects to be carried into their owner's tomb. As one of the gravediggers filled the lamps for the final time and replaced the wicks, he admitted that he was disconcerted by the woman's attitude. "How can she remain unmoved in the midst of the joy that has taken possession of the Danhomênous?"

"I am no less surprised than you are," replied one of his companions. "And yet the youth and beauty of that woman are such that she could even remarry a prince of the royal family and thereby help replenish the population of Danhomê."

"She has apparently not been treated with much consideration since the disappearance of her husband during the first Hounjroto campaign. She only decided to leave this world because she has become an object of loathing for those who were seduced by her beauty," revealed the third gravedigger, glancing furtively over his shoulder and claiming to have been informed about the woman by one of his relatives.

"In that case, she's right!" concluded the first gravedigger. "The earth alone can bury human misery!"

Before reascending, one of them said to Doguicimi: "The heat is becoming oppressive in here. It's much better outside. Although the lamps are full of oil, the flames are flickering for lack of air. It won't be long before they go out. There is still time to climb out, if you like."

He affected a sincere compassion.

The woman had once again turned over on her back, cradling her husband's skull on her chest; her only reply was to turn away her head.

The sound of the songs and the trampling of the ground reverberated in Doguicimi's ears without provoking in her any desire to return and share the joy of the Danhomêmous.

The chief gravedigger was absolutely convinced that the extinguishing of the lamps would vanquish Doguicimi's pride.

At the request of the heir to the throne, Dopêgan descended into the sepulchre for one last inspection. Before returning to the surface, he informed the woman that she could still rejoin her companions and experience the joy of life.

He left and told the assembled dignitaries that Doguicimi had not even glanced in his direction.

A large earthen vessel was lowered to the floor of the shaft. One of the gravediggers wedged the bottom of the vessel into the entrance of the passageway that formed an ante-chamber to the sepulchre. He returned to the surface. Three basketfuls of earth were thrown into the shaft. A volley of sobs immediately burst from the ranks of Toffa's widows, orphans, and servants.

Dopêgan descended the shaft and cocked his ear in the direction of the passageway; he heard nothing. Nonetheless, he shouted, "Doguicimi, do you want to go up?" There was no reply.

Once he had regained the surface, he ordered two more basketfuls of earth thrown into the shaft.

Vidaho's hope was entirely based upon the assumption that the horrors of the grave would persuade Doguicimi to beg that she be allowed to return and experience the joy of life.

He commanded Dopêgan to have the entrance to the passageway cleared and the earthen vessel raised. A stifling odor stuck in the throat of the gravedigger, who could not prevent himself from coughing. The sepulchre was almost completely shrouded in darkness. Yet, by the light of the only lamp that still flickered eerily, the man saw Doguicimi lying as before upon the pallet. He shouted to her, "Vidaho beseeches you to go up and experience the joy of life."

She did not reply.

The gravedigger returned to make his report.

Migan lifted his gaze toward the sky; several sons of the moon[3] had already risen to the middle of the firmament; the glow of many others was beginning to dwindle. In a trenchant tone of voice, the minister observed: "This game has gone on long enough! We have orders to finish everything before the first crowing of the cock!"

They had to comply. The earthen vessel was replaced at the entrance to the side corridor that led to the sepulchre.

Two men were piling dirt into the baskets that were being passed to the site of the grave by a chain of gravediggers. The shaft was filled to the top. Two gravediggers stamped down the dirt; the others accompanied them with funeral laments.

Each pounding blow of their feet hammered at Vidaho's heart.

He was only present in body.

The compacted earth sank about a cubit. More basketfuls of dirt were brought. The gravediggers took up their dance again. This time the hole had been amply filled.

Aroused from his meditations by the solemn voice of Migan, who informed him that the interment was complete, the rejected suitor shook his head.

Staring for one last time at the spot where the woman of his desires had just disappeared, he sighed: "Doguicimi, your attacks against the king filled me at first with hatred toward you, although in the end I was captivated by them. Yet your virtue triumphed over every scheme inspired by the passionate love that burned within me and sought to kindle a companion flame in you. Your quick-wittedness permitted you to thwart the ambushes I had laid to prove you guilty of infidelity toward Toffa so that the king might sentence you to death. Your courage enabled you to endure all the torments that my scorned love devised to exact its revenge, and today this same courage kindles joy in your heart and prompts you to accept the pangs of death in a tomb where you are allowing yourself to be buried alive. Our souls are surely not in harmony with each other. That lies beyond our control. Marrying you would undoubtedly have resulted in disaster for me. Foreseeing such an outcome, my ancestors opposed our union. And yet that only makes me love you all the more, Doguicimi!"

---

[3] "Sons of the moon" is a local expression that refers to the stars, regarded as children of the moon. (author's note)

Epilogue

Doguicimi, your heroism, like that of so many others in Dahomey, reveals the admirable qualities of this race.

Desiring to heighten the drama of your sacrifice, which actually did occur, I imagined that, like a large number of Dahomeyans, Toffa was steeped in prejudice against beings with only "seven pairs of ribs" and that on the eve of his departure for the war of Hounjroto, which also actually took place, he did not conceal from you his doubts about your fidelity, indeed his doubts about the fidelity of all women.

The woman I created eloquently defended her sex against these slanders.

The woman I created was so grief-stricken at the announcement of her husband's disappearance at Hounjroto and so angered by the slanders against his memory that she was aroused to oppose Guézo and wish for his death far from the land of his Fathers as an expiation for his crime.

The woman I created had to endure unremitting assaults upon her virtue by the heir to the throne and by a spy during her husband's captivity, but, aided by the stout defenses with which her upbringing had endowed her, supported by her love for her husband, and protected by her ancestors and her fetishes (that is to say, by her religion), she succeeded in triumphing over those who wanted to make her stray from the path of virtue.

I imagined that queens and co-wives had vowed to bring about her downfall and had schemed against her, not because they were perverse and resented virtue and chastity, but because the Dahomeyan can not bear to see anyone else rise above the average; once someone is noticed, people take aim at him and persist in bringing him down.

I imagined how the hatred of a rejected suitor and that of a scorned intriguant were called down upon the head of my Doguicimi as a result of her integrity and how she expiated her love for Toffa in heroic suffering.

I imagined that, at the very moment when she was fighting heroically to maintain her purity and even in the grave itself, she was being slandered in the vilest manner, because that is often the fate of virtuous individuals.

It is my opinion, Doguicimi, that, ever since you rejoined Toffa after agreeing to confront the horrors of death in a sepulchre, he must have been convinced of your fidelity and the sincerity of your love for him, if he ever truly doubted it.

Today the women of Dahomey can no longer follow your example and make the supreme sacrifice that has immortalized your name, but they can still refuse to participate in an illicit love. It is true that one still finds Ayomayis in this country. Why deny it? But there are also legions of our mothers, that is to say, women whose families raised them with an abhorrence of ever prostituting themselves, those who realize that such immoral behavior is a disgrace as much for themselves as for their husbands and their families. The natural modesty of our mothers was, we have to admit, bolstered by the fear of a salutary punishment on behalf of the ancestors and the fetishes; Dahomeyans were convinced that adultery is always punished by a death meted out by a woman's own ancestors, or by those of her husband in their anger at the shame being heaped upon them by the immoral behavior of their descendants or their daughter-in-law, or by the fetishes that are pitiless in their pursuit of unfaithful wives. This fear is a powerful restraint, and it continues to sustain an integrity of morals among the fetishists of Dahomey, resulting in the fact that the large number of virtuous women more than compensates for the deviance of the others, who are still but an insignificant minority, although their numbers have been growing ever since divorce was made easier under the pretext of emancipating the black woman.

Doguicimi, I also fancied that, when the mission from Europe was received at the court of Guézo, you would have preferred the coming of the Zojagués – the French – who, you thought, seemed to combine the essential qualities that would enable them to stop the endless wars of the Dahomeyan kings, the slave trade, and the human sacrifices that were laying waste to the country more than they were enriching it.

Our elders assure us that our dead continue to interest themselves in everything that happens in our world.

Thus, you are no doubt rejoicing to see that, where the diplomacy of the Glincis proved unproductive, the French flag was to succeed magnificently a half century later, that is to say in bringing a reign of peace, liberty, and humanity to Dahomey.

Cotonu, 22 August 1935

Glossary

Adogouin	a market in Agbomê
Aflémougan	a small double bell that was sounded to order the people to gather in the Great Courtyard of the Palace at Agbomê.
Afomayi	a place of exile for princes and other high dignitaries whose crimes do not merit the death penalty.
Agbé	the sea god of the Danhomênous.
Agassou	a monster that was half-human and half-panther.
Agouda	the Portuguese language or a person from Portugal.
Aja	the West.
Ajahi	a market in Agbomê.
Ajaho	title given to the minister who administered the affairs of the Palace, oversaw extensive foreign and domestic spy networks, and conducted the trial by poison.
Akassa	a maize dough wrapped in leaves. Akassa serves the Danhomênous as a kind of bread.
Akplogan	title given to the minister who served as high priest of the religious cult and lived in the city of Allada.
Alcarraza	an earthenware jug.
Apatam	a temporary shelter with a thatched roof. The apatam is the place where important dignitaries and distinguished guests sit during official ceremonies.
Assen	miniscule parasol that represents a dead person. Assens are displayed at a house specifically constructed for that purpose.
Avoutou	the shot that was fired in the forecourt of the Palace to announce the arrival of the king in the main courtyard.

383

Ayidohouédo	the rainbow, regarded as a fetish and worshipped by the Danhomênous.
Ayo	the East.
Bamboo	a Danhomê unit of measurement, roughly equivalent to five meters.
Bo-savo	the fifth day of the Danhomê calendar.
Boubou	an ample, robelike garment usually worn by men. The boubou was introduced to sub-Saharan Africa by Moslems from the North.
Bozounvodoun	the third day of the Danhomê calendar.
Caloulou	a dish prepared with meat, fish, or vegetables and served with akassa.
Dogba	a drum that served to announce the king's appearance before the people. It was also beaten on the occasion of the king's death.
Fon	the language spoken in Danhomê.
Foofoo	a starchy paste made from pounded cassava roots.
Gaou	title given to the first minister of war.
Glinci	the English language or an Englishman.
Gris-Gris	a small object believed to have magical powers. Gris-gris exist in many forms and are often worn as amulets or carried in small pouches.
Guédévis	the original inhabitants of the Agbomê plain, where they lived before the arrival of the Aladahonous (i.e., the Danhomênous).
Heviossê	lightning, one of the gods of Danhomê.
Houéda	of or belonging to the Houéda country, an area to the West of Danhomê. Houédanous are people from this area.

Houn	the South.
Ké	the North.
Legba	the spirit of evil who performs vulgar tasks for the gods.
Li	the name given to the earth considered as a divinity.
Loco	the sacred tree of Danhomê.
Mahi	Of or belonging to the Mahi country, an area north of Danhomê. The Mahinous (people from the Mahi country) were frequently captured and sold as slaves by the Danhomênous.
Mejo	the first day of the Danhomê calandar.
Mêwou	title given to the minister of the interior, who was charged with administering justice within the large royal family, assuring communication with other parts of the kingdom, and overseeing the affairs of the coastal provinces.
Migan	title given to the first minister, who was charged with administering justice in the population at large, performing human sacrifices, and overseeing the governance of the province of Allada.
Nago	of or belonging to the Yoruba. Nagonous are people from the land of the Yoruba.
Nété	a tree. The seeds of the nété are used to prepare a form of mustard.
Ogou	the god of war and weapons.
Possou	title given to the second minister of war.
Sapodilla	a large tropical tree with reddish wood and evergreen foliage. The sapodilla tree bears edible fruit and is a source of latex.

Sogan	title given to the minister who supervised the king's possessions, including the slaves who worked on the royal plantations.
Soudofi	captives who had been taken in early childhood and raised in Danhomê.
Tohubohu	chaos, confusion.
Tokpo	title given to the minister in charge of agriculture, landholdings, and the sacred waters used for royal ceremonies.
Vidaho	the title accorded the heir to the throne of Danhomê.
Yévogan	the Danhomê Governor of Gléhoué (Ouidah or Whydah). The Yévogan was charged with supervising all trade between Danhomê and the Europeans.
Zado	the name given to the kingdom of Danhomê by the people of the Mahi country. A Zadonou is a man from Zado (i.e., a Danhomênou).
Zogbodo	a market in Agbomê. The day of Zogbodo is devoted to the worship of fetishes.
Zojagué	the French language or a Frenchman.

Note on the Translator

Richard Bjornson is a literary critic and translator who teaches French and Comparative Literature at The Ohio State University. He has spent several years in West Africa. His other translations include works by Mongo Beti, Ferdinand Oyono, René Philombe, François-Borgia Marie Evembe, and Léopold Sédar Senghor.

A former president of the American Literary Translators Association and editor-designate of the influential journal *Research in African Literatures*, Bjornson has written extensively on literature, culture, and the nation-building process in Africa.

Among his other books are *The Picaresque Hero in European Fiction*, *Approaches to Teaching Cervantes' "Don Quixote," Africa and the West* (ed.), *The University of the Future* (ed.), and *African Humanism: Challenges and Aspirations* (ed.). He is currently working on a book entitled *The African Quest for Freedom and Identity: Cameroonian Literature and the National Experience*.

Three Continents Press has previously published three of Bjornson's translations of Cameroonian literature: *Lament for an African Pol* by Mongo Beti, *Tales from Cameroon* by René Philombe, and *Road to Europe* by Ferdinand Oyono.